PEARSON   ALWAYS LEARNING

Inventing Arguments
A Rhetoric and Reader for the University of Maryland's Academic Writing Program

Second Custom Edition

Taken from:
Writing Arguments: A Rhetoric with Readings, Tenth Edition
by John D. Ramage, John C. Bean, and June Johnson

Style: The Basics of Clarity and Grace, Fifth Edition
by Joseph M. Williams

From Inquiry to Argument
by Linda McMeniman

Pearson Education, Inc., 330 Hudson Street, New York, New York 10013
A Pearson Education Company
www.pearsoned.com

Printed in the United States of America

1   16

000200010272042819

PM/KC

 ISBN 10: 1-323-51155-5
ISBN 13: 978-1-323-51155-8

Copyright Acknowledgments

Contents

Chapter 1–14 Taken from *Writing Arguments: A Rhetoric with Readings*, Tenth Edition, by John D. Ramage, John C. Bean, and June Johnson

SECTION ONE

Inventing Arguments: A Rhetoric and Reader

Overview of Argument

Across the country, protests like this one in front of a Burger King in Boston are raising awareness of the poverty-level wages of fast-food workers, who are not represented by unions and who often depend on public assistance such as food stamps to get by every month. While protestors argue for a minimum wage of $15 per hour, opponents argue that raising the minimum wage would increase food prices and reduce the number of jobs. If you were making a brochure or poster in favor of an increased minimum wage for fast-food workers, how effective would this realistic, low-keyed photo be in raising sympathy for the cause? Chapters 2 and 7 explore the issue of a living wage for unskilled workers.

Argument: An Introduction

1

> **What you will learn in this chapter:**
> **1.1** To explain common misconceptions about the meaning of argument
> **1.2** To describe defining features of argument
> **1.3** To understand the relationship of argument to the problem of truth

At the outset of a book on argument, you might expect us to provide a simple definition of argument. Instead, we're going to explain why no universally accepted definition is possible. Over the centuries, philosophers and rhetoricians have disagreed about the meaning of the term and about the goals that arguers should set for themselves. This opening chapter introduces you to some of these controversies.

We begin by showing some common misconceptions about argument while also explaining how arguments can be either implicit or explicit. We then proceed to three defining features of argument: it requires writers or speakers to justify their claims; it is both a product and a process; and it combines elements of truth seeking and persuasion. Finally, we explore more fully the relationship between truth seeking and persuasion by asking questions about the nature of "truth" that arguments seek.

What Do We Mean by Argument?

1.1 To explain common misconceptions about the meaning of argument

Let's begin by examining the inadequacies of two popular images of argument—fight and debate.

Argument Is Not a Fight or a Quarrel

To many, the word *argument* connotes anger and hostility, as when we say, "I just got in a huge argument with my roommate," or "My mother and I argue all the time." What we picture here is heated disagreement, rising pulse rates, and an urge to slam doors. Argument imagined as fight conjures images of shouting talk-show guests, flaming bloggers, or fist-banging speakers.

But to our way of thinking, argument doesn't imply anger. In fact, arguing is often pleasurable. It is a creative and productive activity that engages us at high levels of inquiry and critical thinking, often in conversation with people we like and respect. For your primary image of argument, we invite you to think not of a shouting match on cable news but of a small group of reasonable people seeking the best solution to a problem. We will return to this image throughout the chapter.

Argument Is Not Pro-Con Debate

Another popular image of argument is debate—a presidential debate, perhaps, or a high school or college debate tournament. According to one popular dictionary, *debate* is "a formal contest of argumentation in which two opposing teams defend and attack a given proposition." Although formal debate can develop critical thinking, its weakness is that it can turn argument into a game of winners and losers rather than a process of cooperative inquiry.

For an illustration of this weakness, consider one of our former students, a champion high school debater who spent his senior year debating the issue of prison reform. Throughout the year he argued for and against propositions such as "The United States should build more prisons" and "Innovative alternatives to prison should replace prison sentences for most crimes." We asked him, "What do you personally think is the best way to reform prisons?" He replied, "I don't know. I haven't thought about what I would actually choose."

Here was a bright, articulate student who had studied prisons extensively for a year. Yet nothing in the atmosphere of pro-con debate had engaged him in truth-seeking inquiry. He could argue for and against a proposition, but he hadn't experienced the wrenching process of clarifying his own values and taking a personal stand. As we explain throughout this text, argument entails a desire for truth; it aims to find the best solutions to complex problems. We don't mean that arguers don't passionately support their own points of view or expose weaknesses in views they find faulty. Instead, we mean that their goal isn't to win a game but to find and promote the best belief or course of action.

Arguments Can Be Explicit or Implicit

Before proceeding to some defining features of argument, we should note also that arguments can be either explicit or implicit. An *explicit* argument directly states its controversial claim and supports it with reasons and evidence. An *implicit* argument, in contrast, may not look like an argument at all. It may be a bumper sticker, a billboard, a poster, a photograph, a cartoon, a vanity license plate, a slogan on a T-shirt, an advertisement, a poem, or a song lyric. But like an explicit argument, it persuades its audience toward a certain point of view.

Consider the striking photograph in Figure 1.1—a baby wearing a bib labeled "POISON." This photograph enters a conversation about the safety of toys and other baby products sold in the United States. In recent years, fears about toy safety have

FIGURE 1.1 An implicit argument against phthalates

come mostly from two sources: the discovery that many toys imported from China contained lead paint and the discovery that a substance used to make plastics pliable and soft—called *phthalates* (pronounced "thalates")—may be harmful. Phthalates have been shown to interfere with hormone production in rat fetuses and, based on other rodent studies, may produce some kinds of cancers and other ailments. Because many baby products contain phthalates—bibs, edges of cribs, rubber duckies, and any number of other soft, rubbery toys—parents worry that babies can ingest phthalates by chewing on these toys.

The photograph of the baby and bib makes the argumentative claim that baby products are poisonous; the photograph implicitly urges viewers to take action against phthalates. But this photograph is just one voice in a surprisingly complex conversation. Is the bib in fact poisonous? Such questions were debated during a recent campaign to ban the sale of toys containing phthalates in California. A legislative initiative sparked intense lobbying from both child-advocacy groups and representatives of the toy industry. At issue were a number of scientific questions about the risk posed by phthalates. To what extent do studies on rats apply to humans? How much exposure to phthalates should be considered dangerous? (Experiments on rats used large amounts of phthalates—amounts that, according to many scientists, far exceed anything a baby could absorb by chewing on a toy.) Also at issue is the level of health risks a free market society should be willing to tolerate. The European Union, operating on the "precautionary principle," and citing evidence that such toys *might* be dangerous, has banned toys containing phthalates. The U.S. government sets less strict standards than does the European Union. A federal agency generally doesn't ban a substance unless it has been *proven* harmful to humans, not merely suspected of being harmful. In defense of free markets, the toy and chemical industries accused opponents of phthalates of using "junk science" to produce scary but inaccurate data.

Our point in summarizing the toxic toy controversy is to demonstrate the persuasive roles of both implicit and explicit arguments.

In contrast to the implicit argument made in Figure 1.1, consider the following explicit argument posted by student writer Juan Lucas on a blog site. As an explicit argument, it states its claim directly and supports it with reasons and evidence.

An Argument Against Banning Phthalates

(BLOG POST BY STUDENT JUAN LUCAS)

The campaign to ban phthalates from children's toys uses scare tactics that aren't grounded in good science. The anti-phthalate campaign shocks us with photos of baby bibs labeled "poison." It arouses fear by linking phthalates to possible cancers or abnormalities in hormone production. In contrast, the scientific literature about phthalates is much more guarded and cautious. Political pressure has already led to a 2009 federal ban on phthalates used in toys that can be put in a baby's mouth, such as bottle nipples and teething rings. But based on the scientific evidence, I argue that further banning of phthalates from children's toys is a mistake.

Despite the warnings from the anti-phthalates campaign, the federal Consumer Product Safety Commission, after extensive tests and review of the scientific literature, says that the level of phthalates absorbed from toys is too low to be harmful. No scientific study has yet demonstrated harm to humans. Moreover, humans are exposed to phthalates daily, especially from food packaging, plastic bottles, shower curtains, personal care products, and elsewhere. Banning phthalates in children's toys wouldn't significantly reduce human exposure to phthalates from other sources.

Banning substances on emotional rather than scientific grounds has its own negative consequences. If we try to ban all potentially harmful substances before they have been proven harmful, we will be less watchful against scientifically proven dangers such as lead, coal dust, sulfur dioxide, or mercury in fish. We should place phthalates in the same category as other possible-but-not-proven threats that are part of living in the industrial world: artificial sweeteners, electromagnetic waves, non-organic foods (because of possible pesticide residue), GMO corn and soy beans, and radon in our walls. We should demand rigorous testing of all these threats, but not try to ban them until evidence-based science proves their harmfulness.

We should also keep in mind the impact of too much regulation on people's jobs and the economy in general. The toy industry, a vibrant and important one in our economy (just ask Santa Claus), provides thousands of jobs, and is already highly regulated with safety standards. The use of phthalates, in fact, might make many toys safer by making them softer and less brittle. Ensuring toy safety through strong testing and regulation is absolutely necessary. But let's base our regulations on good science.

■ ■ ■ **FOR WRITING AND DISCUSSION   Implicit and Explicit Arguments   MyWritingLab™**

Any argument, whether implicit or explicit, tries to influence the audience's stance on an issue, moving the audience toward the arguer's claim. Arguments work on us psychologically as well as cognitively, triggering emotions as well as thoughts and ideas. Each of the implicit arguments in Figures 1.2–1.4 makes a claim on its audience, trying to get viewers to adopt its position, perspective, belief, or point of view on an issue.

FIGURE 1.2 Poster related to the GMO controversy

FIGURE 1.3 Photograph of protestors at a New York State Occupy Wall Street Rally

"Do you John promise that your schedule, please put your iPhone away, will never be more important than your times together?"

FIGURE 1.4 Cartoon on social etiquette and digital media

Individual task: For each argument, answer the following questions:

1. What conversation does this argument join? What is the issue or controversy? What is at stake? (Sometimes "insider knowledge" might be required to understand the argument. In such cases, explain to an outsider the needed background information or cultural context.)
2. What is the argument's claim? That is, what value, perspective, belief, or position does the argument ask its viewers to adopt?
3. What is an opposing or alternative view? What views is the argument pushing against?
4. Convert the implicit argument into an explicit argument by stating its claim and supporting reasons in words. How do implicit and explicit arguments work differently on the brains or hearts of the audience?

Group task: Working in pairs or as a whole class, share your answers with classmates. ■ ■ ■

The Defining Features of Argument

1.2 To describe defining features of argument

We turn now to examine arguments in more detail. (Unless we say otherwise, by *argument* we mean explicit arguments that attempt to supply reasons and evidence to support their claims.) This section examines three defining features of such arguments.

Argument Requires Justification of Its Claims

To begin defining argument, let's turn to a humble but universal site of disagreement: the conflict between a parent and a teenager over rules. In what way and in what circumstances do such conflicts constitute arguments?

Consider the following dialogue:

YOUNG PERSON (*racing for the front door while putting coat on*):   Bye. See you later.

PARENT: Whoa! What time are you planning on coming home?

YOUNG PERSON (*coolly, hand still on doorknob*):   I'm sure we discussed this earlier. I'll be home around 2 A.M. (*The second sentence, spoken very rapidly, is barely audible.*)

PARENT (*mouth tightening*):   We did *not* discuss this earlier and you're *not* staying out till two in the morning. You'll be home at twelve.

At this point in the exchange, we have a quarrel, not an argument. Quarrelers exchange antagonistic assertions without any attempt to support them rationally. If the dialogue never gets past the "Yes-you-will/No-I-won't" stage, it either remains a quarrel or degenerates into a fight.

Let us say, however, that the dialogue takes the following turn:

YOUNG PERSON (*tragically*):   But I'm *sixteen years old!*

Now we're moving toward argument. Not, to be sure, a particularly well-developed or cogent one, but an argument all the same. It's now an argument because one of the quarrelers has offered a reason for her assertion. Her choice of curfew is satisfactory, she says, *because* she is sixteen years old, an argument that depends on the unstated assumption that sixteen-year-olds are old enough to make decisions about such matters.

The parent can now respond in one of several ways that will either advance the argument or turn it back into a quarrel. The parent can simply invoke parental authority ("I don't care—you're still coming home at twelve"), in which case argument ceases. Or the parent can provide a reason for his or her view ("You will be home at twelve because your dad and I pay the bills around here!"), in which case the argument takes a new turn.

So far we've established two necessary conditions that must be met before we're willing to call something an argument: (1) a set of two or more conflicting assertions and (2) the attempt to resolve the conflict through an appeal to reason.

But good argument demands more than meeting these two formal requirements. For the argument to be effective, an arguer is obligated to clarify and support the reasons presented. For example, "But I'm sixteen years old!" is not yet a clear support for the assertion "I should be allowed to set my own curfew." On the surface, Young Person's argument seems absurd. Her parent, of all people, knows precisely how old she is. What makes it an argument is that behind her claim lies an unstated assumption—all sixteen-year-olds are old enough to set their own curfews. What Young Person needs to do now is to support that assumption.* In doing so, she must anticipate the sorts of questions the assumption will raise in the mind of her parent: What is the legal status of sixteen-year-olds? How psychologically mature, as opposed to chronologically mature, is Young Person? What is the actual track record of Young Person in being responsible? and so forth. Each of these questions will force Young Person to reexamine and clarify her assumptions about the proper degree of autonomy for sixteen-year-olds. And her responses to those questions should in turn force the parent to reexamine his or her assumptions about the dependence of sixteen-year-olds on parental guidance and wisdom. (Likewise, the parent will need to show why "paying the bills around here" automatically gives the right to set Young Person's curfew.)

As the argument continues, Young Person and Parent may shift to a different line of reasoning. For example, Young Person might say: "I should be allowed to stay out until 2 A.M. because all my friends get to stay out that late." (Here the unstated assumption is that the rules in this family ought to be based on the rules in other families.) The parent might in turn respond, "But I certainly never stayed out that late when I was your age"—an argument assuming that the rules in this family should follow the rules of an earlier generation.

As Young Person and Parent listen to each other's points of view (and begin realizing why their initial arguments have not persuaded their intended audience), both parties find themselves in the uncomfortable position of having to examine their own beliefs and to justify assumptions that they have taken for granted. Here we encounter one of the earliest meanings of the term *to argue,* which is "to clarify." As an arguer begins to clarify her own position on an issue, she also begins to clarify her audience's position. Such clarification helps the arguer see how she might accommodate her audience's views, perhaps by adjusting her own position or by developing reasons that appeal to her audience's values. Thus Young Person might suggest an argument like this:

> I should be allowed to stay out until two on a trial basis because I need enough freedom to demonstrate my maturity and show you I won't get into trouble.

The assumption underlying this argument is that it is good to give teenagers freedom to demonstrate their maturity. Because this reason is likely to appeal to her parent's own values (the parent wants to see his or her daughter grow in maturity) and because it is tempered by the qualifier "on a trial basis" (which reduces some of the threat of Young Person's initial demands), it may prompt productive discussion.

Whether or not Young Person and Parent can work out a best solution, the preceding scenario illustrates how argument leads people to clarify their reasons and provide justifications that can be examined rationally. The scenario also illustrates two specific aspects of argument that we will explore in detail in the next sections: (1) Argument is both a process and a product. (2) Argument combines truth seeking and persuasion.

---

*Later in this text we will call the assumption underlying a line of reasoning its *warrant* (see Chapter 4).

Argument Is Both a Process and a Product

As the preceding scenario revealed, argument can be viewed as a *process* in which two or more parties seek the best solution to a question or problem. Argument can also be viewed as a *product,* each product being any person's contribution to the conversation at a given moment. In an informal discussion, the products are usually short, whatever time a person uses during his or her turns in the conversation. Under more formal settings, an orally delivered product might be a short, impromptu speech (say, during an open-mike discussion of a campus issue) or a longer, carefully prepared formal speech (as in a PowerPoint presentation at a business meeting or an argument at a public hearing for or against a proposed city project).

Similar conversations occur in writing. Roughly analogous to a small-group discussion is an exchange of the kind that occurs regularly online through informal chat groups or more formal blog sites. In an online discussion, participants have more thinking time to shape their messages than they do in a real-time oral discussion. Nevertheless, messages are usually short and informal, making it possible over the course of several days to see participants' ideas shift and evolve as conversants modify their initial views in response to others' views.

Roughly equivalent to a formal speech would be a formal written argument, which may take the form of an academic argument for a college course; a grant proposal; an online posting; a guest column for the op-ed* section of a newspaper; a legal brief; a letter to a member of Congress; or an article for an organizational newsletter, popular magazine, or professional journal. In each of these instances, the written argument (a product) enters a conversation (a process)—in this case, a conversation of readers, many of whom will carry on the conversation by writing their own responses or by discussing the writer's views with others. The goal of the community of writers and readers is to find the best solution to the problem or issue under discussion.

Argument Combines Truth Seeking and Persuasion

In thinking about argument as a product, the writer will find herself continually moving back and forth between truth seeking and persuasion—that is, between questions about the subject matter (What is the best solution to this problem?) and about audience (What do my readers already believe or value? What reasons and evidence will most persuade them?). Back and forth she'll weave, alternately absorbed in the subject of her argument and in the audience for that argument.

Neither of the two focuses is ever completely out of mind, but their relative importance shifts during different phases of the development of a paper. Moreover, different rhetorical situations place different emphases on truth seeking versus persuasion.

Op-ed stands for "opposite-editorial." It is the generic name in journalism for a signed argument that voices the writer's opinion on an issue, as opposed to a news story that is supposed to report events objectively, uncolored by the writer's personal views. Op-ed pieces appear in the editorial-opinion section of newspapers, which generally features editorials by the resident staff, opinion pieces by syndicated columnists, and letters to the editor from readers. The term *op-ed* is often extended to syndicated columns appearing in newsmagazines, advocacy Web sites, and online news services.

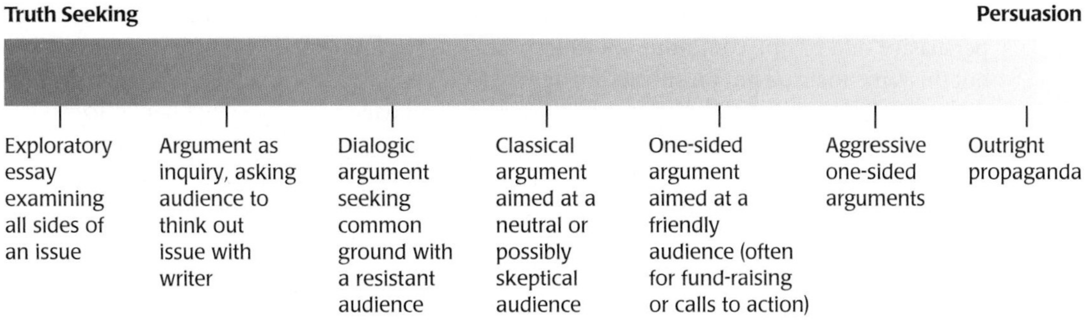

Truth Seeking   **Persuasion**

| Exploratory essay examining all sides of an issue | Argument as inquiry, asking audience to think out issue with writer | Dialogic argument seeking common ground with a resistant audience | Classical argument aimed at a neutral or possibly skeptical audience | One-sided argument aimed at a friendly audience (often for fund-raising or calls to action) | Aggressive one-sided arguments | Outright propaganda |

FIGURE 1.5 Continuum of arguments from truth seeking to persuasion

We could thus place arguments on a kind of continuum that measures the degree of attention a writer gives to subject matter versus audience. (See Figure 1.5.) At the far truth-seeking end of the continuum might be an exploratory piece that lays out several alternative approaches to a problem and weighs the strengths and weaknesses of each with no concern for persuasion. At the other end of the continuum would be outright propaganda, such as a political campaign advertisement that reduces a complex issue to sound bites and distorts an opponent's position through out-of-context quotations or misleading use of data. (At its most blatant, propaganda obliterates truth seeking; it will do anything, including the knowing use of bogus evidence, distorted assertions, and outright lies, to win over an audience.) In the middle ranges of the continuum, writers shift their focuses back and forth between truth seeking and persuasion but with varying degrees of emphasis.

As an example of a writer focusing primarily on truth seeking, consider the case of Kathleen, who, in her college argument course, addressed the definitional question "Is American Sign Language (ASL) a 'foreign language' for purposes of meeting the university's foreign language requirement?" Kathleen had taken two years of ASL at a community college. When she transferred to a four-year college, the chair of the foreign languages department at her new college would not allow her ASL proficiency to count for the foreign language requirement. ASL isn't a "language," the chair said summarily. "It's not equivalent to learning French, German, or Japanese."

Kathleen disagreed, so she immersed herself in developing her argument. While doing research, she focused almost entirely on subject matter, searching for what linguists, neurologists, cognitive psychologists, and sociologists had said about the language of deaf people. Immersed in her subject matter, she was only tacitly concerned with her audience, whom she thought of primarily as her classmates and the professor of her argument class—people who were friendly to her views and interested in her experiences with the deaf community. She wrote a well-documented paper, citing several scholarly articles, that made a good case to her classmates (and the professor) that ASL is indeed a distinct language.

Proud of the big red A the professor had placed on her paper, Kathleen decided for a subsequent assignment to write a second paper on ASL—but this time aiming it directly at the chair of foreign languages and petitioning him to accept her ASL proficiency for the foreign language requirement. Now her writing task fell closer to the persuasive end of our continuum. Kathleen once again immersed herself in research, but this time focused not on subject matter (whether ASL is a distinct language) but on audience. She researched the history of the foreign language requirement at her college and discovered some of the politics behind it (an old foreign language requirement had been dropped in the 1970s and reinstituted in the 1990s, partly—a math professor told her—to boost enrollments in foreign language courses). She also interviewed foreign language teachers to find out what they knew and didn't know about ASL. She discovered that many teachers thought ASL was "easy to learn," so that accepting ASL would allow students a Mickey Mouse way to avoid the rigors of a "real" foreign language class. Additionally, she learned that foreign language teachers valued immersing students in a foreign culture; in fact, the foreign language requirement was part of her college's effort to create a multicultural curriculum.

This new understanding of her target audience helped Kathleen reconceptualize her argument. Her claim that ASL is a real language (the subject of her first paper) became only one section of her second paper, much condensed and abridged. She added sections showing the difficulty of learning ASL (to counter her audience's belief that learning ASL is easy), showing how the deaf community forms a distinct culture with its own customs and literature (to show how ASL would meet the goals of multi-culturalism), and showing that the number of transfer students with ASL credits would be negligibly small (to allay fears that accepting ASL would threaten enrollments in language classes). She ended her argument with an appeal to her college's public emphasis (declared boldly in its mission statement) on eradicating social injustice and reaching out to the oppressed. She described the isolation of deaf people in a world where almost no hearing people learn ASL, and she argued that the deaf community on her campus could be integrated more fully into campus life if more students could "talk" with them. Thus the ideas included in her new argument—the reasons selected, the evidence used, the arrangement and tone—all were determined by her primary focus on persuasion.

Our point, then, is that all along the continuum, writers attempt both to seek truth and to persuade, but not necessarily with equal balance. Kathleen could not have written her second paper, aimed specifically at persuading the chair of foreign languages, if she hadn't first immersed herself in truth-seeking research that convinced her that ASL is indeed a distinct language. Nor are we saying that her second argument was better than her first. Both fulfilled their purposes and met the needs of their intended audiences. Both involved truth seeking and persuasion, but the first focused primarily on subject matter whereas the second focused primarily on audience.

Argument and the Problem of Truth

1.3 To understand the relationship of argument to the problem of truth

The tension that we have just examined between truth seeking and persuasion raises an ancient issue in the field of argument: Is the arguer's first obligation to truth or to winning the argument? And just what is the nature of the truth to which arguers are supposed to be obligated?

In Plato's famous dialogues from ancient Greek philosophy, these questions were at the heart of Socrates' disagreement with the Sophists. The Sophists were professional rhetoricians who specialized in training orators to win arguments. Socrates, who valued truth seeking over persuasion and believed that truth could be discovered through philosophic inquiry, opposed the Sophists. For Socrates, Truth resided in the ideal world of forms, and through philosophic rigor humans could transcend the changing, shadowlike world of everyday reality to perceive the world of universals where Truth, Beauty, and Goodness resided. Through his method of questioning his interlocutors, Socrates would gradually peel away layer after layer of false views until Truth was revealed. The good person's duty, Socrates believed, was not to win an argument but to pursue this higher Truth. Socrates distrusted rhetoricians because they were interested only in the temporal power and wealth that came from persuading audiences to the orator's views.

Let's apply Socrates' disagreement with the Sophists to a modern instance. Suppose your community is divided over the issue of raising environmental standards versus keeping open a job-producing factory that doesn't meet new guidelines for waste discharge. The Sophists would train you to argue any side of this issue on behalf of any lobbying group willing to pay for your services. If, however, you followed the spirit of Socrates, you would be inspired to listen to all sides of the dispute, peel away false arguments, discover the Truth through reasonable inquiry, and commit yourself to a Right Course of Action.

But what is the nature of Truth or Right Action in a dispute between jobs and the environment? The Sophists believed that truth was determined by those in power; thus they could enter an argument unconstrained by any transcendent beliefs or assumptions. When Socrates talked about justice and virtue, the Sophists could reply contemptuously that these were fictitious concepts invented by the weak to protect themselves from the strong. Over the years, the Sophists' relativist beliefs became so repugnant to people that the term *sophistry* became synonymous with trickery in argument.

However, in recent years the Sophists' critique of a transcendent Universal Truth has been taken seriously by many philosophers, sociologists, and other thinkers who doubt Socrates' confident belief that arguments, properly conducted, necessarily arrive at a single Truth. For these thinkers, as for the Sophists, there are often different degrees of truth and different kinds of truths for different situations or cultures. From this perspective, when we consider questions of interpretation or value, we can never demonstrate that a belief or assumption is true—not through scientific observation, not through reason, and not through religious revelation. We get our beliefs, according to these contemporary thinkers, from the shared assumptions of our particular cultures. We are condemned (or liberated) to live in a pluralistic, multicultural world with competing visions of truth.

If we accept this pluralistic view of the world, do we then endorse the Sophists' radical relativism, freeing us to argue any side of any issue? Or do we doggedly pursue some modern equivalent of Socrates' truth?

Our own sympathies are with Socrates, but we admit to a view of truth that is more tentative, cautious, and conflicted than his. For us, truth seeking does not mean finding the "Right Answer" to a disputed question, but neither does it mean a valueless relativism in which all answers are equally good. For us, truth seeking means taking responsibility for determining the "best answer" or "best solution" to the question for the good of the whole community when taking into consideration the interests of all stakeholders. It means making hard decisions in the face of uncertainty. This more tentative view of truth means that you cannot use argument to "prove" your claim, but only to make a reasonable case for your claim. One contemporary philosopher says that argument can hope only to "increase adherence" to ideas, not absolutely convince an audience of the necessary truth of ideas. Even though you can't be certain, in a Socratic sense, that your solution to the problem is the best one available, you must ethically take responsibility for the consequences of your claim and you must seek justice for stakeholders beyond yourself. You must, in other words, forge a personal stance based on your examination of all the evidence and your articulation of values that you can make public and defend.

To seek truth, then, means to seek the best or most just solution to a problem while observing all available evidence, listening with an open mind to the views of all stakeholders, clarifying and attempting to justify your own values and assumptions, and taking responsibility for your argument. It follows that truth seeking often means delaying closure on an issue, acknowledging the pressure of alternative views, and being willing to change one's mind. Seen in this way, learning to argue effectively has the deepest sort of social value: It helps communities settle conflicts in a rational and humane way by finding, through the dialectic exchange of ideas, the best solutions to problems without resorting to violence or to other assertions of raw power.

■ ■ ■   **FOR CLASS DISCUSSION**   Role-Playing Arguments

On any given day, the media provides evidence of the complexity of living in a pluralistic culture. Issues that could be readily decided in a completely homogeneous culture raise questions in a society that has fewer shared assumptions. Choose one of the following cases as the subject for a "simulation game" in which class members present the points of view of the people involved.

Case 1: Political Asylum for German Family Seeking Right to Homeschool Their Children

In 2010 an Evangelical Christian family from Germany, Uwe and Hannelore Romeike and their five children, moved to the United States seeking asylum from political persecution. At the U.S. immigration hearings, the couple argued that if they remained in Germany their decision to homeschool their children would result in fines, possible arrest, and even forced separation from their children. German law forbids homeschooling on the grounds that failure to attend recognized schools will create "parallel societies" whose members will fail to integrate into Germany's open and pluralistic culture. In early 2011, a U.S. federal immigration judge granted political asylum to the family, denouncing the German government's policy against homeschooling. He called it "utterly repellent to everything we believe as Americans." However, in 2013 the Sixth Circuit Court unanimously overturned the original decision and revoked the family's status as political refugees. Stating that the United States cannot give political asylum to every victim of perceived unfairness in another country's laws, the court declared that Germany's ban on homeschooling did not constitute political persecution. The decision led to international debate about the role of homeschooling in a pluralistic society and about the definition of political persecution. In the United States, the Homeschooling Legal Defense Association urged that the case be heard by the United States Supreme Court and sponsored a petition drive supporting the Romeike family.

Your task: Imagine a public hearing on this issue where all stakeholders are invited to present their points of view. The U.S. Immigration Web site offers the following definition of refugee status:

> Refugee status or asylum may be granted to people who have been persecuted or fear they will be persecuted on account of race, religion, nationality, and/or membership in a particular social group or political opinion

Your goal isn't to make your own decision about this case but to bring to imaginative life all the points of view in the controversy. Hold a mock public hearing in which classmates play the following roles: (a) An American parent advocating homeschooling; (b) an American teacher's union representative opposing homeschooling; (c) an attorney arguing that the Romeike family meets the criteria for "refugee status"; (d) an attorney arguing that the Romeike family does not meet the criteria for refugee status; (e) a German citizen supporting the German law against homeschooling; (f) a Romeike parent arguing that they would be persecuted if they returned to Germany; (g) other roles that your class thinks are relevant to this case.

Case 2: HPV Vaccines for Sixth Grade Girls (and Boys)

In 2007 the pharmaceutical company Merke developed a vaccine against the sexually transmitted HPV virus (human papillomavirus), some strains of which can cause cervical cancer as well as genital warts. They launched an extensive television campaign promoting the vaccine (which would bring substantial profits to Merke) and advised that girls should get the vaccine before they reached puberty. Following recommendations from doctors and medical researchers, several states passed laws mandating that the HPV vaccine be included for girls among the other vaccinations required of all children for entry into the sixth or seventh grades (depending on the state). These laws sparked public debate about the benefits versus potential adverse effects of vaccines, and about the state's versus parents' role in determining what vaccines a child should get.

Your task: Imagine a public hearing addressing what your state's laws should be concerning HPV vaccinations for pre-pubescent children. Your goal isn't to make your own decision about this case but to bring to imaginative life all the points of view in the controversy. Hold a mock hearing in which classmates play the following roles: (a) a cancer specialist who supports mandatory HPV vaccination for girls; (b) a public health specialist who also supports expanding the requirement to include boys; (c) a skeptical person concerned about the potential adverse effects of vaccines in general; (d) a religiously conservative parent who believes in abstinence and monogamy and opposes the cultural message of the HPV vaccination.

Conclusion

In this chapter we have explored some of the complexities of argument, showing you why we believe that argument is a matter not of fist banging or of win-lose debate but of finding, through a process of rational inquiry, the best solution to a problem or issue. Good argument requires justification of its claim, is both a process and product, and combines truth seeking with persuasion. We particularly want to emphasize its truth-seeking dimension. We suggest that when you enter an argument you seek out a wide range of views, that you especially welcome views different from your own, that you treat these views respectfully, and that you see them as intelligent and rationally defensible. Although like the Sophists you can use the skills of argument to support any side of any issue, we hope you won't. We hope that, like Socrates, you will use argument for truth seeking and that you will consequently find yourself, on at least some occasions, changing your position on an issue while writing a rough draft (a sure sign that the process of arguing has complicated your views).

At the deepest level, we believe that the skills of reason and inquiry developed through writing arguments can help you get a clearer sense of who you are. If our culture sets you adrift in pluralism, argument can help you take a stand, to say, "These things I believe." In this text we will not pretend to tell you what position to take on any given issue. But as a responsible being, you will often need to take a stand, to define yourself, to say, "Here are the reasons that choice A is better than choice B, not just for me but for you also." If this text helps you base your commitments and actions on reasonable grounds, then it will have been successful.

MyWritingLab™

Visit Ch. 1 Argument: An Introduction in *MyWritingLab* to complete the For Writing and Discussion and to test your understanding of the chapter objectives.

Argument as Inquiry
Reading and Exploring

What you will learn in this chapter:

2.1 To find issues to explore

2.2 To read sources rhetorically by analyzing a text's genre, purpose, and degree of advocacy

2.3 To read to believe an argument's claims

2.4 To read to doubt an argument's claims

2.5 To delay closure by thinking dialectically

In the previous chapter we explained that argument focuses on both truth seeking and persuasion. In this chapter, we focus on inquiry (truth seeking) as the entry point into argumentative conversations. Unfortunately, in today's wired environment these conversations often preclude truth seeking. They are carried on within isolated echo chambers of like-minded participants who believe they already possess the truth. We can observe these echo chambers on politically homogenous Web sites, on cable news channels, or on talk-show debates where participants shout at each other with no interest in listening to alternative views. This reductive trend has elicited the concern of cultural critics, journalists, rhetoricians, scholars, and citizens. Journalist Matt Miller recently posed the questions, "Is it possible in America today to convince anyone of anything he doesn't already believe? … [A]re there enough places where this mingling of minds occurs to sustain a democracy?"*

We believe this "mingling of minds" is essential if we are to understand argument as a search for the best solutions to problems. To do so means to position ourselves as inquirers as well as persuaders. In this chapter we approach argument as an exploratory process in which participants try to suspend judgment and delay closure by engaging thoughtfully with alternative points of view, truly listening to other perspectives, examining their own values and assumptions, and perhaps even changing their views. We value the insight of rhetorician Wayne Booth, who proposes that when we enter an argumentative

---

*Matt Miller, "Is Persuasion Dead?" *New York Times* 4 June 2005, A29.

conversation, we should not ask first "How can I change your mind?" but rather "When should I change my mind?"*

In this chapter, we present some practical strategies for reading and exploring arguments in an open-minded and intellectually responsible way. To illustrate argument as inquiry, we will show you how one student, Trudie Makens, explored the problem of whether fast-food workers and other low-wage laborers should be paid a "living wage" of $15 per hour.

Finding Issues to Explore

2.1 To find issues to explore

Your engagement with a controversial issue might be sparked by personal experience, by conversations with others, or by something you listen to, see, or read. Sometimes you will be confused about the issue, unable to take a stand. At other times, you will have a visceral gut reaction that causes you to take an immediate position, even though you haven't thought through the issue in depth. At the start of the arguing process, the confused or puzzled position is often the stronger one because it promotes inquiry as truth seeking. If you start with a firm stand, you might be less disposed to uncover your issue's complexity and let your position evolve. In this section we examine some strategies you can use to find issues worth exploring.

Do Some Initial Brainstorming

As a first step, make an inventory of issues that interest you. Many of the ideas you develop may become subject matter for arguments that you will write later in this course. The chart on page 19 will help you generate a productive list.

Once you've made a list, add to it as new ideas strike you and return to it each time you are given a new argumentative assignment.

Be Open to the Issues All around You

We are surrounded by argumentative issues. You'll start noticing them everywhere once you get attuned to them. You will be invited into argumentative conversations by posters, bumper stickers, blog sites, newspaper editorial pages, magazine articles, the sports section, movie reviews, song lyrics, and so forth. When you read or listen, watch for "hot spots"—passages or moments that evoke strong agreement, disagreement, or confusion. As an illustration of how arguments are all around us, try the following exercise on the issue of a living wage for low wage workers.

---

*Wayne Booth raised these questions in a featured session with Peter Elbow titled "Blind Skepticism vs. the Rhetoric of Assent: Implications for Rhetoric, Argument, and Teaching," presented at the CCCC annual convention, Chicago, Illinois, March 2002.

Brainstorming Issues to Explore

What You Can Do	How It Works
Make an inventory of the communities to which you belong. Consider classroom communities; clubs and organizations; residence hall, apartment, neighborhood, or family communities; church/synagogue or work communities; communities related to your hobbies or avocations; your city, state, region, nation, and world communities.	Because arguments arise out of disagreements within communities, you can often think of issues for argument by beginning with a list of the communities to which you belong.
Identify controversies within those communities. Think both big and small: <ul><li>Big issue in world community: What is the best way to prevent destruction of rain forests?</li><li>Small issue in residence hall community: Should quiet hours be enforced?</li></ul>	To stimulate thinking, use prompts such as these: <ul><li>People in this community frequently disagree about _____ .</li><li>Within my work community, Person X believes _____ ; however, this view troubles me because _____ .</li><li>In a recent residence hall meeting, I didn't know where I stood on _____ .</li><li>The situation at _____ could be improved if _____ .</li></ul>
Narrow your list to a handful of problematic issues for which you don't have a position; share it with classmates. Identify a few issues that you would like to explore more deeply. When you share with classmates, add their issues to yours.	Sharing your list with classmates stimulates more thinking and encourages conversations. The more you explore your views with others, the more ideas you will develop. Good writing grows out of good talking.
Brainstorm a network of related issues. Any given issue is always embedded in a network of other issues. To see how open-ended and fluid an argumentative conversation can be, try connecting one of your issues to a network of other issues including subissues and side issues.	Brainstorm questions that compel you to look at an issue in a variety of ways. For example, if you explored the controversy over whether toys with phthalates should be banned (see Chapter 1), you might generate questions such as these about related issues: <ul><li>How dangerous are phthalates?</li><li>Is the testing that has been done on rats adequate or accurate for determining the effects on humans?</li><li>Is the European "precautionary principle" a good principle for the United States to follow?</li><li>To what extent are controversies over phthalates similar to controversies over steroids, genetically modified foods, nitrites in cured meat, or mercury in dental fillings?</li></ul>

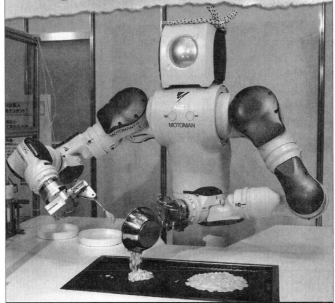

FIGURE 2.1 Full-page ad opposed to raising the minimum wage for fast-food workers

■ ■ ■   **FOR CLASS DISCUSSION** Responding to Visual Arguments about a Living Wage

Suppose, in your initial search for a controversial issue, you encounter visual texts related to raising the minimum wage for fast-food workers: photos of protestors, newspaper ads, cartoons, graphics, and other forms of visual arguments (see protest photo on page 1 and Figures 2.1–2.3). Working individually or in small groups, generate exploratory responses to these questions:

1. What claim is each of these visual texts making?
2. What background information about the problems of minimum-wage workers do these visual texts assume?
3. What network of issues do these visual texts suggest?
4. What puzzling questions do these visual texts raise for you?

FIGURE 2.2 Political cartoon on minimum wage

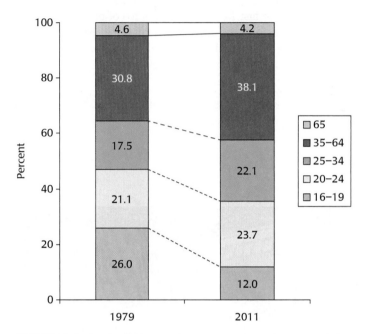

Percentage of Low-Wage Workers By Age Group, 1979 and 2011

FIGURE 2.3 Graph offering employment statistics relevant to minimum wage controversy

Adapted from Schmitt, John, and Janelle Jones, "Low-Wage Workers Are Older and Better Educated than Ever." Center for Economic and Policy Research. April 2012.

Explore Ideas by Freewriting

Freewriting is useful at any stage of the writing process. When you freewrite, you put fingers to keyboard (or pen to paper) and write rapidly *nonstop,* usually five to ten minutes at a stretch, without worrying about structure, grammar, or correctness. Your goal is to generate as many ideas as possible without stopping to edit your work. If you can't think of anything to say, write "relax" or "I'm stuck" over and over until new ideas emerge. Here is how Trudie Makens did a freewrite in response to the protest photo on page 1.

Trudie's Freewrite

Working in the food and service industry as a busser, I relate to the man in the picture holding the sign reading "Stand with Fast Food Workers." It's hard to live off of minimum wage, and if it weren't for my tips, I wouldn't be able to pay some of my bills. And that is with help from my parents since I am a college student. I can't imagine what it would be like for full-time workers in the fast-food industry where orders are taken via counter. I remember when I worked counter service jobs, as a barista and at a dumpling café, no one ever tipped. They didn't feel like they needed too since it was not formal wait service.

My work, and my coworkers' work, was not valued. What some people don't realize is that whether you are working at McDonalds or in an upscale restaurant, you are still working hard to provide good service. If anything, it is harder to work jobs like McDonalds where customers are dismissive and don't value the service they are receiving. Think, relax. Why do people not value the work of fast-food and counter service workers? Because it is considered unskilled labor? A lot of the people I have worked with didn't have the time or money to go to college because they were burdened with the financial strains of having children or caring for sick or elderly relatives. I remember my coworker Maria who was always stressed out because she couldn't pay her rent and had a child to support. A living wage would help people who haven't been lucky enough to inherit wealth to pull themselves out of poverty. And it wouldn't hurt corporations like McDonalds to live with a little less profit.

Explore Ideas by Idea Mapping

Another good technique for exploring ideas is *idea mapping*. When you make an idea map, draw a circle in the center of a page and write some trigger idea (a broad topic, a question, or working thesis statement) in the center of the circle. Then record your ideas on branches and subbranches extending from the center circle. As long as you pursue one train of thought, keep recording your ideas on that branch. But when that line of thinking gives out, start a new branch. Often your thoughts will jump back and forth between branches. That's a major advantage of "picturing" your thoughts; you can see them as part of an emerging design rather than as strings of unrelated ideas.

Idea maps usually generate more ideas, though less well-developed ones, than freewrites. Figure 2.4 shows an idea map that student Trudie Makens created on the issue of minimum wage after class discussion of the visual texts in Figures 2.1–2.3.

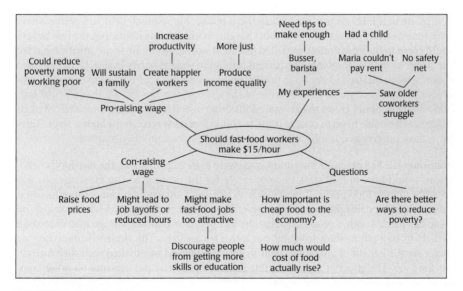

FIGURE 2.4 Trudie's idea map

Explore Ideas by Playing the Believing and Doubting Game

The believing and doubting game, a critical thinking strategy developed by rhetorician Peter Elbow that systematically stretches your thinking, is an excellent way to imagine views different from your own and to anticipate responses to those views.

- **As a believer, your role is to be wholly sympathetic to an idea.** You must listen carefully to the idea and suspend all disbelief. You must identify all the ways in which the idea may appeal to different audiences and all the reasons for believing the idea. The believing game can be difficult, even frightening, if you are asked to believe an idea that strikes you as false or threatening.
- **As a doubter, your role is to be judgmental and critical, finding fault with an idea.** The doubting game is the opposite of the believing game. You do your best to find counterexamples and inconsistencies that undermine the idea you are examining. Again, it can be threatening to doubt ideas that you instinctively want to believe.

When you play the believing and doubting game with an assertion, simply write two different chunks, one chunk arguing for the assertion (the believing game) and one chunk opposing it (the doubting game). Freewrite both chunks, letting your ideas flow without censoring. Or, alternatively, make an idea map with believing and doubting branches. Here is how student writer Trudie Makens played the believing and doubting game with the assertion "Fast-food workers should be paid $15 per hour."

Trudie 's Believing and Doubting Game

Believing: I doubt anyone strives to become a full-time fast-food worker, but many people become stuck in those jobs and can't advance because they don't have a college education or because there are no better jobs available. Sometimes the workers are college students, so an increase in minimum pay would help them not accrue so much debt and perhaps have more time to study because they wouldn't have to work so many hours. But the real benefit would come to the uneducated, unskilled fast-food worker whose financial situation has led him or her to the fast-food job. The current minimum wage is barely livable. If the fast-food worker were to receive $15 per hour, there is far more of a chance for them to support themselves and their family comfortably without the stress of poverty. Even if the full-time fast-food worker does not go on to get more skills or go to college, it becomes more likely their children will be able to go to college if the fast-food worker is receiving a higher wage. Thus, the cycle of poverty as it is inherited generationally is, at least mildly, disrupted.

Doubting: If a $15 per hour minimum wage were to be implemented, the fast-food corporations would have to find ways to compensate for the profit loss. The most obvious way would be to raise food prices. If prices were to rise, fast food would no longer be affordable. This could have damaging and reversing effects on the working class who may rely on cheap fast food. Another problem is that the $15 per hour minimum wage may encourage workers to stay put in their jobs and not strive for a career. The student worker may no longer see the benefit of going into debt to get a degree and be satisfied with their current fast-food job. The effect of more desirable fast-food jobs may put pressure on other companies to raise the hourly wage of their entry-level positions. The rise in wage may, again, have the ripple effect of higher-priced products, thus reducing sales and forcing these companies to lay off some workers. No matter what scenario is dreamt up, it would seem that raising the minimum wage to $15 per hour, even if just for fast-food workers, might have damaging effects on the economy that would diminish any benefits or advantages that theoretically come from receiving a higher wage.

Although Trudie sees the injustice of paying low wages to fast-food workers, she also sees that paying such workers $15 per hour might raise the cost of food, reduce the number of jobs available, or have other negative consequences. Playing the believing and doubting game has helped her articulate her dilemma and see the issue in more complex terms.

■ ■ ■ **FOR WRITING AND DISCUSSION** **Playing the Believing and Doubting Game** MyWritingLab™

Individual task: Choose one or more of the following controversial claims and play the believing and doubting game with it, through either freewriting or idea mapping.

1. A student should report a fellow student who is cheating on an exam or plagiarizing an essay.
2. Federal law should forbid the purchase of assault weapons or high-capacity magazines.
3. Athletes should be allowed to take steroids and human growth hormone under a doctor's supervision.
4. Illegal immigrants already living in the United States should be granted amnesty and placed on a fast track to U.S. citizenship.

Group task: Working in pairs, in small groups, or as a whole class, share your results with classmates. ■ ■ ■

Reading Texts Rhetorically

2.2 To read sources rhetorically by analyzing a text's genre, purpose, and degree of advocacy

Once you become engaged with an issue, you will typically research it to understand the various voices in the conversation, the points of disagreement, the uses of evidence and counter-evidence, and the underlying assumptions and beliefs of different stakeholders. When you find these sources yourself, you will need the skills of library, database, and Web research taught in Part Five of this text. Often, however, the sources you read may be supplied for you in an anthology, textbook, course pack, or course Web site. In this section, we focus on the skills of reading sources rhetorically by analyzing their genre, their author's purpose and intended audience, and the text's degree of advocacy. In later chapters, we discuss rhetorical reading in more depth: Chapter 5 teaches the concept of "angle of vision" based on the way an argumentative text selects and frames evidence; and Chapter 8 teaches you how to write a rhetorical analysis of a text.

Genres of Argument

To situate an argument rhetorically, you should know something about its genre. A *genre* is a recurring type or pattern of argument such as a letter to the editor, a political cartoon, or the home page of an advocacy Web site. Genres are often categorized by recurring features, formats, and styles. The genre of any given argument helps determine its length, tone, sentence complexity, level of informality or formality, use of visuals, kinds of evidence, and the presence or absence of documentation.

When you read arguments reprinted in a textbook such as this one, you lose clues about the argument's original genre. (You should therefore note the information about genre provided in our introductions to readings.) Likewise, you can lose clues about genre when you download articles from the Internet or from licensed databases such as LexisNexis or ProQuest. When you do your own research, you therefore need to be aware of the original genre of the text you are reading—to know, for example, whether the piece was originally a newspaper editorial, a blog, a peer-reviewed scholarly article, or something else.

In the following chart we identify most of the genres of argument through which readers and writers carry on the conversations of a democracy.

Genres of Argument

Genre	Explanation and Examples	Stylistic Features
Personal correspondence	▪ Letters or e-mail messages ▪ Often sent to specific decision makers (complaint letter, request for an action)	▪ Style can range from a formal business letter to an informal note
Letters to the editor	▪ Published in newspapers and some magazines ▪ Provide a forum for citizens to voice views on public issues	▪ Very short (fewer than three hundred words) and time sensitive ▪ Can be summaries of longer arguments, but often focus in "sound bite" style on one point
Newspaper editorials and op-ed pieces	▪ Published on the editorial or op-ed ("opposite-editorial") pages ▪ Editorials promote views of the newspaper owners/editors ▪ Often written in response to political events or social problems in the news	▪ Usually short (500–1,000 words) ▪ Vary from explicit thesis-driven arguments to implicit arguments with stylistic flair ▪ Have a journalistic style (short paragraphs) without detailed evidence ▪ Sources usually not documented

Genre	Explanation and Examples	Stylistic Features
Blogs and postings to chat rooms and electronic bulletin boards	▨ Web-published commentaries, usually on specific topics and often intended to influence public opinion ▨ Blogs (Web logs) are gaining influence as alternative commentaries to the established media	▨ Often blend styles of journalism, personal narrative, and formal argument ▨ Often difficult to determine identity and credentials of blogger
Articles in public affairs or niche magazines	▨ Reflect a wide range of perspectives ▨ Usually written by staff writers or freelancers ▨ Appear in public affairs magazines such as *National Review* or *The Progressive* or in niche magazines for special-interest groups such as *Rolling Stone* (popular culture), *Minority Business Entrepreneur* (business), or *The Advocate* (gay and lesbian issues) ▨ Often reflect the political point of view of the magazine	▨ Often provide hyperlinks to related sites on the Web ▨ Frequently include narrative elements rather than explicit thesis-and-reasons organization ▨ Often provide well-researched coverage of various perspectives on a public issue
Articles in scholarly journals	▨ Peer-reviewed articles published by nonprofit academic journals subsidized by universities or scholarly societies ▨ Characterized by scrupulous attention to completeness and accuracy in treatment of data	▨ Usually employ a formal academic style ▨ Include academic documentation and bibliographies ▨ May reflect the biases, methods, and strategies associated with a specific school of thought or theory within a discipline
Legal briefs and court decisions	▨ Written by attorneys or judges ▨ "Friend-of-the-court" briefs are often published by stakeholders to influence appeals courts ▨ Court decisions explain the reasoning of justices on civic cases (and often include minority opinions)	▨ Usually written in legalese, but use a logical reasons-and-evidence structure ▨ Friend-of-the-court briefs are sometimes aimed at popular audiences

(Continued)

Genre	Explanation and Examples	Stylistic Features
Organizational white papers	▪ In-house documents or PowerPoint presentations aimed at influencing organizational policy or decisions or giving informed advice to clients ▪ Sometimes written for external audiences to influence public opinion favorable to the organization ▪ External white papers are often posted on Web sites or sent to legislators	▪ Usually desktop or Web published ▪ Often include graphics and other visuals ▪ Vary in style from the dully bureaucratic (satirized in *Dilbert* cartoons) to the cogent and persuasive
Public affairs advocacy advertisements	▪ Published as posters, fliers, Web pages, or paid advertisements ▪ Condensed verbal/visual arguments aimed at influencing public opinion ▪ Often have explicit bias and ignore alternative views	▪ Use succinct "sound bite" style ▪ Employ document design, bulleted lists, and visual elements (graphics, photographs, or drawings) for rhetorical effect
Advocacy Web sites	▪ Usually identified by the extension ".org" in the Web site address ▪ Often created by well-financed advocacy groups such as the NRA (National Rifle Association) or PETA (People for the Ethical Treatment of Animals) ▪ Reflect the bias of the site owner	▪ Often contain many layers with hyperlinks to other sites ▪ Use visuals and verbal text to create an immediate visceral response favorable to the site owner's views ▪ Ethically responsible sites announce their bias and purpose in an "About Us" or "Mission Statement" link on the home page
Visual arguments	▪ Political cartoons, usually drawn by syndicated cartoonists ▪ Other visual arguments (photographs, drawings, graphics, ads), usually accompanied by verbal text	▪ Make strong emotional appeals, often reducing complex issues to one powerful perspective (see Chapter 9)

Genre	Explanation and Examples	Stylistic Features
Speeches and PowerPoint presentations	▪ Political speeches, keynote speeches at professional meetings, informal speeches at hearings, interviews, business presentations ▪ Often made available via transcription in newspapers or on Web sites ▪ In business or government settings, often accompanied by PowerPoint slides	▪ Usually organized clearly with highlighted claim, supporting reasons, and transitions ▪ Accompanying PowerPoint slides designed to highlight structure, display evidence in graphics, mark key points, and sometimes provide humor
Documentary films	▪ Formerly nonfiction reporting, documentary films now range widely from efforts to document reality objectively to efforts to persuade viewers to adopt the filmmaker's perspective or take action ▪ Usually cost less to produce than commercial films and lack special effects ▪ Cover topics such as art, science, and economic, political, environmental, and military crises	▪ Often use extended visual arguments, combined with interviews and voice-overs, to influence as well as inform viewers ▪ The filmmaker's angle of vision may dominate, or his or her perspective and values may be more subtle

Authorial Purpose and Audience

A democratic society depends on the lively exchange of ideas—people with stakes in issues and different perspectives advocating for their positions. In reconstructing the rhetorical context of an argument, consider how any given writer is spurred to write by a motivating occasion and by the desire to change the views of a particular audience. Individuals often write arguments addressing personal or workplace issues. For public issues, the following list identifies the wide range of writers, as well as cartoonists, filmmakers, and others, who are apt to produce arguments.

▪ **Lobbyists and advocacy groups.** Lobbyists and advocacy groups commit themselves to a cause, often with passion, and produce avidly partisan arguments aimed at persuading voters, legislators, government agencies, and other decision makers. They often maintain advocacy Web sites, buy advertising space in newspapers and magazines, and lobby legislators face-to-face.

■ **Legislators, political candidates, and government officials.** Whenever new laws, regulations, or government policies are proposed, staffers do research and write white papers recommending positions on an issue. Often these are available on the Web.

■ **Business professionals, labor union leaders, and bankers.** Business spokespeople often try to influence public opinion in ways that support corporate or business interests, whereas labor union officials support wage structures favorable to union members. Typically businesspeople produce "corporate image" advertisements, send white papers to legislators, or write op-ed pieces that frame issues from a business perspective, whereas labor unions produce arguments favorable to workers.

■ **Lawyers and judges.** Many controversial issues are entangled in legal matters. Lawyers write briefs supporting their clients' cases. Sometimes lawyers or legal experts not directly connected to a case, particularly law professors, file "friend-of-the-court" briefs aimed at influencing the decision of judges. Finally, judges write court opinions explaining their decisions on a case.

■ **Media commentators.** Many controversial issues are in the news and attract the attention of media commentators (journalists, editorial writers, syndicated columnists, bloggers, political cartoonists) who write articles and blogs or op-ed pieces on the issue or produce editorial cartoons, filtering their arguments through the perspective of their own political views.

■ **Professional freelance or staff writers.** Some of the most thoughtful analyses of public issues are composed by freelance or staff writers for public forum magazines such as *Atlantic Monthly*, *The Nation*, *Ms.*, *The National Review*, *The New Yorker*, or for online news sites or blogs such as *The Daily Kos* or *Little Green Footballs*. These can range from in-depth background pieces to arguments with a highly persuasive aim.

■ **Think tanks.** Because today many political, economic, and social issues are very complex, policy makers and commentators often rely on research institutions or think tanks to supply statistical studies and in-depth investigation of problems. These think tanks range across the political spectrum, from conservative (the Hoover Institute, the Heritage Foundation) or libertarian (the Cato Institute) to the centrist or liberal (the Brookings Institution, the Pew Foundation, the Economic Policy Institute). They usually maintain many-layered Web sites that include background on research writers, recent publications, and archives of past publications, including policy statements and white papers.

■ **Scholars and academics.** College professors play a public role through their scholarly research, contributing data, studies, and analyses to public debates. Scholarly research differs substantially from advocacy argument in its systematic attempt to arrive at the best answers to questions based on the full examination of relevant data. Scholarly research is usually published in refereed academic journals rather than in popular magazines.

■ **Independent and commercial filmmakers.** Testifying to the growing popularity of film and its power to involve people in issues, documentary filmmakers often reflect on issues of the day, and commercial filmmakers often embed arguments within their dramatic storytelling. The global film industry is adding international perspectives as well.

- **Citizens and students.** Engaged citizens influence social policy through letters, contributions to advocacy Web sites, guest editorials for newspapers, blogs, and speeches in public forums. Students also write for university communities, present their work at undergraduate research conferences, and influence public opinion by writing to political leaders and decision makers.

Determining Degree of Advocacy

As you read any given source connected to your issue, try to determine whether it is a background piece that provides the context for an issue, an overview article that tries to summarize the various positions in the controversy, or an argument that supports a position. If it is an argument, also try to determine its degree of advocacy along the continuum from "truth seeking" to "persuasion" shown in Figure 1.5 (page 11). It is important to know, for example, whether a blog that you are reading appears on Daily Kos (a liberal blog site) or on Little Green Footballs (a conservative blog site). Particularly pay attention to how an argument selects and frames evidence—a rhetorical reading skill that we cover in depth in Chapter 5, pages 95–101.

The background we have just provided about the genres of argument, a writer's purpose and audience, and a text's degree of advocacy will help you situate arguments in their rhetorical context. When you encounter any argumentative text, whether reprinted in a textbook or retrieved through your own library and Web research, use the following guide questions to help you read the text rhetorically. This same skill is covered in more depth in Chapter 8, pages 154–159.

Questions for Reading Texts Rhetorically

1. What genre of argument is this? How do the conventions of that genre help determine the depth, complexity, and even appearance of the argument?
2. Who is the author? What are the author's credentials and what is his or her investment in the issue?
3. What audience is he or she writing for?
4. What motivating occasion prompted the writing? The motivating occasion could be a current event, a crisis, pending legislation, a recently published alternative view, or another ongoing problem.
5. What is the author's purpose? The purpose could range from strong advocacy to inquiring truth seeker (analogous to the continuum from persuasion to truth seeking discussed in Chapter 1, page 11).
6. What information about the publication or source (magazine, newspaper, advocacy Web site) helps explain the writer's perspective or the structure and style of the argument?

7. What is the writer's angle of vision? By angle of vision, we mean the filter, lens, or selective seeing through which the writer is approaching the issue. What is left out from this argument? What does this author not see? (Chapter 5, pages 95–101, discusses how angle of vision operates in the selection and framing of evidence.)

This rhetorical knowledge becomes important in helping you select a diversity of voices and genres of argument when you are exploring an issue. Note how Trudie Makens makes use of her awareness of rhetorical context in her exploratory paper on pages 44–50.

■ ■ ■   **FOR CLASS DISCUSSION**   Placing Readings in Their Rhetorical Context

Find two recent arguments on the subject of minimum wage or on another subject specified by your instructor. Your arguments should (1) represent different genres and (2) represent different kinds of arguers (syndicated newspaper columnists, bloggers, freelance magazine writers, scholars, and so forth). You can find your arguments in any of these places:

- In magazines: news commentary/public affairs magazines or niche magazines
- On the Web: on Web sites for think tanks, advocacy organizations, or blogs
- In newspapers: local, regional, or national

For each argument, answer the "Questions for Reading Texts Rhetorically" on page 31. Then share your findings with classmates.   ■ ■ ■

Reading to Believe an Argument's Claims

2.3 To read to believe an argument's claims

A powerful strategy for reading an argument rhetorically is to follow the spirit of the believing and doubting game, beginning with "believing." When you read to believe an argument, you practice what psychologist Carl Rogers calls *empathic listening*. Empathic listening requires that you see the world through the author's eyes, temporarily adopt the author's beliefs and values, and suspend your scepticism and biases in order to hear what the author is saying.

To illustrate what we mean by reading to believe, we will continue with our example of raising the minimum wage, a highly controversial issue. The following article, "The Pay Is Too Damn Low," is by James Surowiecki, an American journalist who writes the "Financial Page" column in *The New Yorker*, a magazine with a liberal perspective. This article appeared in *The New Yorker* in August 2013. Please read this article carefully in preparation for the exercises and examples that follow.

The Pay Is Too Damn Low

JAMES SUROWIECKI

A few weeks ago, Washington, D.C., passed a living-wage bill designed to make Walmart pay its workers a minimum of $12.50 an hour. Then President Obama called on Congress to raise the federal minimum wage (which is currently $7.25 an hour). McDonald's was widely derided for releasing a budget to help its employees plan financially, since that only underscored how brutally hard it is to live on a McDonald's wage. And last week fast-food workers across the country staged walkouts, calling for an increase in their pay to fifteen dollars an hour. Low-wage earners have long been the hardest workers to organize and the easiest to ignore. Now they're front-page news.

The workers' grievances are simple: low wages, few (if any) benefits, and little full-time work. In inflation-adjusted terms, the minimum wage, though higher than it was a decade ago, is still well below its 1968 peak (when it was worth about $10.70 an hour in today's dollars), and it's still poverty-level pay. To make matters worse, most fast-food and retail work is part time, and the weak job market has eroded what little bargaining power low-wage workers had: their earnings actually fell between 2009 and last year, according to the National Employment Law Project.

Still, the reason this has become a big political issue is not that the jobs have changed; it's that the people doing the jobs have. Historically, low-wage work tended to be done either by the young or by women looking for part-time jobs to supplement family income. As the historian Bethany Moreton has shown, Walmart in its early days sought explicitly to hire underemployed married women. Fast-food workforces, meanwhile, were dominated by teenagers. Now, though, plenty of family breadwinners are stuck in these jobs. That's because, over the past three decades, the U.S. economy has done a poor job of creating good middle-class jobs; five of the six fastest-growing job categories today pay less than the median wage. That's why, as a recent study by the economists John Schmitt and Janelle Jones has shown, low-wage workers are older and better educated than ever. More important, more of them are relying on their paychecks not for pin money or to pay for Friday-night dates but, rather, to support families. Forty years ago, there was no expectation that fast-food or discount-retail jobs would provide a living wage, because these were not jobs that, in the main, adult heads of household did. Today, low-wage workers provide 46 percent of their family's income. It is that change which is driving the demand for higher pay.

The situation is the result of a tectonic shift in the American economy. In 1960, the country's biggest employer, General Motors, was also its most profitable company and one of its best-paying. It had high profit margins and real pricing power, even as it was paying its workers union wages. And it was not alone: firms such as Ford, Standard Oil, and Bethlehem Steel employed huge numbers of well-paid workers while earning big profits. Today, the country's biggest employers are retailers and fast-food chains, almost all of which have built their businesses on low pay—they've striven to keep wages down and unions out—and low prices.

5   This complicates things, in part because of the nature of these businesses. They make plenty of money, but most have slim profit margins: Walmart and Target earn between three and four cents on the dollar; a typical McDonald's franchise restaurant earns around six cents on the dollar before taxes, according to an analysis from Janney Capital Markets. In fact, the combined profits of all the major retailers, restaurant chains, and supermarkets in the Fortune 500 are smaller than the profits of

Apple alone. Yet Apple employs just 76,000 people, while the retailers, supermarkets, and restaurant chains employ 5.6 million. The grim truth of those numbers is that low wages are a big part of why these companies are able to stay profitable while offering low prices. Congress is currently considering a bill increasing the minimum wage to $10.10 over the next three years. That's an increase that the companies can easily tolerate, and it would make a significant difference in the lives of low-wage workers. But that's still a long way from turning these jobs into the kind of employment that can support a middle-class family. If you want to accomplish that, you have to change the entire way these companies do business. Above all, you have to get consumers to accept significantly higher, and steadily rising, prices. After decades in which we've grown used to cheap stuff, that won't be easy.

Realistically, then, a higher minimum wage can be only part of the solution. We also need to expand the earned-income tax credit and strengthen the social-insurance system, including child care and health care (the advent of Obamacare will help in this regard). Fast-food jobs in Germany and the Netherlands aren't much better-paid than in the United States, but a stronger safety net makes workers much better off. We also need many more of the "middle-class jobs" we're always hearing about. A recent McKinsey report suggested that the government should invest almost a trillion dollars over the next five years in repairing and upgrading the national infrastructure, which seems like a good place to start. And we really need the economy as a whole to grow faster, because that would both increase the supply of good jobs and improve the bargaining power of low-wage workers. As Jared Bernstein, an economist at the Center for Budget and Policy Priorities told me, "The best friend that low-wage workers have is a strong economy and a tight job market." It isn't enough to make bad jobs better. We need to create better jobs.

Summary Writing as a Way of Reading to Believe

One way to show that you have listened well to an article is to summarize its argument in your own words. A summary (also called an *abstract,* a *précis,* or a *synopsis*) presents only a text's major points and eliminates supporting details. Writers often incorporate summaries of other writers' views into their own arguments, either to support their own views or to represent alternative views that they intend to oppose. (When opposing someone else's argument, writers often follow the template "Although X contends that [summary of X's argument], I argue that _____.") Summaries can be any length, depending on the writer's purpose, but usually they range from several sentences to one or two paragraphs. To maintain your own credibility, your summary should be as neutral and fair to that piece as possible.

To help you write an effective summary, we recommend the following steps:

Step 1: *Read the argument for general meaning.* Don't judge it. Put your objections aside; just follow the writer's meaning, trying to see the issue from the writer's perspective. Try to adopt the writer's values and belief system. Walk in the writer's shoes.

Step 2: *Reread the article slowly, writing brief* does *and* says *statements for each paragraph (or group of closely connected paragraphs).* A *does* statement identifies a paragraph's function, such as "summarizes an opposing view," "introduces a supporting reason," "gives an example," or "uses statistics to support the previous point."

A *says* statement summarizes a paragraph's content. Your challenge in writing *says* statements is to identify the main idea in each paragraph and translate that idea into your own words, most likely condensing it at the same time. This process may be easier with an academic article that uses long, developed paragraphs headed by clear topic sentences than with more informal, journalistic articles that use shorter, less developed paragraphs. What follows are *does* and *says* statements for the first three paragraphs of Surowiecki's article:

Does/Says Analysis of Surowiecki's Article

Paragraph 1: *Does:* Gives examples of recent news stories about protests of low-wage workers. *Says:* Hard-to-organize, low-wage earners are now in the news demanding an increase in the minimum wage.

Paragraph 2: *Does:* Provides details about the workers' grievances. *Says*: A weakening job market combined with low wages, lack of benefits, and mainly part-time hours keeps low-wage workers at poverty levels.

Paragraph 3: *Does:* Explains the changing demographics of those who hold low-wage jobs. *Says*: In the past, minimum-wage jobs were held primarily by teenagers or by women desiring part-time work to supplement family incomes, but today many primary breadwinners depend on minimum-wage jobs to support a family.

■ ■ ■ **FOR CLASS DISCUSSION** *Writing Does/Says Statements*

Working individually or in small groups, write *does* and *says* statements for the ■ ■ ■ remaining paragraphs of Surowiecki's article.

Step 3: *Examine your* does *and* says *statements to determine the major sections of the argument.* Create a list of the major points (and subpoints) that must appear in a summary in order to represent that argument accurately. If you are visually oriented, you may prefer to make a diagram, flowchart, or scratch outline of the sections of Surowiecki's argument.

Step 4: *Turn your list, outline, flowchart, or diagram into a prose summary.* Typically, writers do this in one of two ways. Some start by joining all their *says* statements into a lengthy paragraph-by-paragraph summary and then prune it and streamline it. They combine ideas into sentences and then revise those sentences to make them clearer and more tightly structured. Others start with a one-sentence summary of the argument's thesis and major supporting reasons and then flesh it out with more supporting ideas. Your goal is to be as neutral and objective as possible by keeping your own response to the writer's ideas out of your summary. To be fair to the writer, you also need to cover all the writer's main points and give them the same emphasis as in the original article.

Step 5: *Revise your summary until it is the desired length and is sufficiently clear, concise, and complete.* Your goal is to spend your words wisely, making every word count. In a summary of several hundred words, you will often need transitions to indicate structure and create a coherent flow of ideas: "Surowiecki's second point is that…," or "Surowiecki concludes by…." However, don't waste words with meaningless transitions such as "Surowiecki goes on to say…." When you incorporate a summary into your own essay, you must distinguish that author's views from your own by using *attributive tags* (expressions such as "Surowiecki asserts" or "according to Surowiecki"). You must also put any directly borrowed wording in quotation marks. Finally, you must cite the original author using appropriate conventions for documenting sources.

What follows are two summaries of Surowiecki's article—a one-paragraph version and a one-sentence version—by student writer Trudie Makens. Trudie's one-paragraph version illustrates the MLA documentation system, in which page numbers for direct quotations are placed in parentheses after the quotation and complete bibliographic information is placed in a Works Cited list at the end of the paper.

Trudie's One-Paragraph Summary of Surowiecki's Argument

In his *New Yorker* article "The Pay Is Too Damn Low," James Surowiecki analyzes the grievances of workers at fast-food franchises, Walmart, or Target. In the past, it didn't matter that these jobs were low-pay, part-time, and without benefits because they were held mainly by teenagers or married women seeking to supplement a husband's wages. But today, says Surowiecki, a growing number of primary breadwinners rely on these poverty-level wages to support families. The problem stems from a "tectonic shift in the American economy." While in 1960, "firms such as Ford, Standard Oil, and Bethlehem Steel employed huge numbers of well-paid workers while earning big profits," nowadays America's biggest employers are fast-food and retail companies with low profit margins. These companies depend on low-wage workers to keep prices cheap for the American consumer. Paying living wages to workers would completely change the business model, resulting in steadily rising prices. According to Surowiecki raising the minimum wage is only one tool for fighting poverty. America also needs to create a social insurance system like that of Germany or the Netherlands. Surowiecki calls for an increase in earned income tax credit, universal health insurance, affordable child care, and investment of almost a trillion dollars in infrastructure to create good middle-class jobs.

Work Cited

Surowiecki, James. "The Pay Is Too Damn Low." *The New Yorker,* 12 Aug. 2013, www.newyorker.com/magazine/2013/08/12/the-pay-is-too-damn-low.

Trudie's One-Sentence Summary of Surowiecki's Argument

In his *New Yorker* article, "The Pay Is Too Damn Low," James Surowiecki argues that raising the minimum wage is only a partial solution to the problem of poverty and needs to be supplemented with a European-style social security network including an increase in earned income tax credit, universal health insurance, affordable child care, and investment of almost a trillion dollars in infrastructure to create good middle-class jobs.

Practicing Believing: Willing Your Own Belief in the Writer's Views

Although writing an accurate summary of an argument shows that you have listened to it effectively and understood it, summary writing by itself doesn't mean that you have actively tried to enter the writer's worldview. Before we turn in the next section to doubting an argument, we want to stress the importance of believing it. Rhetorician Peter Elbow reminds us that before we critique a text, we should try to "dwell with" and "dwell in" the writer's ideas—play the believing game—in order to "earn" our right to criticize.* He asserts, and we agree, that this use of the believing game to engage with strange, threatening, or unfamiliar views can lead to a deeper understanding and may provide a new vantage point on our own knowledge, assumptions, and values. To believe a writer and dwell with his or her ideas, find places in the text that resonate positively for you, look for values and beliefs you hold in common (however few), and search for personal experiences and values that affirm his or her argument.

Reading to Doubt

2.4 To read to doubt an argument's claims

After willing yourself to believe an argument, will yourself to doubt it. Turn your mental energies toward raising objections, asking questions, expressing skepticism, and withholding your assent. When you read as a doubter, you question the writer's logic, the writer's evidence and assumptions, and the writer's strategies for developing the argument. You also think about what is *not* in the argument by noting what the author has glossed over, left unexplained, or left out entirely. You add a new layer of marginal notes, articulating what is bothering you, demanding proof, doubting evidence, challenging the author's assumptions and values, and so forth. Writing your own notes helps you read a text actively, bringing your own voice into conversation with the author.

■ ■ ■ **FOR CLASS DISCUSSION** Raising Doubts about Surowiecki's Argument

Return now to Surowiecki's article and read it skeptically. Raise questions, offer objections, and express doubts. Then, working as a class or in small groups, list all the doubts you have about Surowiecki's argument.   ■ ■ ■

Now that you have doubted Surowiecki's article, compare your questions and doubts to some raised by student writer Trudie Makens.

Trudie's Doubts about Surowiecki's Article

- In his second paragraph, Surowiecki outlines three workers' grievances: "low wages, few (if any) benefits, and little full-time work." But increasing the minimum wage addresses only one of the grievances. A higher minimum wage might make it less likely for a worker to receive benefits or obtain full-time rather than part-time work. Moreover, with a higher wage, large companies may try to maintain profits by cutting jobs.

---

*Peter Elbow, "Bringing the Rhetoric of Assent and the Believing Game Together—Into the Classroom," *College English,* 67.4 (March 2005), 389.

- Surowiecki asserts that large retailers and fast-food companies would absorb the cost of a higher minimum wage by raising prices on consumer goods. But if low-wage workers are also consumers, won't higher prices on previously cheap products defeat the benefits of a higher wage?

- Though he ends his article by calling for a multifaceted solution to poverty, he does so without offering a way to accomplish this goal. Where would the money come from in order to expand the earned income tax credit, strengthen the United States' current social insurance system, or invest in infrastructure? Further, how would the United States effectively implement and sustain these nationwide social programs without upsetting the already delicate economy?

- In his article Surowiecki mentions several studies, but there is no way to tell if these are widely respected studies or controversial ones. Would other studies, for example, conclude that low-wage workers today are responsible for 46 percent of their family's income?

These are only some of the objections that might be raised against Surowiecki's argument. The point here is that doubting as well as believing is a key part of the exploratory process and purpose. *Believing* takes you into the views of others so that you can expand your views and perhaps see them differently and modify or even change them. *Doubting* helps protect you from becoming overpowered by others' arguments and teaches you to stand back, consider, and weigh points carefully. It also leads you to new questions and points you might want to explore further.

Thinking Dialectically

2.5 To delay closure by thinking dialectically

This chapter's final strategy—thinking dialectically to bring texts into conversation with each other—encompasses all the previous strategies and can have a powerful effect on your growth as a thinker and arguer. The term *dialectic* is associated with the German philosopher Georg Wilhelm Friedrich Hegel, who postulated that each thesis prompts an opposing thesis (which he calls an "antithesis") and that the conflict between these views can lead thinkers to a new claim (a "synthesis") that incorporates aspects of both views. Dialectic thinking is the philosophical underpinning of the believing and doubting game, pushing us toward new and better ideas. As Peter Elbow puts it, "Because it's so hard to let go of an idea we are holding (or more to the point, an idea that's holding us), our best hope for leverage in learning to doubt such ideas is *to take on different ideas.*"*

This is why expert thinkers actively seek out alternative views—not to shout them down but to listen to them. If you were an arbitrator, you wouldn't settle a dispute between A and B on the basis of A's testimony only. You would also insist on hearing B's side of the story (and perhaps also C's and D's if they are stakeholders in the dispute). Dialectic thinking means playing ideas against each other, creating a tension that forces you to keep expanding your perspective. It helps you achieve the "mingling of minds" that we discussed in the introduction to this chapter.

---

*Peter Elbow, "Bringing the Rhetoric of Assent and the Believing Game Together—Into the Classroom," *College English* 67.4 (March 2005), 390.

As you listen to differing views, try to identify sources of disagreement among arguers, which often fall into two categories: (1) disagreement about the facts of the case and (2) disagreement about underlying values, beliefs, or assumptions. We saw these disagreements in Chapter 1 in the conversation about phthalates in children's toys. At the level of facts, disputants disagreed about the amount of phthalates a baby might ingest when chewing a rubber toy or about the quantity of ingested phthalates needed to be harmful. At the level of values, disputants disagreed on the amount of risk that must be present in a free market economy before a government agency should ban a substance. As you try to determine your own position on an issue, consider what research you might have to do to resolve questions of fact; also try to articulate your own underlying values, beliefs, and assumptions.

As you consider multiple points of view on an issue, try using the following questions to promote dialectic thinking:

Questions to Promote Dialectic Thinking

1. What would writer A say to writer B?
2. After I read writer A, I thought _____; however, after I read writer B, my thinking on this issue had changed in these ways: _____.
3. To what extent do writer A and writer B disagree about facts and interpretations of facts?
4. To what extent do writer A and writer B disagree about underlying beliefs, assumptions, and values?
5. Can I find any areas of agreement, including shared values and beliefs, between writer A and writer B?
6. What new, significant questions do these texts raise for me?
7. After I have wrestled with the ideas in these two texts, what are my current views on this issue?

Responding to questions like these—either through class discussion or through exploratory writing—can help you work your way into a public controversy. Earlier in this chapter you read James Surowiecki's article expressing liberal support for raising the minimum wage and enacting other government measures to help the poor. Now consider an article expressing a quite different point of view, an opinion piece written by Michael Saltsman, the research director at the Employment Policies Institute—a pro-business, free market think tank opposed to raising the minimum wage. It appeared in *The Huffington Post* on April 26, 2013. We ask you to read the article and then use the preceding questions to stimulate dialectic thinking about Surowiecki versus Saltsman.

■ ■ ■   **FOR WRITING AND DISCUSSION** Practicing Dialectic Thinking with   MyWritingLab™
                                                            Two Articles

Individual task: Freewrite your responses to the preceding questions, in which Surowiecki is writer A and Saltsman is writer B. **Group task:** Working as a whole class or in small groups, share your responses to the two articles, guided by the dialectic questions.   ■ ■ ■

To Help the Poor, Move Beyond "Minimum" Gestures

MICHAEL SALTSMAN

Actor and director Ben Affleck made news this week with the announcement that he'll spend five days living on just $1.50—the U.S.-dollar daily equivalent of extreme poverty, according to the Global Poverty Project.

Affleck's heart is in the right place, but his actions won't provide a measurable benefit for people who actually live in poverty. On that score, Affleck's actions are not unlike a series of recently-introduced proposals to raise the federal minimum wage—well-intentioned but ultimately empty gestures that will do little to raise poor families out of poverty.

For poverty-reducing policies to benefit the poor, the benefits first have to be properly targeted to people living in poverty. On this count, a higher minimum wage fails miserably. Census Bureau data shows that over 60 percent of people living below the poverty line don't work. They don't need a raise—they need a job.

Among those who do earn the minimum wage, a majority actually don't live in poverty. According to a forthcoming Employment Policies Institute analysis of Census Bureau data, over half of those covered by President Obama's $9 proposal live in households with income at least twice the poverty level—and one-third are in households with an income three times or greater than the poverty level.

5   That's because nearly 60 percent of affected employees aren't single earners, according to the EPI report—they're living in households where a parent or a spouse often earns an income far above the minimum. (The average family income of this group is $50,789.) By contrast, we found that only nine percent of people covered by President Obama's $9 minimum wage are single parents with children.

It's for reasons like these that the majority of academic research shows little connection between a higher minimum wage and reductions in poverty. For instance, economists from American and Cornell Universities examined data from the 28 states that raised their minimum wages between 2003 and 2007, and found no associated reductions in poverty.

Of course, poor targeting isn't the only problem. The vast majority of economic research—including 85 percent of the most credible studies from the last two decades—finds that job loss for the least-skilled employees follows on the heels of minimum wage hikes.

That's why better-targeted policies like the Earned Income Tax Credit (EITC) deserve the support of politicians and public figures who want to do something about poverty. It's been empirically proven to boost employment and incomes, without the unintended consequences of a wage hike. Accounting for the EITC, the full-time hourly wage for many minimum wage earners is already above the $9 figure that President Obama has proposed.

Three Ways to Foster Dialectic Thinking

In this concluding section, we suggest three ways to stimulate and sustain the process of dialectic thinking: Effective discussions in class, over coffee, or online; a reading log in which you make texts speak to each other; or a formal exploratory essay. We'll look briefly at each in turn.

Effective Discussions   Good, rich talk is one of the most powerful ways to stimulate dialectic thinking and foster a "mingling of minds." The key is to keep these discussions from being shouting matches or bully pulpits for those who like to dominate the air-time. Discussions are most productive if people are willing to express different points of view or to role-play those views for the purpose of advancing the conversation. Try Rogerian listening, in which you summarize someone else's position before you offer your own, different position. (See Chapter 7 for more explanation of Rogerian listening.) Probe deeply to discover whether disagreements are primarily about facts and evidence or about underlying values and beliefs. Be respectful of others' views, but don't hesitate to point out where you see problems or weaknesses. Good discussions can occur in class, in late-night coffee shops, or in online chat rooms or on discussion boards.

Reading Logs   In our classes, we require students to keep reading logs or journals in which they use freewriting and idea mapping to explore their ideas as they encounter multiple perspectives on an issue. One part of a journal or reading log should include summaries of each article you read. Another part should focus on your own dialectic thinking as you interact with your sources while you are reading them. Adapt the questions for promoting dialectic thinking on page 39.

A Formal Exploratory Essay   A formal exploratory essay tells the story of an intellectual journey. It is both a way of promoting dialectical thinking and a way of narrating one's struggle to negotiate multiple views. The keys to writing successful exploratory essays are: (1) choosing an issue to explore on which you don't yet have an answer or position (or on which you are open to changing your mind); (2) wrestling with an issue or problem by resisting quick, simple answers and by exploring diverse perspectives; and (3) letting your thinking evolve and your own stance on the issue grow out of this exploration.

Exploratory essays can be powerful thinking and writing experiences in their own right, but they can also be a valuable precursor to a formal argument. Many instructors assign a formal exploratory paper as the first stage of a course research project—what we might call a "thesis-seeking" stage. (The second stage is a formal argument that converts your exploratory thinking into a hierarchically organized argument using reasons and evidence to support your claim.) Although often used as part of a research project, exploratory essays can also be low-stakes reflective pieces narrating the evolution of a writer's thinking during a class discussion.

An exploratory essay includes these thinking moves and parts:

- The essay is opened and driven by the writer's issue question or research problem—not a thesis.
- The introduction to the essay presents the question and shows why it interests the writer, why it is significant, and why it is problematic rather than clear-cut or easy to resolve.

■ The body of the essay shows the writer's inquiry process. It demonstrates how the writer has kept the question open, sincerely wrestled with different views on the question, accepted uncertainty and ambiguity, and possibly redefined the question in the midst of his or her reading and reflection on multiple perspectives.

■ The body of the essay includes summaries of the different views or sources that the writer explored and often includes believing and doubting responses to them.

■ In the essay's conclusion, the writer may clarify his or her thinking and discover a thesis to be developed and supported in a subsequent argument. But the conclusion can also remain open because the writer may not have discovered his or her own position on the issue and may acknowledge the need or desire for more exploration.

One of the writing assignment options for this chapter is a formal exploratory paper. Trudie Makens's exploratory essay on pages 44–50 shows how she explored different voices in the controversy over raising the minimum wage to $15 per hour.

Conclusion

This chapter has focused on inquiry as a way to enrich your reading and writing of arguments. This chapter has offered five main strategies for deep reading: (1) Use a variety of questions and prompts to find an issue to explore; (2) read sources rhetorically by placing them in their rhetorical context; (3) read as a believer; (4) read as a doubter; and (5) think dialectically. This chapter has also shown you how to summarize an article and incorporate summaries into your own writing, using attributive tags to distinguish the ideas you are summarizing from your own. It has explained why a reading's rhetorical context (purpose, audience, and genre) must be considered in any thoughtful response to an argument. Finally, it has emphasized the importance of dialectic thinking and has offered the exploratory essay as a way to encourage wrestling with multiple perspectives rather than seeking early closure.

WRITING ASSIGNMENT   An Argument Summary or a Formal Exploratory Essay   MyWritingLab™

Option 1: An Argument Summary Write a 250-word summary of an argument selected by your instructor. Then write a one-sentence summary of the same argument. Use as models Trudie Makens's summaries of James Surowiecki's argument on raising the minimum wage (page 36).

Option 2: A Formal Exploratory Essay Write an exploratory essay in which you narrate in first-person, chronological order the evolution through time of your thinking about an issue or problem. Rather than state a thesis or claim, begin with a question or problem. Then describe your inquiry process as you worked your way through sources or different views. Follow the guidelines for an exploratory paper shown on page 43. When you cite the sources you have considered, be sure to use attributive tags so that the reader can distinguish between your own ideas and those of the sources you have summarized. If you use research sources, use MLA documentation for citing ideas and quotations and for creating a Works Cited at the end.

Organization Plan for an Exploratory Essay

Introduction (one to several paragraphs)	• Establish that your question is complex, problematic, and significant. • Show why you are interested in it. • Present relevant background on your issue. Begin with your question or build up to it, using it to end your introductory section.
Body section 1: First view or source	• Introduce your first source and show why you started with it. • Provide rhetorical context and information about it. • Summarize the source's content and argument. • Offer your response to this source, including both believing and doubting points. • Talk about what this source contributes to your understanding of your question: What did you learn? What value does this source have for you? What is missing from this source that you want to consider? Where do you want to go from here?
Body section 2: Second view or source	• Repeat the process with a new source selected to advance the inquiry. • Explain why you selected this source (to find an alternative view, pursue a subquestion, find more data, and so forth). • Summarize the source's argument. • Respond to the source's ideas. Look for points of agreement and disagreement with other sources. • Show how your cumulative reading of sources is shaping your thinking or leading to more questions.
Body sections 3, 4, 5, etc.	• Continue exploring views or sources.
Conclusion	• Wrap up your intellectual journey and explain where you are now in your thinking and how your understanding of your problem has changed. • Present your current answer to your question based on all that you have learned so far, or explain why you still can't answer your question, or explain what research you might pursue further.

Explanation and Organization

An exploratory essay could grow out of class discussion, course readings, field work and interviews, or simply the writer's role-playing of alternative views. In all cases, the purpose of an exploratory paper is not to state and defend a thesis. Instead, its purpose is to think dialectically about multiple perspectives, narrating the evolution through time of the writer's thought process. Many students are inspired by the open, "behind-the-scenes" feel of an exploratory essay. They enjoy taking readers on the same intellectual and emotional journey they have just traveled. A typical organization plan for an exploratory essay is shown on page 43. ■

Reading

What follows is Trudie Makens's exploratory essay on the subject of raising the minimum wage. Her research begins with the articles by Surowiecki and Saltsman that you have already read and discussed. She then moves off in her own direction.

Title as question indicates an exploratory purpose.

Should Fast-Food Workers Be Paid $15 per Hour?

TRUDIE MAKENS (STUDENT)

Introduction identifies the issue, explains the writer's interest in it, and acknowledges its complexity.

Having worked as a busser in a pizza restaurant, a part-time barista, and a server at a dumpling cafe, I was immediately attracted to our class discussions of minimum wage, sparked by recent protests of fast-food workers demanding pay of $15 per hour. My first job as a barista exposed me to the harsh reality of living on today's existing minimum wage as I witnessed my coworker Maria lose her home because she couldn't pay rent and support her kids at the same time. As a single mother of two, Maria had to bounce from relative to relative putting a strain on her family relations, her image of herself as an able provider, and her children. I am lucky because, as a student, I am blessed to have my family operate as a safety net for me. If I am ever short on a bill or get sick or hurt, my parents will assist me financially. Many of the individuals I have worked with do not have that same safety net. These individuals are often older and have children or are beginning a family. Understanding the hardships of minimum-wage jobs, I entered our class discussions in support of the $15/hour demand because this pay rate would give workers a living wage. However, despite my personal affinities with these workers, I also understood that raising the minimum wage might have negative consequences for our economy. I wanted to explore this issue in more depth so I decided to pose my research question as "Should fast-food workers be paid a living wage of $15 per hour?"

My exploration began with an article that our instructor assigned to the whole class: "The Pay Is Too Damn Low" by James Surowiecki from *The New Yorker*. In the past, according to Surowiecki, it didn't matter that jobs at Walmart, Target, or fast-food franchises were low-pay, part-time, and without benefits because they were held mainly by teenagers or married women seeking to supplement a husband's wages. But today, says Surowiecki, a growing number of primary breadwinners rely on these poverty-level wages to support families. The problem stems from a "tectonic shift in the American economy." While in 1960, "firms such as Ford, Standard Oil, and Bethlehem Steel employed huge numbers of well-paid workers while earning big profits," nowadays America's biggest employers are fast-food and retail companies with low profit margins. While Surowiecki acknowledges that these retail companies and food franchises depend on low-wage workers to keep prices cheap for the American consumer, he still supports increasing the minimum wage but sees it as only one tool for fighting poverty. He argues that America also needs to create a European-style safety net system and calls for an increase in earned income tax credit, universal health insurance, affordable child care, and investment of almost a trillion dollars in infrastructure to create good middle-class jobs.

Surowiecki's concluding remarks about a safety net system resonated with me. I understood that what protected me from a financial crisis was my family acting like a safety net. The government, Surowiecki argues, should perform the same function for low-wage earners through such programs as childcare and health care. He points to Germany and the Netherlands, arguing the stronger safety net put in place for workers by these European governments provides a better economic and social situation for low-wage workers, even though they are paid around the same amount as United States low-wage workers. Surowiecki also addressed some of my concerns regarding the economic consequences of implementing a living wage. Even though some low-wage jobs might be eliminated and food costs might go up, government investment in infrastructure might create more high-paying, middle-class jobs, resulting in a net benefit. But I still wasn't convinced or completely satisfied. How exactly would the government raise the money for a redesigned social insurance system? Would the country accept the needed higher taxes? While Surowiecki had convinced me that the government had

Writer states her research question.

Writer identifies her first source.

Writer summarizes the article.

Writer shows how this article has advanced her thinking by strengthening her previous mention of "safety nets."

Writer includes doubting points by identifying problems not resolved in first source.

an important role to play in creating the conditions for a living wage, I still was unclear on how the government could effectively do so without detrimentally upsetting the economy.

Writer shows rhetorical thinking by purposely seeking an argument from a business perspective; she identifies conservative credentials of author and summarizes his argument.

Writer summarizes second source.

I wanted to know more about raising the minimum wage from the business perspective, so I Googled "living wage" and found an anti-minimum wage article from Michael Saltsman, the research director of the Employment Policy Institute. The opinion piece was published online in *The Huffington Post* and entitled, "To Help the Poor, Move Beyond 'Minimum' Gestures." I also found a full-page ad from the same conservative institute depicting a robot doing the work of a fast-food employee. Saltsman believes that despite the good intentions of living wage proponents a higher federal minimum wage will do more harm than good. Within his piece, Saltsman equates the symbolic value of Ben Affleck's pledge to live five days on $1.50, "the U.S.-dollar equivalent of extreme poverty," to proposals for a higher federal minimum wage. Both, according to Saltsman, are "ultimately empty gestures" that do little to lift families out of poverty. What the poor need, Saltsman asserts, is "not a raise" but a job. Saltsman claims that over "60% of people living below the poverty line don't work" and those who do earn a minimum wage don't live in poverty households. Even if a member of the working poor were to receive a living wage, Saltsman argues, "job loss for the least-skilled employees follows on the heels of a minimum wage hike." What helps to reduce poverty, according to Saltsman, is not a higher minimum wage but the Earned Income Tax Credit, "empirically proven to boost employment and incomes" and thus providing "a measurable difference for the poor."

Writer includes both believing and doubting points.

Writer shows dialectic thinking by comparing and contrasting views of first two sources.

5   Prior to reading Saltsman, I had not fully considered the potential that workers would be laid off because it would be cheaper for businesses to use robots or other automation than to employ higher-wage workers. Though Saltsman got me thinking about the dangers of job displacement, I wasn't convinced by his argument that an increased minimum wage would primarily benefit people who didn't need it such as teenagers or second earners in an already middle-class family. I could see that an increased minimum wage wouldn't help the 60 percent of the poor who were unemployed, but I also realized that the Earned Income Tax Credit wouldn't help the unemployed either because it goes only to poor people who report income. (I Googled "earned income tax credit" just to make sure I understood how it works by giving a boost of income to poor but working tax filers.) Though Saltsman persuaded me to consider the negative economic consequences of a living wage, I wasn't convinced the living wage was entirely ineffective. I thought back to Surowiecki who, unlike Saltsman, saw a living wage as one component in a larger solution to reduce poverty. Both recommended an expanded

Earned Income Tax Credit, but Surowiecki went further and also encouraged a stronger social-insurance system in addition to a higher minimum wage. Neither article persuaded me the living wage was either fully beneficial or fully injurious. To clarify my position, I needed to do more research.

Writer again seeks sources purposefully; she shows how she found the source and places it in rhetorical context.

Writer summarizes the article.

I wanted another economist's perspective, so I typed in "economic impact and living wage" into ProQuest, an interdisciplinary research database. One of the articles that caught my attention was "Living Wage: Some Gain, Neediest Lose Out." The article was an interview with labor economist Richard Toikka by author Charles Oliver featured in *Investor's Business Daily,* a conservative financial newspaper focused on stock and bond investments. In the interview, Oliver prompts Toikka to discuss the unintended consequences of a higher minimum wage. Toikka asserts that in order to absorb the cost of a higher wage, companies seek to hire higher-skilled workers who require less training, and thus cost the company less money. With a higher wage offered, Toikka argues, more high-skilled workers, such as college students, seek these jobs, increasing "the competition low skilled workers face." Thus an increased minimum wage reduces the number of low-skilled jobs available. Toikka also makes the same argument as Saltsman, concluding that the benefits of a higher wage don't go towards the families who need it, but instead to second-earners who aren't living below the poverty line. Toikka cites a survey among labor economists asked to rate the efficiency of anti-poverty measures, and "69% said living wages weren't at all efficient in meeting the needs of poor families." The more efficient way to combat poverty, Toikka argues, is not a living wage but an expansion of the Earned Income Tax Credit.

Writer shows how the pro-business sources have complicated her initial tentative position.

Writer uses believing and doubting strategies to think dialectically, looking for a synthesis.

Putting Toikka in conversation with Saltsman, I began to understand and heed the warnings of both economists. Though well-intentioned, increasing the minimum wage by itself is not apt to reduce poverty and would ultimately injure the poor rather than helping. If a living wage does lead to heightened competition and employers slashing jobs, then perhaps a living wage is ineffective and therefore should be abandoned in favor of the Earned Income Tax Credit. So far, all the articles agreed the Earned Income Tax Credit was a good way to reduce poverty, even though it too benefits only those with jobs. Even so, I couldn't help but think that abandoning a living wage was a concession to a flawed economic system that doesn't value the working poor or the impoverished unemployed enough. I thought back to Surowiecki when he praised Germany and the Netherlands for providing a strong social insurance system that served as a safety net for those in low-wage jobs. If Europe can ensure dignity and security to its citizens, then why can't the United States? Although 69 percent of labor economists say that a living wage is an inefficient way to alleviate poverty, we don't know what they would say if the government also invested in infrastructure to create well-paying jobs. Right now, it seems from my readings, that the current market doesn't value low-wage workers. What is valued in our economy is capital, profit, and cheap goods, all of which come at the expense of millions of workers. Is the structure of the economy where wealth is unequally distributed and workers are exploited really inevitable? Or is it an economic trend that can be reversed? I wanted to believe the latter, so I returned to ProQuest to find another article addressing the economic impact of a living wage but from a pro-labor perspective.

Writer purposefully seeks a different perspective.

In my search, I found an article entitled "The Task Rabbit Economy," authored by Robert Kuttner and published in the progressive magazine *The American Prospect.* Kuttner begins by describing a successful San Francisco company whose Web site matches people who have an odd job they need done with people who will do the work for a fee. The company, named the Task Rabbit, is like an online temp agency that operates by having would-be workers bid against each other, driving the price down for their labor. Kuttner argues that Task Rabbit's business model, which produces cheap labor, is analogous to our current economy, where workers have lost "bargaining power" and work has become casual and unstable (46). Kuttner argues that this low-wage economy has produced less economic growth, less prosperity, and more unemployment than earlier eras when there was more job stability and higher wages. According to Kuttner, the claim made by labor economists that a higher minimum wage leaves low-skilled workers without a job ignores how an unregulated labor market has allowed corporations to "weaken labor...and extract abnormal profits" (47). Kuttner draws on the economy of Sweden to provide an example where a living wage, full employment, and a "deliberate effort to narrow wage gaps" has been implemented effectively (48). What's more, Kuttner addresses the concern of rising prices by citing a Demos study that found raising wages so retail workers "earned at least $25,000 a year" only cost large retailers "1 percent of the $2.17 trillion annual sales" (52). Kuttner closes out his article by emphasizing that "organized labor" is what will change the labor market, using both collective bargaining and "political force" (55).

Writer identifies next source and places it in rhetorical context.

Writer summarizes the article.

Kuttner's article moved me in a way that Toikka and Saltsman's pieces could not. Instead of accepting an economic system where low-wage workers are exploited for stockholder profits and cheap goods, Kuttner criticizes the labor market for its failure to value workers. Kuttner acknowledges that a higher minimum wage will upset the

Writer shows how this source has advanced and solidified her own thinking.

present economy, but he argues that the present economic system isn't inevitable but the result of large employers choosing to value capital over people without strong governmental policies protecting labor and the poor. Moreover, Kuttner's article illuminates the inefficiency of our economy. The studies Kuttner references reveal that the United States was better off in the years after World War II, when jobs were stable, plentiful, and paid a living wage. Most of all, I appreciated Kuttner's concluding call to action, and his assurance that such action will not lead to economic suicide but create the "dynamic, supple, and innovative" economy our nation strives for. According to Kuttner, we can choose to allow the market to continue unregulated, or, through organizing workers, we can push towards policies that value people—their rights, health, and dignity. As I read Kuttner, I wondered what current labor movements are in existence today and the progress they are making in their fight to gain rights and a living wage. I, again, turned to ProQuest.

Writer again shows purposeful search for next source.

Writer identifies next source and places it 10 in rhetorical context.

My search handed me a long list of results, but I found one article that provided a relevant look into a labor campaign organized by Walmart sales associates. Titled "Job Insecurity," the article was written by Kevin Clarke and published in the Catholic magazine *America*. Clarke begins by introducing William Fletcher, a twenty-three-year-old retail sales associate at Walmart. According to Fletcher, he loves his job and "working with the public" but, he says, he and other employees constantly struggle with "low wages, chaotic scheduling, and insensitive management." Both Fletcher and Clarke wonder why being a retail sales associate for Walmart warrants not receiving enough to "have a home, have health insurance, have all the basic things in life." In order to improve his working conditions, Fletcher joined Organization United for Respect at Walmart, or OUR Walmart. OUR Walmart, Clarke states, is "part of an emerging labor phenomenon of non-union activism against Walmart and other powerful, profitable U.S. corporations that maintain large, low paid work forces." Walmart, according to both Fletcher and Clarke, is a trend-setting company. If labor conditions improve at Walmart, other companies could follow suit. The organization draws from the tactics of "community organizing and the civil rights movement." Unfortunately, Clarke states, Walmart management continues to thwart protests or walkouts. Despite obstacles, OUR Walmart persists, marking a major moment in the contemporary labor movement. The article ends with Clarke's appeal to the Catholic social justice tradition of solidarity with the poor. He notes that Walmart sales associates depend on government support programs such as food stamps and housing assistance. He reminds his readers that our continual search for the cheapest goods makes us partially guilty for

Writer pulls together
the results of her
dialectic thinking,
which has resulted in a
synthesis.

the exploitation of workers. He urges us to shop conscientiously and thoughtfully.

I reached the end of the article feeling shocked. In lieu of everything I read from Kuttner, I was amazed that Walmart could dismiss the demands of OUR Walmart. Clarke states the owners of Walmart, the Walton family, possess "48% of Walmart stock and [are] the richest family on earth, with over $107 billion in net worth." Hearing numbers like these confirmed my forming conviction that the unregulated labor market dangerously exploits workers in order to gain cheap labor, cheap goods, and bloated profits. What's more, Walmart actively tries to scare workers from organizing—threatening to take away their jobs. Though there is much more to read and learn about the growing labor movement in the United States, Clarke's article, as well as Surowiecki, Saltsman, Toikka, and Kuttner's pieces, allowed me to round out my position on a higher minimum wage. As I end my exploratory paper, I understand that a living wage is possible and should be provided to service workers as a basic human right. But it also needs to be supplemented with the kinds of social insurance systems stressed by Surowiecki and Kuttner.

Final sentences reveal
synthesis that goes
beyond original lean-
ings in first paragraph.

Works Cited

Clarke, Kevin. "Job Insecurity." *America,* 18 Feb. 2013, americamagazine.org/issue/article/job-insecurity.

Kuttner, Robert. "The Task Rabbit Economy." *The American Prospect,* 24 Sept. 2013, pp. 45-55.

Oliver, Charles. "Living Wage: Some Gain, Neediest Lose Out." *Investor's Business Daily,* 5 Sept. 2000. *ProQuest,* 10 Jan. 2014, search.proquest.com/docview/1026806044/fulltext/DA48476F0F254E4CPQ/1?accountid=10226.

Saltsman, Michael. "To Help the Poor, Move Beyond 'Minimum' Gestures." *The Huffington Post,* 26 Apr. 2013, updated 26 June 2013, www.huffingtonpost.com/michael-saltsman/earned-income-tax-credit-minimum-wage_b_3165459.html.

Surowiecki, James. "The Pay Is Too Damn Low." *The New Yorker,* 12 Aug. 2013, p. 35.

Writer compiles an
MLA-formatted "Works
Cited" page that lists
alphabetically all the
sources discussed in
the paper.

MyWritingLab™

Visit Ch. 2 Argument as Inquiry: Reading and Exploring in *MyWritingLab* to complete the For Writing and Discussion and Writing Assignments and to test your understanding of the chapter objectives.

PART TWO
Writing an Argument

This still from the *Tomb Raider* video game series features main character Lara Croft engaged in one of her typical combats with humans, beasts, or supernatural creatures. Lara, an adventurer and archaeologist, represents both a sexualized and an empowered woman. Women and violent video games are the focus of student Carmen Tieu's argument developed in Chapters 3–5; however, Carmen explores gender roles from the perspective of a woman playing a "male" video game, *Halo*.

The Core of an Argument
A Claim with Reasons

3

What you will learn in this chapter:

3.1 To describe the key elements of classical argument

3.2 To explain the rhetorical appeals

3.3 To distinguish between issue and information questions and between genuine and pseudo-arguments

3.4 To describe the basic frame of an argument

In Part One we explained that argument combines truth seeking with persuasion. Part One, by highlighting the importance of exploration and inquiry, emphasizes the truth-seeking dimension of argument. The suggested writing assignments in Part One included a variety of exploratory tasks: freewriting, playing the believing and doubting game, and writing a formal exploratory essay. In Part Two we show you how to convert your exploratory ideas into a thesis-governed classical argument that uses effective reasons and evidence to support its claims. Each chapter in Part Two focuses on a key skill or idea needed for responsible and effective persuasion.

The Classical Structure of Argument

3.1 To describe the key elements of classical argument

Classical argument is patterned after the persuasive speeches of ancient Greek and Roman orators. In traditional Latin terminology, the main parts of a persuasive speech are the *exordium*, in which the speaker gets the audience's attention; the *narratio*, which provides needed background; the *propositio*, which is the speaker's claim or thesis; the *partitio*, which forecasts the main parts of the speech; the *confirmatio*, which presents the speaker's arguments supporting the claim; the *confutatio*, which summarizes and rebuts opposing views; and the *peroratio*, which concludes the speech by summing up the argument, calling for action, and leaving a strong, lasting impression. (Of course, you don't need to remember these tongue-twisting Latin terms. We cite them only to assure you that in writing a classical argument, you are joining a time-honored tradition that links back to the origins of democracy.)

Let's go over the same territory again using more contemporary terms. We provide an organization plan below showing the structure of a classical argument, which shows these typical sections:

▥ **The introduction.** Writers of classical argument typically begin by connecting the audience to the issue by showing how it arises out of a current event or by using an illustrative story, memorable scene, or startling statistic—something that grabs the audience's attention. They continue the introduction by focusing the issue—often by stating it directly as a question or by briefly summarizing opposing views—and providing needed background and context. They conclude the introduction by presenting their claim (thesis statement) and forecasting the argument's structure.

(continued)

Organization Plan for an Argument with a Classical Structure

• *Exordium* • *Narratio* • *Propositio* • *Partitio*	**Introduction (one to several paragraphs)**	• Attention grabber (often a memorable scene) • Explanation of issue and needed background • Writer's thesis (claim) • Forecasting passage
• *Confirmatio*	**Presentation of writer's position**	• Main body of essay • Presents and supports each reason in turn • Each reason is tied to a value or belief held by the audience
• *Confutatio*	**Summary of opposing views**	• Summary of views differing from writer's (should be fair and complete)
	Response to opposing views	• Refutes or concedes to opposing views • Shows weaknesses in opposing views • May concede to some strengths
• *Peroratio*	**Conclusion**	• Brings essay to closure • Often sums up argument • Leaves strong last impression • Often calls for action or relates topic to a larger context of issues

- **The presentation of the writer's position.** The presentation of the writer's own position is usually the longest part of a classical argument. Here writers present the reasons and evidence supporting their claims, typically choosing reasons that tie into their audience's values, beliefs, and assumptions. Usually each reason is developed in its own paragraph or sequence of paragraphs. When a paragraph introduces a new reason, writers state the reason directly and then support it with evidence or a chain of ideas. Along the way, writers guide their readers with appropriate transitions.

- **The summary and critique of alternative views.** When summarizing and responding to opposing views, writers have several options. If there are several opposing arguments, writers may summarize all of them together and then compose a single response, or they may summarize and respond to each argument in turn. As we will explain in Chapter 7, writers may respond to opposing views either by refuting them or by conceding to their strengths and shifting to a different field of values.

- **The conclusion.** Finally, in their conclusion, writers sum up their argument, often restating the stakes in the argument and calling for some kind of action, thereby creating a sense of closure and leaving a strong final impression.

In this organization, the body of a classical argument has two major sections—the one presenting the writer's own position and the other summarizing and responding to alternative views. The organization plan and our discussion have the writer's own position coming first, but it is possible to reverse that order. (In Chapter 7 we consider the factors affecting this choice.)

For all its strengths, an argument with a classical structure may not always be your most persuasive strategy. In some cases, you may be more effective by delaying your thesis, by ignoring alternative views altogether, or by showing great sympathy for opposing views (see Chapter 7). Even in these cases, however, the classical structure is a useful planning tool. Its call for a thesis statement and a forecasting statement in the introduction helps you see the whole of your argument in miniature. And by requiring you to summarize and consider opposing views, the classical structure alerts you to the limits of your position and to the need for further reasons and evidence. As we will show, the classical structure is a particularly persuasive mode of argument when you address a neutral or undecided audience.

Classical Appeals and the Rhetorical Triangle

3.2 To explain the rhetorical appeals | Besides developing a template or structure for an argument, classical rhetoricians analyzed the ways that effective speeches persuaded their audiences. They identified three kinds of persuasive appeals, which they called *logos, ethos,* and *pathos.* These appeals can be understood within a rhetorical context illustrated by a triangle with points labeled *message, writer or speaker,* and *audience* (see Figure 3.1). Effective arguments pay attention to all three points on this *rhetorical triangle.*

Message
LOGOS: *How can I make the argument
internally consistent and logical?
How can I find the best reasons and
support them with the best evidence?*

Audience
PATHOS: *How can I make the reader
open to my message? How can I best
appeal to my reader's values and
interests? How can I engage my
reader emotionally and imaginatively?*

Writer or Speaker
ETHOS: *How can I present myself
effectively? How can I enhance my
credibility and trustworthiness?*

FIGURE 3.1 The rhetorical triangle

As Figure 3.1 shows, each point on the triangle corresponds to one of the three persuasive appeals:

- *Logos* (Greek for "word") focuses attention on the quality of the message—that is, on the internal consistency and clarity of the argument itself and on the logic of its reasons and support. The impact of logos on an audience is referred to as its logical appeal.
- *Ethos* (Greek for "character") focuses attention on the writer's (or speaker's) character as it is projected in the message. It refers to the credibility of the writer. *Ethos* is often conveyed through the writer's investment in his or her claim, through the fairness with which the writer considers alternative views, through the tone and style of the message, and even through the message's professional appearance on paper or screen, including correct grammar, flawless proofreading, and appropriate formats for citations and bibliography. In some cases, *ethos* is also a function of the writer's reputation for honesty and expertise independent of the message. The impact of *ethos* on an audience is referred to as the *ethical appeal* or *appeal from credibility.*
- *Pathos* (Greek for "suffering" or "experience") focuses attention on the values and beliefs of the intended audience. It is often associated with emotional appeal. But *pathos* appeals more specifically to an audience's imaginative sympathies—their capacity to feel and see what the writer feels and sees. Thus, when we turn the abstractions of logical discourse into a tangible and immediate story, we are making

a pathetic appeal. Whereas appeals to *logos* and *ethos* can further an audience's intellectual assent to our claim, appeals to *pathos* engage the imagination and feelings, moving the audience to a deeper appreciation of the argument's significance.

A related rhetorical concept, connected to the appeals of *logos, ethos,* and *pathos,* is that of *kairos,* from the Greek word for "right time," "season," or "opportunity." This concept suggests that for an argument to be persuasive, its timing must be effectively chosen and its tone and structure in right proportion or measure. You may have had the experience of composing an argumentative e-mail and then hesitating before clicking the "send" button. Is this the right moment to send this message? Is my audience ready to hear what I'm saying? Would my argument be more effective if I waited for a couple of days? If I send this message now, should I change its tone and content? This attentiveness to the unfolding of time is what is meant by *kairos.* We will return to this concept in Chapter 6, when we consider *ethos* and *pathos* in more depth.

Given this background on the classical appeals, let's turn now to *logos*—the logic and structure of arguments.

Issue Questions as the Origins of Argument

3.3 To distinguish between issue and information questions and between genuine and pseudo-arguments

At the heart of any argument is an issue, which we can define as a controversial topic area such as "the labeling of genetically modified foods" or "racial profiling," that gives rise to differing points of view and conflicting claims. A writer can usually focus an issue by asking an issue question that invites at least two alternative answers. Within any complex issue—for example, the issue of abortion—there are usually a number of separate issue questions: Should abortions be legal? Should the federal government authorize Medicaid payments for abortions? When does a fetus become a human being (at conception? at three months? at quickening? at birth?)? What are the effects of legalizing abortion? (One person might stress that legalized abortion leads to greater freedom for women. Another person might respond that it lessens a society's respect for human life.)

Difference between an Issue Question and an Information Question

Of course, not all questions are issue questions that can be answered reasonably in two or more differing ways; thus not all questions can lead to effective arguments. Rhetoricians have traditionally distinguished between *explication,* which is writing that sets out to inform or explain, and *argumentation,* which sets out to change a reader's mind. On the surface, at least, this seems like a useful distinction. If a reader is interested in a writer's question mainly to gain new knowledge about a subject, then the writer's essay could be considered explication rather than argument. According to this view, the following questions about teenage pregnancy might be called information questions rather than issue questions:

> How does the teenage pregnancy rate in the United States compare with the rate in Sweden? If the rates are different, why?

Although both questions seem to call for information rather than for argument, we believe that the second one would be an issue question if reasonable people disagreed on the answer. Thus, different writers might agree that the teenage pregnancy rate in the United States is seven times higher than the rate in Sweden. But they might disagree about why. One writer might emphasize Sweden's practical, secular sex-education courses, leading to more consistent use of contraceptives among Swedish teenagers. Another writer might point to the higher use of oral contraceptives among teenage girls in Sweden (partly a result of Sweden's generous national health program) and to less reliance on condoms for preventing pregnancy. Another might argue that moral decay in the United States or a breakdown of the traditional family is at fault. Thus, underneath the surface of what looks like a simple explication of the "truth" is really a controversy.

How to Identify an Issue Question

You can generally tell whether a question is an issue question or an information question by examining your purpose in relationship to your audience. If your relationship to your audience is that of teacher to learner, so that your audience hopes to gain new information, knowledge, or understanding that you possess, then your question is probably an information question. But if your relationship to your audience is that of advocate to decision maker or jury, so that your audience needs to make up its mind on something and is weighing different points of view, then the question you address is an issue question.

Often the same question can be an information question in one context and an issue question in another. Let's look at the following examples:

- **How does a diesel engine work?** (This is probably an information question, because reasonable people who know about diesel engines will probably agree on how they work. This question would be posed by an audience of new learners.)
- **Why is a diesel engine more fuel efficient than a gasoline engine?** (This also seems to be an information question, because all experts will probably agree on the answer. Once again, the audience seems to be new learners, perhaps students in an automotive class.)
- **What is the most cost-effective way to produce diesel fuel from crude oil?** (This could be an information question if experts agree and you are addressing new learners. But if you are addressing engineers and one engineer says process X is the most cost-effective and another argues for process Y, then the question is an issue question.)
- **Should the present highway tax on diesel fuel be increased?** (This is certainly an issue question. One person says yes; another says no; another offers a compromise.)

■ ■ ■ **FOR CLASS DISCUSSION** Information Questions versus Issue Questions

Working as a class or in small groups, try to decide which of the following questions are information questions and which are issue questions. Many of them could be either, depending on the rhetorical context. For such questions, create hypothetical contexts to show your reasoning.

1. What percentage of public schools in the United States are failing?
2. Which causes more traffic accidents, drunk driving or texting while driving?
3. What is the effect on children of playing first-person-shooter games?
4. Is genetically modified corn safe for human consumption?
5. Should people get rid of their land lines and have only cell phones?

Difference between a Genuine Argument and a Pseudo-Argument

Although every argument features an issue question with alternative answers, not every dispute over answers is a rational argument. Rational arguments require two additional factors: (1) reasonable participants who operate within the conventions of reasonable behavior and (2) potentially sharable assumptions that can serve as a starting place or foundation for the argument. Lacking one or both of these conditions, disagreements remain stalled at the level of pseudo-arguments.

Pseudo-Arguments: Committed Believers and Fanatical Skeptics

A reasonable argument assumes the possibility of growth and change; disputants may modify their views as they acknowledge strengths in an alternative view or weaknesses in their own. Such growth becomes impossible—and argument degenerates to pseudo-argument—when disputants are fanatically committed to their positions. Consider the case of the fanatical believer and the fanatical skeptic.

From one perspective, committed believers are admirable persons, guided by unwavering values and beliefs. Committed believers stand on solid rock, unwilling to compromise their principles or bend to the prevailing winds. But from another perspective, committed believers can seem rigidly fixed, incapable of growth or change. When committed believers from two clashing belief systems try to engage in dialogue with each other, a truth-seeking exchange of views becomes difficult. They talk past each other; dialogue is replaced by monologue from within isolated silos. Once committed believers push each other's buttons on global warming, guns, health care, taxes, religion, or some other issue, each disputant resorts to an endless replaying of the same prepackaged arguments. Disagreeing with a committed believer is like ordering the surf to quiet down. The only response is another crashing wave.

In contrast to the committed believer, the fanatical skeptic dismisses the possibility of ever believing anything. Skeptics often demand proof where no proof is possible. So what if the sun has risen every day of recorded history? That's no proof that it will rise tomorrow. Short of absolute proof, which never exists, fanatical skeptics accept nothing. In a world where the most we can hope for is increased audience adherence to our ideas, the skeptic demands an ironclad, logical demonstration of our claim's rightness.

A Closer Look at Pseudo-Arguments: The Lack of Shared Assumptions

As we have seen, rational argument degenerates to pseudo-argument when there is no possibility for listening, learning, growth, or change. In this section, we look more closely at a frequent cause of pseudo-arguments: lack of shared assumptions.

Shared Assumptions and the Problem of Ideology   As our discussion of committed believers suggests, reasonable argument is difficult when the disputants have differing "ideologies," which is an academic word for belief systems or worldviews. We all have our own ideologies. We all look at the world through a lens shaped by our life's experiences. Our beliefs and values are shaped by our family background, our friends, our culture, our particular time in history, our race or ethnicity, our gender or sexual orientation, our social class, our religion, our education, and so forth. Because we tend to think that our particular lens for looking at the world is natural and universal rather than specific to ourselves, we must be aware that persons who disagree with us may not share our deepest assumptions and beliefs. To participate in rational argument, we and our audience must seek shared assumptions—certain principles or values or beliefs that can serve as common ground.

The failure to find shared assumptions often leads to pseudo-arguments, particularly if one disputant makes assumptions that the other disputant cannot accept. Such pseudo-arguments often occur in disputes arising from politics or religion. For example, consider differences within the Christian community over how to interpret the Bible. Some Christian groups choose a straightforward, literal interpretation of the Bible as God's inerrant word, while other groups read some passages metaphorically or mythically and focus on the paradoxes, historical contexts, and interpretive complexities of the Bible; still other Christian groups read it as an ethical call for social justice. Members of these different Christian groups may not be able to argue rationally about, say, evolution or gay marriage because they have very different ways of reading Biblical passages and invoking the authority of the Bible. Similarly, within other religious traditions, believers may also differ about the meaning and applicability of their sacred texts to scientific issues and social problems.

Similar disagreements about assumptions occur in the political arena as well. Our point is that certain religious or political beliefs or texts cannot be evoked for evidence or authority when an audience does not assume the belief's truth or does not agree on the way that a given text should be read or interpreted.

Shared Assumptions and the Problem of Personal Opinions   Lack of shared assumptions also dooms arguments about purely personal opinions—for example, someone's claim that opera is boring or that pizza is better than nachos. Of course, a pizza-versus-nachos argument might be possible if the disputants assume a shared criterion about nutrition. For example, a nutritionist could argue that pizza is better than nachos because pizza provides more balanced nutrients per calorie. But if one of the disputants responds, "Nah, nachos are better than pizza because nachos taste

better," then he makes a different assumption—"My sense of taste is better than your sense of taste." This is a wholly personal standard, an assumption that others are unable to share.

■ ■ ■ **FOR WRITING AND DISCUSSION** Reasonable Arguments versus   MyWritingLab™
                                Pseudo-Arguments

The following questions can all be answered in alternative ways. However, not all of them will lead to reasonable arguments. Your goal is to show your understanding of the difference between reasonable arguments and pseudo-arguments.

Individual task: Which of the following questions will lead to reasonable arguments and which will lead only to pseudo-arguments? Imagining someone who disagrees with you, explain why you think the question is arguable (or not) in a short written passage.

1. Are the *Star Wars* films good science fiction?
2. Is it ethically justifiable to capture dolphins or orca whales and train them for human entertainment?
3. Should cities subsidize professional sports venues?
4. Is this abstract oil painting created by a monkey smearing paint on a canvas a true work of art?
5. Are nose rings and tongue studs attractive?

Group task: Working in pairs, small groups, or as a whole class, share your reasoning about these questions with classmates.   ■ ■ ■

Frame of an Argument: A Claim Supported by Reasons

3.4 To describe the basic frame of an argument

We said earlier that an argument originates in an *issue question,* which by definition is any question that provokes disagreement about the best answer. When you write an argument, your task is to take a position on the issue and to support it with reasons and evidence. The *claim* of your essay is the position you want your audience to accept. To put it another way, your claim is your essay's *thesis statement,* a one-sentence summary answer to your issue question. Your task, then, is to make a claim and support it with reasons.

What Is a Reason?

A *reason* (also called a *premise*) is a claim used to support another claim. In speaking or writing, a reason is usually linked to the claim with connecting words such as *because, since, for, so, thus, consequently,* and *therefore,* indicating that the claim follows logically from the reason.

Let us take an example of a controversial issue that frequently gets reported in the news—the public debate over keeping large sea mammals such as dolphins, porpoises, and orcas (killer whales) in captivity in marine parks where they entertain large crowds with their performances. This issue has many dimensions, including safety concerns for both the animals and their human trainers, as well as moral, scientific, legal, and economic concerns. Recent popular documentary films have heightened the public's awareness of the dangers of captivity to both the animals and the humans who work with them. *The Cove* (2009) exposes the gory dolphin hunts in Japan in which dolphins are killed en masse by fishermen and some are captured for display in shows around the world. *Blackfish* (2012) tells the history of the orca Tilicum who, in 2010, killed his trainer, Dawn Blancheau, at SeaWorld in Orlando, Florida. Recently a flurry of legal efforts to release the captive orca Lolita back into the wild has joined the larger battle among advocacy, governmental, scientific, and commercial groups over wild animals in captivity. In one of our recent classes, students heatedly debated the ethics of capturing wild dolphins and training them to perform in marine parks. Another student cited the personal experience of his sister's internship at SeaWorld San Diego where she worked on sea mammal rescue and rehabilitation, one of the projects of the marine park. In response, another student mentioned the millions of dollars these marine parks make on their dolphin and orca shows as well as on the stuffed animals, toys, magnets, T-shirts, and hundreds of other lucrative marine park souvenirs. Here are the frameworks the class developed for two alternative positions on this issue:

One View

CLAIM: The public should not support marine parks.

REASON 1: Marine parks stressfully separate dolphins and orcas from their natural habitat.

REASON 2: The education these parks claim to offer about marine mammals is just a series of artificial, exploitive tricks taught through behavior modification.

REASON 3: The motive behind these parks is big business profit.

REASON 4: Marine parks encourage artificial breeding programs and inhumane hunts and captures.

REASON 5: Marine parks promote an attitude of human dominance over animals.

Alternative View

CLAIM: The public should continue to enjoy marine parks.

REASON 1: These parks observe accreditation standards for animal welfare, health, and nutrition.

REASON 2: These marine parks enable scientists and veterinarians to study animal behavior in ways not possible with field studies in the wild.

REASON 3: These marine parks provide environmental education and memorable entertainment.

REASON 4: Marine parks use some of their profits to support research, conservation, and rescue and rehabilitation programs.

REASON 5: In their training of dolphins and orcas, these marine parks reinforce natural behaviors, exercise the animals' intelligence, and promote beneficial bonding with humans.

Formulating a list of reasons in this way breaks your argumentative task into a series of subtasks. It gives you a frame for building your argument in parts. In the previous example, the frame for the argument opposing commercial use of sea mammals suggests five different lines of reasoning a writer might pursue. A writer might use all five reasons or select only two or three, depending on which reasons would most persuade the intended audience. Each line of reasoning would be developed in its own separate section of the argument. For example, you might begin one section of your argument with the following sentence: "The public should not support marine parks because they teach dolphins and orcas clownish tricks and artificial behaviors, which they pass off as 'education about these animals.'" You would then provide examples of the tricks and stunts that dolphins and orcas are taught, explain how these contrast with their natural behaviors, and offer examples of erroneous facts or information about these animals supplied by these programs. You might also need to support the underlying assumption that it is good to acquire *real knowledge* about sea mammals in the wild. (How one articulates and supports the underlying assumptions of an argument will be developed in Chapter 4 when we discuss warrants and backing.) You would then proceed in the same way for each separate section of your argument.

To summarize our point in this section, the frame of an argument consists of the claim (the thesis statement of the essay), which is supported by one or more reasons, which are in turn supported by evidence or sequences of further reasons.

■ ■ ■ **FOR CLASS DISCUSSION**   Using Images to Support an Argument

In Chapter 1, we talked about implicit and explicit arguments and introduced you to some visual arguments. This exercise asks you to consider how images can shape or enhance an argument. Imagine that your task is to argue why a nonprofit group in your city should (or should not) offer as a fund-raising prize a trip to SeaWorld in Orlando, Florida, San Antonio, Texas, or San Diego, California. Examine the photographs of orcas in Figures 3.2 and 3.3 and describe the implicit argument that each photo seems to make about these whales. How might one or both of these photos be used to support an argument for or against the prize trip to SeaWorld? What reasons for going (or not going) to SeaWorld are implied by each photo? Briefly sketch out your argument for your group and explain your choice of photograph to support your position.   ■ ■ ■

Expressing Reasons in Because Clauses

Chances are that when you were a child, the word *because* contained magical explanatory powers. Somehow *because* seemed decisive. It persuaded people to accept your view of the world; it changed people's minds. Later, as you got older, you discovered that *because* only introduced your arguments and that it was the reasons following *because* that made the difference. Still, *because* introduced you to the powers potentially residing in the adult world of logic.

FIGURE 3.2 Orca performance at a marine park

FIGURE 3.3 Jumping orcas

Of course, there are many other ways to express the logical connection between a reason and a claim. Our language is rich in ways of stating *because* relationships:

- The public should not support marine parks because these parks stressfully separate dolphins and orcas from their natural habitat.
- Marine parks stressfully separate dolphins and orcas from their natural habitat. Therefore the public should not support them.
- Marine parks stressfully separate dolphins and orcas from their natural habitat, so the public should not support them.
- One reason that the public should not support marine animal parks is that they stressfully separate dolphins and orcas from their natural habitat.
- My argument that the public should not support marine animal parks is based mainly on the grounds that they stressfully separate dolphins and orcas from their natural habitat.

Even though logical relationships can be stated in various ways, writing out one or more *because* clauses seems to be the most succinct and manageable way to clarify an argument for oneself. We therefore suggest that sometime in the writing process, you create a *working thesis statement* that summarizes your main reasons as because clauses attached to your claim.* Just when you compose your own working thesis statement depends largely on your writing process. Some writers like to plan out their whole argument from the start and often compose their working thesis statements with *because* clauses before they write their rough drafts. Others discover their arguments as they write. And sometimes it is a combination of both. For these writers, an extended working thesis statement is something they might write halfway through the composing process as a way of ordering their argument when various branches seem to be growing out of control. Or they might compose a working thesis statement at the very end as a way of checking the unity of the final product.

Whenever you write your extended thesis statement, the act of doing so can be simultaneously frustrating and thought provoking. Composing *because* clauses can be a powerful discovery tool, causing you to think of many different kinds of arguments to support your claim. But it is often difficult to wrestle your ideas into the *because* clause shape, which sometimes seems to be overly tidy for the complex network of ideas you are trying to work with. Nevertheless, trying to summarize your argument as a single claim with reasons should help you see more clearly what you have to do.

---

*A working thesis statement opposing the commercial use of captured dolphins and orcas might look like this: The public should not support marine parks because marine parks stressfully separate dolphins and orcas from their natural habitat; because they are mainly big businesses driven by profit; because they create inaccurate and incomplete educational information about dolphins and orcas; because they encourage inhumane breeding programs and hunts and captures; and because they promote an attitude of human dominance over animals. You might not put a bulky thesis statement like this into your essay; rather, a working thesis statement is a behind-the-scenes way of summarizing your argument so that you can see it whole and clear.

■ ■ ■   **FOR CLASS DISCUSSION**   Developing Claims and Reasons

Try this group exercise to help you see how writing *because* clauses can be a discovery procedure. Divide into small groups. Each group member should contribute an issue that he or she would like to explore. Discussing one person's issue at a time, help each member develop a claim supported by several reasons. Express each reason as a *because* clause. Then write out the working thesis statement for each person's argument by attaching the *because* clauses to the claim. Finally, try to create *because* clauses in support of an alternative claim for each issue. Recorders should select two or three working thesis statements from the group to present to the class as a whole.   ■ ■ ■

Conclusion

This chapter has introduced you to the structure of classical argument, to the rhetorical triangle (message, writer or speaker, and audience), and to the classical appeals of *logos, ethos*, and *pathos*. It has also shown how arguments originate in issue questions, how issue questions differ from information questions, and how arguments differ from pseudo-arguments. At the heart of this chapter we explained that the frame of an argument is a claim supported by reasons. As you generate reasons to support your own arguments, it is often helpful to articulate them as *because* clauses attached to the claim.

In the next chapter we will see how to support a reason by examining its logical structure, uncovering its unstated assumptions, and planning a strategy of development.

WRITING ASSIGNMENT   An Issue Question and Working Thesis Statements   MyWritingLab™

Decide on an issue and a claim for a classical argument that you would like to write. Write a one-sentence question that summarizes the controversial issue that your claim addresses. Then draft a working thesis statement for your proposed argument. Organize the thesis as a claim with bulleted *because* clauses for reasons. You should have at least two reasons, but it is okay to have three or four. Also include an opposing thesis statement—that is, a claim with *because* clauses for an alternative position on your issue.

Recall that in Part One we emphasized exploratory writing as a way of resisting closure and helping you wrestle with multiple perspectives. Now we ask you to begin a process of closure by developing a thesis statement that condenses your argument into a claim with supporting reasons. However, as we emphasize throughout this text, drafting itself is an exploratory process. Writers almost always discover new ideas when they write a first draft; as they take their writing project through multiple drafts, their views may change substantially. Often, in fact, honest writers can change positions on an issue by discovering that a counterargument is stronger than their own. So the working thesis statement that you submit for this assignment may evolve substantially once you begin to draft.

In this chapter, as well as in Chapters 4 and 5, we will follow the process of student writer Carmen Tieu as she constructs an argument on violent video games. During earlier exploratory writing, she wrote about a classroom incident in which her professor had described video game playing as gendered behavior (overwhelmingly male). The professor indicated his dislike for such games, pointing to their antisocial, dehumanizing values. In her freewrite, Carmen described her own enjoyment of violent video games—particularly first-person-shooter games—and explored the pleasure that she derived from beating boys at Halo 2. She knew that she wanted to write an argument on this issue. What follows is Carmen's submission for this assignment.

Carmen's Issue Question and Working Thesis Statements

Issue Question: Should girls be encouraged to play first-person-shooter video games?

My claim: First-person-shooter (FPS) video games are great activities for girls,

- because beating guys at their own game is empowering for girls
- because being skilled at FPS games frees girls from feminine stereotypes
- because they give girls a different way of bonding with males
- because they give girls new insights into a male subculture

Opposing claim: First-person-shooter games are a bad activity for anyone, especially girls,

- because they promote antisocial values such as indiscriminate killing
- because they amplify the bad, macho side of male stereotypes
- because they waste valuable time that could be spent on something constructive
- because FPS games could encourage women to see themselves as objects ■

MyWritingLab™

Visit Ch. 3 The Core of an Argument: A Claim with Reasons in *MyWritingLab* to complete the For Writing and Discussion and Writing Assignments and to test your understanding of the chapter objectives.

The Logical Structure of Arguments

4

What you will learn in this chapter:

4.1 To explain the logical structure of argument in terms of claim, reason, and assumption granted by the audience

4.2 To use the Toulmin system to describe an argument's logical structure

4.3 To use the Toulmin system to generate ideas for your argument and test it for completeness

---

In Chapter 3 you learned that the core of an argument is a claim supported by reasons and that these reasons can often be stated as *because* clauses attached to a claim. In the present chapter we examine the logical structure of arguments in more depth.

An Overview of *Logos*: What Do We Mean by the "Logical Structure" of an Argument?

4.1 To explain the logical structure of argument in terms of claim, reason, and assumption granted by the audience

As you will recall from our discussion of the rhetorical triangle, *logos* refers to the strength of an argument's support and its internal consistency. *Logos* is the argument's logical structure. But what do we mean by "logical structure"?

Formal Logic versus Real-World Logic

First of all, what we *don't* mean by logical structure is the kind of precise certainty you get in a philosophy class in formal logic. Logic classes deal with symbolic assertions that are universal and unchanging, such as "If all ps are qs and if r is a p, then r is a q." This statement is logically certain so long as p, q, and r are pure abstractions. But in the real world, p, q, and r turn into actual things, and the relationships among them suddenly become fuzzy. For example, p might be a class of actions called "Sexual Harassment," while q could be the class called "Actions That Justify Getting Fired from One's Job." If r is the class "Telling Off-Color Stories," then the logic of our p–q–r statement suggests that telling off-color stories (r) is an instance of sexual harassment (p), which in turn is an action justifying getting fired from one's job (q).

Now, most of us would agree that sexual harassment is a serious offense that might well justify getting fired. In turn, we might agree that telling off-color stories, if the jokes are sufficiently raunchy and are inflicted on an unwilling audience, constitutes sexual harassment. But few of us would want to say categorically that all people who tell off-color stories are harassing their listeners and ought to be fired. Most of us would want to know the particulars of the case before making a final judgment.

In the real world, then, it is difficult to say that *r*s are always *p*s or that every instance of a *p* results in *q*. That is why we discourage students from using the word *prove* in claims they write for arguments (as in "This paper will prove that euthanasia is wrong"). Real-world arguments seldom *prove* anything. They can only make a good case for something, a case that is more or less strong, more or less probable. Often the best you can hope for is to strengthen the resolve of those who agree with you or weaken the resistance of those who oppose you.

The Role of Assumptions

A key difference, then, between formal logic and real-world argument is that real-world arguments are not grounded in abstract, universal statements. Rather, as we shall see, they must be grounded in beliefs, assumptions, or values granted by the audience. A second important difference is that in real-world arguments, these beliefs, assumptions, or values are often unstated. So long as writer and audience share the same assumptions, it's fine to leave them unstated. But if these underlying assumptions aren't shared, the writer has a problem.

To illustrate the nature of this problem, consider one of the arguments we introduced in the last chapter.

> The public should not support marine parks because they stressfully separate dolphins and orcas from their natural habitat.

On the face of it, this is a plausible argument. But the argument is persuasive only if the audience agrees with the writer's assumption that it is wrong to separate wild animals from their natural habitats and social groups. What if you believed that confinement of wild animals is not always harmful or stressful to the animals, that the knowledge derived from the capture of wild animals enables humans to preserve the natural environment for these animals, and that the benefits to be gained from the captivity of a small number of wild animals outweigh the animals' loss of freedom? If this were the case, you might believe that marine parks have positive consequences so long as they strive to provide humane conditions for the animals, with minimal stress. If these were your beliefs, the argument wouldn't work for you because you would reject the underlying assumption. To persuade you with this line of reasoning, the writer would have to defend this assumption, showing why it is unwise or unethical to remove animals from their free and wild conditions.

The Core of an Argument: The Enthymeme

The previous core argument ("The public should not support marine parks because they stressfully separate dolphins and orcas from their natural habitat") is an incomplete logical structure called an *enthymeme*. Its persuasiveness depends on an underlying assumption or belief that the audience must accept. To complete the enthymeme and make it effective, the audience must willingly supply a missing premise—in this case, that it is wrong to separate wild animals from their natural environments. The Greek philosopher Aristotle showed how successful enthymemes root the speaker's argument in assumptions, beliefs, or values held by the audience. The word *enthymeme* comes from the Greek *en* (meaning "in") and *thumos* (meaning "mind"). Listeners or readers must have in mind an assumption, belief, or value that lets them willingly supply the missing premise. If the audience is unwilling to supply the missing premise, then the argument fails. Our point is that successful arguments depend both on what the arguer says and on what the audience already has "in mind."

To clarify the concept of "enthymeme," let's go over this same territory again, this time more slowly, examining what we mean by "incomplete logical structure." The sentence "The public should not support marine parks because they stressfully separate dolphins and orcas from their natural habitat" is an enthymeme. It combines a claim (the public should not support marine parks) with a reason expressed as a *because* clause (because they stressfully separate dolphins and orcas from their natural habitat). To render this enthymeme logically complete, the audience must willingly supply a missing assumption—that it is wrong to separate wild animals from their natural habitats. If your audience accepts this assumption, then you have a starting place on which to build an effective argument. If your audience doesn't accept this assumption, then you must supply another argument to support it, and so on until you find common ground with your audience.

To sum up:

1. Claims are supported with reasons. You can usually state a reason as a *because* clause attached to a claim (see Chapter 3).
2. A *because* clause attached to a claim is an incomplete logical structure called an enthymeme. To create a complete logical structure from an enthymeme, the underlying assumption (or assumptions) must be articulated.
3. To serve as an effective starting point for the argument, this underlying assumption should be a belief, value, or principle that the audience grants.

Let's illustrate this structure by putting the previous example into schematic form.

ENTHYMEME

CLAIM The public should not support marine parks

REASON because they stressfully separate dolphins and orcas from their natural habitat.

Audience must supply this assumption ———→

UNDERLYING ASSUMPTION
It is wrong to separate wild animals from their natural habitats.

The Power of Audience-Based Reasons

Aristotle's concept of the enthymeme focuses on the writer's need to create what we can now call "audience-based reasons" as opposed to "writer-based reasons." A reason that is persuasive to you might not be persuasive to your audience. Finding audience-based reasons means finding arguments effectively anchored within your audience's beliefs and values. To illustrate the difference between an audience-based reason and a writer-based reason, suppose that you are a vegetarian persuaded mainly by ethical arguments against causing needless suffering to animals. Suppose further that you wanted to persuade others to become vegetarians or at least to reduce their consumption of meat. Your "writer-based reason" for vegetarianism could be stated as follows:

> You should become a vegetarian because doing so will help reduce the needless suffering of animals.

The underlying assumption here is that it is wrong to cause the suffering of animals. This writer-based reason might also be an audience-based reason for persons who are wrestling with the moral dimension of animal suffering. But this assumption might not resonate with people who have made their own peace with eating meat. How might you use audience-based reasons to appeal to these meat-eaters? Here are two more possible enthymemes:

> You should become a vegetarian because doing so may help you lower your cholesterol.

> You should become a vegetarian because doing so will significantly lower your carbon footprint.

These arguments hook into the assumption that it is good to lower one's cholesterol (health values) or that it is good to lower one's carbon footprint (environmental values). All three of the arguments—whether based on ethics, health, or the environment—might further the practice of vegetarianism or at least reduce the amount of meat consumed, but they won't appeal equally to all audiences. From the perspective of logic alone, all three arguments are equally sound. But they will affect different audiences differently.

■ ■ ■ ■ **FOR CLASS DISCUSSION** Identifying Underlying Assumptions and Choosing Audience-Based Reasons

Part 1: Working individually or in small groups, identify the unstated assumption that the audience must supply in order to make the following enthymemes persuasive.

Example

Enthymeme: Rabbits make good pets because they are gentle.

Underlying assumption: Gentle animals make good pets.

1. We shouldn't elect Joe as committee chair because he is too bossy.
2. Airport screeners should use racial profiling because doing so will increase the odds of stopping terrorists.

3. Racial profiling should not be used by airport screeners because it violates a person's civil rights.
4. We should strengthen the Endangered Species Act because doing so will preserve genetic diversity on the planet.
5. The Endangered Species Act is too stringent because it severely damages the economy.

Part 2: In the following items, decide which of the two reasons offered would be more persuasive to the specified audience. How might the reason not chosen be effective for a different kind of audience? Be prepared to explain your reasoning.

1. Audience: people who advocate a pass/fail grading system on the grounds that the present grading system is too competitive
   a. We should keep the present grading system because it prepares people for the dog-eat-dog pressures of the business world.
   b. We should keep the present grading system because it tells students that certain standards of excellence must be met if individuals are to reach their full potential.
2. Audience: environmentalists
   a. We should support fracking for natural gas because doing so will help reduce our dependence on foreign sources of oil.
   b. We should support fracking for natural gas because doing so will provide a greener "bridge fuel" that will give us time to develop better renewable technologies.
3. Audience: conservative proponents of "family values"
   a. Same-sex marriages should be legalized because doing so will promote public acceptance of homosexuality.
   b. Same-sex marriages should be legalized because doing so will make it easier for gay people to establish and sustain long-term, stable relationships.

Adopting a Language for Describing Arguments: The Toulmin System

4.2 To use the Toulmin system to describe an argument's logical structure

Understanding a new field usually requires us to learn a new vocabulary. For example, if you were taking biology for the first time, you'd have to learn dozens and dozens of new terms. Luckily, the field of argument requires us to learn a mere handful of new terms. A particularly useful set of argument terms, one we'll be using occasionally throughout the rest of this text, comes from philosopher Stephen Toulmin. In the 1950s, Toulmin rejected the prevailing models of argument based on formal logic in favor of a very audience-based courtroom model.

Toulmin's courtroom model differs from formal logic in that it assumes that (1) all assertions and assumptions are contestable by "opposing counsel" and that (2) all final "verdicts" about the persuasiveness of the opposing arguments will be rendered by a neutral third party, a judge, or jury. As writers, keeping in mind the "opposing counsel" forces us to anticipate counterarguments and to question our assumptions. Keeping in mind the judge and jury reminds us to answer opposing arguments fully, without rancor, and to present positive reasons for supporting our case as well as negative reasons for disbelieving the opposing case. Above all else, Toulmin's model reminds us not to construct an argument that appeals only to those who already agree with us. In short, it helps arguers tailor arguments to their audiences.

The system we use for analyzing arguments combines Toulmin's language with Aristotle's concept of the enthymeme. It builds on the system you have already been practicing. We simply need to add a few key terms from Toulmin. The first term is Toulmin's *warrant,* the name we will now use for the underlying assumption that turns an enthymeme into a complete, logical structure as shown below.

Toulmin derives his term *warrant* from the concept of "warranty" or "guarantee." The warrant is the value, belief, or principle that the audience has to hold if the soundness of the argument is to be guaranteed or warranted. We sometimes make similar use of this word in ordinary language when we say, "That is an unwarranted conclusion," meaning one has leaped from information about a situation to a conclusion about that situation without any sort of general principle to justify or "warrant" that move. Thus the warrant—once accepted by the audience—"guarantees" the soundness of the argument.

ENTHYMEME

CLAIM The public should not support marine parks

REASON because they stressfully separate dolphins and orcas from their natural habitat.

Audience must supply this warrant ────────┐
                                            ↓

WARRANT
It is wrong to separate wild animals from their natural habitats.

But arguments need more than claims, reasons, and warrants. These are simply one-sentence statements—the frame of an argument, not a developed argument. To give body and weight to our arguments and make them convincing, we need what Toulmin calls *grounds* and *backing.* Let's start with grounds. Grounds are the supporting evidence that causes an audience to accept your reason. Grounds are facts, data, statistics, causal links, testimony, examples, anecdotes—the blood and muscle that flesh out the skeletal frame of your enthymeme. Toulmin suggests that grounds are "what you have to go on" in an argument—the stuff you can point to and present before a jury. Here is how grounds fit into our emerging argument schema:

ENTHYMEME

CLAIM The public should not support marine parks

REASON because they stressfully separate dolphins and orcas from their natural habitat.

Grounds support the reason → **GROUNDS**

Evidence and arguments showing stressful difference between dolphin and orca behavior in the wild and in captivity:

• In the wild, dolphins and orcas swim in pods, dolphins around forty miles a day, and orcas around sixty miles a day, in the open ocean whereas marine park tanks provide only a tiny fraction of that space.

• Evidence that separation from their family members and pods in their natural habitats creates emotional distress that can't be remedied by the presence of randomly selected other dolphins and orcas in these marine parks.

• Statistics that the stress caused by confinement and the echoes and noise of concrete pools, audiences, and music often results in the animals needing medication.

• Statistics that show that dolphins and orcas don't live as long in captivity as in their natural habitat.

In many cases, successful arguments require just these three components: a claim, a reason, and grounds. If the audience already accepts the unstated assumption behind the reason (the warrant), then the warrant can safely remain in the background, unstated and unexamined. But if there is a chance that the audience will question or doubt the warrant, then the writer needs to back it up by providing an argument in its support. *Backing* is the argument that supports the warrant. It may require no more than one or two sentences or as much as a major section in your argument. Its goal is to persuade the audience to accept the warrant. Here is how *backing* is added to our schema:

WARRANT

It is wrong to separate wild animals from their natural habitats.

Backing supports the warrant → **BACKING**

Arguments showing why it is unwise, unethical, or otherwise wrong to separate wild animals from their natural environments:

• Examples of wild animals (those in aquariums and zoos) that do not thrive in artificially constructed environments, that don't live long, or that suffer psychological stress from confinement

• An ecological argument about the beauty of animals in the wild and of the complexity of the natural webs of which animals are a part

• A philosophical argument that humans shouldn't treat animals as instruments for their own enjoyment or profit

Toulmin's system next asks us to imagine how a resistant audience would try to refute our argument. Specifically, the adversarial audience might challenge our reason and grounds by arguing that dolphins and orcas in captivity are not as stressed as we claim (evidence provided by veterinarians, caretakers, or animal trainers verifying that most sea mammals in captivity are in good health). Or the adversary might attack our warrant and backing by showing how the captivity of some wild animal might save the species from extinction or how animals are often saved from illness and predators by caring humans. An adversary might attack our philosophical or spiritual arguments by saying that the same reasoning, taken to its logical conclusion, would eliminate zoos and require all humans to become vegetarians or vegans. An adversary might even argue that dolphins and orcas enjoy being with humans and have the same capacity to be animal companions as dogs or horses.

In the case of the argument opposing dolphins in captivity, an adversary might offer one or more of the following rebuttals.

Writer must anticipate these attacks from skeptics

ENTHYMEME

CLAIM The public should not support marine parks

REASON because they stressfully separate dolphins and orcas from their natural habitat.

GROUNDS

Evidence and arguments showing stressful difference between dolphin behavior in the wild and in captivity:

- In the wild, dolphins swim in pods around forty miles a day in the open ocean whereas marine park tanks provide only a tiny fraction of that space.
- Evidence that the echoes from concrete pools, music of dolphin shows, and the applause and noise of audiences are stressful and harmful
- Statistics about the excessive number of performances or about the levels of stress hormones produced in dolphins

"POSSIBLE CONDITIONS OF REBUTTAL
A skeptic can attack the reason and grounds":

- Argument that these programs must observe strict accreditation standards for animal welfare, health, and education
- Marine parks exercise dophins' and orcas' intelligence and abilities and build on their natural behaviors.
- Many dolphins and orcas have been bred in captivity, so they aren't "wild."
- The education and entertainment provided by marine parks promote public concern for dolphins and orcas.

WARRANT

It is wrong to separate wild animals from their natural habitats.

BACKING

Arguments showing why it is unwise, unethical, or otherwise wrong to separate wild animals from their natural environments:

- Examples of wild animals (those in aquariums and zoos) that do not thrive in artificially constructed environments, that don't live long, or that suffer psychological stress from confinement
- An ecological argument about the beauty of animals in the wild and of the complexity of the natural webs of which animals are a part
- A philosophical argument that humans shouldn't treat animals as instruments for their own enjoyment or profit

"POSSIBLE CONDITIONS OF REBUTTAL
A skeptic can attack the warrant and backing."

- The natural habitat is not always the best environment for wild animals.
- Captivity may actually preserve some species.
- Scientists have been able to conduct valuable studies of dolphins and learn more about orcas in captivity, which would have been impossible in the wild.

As this example shows, adversarial readers can question an argument's reasons and grounds or its warrant and backing or sometimes both. Conditions of rebuttal remind writers to look at their arguments from the perspective of skeptics. The same principle can be illustrated in the following analysis of an argument that the minimum wage for fast-food workers should be raised to $15/hour.

ENTHYMEME

CLAIM The federal government should mandate a minimum living wage of $15/hour

REASON because such a wage will reduce poverty.

GROUNDS

- Statistical data showing that $15/hour will support a family of four at an above-poverty level

- Statistical data about the numbers of people affected by a higher minimum wage

CONDITIONS OF REBUTTAL ATTACKING GROUNDS

Raising minimum wage doesn't directly target the poor:

- Only about 20 percent of those receiving the minimum wage have incomes below the poverty line; the remaining 80 percent are often teenagers or second earners who come from families above the poverty line.

- Of those below the poverty line, 60 percent do not have jobs and would not benefit from a minimum wage. (The poor need jobs, not raises.)

- There are better ways to reduce poverty than increasing the minimum wage.

WARRANT

Policies that reduce poverty are good.

BACKING

Arguments showing how reducing the number of poor people reduces the ills associated with poverty.

- Data about crime rates in poor neighborhoods

- Data about poor education and health outcomes among poor people

- Data about the need for taxpayer assistance for those working at current minimum wage (food stamps, housing assistance)

CONDITIONS OF REBUTTAL ATTACKING WARRANT

Policies aimed at reducing poverty are good only if they don't bring harmful consequences that outweigh the good. Raising minimum wage brings many harmful consequences:

- Increases cost of goods to consumers

- Leads to fewer jobs as companies automate, hire fewer workers, or move to new locations

- Causes many small businesses to close their doors

Toulmin's final term, used to limit the force of a claim and indicate the degree of its probable truth, is *qualifier*. The qualifier reminds us that real-world arguments almost never prove a claim. We may say things such as *very likely, probably,* or *maybe* to indicate the strength of the claim we are willing to draw from our grounds and warrant. Thus if there are exceptions to your warrant or if your grounds are not very strong, you will have to qualify your claim. For example, you might say, "Except for limited cases of scientific research, dolphins and orcas should not be held in captivity," or "We should consider raising the minimum wage because doing so may be one possible way to reduce poverty." In our future displays of the Toulmin scheme we will omit the qualifiers, but you should always remember that no argument is 100 percent conclusive.

■ ■ ■   **FOR CLASS DISCUSSION**   Developing Enthymemes with the Toulmin Schema

Working individually or in small groups, imagine that you have to write arguments developing the five enthymemes listed in the For Class Discussion exercise on pages 70–71. Use the Toulmin schema to help you determine what you need to consider when developing each enthymeme. We suggest that you try a four-box diagram structure as a way of visualizing the schema. We have applied the Toulmin schema to the first enthymeme: "We shouldn't elect Joe as committee chair because he is too bossy."

ENTHYMEME

CLAIM We shouldn't elect Joe as committee chair
REASON because he is too bossy.

GROUNDS

Evidence of Joe's bossiness:

• Examples of the way he dominates meetings—doesn't call on people, talks too much

• Testimony about his bossiness from people who have served with him on committees

• Anecdotes about his abrasive style

CONDITIONS OF REBUTTAL
Attacking the reason and grounds

Evidence that Joe is not bossy or is only occasionally bossy:

• Counterevidence showing his collaborative style

• Testimony from people who have liked Joe as a leader and claim he isn't bossy; testimony about his cooperativeness and kindness

• Testimony that anecdotes about Joe's bossiness aren't typical

WARRANT
Bossy people make bad committee chairs.

BACKING
Problems caused by bossy committee chairs:

• Bossy people don't inspire cooperation and enthusiam.

• Bossy people make others angry.

• Bossy people tend to make bad decisions because they don't incorporate advice from others.

CONDITIONS OF REBUTTAL
Attacking the warrant and backing

• Arguments that bossiness can be a good trait

  • Sometimes bossy people make good chairpersons.

  • This committee needs a bossy person who can make decisions and get things done.

• Argument that Joe has other traits of good leadership that outweigh his bossiness

■ ■ ■

Using Toulmin's Schema to Plan and Test Your Argument

4.3 To use the Toulmin system to generate ideas for your argument and test it for completeness

So far we have seen that a claim, a reason, and a warrant form the frame for a line of reasoning in an argument. Most of the words in an argument, however, are devoted to grounds and backing.

Hypothetical Example: Cheerleaders as Athletes

For an illustration of how a writer can use the Toulmin schema to generate ideas for an argument, consider the following case. In April 2005, the Texas House of Representatives passed a bill banning "sexually suggestive" cheerleading. Across the nation, evening television show comedians poked fun at the bill, while newspaper editorialists debated its wisdom and constitutionality. In one of our classes, however, several students, including one who had earned a high school varsity letter in competitive cheerleading, defended the bill by contending that provocative dance moves hurt the athletic image of cheerleading. In the following example, which draws on ideas developed in class discussion, we create a hypothetical student writer (we'll call her Chandale) who argues in defense of the Texas bill. Chandale's argument is based on the following enthymeme:

> The bill banning suggestive dancing for high school cheerleaders is a good law because it promotes a view of female cheerleaders as athletes.

Chandale used the Toulmin schema to brainstorm ideas for developing her argument. Here are her notes:

Chandale's Planning Notes Using the Toulmin Schema

Enthymeme: The bill banning suggestive dancing for high school cheerleaders is a good law because it promotes a view of female cheerleaders as athletes.

Grounds: First, I've got to use evidence to show that cheerleaders are athletes.

- Cheerleaders at my high school are carefully chosen for their stamina and skill after exhausting two-week tryouts.
- We begin all practices with a mile run and an hour of warm-up exercises—we are also expected to work out on our own for at least an hour on weekends and on days without practice.
- We learned competitive routines and stunts consisting of lifts, tosses, flips, catches, and gymnastic moves. This requires athletic ability! We'd practice these stunts for hours each week.
- Throughout the year cheerleaders have to attend practices, camps, and workshops to learn new routines and stunts.
- Our squad competed in competitions around the state.
- Competitive cheerleading is a growing movement across the country—University of Maryland has made it a varsity sport for women.
- Skimpy uniforms and suggestive dance moves destroy this image by making women eye candy like the Dallas Cowboys cheerleaders.

Warrant: It is a good thing to view female cheerleaders as athletes.

Backing: Now I need to make the case that it is good to see cheerleaders as athletes rather than as eye candy.

- Athletic competition builds self-esteem, independence, and a powerful sense of achievement. It also contributes to health, strength, and conditioning.
- Competitive cheerleading is one of the few sports where teams are made up of both men and women. (Why is this good? Should I use this?)
- The suggestive dance moves turn women into sex objects whose function is to be gazed at by men, which suggests that women's value is based on their beauty and sex appeal.

- We are talking about HIGH SCHOOL cheerleading—it is a very bad early influence on girls to model themselves on Dallas Cowboys cheerleaders or sexy MTV videos of rock stars.
- Junior high girls want to do what senior high girls do—suggestive dance moves promote sexuality way too early.

Conditions of Rebuttal: Would anybody try to rebut my reasons and grounds that cheerleading is an athletic activity?

- No. I think it is obvious that cheerleading is an athletic activity once they see my evidence.
- However, they might not think of cheerleading as a sport. They might say that the University of Maryland just declared it a sport as a cheap way to meet Title IX federal rules to have more women's sports. I'll have to make sure that I show this is really a sport.
- They also might say that competitive cheerleading shouldn't be encouraged because it is too dangerous—lots of serious injuries, including paralysis, have been caused by mistakes in doing flips, lifts, and tosses. If I include this, maybe I could say that other sports are dangerous also, and it is in fact danger that makes this sport so exciting.

Would anyone doubt my warrant and backing that it is good to see female cheerleaders as athletes?

- Yes, all those people who laughed at the Texas legislature think that people are being too prudish and that banning suggestive dance moves violates free expression. I'll need to make my case that it is bad for young girls to see themselves as sex objects too early.

The information that Chandale lists under "grounds" is what she sees as the facts of the case—the hard data she will use as evidence to support her contention that cheerleading is an athletic activity. The paragraph that follows shows how this argument might look when placed in written form.

First Part of Chandale's Argument

Summarizes opposing view

States her claim

For grounds, uses personal experience details to show that cheerleading is an athletic activity

    Although evening television show comedians have made fun of the Texas legislature's desire to ban "suggestive" dance moves from cheerleading routines, I applaud this bill because it promotes a healthy view of female cheerleaders as athletes rather than showgirls. I was lucky enough to attend a high school where cheerleading is a sport, and I earned a varsity letter as a cheerleader. To get on my high school's cheerleading squad, students have to go through an exhausting two-week tryout of workouts and instruction in the basic routines; then they are chosen based on their stamina and skill. Once on the squad, cheerleaders begin all practices with a mile run and an hour of grueling warm-up exercises, and they are expected to exercise on their own on weekends. As a result of this regimen, cheerleaders achieve and maintain a top level of physical fitness. In addition, to get on the squad, students must be able to do handstands, cartwheels, handsprings, high jumps, and the splits. Each year the squad builds up to its complex routines and stunts consisting of lifts, tosses, flips, catches, and gymnastic moves that only trained athletes can do. In tough competitions at the regional and state levels, the cheerleading squad demonstrates its athletic talent. This view of cheerleading as a competitive sport is also spreading to colleges. As reported recently in a number of newspapers, the University of Maryland has made cheerleading a varsity sport, and many other universities are following suit. Athletic performance of this caliber is a far cry from the sexy dancing that many high school girls often associate with cheerleading. By banning suggestive dancing in cheerleading routines, the Texas legislature creates an opportunity for schools to emphasize the athleticism of cheerleading.

Provides more grounds by showing emerging views of cheerleading as a competitive sport

As you can see, Chandale has plenty of evidence for arguing that competitive cheerleading is an athletic activity quite different from sexy dancing. But how effective is this argument as it stands? Is this all she needs? The Toulmin schema encourages writers to include—if needed for the intended audience—explicit support for their warrants as well as attention to conditions for rebuttal. Because the overwhelming national response to the Texas law was ridicule at the perceived prudishness of the legislators, Chandale decides to expand her argument as follows:

Continuation of Chandale's Argument

Supplies warrant: It is good to see cheerleaders as athletic and bad to see them as sex objects

This emphasis on cheerleaders as athletes rather than sexy dancers is good for girls. The erotic dance moves that many high school cheerleaders now incorporate into their routines show that they are emulating the Dallas Cowboys cheerleaders or pop stars on MTV. Our already sexually saturated culture (think of the suggestive clothing marketed to little girls) pushes girls and women to measure their value by their beauty and sex appeal. It would be far healthier, both physically and psychologically, if high school cheerleaders were identified as athletes. For women and men both, competitive cheerleading can build self-esteem, pride in teamwork, and a powerful sense of achievement, as well as promote health, strength, and fitness.

Supplies backing: Shows benefits that come from seeing cheerleaders as athletes

Anticipates an
objection

Responds to objection
by supplying more
evidence that
cheerleading is a sport;
in fact it is a dangerous
sport

Sums up by returning
to claim

Some people might object to competitive cheerleading by saying that cheerleading isn't really a sport. Some have accused the University of Maryland of making cheerleading a varsity sport only as a cheap way of meeting Title IX requirements. But anyone who has watched competitive cheerleading, and imagined what it would be like to be thrown high into the air, knows instinctively that this is a sport indeed. In fact, other persons might object to competitive cheerleading because it is too dangerous, with potential for very severe injuries, including paralysis. Obviously the sport is dangerous—but so are many sports, including football, gymnastics, diving, and trampoline. The danger and difficulty of the sport is part of its appeal. Part of what can make cheerleaders as athletes better role models for girls than cheerleaders as erotic dancers is the courage and training needed for success. Of course, the Texas legislators might not have had athleticism in mind when they banned suggestive dancing. They might only have been promoting their vision of morality. But at stake are the role models we set for young girls. I'll pick an athlete over a Dallas Cowboys cheerleader every time.

Our example suggests how a writer can use the Toulmin schema to generate ideas for an argument. For evidence, Chandale draws primarily on her personal experiences as a cheerleader/athlete and on her knowledge of popular culture. She also draws on her reading of several newspaper articles about the University of Maryland making cheerleading a varsity sport. (In an academic paper rather than a newspaper editorial, she would need to document these sources through formal citations.) Although many arguments depend on research, many can be supported wholly or in part by your own personal experiences, so don't neglect the wealth of evidence from your own life when searching for data. (A more detailed discussion of evidence in arguments occurs in Chapter 5.)

Extended Student Example: Girls and Violent Video Games

Let's look at one more example of how the Toulmin system can help you generate ideas for your argument. In this case we will look at a complete example from student writer Carmen Tieu, whose evolving argument about girls and violent video games was introduced in the last chapter. Carmen's assignment was to write a "supporting reasons" argument, which is a shortened form of the classical argument described on pages 53–54. It has all the features of a classical argument except for the requirement to summarize and rebut opposing views. In planning her argument, Carmen decided to use four lines of reasoning, as shown in her *because* clauses listed on page 66. She began by creating a basic Toulmin frame for each reason:

Carmen's Toulmin Frames

My claim: Playing first-person-shooter (FPS) video games is good for girls

1. **Reason**: because playing FPS lets girls beat guys at their own game. **Warrant:** It is good for girls to beat guys at their own game.
2. **Reason:** because playing FPS games frees girls from feminine stereotypes. **Warrant:** It is good for girls to be freed from feminine stereotypes.
3. **Reason:** because playing FPS games gives girls a different way of bonding with males. **Warrant:** It is good for girls to find a different way of bonding with boys.
4. **Reason:** because playing FPS games gives girls new insights into a male subculture. **Warrant:** It is good for girls to get new insights into a male subculture.

As Carmen began drafting her essay, she was confident she could support her first three lines of reasoning. For reason 1 she could use evidence (grounds) from personal experience to show how she learned to beat guys at video games. She could also support her warrant by showing how beating boys made her feel empowered. For reason 2, she decided that she primarily needed to support her warrant (backing). It is obvious that playing FPS games breaks feminine stereotypes. What she had to show was why it was good or valuable to be freed from feminine stereotypes. Reason 3, she felt, needed support for both the reason and the warrant. She had to show how these games gave her a different way of bonding with males (grounds) and then why this different way was a good thing (backing). Carmen felt that her reason 4 was the most complex. Here are her more detailed planning notes for reason 4:

Carmen's Planning Notes for Reason 4

Enthymeme: First-person-shooter (FPS) video games are great activities for girls because playing these games gives girls new insights into male subculture.

Grounds: I've got to show the insights into male subculture I gained.

- The guys who play these video games are intensely competitive.
  - They can play for hours without stopping—intense concentration.
  - They don't multitask—no small talk during the games; total focus on playing.
  - They take delight in winning at all costs—they boast with every kill; they call each other losers.
- They often seem homophobic or misogynist.
  - They put each other down by calling opponents "faggot" and "wussy," or other similar names that are totally obscene.
  - They associate victory with being macho.

Warrant: It is beneficial for a girl to get these insights into male subculture.

Backing: How can I show these benefits?

- It was a good learning experience to see how girls' way of bonding is very different from that of boys; girls tend to be nicer to each other rather than insulting each other. Although I enjoy winning at FPS games, as a girl I feel alienated from this male subculture.

- The game atmosphere tends to bring out these homophobic traits; guys don't talk this way as much when they are doing other things.
- This experience helped me see why men may progress faster than women in a competitive business environment—men seem programmed to crush each other and they devote enormous energy to the process.
- What else can I say? I need to think about this further.

Based on these planning notes, Carmen's composed argument went through several drafts. Here is her final version.

Title makes persuasive claim

Why Violent Video Games Are Good for Girls

CARMEN TIEU (STUDENT)

Attention-grabbing scene

It is ten o'clock P.M., game time. My entire family knows by now that when I am home on Saturday nights, ten P.M. is my gaming night when I play my favorite first-person-shooter games, usually *Halo 3,* on Xbox Live. Seated in my mobile chair in front of my family's 42-inch flat screen HDTV, I log onto Xbox Live. A small message in the bottom of the screen appears with the words "Kr1pL3r is online," alerting me that one of my male friends is online and already playing. As the game loads, I send Kr1pL3r a game invite, and he joins me in the pre-game room lobby.

Continues scene and provides more background

In the game room lobby, all the players who will be participating in the match are chatting aggressively with each other: "Oh man, we're gonna own you guys so bad." When a member of the opposing team notices my gamer tag, "embracingapathy," he begins to insult me by calling me various degrading, gay-associated names: "Embracing apa-what? Man, it sounds so emo. Are you some fag? I bet you want me so bad. You're gonna get owned!" Players always assume from my gamer tag that I am a gay male, never a female. The possibility that I am a girl is the last thing on their minds. Of course, they are right that girls seldom play first-person-shooter games. Girls are socialized into activities that promote togetherness and talk, not high-intensity competition involving fantasized shooting and killing. The violent nature of the games tends to repulse girls.

Sums up opposing views

Opponents of violent video games typically hold that these games are so graphically violent that they will influence players to become amoral and sadistic. Feminists also argue that violent video games often objectify women by portraying them as sexualized toys for men's gratification. Although I understand these objections, I argue that playing first-person-shooter games can actually

States claim

be good for girls.

States first reason

First, playing FPS games gives girls the chance to beat guys at their own game. When I first began playing *Halo 2,* I was horrible. My male friends constantly put me down for my lack of skills, constantly telling me that I was awful, "but for a girl, you're good." But it didn't take much practice until I learned to operate the two joy sticks with precision and with quick instinctual reactions. While guys and girls can play many physical games together, such as basketball or touch football, guys will always have the advantage because on average they are taller, faster, and stronger than females. However, when it comes to video games, girls can compete equally because physical strength isn't required, just quick reaction time and manual dexterity—skills that women possess in abundance. The adrenaline rush that I receive from beating a bunch of testosterone-driven guys at something they supposedly excel at is empowering and exciting; I especially savor the look of horror on their faces when I completely destroy them.

Since female video gamers are so rare, playing shooter games allows girls to be freed from feminine stereotypes and increases their confidence. Culture generally portrays females as caring, nonviolent, and motherly beings who are not supposed to enjoy FPS games with their war themes and violent killings. I am in no way rejecting these traditional female values since I myself am a compassionate, tree-hugging vegan. But I also like to break these stereotypes. Playing video games offers a great way for females to break the social mold of only doing "girly" things and introduces them to something that males commonly enjoy. Playing video games with sexist males has also helped me become more outspoken. Psychologically, I can stand up to aggressive males because I know that I can beat them at their own game. The confidence I've gotten from excelling at shooter games may have even carried over into the academic arena because I am majoring in chemical engineering and have no fear whatsoever of intruding into the male-dominated territory of math and science. Knowing that I can beat all the guys in my engineering classes at *Halo* gives me that little extra confidence boost during exams and labs.

Another reason for girls to play FPS games is that it gives us a different way of bonding with guys. Once when I was discussing my latest *Halo 3* matches with one of my regular male friends, a guy whom I didn't know turned around and said, "You play *Halo*? Wow, you just earned my respect." Although I was annoyed that this guy apparently didn't respect women in general, it is apparent that guys will talk to me differently now that I can play video games. From a guy's perspective I can also appreciate why males find video games so addicting. You get joy from perfecting your skills so that your high-angle grenade kills

States first reason

For grounds, uses personal narrative to show how she can beat guys

Briefly backs warrant by showing the good feeling of empowerment

States second reason

Details focus on backing for warrant: It is good for girls to be freed from feminine stereotypes

Provides third reason 5

Uses a narrative example for grounds; shows how FPS games give her a different way of bonding with males become a thing of beauty. While all of these skills may seem trivial to some, the acknowledgment of my skills from other players leaves me with a perverse sense of pride in knowing that I played the game better than everyone else. Since I have started playing, I have also noticed that it is much easier to talk to males about lots of different subjects. Talking video games with guys is a great ice-breaker that leads to different kinds of friendships outside the realm of romance and dating.

Finally, playing violent video games can be valuable for girls because it gives them insights into a disturbing part of male subculture. When the testosterone starts kicking in, guys become blatantly homophobic and misogynistic. Any player, regardless of gender, who cannot play well (as measured by having a high number of kills and a low number of deaths) is made fun of by being called gay, a girl, or worse. Even when some guys finally meet a female player, they will also insult her by calling her a lesbian or an ugly fat chick that has no life. Their insults towards the girl will dramatically increase if she beats them because they feel so humiliated. In their eyes, playing worse than a girl is embarrassing because girls are supposed to be inept at FPS games. Whenever I play *Halo* better than my male friends, they often comment on how "it makes no sense that we're getting owned by Carmen."

When males act like such sexist jerks it causes one to question if they are always like this. My answer is no because I know, first hand, that when guys like that are having one-on-one conversations with a female, they show a softer side, and the macho side goes away. They don't talk about how girls should stay in the kitchen and make them dinner, but rather how they think it is cool that they share a fun, common interest with a girl. But when they are in a group of males their fake, offensive macho side comes out. I find this phenomenon troubling because it shows a real problem in the way boys are socialized. To be a real "man" around other guys, they have to put down women and gays in activities involving aggressive behavior where men are supposed to excel. But they don't become macho and aggressive in activities like reading and writing, which they think of as feminine. I've always known that guys are more physically aggressive than women, but until playing violent video games I had never realized how this aggression is related to misogyny and homophobia. Perhaps these traits aren't deeply ingrained in men but come out primarily in a competitive male environment. Whatever the cause, it is an ugly phenomenon, and I'm glad that
I learned more about it. Beating guys at FPS games has made me a more confident woman while being more aware of gender differences in the way men and women are socialized. I joined the guys in playing *Halo,* but I didn't join their subculture of ridiculing women and gays.

The Thesis-Governed "Self-Announcing" Structure of Classical Argument

Like the complete classical argument explained on pages 70–71, Carmen's supporting-reasons argument has a thesis-governed structure in which she states her claim near the end of the introduction, begins body paragraphs with clearly stated reasons, and uses effective transitions throughout to keep her reader on track. This kind of tightly organized structure is sometimes called a *self-announcing* or *closed-form* structure because the writer states his or her claim before beginning the body of the argument and forecasts the structure that is to follow. In contrast, an *unfolding* or *open-form* structure often doesn't give away the writer's position until late in the essay. (We discuss delayed-thesis arguments in Chapter 7.) A general rule of thumb for arguments using more than one line of reasoning is to place your most important or interesting reason last, where it will have the greatest impact on your readers.

In writing a self-announcing argument, students often ask how much of the argument to summarize in the thesis statement. Consider Carmen's options:

- She might announce only her claim:

  Playing first-person-shooter games can be good for girls.

- She might forecast a series of parallel reasons:

  There are several reasons that playing first-person-shooter games can be good for girls.

- She might forecast the actual number of reasons:

  I will present four reasons that playing first-person-shooter games can be good for girls.

- Or she might forecast the whole argument by including her *because* clauses with her claim:

  Playing first-person-shooter games can be good for girls because it lets girls feel empowered by beating guys at their own game, because it frees girls from feminine stereotypes, because it gives girls a different way of bonding with males, and because it gives girls new insights into a male subculture.

This last thesis statement forecasts not only the claim, but also the supporting reasons that will serve as topic sentences for key paragraphs throughout the body of the paper.

No formula can tell you precisely how much of your argument to forecast in the introduction. However, these suggestions can guide you. In writing a self-announcing argument, forecast only what is needed for clarity. In short arguments, readers often need only your claim. In longer arguments, however, or in especially complex ones, readers appreciate your forecasting the complete structure of the argument (claim with reasons). Also, as we explain in later chapters, the directness of classical argument is not always the best way to reach all audiences. On many occasions more open-form or delayed-thesis approaches are more effective.

■ ■ ■   **FOR WRITING AND DISCUSSION**   **Reasons, Warrants, and Conditions** MyWritingLab™
                                                        of Rebuttal

Individual task:

1. Choose one of the following reasons. Then write a passage that provides grounds to support the reason. Use details from personal experience or imagine plausible, hypothetical details.
    a. For college students, Web surfing or checking social media can be harmful because it causes you to waste so much study time.
    b. Rap has a bad influence on teenagers because it celebrates angry violence.
    c. The university's decision to charge more for parking permits for solo drivers is a good environmental plan because it encourages students to use public transportation.

2. Now create an argument to support the warrant for the reason you chose in 1. The warrants for each of the arguments are stated below.
    a. Support this warrant: Wasting study time is harmful for college students.
    b. Support this warrant: It is bad to celebrate angry violence.
    c. Support this warrant: It is good for the environment to encourage students to use public transportation.

Group task: Working in pairs, small groups, or as a whole class, share your strategies   ■ ■ ■
for supporting your chosen reason and warrant.

Conclusion

Chapters 3 and 4 have provided an anatomy of argument. They have shown that the core of an argument is a claim with reasons that usually can be summarized in one or more *because* clauses attached to the claim. Often, it is as important to articulate and support the underlying assumptions in your argument (warrants) as it is to support the stated reasons because a successful argument should be rooted in your audience's beliefs and values. In order to plan an audience-based argument strategy, arguers can use the Toulmin schema to help them discover grounds, warrants, and backing for their arguments and test them through conditions of rebuttal.

A Note on the Informal Fallacies

The Toulmin system explained in this chapter is a response to the problem of uncertainty or inconclusiveness in real-world arguments, where we have to deal with probability as opposed to the certainty of formal logic. In the real world, we seldom encounter arguments that are absolutely conclusive. We can say that an argument is more or less "persuasive" or "non-persuasive" to certain audiences but not that it proves its case conclusively.

Another response to the problem of conclusiveness is the class of reasoning problems known as the informal fallacies. (You have probably at least heard of some of them with their exotic, Latinate, or sometimes funny names—hasty generalization, *post hoc ergo propter hoc*, slippery slope, or poisoning the well.) They are called "informal" because, like the Toulmin system, they don't focus on the form of the syllogism. Although the fallacies are not useful for helping writers plan and test their own arguments, they can often help us name what is uncertain or illogically seductive in someone else's argument. They function as a kind of compendium of the ways that flawed arguments can nevertheless seem persuasive on the surface. In this text we discuss selected fallacies at moments when they are illuminating and relevant to the material at hand.

WRITING ASSIGNMENT   **Plan of an Argument's Details**   MyWritingLab™

This assignment asks you to return to the working thesis statement that you created for the brief writing assignment in Chapter 3. From that thesis statement extract one of your enthymemes (your claim with one of your *because* clauses). Write out the warrant for your enthymeme. Then use the Toulmin schema to brainstorm the details you might use (grounds, backing, conditions of rebuttal) to convert your enthymeme into a fleshed-out argument. Use as your model Chandale's planning notes on pages 77–78 or Carmen's planning notes on pages 81–82. Note that this is a process-oriented brainstorming task aimed at helping you generate ideas for an argument in progress. You may end up changing your ideas substantially as you compose the actual argument. (An assignment to write a complete "supporting reasons" argument like Carmen's comes at the end of the next chapter on uses of evidence.) ■

MyWritingLab™

Visit Ch. 4 The Logical Structure of Arguments in *MyWritingLab* to complete the For Writing and Discussion and Writing Assignments and to test your understanding of the chapter objectives.

Using Evidence Effectively

5

What you will learn in this chapter:

5.1 To explain the different kinds of evidence

5.2 To make your evidence persuasive by using the STAR criteria and other strategies

5.3 To understand evidence rhetorically by explaining how the selection and framing of evidence reveals an angle of vision

In Chapters 3 and 4 we introduced you to the concept of *logos*—the logical structure of reasons and evidence in an argument—and showed you how an effective argument advances the writer's claim by linking its supporting reasons to one or more assumptions, beliefs, or values held by the intended audience. In this chapter, we turn to the uses of evidence in argument. By "evidence," we mean all the verifiable data and information a writer might use as support for an argument. In Toulmin's terms, evidence is part of the "grounds" or "backing" of an argument in support of reasons or warrants. By understanding evidence rhetorically, you will better understand how to use evidence ethically, responsibly, and persuasively in your own arguments.

Kinds of Evidence

5.1 To explain the different kinds of evidence

Writers have numerous options for the kinds of evidence they can use in an argument, including personal experience, observations, interviews, questionnaires, field or laboratory research, or findings derived from researching primary or secondary sources found in libraries, databases, or the World Wide Web. Carmen Tieu's argument in the last chapter is based on personal experience. More commonly, college arguments require library and Internet research—what professors call "information literacy." The skills and knowledge needed for information literacy are explained in Part Five, where we show you how to find and evaluate sources, incorporate them into your own argument, and cite and document them properly. This chapter focuses more basically on how evidence functions rhetorically in an argument and how it is selected and framed.

We will begin by categorizing different kinds of evidence, illustrating how each kind might be incorporated into an argument, and suggesting the strengths and limitations of each.

Data from Personal Experience   One powerful kind of evidence comes from personal experience:

Example	Strengths and Limitations
Despite recent criticism that Ritalin is overprescribed for hyperactivity and attention-deficit disorder, it can often seem like a miracle drug. My little brother is a perfect example. Before he was given Ritalin, he was a terror in school.... [Tell the "before" and "after" story of your little brother.]	▪ Personal-experience examples help readers identify with writer; they show writer's personal connection to the issue. ▪ Vivid stories capture the imagination and appeal to *pathos*. ▪ Skeptics may sometimes argue that personal-experience examples are insufficient (writer is guilty of hasty generalization), not typical, or not adequately scientific or verifiable.

Data from Observation or Field Research   You can also develop evidence by personally observing a phenomenon or by doing your own field research:

Example	Strengths and Limitations
The intersection at Fifth and Montgomery is particularly dangerous because pedestrians almost never find a comfortable break in the heavy flow of cars. On April 29, I watched fifty-seven pedestrians cross the street. Not once did cars stop in both directions before the pedestrian stepped off the sidewalk onto the street. [Continue with observed data about danger.]	▪ Field research gives the feeling of scientific credibility. ▪ It increases typicality by expanding database beyond example of one person. ▪ It enhances the *ethos* of the writer as personally invested and reasonable. ▪ Skeptics may point to flaws in how observations were conducted, showing how data are insufficient, inaccurate, or nontypical.

Data from Interviews, Questionnaires, Surveys   You can also gather data by interviewing stakeholders in a controversy, creating questionnaires, or doing surveys.

Example	Strengths and Limitations
Another reason to ban laptops from classrooms is the extent to which laptop users disturb other students. In a question-naire that I distributed to fifty students in my residence hall, a surprising 60 percent said that they are annoyed by fellow stu-dents checking Facebook, sending e-mail, paying their bills, or surfing the Web while pretending to take notes in class. Additionally, I interviewed five students who gave me specific examples of how these distractions interfere with learning. [Report the examples.]	▪ Interviews, questionnaires, and surveys enhance the sufficiency and typicality of evidence by expanding the database beyond the experiences of one person. ▪ Quantitative data from questionnaires and surveys often increase the scientific feel of the argument. ▪ Surveys and questionnaires often uncover local or recent data not available in published research. ▪ Interviews can provide engaging personal stories, thus enhancing *pathos*. ▪ Skeptics can raise doubts about research methodology, questionnaire design, or typicality of interview subjects.

Data from Library or Internet Research   For many arguments, evidence is derived from reading, particularly from library or Internet research. Part Five of this text helps you conduct effective research and incorporate research sources into your arguments:

Example	Strengths and Limitations
The belief that a high-carbohydrate, low-fat diet is the best way to lose weight has been challenged by research conducted by Walter Willett and his colleagues in the department of nutrition at the Harvard School of Public Health. Willett's research suggests that complex carbohydrates such as pasta and potatoes spike glucose levels, increasing the risk of diabetes. Additionally, some fats— especially monounsaturated and polyun-saturated fats found in nuts, fish, and most vegetable oils—help lower "bad" cholesterol levels (45).*	▪ Researched evidence is often powerful, especially when sources are respected by your audience; writers can spotlight source's credentials through attributive tags. ▪ Researched data may take the form of facts, examples, quotations, summaries of research studies, and so forth. ▪ Skeptics might doubt the accuracy of facts, the credentials of a source, or the research design of a study. They might also cite studies with different results. ▪ Skeptics might raise doubts about sufficiency, typicality, or relevance of your research data.

Testimony   Writers frequently use testimony when direct data are either unavailable or highly technical or complex. Testimonial evidence can come from research or from interviews:

---

*Parenthetical citations in this example and the next follow the MLA documentation system.

Example	Strengths and Limitations
Although the Swedish economist Bjorn Lomborg claims that acid rain is not a significant problem, many environmentalists disagree. According to David Bellamany, president of the Conservation Foundation, "Acid rain does kill forests and people around the world, and it's still doing so in the most polluted places, such as Russia" (qtd. in *BBC News*).	■ By itself, testimony is generally less persuasive than direct data. ■ Persuasiveness can be increased if source has impressive credentials, which the writer can state through attributive tags introducing the testimony. ■ Skeptics might undermine testimonial evidence by questioning credentials of source, showing source's bias, or quoting a countersource.

Statistical Data   Many contemporary arguments rely heavily on statistical data, often supplemented by graphics such as tables, pie charts, and graphs. (See Chapter 9 for a discussion of the use of graphics in argument.)

Example	Strengths and Limitations
Americans are delaying marriage at a surprising rate. In 1970, 85 percent of Americans between ages twenty-five and twenty-nine were married. In 2010, however, only 45 percent were married (U.S. Census Bureau).	■ Statistics can give powerful snapshots of aggregate data from a wide database. ■ They are often used in conjunction with graphics (see pages 200–206). ■ They can be calculated and displayed in different ways to achieve different rhetorical effects, so the reader must be wary (see page 101). ■ Skeptics might question statistical methods, research design, and interpretation of data.

Hypothetical Examples, Cases, and Scenarios   Arguments occasionally use hypothetical examples, cases, or scenarios, particularly to illustrate conjectured consequences of an event or to test philosophical hypotheses:

Example	Strengths and Limitations
Consider what might happen if we continue to use biotech soybeans that are resistant to herbicides. The resistant gene, through cross-pollination, might be transferred to an ordinary weed, creating an out-of-control superweed that herbicides couldn't kill. Such a superweed could be an ecological disaster.	■ Scenarios have strong imaginative appeal. ■ They are persuasive only if they seem plausible. ■ A scenario narrative often conveys a sense of "inevitability" even if the actual scenario is unlikely; hence rhetorical effect may be illogical. ■ Skeptics might show the implausibility of the scenario or offer an alternative scenario.

Reasoned Sequence of Ideas   Sometimes arguments are supported with a reasoned sequence of ideas rather than with concrete facts or other forms of empirical evidence. The writer's concern is to support a point through a logical progression of ideas. Such arguments are conceptual, supported by linked ideas, rather than evidential. This kind of support occurs frequently in arguments and is often intermingled with evidential support.

Example	Strengths and Limitations
Embryonic stem cell research, despite its promise in fighting diseases, may have negative social consequences. This research encourages us to place embryos in the category of mere cellular matter that can be manipulated at will. Currently we reduce animals to this category when we genetically alter them for human purposes, such as engineering pigs to grow more human-like heart valves for use in transplants. Using human embryos in the same way—as material that can be altered and destroyed at will—may benefit society materially, but this quest for greater knowledge and control involves a reclassifying of embryos that could potentially lead to a devaluing of human life.	▪ These sequences are often used in causal arguments to show how causes are linked to effects or in definitional or values arguments to show links among ideas. ▪ They have great power to clarify values and show the belief structure on which a claim is founded. ▪ They can sketch out ideas and connections that would otherwise remain latent. ▪ Their effectiveness depends on the audience's acceptance of each link in the sequence of ideas. ▪ Skeptics might raise objections at any link in the sequence, often by pointing to different values or outlining different consequences.

The Persuasive Use of Evidence

5.2 To make your evidence persuasive by using the STAR criteria and other strategies

We turn now from kinds of evidence to strategies for making evidence as convincing and persuasive as possible. Consider a target audience of educated, reasonable, and careful readers who approach an issue with healthy skepticism, open-minded but cautious. What demands would such readers make on a writer's use of evidence? To begin to answer that question, let's look at some general principles for using evidence persuasively.

Apply the STAR Criteria to Evidence

Our open-minded but skeptical audience would first of all expect the evidence to meet what rhetorician Richard Fulkerson calls the STAR criteria:*

> **S**ufficiency: Is there enough evidence?
>
> **T**ypicality: Is the chosen evidence representative and typical?
>
> **A**ccuracy: Is the evidence accurate and up-to-date?
>
> **R**elevance: Is the evidence relevant to the claim?
>
> Let's examine each in turn.

---

*Richard Fulkerson, *Teaching the Argument in Writing* (Urbana, IL: National Council of Teachers of English, 1996), 44–53. In this section, we are indebted to Fulkerson's discussion.

Sufficiency of Evidence   How much evidence you need is a function of your rhetorical context. In a court trial, opposing attorneys often agree to waive evidence for points that aren't in doubt in order to concentrate on contested points. The more a claim is contested or the more your audience is skeptical, the more evidence you may need to present. If you provide too little evidence, you may be accused of *hasty generalization,* a reasoning fallacy in which a person makes a sweeping conclusion based on only one or two instances. On the other hand, if you provide too much evidence your argument may become overly long and tedious. You can guard against having too little or too much evidence by appropriately qualifying the claim your evidence supports.

> **Strong claim:** Working full-time seriously harms a student's grade point average. (much data needed—probably a combination of examples and statistical studies)
>
> **Qualified claim**: Working full-time often harms a student's grade point average. (a few representative examples may be enough)

Typicality of Evidence   Whenever you select evidence, readers need to believe the evidence is typical and representative rather than extreme instances. Suppose that you want to argue that students can combine full-time work with full-time college and cite the case of your friend Pam, who pulled a straight-A grade point average while working forty hours per week as a night receptionist in a small hotel. Your audience might doubt the typicality of Pam's case since a night receptionist can often use work hours for studying. What about more typical jobs, they'll ask, where you can't study while you work?

Accuracy of Evidence   Evidence can't be used ethically unless it is accurate and up-to-date, and it can't be persuasive unless the audience believes in the credibility of the writer's sources. We'll develop this point more fully later in this section.

Relevance of Evidence   Finally, evidence will be persuasive only if the reader considers it relevant to what is at stake in the dispute. Consider the following student argument: "I deserve an A in this course because I worked exceptionally hard." The student then cites substantial evidence of how hard he worked—a log of study hours, copies of multiple drafts of papers, testimony from friends, and so forth. But what is at stake here is the underlying assumption (warrant) that grades should be based on effort, not quality of work. The student provides ample evidence to support the reason ("I worked exceptionally hard") but this evidence is irrelevant for the warrant ("People who work exceptionally hard deserve an A"). Although some instructors may give partial credit for effort, the criterion for grades is usually the quality of the student's performance, not the student's time spent studying.

Establish a Trustworthy Ethos

Besides supplying evidence that meets the STAR criteria, you can make your evidence more persuasive by being fair, honest, and open to uncertainty (the appeal to *ethos*— see Chapter 6, pages 106–107). To establish your readers' confidence, you must first tell them the source of your evidence. If your evidence comes from personal experience or observation, your prose needs to make that clear. If your evidence comes from others (say through interviews or library/Internet research), you must indicate these sources through attributive tags (phrases like "according to T. Alvarez" or "as stated by a recent EPA report"). For academic papers, you must also cite and document your sources using an appropriate style for in-text citations and concluding bibliography. Finally, you need to be fair in the way you select evidence from your research sources. For example, it is unethical to take quotations out of context or to write an unfair summary that oversimplifies or distorts a source author's intended meaning.

Be Mindful of a Source's Distance from Original Data

When you support an argument through library/Internet research, you often encounter sources that report evidence from a second- or third-hand perspective. You need to imagine where your source author found the information that you now want to use in your own argument. How might you trace the process that led from the original data to your source author's use of it? Let's take as an example a passage from James Surowiecki's article on the minimum wage reprinted in Chapter 2. Because this is a magazine article rather than an academic paper, it contains no footnotes or bibliography, but Surowiecki nevertheless uses attributive tags to identify his main sources. Here is a passage from page 33:

Passage from "The Pay Is Too Damn Low" by James Surowiecki

Attributive tag (cites this study as his source)

Purported factual statement that we are examining

[O]ver the past three decades, the U.S. economy has done a poor job of creating good middle-class jobs; five of the six fastest-growing job categories today pay less than the median wage. That's why, as a recent study by the economists John Schmitt and Janelle Jones has shown, low-wage workers are older and better educated than ever. More important, more of them are relying on their paychecks not for pin money or to pay for Friday-night dates but, rather, to support families.

Much of Surowiecki's argument for increasing the minimum wage depends on evidence that low-wage workers are "older and better educated than ever." But we might ask, How does Surowiecki know about the age and education of low-wage workers? Why should we trust him? Using an attributive tag, he identifies his source as a recent study by economists John Schmitt and Janelle Jones. We plugged these names into a Google search and quickly located the source: A white paper titled, "Low-wage Workers Are Older and Better Educated than Ever," dated April 2012, from the Center for Economic and Policy Research, which, according to its Web site, is a nonprofit, nonpartisan research center aimed at providing factual economic data for public policy makers.

So where did Schmitt and Jones get their data? They cite statistical tables compiled by the "Current Population Survey," which is a joint effort of the Census Bureau and Bureau of Labor Statistics. Based on these original data, Schmitt and Jones constructed two graphs showing shifts in distribution of low-wage workers by age and then by education from 1971 to 2011. One of these graphs, for example, shows that in 1979, 26 percent of low-wage jobs were held by teenagers, but by 2011 only 12 percent were teenagers. (You can see this graph in Chapter 2, Figure 2.3, page 22). Conversely, the second graph shows that in 1979 only 25 percent of low-wage job holders had completed at least some college, but by 2011, 43 percent had completed some college.

Let's summarize the process we have just traced: The original data came from government statistics collected by the Census Bureau and the Bureau of Labor Statistics. Schmitt and Jones then converted these data into detailed graphs. Surowiecki then summarized the message of the graphs into his single sentence. If you were then to cite Surowiecki as your source for this same information, you would be depending on a chain of trust stretching from the original data through Schmitt and Jones and Surowiecki to you. Of course, you can't be expected to trace all your research-gathered evidence back to the original data, but you need to imagine that it is possible to do so. Ideally, the closer you can get to the original data, the more trustworthy your evidence. Often, unfortunately, fact-checkers employed by news sources or nonprofit organizations discover that purportedly accurate information cannot be traced back to a credible original source. They might show that the information is not factual at all, that it is derived from flawed or discredited studies, that it has been distorted unfairly, or that sometimes it has even been invented in the service of propaganda. *Politifact.com*, a nationally respected fact-checker, uses a "truth-o-meter" to rank purported evidential statements along a scale from "True" to "False," with the most egregiously false statements earning their famous "Pants-on-Fire" award. To develop a respected *ethos*, you need to develop your own internal truth-o-meter by being aware of a source's distance from the original data and by occasionally tracing back a piece of evidence to its origins.

Rhetorical Understanding of Evidence

5.3 To understand evidence rhetorically by explaining how the selection and framing of evidence reveals an angle of vision

In the previous section we presented some principles for persuasive use of evidence. We now ask you to look more closely at the rhetorical context in which evidence operates.

Angle of Vision and the Selection and Framing of Evidence

When we enter the argumentative arena, we come as complex, whole persons, not as disembodied computers that reach claims through a value-free calculus. We enter with our own ideologies, beliefs, values, and guiding assumptions as formed by our particular lived lives. These differences help explain why one person's terrorist might be another person's freedom fighter or why a hand gun in a drawer might be one person's defense against intruders and another person's child accident waiting to happen. In writing about guns, a believer in Second Amendment rights is apt to cite evidence that having a gun can stop a violent intruder or prevent a rape. Conversely, proponents of gun control are apt to cite evidence about accidental deaths or suicides. In an argument, evidence is always selected to further the arguer's claim and is never simply an inert, neutral "fact."

These guiding beliefs and values work together to create a writer's "angle of vision." By this term we mean a perspective, bias, lens, filter, frame, or screen that helps determine what a writer sees or doesn't see. This angle of vision makes certain items stand out in a field of data and other items become invisible. It both determines and reveals the writer's view of which data are important and which are trivial, which are significant, and which can be ignored.

To illustrate how angle of vision creates this kind of selective seeing, consider how two hypothetical speakers might select different data about homeless people when presenting speeches to their city council. The first speaker argues that the city should increase its services to the homeless. The second asks the city to promote tourism more aggressively. Their differing angles of vision will cause the two speakers to select different data about homeless people and to frame these data in different ways. Because the first speaker wants to increase the council's sympathy for the homeless, she frames homeless people positively by telling the story of one homeless man's struggle to find shelter and nutritious food. Her speech focuses primarily on the low number of tax dollars devoted to helping the homeless. In contrast, the second speaker, using data about lost tourist income, might frame the homeless as "panhandlers" by telling the story of obnoxious, urine-soaked winos who pester shoppers for handouts. As arguers, both speakers want their audience to see the homeless from their own angles of vision. Consequently, lost tourist dollars don't show up at all in the first speaker's argument, whereas the story of a homeless man's night in the cold doesn't show up in the second speaker's argument. As this example shows, one goal writers have in selecting and framing evidence is to bring the reader's view of the subject into alignment with the writer's angle of vision. The writer selects and frames evidence to limit and control what the reader sees.

To help you better understand the concepts of selection and framing, we offer the following exercise based on different angles of vision regarding "festival seating" at rock concerts. Because of nationally reported injuries and near-death experiences resulting from stage diving and crowd surfing at rock concerts, many cities have tried to ban festival seating that allows for the spontaneous creation of mosh pits. Critics of mosh pits have pointed to the injuries caused by crowd surfing and to the ensuing lawsuits against concert venues. Meanwhile, supporters cite the almost ecstatic enjoyment of crowd-surfing rock fans who seek out concerts with "festival seating."

Suppose that your city has scheduled a public hearing on a proposed ordinance to ban mosh pits at rock concerts. Among the possible data and evidence available to various speakers are the following:

- Some bands, such as Nine Inch Nails, specify festival seating that allows a mosh pit area.
- A female mosher writing on the Internet says: "I experience a shared energy that is like no other when I am in the pit with the crowd. It is like we are all a bunch of atoms bouncing off of each other. It's great. Hey, some people get that feeling from basketball games. I get mine from the mosh pit."

- A student conducted a survey of fifty students on her campus who had attended rock concerts in the last six months. Of the respondents, 80 percent thought that mosh pits should be allowed at concerts.
- Narrative comments on these questionnaires included the following:
    - Mosh pits are a passion for me. I get an amazing rush when crowd surfing.
    - I don't like to be in a mosh pit or do crowd surfing. But I love festival seating and like to watch the mosh pits. For me, mosh pits are part of the ambience of a concert.
    - I know a girl who was groped in a mosh pit, and she'll never do one again. But I have never had any problems.
    - Mosh pits are dangerous and stupid. I think they should be outlawed.
    - If you are afraid of mosh pits, just stay away. Nobody forces you to go into a mosh pit! It is ridiculous to ban them because they are totally voluntary. They should just post big signs saying, "City assumes no responsibility for accidents occurring in mosh pit area."
- On September 14, 2013, six people were taken to hospitals with injuries after a mosh pit broke out at the Riot Fest music festival in Chicago.
- According to a 2008 ABC news special, a company specializing in crowd management at rock festivals estimated that "10,000 people have been injured in and around mosh pits in the last decade." The company said further that "most injuries incurred from mosh pits aren't actually by the moshers but by innocent bystanders."
- In 2005, a blogger reported breaking his nose on an elbow; another described having his lip ring pulled out. Another blogger on the same site described having his lip nearly sliced off by the neck of a bass guitar. The injury required seventy-eight stitches. In May 2008, fifty people were treated at emergency rooms for mosh pit injuries acquired at a Bamboozle concert in New Jersey.
- Twenty-four concert deaths were recorded in 2001, most of them in the area closest to the stage where people are packed in.
- A twenty-one-year-old man suffered cardiac arrest at a Metallica concert in Indiana and is now in a permanent vegetative state. Because he was jammed into the mosh pit area, nobody noticed he was in distress.
- A teenage girl suffered brain damage and memory loss at a 1998 Pearl Jam concert in Rapid City, South Dakota. According to her attorney, she hadn't intended to body surf or enter the mosh pit but "got sucked in while she was standing at its fringe."
- The Web site Wikihow offers tips on staying safe in a mosh pit. According to the site, "While it may seem otherwise, moshing is by no means a way to hurt someone. Moshing is about releasing aggression, and having fun while enjoying some awesome music."

■ ■ ■ **FOR WRITING AND DISCUSSION Creating Contrasting Angles** MyWritingLab™
of Vision

Individual task: Compose two short speeches, one supporting the proposed city ordinance to ban mosh pits and one opposing it. How you use these data is up to you, but be able to explain your reasoning in the way you select and frame your evidence.

Group task: Working in pairs or as a whole class, share your speeches with class-mates. Then, after you have shared examples of different speeches, explain the approaches that different classmates employed. What principle of selection was used? If arguers included evidence contrary to their positions, how did they handle it, respond to it, minimize its importance, or otherwise channel its rhetorical effect? ■ ■ ■

EXAMINING VISUAL ARGUMENTS

MyWritingLab™

Crowd surfing in a mosh pit

Angle of Vision

Angle of vision can be conveyed visually as well as verbally. These photos display different angles of vision toward mosh pits. Suppose you were writing a blog in support of festival seating and mosh pits. Which image would you include in your posting? Why? Suppose alternatively that you were blogging against mosh pits, perhaps urging local officials to outlaw them. Which image would you choose? Why?

Analyze the visual features of these photographs in order to explain how they are constructed to create alternative angles of vision on mosh pits.

An alternative view of a mosh pit

Rhetorical Strategies for Framing Evidence

What we hope you learned from the preceding exercises is that an arguer consciously selects evidence from a wide field of data and then frames these data through rhetorical strategies that emphasize some data, minimize others, and guide the reader's response. Now that you have a basic idea of what we mean by framing of evidence, here are some strategies writers can use to guide what the reader sees and feels.

Strategies for Framing Evidence

- **Controlling the space given to supporting versus contrary evidence:** Depending on their audience and purpose, writers can devote most of their space to supporting evidence and minimal space to contrary evidence (or omit it entirely). Thus people arguing in favor of mosh pits may have used lots of evidence supporting mosh pits, including enthusiastic quotations from concertgoers, while omitting (or summarizing very rapidly) the data about the dangers of mosh pits.
- **Emphasizing a detailed story versus presenting lots of facts and statistics:** Often, writers can choose to support a point with a memorable individual case or with aggregate data such as statistics or lists of facts. A memorable story can have a strongly persuasive effect. For example, to create a negative view of mosh pits, a writer might tell the heartrending story of a teenager suffering permanent brain damage from being dropped on a mosh pit floor. In contrast, a supporter of mosh pits might tell the story of a happy music lover turned on to the concert scene by the rush of crowd surfing. A different strategy is to use facts and statistics rather than case narratives—for example, data about the frequency of mosh pit accidents, financial consequences of lawsuits, and so forth. The single-narrative case often has a more powerful rhetorical effect, but it is always open to the charge that it is an insufficient or nonrepresentative example. Vivid anecdotes make for interesting reading, but by themselves they may not be compelling logically. In contrast, aggregate data, often used in scholarly studies, can provide more compelling, logical evidence but sometimes make the prose wonkish and dense.
- **Providing contextual and interpretive comments when presenting data:** When citing data, writers can add brief contextual or interpretive comments that act as lenses over the readers' eyes to help them see the data from the writer's perspective. Suppose you want to support mosh pits, but also want to admit that mosh pits are dangerous. You could make that danger seem irrelevant or inconsequential by saying: "It is true that occasional mosh pit accidents happen, just as accidents happen in any kind of recreational activity such as swimming or weekend softball games." The concluding phrase frames the danger of mosh pits by comparing it to other recreational accidents that don't require special laws or regulations. The implied argument is this: banning mosh pits because of an occasional accident would be as silly as banning recreational swimming because of occasional accidents.

- **Putting contrary evidence in subordinate positions:** Just as a photographer can place a flower at the center of a photograph or in the background, a writer can place a piece of data in a subordinate or main clause of a sentence. Note how the structure of the following sentence minimizes emphasis on the rarity of mosh pit accidents: "Although mosh pit accidents are rare, the danger to the city of multi-million-dollar liability lawsuits means that the city should nevertheless ban them for reasons of fiscal prudence." The factual data that mosh pit accidents are rare is summarized briefly and tucked away in a subordinate *although* clause, while the writer's own position is elaborated in the main clause where it receives grammatical emphasis. A writer with a different angle of vision might say, "Although some cities may occasionally be threatened with a lawsuit, serious accidents resulting from mosh pits are so rare that cities shouldn't interfere with the desires of music fans to conduct concerts as they please."
- **Choosing labels and names that guide the reader's response to data:** One of the most subtle ways to control your readers' response to data is to choose labels and names that prompt them to see the issue as you do. If you like mosh pits, you might refer to the seating arrangements in a concert venue as "festival seating, where concertgoers have the opportunity to create a free-flowing mosh pit." If you don't like mosh pits, you might refer to the seating arrangements as "an accident-inviting use of empty space where rowdies can crowd together, slam into each other, and occasionally punch and kick." The labels you choose, along with the connotations of the words you select, urge your reader to share your angle of vision.
- **Using images (photographs, drawings) to guide the reader's response to data:** Another strategy for moving your audience toward your angle of vision is to include a photograph or drawing that portrays a contested issue from your perspective. Consider how the photographs on page 98 make arguments about mosh pits. Most people agree that the first photo supports a positive view of mosh pits. The crowd looks happy and relaxed (rather than rowdy or out of control), and the young woman lifted above the crowd smiles broadly, her body relaxed, her arms extended. In contrast, the second photo emphasizes muscular men (rather than a smiling and relaxed woman) and threatens danger rather than harmony. The crowd seems on the verge of turning ugly. (See Chapter 9 for a complete discussion of the use of visuals in argument.)
- **Revealing the value system that determines the writer's selection and framing of data:** Ultimately, how a writer selects and frames evidence is linked to the system of values that organize his or her argument. If you favor mosh pits, you probably favor maximizing the pleasure of concertgoers, promoting individual choice, and letting moshers assume the risk of their own behavior. If you want to forbid mosh pits, you probably favor minimizing risks, protecting the city from lawsuits, and protecting individuals from the danger of their own out-of-control actions. Sometimes you can foster connections with your audience by openly addressing the underlying values that you hope your audience shares with you. You can often frame your selected data by stating explicitly the values that guide your argument.

Special Strategies for Framing Statistical Evidence

Numbers and statistical data can be framed in so many ways that this category of evidence deserves its own separate treatment. By recognizing how writers frame numbers to support the story they want to tell, you will always be aware that other stories are also possible. Ethical use of numbers means that you use reputable sources for your basic data, that you don't invent or intentionally distort numbers for your own purposes, and that you don't ignore alternative points of view. Here are some of the choices writers make when framing statistical data:

- **Raw numbers versus percentages.** You can alter the rhetorical effect of a statistic by choosing between raw numbers and percentages. In the summer of 2002, many American parents panicked over what seemed like an epidemic of child abductions. If you cited the raw number of these abductions reported in the national news, this number, although small, could seem scary. But if you computed the actual percentage of American children who were abducted, that percentage was so infinitesimally small as to seem insignificant. You can apply this framing option directly to the mosh pit case. To emphasize the danger of mosh pits, you can say that twenty-four deaths occurred at rock concerts in a given year. To minimize this statistic, you could compute the percentage of deaths by dividing this number by the total number of people who attended rock concerts during the year, certainly a number in the several millions. From the perspective of percentages, the death rate at concerts is extremely low.

- **Median versus mean.** Another way to alter the rhetorical effect of numbers is to choose between the median and the mean. The mean is the average of all numbers on a list. The median is the middle number when all the numbers are arranged sequentially from high to low. In 2006 the mean annual income for retired families in the United States was $41,928—not a wealthy amount but enough to live on comfortably if you owned your own home. However, the median income was only $27,798, a figure that gives a much more striking picture of income distribution among older Americans. This median figure means that half of all retired families in the United States had annual incomes of $27,798 or less. The much higher mean income indicates that many retired Americans are quite wealthy. This wealth raises the average of all incomes (the mean) but doesn't affect the median.

- **Unadjusted versus adjusted numbers.** Suppose your boss told you that you were getting a 5 percent raise. You might be happy—unless inflation rates were running at 6 percent. Economic data can be hard to interpret across time unless the dollar amounts are adjusted for inflation. This same problem occurs in other areas. For example, comparing grade point averages of college graduates in 1970 versus 2012 means little unless one can somehow compensate for grade inflation.

- **Base point for statistical comparisons.** Suppose you create a graph of global average temperatures from 1998 to the present. This graph, with 1998 as a base starting point, will suggest that the earth is cooling slightly, not heating up. However, if you begin the graph in 1980, the line, though fluctuating, rises steadily. (See graph on page 248). One's choice of the base point for a comparison often makes a significant rhetorical difference.

■ ■ ■   **FOR CLASS DISCUSSION**   Using Strategies to Frame Statistical Evidence

A proposal to build a publicly funded sports stadium in a major American city yielded a wide range of statistical arguments. All of the following statements are reasonably faithful to the same facts:

- The stadium would be paid for by raising the sales tax from 8.2 percent to 8.3 percent during a twenty-year period.
- The sales tax increase is one-tenth of 1 percent.
- This increase represents an average of $7.50 per person per year—about the price of a large special coffee drink and a pastry.
- This increase represents $750 per five-person family over the twenty-year period of the tax.
- For a family building a new home in this city, this tax will increase building costs by $200.
- This is a $250 million tax increase for city residents.

How would you describe the costs of the proposed ballpark if you opposed the proposal?
How would you describe the costs if you supported the proposal?   ■ ■ ■

Creating a Plan for Gathering Evidence

We conclude this chapter with a list of brainstorming questions that may help you think of possible sources for evidence in your own argument. As you begin contemplating an argument, you can use the following checklist to help you think of possible sources for evidence.

A Checklist for Brainstorming Sources of Evidence

- What personal experiences have you had with this issue? What details from your life or the lives of your friends, acquaintances, or relatives might serve as examples or other kinds of evidence?
- What observational studies would be relevant to this issue?
- What people could you interview to provide insights or expert knowledge on this issue?
- What questions about your issue could be addressed in a survey or questionnaire?
- What useful information on this issue might encyclopedias or specialized references in your university library provide?
- What evidence might you seek on this issue using licensed databases to search for relevant articles from magazines, newspapers, and scholarly journals?
- How might an Internet search engine help you research this issue?
- What evidence might you find on this issue from reliable statistical resources such as U.S. Census Bureau data, the Centers for Disease Control, or *Statistical Abstract of the United States*?

Conclusion

Effective use of evidence is an essential skill for arguers. In this chapter we showed you various kinds of evidence ranging from personal experience to library/Internet research. We then discussed ways you can make your evidence persuasive by applying the STAR criteria, developing a trustworthy *ethos*, and being mindful of a secondary source's distance from the original data. We next examined how a writer's angle of vision influences his or her selection and framing of evidence. Finally, we described framing strategies for emphasizing evidence, de-emphasizing it, and guiding your reader's response to it.

WRITING ASSIGNMENT   A Supporting-Reasons Argument   MyWritingLab™

Write an argument that uses at least two reasons to support your claim. Your argument should include all the features of a classical argument except that you can omit the section on summarizing and responding to opposing views, which we will cover in Chapter 7. This assignment builds on the brief writing assignments in Chapter 3 (create a thesis statement for an argument) and Chapter 4 (brainstorm support for one of your enthymemes using the Toulmin schema). Like a complete classical argument, a supporting-reasons argument has a thesis-governed structure in which you state your claim at the end of the introduction, begin body paragraphs with clearly stated reasons, and use effective transitions throughout to keep your reader on track. In developing your own argument, place your most important, persuasive, or interesting reason last, where it will have the greatest impact on your readers. A model for a supporting-reasons argument is Carmen Tieu's "Why Violent Video Games Are Good for Girls" on pages 82–84. ■

MyWritingLab™

Visit Ch. 5 Using Evidence Effectively in *MyWritingLab* to complete the For Writing and Discussion, Examining Visual Arguments, and Writing Assignments and to test your understanding of the chapter objectives.

Moving Your Audience
Ethos, Pathos, and *Kairos*

6

What you will learn in this chapter:

6.1 To explain how the classical appeals of *logos, ethos,* and *pathos* work together to move your audience

6.2 To create effective appeals to *ethos*

6.3 To create effective appeals to *pathos*

6.4 To be mindful of *kairos* or the "timeliness" of your argument

6.5 To explain how images make visual appeals to *logos, ethos, pathos,* and *kairos*

6.6 To explain how audience-based reasons appeal to *logos, ethos, pathos,* and *kairos*

In Chapters 4 and 5 we focused on *logos*—the logical structure of reasons and evidence in argument. Even though we have treated *logos* in its own chapters, an effective arguer's concern for *logos* is always connected to *ethos* and *pathos* (see the rhetorical triangle introduced in Chapter 3, page 55) and always considers the *kairos*, or timeliness of the argument. This chapter explains how arguers can create effective appeals from *ethos, pathos,* and *kairos*. It also explains the crucial role played by concrete language, examples, narrative stories, and use of images in enhancing ethical and emotional appeals. We conclude by showing how audience-based reasons enhance *logos* while also appealing to *ethos* and *pathos*.

Logos, Ethos, and *Pathos* as Persuasive Appeals: An Overview

6.1 To explain how the classical appeals of *logos, ethos,* and *pathos* work together to move your audience

At first, one may be tempted to think of *logos, ethos,* and *pathos* as "ingredients" in an essay, like spices you add to a casserole. But a more appropriate metaphor might be that of different lamps and filters used on theater spotlights to vary lighting effects on a stage. Thus if you switch on a *pathos* lamp (possibly through using more concrete language or vivid examples), the resulting image will engage the audience's sympathy and emotions more deeply. If you overlay an *ethos* filter (perhaps by adopting a different tone toward your audience), the projected image of the writer as a person will be subtly altered. If you switch on a *logos* lamp (by adding, say, more data for evidence), you will draw the reader's attention to the logical appeal of the argument. Depending on how you modulate the lamps and filters, you shape and color your readers' perception of you and your argument.

Our metaphor is imperfect, of course, but our point is that *logos, ethos,* and *pathos* work together to create an impact on the reader. Consider, for example, the different impacts of the following arguments, all having roughly the same logical appeal.

1. People should adopt a vegetarian diet because doing so will help prevent the cruelty to animals caused by factory farming.
2. If you are planning to eat chicken tonight, please consider how much that chicken suffered so that you could have a tender and juicy meal. Commercial growers cram the chickens so tightly together into cages that they never walk on their own legs, see sunshine, or flap their wings. In fact, their beaks must be cut off to keep them from pecking each other's eyes out. One way to prevent such suffering is for more and more people to become vegetarians.
3. People who eat meat are no better than sadists who torture other sentient creatures to enhance their own pleasure. Unless you enjoy sadistic tyranny over others, you have only one choice: become a vegetarian.
4. People committed to justice might consider the extent to which our love of eating meat requires the agony of animals. A visit to a modern chicken factory—where chickens live their entire lives in tiny, darkened coops without room to spread their wings—might raise doubts about our right to inflict such suffering on sentient creatures. Indeed, such a visit might persuade us that vegetarianism is a more just alternative.

Each argument has roughly the same logical core:

ENTHYMEME

CLAIM People should adopt a vegetarian diet

REASON because doing so will help prevent the cruelty to animals caused by factory farming.

GROUNDS

• Evidence of suffering in commercial chicken farms, where chickens are crammed together and lash out at one another

• Evidence that only widespread adoption of vegetarianism will end factory farming

WARRANT

If we have an alternative to making animals suffer, we should use it.

But the impact of each argument varies. The difference between arguments 1 and 2, most of our students report, is the greater emotional power of argument 2. Whereas argument 1 refers only to the abstraction "cruelty to animals," argument 2 paints a vivid picture of chickens with their beaks cut off to prevent their pecking each other blind. Argument 2 makes a stronger appeal to *pathos* (not necessarily a stronger argument), stirring feelings by appealing simultaneously to the heart and to the head.

The difference between arguments 1 and 3 concerns both *ethos* and *pathos*. Argument 3 appeals to the emotions through highly charged words such as *torture, sadists,* and *tyranny.* But argument 3 also draws attention to its writer, and most of our students report not liking that writer very much. His stance is self-righteous and insulting. In contrast, argument 4's author establishes a more positive *ethos.* He establishes rapport by assuming his audience is committed to justice and by qualifying his argument with the conditional term *might.* He also invites sympathy for the chickens' plight—an appeal to *pathos*—by offering a specific description of chickens crammed into tiny coops.

Which of these arguments is best? The answer depends on the intended audience. Arguments 1 and 4 seem aimed at receptive audiences reasonably open to exploration of the issue, whereas arguments 2 and 3 seem designed to shock complacent audiences or to rally a group of True Believers. Even argument 3, which is too abusive to be effective in most instances, might work as a rallying speech at a convention of animal liberation activists.

Our point thus far is that *logos, ethos,* and *pathos* are different aspects of the same whole, different lenses for intensifying or softening the light beam you project onto the screen. Every choice you make as a writer affects in some way each of the three appeals. The rest of this chapter examines these choices in more detail.

How to Create an Effective *Ethos*: The Appeal to Credibility

6.2 To create effective appeals to *ethos*

The ancient Greek and Roman rhetoricians recognized that an argument would be more persuasive if the audience trusted the speaker. Aristotle argued that such trust resides within the speech itself, not in the prior reputation of the speaker. In the speaker's manner and delivery, tone, word choice, and arrangement of reasons, in the sympathy with which he or she treats alternative views, the speaker creates a trustworthy persona. Aristotle called the impact of the speaker's credibility the appeal from *ethos.* How does a writer create credibility? We suggest four ways:

- **Be knowledgeable about your issue.** The first way to gain credibility is to *be credible*—that is, to argue from a strong base of knowledge, to have at hand the examples, personal experiences, statistics, and other empirical data needed to make a sound case. If you have done your homework, you will command the attention of most audiences.
- **Be fair.** Besides being knowledgeable about your issue, you need to demonstrate fairness and courtesy to alternative views. Because true argument can occur only where people may reasonably disagree with one another, your *ethos* will be

strengthened if you demonstrate that you understand and empathize with other points of view. There are times, of course, when you may appropriately scorn an opposing view. But these times are rare, and they mostly occur when you address audiences predisposed to your view. Demonstrating empathy to alternative views is generally the best strategy.

- **Build a bridge to your audience.** A third means of establishing credibility—building a bridge to your audience—has been treated at length in our earlier discussions of audience-based reasons. By grounding your argument in shared values and assumptions, you demonstrate your goodwill and enhance your image as a trustworthy person respectful of your audience's views. We mention audience-based reasons here to show how this aspect of *logos*—finding the reasons that are most rooted in the audience's values—also affects your *ethos* as a person respectful of your readers' views.

- **Demonstrate professionalism.** Finally, you can enhance your *ethos* by the professionalism revealed in your manuscript itself: Appropriate style, careful editing and proofreading, accurate documentation, and adherence to the genre conventions expected by your audience all contribute to the image of the person behind the writing. If your manuscript is sloppy, marred by spelling or grammatical errors, or inattentive to the tone and style of the expected genre, your own credibility will be damaged.

How to Create *Pathos*: The Appeal to Beliefs and Emotions

6.3 To create effective appeals to *pathos*

Before the federal government outlawed unsolicited telephone marketing, newspapers published flurries of articles complaining about annoying telemarketers. Within this context, a United Parcel Service worker, Bobbi Buchanan, wanted to create sympathy for telemarketers. She wrote a *New York Times* op-ed piece entitled "Don't Hang Up, That's My Mom Calling," which begins as follows:

> The next time an annoying sales call interrupts your dinner, think of my 71-year-old mother, LaVerne, who works as a part-time telemarketer to supplement her social security income. To those Americans who have signed up for the new national do-not-call list, my mother is a pest, a nuisance, an invader of privacy. To others, she's just another anonymous voice on the other end of the line. But to those who know her, she's someone struggling to make a buck, to feed herself and pay her utilities—someone who personifies the great American way.

The editorial continues with a heartwarming description of LaVerne. Buchanan's rhetorical aim is to transform the reader's anonymous, depersonalized image of telemarketers into the concrete image of her mother: a "hardworking, first generation American; the daughter of a Pittsburgh steelworker; survivor of the Great Depression; the widow of a World War II veteran; a mother of seven, grandmother of eight, great-grandmother of three...." The intended effect is to alter our view of telemarketers through the positive emotions triggered by our identification with LaVerne.

By urging readers to think of "my mother, LaVerne" instead of an anonymous telemarketer, Buchanan illustrates the power of *pathos,* an appeal to the reader's emotions. Arguers create pathetic appeals whenever they connect their claims to readers' values, thus triggering positive or negative emotions depending on whether these values are affirmed or transgressed. Pro-life proponents appeal to *pathos* when they graphically describe the dismemberment of a fetus during an abortion. Proponents of improved women's health and status in Africa do so when they describe the helplessness of wives forced to have unprotected sex with husbands likely infected with HIV. Opponents of oil exploration in the Arctic National Wildlife Refuge (ANWR) do so when they lovingly describe the calving grounds of caribou.

Are such appeals legitimate? Our answer is yes, if they intensify and deepen our response to an issue rather than divert our attention from it. Because understanding is a matter of feeling as well as perceiving, *pathos* can give access to nonlogical, but not necessarily nonrational, ways of knowing. *Pathos* helps us see what is deeply at stake in an issue, what matters to the whole person. Appeals to *pathos* help readers walk in the writer's shoes. That is why arguments are often improved through the use of stories that make issues come alive or sensory details that allow us to see, feel, and taste the reality of a problem.

Appeals to *pathos* become illegitimate, we believe, when they confuse an issue rather than clarify it. Consider the case of a student who argues that Professor Jones ought to raise his grade from a D to a C, lest he lose his scholarship and be forced to leave college, shattering the dreams of his dear old grandmother. To the extent that students' grades should be based on performance or effort, the student's image of the dear old grandmother is an illegitimate appeal to *pathos* because it diverts the reader from rational to irrational criteria. The weeping grandmother may provide a legitimate motive for the student to study harder but not for the professor to change a grade.

Although it is difficult to classify all the ways that writers can create appeals from *pathos,* we will focus on four strategies: concrete language; specific examples and illustrations; narratives; and connotations of words, metaphors, and analogies. Each of these strategies lends "presence" to an argument by creating immediacy and emotional impact.

Use Concrete Language

Concrete language—one of the chief ways that writers achieve voice—can increase the liveliness, interest level, and personality of a writer's prose. When used in argument, concrete language typically heightens *pathos.* For example, consider the differences between the first and second drafts of the following student argument:

First Draft

People who prefer driving a car to taking a bus think that taking the bus will increase the stress of the daily commute. Just the opposite is true. Not being able to find a parking spot when in a hurry to be at work or school can cause a person stress. Taking the bus gives a person time to read or sleep, etc. It could be used as a mental break.

Second Draft (Concrete Language Added)

Taking the bus can be more relaxing than driving a car. Having someone else behind the wheel gives people time to chat with friends or study for an exam. They can check Facebook and Twitter, send text messages, doze off, read the daily newspaper, or get lost in a novel rather than foam at the mouth looking for a parking space.

In this revision, specific details enliven the prose by creating images that trigger positive feelings. Who wouldn't want some free time to doze off or to get lost in a novel?

Use Specific Examples and Illustrations

Specific examples and illustrations serve two purposes in an argument. They provide evidence that supports your reasons; simultaneously, they give your argument presence and emotional resonance. Note the flatness of the following draft arguing for the value of multicultural studies in a university core curriculum:

First Draft

Another advantage of a multicultural education is that it will help us see our own culture in a broader perspective. If all we know is our own heritage, we might not be inclined to see anything bad about this heritage because we won't know anything else. But if we study other heritages, we can see the costs and benefits of our own heritage.

Now note the increase in "presence" when the writer adds a specific example:

Second Draft (Example Added)

Another advantage of multicultural education is that it raises questions about traditional Western values. For example, owning private property (such as buying your own home) is part of the American dream. However, in studying the beliefs of American Indians, students are confronted with a very different view of private property. When the U.S. government sought to buy land in the Pacific Northwest from Chief Sealth, he is alleged to have replied:

> The president in Washington sends words that he wishes to buy our land. But how can you buy or sell the sky? The land? The idea is strange to us. If we do not own the freshness of the air and the sparkle of the water, how can you buy them?[...] We are part of the earth and it is part of us.[...] This we know: The earth does not belong to man, man belongs to the earth.

Our class was shocked by the contrast between traditional Western views of property and Chief Sealth's views. One of our best class discussions was initiated by this quotation from Chief Sealth. Had we not been exposed to a view from another culture, we would have never been led to question the "rightness" of Western values.

The writer begins his revision by evoking a traditional Western view of private property, which he then questions by shifting to Chief Sealth's vision of land as open, endless, and unobtainable as the sky. Through the use of a specific example, the writer brings to life his previously abstract point about the benefit of multicultural education.

Use Narratives

A particularly powerful way to evoke *pathos* is to tell a story that either leads into your claim or embodies it implicitly and that appeals to your readers' feelings and imagination. Brief narratives—whether true or hypothetical—are particularly effective as opening attention grabbers for an argument. To illustrate how an introductory narrative (either a story or a brief scene) can create pathetic appeals, consider the following first paragraph to an argument opposing jet skis:

> I dove off the dock into the lake, and as I approached the surface I could see the sun shining through the water. As my head popped out, I located my cousin a few feet away in a rowboat waiting to escort me as I, a twelve-year-old girl, attempted to swim across the mile-wide, pristine lake and back to our dock. I made it, and that glorious summer day is one of my most precious memories. Today, however, no one would dare attempt that swim. Jet skis have taken over this small lake where I spent many summers with my grandparents. Dozens of whining jet skis crisscross the lake, ruining it for swimming, fishing, canoeing, rowboating, and even water-skiing. More stringent state laws are needed to control jet skiing because it interferes with other uses of lakes and is currently very dangerous.

This narrative makes a case for a particular point of view toward jet skis by winning our identification with the writer's experience. She invites us to relive that experience with her while she also taps into our own treasured memories of summer experiences that have been destroyed by change.

Opening narratives to evoke *pathos* can be powerfully effective, but they are also risky. If they are too private, too self-indulgent, too sentimental, or even too dramatic and forceful, they can backfire on you. If you have doubts about an opening narrative, read it to a sample audience before using it in your final draft.

Use Words, Metaphors, and Analogies with Appropriate Connotations

Another way of appealing to *pathos* is to select words, metaphors, or analogies with connotations that match your aim. We have already described this strategy in our discussion of the "framing" of evidence (Chapter 5, pages 99–100). By using words with particular connotations, a writer guides readers to see the issue through the writer's angle of vision. Thus if you want to create positive feelings about a recent city council decision, you can call it "bold and decisive"; if you want to create negative feelings, you can call it "short-sighted and autocratic." Similarly, writers can use favorable or unfavorable metaphors and analogies to evoke different imaginative or emotional responses. A tax bill might be viewed as a "potentially fatal poison pill" or as "unpleasant but necessary economic medicine." In each of these cases, the words create an emotional as well as intellectual response.

■ ■ ■   **FOR CLASS DISCUSSION**   Incorporating Appeals to *Pathos*

Outside class, rewrite the introduction to one of your previous papers (or a current draft) to include more appeals to *pathos*. Use any of the strategies for giving your argument presence: concrete language, specific examples, narratives, metaphors, analogies, and connotative words. Bring both your original and your rewritten introductions to class. In pairs or in groups, discuss the comparative effectiveness of these introductions in trying to reach your intended audience.

■ ■ ■

Kairos: The Timeliness and Fitness of Arguments

6.4 To be mindful of *kairos* or the "timeliness" of your argument

To increase your argument's effectiveness, you need to consider not only its appeals to *logos, ethos,* and *pathos,* but also its *kairos*—that is, its timing, its appropriateness for the occasion. *Kairos* is one of those wonderful words adopted from another language (in this case, ancient Greek) that is impossible to define, yet powerful in what it represents. In Greek, *kairos* means "right time," "season," or "opportunity." It differs subtly from the ordinary Greek word for time, *chronos,* the root of our words "chronology" and "chronometer." You can measure *chronos* by looking at your watch, but you measure *kairos* by sensing the opportune time through psychological attentiveness to situation and meaning. To think *kairotically* is to be attuned to the total context of a situation in order to act in the right way at the right moment. By analogy, consider a skilled base runner who senses the right moment to steal second, a wise teacher who senses the right moment to praise or critique a student's performance, or a successful psychotherapist who senses the right moment to talk rather than listen in a counseling session. *Kairos* reminds us that a rhetorical situation is not stable and fixed, but evolves as events unfold or as audiences experience the psychological ebbs and flows of attention and care. Here are some examples that illustrate the range of insights contained by the term *kairos*:

■ If you write a letter to the editor of a newspaper or post a response to a blog, you usually have a one- or two-day window before a current event becomes "old news" and is no longer interesting. An out-of-date response will go unread, not because it is poorly written or argued but because it misses its *kairotic* moment. (Similar instances of lost timeliness occur in class discussions: On how many occasions have you wanted to contribute an idea to class discussion, but the professor doesn't acknowledge your raised hand? When you finally are called on, the *kairotic* moment has passed.)

■ Bobbi Buchanan's "Don't Hang Up, That's My Mom Calling," which we used to illustrate *pathos* (page 107), could have been written only during a brief historical period when telemarketing was being publicly debated. Moreover, it could have been written only late in that period, after numerous writers had attacked telemarketers. The piece was published in the *New York Times* because the editor received it at the right *kairotic* moment.

■ A sociology major is writing a senior capstone paper for graduation. The due date for the paper is fixed, so the timing of the paper isn't at issue. But *kairos* is still relevant. It urges the student to consider what is appropriate for such a paper. What is the "right way" to produce a sociology paper at this moment in the history of the discipline? Currently, what are leading-edge versus trailing-edge questions in sociology? What theorists are now in vogue? What research methods would most impress a judging committee? How would a good capstone paper written in 2015 differ from one written a decade earlier?

As you can see from these examples, *kairos* concerns a whole range of questions connected to the timing, fitness, appropriateness, and proportions of a message within an evolving rhetorical context. There are no rules to help you determine the *kairotic* moment for your argument, but being attuned to *kairos* will help you "read" your audience and rhetorical situation in a dynamic way.

Often you can establish the *kairos* of your argument in the opening sentences of your introduction. An introduction might mention a recent news event, political speech, legislative bill, or current societal problem that the audience may have experienced, thereby using awareness of *kairos* to connect with the audience's interests, knowledge, and experience. Elsewhere in your argument, attention to *kairos* can infuse currency and immediacy by establishing the stakes in the argument and enlist the audience's concern. For example, if you were going to argue that your university's policy on laptops in the classroom is too restrictive, you might enhance your argument by mentioning several recent editorials in your campus newspaper on this subject. If you were going to argue for increased urban gardening in your city, you might site a recent TED talk on successful experiments with urban gardening. If you are creating a text that includes images, you might also establish *kairos* through a photograph or cartoon that signals appropriate currency. Thinking about *kairos* helps you focus on the public conversation your argument is joining and on the interests, knowledge, and values of your audience.

■ ■ ■   **FOR CLASS DISCUSSION** Analyzing an Argument from the Perspectives
of *Logos, Ethos, Pathos,* and *Kairos*

Your instructor will select an argument for analysis. Working in small groups or as a whole class, analyze the assigned argument first from the perspective of *kairos* and then from the perspectives of *logos, ethos,* and *pathos.*

1. As you analyze the argument from the perspective of *kairos,* consider the following questions:
   a. What is the motivating occasion for this argument? That is, what causes this writer to put pen to paper or fingers to keyboard?

    b. What conversation is the writer joining? Who are the other voices in this conversation? What are these voices saying that compels the writer to add his or her own voice? How was the stage set to create the *kairotic* moment for this argument?

    c. Who is the writer's intended audience and why?

    d. What is the writer's purpose? Toward what view or action is the writer trying to persuade his or her audience?

    e. To what extent can various features of the argument be explained by your understanding of its *kairotic* moment?

  2. Now analyze the same argument for its appeals to *logos, ethos,* and *pathos.* How successful is this argument in achieving its writer's purpose?   ■ ■ ■

Using Images to Appeal to *Logos, Ethos, Pathos,* and *Kairos*

6.5 To explain how images make visual appeals to *logos, ethos, pathos,* and *kairos*

One of the most powerful ways to move your audience is to use photos or other images that can appeal to *logos, ethos, pathos,* and *kairos* in one glance. (Chapter 9 focuses exclusively on visual rhetoric—the persuasive power of images.) Although many written arguments do not lend themselves to visual illustrations, we suggest that when you construct arguments you consider the potential of visual support. Imagine that your argument were to be delivered as a PowerPoint presentation or appear in a newspaper, in a magazine, or on a Web site where space would be provided for one or two visuals. What photographs or drawings might help persuade your audience toward your perspective?

When images work well, they make particularly powerful appeals to *pathos* analogous to the verbal strategies of concrete language, specific illustrations, narratives, and connotative words. The challenge in using visuals is to find material that is straightforward enough to be understood without elaborate explanations, that is timely and relevant, and that clearly adds impact to a specific part of your argument. As an example, suppose you are writing an argument supporting fund-raising efforts to help a third-world country that has recently experienced a natural catastrophe. To add a powerful appeal to *pathos,* you might consider incorporating into your argument the photograph shown in Figure 6.1 of the devastation and personal loss caused by typhoon Haiyan in the Philippines in 2013. A photograph such as this one can evoke a strong emotional and imaginative response as well as make viewers think.

■ ■ ■ **FOR WRITING AND DISCUSSION Analyzing Images as Appeals**   MyWritingLab™
                                              to *Pathos*

Individual task: Use the following questions to analyze the photo in Figure 6.1.

  1. How would you describe the emotional/imaginative impact of Figure 6.1? What details of the photo specifically create its appeal to *pathos*?

  2. Many disaster-relief photos seek to convey the magnitude of the destruction and suffering, sometimes shockingly, by depicting destroyed buildings, mangled

FIGURE 6.1 Photo after Typhoon Haiyan in the Philippines

bodies, and images of human misery. How is your response to Figure 6.1 similar to or different from your response to commonly encountered close-up photographs of grief-stricken victims or to distance shots of widespread destruction? To what extent is Figure 6-1's story—told from the perspective of a child—different from the more typical photographs of destroyed buildings or anguished faces?

3. After searching the Web for other photos taken after typhoon Haiyan, write a rationale for why you would, or would not, choose this photo to accompany a proposal argument appealing for support for people in this region of the Philippines.

Group task: Share your individual analysis and rationale with others in your class.

EXAMINING VISUAL ARGUMENTS

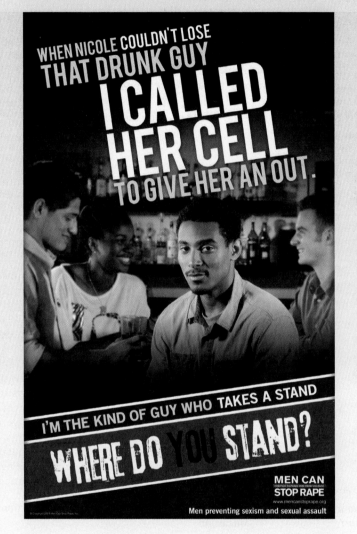

Logos, Ethos, Pathos, and *Kairos*

Efforts to combat sexual assault and the culture of date rape on campuses have figured prominently in public conversation recently, with discussions booming on the Web sites of newly formed organizations and stories of rallies on university campuses appearing on news sites. As this advocacy poster shows, the need to bolster bystander intervention is a critical piece in addressing this problem.

How does this advocacy poster attempt to move its audience? Analyze the poster's visual and verbal appeals to *logos, ethos, pathos,* and *kairos.*

How Audience-Based Reasons Appeal
To *Logos, Ethos, Pathos,* and *Kairos*

6.6 To explain how audience-based reasons appeal to *logos ethos, pathos,* and *kairos*

We conclude this chapter by returning to the concept of audience-based reasons that we introduced in Chapter 4. Audience-based reasons enhance *logos* because they build on underlying assumptions (warrants) that the audience is likely to accept. But they also enhance *ethos, pathos,* and *kairos* by helping the audience identify with the writer, by appealing to shared beliefs and values, and by conveying a shared sense of an issue's timeliness. To consider the needs of your audience, you can ask yourself the following questions:

Questions for Analyzing Your Audience

What to Ask	Why to Ask It
1. *Who is your audience?*	Your answer will help you think about audience-based reasons.
	▪ Are you writing to a single person, a committee, or the general readership of a newspaper, magazine, blog site, and so forth?
	▪ Are your readers academics, professionals, fellow students, general citizens, or people with specialized background and interests?
	▪ Can you expect your audience to be politically and culturally liberal, middle of the road, conservative, or all over the map? What about their religious views?
	▪ How do you picture your audience in terms of social class, ethnicity, gender, sexual orientation, age, and cultural identity?
	▪ To what extent does your audience share your own interests and cultural position? Are you writing to insiders or outsiders with regard to your own values and beliefs?
2. *How much does your audience know or care about your issue?*	Your answer can especially affect your introduction and conclusion:
	▪ Do your readers need background on your issue or are they already in the conversation?
	▪ If you are writing to specific decision makers, are they currently aware of the problem you are addressing? If not, how can you get their attention?
	▪ Does your audience care about your issue? If not, how can you get them to care?

What to Ask	Why to Ask It
3. *What is your audience's current attitude toward your issue?*	Your answer will help you decide the structure and tone of your argument.
	▪ Are your readers already supportive of your position? Undecided? Skeptical? Strongly opposed?
	▪ What other points of view besides your own will your audience be weighing?
4. *What will be your audience's likely objections to your argument?*	Your answer will help determine the content of your argument and will alert you to extra research you may need.
	▪ What weaknesses will audience members find?
	▪ What aspects of your position will be most threatening to them and why?
	▪ How are your basic assumptions, values, or beliefs different from your audience's?
5. *What values, beliefs, or assumptions about the world do you and your audience share?*	Your answer will help you find common ground with your audience.
	▪ Despite different points of view on this issue, where can you find common links with your audience?
	▪ How might you use these links to build bridges to your audience?

To see how a concern for audience-based reasons can enhance *ethos* and *pathos,* suppose that you support racial profiling (rather than random selection) for determining who receives intensive screening at airports. Suppose further that you are writing a guest op-ed column for a liberal campus newspaper and imagine readers repulsed by the notion of racial profiling (as indeed you are repulsed too in most cases). It's important from the start that you understand and acknowledge the interests of those opposed to your position. The persons most likely targeted by racial profiling would be Middle Eastern males as well as black males with African passports, particularly those from African nations with large Islamic populations. These persons will be directly offended by racial profiling at airports. From the perspective of social justice, they can rightfully object to the racial stereotyping that lumps all people of Arabic, Semitic, or African appearance into the category "potential terrorists." Similarly, African Americans and Hispanics, who frequently experience racial profiling by police in U.S. cities, may object to further extension of this hated practice. Also, most political liberals, as well as many moderates and conservatives, may object to the racism inherent in selecting people for airport screening on the basis of ethnicity or country of origin.

What shared values might you use to build bridges to those opposed to racial profiling at airports? You need to develop a strategy to reduce your audience's fears and to link your reasons to their values. Your thinking might go something like this:

Problem: How can I create an argument rooted in shared values? How can I reduce fear that racial profiling in this situation endorses racism or will lead to further erosion of civil liberties?

Bridge-building goals: I must try to show that my argument's goal is to increase airline safety by preventing terrorism like that of 9/11/01. My argument must show my respect for Islam and for Arabic and Semitic peoples. I must also show my rejection of racial profiling as normal police practice.

Possible strategies:

- Stress the shared value of protecting innocent people from terrorism.
- Show how racial profiling significantly increases the efficiency of secondary searches. (If searches are performed at random, then we waste time and resources searching people who are statistically unlikely to be terrorists.)
- Argue that airport screeners must also use indicators other than race to select people for searches (for example, traits that might indicate a domestic terrorist).
- Show my respect for Islam.
- Show sympathy for people selected for searching via racial profiling and acknowledge that this practice would normally be despicable except for the extreme importance of airline security, which overrides personal liberties in this case.
- Show my rejection of racial profiling in situations other than airport screening—for example, stopping African Americans for traffic violations more often than whites and then searching their cars for drugs or stolen goods.
- Perhaps show my support of affirmative action, which is a kind of racial profiling in reverse.

These thinking notes allow you to develop the following plan for your argument.

- Airport screeners should use racial profiling rather than random selection to determine which people undergo intensive screening
  - because doing so will make more efficient use of airport screeners' time, increase the odds of finding terrorists, and thus lead to greater airline safety (*WARRANT: Increased airline safety is good;* or, at a deeper level, *The positive consequences of increasing airline safety through racial profiling outweigh the negative consequences.*)
  - because racial profiling in this specific case does not mean allowing it in everyday police activities nor does it imply disrespect for Islam or for Middle Eastern or African males (WARRANT: *Racial profiling is unacceptable in everyday police practices. It is wrong to show disrespect for Islam or Middle Eastern or African males.*)

As this plan shows, your strategy is to seek reasons whose warrants your audience will accept. First, you will argue that racial profiling will lead to greater airline safety, allowing you to stress that safe airlines benefit all passengers. Your concern is the lives of hundreds of passengers as well as others who might be killed in a terrorist attack. Second, you plan to reduce adversaries' resistance to your proposal by showing that the consequences aren't as severe as they might fear. Using racial profiling in airports would not justify using it in urban police work (a practice you find despicable) and it would not imply disrespect for Islam or Middle Eastern or African males. As this example shows, your focus on audience—on the search for audience-based reasons— shapes the actual invention of your argument from the start. It also encourages you to fuse concerns for *ethos* and *pathos* into your foundational planning for your argument as you think about how to reach your audience and how to establish yourself as sympathetic, fair, and concerned about social justice and the public good.

■ ■ ■ **FOR WRITING AND DISCUSSION** Planning an Audience-Based   MyWritingLab™
                                        Argumentative Strategy

Individual task:

1. Choose one of the following cases and plan an audience-based argumentative strategy. Follow the thinking process used by the writer of the racial-profiling argument: (1) state several problems that the writer must solve to reach the audience, and (2) develop possible solutions to those problems.

   a. An argument for the right of software companies to continue making and selling violent video games: aim the argument at parents who oppose their children playing these games.

   b. An argument to reverse grade inflation by limiting the number of As and Bs a professor can give in a course: aim the argument at students who fear getting lower grades.

   c. An argument supporting the legalization of cocaine: aim the argument at readers of *Reader's Digest,* a conservative magazine that supports the current war on drugs.

Group task: Share your planning notes with other members of your class, and discuss how your sketched argument would make appeals to *ethos* and *pathos* as well as to *logos*. ■ ■ ■

Conclusion

In this chapter, we have explored ways that writers can strengthen the persuasiveness of their arguments by creating appeals to *ethos* and *pathos,* by being attentive to *kairos,* by thinking visually, and by building bridges to their readers through audience-based reasons. Arguments are more persuasive if readers trust the credibility of the writer and if the argument appeals to readers' hearts and imaginations as well as to their intellects. Attentiveness to *kairos* keeps the writer attuned to the dynamics of a rhetorical situation in order to create the right message at the right time. Sometimes images such as drawings or photographs may reinforce the argument by evoking strong emotional responses, thus enhancing *pathos*. Finally, all these appeals come together when the writer explicitly focuses on finding audience-based reasons.

WRITING ASSIGNMENT Revising a Draft for *Ethos, Pathos,*   MyWritingLab™
                          and Audience-Based Reasons

Part 1: Choose an argument that you have previously written or that you are currently drafting. Revise the argument with explicit focus on increasing its appeals to *logos, ethos, pathos,* and *kairos* via audience-based reasons and other strategies. Consider especially how you might improve *ethos* by building bridges to the audience or improve *pathos* through concrete language, specific examples, metaphors, or connotations of words. Finally, consider the extent to which your reasons are audience-based.

Or

Multimodal option: Imagine an argument that you have previously written or are currently drafting that could be enhanced with effective photographs or images. Revise your argument to include these images, perhaps creating a desktop published document that wraps text around visuals chosen to enhance *pathos.* Other multimodal possibilities include transforming your argument into a speech supported by Power-Point images (see Chapter 14, pages 333–334), into a poster argument (see Chapter 9, page 196 and Chapter 14, page 332), or even into a podcast that includes music.

Part 2: Attach to your revision or transformed project a reflective letter explaining the choices you made in revising your original argument or in transforming it using a multimodal approach. Describe for your instructor the changes or transformations you made and explain how or why your new version enhances your argument's effectiveness at moving its audience. ■

MyWritingLab™

Visit Ch. 6 Moving Your Audience: *Ethos, Pathos,* and *Kairos* in *MyWritingLab* to complete the For Writing and Discussion, Examining Visual Arguments, and Writing Assignments and to test your understanding of the chapter objectives.

Responding to Objections and Alternative Views

7

What you will learn in this chapter:

7.1 To explain the differences between one-sided, multisided, and dialogic argument

7.2 To determine the degree of your audience's resistance to your views in order to shape the content, structure, and tone of your argument

7.3 To use one-sided argument to appeal to supportive audiences

7.4 To use classical argument to appeal to neutral or undecided audiences, using refutation and concession

7.5 To use dialogic, delayed thesis argument to appeal to resistant audiences

7.6 To use Rogerian communication to open up new channels of understanding between you and an opposing audience

In the previous chapter we discussed strategies for moving your audience through appeals to *ethos, pathos,* and *kairos.* In this chapter we examine strategies for addressing opposing or alternative views—whether to omit them, refute them, concede to them, or incorporate them through compromise and conciliation—and we explain when a very different, collaborative approach would be appropriate, when your audience holds views that clash with yours.

One-Sided, Multisided, and Dialogic Arguments

7.1 To explain the differences between one-sided, multisided, and dialogic argument

Arguments are said to be one-sided, multisided, or dialogic:

- *A one-sided argument* presents only the writer's position on the issue without summarizing and responding to alternative viewpoints.

- *A multisided argument* presents the writer's position, but also summarizes and responds to possible objections and alternative views.

- *A dialogic argument* has a much stronger component of inquiry in which the writer presents herself as uncertain or searching, the audience is considered a partner in the dialogue, and the writer's purpose is to seek common ground, perhaps leading to a consensual solution to a problem. (See our discussion in Chapter 1 of argument as truth seeking versus persuasion, pages 10–12.)

One-sided and *multisided* arguments often take an adversarial stance in that the writer regards alternative views as flawed or wrong and supports her own claim with a strongly persuasive intent. Although multisided arguments can be adversarial, they can also be made to feel *dialogic*, depending on the way the writer introduces and responds to alternative views.

At issue, then, is the writer's treatment of alternative views. Does the writer omit them (a one-sided argument), summarize them in order to rebut them (an adversarial kind of multisided argument), or summarize them in order to acknowledge their validity, value, and force (a more dialogic kind of multisided argument)? Each of these approaches can be appropriate for certain occasions, depending on your purpose, your confidence in your own stance, and your audience's resistance to your views.

How can you determine the kind of argument that would be most effective in a given case? As a general rule, one-sided arguments occur commonly when an issue is not highly contested. If the issue is highly contested, then one-sided arguments tend to strengthen the convictions of those who are already in the writer's camp, but alienate those who aren't. In contrast, for those initially opposed to a writer's claim, a multisided argument shows that the writer has considered other views, and thus reduces some initial hostility. An especially interesting effect can occur with neutral or undecided audiences. In the short run, one-sided arguments are often persuasive to a neutral audience, but in the long run, multisided arguments have more staying power. Neutral audiences who have heard only one side of an issue tend to change their minds when they hear alternative arguments. By anticipating and rebutting opposing views, a multisided argument diminishes the surprise and force of subsequent counterarguments. If we move from neutral to highly resistant audiences, adversarial approaches—even multisided ones—are seldom effective because they increase hostility and harden the differences between writer and reader. In such cases, more dialogic approaches have the best chance of establishing common ground for inquiry and consensus.

In the rest of this chapter we will show you how your choice of writing one-sided, multisided, or dialogic arguments is a function of how you perceive your audience's resistance to your views, your level of confidence in your own views, and your purpose—to persuade your audience or open up dialogue.

Determining Your Audience's Resistance to Your Views

7.2 To determine the degree of your audience's resistance to your views in order to shape the content, structure, and tone of your argument

When you write an argument, you must always consider your audience's point of view. One way to imagine your relationship to your audience is to place it on a scale of resistance ranging from strong support of your position to strong opposition (see Figure 7.1). At the "Accord" end of this scale are like-minded people who basically agree with your position on the issue. At the "Resistance" end are those who strongly disagree with you, perhaps unconditionally, because their values, beliefs, or assumptions sharply differ from your own. Between "Accord" and "Resistance" lies a range of opinions. Close to your position will be those leaning in your direction but with less conviction than you have.

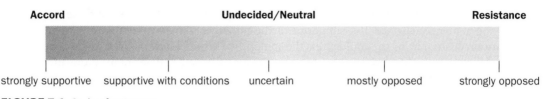

FIGURE 7.1 Scale of resistance

Close to the resistance position will be those basically opposed to your view but willing to listen to your argument and perhaps willing to acknowledge some of its strengths. In the middle are those undecided people who are still sorting out their feelings, seeking additional information, and weighing the strengths and weaknesses of alternative views.

Seldom, however, will you encounter an issue in which the range of disagreement follows a simple line from accord to resistance. Often resistant views fall into different categories so that no single line of argument appeals to all those whose views are different from your own. You thus have to identify not only your audience's resistance to your ideas but also the causes of that resistance.

Consider, for example, the issues surrounding publicly financed sports stadiums. In one city, a ballot initiative asked citizens to agree to an increase in sales taxes to build a new retractable-roof stadium for its baseball team. Supporters of the initiative faced a complex array of resisting views (see Figure 7.2). Opponents of the initiative could be placed into four categories. Some simply had no interest in sports, cared nothing about baseball, and saw no benefit in building a huge, publicly financed sports facility. Another group loved baseball and followed the home team passionately, but was philosophically opposed to subsidizing rich players and owners with taxpayer money. This group argued that the whole sports industry needed to be restructured so that stadiums were paid for out of sports revenues. Still another group was opposed to tax hikes in general. It focused on the principle of reducing the size of government and of using tax revenues only for essential services. Finally, another powerful group supported baseball and supported the notion of public funding of a new stadium but opposed the kind of retractable-roof stadium specified in the initiative. This group wanted an old-fashioned, open-air stadium like Baltimore's Camden Yards or Cleveland's Jacobs Field.

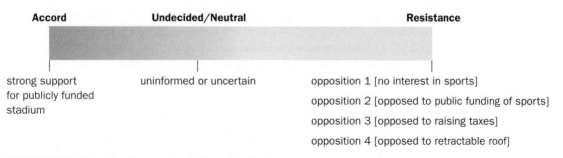

FIGURE 7.2 Scale of resistance, baseball stadium issue

Writers supporting the initiative found it impossible to address all of these resisting audiences at once. If a supporter of the initiative wanted to aim an argument at sports haters, he or she could stress the spinoff benefits of a new ballpark (for example, the new ballpark would attract tourist revenue, renovate a deteriorating downtown neighborhood, create jobs, make sports lovers more likely to vote for public subsidies of the arts, and so forth). But these arguments would be irrelevant to those who wanted an open-air stadium, who opposed tax hikes categorically, or who objected to public subsidy of millionaires.

The baseball stadium example illustrates the difficulty of adapting your argument to your audience's position on the scale of resistance. Yet doing so is important because you need a stable vision of your audience before you can determine an effective content, structure, and tone for your argument. As we showed in Chapter 4, effective content derives from choosing audience-based reasons that appeal to your audience's values, assumptions, and beliefs. As we show in the rest of this chapter, an effective structure and tone are often a function of where your audience falls on the scale of resistance. The next sections show how you can adjust your arguing strategy depending on whether your audience is supportive, neutral, or hostile.

Appealing to a Supportive Audience: One-Sided Argument

7.3 To use one-sided argument to appeal to supportive audiences

One-sided arguments commonly occur when an issue isn't highly contested and the writer's aim is merely to put forth a new or different point of view. When an issue is contested, however, one-sided arguments are used mainly to stir the passions of supporters—to convert belief into action by inspiring a party member to contribute to a senator's campaign or a bored office worker to sign up for a change-your-life weekend seminar.

Typically, appeals to a supportive audience are structured as one-sided arguments that either ignore opposing views or reduce them to "enemy" stereotypes. Filled with motivational language, these arguments list the benefits that will ensue from the reader's donations to the cause and the horrors just around the corner if the other side wins. One of the authors of this text received a fund-raising letter from an environmental lobbying group declaring, "It's crunch time for the polluters and their pals on Capitol Hill." The "corporate polluters" and "anti-environment politicians," the letter continues, have "stepped up efforts to roll back our environmental protections—relying on large campaign contributions, slick PR firms and well-heeled lobbyists to get the job done before November's election." This letter makes the reader feel like part of an in-group of good guys fighting the big business "polluters." Nothing in the letter examines environmental issues from business's perspective or attempts to examine alternative views fairly. Because the intended audience already believes in the cause, nothing in the letter invites readers to consider the issues more thoroughly. Rather, the letter's goal is to solidify support, increase the fervor of belief, and inspire action. Most appeal arguments make it easy to act, ending with an 800 phone number to call, a Web site to visit, an online petition to sign, or a congressperson's address to write to.

Appealing to a Neutral or Undecided Audience: Classical Argument

7.4 To use classical argument to appeal to neutral or undecided audiences, using refutation and concession

The in-group appeals that motivate an already supportive audience can repel a neutral or undecided audience. Because undecided audiences are like jurors weighing all sides of an issue, they distrust one-sided arguments that caricature other views. Generally the best strategy for appealing to undecided audiences is the classically structured argument described in Chapter 3 (pages 53–54).

What characterizes the classical argument is the writer's willingness to summarize opposing views fairly and to respond to them openly—either by trying to refute them or by conceding to their strengths and then shifting to a different field of values. Let's look at these strategies in more depth.

Summarizing Opposing Views

The first step toward responding to opposing views in a classical argument is to summarize them fairly. Follow the *principle of charity*, which obliges you to avoid loaded, biased, or "straw man" summaries that oversimplify or distort opposing arguments, making them easy to knock over.

Consider the difference between an unfair and a fair summary of an argument. In the following example, a hypothetical supporter of genetically engineered foods intends to refute the argument of organic-food advocate Lisa Turner, who opposes all forms of biotechnology.

Unfair Summary of Turner's Argument

In a biased article lacking scientific understanding of biotechnology, natural-foods huckster Lisa Turner parrots the health food industry's party line that genetically altered crops are Frankenstein's monsters run amok. She ignorantly claims that consumption of biotech foods will lead to worldwide destruction, disease, and death, ignoring the wealth of scientific literature showing that genetically modified foods are safe. Her misinformed attacks are scare tactics aimed at selling consumers on overpriced "health food" products to be purchased at boutique organic-food stores.

Fair Summary of Turner's Argument

In an article appearing in a nutrition magazine, health food advocate Lisa Turner warns readers that much of our food today is genetically modified using gene-level techniques that differ completely from ordinary crossbreeding. She argues that the potential, unforeseen, harmful consequences of genetic engineering offset the possible benefits of increasing the food supply, reducing the use of pesticides, and boosting the nutritional value of foods. Turner asserts that genetic engineering is imprecise, untested, unpredictable, irreversible, and also uncontrollable because of animals, insects, and winds.

In the unfair summary, the writer distorts and oversimplifies Turner's argument, creating a straw man argument that is easy to knock over because it doesn't make the opponent's best case. In contrast, the fair summary follows the "principle of charity," allowing the strength of the opposing view to come through clearly.

■ ■ ■   **FOR WRITING AND DISCUSSION**   Distinguishing Fair from   MyWritingLab™
                                            Unfair Summaries

Individual task: Use the following questions to analyze the differences between the two summaries of Lisa Turner's article.

1. What makes the first summary unfair? How can you tell?
2. In the unfair summary, what strategies does the writer use to make the opposing view seem weak and flawed? In the fair summary, how is the opposing view made strong and clear?
3. In the unfair summary, how does the writer attack Turner's motives and credentials? This attack is sometimes called an *ad hominem* argument in that it attacks the arguer rather than the argument. How does the writer treat Turner differently in the fair summary?
4. Do you agree with our view that arguments are more persuasive if the writer summarizes opposing views fairly rather than unfairly? Why?

Group task: As a group, write a fair and an unfair summary of an argument that your   ■ ■ ■
instructor gives you, using the strategies you analyzed in the Turner examples.

Refuting Opposing Views

Once you have summarized opposing views, you can either refute them or concede to their strengths. In refuting an opposing view, you attempt to convince readers that its argument is logically flawed, inadequately supported, or based on erroneous assumptions. In refuting an argument, you can rebut (1) the writer's stated reason and grounds, (2) the writer's warrant and backing, or (3) both. Put in less specialized language, you can rebut a writer's reasons and evidence or the writer's underlying assumptions. Suppose, for example, that you wanted to refute this argument:

> Students should limit the number of internships they take because internships are time-consuming.

We can clarify the structure of this argument by showing it in Toulmin terms:

One way to refute this argument is to rebut the stated reason that internships are time-consuming. Your rebuttal might go something like this:

ENTHYMEME

CLAIM: Students should limit the number of internships they take

REASON: because internships are time-consuming.

I disagree that internships are time-consuming. In fact, organizations and businesses are usually very upfront, realistic, and flexible in the weekly hours that they ask of students. The examples that you cite of overly demanding internships are exceptions. Furthermore, these internships have since been re-tailored to students' schedules. [The writer could then provide examples of realistic, limited-time internships.]

WARRANT

Time-consuming internships are bad for students.

Or you could concede that internships are time-consuming but rebut the argument's warrant that using time in these apprentice situations is bad for students:

> I agree that internships take sizable chunks of students' time, but investment in real-world work environments is a worthwhile use of students' time. Through this investment, students clarify their professional goals, log work experience, and gain references. Without interning in these work environments, students would miss important career preparation.

Let's now illustrate these strategies in a more complex situation. Consider the controversy inspired by a *New York Times Magazine* article titled "Recycling Is Garbage." Its author, John Tierney, argued that recycling is not environmentally sound and that it is cheaper to bury garbage in a landfill than to recycle it. Tierney argued that recycling wastes money; he provided evidence that "every time a sanitation department crew picks up a load of bottles and cans from the curb, New York City loses money." In Toulmin's terms, one of Tierney's arguments is structured as shown below.

A number of environmentalists responded angrily to Tierney's argument, challenging either his reason, his warrant, or both. Those refuting the reason offered counterevidence showing that recycling isn't as expensive as Tierney claimed. Those refuting the warrant said that even if the costs of recycling are higher than the costs of burying wastes in a landfill, recycling still benefits the environment by reducing the amount of virgin materials taken from nature. These critics, in effect, offered a new warrant: Conserving the world's resources is an important goal of garbage disposal.

ENTHYMEME

CLAIM Recycling is bad policy

REASON because it costs more to recycle material than to bury it in a landfill.

GROUNDS

• Evidence of the high cost of recycling [Tierney says it costs New York City $200 more per ton for recyclables than trash.]

WARRANT

We should dispose of garbage in the least expensive way.

Strategies for Rebutting Evidence

Whether you are rebutting an argument's reasons or its warrant, you will frequently need to question a writer's use of evidence. Here are some strategies you can use:

■ **Deny the truth of the data.** Arguers can disagree about the facts of a case. If you have reasons to doubt a writer's facts, call them into question.

- **Cite counterexamples and countertestimony.** You can often rebut an argument based on examples or testimony by citing counterexamples or countertestimony that denies the conclusiveness of the original data.
- **Cast doubt on the representativeness or sufficiency of examples.** Examples are powerful only if they are believed to be representative and sufficient. Many environmentalists complained that John Tierney's attack on recycling was based too largely on data from New York City and that it didn't accurately take into account more positive experiences of other cities and states. When data from outside New York City were examined, the cost-effectiveness and positive environmental impact of recycling seemed more apparent.
- **Cast doubt on the relevance or recency of the examples, statistics, or testimony.** The best evidence is up-to-date. In a rapidly changing universe, data that are even a few years out-of-date are often ineffective. For example, as the demand for recycled goods increases, the cost of recycling will be reduced. Out-of-date statistics will skew any argument about the cost of recycling.
- **Question the credibility of an authority.** If an opposing argument is based on testimony, you can undermine its persuasiveness if you show that a person being cited lacks current or relevant expertise in the field.
- **Question the accuracy or context of quotations.** Evidence based on testimony is frequently distorted by being either misquoted or taken out of context. Often scientists qualify their findings heavily, but these qualifications are omitted by the popular media. You can thus attack the use of a quotation by putting it in its original context or by restoring the qualifications in its original source.
- **Question the way statistical data were produced or interpreted.** Chapter 5 provides fuller treatment of how to question statistics. In general, you can rebut statistical evidence by calling into account how the data were gathered, treated mathematically, or interpreted. It can make a big difference, for example, whether you cite raw numbers or percentages or whether you choose large or small increments for the axes of graphs.

Conceding to Opposing Views

In writing a classical argument, a writer must sometimes concede to an opposing argument rather than refute it. Sometimes you encounter portions of an argument that you simply can't refute. For example, suppose that you are a libertarian who supports the legalization of hard drugs such as cocaine and heroin. Adversaries argue that legalizing hard drugs will increase the number of drug users and addicts. You might dispute the size of their numbers, but you reluctantly agree that they are right. Your strategy is thus not to refute the opposing argument but to concede to it by admitting that legalization of hard drugs will promote heroin and cocaine addiction. Having made that concession, your task is then to show that the benefits of drug legalization, such as a reduction in crime and the emptying out of America's prisons, still outweigh the costs you've just conceded.

As this example shows, the strategy of a concession argument is to switch from the field of values employed by the writer you disagree with to a different field of values more favorable to your position. You don't try to refute the writer's stated reason and grounds (by arguing that legalization will *not* lead to increased drug usage and addiction) or the writer's warrant (by arguing that increased drug use and addiction is not a problem). Rather, you shift the argument to a new field of values by introducing a new warrant, one that you think your audience can share (that the benefits of legalization outweigh the costs of increased addiction). To the extent that opponents of legalization share your desire to stop drug-related crime, shifting to this new field of values is a good strategy. Although it may seem that you weaken your own position by conceding to an opposing argument, you may actually strengthen it by increasing your credibility and gaining your audience's goodwill. Moreover, conceding to one part of an opposing argument doesn't mean that you won't refute other parts of that argument.

Example of a Student Essay Using Refutation Strategy

The following student essay, which grew out of Trudie's exploratory essay in Chapter 2, illustrates how a classical argument appealing to a neutral or even mildly resistant audience engages with alternative views. Note the use of both concession and rebuttal strategies.

Bringing Dignity to Workers: Make the Minimum Wage a Living Wage

TRUDIE MAKENS (STUDENT)

Uses personal example to illustrate problems of low-wage workers

Having worked as a busser in a pizza restaurant, a part-time barista, and a server at a dumpling cafe I have worked a number of minimum-wage jobs. My coworkers have ranged from students like myself to single parents and primary providers for their families. As a student, I have always had my parents as a safety net protecting me from financial hardship. However, my coworkers whose only income is their minimum wage endured financial hardships daily. I witnessed one of my coworkers, Maria, lose her home trying to balance supporting her two children and paying her rent. At work, Maria would describe her anxiety as she bounced from relative to relative, straining her family relations and image of herself as an able provider. Without a living wage or the government's providing social insurance programs to ensure financial security for all citizens, families like Maria's are locked into poverty. Raising the federal minimum wage to a livable standard is an important and necessary step to eradicate poverty and ensure dignified living for individuals and families.

Thesis statement

Yet some argue that a higher federal minimum wage will do more harm than good. Michael Saltsman, the research director of the

Forecasts rebuttal of three opposing views raised by Saltsman

Summarizes Saltsman's first objection to minimum wage

Rebuts argument by citing more recent research

Summarizes Saltsman's second objection

Concedes that higher minimum wage won't help jobless, but shifts to other benefits that Saltsman ignores

Summarizes Saltsman's last argument.

Rebuts this argument by showing weaknesses in the Earned Income Tax Credit approach.

Uses conclusion to summarize additional measures (besides higher minimum wage) to combat poverty.

Employment Policy Institute, elaborates the pro-business objections to a minimum wage in several op-ed pieces published in national print or online newspapers. Saltsman primarily makes three arguments against raising the minimum wage. Each of them, I contend, is weak or flawed.

First, Saltsman warns that raising the minimum wage will force businesses to cut jobs. In order to maintain profit and to keep prices low, Saltsman argues, businesses will pay for a higher wage by slashing the number of workers. Worse, businesses may cut entire departments in favor of automation such as having fast-food customers order their meals from computer touch screens. Saltsman's argument, however, depends on older studies that, according to University of California economist Michael Reich, are "fundamentally flawed" (Maclay). In a study published in 2010, Reich and his coauthors find that these earlier studies fail to account for all the critical variables besides wages that influence employment levels. By comparing employment levels between states with higher versus lower minimum-wage levels, Reich and his colleagues provide empirical evidence that raising the minimum wage produces no "adverse employment effects" (954).

Saltsman's second objection to a higher minimum wage is that it targets the wrong people and thus won't reduce overall poverty levels. According to Saltsman, a majority of people living in poverty are unemployed while a majority of minimum-wage workers are from households above the poverty line. Although Saltsman may be correct that a higher minimum-wage won't help a jobless person, he ignores the benefits of a living wage to the working poor who would be lifted out of poverty. Moreover, a higher minimum wage might itself stimulate jobs because minimum-wage workers with more money in their pockets are apt to spend it, increasing demand for goods.

5   Finally Saltsman argues that the minimum wage is less effective at reducing poverty than the Earned Income Tax Credit, which boosts the income of low-wage workers while not giving any income boost to workers who are already above the poverty level. However, the Earned Income Tax Credit, like the minimum wage, does nothing for the jobless poor. Moreover, the Earned Income Tax Credit puts the burden of poverty relief on taxpayers rather than employers and corporate shareholders, doing little to shift the economy in an equitable direction. We need both an increased minimum wage and the Earned Income Tax Credit.

It seems clear that to combat poverty, the United States needs a many-pronged effort with a hike in the minimum wage being only one of the prongs. Although a higher minimum wage will not by itself eliminate poverty, it will certainly help. It needs to be combined with investments in infrastructure to create jobs, with affordable higher education, with better job training, and with other safety-net systems such as those in place in Europe to give dignity to all citizens. Rather than our government and market system prioritizing corporations and profit, the rights and dignity of workers should be held foremost important. Raising the minimum wage to a living wage will help change the structure of a market system that often exploits workers.

Works Cited

Maclay, Kathleen. "Minimum Wage Hikes Don't Eliminate Jobs, Study Finds." *UC Berkeley News Center,* 1 Dec. 2010, news.berkeley.edu/2010/12/01/minimumwagejobs.

Reich, Michael, et al. "Minimum Wage Effects across State Borders: Estimates Using Contiguous Counties." *Review of Economics and Statistics,* vol. 92, no. 4, 2010, pp. 945-64.

Saltsman, Michael. "The Wrong Way to Reduce Poverty." *USA Today,* 20 Sept. 2013, www.usatoday.com/story/opinion/2013/09/20/minimum-wages-poverty-column/2839003.

---. "To Help the Poor, Move Beyond 'Minimum' Gestures." *The Huffington Post,* 26 Apr. 2013, updated 26 June 2013, www.huffingtonpost.com/michael-saltsman/earned-income-tax-credit-minimum-wage_b_3165459.html.

■ ■ ■   **FOR WRITING AND CLASS DISCUSSION**   Refutation Strategies

Individually or in groups, examine each of the following arguments, imagining how the claim and reason could be fleshed out with grounds and backing. Then attempt to refute each argument. Suggest ways to rebut the reason, or the warrant, or both, or to concede to the argument and then switch to a different field of values.

a. The criminal justice system should reduce sentences for low-level, nonviolent offenders because this change will save taxpayers' money.
b. Majoring in engineering is better than majoring in music because engineers make more money than musicians.
c. The SAT exam for college entrance should be not be required by colleges and universities because high school grades are a better predictor of student success than SAT scores.
d. The United States should build more nuclear reactors because nuclear reactors will provide substantial electrical energy without emitting greenhouse gases.
e. People should be allowed to own handguns because owning handguns helps them protect their homes against potentially violent intruders.   ■ ■ ■

Appealing to a Resistant Audience: Dialogic Argument

7.5 To use dialogic, delayed-thesis argument to appeal to resistant audiences

We now turn to an approach to argument that envisions a less confrontational role for the writer and a more collaborative relationship between the writer and a resistant audience. This approach, often called dialogic argument, emphasizes an exploratory, "let's think this out together" structure and tone. In today's public sphere, dialogic argument could be particularly important because it resists the impulsive and superficial comments, often posted on online forums, with no regard for the audience. Syndicated columnist Frank Bruni asserts that Twitter and other social media promote a style of communication that fosters the online publishing of "unformed thoughts, half-baked wit or splenetic reactions" before people take time to deliberate about issues or consider their audience. Citing the research of social psychologist Jonathan Haidt, Bruni writes that "people are more likely to be moved by information that challenges their prejudices if they're prevented from responding to it straight away and it has time to sink in, to steep."* Dialogic argument offers both writers and audiences this calm thinking time to live with opposing views, consider reasons on different sides of an issue, and weigh the evidence.

Let's think about the instances when writers would want to enlist dialogic argument. Whereas classical argument is effective for neutral or undecided audiences, it is often less effective for audiences strongly opposed to the writer's views or for arguments that lean toward the inquiry end of the argument continuum. Because resistant audiences hold values, assumptions, or beliefs widely different from the writer's, they are often unswayed by classical argument, which attacks their worldview too directly. Writers, too, may recognize that progress toward communication on some values-laden issues may require them to take a more open, problem-solving approach. On issues such as abortion, gun control, certain environmental regulations, or the role of religion in the public sphere, the distance between a writer and a resistant audience can be so great that dialogue seems impossible. In these cases the writer's goal may be simply to open dialogue by seeking common ground—that is, by finding places where the writer and audience agree. For example, pro-choice and pro-life advocates may never agree on a woman's right to an abortion, but they may share common ground in wanting to reduce teenage pregnancy. There is room, in other words, for conversation, if not for agreement.

Because of these differences in basic beliefs and values, the goal of dialogic argument is seldom to convert resistant readers to the writer's position. The best a writer can hope for is to reduce somewhat the level of resistance, perhaps by increasing the reader's willingness to listen as preparation for future dialogue. In this section and the next, we introduce you to two strategies for reducing the resistance of hostile audiences—a dialogic argument with a delayed thesis and Rogerian communication, a listening and thinking strategy that can enlarge the writer's as well as the reader's view of a conflicted issue.

Creating a Dialogic Argument with a Delayed Thesis

Unlike a classical argument, a delayed-thesis argument assumes an exploratory approach to a subject. With some issues, you may want to convey that you are still thinking out your position, finding your way through a thicket of alternative views and the complexities of the issue. You yourself may be pulled in multiple directions and may have arrived at your position after pondering different views. In addition, your readers' resistance to your views means that they may be turned off if you forthrightly plunge into your claim and reasons. Under these rhetorical conditions, a delayed-thesis argument enables you to engage your audience in a dialogic exploration of the problem before you argue a thesis.

*Frank Bruni, "Tweet Less, Read More in 2014," *Seattle Times* 2 January 2014. A11.

Instead of declaring a claim and reasons early in the argument, you may work your way slowly to your claim, devoting a large part of the argument to examining different views and re-creating your own inquiry into the subject.

Let's look at an example of a delayed-thesis argument, examining its form and its emotional impact. (For another example of a delayed-thesis argument, see Ellen Goodman's commentary piece "Womb for Rent—for a Price" on pages 169–170.) The following op-ed piece by syndicated columnist Ross Douthat appeared in the *New York Times* during the public debates about building a Muslim community center near Ground Zero in lower Manhattan. Note how Douthat takes a nonthreatening tone and pulls readers into his exploration of the issue.

Islam in Two Americas*

ROSS DOUTHAT

Writer frames the controversy as a conflict of American identities, two divergent ways that the country thinks of itself.

There's an America where it doesn't matter what language you speak, what god you worship or how deep your New World roots run. An America where allegiance to the Constitution trumps ethnic differences, language barriers and religious divides. An America where the newest arrival to our shores is no less American than the ever-so-great granddaughter of the Pilgrims.

But there's another America as well, one that understands itself as a distinctive culture, rather than just a set of political propositions. This America speaks English, not Spanish or Chinese or Arabic. It looks back to a particular religious heritage: Protestantism originally, and then a Judeo-Christian consensus that accommodated Jews and Catholics as well.

Writer establishes the problem and its timeliness and invites his readers to contemplate it with him.

These two understandings of America, one constitutional and one cultural, have been in tension throughout our history. They're in tension in the controversy over the Islamic mosque and cultural center scheduled to go up two blocks from ground zero.

Writer explores the problem from several perspectives: first, the inclusive constitutional America, which defends the right of all religious groups to worship as they please.

The first America views the project as the consummate expression of our nation's high ideals. "This is America," President Barack Obama intoned last week, "and our commitment to religious freedom must be unshakeable." The construction of the mosque, Mayor Michael Bloomberg told New Yorkers, is as important a test of the principle of religious freedom "as we may see in our lifetimes."

5   The second America begs to differ. It sees the project as an affront to the memory of 9/11, and a sign of disrespect for the values of a country

where Islam has only recently become part of the public consciousness. And beneath these concerns lurks the darker suspicion that Islam in any form may be incompatible with the American way of life.

Both understandings of this country have wisdom to offer, and both have been necessary to the American experiment's success. During the great waves of 19th-century immigration, the insistence that new arrivals adapt to Anglo-Saxon culture was crucial to their swift assimilation.

The same was true in religion. The steady pressure to conform to American norms eventually persuaded the Mormons to abandon polygamy, smoothing their assimilation into the American mainstream. Nativist concerns about Catholicism's illiberal tendencies inspired American Catholics to prod their church toward a recognition of the virtues of democracy, making it possible for generations of immigrants to feel unambiguously Catholic and American.

So it is today with Islam. The first America is correct to insist on Muslims' absolute right to build and worship where they wish. But the second America is right to press for something more from Muslim Americans—particularly from figures like Feisal Abdul Rauf, the imam behind the mosque—than simple protestations of good faith.

Too often, American Muslim institutions have turned out to be entangled with ideas and groups that most Americans rightly consider beyond the pale. Too often, American Muslim leaders strike ambiguous notes when asked to disassociate themselves completely from illiberal causes.

10 For Muslim Americans to integrate fully into our national life, they'll need leaders who don't describe America as "an accessory to the crime" of 9/11 (as Rauf did shortly after the 2001 attacks), or duck questions about whether groups like Hamas count as terrorist organizations (as Rauf did in June). They'll need leaders whose antennas are sensitive enough to recognize that the quest for inter-religious dialogue is ill served by throwing up a high-profile mosque two blocks from the site of a mass murder committed in the name of Islam.

They'll need leaders, in other words, who understand that while the ideals of the first America protect the *e pluribus,* it's the demands the second America makes of new arrivals that help create the *unum.*

In this delayed-thesis argument, Ross Douthat, a conservative columnist writing for the liberal *New York Times,* asks readers to think with him about the fierce clash of views over building a Muslim community center near Ground Zero. Douthat wants to reach typical *New York Times* readers, who are apt to support the Muslim project based on their liberal views of tolerance and religious freedom. Douthat enters this public debate calmly, admits the legitimacy of different opposing views, and only toward the end of the argument states his own position.

If Douthat had chosen to write a classical argument, he would have declared his position in the first paragraph, perhaps with a thesis statement like this:

> Muslim Americans should not build their community center near Ground Zero because doing so represents disrespect for America's core cultural identity and insensitivity to Americans' national pain caused by Islamic terrorists.

With this thesis, readers would have no initial doubt where Douthat stands. However, this in-your-face thesis would activate the emotional objections of readers who support the Islamic community center and might prevent them from even reading the piece. In contrast, both liberal and conservative readers can get drawn into the building momentum of Douthat's delayed-thesis version and appreciate its subtlety and surprise.

Writing a Delayed-Thesis Argument

Clearly, where you place your claim can affect your argument's impact on its audience. We should note, however, that a delayed-thesis argument is not simply a classical argument turned upside down. Instead, it promotes dialogue with the audience rather than compels readers to accept the writer's views. It strives to enrich and complicate the discussion as well as present a view of an issue. It entails some risk to the writer because it leaves space only at the end of the argument for developing the writer's claim. However, it may lead the writer and readers to a deeper understanding of the issue, provide clarification, and promote further discussion. Although there is no set form, the organization plan below shows characteristic elements often found in delayed-thesis arguments.

Organization Plan for a Delayed-Thesis Argument

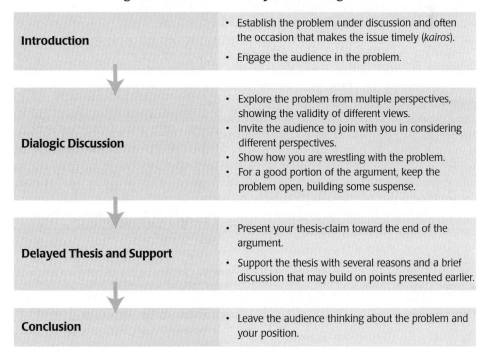

Introduction	• Establish the problem under discussion and often the occasion that makes the issue timely (*kairos*). • Engage the audience in the problem.
Dialogic Discussion	• Explore the problem from multiple perspectives, showing the validity of different views. • Invite the audience to join with you in considering different perspectives. • Show how you are wrestling with the problem. • For a good portion of the argument, keep the problem open, building some suspense.
Delayed Thesis and Support	• Present your thesis-claim toward the end of the argument. • Support the thesis with several reasons and a brief discussion that may build on points presented earlier.
Conclusion	• Leave the audience thinking about the problem and your position.

A More Open-Ended Approach: Rogerian Communication

7.6 To use Rogerian communication to open up new channels of understanding between you and an opposing audience

We now turn to a more complex kind of dialogic method: *Rogerian communication*. We use the term "communication" rather than "argument" because, as we will explain in more detail shortly, this strategy focuses on mutual listening and growth more than on persuasion. All dialogic arguments emphasize problem solving, collaborative thinking, and negotiation with a resistant audience. But Rogerian communication, besides delaying its thesis, works to change the writer as well as the reader. Rogerian communication is named after psychotherapist Carl Rogers, who developed a communication strategy for helping people resolve differences.* The Rogerian strategy emphasizes "empathic listening," which Rogers defined as the ability to see an issue sympathetically from another person's perspective or "frame of reference." He trained people to withhold judgment of another person's ideas until after they had listened attentively to the other person, understood that person's reasoning, appreciated that person's values, and respected that person's humanity—in short, walked in that person's shoes. What Carl Rogers understood is that traditional methods of argumentation are threatening. Because Rogerian communication stresses the psychological as well as the logical dimensions of argument, it is particularly effective when dealing with emotion-laden issues.

With Rogerian communication, the writer tries to reduce the sense of difference between writer and reader by releasing her tight hold on her own views. Particularly, she tries to show that *both writer and resistant audience share many basic values.* This search for common ground often has the psychological effect of enlarging, complicating, or deepening the writer's own worldview. By acknowledging that she has empathy for the audience's views, the writer makes it easier for the audience to listen to her views. Ideally, this mutual listening leads to a compromise or synthesis or, at the least, better understanding and more open channels of communication.

Essential to successful Rogerian communication, besides the art of listening, is the ability to point out areas of agreement between the writer's and reader's positions. For example, if you, as a supporter of alternative energy, oppose offshore or wilderness drilling and are arguing with someone who is in favor of maximizing oil exploration, you are caught in an impasse. However, if the problem you are both confronting is that of increasing available energy resources, you might reduce tension and establish conditions for problem solving. You might begin this process by summarizing your reader's position sympathetically, stressing your shared values. You

---

*See Carl Rogers's essay "Communication: Its Blocking and Its Facilitation" in his book *On Becoming a Person* (Boston: Houghton Mifflin, 1961), 329–37. For a fuller discussion of Rogerian argument, see Richard Young, Alton Becker, and Kenneth Pike, *Rhetoric: Discovery and Change* (New York: Harcourt Brave, 1972).

might say, for example, that you also value energy independence, that you appreciate recent advances in safe drilling technology, and that you are disturbed by people who deny our country's vast energy needs. You also agree that it is unrealistic to pretend that we can dispense with our oil needs overnight. Your effort to understand your audience's views and to build bridges between you and your audience will encourage dialogue and make it more likely that your audience will listen when you offer your perspective.

Rogers's communication strategies have been the subject of intense debate among scholars. On the one hand, some rhetoricians don't like the term "Rogerian *argument*," preferring instead "Rogerian *rhetoric*" or "Rogerian *communication*." These theorists say that Rogerian listening isn't a form of argument or persuasion at all. Rather, its goal is increased mutual understanding and enlarged perspectives on reality for both writer and audience. According to rhetorician Nathaniel Teich, Rogerian rhetoric seeks to foster discovery of others' perspectives and revision of both parties' worldviews.*

In contrast to this perspective, other scholars view Rogerian argument as a means of manipulating resistant audiences. According to this view, the best way to persuade a hostile audience is to adopt a nonthreatening tone and approach, treat the opponent views sympathetically, and then lure the opponent into accepting your views. The problem with this perspective is that it is purely instrumental and reduces Rogerian argument to a technique, a clever means to an end.

Our view of Rogerian communication forges a middle path between these two perspectives. Throughout this text, we emphasize that argument includes inquiry. (See particularly Chapters 1 and 2.) Here we treat Rogerian communication as dialogic inquiry in which the writer negotiates with the audience in a mutual search for provisional solutions.

Rogerian Communication as Growth for the Writer

One of the key features of Rogerian communication is the open relationship it establishes between the writer and the subject; it recasts argument as a process of growth for the writer. Because Rogerian communication asks the writer to listen to the opponent's views—views that the writer may find uncomfortable or threatening—it promotes inquiry and self-reflection, a more tentative and exploratory approach to the subject than the writer takes in classical argument or delayed-thesis argument. Rogerian communication urges writers to play Peter Elbow's "believing game," where the writer must try "to get inside the head of someone" who holds unwelcome ideas.†

---

*For one of the most thorough analyses of Carl Rogers's influence on rhetoric and composition, see Nathaniel Teich's scholarly anthology *Rogerian Perspectives: Collaborative Rhetoric for Oral and Written Communication* (Norwood, NJ: Ablex Publishing Corporation, 1992).

†For more suggestions on how to encourage empathic listening, see Elbow's "Bringing the Rhetoric of Assent and the Believing Game Together—and into the Classroom," *College English* 67.4 (March 2005), 389.

(See our discussion of the believing and doubting game in Chapter 2, pages 24–25.) This "dwelling in" unappealing ideas often compels writers to articulate their own values and to achieve a new understanding of them. Extending Elbow's strategy and emphasizing the connection between values and identity, rhetorician James Baumlin argues that Rogerian rhetoric creates "a realm of plural selves or identities" in the process of taking on "another's beliefs and worldview" through role-playing.* Rogerian communication thus promotes a writer's self-examination and exploration of multiple perspectives on a problem. This double process of exploration and reflection can in turn lead to a change of mind or at least a deeper understanding of a problem.

Rogerian Communication as Collaborative Negotiation

A second key feature of Rogerian communication is its altered argumentative purpose and attitude toward the audience. In the absence of the possibility of persuading a resistant audience to accept the writer's views, the writer seeks different goals through a relationship with the audience. These goals include reducing antagonism toward those with different beliefs, initiating small steps in understanding, cultivating mutual respect, and encouraging further problem solving—in short, nurturing conditions for future exchanges. The focus shifts from persuasion toward collaborative negotiation. Thus Rogerian communication particularly lends itself to rhetorical situations involving complex, emotionally volatile issues. Rogerian communication is appropriate whenever writers are seeking to open up dialogue with a resistant audience and are themselves willing to work toward a synthesis of views.

Writing Rogerian Communication

A major thrust of Rogerian communication is building bridges between writer and audience. Because Rogers's principles originated as a communication strategy between two parties in conversation, Rogerian communication most commonly takes the form of a letter or an open letter directed to a specific person or group. For example, the audience for a Rogerian letter might be a particular person whom the writer already knows, a speaker the writer has recently heard, or the author of an article that the writer has recently read. In all these cases, the writer is disturbed by the audience's views and hopes to open up dialogue. Rogerian communication will most likely include the features shown in the chart on the next page, although not necessarily in any set form.

---

*For more discussion of the relationship between role-playing, understanding, and identity, see James S. Baumlin's "Persuasion, Rogerian Rhetoric, and Imaginative Play," *Rhetoric Society Quarterly* 17.1 (Winter 1987), 36.

Organization Plan for Rogerian Communication

Introduction	• Address the audience and identify the problem that you and your audience want to solve. • Possibly, show the timeliness (*kairos*) of the problem. • Try to establish a friendly or cordial relationship with the audience. • Possibly include information that shows your familiarity with the audience.
Summary of the Audience's Views	• Summarize the audience's views in a fair and neutral way that the audience would accept. • Show that you understand the audience's position. • Also show an understanding of, and respect for, the audience's values and beliefs; the goal of this "saying back" (Rogers's term) is to summarize these views in a way that will be entirely acceptable to the audience.
Common Ground	• Identify common ground you share with your audience. • Demonstrate your growth through empathic consideration of views that you would otherwise find threatening or unwelcome. • Show understanding of the audience's views by "indwelling" with them and perhaps by extending them to other situations through new examples. • Show how your views have been enlarged by empathic listening to the audience's ideas.
Contribution of New Points to the Negotiation	• Respectfully propose your own way of looking at this issue. • Through a respectful and inquiring tone, encourage the audience to listen and work with you to solve the problem.
Conclusion	• Possibly propose a synthesis of the two positions, discuss how both parties gain from an enlarged vision, or invite the audience to ongoing negotiation.

In the following example of a Rogerian letter, student writer Colleen Fontana responds to an article written by Robert A. Levy, a senior fellow for constitutional studies at the Cato Institute, a libertarian think tank. In this open letter, Colleen conducts a collaborative discussion directed toward solving the problem of gun violence.* Annotations in the margins indicate how Colleen is practicing Rogerian principles.

An Open Letter to Robert Levy in Response to His Article "They Never Learn"

COLLEEN FONTANA (STUDENT)

Dear Robert Levy,

Writer addresses the audience.

My recent interest in preventing gun violence led me to find your article "They Never Learn" in *The American Spectator* about the mass shooting at Virginia Tech in 2007. I was struck by the similarities between that incident and the recent shooting in Tucson, Arizona, where a young man gunned down U.S. Representative Gabrielle Giffords and nineteen others in a supermarket parking lot. Although your article came several years before this Arizona incident, we can see that gun violence remains an enduring issue. I have long struggled with the question of how we can reduce gun-related violence without detracting from an individual's right to own a gun. Your article shed new light on this question for me.

Writer identifies the problem, shows its current timeliness (kairos), and establishes a cordial relationship with the audience.

Your article stresses the need for something different from our nation's current gun policies. You assert that the solution lies not in stricter gun control policies, but rather in "liberalized laws." According to you, Mr. Levy, it was primarily the existence of anti-gun laws on the Virginia Tech campus that prevented an armed citizen from saving the victims of the 2007 shooting. You comment that "gun control does not work. It just prevents weaker people from defending themselves against stronger predators." Your article gives detailed examples of studies that have substantiated that stricter gun laws have not resulted in lower murder rates. You also cite evidence that fewer crimes are likely to happen if the victim brandishes a gun, even if he or she never fires it. According to your article, stricter gun laws are doing nothing to help society, and your solution lies in relaxed laws, allowing more responsible citizens to carry concealed weapons.

In neutral, fair terms, the writer summarizes the audience's previous argument, the article to which she is responding.

Living on a college campus myself, I identify immediately with your concern for preventing school shootings. I appreciate that you are

---

*We are indebted to Doug Brent for his insight that Rogerian arguments can often be addressed to the author of an article that a reader finds disturbing. See "Rogerian Rhetoric: Ethical Growth Through Alternative Forms of Argumentation." In *Argument Revisited; Argument Redefined,* eds. Barbara Emmel, Paula Resch, and Deborah Tenney (Thousand Oaks, CA: Sage, 1996), 81.

concerned with the safety of the students and the public, and I agree that there exists a need for greater safety on school campuses. I also agree that current gun laws are not effective, as is shown by the number of gun-related deaths that happen annually. Even though such laws exist, they are not likely to stop "crazed fanatics undeterred by laws against murder," as you say, from committing certain crimes. I particularly agree with you when you discuss the right of self-defense. I struggle with laws that forbid carrying a gun because I believe in the right of self-defense. As you mentioned in your article, instances do occur in which civilians carrying guns have the ability to save themselves and others. Although I have not experienced this situation personally, I have read of brave acts of self-defense and intervention. For example, my research turned up an article by John Pierce on MonachusLex.com, "It Takes a Gun to Stop a Gunman." In this article Pierce describes an occurrence in Richmond, Virginia, in July of 2009 where a store owner and several customers were saved from an armed robber by a civilian in the store who happened to be carrying a firearm. Even though Pierce is a long-time gun rights advocate and an NRA-certified instructor, the points he brought up were striking. If that civilian hadn't been carrying a gun in that store on that day, then everyone in the store might have been killed by the robber. This realization resonates with me. I imagine myself in that store, and I know I would have been quite grateful that he was carrying a weapon that saved my life. Reading this story has forced me to think of the responsibility many gun-owning citizens must feel—a responsibility to protect not only themselves but those around them as well. A similar event happened recently in New York where a person attempting to rob a jewelry shop was shot by the owner in an act of self-defense. His neighbors regard him as a hero (Kilgannon).

While I agree with you that self-defense is an important right and that armed citizens can sometimes prevent the death of innocent people, I wonder whether the possibility of allowing more guns in public through liberalized gun laws is the best solution. Is there a chance more guns in the hands of more people would foster a more danger-prone climate both from accidents and from sudden fits of rage? I was surprised to learn in a recent *New York Times* article by Charles M. Blow that for every ten people in America there are nine guns. Among major nations, according to a U.N. study, we have both the highest ratio of guns to people and the highest incidence of violence. If liberalizing gun ownership will lead to even more guns, then my concern is that there will be a higher chance of children finding a loaded gun in a parent's bed stand or of deaths caused by gang warfare or from momentary rage in an escalating fight between neighbors. Such danger could also exist on school campuses if guns were allowed. On a campus where drinking nurtures the party scene, I worry that rowdy people waving a gun perhaps as a joke might turn a party into a tragedy. Do you have any ideas, Mr. Levy, for reducing gun accidents or irresponsible use of firearms if they are widely available?

5   I found your point about owning a firearm for self-defense really thought provoking. But even if Virginia Tech had allowed guns on campus, what are the odds that an armed student or teacher would have been at the right place at the right time with an actual chance of shooting the gunman? Only in the movies are good guys and heroes *always* on the spot and capable of taking the right action to protect potential victims. Although I can really see your point about using handguns for self-defense, I don't think self-defense can be used as a justification for assault weapons or automatic weapons with large clips. If guns were freely allowed on campuses, perhaps massacres such as Virginia Tech might occur more often. Or is there a way to allow people to carry concealed handguns on campus but still to forbid rifles, shotguns, or other weapons more useful for massacres than for self-defense?

After reading your article I have more understanding of the arguments in favor of guns, and I continue to ponder the ethical and practical issues of gun control versus the right to self-defense. You have underscored for me the importance of our continuing to seek means of preventing these terrible massacres from happening in our nation's schools. You have also opened my eyes to the fact that no amount of enforcement of gun laws can deter determined people from using guns to harm others. I am not sure, however, that your proposal to eliminate gun control laws is the best solution, and I am hoping that you might be willing to consider some of my reasons for fearing guns, especially assault weapons and automatic weapons that can be fired like machine guns. Perhaps we could both agree that pursuing responsible gun ownership is a step in the right direction so that we reduce the number of accidents, keep guns away from children, and reduce access to guns capable of unleashing mass murder. I am hopeful that with our common concern over the current ineffectiveness of gun laws and the desire for safety in our schools, we can find a reasonable solution while still preserving the human right of self-defense.

Sincerely,

Colleen Fontana

Writer expresses a second concern, one that Levy did not mention: assault weapons.

Writer concludes her letter with a reiteration of the mutual concerns she shares with her audience; she acknowledges how her perspectives have been widened by Levy's views; she seeks to keep the channel of communication open; and she expresses interest in further problem solving.

Works Cited

Blow, Charles M. "Obama's Gun Play." *The New York Times,* 21 Jan. 2011, www.nytimes.com/2011/01/22/opinion/22blow.html?_r=0.

Kilgannon, Cory. "After Shooting, Merchant Is Hero of Arthur Avenue." *The New York Times,* 12 Feb. 2011, www.nytimes.com/2011/02/18/nyregion/18arthur.html.

Levy, Robert A. "They Never Learn." *The American Spectator,* 25 Apr. 2007, spectator.org/articles/45477/they-never-learn.

Pierce, John. "It Takes a Gun to Stop a Gunman." *MonachusLex.com,* 15 July 2009, monachuslex.com/?p=262.

■ ■ ■   **FOR WRITING AND DISCUSSION**   **Listening Empathically and**   MyWritingLab™
Searching for Common Ground

The heated national debate over immigration reform is highlighted in the photos shown in Figures 7.3–7.6. One of the most contentious parts of the immigration debate concerns deportation of illegals by the U.S. Immigration and Customs Enforcement. Intended to be enforced primarily on illegal immigrants guilty of crimes, this practice has swept up many illegals who have been peacefully raising families and working in the United States, often for many years. Illegals are often

FIGURE 7.3 Demonstrators in Tacoma, Washington, protest immigrant deportations as inhumane

FIGURE 7.4 Demonstrators in Phoenix support Arizona's tough law against illegal immigration

FIGURE 7.5 A rally on Capitol Hill opposes immigration reform with amnesty

FIGURE 7.6 Demonstrators urge executive support of immigrant family unity

detained in harsh prison-like conditions before they are deported. Another part of the immigration debate focuses on illegal immigrants' impact on American jobs. Usually, stakeholders who believe illegal immigrants are displacing American workers also oppose creating a path to citizenship for illegals. The photos portray protestors taking strong, emotional stands on the problem of illegal immigration and the treatment of illegal immigrants.

Individual task: Among the photos, choose one that represents the position on immigration with which you most disagree. Then imagine that you are conducting a Rogerian discussion with the people in the photo and follow these thinking and writing steps:

1. What are your own views about how the United States should handle the problem of 11 million illegal immigrants in the country? In what ways have you benefitted from the presence of illegal workers? Should the government try to establish a path to citizenship for them? Evict them from the country? Deport only those who have a criminal record? Explore your own values.
2. Write a summary of the views you think the people in your chosen photo hold. Write your summary in fair, neutral language that indicates your understanding and that would make your summary acceptable to the people you oppose.
3. Then write a common-grounds paragraph in which you go beyond summary to show your respectful understanding of the values held by these people. Consider how these views might be valid. Demonstrate your empathy, and add an example of your own that shows how your views and those of the people in the photo could intersect.

Group task: As you share your summaries and common-grounds paragraphs with members of your class, role-play being the people in the photo with whom the writer is trying to seek common values and a basis for collaborative problem solving. From your assumed role, comment on how well the writer has understood and identified with your views and values.

Conclusion

This chapter explains strategies for addressing alternative views. When intending to engage supportive audiences in a cause, writers often compose one-sided arguments. Neutral or undecided audiences generally respond most favorably to classical argument, which uses strong reasons in support of its claim while openly summarizing alternative views and responding to them through rebuttal or concession. Strongly resistant audiences typically respond most favorably to dialogic strategies, such as delayed-thesis or Rogerian communication, which seeks common ground with an audience, aims at reducing hostility, and takes a more inquiring or conciliatory stance. Rogerian communication, especially, envisions both writer and reader undergoing mutual change.

Option 1: A Classical Argument Write a classical argument following the explanations in Chapter 3, pages 52–54, and using the guidelines for developing such an argument throughout Chapters 3–7. Depending on your instructor's preferences, this argument could be on a new issue, or it could be a final stage of an argument in progress throughout Part Two. This assignment expands the supporting-reasons assignment from Chapter 5 by adding sections that summarize opposing views and respond to them through refutation or concession. For an example of a classical argument, see "The Dangers of Digital Distraction" by Lauren Shinozuka (pages 145–148). Note how Lauren uses research to show that she is joining a larger public conversation on her generation's use of digital technology.

Option 2: A Rogerian Letter Write a Rogerian letter addressed to a specific person, either someone you know, someone you have heard deliver a speech, or the author of an article that has disturbed you. As you generate ideas for your letter, take stock of what you know about your audience and summarize his or her views in a way that your audience would find satisfactory. As you explore what your audience values and believes in, also explore how your own values differ. Where do you agree with your audience? Under what conditions would you find your audience's values acceptable? Follow the suggestions in the chart that explains the elements of a Rogerian letter on page 139 for determining a purpose and structure for your letter. Depending on the distance between your views and your audience's, your goal may be simply to encourage your audience to be willing to consider your perspective. For examples of Rogerian communication, see Colleen Fontana's "Open Letter to Robert Levy" on pages 140–142 and Monica Allen's "An Open Letter to Christopher Eide in Response to His Article 'High-Performing Charter Schools Can Close the Opportunity Gap'" on pages 149–152. Your instructor may ask you to attach a reflective response in which you describe how your experience of writing this Rogerian letter differed from your experience of writing classical arguments. ■

READINGS

Our first student essay illustrates a classical argument. This essay grew out of Lauren's own wrestling with her immersion in social media. She decided to persuade her peers to see the problem her way with the goal that they will join her in new awareness and new habits.

The Dangers of Digital Distractedness

LAUREN SHINOZUKA (STUDENT)

We are the Net Generation, the Facebook Generation—digital natives. Cultural critics praise us for our digital skills, our facility with multimedia, and our ability to interact electronically with others through collaboration and co-creation. But at what cost? If we are honest, the following anti-social scene is familiar. You are sitting at a table with friends, and then you hear various pings and look up to see every one of your friends with squinted eyes, checking social media apps and text messages, scrolling away on their phones and furiously punching a reply. What kind of togetherness is this? We seem to feel some urgency or need to know what the world wants from us in that moment, prompting us to check our smartphones every six and a half minutes a day. Rather than being skillfully technologically interactive, I argue that our behavior represents dependence, even addiction, that has deep, pervasive consequences. It harms us by promoting an unproductive habit of multitasking, by dehumanizing our relationships, and by encouraging a distorted self-image.

I can hear my peers immediately rejecting these claims as too extreme and too critical, and I acknowledge that a good case can be made for our digital savvy and the benefits that brings. Armed with smartphones and laptops, we believe we are masters of technology because we can access so much information easily and immediately. Thanks to our cell phones, all of our friends are only a mere click or swipe away for starting a conversation or sending an invitation to meet up. I also have to admit that our digital knowledge gives us on-the-job advantages. At my part-time job at a high-end retail store, I constantly use a mobile point-of-sale system to ring up customers for fast and easy "on-the-spot checkout," receiving compliments for my competence. With my comfort with the company's technology, I can troubleshoot easily and help other employees. Because technology facilitates much of what we do and keeps us plugged into the rest of the world, I recognize that it can be difficult to see the negative aspects of our relationship to digital technology, but it is time for serious self-examination.

In college, we tell ourselves that multitasking with technology helps us use our time wisely, but in actuality we become even less productive. I notice that while I study, I feel the need to stop every five or ten minutes to check my phone, or log on to a Web site and allow myself to get distracted before going back to my task. These momentary distractions eat away at my time; when I sit down to write a paper at 9 P.M. I am often startled to find that it is suddenly 12 A.M. and I have less than a page written. We Millennials think we are so cutting edge with our multitasking, yet we get little done with our time. We submerge ourselves into a technological bubble consisting of laptops and music and cell phones, convinced that by arming ourselves with these tools, we can really do it all. In actuality, as writer John Hamilton explains in his report for National Public Radio, our brains cannot "focus on more than one thing at a time." Hamilton cites MIT neuroscientist Earl Miller who says that our minds are "not paying attention to…two things simultaneously, but switching between them very rapidly"; thus, multitasking in itself is a myth. Furthermore, as we continue to overload our brains with multiple tasks, we also begin to reshape our thought processes. Technology—the Internet in particular—helps us avoid the hard work of concentration and contemplation. In the article "Is Google Making Us Stupid?" nonfiction business and technology writer Nicholas Carr describes this way we take in and distribute information as a "swiftly moving stream of particles." We skim rather than read; we rapidly switch tasks rather than truly multitask. I recognize this superficial way of operating in the world in my own behavior. I often turn to Google for an immediate answer to a question I have: Who's the current Speaker of the House? How many ounces are in a cup? Then I click on the first link I see, and more often than not, I see the little subheading that states, "You've visited this page X times." I realize my mental instincts tell me that it's much easier to Google an answer multiple times rather than just *learn* the information. Because I constantly overindulge in my technology, I have engrained the habits of skimming streams of information, constantly bouncing from one task to another, but never stopping to bask in its depths.

Our obsession with technology and social media not only reshapes the way we think, but also fosters a type of false superficial friendship with people we barely know, dehumanizing the kinds of relationships we have. Since coming to college, I've had hundreds of new Facebook friends and dozens of new followers on Twitter. To be fair, a number of these people are truly my good friends, but most of these "friendships" came from a one-time meeting at a party or a class I had with them during my sophomore year. Although some will insist on the vital role social media plays in keeping them connected to distant family and friends, we need to address more directly the extent and pervasive effects of our more common arbitrary cyber friendships. Last summer, while I taught a program at a local elementary school, I would occasionally post a Facebook status of something funny that happened that day, or a picture of my class. Back home later for a short vacation, I ran into a girl from high school whom I hadn't seen in four years and barely knew then. When we stopped to chat, she asked me all about my summer program, and commented that all my students were so cute! After our chat, I left feeling perturbed and uneasy. Immediately, I thought she was so "creepy," but I realized that ultimately I chose to share my life with the rest of the world. Speaking about these digital relationships, Sherry Turkle, MIT professor and author of *Alone Together: Why We Expect More from Technology and Less from Each Other,* labels our behavior "a Goldilocks effect": "we can't get enough of one another if we can use technology to keep one another at distances we can control: not too close, not too far, just right." That moment when my distant "friend" reached out to me about my summer felt so disturbing because she crossed that Goldilocks line through a personal face-to-face conversation. I am embarrassed to say that I was comfortable only when she was one of the masses; I didn't want to engage in a true interpersonal connection.

5   This lack of intimacy through false relationships leads to the creation of a distorted identity. We begin to form a social identity through our conscious decisions of what we choose to share with the rest of the digital world. We want to post pretty pictures that will garner us a number of "likes," and we want to tweet something witty or profound so others will retweet us. When I began to reevaluate my own social media identity, I found that I consciously try to word my Facebook status in order for people to find it funny, and I'm obsessed with editing my pictures with the right filters to achieve that hipster artist effect. I realized that I was interpreting my own life experiences in such a way that I would seem interesting or entertaining to all of my "friends," as if I were performing for an audience I was trying to please. That image of myself is dishonest: It conveys the person I want people to think I am, not the real me.

We see this willful self-distortion in a growing trend called "catfishing": an Internet phenomenon where one person creates a false online identity to engage in a romantic relationship with another person physically far removed. The "catfisher" uses fake pictures of attractive people and an image of talent to create a different person. Coined by a documentary of the same name, *Catfish*, a reality show spin-off, features these long-distance lovers traveling across the country for a chance to meet who really is on the other side of the screen. Often that person's appearance and even gender and motives are strikingly at odds with the self-portrayal. While it is easy for us to judge negatively these extreme cases of catfishing, Molly McHugh, writer for *Digital Trends*, points out what she calls the "slippery slope of catfishdom." These cases may seem extreme, but to an extent, all of us who embrace social media are indeed "catfish" as well. We succumb to what McHugh calls the "aspirational beast" of social media, bending the truth online to some degree in order to portray the self that we want to be. With our growing reliance on social media and technology, the tendency for our romantic relationships to blend into our digital selves becomes even more prevalent. When we continue to mix this intimate, personal self with the demands and desires of social media, we produce tragic, ill-formed identities that no longer resemble our true selves.

Of course, we may draw a sharp distinction between our own digital dependence and the growing number of young users who are actual technological addicts. (According to Carolyn Gregoire's *Huffington Post* article, there is now an inpatient Internet rehabilitation center designed specifically for true addicts.) However, our own participation in the more wide-spread digital craze remains a serious problem too. Yet by taking the first step of making the unconscious conscious, I believe we can combat the digital damage in our lives. I have begun by taking several steps. I purposefully put my phone across the table so I physically need to get up to check it; I only let myself binge-check all my social media apps just before going to bed rather than ten times a day, and I have stopped trying to take pictures of every pretty meal I consume or sunset I see because I know that those are my own special moments, not some glamorous, envious image I want to project. I have begun to avoid friends who find their phones more interesting than the immediate world around them, and this new company has made it easier to break away from my own addiction. I am trying to rehumanize my friendships, and I am finding solace in deep reading once more without the distractions of cell phone vibrations. I invite members of my generation to join me, so we can be together, no longer alone together.

Works Cited

Carr, Nicholas. "Is Google Making Us Stupid?: What the Internet Is Doing to Our Brains." *The Atlantic,* July-Aug. 2008, www.theatlantic.com/magazine/archive/2008/07/is-google-making-us-stupid/306868.

Gregoire, Carolyn. "Welcome to Internet Rehab." *The Huffington Post,* 25 Sept. 2013, updated 25 Oct. 2013, www.huffingtonpost.com/2013/09/25/this-is-where-people-are-_n_3976240.html.

Hamilton, John. "Think You're Multitasking? Think Again." *National Public Radio,* 2 Oct. 2008, www.npr.org/templates/story/story.php?storyId=95256794.

McHugh, Molly. "It's Catfishing Season! How to Tell Lovers from Liars Online, and More." *Digital Trends,* 23 Aug. 2013, www.digitaltrends.com/web/its-catfishing-season-how-to-tell-lovers-from-liars-online-and-more.

Turkle, Sherry. "The Flight from Conversation." *The New York Times,* 21 Apr. 2012, www.nytimes.com/2012/04/22/opinion/sunday/the-flight-from-conversation.html.

To illustrate a conciliatory or Rogerian approach to an issue, we show you student writer Monica Allen's Rogerian letter written for this assignment. Monica's letter grew out of her research on charter schools and educational reform in preparation for writing her own proposal argument later. In this Rogerian letter, she listens carefully to a proponent of charter schools whose views were very different from her own. Monica writes in the hope of opening up a deeper problem-solving conversation.

An Open Letter to Christopher Eide in Response to His Article "High-Performing Charter Schools Can Close the Opportunity Gap"

MONICA ALLEN (STUDENT)

Dear Mr. Eide,

I want to thank you for your article "High-Performing Charter Schools Can Close the Opportunity Gap," which contributes to the national conversation about the role of charter schools in education reform. Like you, I am concerned about whether publically run, privately funded charter schools can provide innovative new approaches to increase the quality of education for minority and economically disadvantaged students. I have been wrestling with the claims that charter schools can help reduce this troubling opportunity gap. Your helpful article has deepened my understanding of charter schools and has given me much to think about.

Your article proposes legislation specifically designed to create high-performing, effective charter schools. What is most exciting in your article is your suggestion that this legislation has the potential to close the opportunity gap. Citing the Stanford Center for Research on Education (CREDO) study and national charter efforts like the Knowledge is Power Program (KIPP), which focus on achievement gains in particular for low-income students in some charter schools, you believe that increased charter education will enable our nation to better educate academically underserved students. Ultimately, you want to look beyond the inconsistent results charter schools have historically shown nationwide and urge our state to focus its charter school innovation on improving opportunities for its students suffering most from the opportunity gap.

Your encouraging article speaks to the belief I share with you that the highest priority in educational innovation needs to be closing the opportunity gap. As education researcher Sean Reardon has shown in "The Widening Income Achievement Gap," the differences in opportunities and outcomes between low- and high-income background students have continued to widen throughout the past three decades. Clearly, we are in desperate need of more and better educational improvement. I share your concern that charter schools, focusing on the wrong objectives, could become a force that widens, rather than narrows, the opportunity gap. I particularly appreciate your commitment to concentrating reform efforts where they are needed most—with students from low-income backgrounds who are disproportionately left behind in traditional public schools. As an English Language Learning tutor and teacher, I am encouraged that the CREDO study you cite indicates that some charter schools produce better gains for ELL students than do traditional public schools. I am grateful that you advocate for underserved students, such as English Language Learners, and am now much more interested in understanding the charter movement because of your conviction that it can address our most pressing educational issue.

Your article also answers some of my prior concerns about charter schools, making me more open to charter education. In particular, I have been wary of the inconsistent performance of charter schools nationwide, and so I appreciate that you support rigorous legislation to hold charter schools accountable to the highest standards possible. Your article also helped dispel some of my concerns that charter schools tend to serve disproportionately higher income students and thereby segregate our schools into high-income charters and low-income traditional public schools. It led me to do more research about charter schools' student demographics and to find that there are many examples of charters serving primarily low-income groups of students. Finally, I appreciated your article's urgency. I, too, believe that the needs of disproportionally poorly educated, low-income students today make this issue a pressing one that calls for immediate action.

5   Because your article awakened me to the social benefits that charter schools can provide, I'd like to share with you four reservations in the hopes that, together, people like us who hold different perspectives on charter schools can learn from one another and better close our education opportunity gap.

First, I share your belief that charter schools offer needed opportunities to be education laboratories—places whose freedom from bureaucracy enables them to test out new strategies that can inform widespread practices. However, are charter schools really experimental? Adamant charter school supporter and Columbia University researcher Priscilla Wohlstetter writes that despite her belief in the prospects of charter schools generally, "most [charter schools] do little to tap the potential of unique, innovative strategies. For all the hype, charters typically borrow familiar classroom strategies (back-to-basics, project-based learning, college prep) from private and traditional public schools." I share Wohlstetter's concern that while the education laboratory concept has popularized charter schools, research demonstrates they have not functioned as such in our education system. Though I am encouraged by your commitment to highly regulated charter schools, I am unsure whether state legislation that only regulates based on the test results of charter school students really ensures that charters deliver what they intend to. Perhaps we should explore other means to measure innovation to ensure that the investment of public funds in charter schools results in gains for the education system as a whole, in part by demonstrating that charter schools can teach us how to teach better. That would be a partnership between public and charter education that I believe we all hope to see.

A second question I have is whether charter schools will make innovative learning more accessible to students who are traditionally underserved. While the CREDO study you cite shows some promising results, Jean Allen, head of the Center for Education Reform, has questioned the conclusiveness of the data (Sanchez). Indeed, researchers across the board believe that the jury is very much still out on the question of whether charter school students really learn as much as traditional public school students, which is why the National Alliance for Public Charter Schools and Harvard University just started afresh with a comprehensive study last fall. I am concerned that we may be implementing a system that has yet to be effectively tested. I do think the anecdotal evidence you cite about KIPP schools is extremely exciting and deserves public attention, because KIPP schools serve a majority of low-income student populations *and* are outperforming traditional public schools near them. But shouldn't we also consider that KIPP schools rely heavily on significant private donations and are unique among charters in this way? To me, it makes sense that KIPP schools outperform other local schools when their operating budgets are 30–50 percent higher (Di Carlo). Could we agree that this income disparity and school funding as a significant predictor of student success calls for more investigation?

I also have a third, more fundamental question with respect to charter schools. I wonder whether in the enthusiasm to innovate our schools, we will lose sight of that which makes American education innovative at its core—its commitment to democratic education. I am concerned that charter schools focusing on low-income student bodies might contribute to the non-democratic socio-economic and ethnic segregation of our schools. I believe that the segregation of schools into the haves and have-nots is one of the largest issues facing our national education system. Could charter schools that concentrate on serving low-income and traditionally underserved ethnic groups unintentionally widen the gap? Along with education activist and writer Jonathan Kozol (Cody), I fear that charter schools with names like "Black Success Academy" and "The African-American Academy for Leadership and Enterprise" divert attention from what really needs to be attended to—the de-segregating of our already divided schools and our school funding on lines of race and socio-economic status. While I, like you, want us to do everything we can immediately to improve the chances for underserved students, I am most interested in focusing our efforts on equalizing our schools' demographics and budgets. How can charters and traditional public schools work together to do this?

Finally, Mr. Eide, I also wonder whether privatizing education will ultimately be in the best interest of students on the low spectrum of the opportunity gap. Public education promises public responsibility to educate each of its students for successful vocational and civic lives. Right now, you and I both know that the American public has not been living up to that responsibility. How can we do better? I am concerned that privatizing education removes not only the public investment in education (namely, tax dollars) from public hands, but diminishes our sense of responsibility and capacity to be a nation that educates all its citizens. I wonder whether, in the long run, the students who stand to lose the most from the public's loss of responsibility to educate all are those who are the most vulnerable. How can charter and traditional schools work together to build public confidence in the civic power of education?

10   Because my own home state will soon be instituting new charter schools, I am thankful for having read your article. Clearly, people who hold different views about

the potential of charter schools have much to learn from one another. I hope to see my home state pioneer cutting-edge methods for charter school regulation and to build relationships between charter and public school communities so that the existence of charter schools in our state has a large-scale impact. I am very glad to have read your article and to know that many advocates of charter schools are committed to equalizing opportunity in education.

Regards,

Monica Allen

Works Cited

Cody, Anthony. "Confronting the Inequality Juggernaut: A Q&A with Jonathan Kozol." *Education Week: Teacher,* 18 July 2011, blogs.edweek.org/teachers/living-in-dialogue/2011/07/time_to_get_off_our_knees_why.html.

Di Carlo, Matthew. "Controversial Consensus on KIPP Charter Schools." *Albert Shanker Institute,* 12 Mar. 2013, www.shankerinstitute.org/blog/controversial-consensus-kipp-charter-schools.

Eide, Christopher. "High-Performing Charter Schools Can Close the Opportunity Gap." *The Seattle Times,* 11 July 2012, www.seattletimes.com/opinion/high-performing-charter-schools-can-close-the-opportunity-gap.

Reardon, Sean F. "The Widening Income Achievement Gap." *Educational Leadership,* vol. 70, no. 8, 2013, pp. 10-16.

Sanchez, Claudio. "The Charter School vs. Public School Debate Continues." *NPR Education,* 16 July 2013, www.npr.org/2013/07/16/201109021/the-charter-school-vs-public-school-debate-continues.

Wohlstetter, Priscilla. "The Debate Must Move On: Charter Schools Are Here to Stay." *WNYC: School Book,* 9 Dec. 2013, www.wnyc.org/story/charter-schools-are-here-stay-now-lets-have-useful-conversation-about-them.

MyWritingLab™

Visit Ch. 7 Responding to Objections and Alternative Views in *MyWritingLab* to complete the For Writing and Discussion and Writing Assignments and to test your understanding of the chapter objectives.

PART THREE
Analyzing Arguments

Increasingly, countries are employing hydraulic fracturing (called fracking), which extracts natural gas from deeply buried shale, to meet their energy needs. Burning natural gas is cleaner than burning gasoline, oil, and coal and emits less carbon dioxide. However, each fracking site uses millions of gallons of water, leaves contaminated waste water, and often emits methane. Also environmentalists fear that fracking may contaminate aquifers. This photo depicts anti-fracking views in a protest near Manchester, England, in January 2014. To what extent does the garb of the protestors make effective appeals to *logos* and *pathos* to turn viewers against fracking?

Analyzing Arguments Rhetorically

What you will learn in this chapter:

8.1 To explain what it means to *think rhetorically* about texts

8.2 To conduct a rhetorical analysis of a specific text

In Part Two of this book, we explained thinking and writing strategies for composing your own arguments. Now in Part Three we show you how to use your new rhetorical knowledge to conduct in-depth analyses of other people's arguments. To analyze an argument rhetorically means to examine closely how it is composed and what makes it effective or ineffective for its targeted audience. A rhetorical analysis identifies the text under scrutiny, summarizes its main ideas, presents some key points about the text's rhetorical strategies for persuading its audience, and elaborates on these points.

Becoming skilled at analyzing arguments rhetorically will have multiple payoffs for you. Rhetorical analyses are common assignments in courses in critical thinking and argument. Additionally, thinking rhetorically about texts is crucial for writing the "literature review" section of research assignments across the disciplines. Furthermore, rhetorical analysis also plays a major role in constructing your own arguments, especially in your decisions about reputable evidence and in sections where you summarize and respond to opposing views. This chapter focuses on the rhetorical analysis of written arguments, and the next one (Chapter 9) equips you to analyze visual arguments.

Thinking Rhetorically about a Text

8.1 To explain what it means to *think rhetorically* about texts

Before we turn directly to rhetorical analysis of specific texts, let's focus on the key word *rhetoric*. In popular usage, *rhetoric* often means empty or deceptive language, as in, "Well, that's just rhetoric." Another related meaning of *rhetoric* is decorative or artificial language. The Greek Stoic philosopher Epictetus likened rhetoric to hairdressers fixing hair*—a view that sees rhetoric as superficial decoration.

---

*Chaim Perelman, "The New Rhetoric: A Theory of Practical Reasoning." In *Professing the New Rhetorics: A Sourcebook,* eds. Theresa Enos and Stuart C. Brown (Englewood Cliffs, NJ: Prentice Hall, 1994), 149.

Most contemporary rhetoricians, however, adopt the larger view of rhetoric articulated by Greek philosopher Aristotle: the art of determining what will be persuasive in every situation. Contemporary rhetorician Donald C. Bryant has described rhetoric in action as "the function of adjusting ideas to people and of people to ideas."* Focusing on this foundational meaning of rhetoric, this chapter shows you how to analyze a writer's motivation, purpose, and rhetorical choices for persuading a targeted audience. This chapter draws primarily on rhetorical concepts with which you are already familiar: audience-based reasons, the STAR criteria for evidence, and the classical appeals of *logos, ethos,* and *pathos.*

Questions for Rhetorical Analysis

Conducting a rhetorical analysis asks you to bring to bear on an argument your knowledge of argument and your repertoire of reading strategies. The chart of questions for analysis on pages 155–157 can help you examine an argument in depth. Although a rhetorical analysis will not include answers to all of these questions, using some of these questions in your thinking stages can give you a thorough understanding of the argument while helping you generate insights for your own rhetorical analysis essay.

Questions for Rhetorical Analysis

What to Focus On	Questions to Ask	Applying These Questions
The *kairotic* moment and writer's motivating occasion	▪ What motivated the writer to produce this piece? ▪ What social, cultural, political, legal, or economic conversations does this argument join?	▪ Is the writer responding to a bill pending in Congress, a speech by a political leader, or a local event that provoked controversy? ▪ Is the writer addressing cultural trends such as the impact of science or technology on values?
Rhetorical context: Writer's purpose and audience	▪ What is the writer's purpose? ▪ Who is the intended audience? ▪ What assumptions, values, and beliefs would readers have to hold to find this argument persuasive? ▪ How well does the text suit its particular audience and purpose?	▪ Is the writer trying to change readers' views by offering a new interpretation of a phenomenon, calling readers to action, or trying to muster votes or inspire further investigations? ▪ Does the audience share a political or religious orientation with the writer?

(Continued)

---

*Donald C. Bryant, "Rhetoric: Its Functions and Its Scope." In *Professing the New Rhetorics: A Sourcebook,* eds. Theresa Enos and Stuart C. Brown (Englewood Cliffs, NJ: Prentice Hall, 1994), 282.

What to Focus On	Questions to Ask	Applying These Questions
Rhetorical context: Writer's identity and angle of vision	■ Who is the writer and what is his or her profession, background, and expertise? ■ How does the writer's personal history, education, gender, ethnicity, age, class, sexual orientation, and political leaning influence the angle of vision? ■ What is emphasized and what is omitted in this text? ■ How much does the writer's angle of vision dominate the text?	■ Is the writer a scholar, researcher, scientist, policy maker, politician, professional journalist, or citizen blogger? ■ Is the writer affiliated with conservative or liberal, religious or lay publications? ■ Is the writer advocating a stance or adopting a more inquiry-based mode? ■ What points of view and pieces of evidence are "not seen" by this writer?
Rhetorical context: Genre	■ What is the argument's original genre? ■ What is the original medium of publication? How does the genre and the argument's place of publication influence its content, structure, and style?	■ How popular or scholarly, informal or formal is this genre? ■ Does the genre allow for in-depth or only sketchy coverage of an issue? ■ (See Chapter 2, pages 26–29, for detailed explanations of genre.)
Logos **of the argument**	■ What is the argument's claim, either explicitly stated or implied? ■ What are the main reasons in support of the claim? Are the reasons audience-based? ■ How effective is the writer's use of evidence? How is the argument supported and developed? ■ How well has the argument recognized and responded to alternative views?	■ Is the core of the argument clear and soundly developed? Or do readers have to unearth or reconstruct the argument? ■ Is the argument one-sided, multisided, or dialogic? ■ Does the argument depend on assumptions the audience may not share? ■ What evidence does the writer employ? Does this evidence meet the STAR criteria? (See pages 92–93.)
Ethos **of the argument**	■ What *ethos* does the writer project? ■ How does the writer try to seem credible and trustworthy to the intended audience? ■ How knowledgeable does the writer seem in recognizing opposing or alternative views and how fairly does the writer respond to them?	■ If you are impressed or won over by this writer, what has earned your respect? ■ If you are filled with doubts or skepticism, what has caused you to question this writer? ■ How important is the character of the writer in this argument?

What to Focus On	Questions to Ask	Applying These Questions
Pathos of the argument	▪ How effective is the writer in using audience-based reasons? ▪ How does the writer use concrete language, word choice, narrative, examples, and analogies to tap readers' emotions, values, and imaginations?	▪ What examples, connotative language, and uses of narrative or analogy stand out for you in this argument? ▪ Does this argument rely heavily on appeals to *pathos?* Or is it more brainy and logical?
Writer's style	▪ How do the writer's language choices and sentence length and complexity contribute to the impact of the argument? ▪ How well does the writer's tone (attitude toward the subject) suit the argument?	▪ How readable is this argument? ▪ Is the argument formal, scholarly, journalistic, informal, or casual? ▪ Is the tone serious, mocking, humorous, exhortational, confessional, urgent, or something else?
Design and visual elements	▪ How do design elements—layout, font sizes and styles, and use of color—influence the effect of the argument? (See Chapter 9 for a detailed discussion of these elements.) ▪ How do graphics and images contribute to the persuasiveness of the argument?	▪ Do design features contribute to the logical or the emotional/imaginative appeals of the argument? ▪ How would this argument benefit from visuals and graphics or some different document design?
Overall persuasiveness of the argument	▪ What features of this argument contribute most to making it persuasive or not persuasive for its target audience and for you yourself? ▪ How would this argument be received by different audiences? ▪ What features contribute to the rhetorical complexity of this argument? ▪ What is particularly memorable, disturbing, or problematic about this argument? ▪ What does this argument contribute to its *kairotic* moment and the argumentative controversy of which it is a part?	▪ For example, are appeals to *pathos* legitimate and suitable? Does the quality and quantity of the evidence help build a strong case or fall short? ▪ What specifically would count as a strength for the target audience? ▪ If you differ from the target audience, how do you differ and where does the argument derail for you? ▪ What gaps, contradictions, or unanswered questions are you left with? ▪ How does this argument indicate that it is engaged in a public conversation? How does it "talk" to other arguments you have read on this issue?

■ ■ ■   **FOR WRITING AND DISCUSSION** Practicing Rhetorical Analysis   MyWritingLab™

In the following exercise, consider the strategies used by two different writers to persuade their audiences to act to stop climate change. The first is from the opening paragraphs of an editorial in the magazine *Creation Care: A Christian Environmental Quarterly*. The second is from the Web site of the Sierra Club, an environmental action group.

Individual task: Read the following passages carefully, and then write out your exploratory answers to the questions that follow. Refer to the chart "Questions for Rhetorical Analysis" on pages 155–157 to help you in your examination of how the key features of these texts contribute to their impact on readers.

Passage 1

As I sit down to write this column, one thing keeps coming to me over and over: "Now is the time; now is the time."

In the New Testament the word used for this type of time is *kairos*. It means "right or opportune moment." It is contrasted with *chronos,* or chronological time as measured in seconds, days, months, or years. In the New Testament *kairos* is usually associated with decisive action that brings about deliverance or salvation.

The reason the phrase, "Now is the time" kept coming to me over and over is that I was thinking of how to describe our current climate change moment.

The world has been plodding along in chronological time on the problem of climate change since around 1988. No more.

Simply put: the problem of climate change has entered *kairos* time; its *kairos* moment has arrived. How long will it endure? Until the time of decisive action to bring about deliverance comes—or, more ominously, until the time when the opportunity for decisive action has passed us by. Which will we choose? Because we do have a choice.

—Rev. Jim Ball, Ph.D., "It's *Kairos* Time for Climate Change: Time to Act," *Creation Care: A Christian Environmental Quarterly* (Summer 2008), 28.

Passage 2

[Another action that Americans must take to combat global warming is to transition] to a clean energy economy in a just and equitable way. Global warming is among the greatest challenges of our time, but also presents extraordinary opportunities to harness home-grown clean energy sources and encourage technological innovation. These bold shifts toward a clean energy future can create hundreds of thousands of new jobs and generate billions of dollars in capital investment. But in order to maximize these benefits across all sectors of our society, comprehensive global warming legislation must auction emission allowances to polluters and use these public assets for public benefit programs.

Such programs include financial assistance to help low and moderate-income consumers and workers offset higher energy costs as well as programs that assist with adaptation efforts in communities vulnerable to the effects of climate change. Revenue generated from emissions allowances should also aid the expansion of renewable and efficient energy technologies that quickly, cleanly, cheaply, and safely reduce our dependence on fossil fuels and curb global warming. Lastly, it is absolutely vital that comprehensive global warming legislation not preempt state authority to cut greenhouse gas emissions more aggressively than mandated by federal legislation.

—Sierra Club, "Global Warming Policy Solutions," 2008, http://www.sierraclub.org/

1. How do the strategies of persuasion differ in these two passages? Explain these differences in terms of targeted audience, original genre, writer's purpose, and writer's angle of vision.
2. How would you describe the relationship between *logos* and *pathos* in each text?
3. How would you describe the writer's style in each?
4. How effective would either argument be for readers outside the intended audience?

Group task: Share your responses to the above questions with class members. Explain your points with specific examples from the texts.

Conducting a Rhetorical Analysis

8.2 To conduct a rhetorical analysis of a specific text

To illustrate rhetorical analysis (both in this section and in the student example at the end of the chapter), we will analyze two articles on reproductive technology, a subject that continues to generate arguments in the public sphere. By *reproductive technology* we mean scientific advances in the treatment of infertility such as egg and sperm donation, artificial insemination, in vitro fertilization, and surrogate motherhood. Our first article, from over a decade ago, springs from the early and increasing popularity of these technological options. Our second article—to be used in our later student example—responds to the recent globalization of this technology.

At this point, please read our first article, "Egg Heads" by Kathryn Jean Lopez, and then proceed to the discussion questions that follow. Lopez's article was originally published in the September 1, 1998, issue of the biweekly conservative news commentary magazine *National Review*.

Egg Heads

KATHRYN JEAN LOPEZ

Filling the waiting room to capacity and spilling over into a nearby conference room, a group of young women listen closely and follow the instructions: Complete the forms and return them, with the clipboard, to the receptionist. It's all just as in any medical office. Then they move downstairs, where the doctor briefs them. "Everything will be pretty much normal," she explains. "Women complain of skin irritation in the local area of injection and bloating. You also might be a little emotional. But, basically, it's really bad PMS."

This is not just another medical office. On a steamy night in July, these girls in their twenties are attending an orientation session for potential egg donors at a New Jersey fertility clinic specializing in in-vitro fertilization. Within the walls of IVF

New Jersey and at least two hundred other clinics throughout the United States, young women answer the call to give "the gift of life" to infertile couples. Egg donation is a quietly expanding industry, changing the way we look at the family, young women's bodies, and human life itself.

It is not a pleasant way to make money. Unlike sperm donation, which is over in less than an hour, egg donation takes the donor some 56 hours and includes a battery of tests, ultrasound, self-administered injections, and retrieval. Once a donor is accepted into a program, she is given hormones to stimulate the ovaries, changing the number of eggs matured from the usual one per month up to as many as fifty. A doctor then surgically removes the eggs from the donor's ovary and fertilizes them with the designated sperm.

Although most programs require potential donors to undergo a series of medical tests and counseling, there is little indication that most of the young women know what they are getting themselves into. They risk bleeding, infection, and scarring. When too many eggs are matured in one cycle, it can damage the ovaries and leave the donor with weeks of abdominal pain. (At worst, complications may leave her dead.) Longer term, the possibility of early menopause raises the prospect of future regret. There is also some evidence of a connection between the fertility drugs used in the process and ovarian cancer.

5 But it's good money—and getting better. New York's Brooklyn IVF raised its "donor compensation" from $2,500 to $5,000 per cycle earlier this year in order to keep pace with St. Barnabas Medical Center in nearby Livingston, New Jersey. It's a bidding war. "It's obvious why we had to do it," says Susan Lobel, Brooklyn IVF's assistant director. Most New York–area IVF programs have followed suit.

Some infertile couples and independent brokers are offering even more for "reproductive material." The International Fertility Center in Indianapolis, Indiana, for instance, places ads in the *Daily Princetonian* offering Princeton girls as much as $35,000 per cycle. The National Fertility Registry, which, like many egg brokerages, features an on-line catalogue for couples to browse in, advertises $35,000 to $50,000 for Ivy League eggs. While donors are normally paid a flat fee per cycle, there have been reports of higher payments to donors who produce more eggs.

College girls are the perfect donors. Younger eggs are likelier to be healthy, and the girls themselves frequently need money—college girls have long been susceptible to classified ads offering to pay them for acting as guinea pigs in medical research. One 1998 graduate of the University of Colorado set up her own website to market her eggs. She had watched a television show on egg donation and figured it "seemed like a good thing to do"—especially since she had spent her money during the past year to help secure a country-music record deal. "Egg donation would help me with my school and music expenses while helping an infertile couple with a family." Classified ads scattered throughout cyberspace feature similar offers.

The market for "reproductive material" has been developing for a long time. It was twenty years ago this summer that the first test-tube baby, Louise Brown, was born. By 1995, when the latest tally was taken by the Centers for Disease Control, 15 percent of mothers in this country had made use of some form of assisted-reproduction technology in conceiving their children. (More recently, women past menopause have begun to make use of this technology.) In 1991 the American Society for Reproductive Medicine was aware of 63 IVF programs offering egg donation. That number had jumped to 189 by 1995 (the latest year for which numbers are available).

Defenders argue that it's only right that women are "compensated" for the inconvenience of egg donation. Brooklyn IVF's Dr. Lobel argues, "If it is unethical to accept payment for loving your neighbor, then we'll have to stop paying babysitters." As long as donors know the risks, says Glenn McGee of the

University of Pennsylvania's Center for Bioethics, this transaction is only "a slightly macabre version of adoption."

Not everyone is enthusiastic about the "progress." Egg donation "represents another rather large step into turning procreation into manufacturing," says the University of Chicago's Leon Kass. "It's the dehumanization of procreation." And as in manufacturing, there is quality control. "People don't want to say the word any more, but there is a strong eugenics issue inherent in the notion that you can have the best eggs your money can buy," observes sociology professor Barbara Katz Rothman of the City University of New York.

10   The demand side of the market comes mostly from career-minded baby-boomers, the frontierswomen of feminism, who thought they could "have it all." Indeed they *can* have it all—with a little help from some younger eggs. (Ironically, feminists are also among its strongest critics; *The Nation*'s Katha Pollitt has pointed out that in egg donation and surrogacy, once you remove the "delusion that they are making babies for other women," all you have left is "reproductive prostitution.")

Unfortunately, the future looks bright for the egg market. Earlier this year, a woman in Atlanta gave birth to twins after she was implanted with frozen donor eggs. The same technology has also been successful in Italy. This is just what the egg market needed, since it avoids the necessity of coordinating donors' cycles with recipients' cycles. Soon, not only will infertile couples be able to choose from a wider variety of donor offerings, but in some cases donors won't even be needed. Young women will be able to freeze their own eggs and have them thawed and fertilized once they are ready for the intrusion of children in their lives.

There are human ovaries sitting in a freezer in Fairfax, Virginia. The Genetics and IVF Institute offers to cut out and remove young women's ovaries and cryopreserve the egg-containing tissue for future implantation. Although the technology was originally designed to give the hope of fertility to young women undergoing treatment for cancer, it is now starting to attract the healthy. "Women can wait to have children until they are well established in their careers and getting a little bored, sometime in their forties or fifties," explains Professor Rothman. "Basically, motherhood is being reduced to a good leisure-time activity."

Early this summer, headlines were made in Britain, where the payment of egg donors is forbidden, when an infertile couple traveled to a California clinic where the woman could be inseminated with an experimental hybrid egg. The egg was a combination of the recipient's and a donor's eggs. The clinic in question gets its eggs from a Beverly Hills brokerage, the Center for Surrogate Parenting and Egg Donation, run by Karen Synesiou and Bill Handel, a radio shock-jock in Los Angeles. Miss Synesiou recently told the London *Sunday Times* that she is "interested in redefining the family. That's why I came to work here."

The redefinition is already well under way. Consider the case of Jaycee Buzzanca. After John and Luanne Buzzanca had tried for years to have a child, an embryo was created for them, using sperm and an egg from anonymous donors, and implanted in a surrogate mother. In March 1995, one month before the baby was born, John filed for divorce. Luanne wanted child support from John, but he refused—after all, he's not the father. Luanne argued that John is Jaycee's father legally. At this point the surrogate mother, who had agreed to carry a baby for a stable two-parent household, decided to sue for custody.

15   Jaycee was dubbed "Nobody's Child" by the media when a California judge ruled that John was not the legal father nor Luanne the legal mother (neither one was genetically related to Jaycee, and Luanne had not even borne her). Enter Erin Davidson, the egg donor, who claims the egg was used without her permission. Not to be left out, the sperm donor jumped into the ring, saying that his sperm was used without his permission, a claim he later dropped. In March of this year, an appeals

court gave Luanne custody and decided that John is the legal father, making him responsible for child support. By contracting for a medical procedure resulting in the birth of a child, the court ruled, a couple incurs "the legal status of parenthood." (John lost an appeal in May.) For Jaycee's first three years on earth, these people have been wrangling over who her parents are.

In another case, William Kane left his girl-friend, Deborah Hect, 15 vials of sperm before he killed himself in a Las Vegas hotel in 1991. His two adult children (represented by their mother, his ex-wife) contested Miss Hect's claim of owner-ship. A settlement agreement on Kane's will was eventually reached, giving his children 80 percent of his estate and Miss Hect 20 percent. Hence she was allowed three vials of his sperm. When she did not succeed in conceiving on the first two tries, she filed a petition for the other 12 vials. She won, and the judge who ruled in her favor wrote, "Neither this court nor the decedent's adult children possess reason or right to prevent Hect from implement-ing decedent's pre-eminent interest in realizing his 'fundamental right' to procreate with the woman of his choice." One day, donors may not even have to have lived. Researchers are experimenting with us-ing aborted female fetuses as a source of donor eggs.

And the market continues to zip along. For over-seas couples looking for donor eggs, Bill Handel has the scenario worked out. The couple would mail him frozen sperm of their choice (presumably from the recipient husband); his clinic would use it to fertilize donor eggs, chosen from its catalogue of offerings, and reply back within a month with a fro-zen embryo ready for implantation. (Although the sperm does not yet arrive by mail, Handel has sent out embryos to at least one hundred international customers.) As for the young women at the New Jersey clinic, they are visibly upset by one aspect of the egg-donation process: they can't have sexual intercourse for several weeks after the retrieval. For making babies, of course, it's already obsolete.

■ ■ ■   **FOR CLASS DISCUSSION** Identifying Rhetorical Features

Working in groups or as a whole class, develop responses to the following questions:

1. How does Lopez appeal to *logos*? What is her main claim and what are her reasons?
2. What does she use for evidence? What ideas would you have to include in a short summary?
3. What appeals to *pathos* does Lopez make in this argument? How well are these suited to the conservative readers of the *National Review*?
4. How would you characterize Lopez's *ethos*? Does she seem knowledgeable and credible? Does she seem fair to stakeholders in this controversy?
5. Choose an additional focus from the "Questions for Rhetorical Analysis" on pages 155–157 to apply to "Egg Heads." How does this question expand your understand-ing of Lopez's argument?
6. What strikes you as problematic, memorable, or disturbing in this argument?   ■ ■ ■

Our Own Rhetorical Analysis of "Egg Heads"

Now that you have identified some of the rhetorical features of "Egg Heads," we offer our own notes for a rhetorical analysis of this argument.

Rhetorical Context   As we began our analysis, we reconstructed the rhetorical context in which "Egg Heads" was published. In the late 1990s, a furious debate about egg donation rippled through college and public newspapers, popular journalism, Web sites, and scholarly commentary. This debate had been kicked off by several couples placing ads in the newspapers of the country's most prestigious colleges, offering up to $50,000 for the eggs of brilliant, attractive, athletic college women. Coinciding with these consumer demands, advances in reproductive technology provided an increasing number of complex techniques to surmount the problem of infertility, including fertilizing eggs in petri dishes and implanting them into women through surgical procedures. These procedures could use either a couple's own eggs and sperm or donated eggs and sperm. All these social and medical factors created the *kairotic* moment for Lopez's article and motivated her to protest the increasing use of these procedures. (Egg donation, surrogate motherhood, and the potential dehumanizing of commercial reproduction continue to be troubling and unresolved controversies across many genres, as you will see when you read Ellen Goodman's op-ed piece at the end of this chapter and student Zachary Stumps's rhetorical analysis of it.)

Genre and Writer   When we considered the genre and writer of this article and its site of publication, we noted that this article appeared in the *National Review*, which describes itself as "America's most widely read and influential magazine and Web site for Republican/conservative news, commentary, and opinion." It reaches "an affluent, educated, and highly responsive audience of corporate and government leaders, the financial elite, educators, journalists, community and association leaders, as well as engaged activists all across America" (http://www.nationalreview.com). According to our Internet search, Kathryn Jean Lopez is known nationally for her conservative journalistic writing on social and political issues. Currently the editor-at-large of *National Review Online*, she has also published in the *Wall Street Journal,* the *New York Post*, and the *Washington Times.* This information told us that in her article "Egg Heads," Lopez is definitely on home territory, aiming her article at a conservative audience.

Logos   Turning to the *logos* of Lopez's argument, we decided that the logical structure of Lopez's argument is clear throughout the article. Her claim is that egg donation and its associated reproductive advances have harmful, long-reaching consequences for society. Basically, she argues that egg donation and reproductive technology represent bad scientific developments for society because they are potentially harmful to the long-range health of egg donors and because they lead to an unnatural dehumanizing of human sexuality. She states a version of this last point at the end of the second paragraph: "Egg donation is a quietly expanding industry, changing the way we look at the family, young women's bodies, and human life itself" (page 160).

   The body of her article elaborates on each of these reasons. In developing her reason that egg donation endangers egg donors, Lopez lists the risks but doesn't supply supporting evidence about the frequency of these problems: damage to the ovaries, persistent pain, early menopause, possible ovarian cancer, and even death. She supports her claim about "the expanding industry" by showing how the procedures have become commercialized. To show the popularity of these procedures as well as their commercial value, she quotes a variety of experts such as directors of in vitro clinics, fertility centers, bioethicists, and the American Society for Reproductive Medicine. She also cleverly bolsters her own case by showing that even liberal cultural critics agree with her views about the big ethical questions raised by the reproductive-technology business. In addition to quoting experts, Lopez has sprinkled impressive numbers and vivid examples throughout the body of her argument that give her argument momentum as it progresses from the potential harm to young egg donors to a number of case studies that depict increasingly disturbing ethical problems.

Pathos   Much of the impact of this argument, we noted, comes from Lopez's appeals to *pathos*. By describing in detail the waiting rooms for egg donors at fertility clinics, Lopez relies heavily on pathetic appeals to move her audience to see the physical and social dangers of egg donation. She conveys the growing commercialism of reproductive technology by giving readers an inside look at the egg-donation process as these young college women embark on the multistep process of donating their eggs. These young women, she suggests in her title "Egg Heads," are largely unaware of the potential physical dangers to themselves and of the ethical implications and consequences of their acts. She asserts that they are driven largely by the desire for money. Lopez also appeals to *pathos* in her choice of emotionally loaded and often cynical language, which creates an angle of vision opposing reproductive technology: "turning procreation into manufacturing"; "reproductive prostitution"; "the intrusion of children in their lives"; "motherhood…reduced to a good leisure-time activity"; "aborted female fetuses as a source of donor eggs"; and intercourse as an "obsolete" way to make babies (pages 160–162).

Audience   Despite Lopez's success at spotlighting serious medical and ethical questions, her lack of attention to alternative views and the alarmism of her language caused us to wonder: Who might find this argument persuasive and who would challenge it? What is noticeably missing from her argument—and apparently from her worldview—is the perspective of infertile couples hoping for a baby. Pursuing our question, we decided that a provocative feature of this argument—one worthy of deeper analysis—is the disparity between how well this argument is suited to its target audience and yet how unpersuasive it is for readers who do not share the assumptions, values, and beliefs of this primary audience.

To Lopez's credit, she has attuned her reasons to the values and concerns of her conservative readers of the *National Review*, who believe in traditional families, gender differences, and gender roles. Opposed to feminism as they understand it, this audience sanctions careers for women only if women put their families first. Lopez's choice of evidence and her orchestration of it are intended to play to her audience's fears that science has uncontrollably fallen into the hands of those who have little regard for the sanctity of the family or traditional motherhood. For example, in playing strongly to the values of her conservative readers, Lopez belabors the physical, social, and ethical dangers of egg donation, mentioning worst-case scenarios; however, these appeals to *pathos* will most likely strike other readers who do some investigating into reproductive technology as overblown. She emphasizes the commercialism of the process as her argument moves from college girls as egg donors to a number of sensationalist case studies that depict intensifying ethical ambiguity. In other words, both the *logos* and the *pathos* of her argument skillfully focus on details that tap her target audience's values and beliefs and feed that audience's fears and revulsion.

Use of Evidence   For a broader or skeptical audience, the alarmism of Lopez's appeals to *pathos,* her use of atypical evidence, and her distortion of the facts weaken the *logos* and *ethos* of her argument. First, Lopez's use of evidence fails to measure up to the STAR criteria (that evidence should be sufficient, typical, accurate, and relevant). She characterizes all egg donors as young women seeking money. But she provides little evidence that egg donors are only out to make a buck. She also paints these young women as shortsighted, uninformed, and foolish. Lopez weakens her *ethos* by not considering the young women who have researched the process and who may be motivated, at least in part, by compassion for couples who can't conceive on their own. Lopez also misrepresents the people who are using egg donation, placing them all into two groups: (1) wealthy couples eugenically seeking designer babies with preordered special traits and (2) feminist career women. She directs much of her criticism toward this latter group: "The demand side of the market comes mostly from career-minded baby-boomers, the frontierswomen of feminism, who thought they could 'have it all'" (page 161). However, readers who do a little research on their own, as we did, will learn that infertility affects one in seven couples; that it is often a male and a female problem, sometimes caused by an incompatibility between the husband's and the wife's reproductive material; and that most couples who take the big step of investing in these expensive efforts to have a baby have been trying to get pregnant for a number of years. Rather than being casual about having children, they are often deeply desirous of children and depressed about their inability to conceive. In addition, far from being the sure thing and quick fix that Lopez suggests, reproductive technology has a success rate of only 50 percent overall and involves a huge investment of time, money, and physical discomfort for women receiving donor eggs.

Another way that Lopez violates the STAR criteria is her choice of extreme cases. For readers outside her target audience, her argument appears riddled with straw man and slippery-slope fallacies. Her examples become more bizarre as her tone becomes more hysterical. Here are some specific instances of extreme, atypical cases:

- her focus on career women casually and selfishly using the service of young egg donors
- the notorious case of Jaycee Buzzanca, dubbed "Nobody's Child" because her adoptive parents who commissioned her creation divorced before she was born
- the legal contest between a dead man's teen girlfriend and his ex-wife and adult children over his vials of sperm
- the idea of taking eggs from aborted female fetuses

By keeping invisible the vast majority of ordinary couples who go to fertility clinics out of last-hope desperation, Lopez uses extreme cases to create a "brave new world" intended to evoke a vehement rejection of these reproductive advances. These skeptical readers would offer the alternative view of the sad, ordinary couples of all ages sitting week after week in fertility clinics, hoping to conceive a child through the "miracle" of these reproductive advances and grateful to the young women who have contributed their eggs.

Concluding Points   In short, we concluded that Lopez's angle of vision, although effectively in sync with her conservative readers of the *National Review,* exaggerates and distorts her case against these reproductive advances. Lopez's traditional values and slanting of the evidence undermine her *ethos,* limit the value of this argument for a wider audience, and compel that audience to seek out alternative sources for a more complete view of egg donation.

Conclusion

To analyze a text rhetorically means to determine how it works: what effect it has on readers and how it achieves or fails to achieve its persuasiveness. Assignments involving rhetorical analysis are present in courses across the curriculum, and analyzing texts rhetorically is a major step in constructing your own arguments. In this chapter, we showed you how to apply your understanding of argument concepts, such as the influence of genre and appeals to *logos, ethos,* and *pathos,* to the examination of the strength of verbal texts. We conclude with a student's rhetorical analysis written for the assignment in this chapter.

WRITING ASSIGNMENT   **A Rhetorical Analysis**   MyWritingLab™

Write a thesis-driven rhetorical analysis essay in which you examine the rhetorical effectiveness of an argument specified by your instructor. Unless otherwise stated, direct your analysis to an audience of your classmates. In your introduction, establish the argumentative conversation to which this argument is contributing. Briefly summarize the argument and present your thesis highlighting two or more rhetorical features of the argument that you find central to the effectiveness or ineffectiveness of this argument. To develop and support your own points, you will need to include textual evidence in the form of examples or short quotations from the argument. Use attributive tags to distinguish your ideas from those of the writer of the argument. Use MLA documentation to cite points and quotations in your essay and in a Works Cited list at the end. Use your rhetorical analysis to share your interpretation of this argument's important features with your audience. Zachary Stumps's analysis of Ellen Goodman's "Womb for Rent" on pages 171–174 is an example of this assignment.

Generating Ideas for Your Rhetorical Analysis

To develop ideas for your essay, you might follow these steps:

Step	How to Do It
Familiarize yourself with the article you are analyzing.	Read your article several times. Divide it into sections to understand its structure.
Place the article in its rhetorical context.	Follow the strategies in Chapter 2 and use the "Questions for Rhetorical Analysis" on pages 155–157.
Summarize the article.	Follow the steps in Chapter 2 on pages 34–36. You may want to produce a longer summary of 150–200 words as well as a short, one-sentence summary.
Reread the article, identifying "hot spots."	Note hot spots in the article—points that impress you, disturb you, confuse you, or puzzle you.
Use the "Questions for Rhetorical Analysis" on pages 157–159.	Choose several of these questions and freewrite responses to them.
From your notes and freewriting, identify the focus for your analysis.	Choose several features of the article that you find particularly important and that you want to discuss in depth in your essay. Identify points that will bring something new to your readers and that will help them see this article with new understanding. You may want to list your ideas and then look for ways to group them together around main points.
Write a thesis statement for your essay.	Articulate your important points in one or two sentences, setting up these points clearly for your audience.

In finding a meaningful focus for your rhetorical analysis essay, you will need to create a focusing thesis statement that avoids wishy-washy formulas such as, "This argument has some strengths and some weaknesses." To avoid a vapid thesis statement, focus on the complexity of the argument, the writer's strategies for persuading the target audience, and the features that might impede its persuasiveness for skeptics. These thesis statements articulate how their writers see the inner workings of these arguments as well as the arguments' contributions to their public conversations.

Lopez's angle of vision, although effectively in sync with her conservative readers of the *National Review*, exaggerates and distorts her case against these reproductive advances, weakening her *ethos* and the value of her argument for a wider audience. [This is the thesis we would use if we were writing a stand-alone essay on Lopez.]

In his *New Yorker* article "The Pay Is Too Damn Low," Surowiecki adopts an angle of vision empathic to low-wage workers rather than owners; by linking an increase in minimum wage with other liberal causes such as universal health care, investment in infrastructure, and establishing European-style safety nets, Surowiecki appeals to his liberal audience but may alienate the business community by under-representing economic arguments opposing the minimum wage.

To make your rhetorical analysis of your article persuasive, you will need to develop each of the points stated or implied in your thesis statement using textual evidence, including short quotations. Your essay should show how you have listened carefully to the argument you are analyzing, summarized it fairly, and probed it deeply.

Organizing Your Rhetorical Analysis

The organization plan below provides a possible structure for your rhetorical analysis. ■

Organization Plan for a Rhetorical Analysis of an Argument

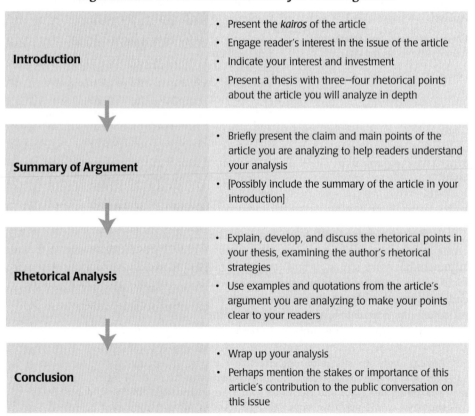

Introduction	• Present the *kairos* of the article • Engage reader's interest in the issue of the article • Indicate your interest and investment • Present a thesis with three–four rhetorical points about the article you will analyze in depth
Summary of Argument	• Briefly present the claim and main points of the article you are analyzing to help readers understand your analysis • [Possibly include the summary of the article in your introduction]
Rhetorical Analysis	• Explain, develop, and discuss the rhetorical points in your thesis, examining the author's rhetorical strategies • Use examples and quotations from the article's argument you are analyzing to make your points clear to your readers
Conclusion	• Wrap up your analysis • Perhaps mention the stakes or importance of this article's contribution to the public conversation on this issue

READINGS

Our first reading is by Pulitzer Prize–winning columnist, author, and speaker Ellen Goodman. This op-ed piece is analyzed rhetorically by student Zachary Stumps in our second reading.

Womb for Rent

ELLEN GOODMAN

By now we all have a story about a job outsourced beyond our reach in the global economy. My own favorite is about the California publisher who hired two reporters in India to cover the Pasadena city government. Really.

There are times as well when the offshoring of jobs takes on a quite literal meaning. When the labor we are talking about is, well, labor.

In the last few months we've had a full nursery of international stories about surrogate mothers. Hundreds of couples are crossing borders in search of lower-cost ways to fill the family business. In turn, there's a new coterie of international workers who are gestating for a living.

Many of the stories about the globalization of baby production begin in India, where the government seems to regard this

as, literally, a growth industry. In the little town of Anand, dubbed "The Cradle of the World," 45 women were recently on the books of a local clinic. For the production and delivery of a child, they will earn $5,000 to $7,000, a decade's worth of women's wages in rural India.

But even in America, some 5 women, including Army wives, are supplementing their income by contracting out their wombs. They have become surrogate mothers for wealthy couples from European countries that ban the practice.

This globalization of baby-making comes at the peculiar intersection of a high reproductive technology and a low-tech work force. The biotech business was created in the same petri dish as Baby Louise, the first IVF baby. But since then, we've seen

conception outsourced to egg donors and sperm donors. We've had motherhood divided into its parts from genetic mother to gestational mother to birth mother and now contract mother.

We've also seen the growth of an international economy. Frozen sperm is flown from one continent to another. And patients have become medical tourists, searching for cheaper health care whether it's a new hip in Thailand or an IVF treatment in South Africa that comes with a photo safari thrown in for the same price. Why not then rent a foreign womb?

I don't make light of infertility. The primal desire to have a child underlies this multinational Creation, Inc. On one side, couples who choose surrogacy want a baby with at least half their own genes. On the other side, surrogate mothers, who are rarely implanted with their own eggs, can believe that the child they bear and deliver is not really theirs.

As one woman put it, "We give them a baby and they give us much-needed money. It's good for them and for us." A surrogate in Anand used the money to buy a heart operation for her son. Another raised a dowry for her daughter. And before we talk about the "exploitation" of the pregnant woman, consider her alternative in Anand: a job crushing glass in a factory for $25 a month.

10   Nevertheless, there is—and there should be—something uncomfortable about a free market approach to baby-making. It's easier to accept surrogacy when it's a gift from one woman to another. But we rarely see a rich woman become a surrogate for a poor

family. Indeed, in Third World countries, some women sign these contracts with a fingerprint because they are illiterate.

For that matter, we have not yet had stories about the contract workers for whom pregnancy was a dangerous occupation, but we will. What obligation does a family that simply contracted for a child have to its birth mother? What control do—should— contractors have over their "employees'" lives while incubating "their" children? What will we tell the offspring of this international trade?

"National boundaries are coming down," says bioethicist Lori Andrews, "but we can't stop human emotions. We are expanding families and don't even have terms to deal with it."

It's the commercialism that is troubling. Some things we cannot sell no matter how good "the deal." We cannot, for example, sell ourselves into slavery. We cannot sell our children. But the surrogacy business comes perilously close to both of these deals. And international surrogacy tips the scales.

So, these borders we are crossing are not just geographic ones. They are ethical ones. Today the global economy sends everyone in search of the cheaper deal as if that were the single common good. But in the biological search, humanity is sacrificed to the economy and the person becomes the product. And, step by step, we come to a stunning place in our ancient creation story. It's called the marketplace.

Critiquing "Womb for Rent"   MyWritingLab™

1. What is Goodman's main claim and what are her reasons? In other words, what ideas would you have to include in a short summary?
2. What appeals to *pathos* does Goodman make in this argument? How do these appeals function in the argument?
3. Choose an additional focus from the "Questions for Rhetorical Analysis" to apply to "Womb for Rent" How does this question affect your perspective of Goodman's argument?
4. What strikes you as problematic, memorable, or disturbing in this argument?

Our second reading shows how student writer Zachary Stumps analyzed the Ellen Goodman article.

A Rhetorical Analysis of Ellen Goodman's "Womb for Rent"

ZACHARY STUMPS (STUDENT)

Introduction provides context and poses issue to be addressed.

With her op-ed piece "Womb for Rent," published in the *Seattle Times* (and earlier in the *Washington Post*), syndicated columnist Ellen Goodman enters the murky debate about reproductive technology gone global. Since Americans are outsourcing everything else, "Why not then rent a foreign womb?" she asks. Goodman, a Pulitzer Prize–winning columnist for the Washington Post Writers Group, is known for helping readers understand the "tumult of social change and its impact on families," and for shattering "the mold of men writing exclusively about politics" ("Ellen Goodman"). This op-ed piece continues her tradition of examining social change from the perspective of family issues.

Provides background on Goodman

Summarizes the op-ed piece

Goodman launches her short piece by asserting that one of the most recent and consequential "jobs" to be outsourced is having babies. She explains how the "globalization of baby production" is thriving because it brings together the reproductive desires of people in developed countries and the bodily resources of women in developing countries such as India. Briefly tracing how both reproductive technology and medical tourism have taken advantage of global possibilities, Goodman acknowledges that the thousands of dollars Indian women earn by carrying the babies of foreign couples represent a much larger income than these women could earn in any other available jobs.

After appearing to legitimize this global exchange, however, Goodman shifts to her ethical concerns by raising some moral questions that she says are not being addressed in this trade. She concludes with a full statement of her claim that this global surrogacy is encroaching on human respect and dignity, exploiting business-based science, and turning babies into products.

Thesis paragraph

In this piece, Goodman's delay of her thesis has several rhetorical benefits: it gives Goodman space to present the perspective of poor women, enhanced by her appeals to *pathos,* and it invites readers to join her journey into the complex contexts of this issue; however, this strategy is also risky because it limits the development of her own argument.

Develops first point in thesis: use of *pathos* in exploring perspective of poor women

5   Instead of presenting her thesis up front, Goodman devotes much of the first part of her argument to looking at this issue from the perspective of foreign surrogate mothers. Using the strategies of *pathos*

to evoke sympathy for these women, she creates a compassionate and progressive-minded argument that highlights the benefits to foreign surrogate mothers. She cites factual evidence showing that the average job for a woman in Anand, India, yields a tiny "$25 a month" gotten through the hard work of "crushing glass in a factory," compared to the "$5,000 to $7,000" made carrying a baby to term. To carry a baby to term for a foreign couple represents "a decade's worth of women's wages in rural India." Deepening readers' understanding of these women, Goodman cites one woman who used her earnings to finance her son's heart operation and another who paid for her daughter's dowry. In her fair presentation of these women, Goodman both builds her own positive *ethos* and adds a dialogic dimension to her argument by helping readers walk in the shoes of otherwise impoverished surrogate mothers.

Develops second point in thesis: the complex contexts of this issue—outsourcing and medical tourism

The second rhetorical benefit of Goodman's delayed thesis is that she invites readers to explore this complex issue of global surrogacy with her before she declares her own view. To help readers understand and think through this issue, she relates it to two other familiar global topics: outsourcing and medical tourism. First, she introduces foreign surrogacy as one of the latest forms of outsourcing: "This globalization of baby-making comes at the peculiar intersection of a high reproductive technology and a low-tech work force." Presenting these women as workers, she explains that women in India are getting paid for "the production and delivery of a child" that is analogous to the production and delivery of sneakers or bicycle parts. Goodman also sets this phenomenon in the context of global medical tourism. If people can pursue lower-cost treatment for illnesses and health conditions in other countries, why shouldn't an infertile couple seeking to start a family not also have such access to these more affordable and newly available means? This reasoning provides a foundation for readers to begin understanding the many layers of the issue.

Shows how the delayed-thesis structure creates two perspectives in conflict

The result of Goodman's delayed-thesis strategy is that the first two-thirds of this piece seem to justify outsourcing surrogate motherhood. Only after reading the whole op-ed piece can readers see clearly that Goodman has been dropping hints about her view all along through her choice of words. Although she clearly sees how outsourcing surrogacy can help poor women economically, her use of market language such as "production," "delivery," and "labor" carry a double meaning. On first reading of this op-ed piece, readers don't know if Goodman's punning is meant to be catchy and entertaining or serves another purpose. This other purpose becomes clear in the last third of the article when Goodman forthrightly asserts her criticism of the commercialism of the global marketplace that promotes worldwide searching for a "cheaper deal": "humanity is sacrificed to the economy and the person becomes the product." This is a bold and big claim, but does the final third of her article support it?

In the final five paragraphs of this op-ed piece, Goodman begins to develop the rational basis of her argument; however, the brevity of the op-ed genre and her choice not to state her view openly initially have left Goodman with little space to develop her own claim. The result is that she presents some profound ideas very quickly. Some of the ethically complex ideas she introduces but doesn't explore much are these:

- The idea that there are ethical limits on what can be "sold."
- The idea that surrogate motherhood might be a "dangerous occupation."
- The idea that children born from this "international trade" may be confused about their identities.

Goodman simply has not left herself enough space to develop these issues and perhaps leaves readers with questions rather than with changed views. I am particularly struck by several questions. Why have European countries banned surrogacy in developing countries and why has the United States not banned this practice? Does Goodman intend to argue that the United States should follow Europe's lead? She could explore more how this business of finding illiterate women to bear children for the wealthy continues to exploit third-world citizens much as sex tourism exploits women in the very same countries. It seems to perpetuate a tendency for the developed world to regard developing countries as a poor place of lawlessness where practices outlawed in the rest of the world (e.g., child prostitution, slave-like working conditions) are somehow tolerable. Goodman could have developed her argument more to state explicitly that a woman who accepts payment for bearing a baby becomes an indentured servant to the family. Yet another way to think of this issue is to see that the old saying of "a bun in the oven" is more literal than metaphoric when a woman uses her womb as a factory to produce children, a body business not too dissimilar to the commercialism of prostitution. Goodman only teases readers by mentioning these complex problems without producing an argument.

10   Still, although Goodman does not expand her criticism of outsourced surrogate motherhood or explore the issues of human dignity and rights, this argument does introduce the debate on surrogacy in the global marketplace, raise awareness, and begin

to direct the conversation toward a productive end of seeking a responsible, healthy, and ethical future. Her op-ed piece lures readers into contemplating deep, perplexing ethical and economic problems and lays a foundation for readers to create an informed view of this issue.

Works Cited

Uses MLA format to list sources cited in the essay

"Ellen Goodman." *Washingtonpost.com,* www.washingtonpost.com/wp-srv/post/writersgroup/biogoodman.htm. Accessed 8 Apr. 2016.

Goodman, Ellen. "Womb for Rent." *The Washington Post,* 11 Apr. 2008, p. B6.

MyWritingLab™

Visit Ch. 8 Analyzing Arguments Rhetorically in *MyWritingLab* to complete the For Writing and Discussion, Critiquing, and Writing Assignments and to test your understanding of the chapter objectives.

Analyzing Visual Arguments

9

To see how images can make powerful arguments, consider the rhetorical persuasiveness of the "polar bear" marching in a small town parade (Figure 9.1). Sponsored by local environmentalists advocating action against climate change, the polar bear uses arguments from *logos* (drawing on audience knowledge

FIGURE 9.1 A visual argument about climate change

175

that climate change threatens polar bears), *pathos* (evoking the bears' vulnerability), and *ethos* (conveying the commitment of the citizens group). Delighting children and adults alike, the bear creates a memorable environmental argument.

When an image such as the parade photograph is joined with words, the resulting text is often called a "multimodal argument." The word *multimodal* combines the concept of "multi" (more than one) and "modality" (a channel, medium, or mode of communication). Multimodal arguments published on the Web might take the form of videos, podcasts, blogs, and advocacy Web pages with arguments blending texts and images, all of which make complex rhetorical appeals to viewers. In static print texts, the visual element of a multimodal text might be an image, drawing, or graph, but it might also include purposeful uses of fonts, type size, and document design. This chapter focuses on the visual component of such multimodal texts.

Understanding Design Elements in Visual Argument

9.1 To explain the elements of design in visual arguments

To understand how visual images can produce an argument, you need to understand the design elements that work together to create a visual text. In this section we'll explain and illustrate the four basic components of visual design: use of type, use of space and layout, use of color, and use of images and graphics.

Use of Type

Type is an important visual element of written arguments. Variations in type, such as size, boldface, italics, or all caps, can direct a reader's attention to an argument's structure and highlight main points. In arguments designed specifically for visual impact, such as posters or advocacy advertisements, type is often used in eye-catching and meaningful ways. In choosing type, you need to consider the typeface or font style, the size of the type, and formatting options. The main typefaces or fonts are classified as serif, sans serif, and specialty type. Serif type has little extensions on the letters. (This text is set in serif type.) Sans serif type lacks these extensions. Specialty type includes script fonts and special symbols. In addition to font style, type comes in different sizes. It is measured in points, with 1 point equal to $\frac{1}{72}$ of an inch. Most text-based arguments consisting mainly of body text are written in 10- to 12-point type, whereas more image-based arguments may use a mixture of type sizes that interacts with the images for persuasive effect. Type can also be formatted using bold, italics, underlining, or shading for emphasis. Table 9.1 shows examples of type styles, as well as their typical uses.

The following basic principles for choosing type for visual arguments can help you to achieve your overall goals of readability, visual appeal, and suitability.

Principles for Choosing Type for Visual Arguments

1. If you are creating a poster or advocacy advertisement, you will need to decide how much of your argument will be displayed in words and how much in images. For the text portions, choose *display type* (sans serif) or specialty fonts for titles, headings, and slogans, and *body* or *text type* (serif) for longer passages of text.

TABLE 9.1 Examples and Uses of Type Fonts

Font Style	Font Name	Example	Use
Serif fonts	Times New Roman Courier New Bookman Old Style	Use type wisely. Use type wisely. Use type wisely.	Easy to read; good for long documents, good for *body type*, or the main verbal parts of a document
Sans serif fonts	Arial Century Gothic	Use type wisely. Use type wisely.	Tiring to read for long stretches; good for *display type* such as headings, titles, and slogans
Specialty fonts	*Zapf Chancery* Onyx MT	*Use type wisely.* Use type wisely.	Difficult to read for long stretches; effective when used sparingly for playful or decorative effect

2. Make type functional and appealing by using only two or three font styles per document.
3. Use consistent patterns of type (similar type styles, sizes, and formats) to indicate relationships among similar items or different levels of importance.
4. Choose type to project a specific impression (a structured combination of serif and sans serif type to create a formal, serious, or businesslike impression; sans serif and specialty type to create a casual, informal, or playful impression, and so forth).

Besides these general principles, rhetorical considerations of genre and audience expectations should govern decisions about type. Text-based arguments in scholarly publications generally use plain, conservative fonts with little variation, whereas text-based arguments in popular magazines may use more variations in font style and size, especially in headings and opening leads. Visual arguments such as posters, fliers, and advocacy ads exploit the aesthetic potential of type.

Use of Space or Layout

A second component of visual design is layout, which is critical for creating the visual appeal of an argument and for conveying meaning. Even visual arguments that are mainly textual should use space very purposefully. By spacing and layout we mean all of the following points:

- Page size and type of paper
- Proportion of text to white space
- Proportion of text to image(s) and graphics
- Arrangement of text on page (space, margins, columns, size of paragraphs, spaces between paragraphs, justification of margins)

- Use of highlighting elements such as bulleted lists, tables, sidebars, and boxes
- Use of headings and other means of breaking text into visual elements

In arguments that don't use visuals directly, the writer's primary visual concern is document design, in which the writer tries to meet the conventions of a genre and the expectations of the intended audience. For example, Julee Christianson's researched argument on pages 266–271 is designed to meet the document conventions of the American Psychological Association (APA). Note the use of a plain, conventional typeface (for easy reading); double spacing and one-inch margins (to leave room for editorial marking and notations); and special title page, headers, and page number locations (to meet expectations of readers familiar with APA documents, which all look exactly the same).

But in moving from verbal-only arguments to visual arguments that use visual elements for direct persuasive effect—for example, posters, fliers, or advocacy ads—creative use of layout is vital. Here are some ideas to help you think about the layout of a visual argument.

Principles for Laying Out Parts of a Visual Text

1. Choose a layout that avoids clutter and confusion by limiting how much text and how many visual items you put on a page.
2. Focus on creating coherence and meaning with layout.
3. Develop an ordering or structuring principle that clarifies the relationships among the parts.
4. Use layout and spacing to indicate the importance of items and to emphasize key ideas. Because Western readers read from left to right and top to bottom, top and center are positions that readily draw readers' eyes.

An Analysis of a Visual Argument Using Type and Spatial Elements

To illustrate the persuasive power of type and layout, we ask you to consider Figure 9.2, which shows a public affairs ad sponsored by the Ad Council and an advocacy organization, StopBulllying.gov. This advocacy piece, which is part of an ongoing campaign to curtail bullying among young people, is aimed at parents, urging them to encourage their children to be active in opposing bullying.

This ad demonstrates how use of type can create powerful visual and verbal rhetorical effects to convey its argument. The ad's creators chose to use lettering—not an image—to illustrate bullying. The type style, presentation of the letters, and words themselves create a strange effect—simultaneously personal and impersonal—that draws viewers into the ad more than an image would. The type style and font make strong appeals to *pathos* through the blend of the shocking abusive language and disturbing lettering style. The words "dumb," "piece," and "trash" are all harshly derogatory. The direct address to the viewer in the word "you" conveys that bullying is an attack, sometimes verbal, and often physical. Note how the blurring of the message in the large bold type makes a visual statement about the act of bullying and about both perception and psychological damage. These large, heavy, blurred letters convey multiple messages.

FIGURE 9.2 Anti-bullying public affairs ad

Bullying can be crude and forceful, but it is often carried on covertly where authority figures cannot see or stop it. The lettering itself bullies the viewers while at the same time reinforcing the idea that not everyone is aware of bullying. The blurring of these letters also suggests that bullying harmfully washes out the personhood of victims. In addition, the ad makes it look as though these dark letters have smudged and stained the yellow background, suggesting that bullying harms the social environment.

The layout of this ad also contributes to the *logos* and *ethos* of the ad. The shock of reading the bold message propels readers to the black sidebar in the lower right side of the ad, where the message in smaller type interprets and explains the message of the blurred letters. The text speaks directly to parents' unawareness of the hostility of their kids' environment and makes an urgent appeal to parental responsibility. While the lettering and layout convey the causal reasons behind the need for action, the message in the smaller letters states the proposal claim: Instruct your kids how to be more than passive observers of bullying: "Teach your kids to be more than a bystander." In addition to delivering a strong message, this ad conveys a positive *ethos* by demonstrating knowledge of the problem and directing readers to authoritative sources of information that will help in engaging with this serious social issue.

Use of Color

A third important element of visual design is use of color, which can contribute significantly to the visual appeal of an argument and move readers emotionally and imaginatively. In considering color in visual arguments, writers are especially controlled by genre conventions. For example, academic arguments use color minimally, whereas popular magazines often use color lavishly. The appeal of colors to an audience and the associations that colors have for an audience are also important. For instance, the psychedelic colors of 1960s rock concert posters would probably not be effective in poster arguments directed toward conservative voters. Color choices in visual arguments often have crucial importance, including the choice of making an image black-and-white when color is possible. As you will see in our discussions of color throughout this chapter, makers of visual arguments need to decide whether color will be primarily decorative (using colors to create visual appeal), functional (for example, using colors to indicate relationships), realistic (using colors like a documentary photo), aesthetic (for example, using colors that are soothing, exciting, or disturbing), or some intentional combination of these.

Use of Images and Graphics

The fourth design element includes images and graphics, which can powerfully condense information into striking and memorable visuals; clarify ideas; and add depth, liveliness, and emotion to your arguments. A major point to keep in mind when using images is that a few simple images may be more powerful than complicated and numerous images. Other key considerations are (1) how you intend an image to work in your argument (for example, to convey an idea, illustrate a point, or evoke an emotional response) and (2) how you will establish the relationship between the image or graphic and the verbal text. Because using images and graphics effectively is especially challenging, we devote the rest of this chapter to explaining how images and graphics can be incorporated into visual arguments. We treat the use of photographs and drawings in the next main section and the use of quantitative graphics in the final section.

An Analysis of a Visual Argument Using All the Design Components

Before we discuss the use of images and graphics in detail, we would like to illustrate how all four of the design components—use of type, layout, color, and images— can reinforce and support each other to achieve a rhetorical effect. Consider the

To show you all of the seriously ill children that local health worker Khalada Yesmin helped save this year, we'd need 122 more pages.

HELP ONE. **SAVE MANY.**
See where the good goes at **GoodGoes.org**

Save the Children.

FIGURE 9.3 Save the Children advocacy ad

"Save the Children" advocacy ad from an April 2011 edition of *Newsweek* (Figure 9.3). This advocacy ad highlights the design features of image, color, and layout, with type used to interpret and reinforce the message delivered by the other features. The layout of the page highlights the connection between the adorable baby on the left side of the page and the female health care worker on the right. The "story" of the ad is told in unobtrusive text (in small white font), which leads the readers' eyes from the baby's face to the heart of the health worker. Interestingly from a design perspective, a third figure, probably the baby's mother, is just partly visible in the form of hands holding the baby. The text itself celebrates the effectiveness of this local health healer, identified by name: "To show you all of the seriously ill children that local health worker Khalada Yesmin helped save this year, we'd need 122 more pages." At the bottom of the page, text conveys the call to action in the form of memorable tag lines "HELP ONE. SAVE MANY"; and "See where the good goes at GoodGoes.org."

This advocacy ad works on readers by blending three themes—the universal appeal of babies; the beneficial effects of educating local workers, particularly women; and the symbolic meaning of helping/healing hands—to convey how those of us in the developed world can provide aid that empowers people in developing countries to help themselves. These themes are portrayed through various visual strategies. In this ad, a baby, the health worker, and a third figure outside the frame of the photo (probably the baby's mother) sit on a woven mat, inside a structure. (Information on the Web site for "Save the Children" and the clothing of the people suggest that this scene takes place in Bangladesh.) The use of bright colors, creating a feeling of warmth and love, the arrangement of the figures, and the close-up shots of the baby and health worker draw viewers into the scene. The close-up, slightly low-angle shot accentuates faces, hands, feet, and traditional clothing. The blurred background suggests palm trees and the doorway to a house. The building is, most likely, the home of the mother and baby, which the health worker is visiting on her rounds. The baby, wearing an orange-beaded blouse or smock, pink shorts or skirt, and a necklace of purple beads, sits and smiles alertly at the health worker, in dark clothing and a red headscarf, who is engrossed in taking the baby's temperature. She seems to be holding the thermometer under the baby's arm with one hand and holding a watch with the other. Her focus on her task conveys her expertise; she knows what she is doing, an idea reinforced by the caption, which tells us that this health worker, Khalada Yesmin, "has helped 122 sick children this year." This caption and the prominence of hands in this photo—Khalada Yesmin's hands, the baby's hand, and the mother's hands supporting the baby—accentuate the idea of direct, grassroots aid that is improving the lives of mothers and children in a community through compassion and knowledge. The slogans at the bottom of the ad "Help one. Save many" and "See where the good goes" extend this network of help to viewers of the ad. If we contribute money to the training and medical supplies of health workers like Khalada Yesmin, we will help expand the web of aid.

In choosing to make this ad portray a positive, upbeat scene of medical success, instead of portraying scenes of pneumonia, malaria, malnutrition, or other diseases that the "seriously ill" children mentioned suffer from, the designers of this ad gave a memorable embodiment to the ideas in the words "help," "save," and "good." Perhaps most importantly, unlike some global ads, this one empowers people in the developing world. Rather than depict them as victims or helpless people in backward countries, this ad shows them—through the image of Khalada Yesmin and the eagerness of the people she is helping—as primary agents in the improvements in their lives. Rather than take control and rush in to solve problems, viewers in developed countries are invited to contribute to this success, figuratively lending a hand through financial support.

■ ■ ■ **FOR WRITING AND DISCUSSION Analyzing an Advocacy Ad**   MyWritingLab™

Individual Task: Using your knowledge of type, layout, color, and image, write a paragraph that analyzes the Buzzed Driving ad sponsored by the Ad Council and the National Highway and Traffic Safety Administration (Figure 9.4). The following questions can guide your response:

1. What story does this ad tell? What is the core argument of this ad?
2. How does this ad use type, layout, image, and color for persuasive effect?
   - Layout and Image: Does the image convey an idea, illustrate a point, or evoke an emotional response? Why do you think the ad makers chose to give spatial preference to the image?

FIGURE 9.4 Advocacy ad against drunk driving

- Color: Is the use of color in this ad decorative, realistic, aesthetic, or some combination of these? How does the use of color contribute to the message of the ad?
  - Type: What is the relationship between the image and the type? Look at the words and ideas in each line of type. What is the effect of using different font sizes?
  3. How does this ad appeal to *logos, ethos,* and *pathos*?

Group Task: Working in pairs or as a whole class, share your analysis of this advocacy ad. Consider alternative designs for ads warning against driving under the influence of alcohol. What other images, layouts, use of type, and color might be effective in conveying the same message as this ad?

The Compositional Features of Photographs and Drawings

9.2 To analyze the compositional features of photographs and drawings rhetorically

Now that we have introduced you to the four major elements of visual design—type, layout, color, and images—we turn to an in-depth discussion of photographic images and drawings. Used with great shrewdness in product advertisements, photos and drawings can be employed with equal shrewdness in posters, fliers, advocacy ads, and Web sites. When an image is created specifically for an argument, almost nothing is left to chance. Although such images are often made to seem spontaneous and "natural," they are almost always composed; designers consciously select the details of staging and composition as well as manipulate camera techniques (filters, camera angle, lighting) and digital or chemical development techniques (airbrushing, merging of images). Even news photography can have a composed feel. For example, public officials often try to control the effect of photographs by creating "photo ops" (photographing opportunities), wherein reporters are allowed to photograph an event only during certain times and from certain angles. Political photographs appearing in newspapers are often press releases officially approved by the politician's staff. To analyze a photograph or drawing, or to create visual images for your own arguments, you need to think both about the composition of the image and about the camera's relationship to the subject. Because drawings produce a perspective on a scene analogous to that of a camera, design considerations for photographs can be applied to drawings as well. The following list of questions can guide your analysis of any persuasive image.

- **Type of photograph or drawing**: Is the image documentary-like (representing a real event), fiction-like (intending to tell a story or dramatize a scene), or conceptual (illustrating or symbolizing an idea or theme)? The photos of the protest for higher wages for fast-food workers on page 1 and of the anti-fracking march on page 153 are documentary photos capturing real events in action. In contrast, the cartoonish drawing of the fly in the health poster in

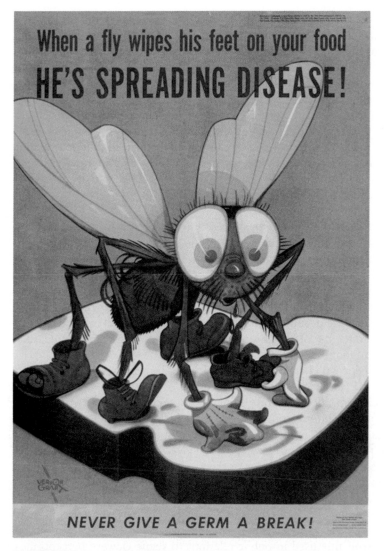

FIGURE 9.5 Health poster from the War Department in World War II

Figure 9.5 is both a fictional narrative telling a story and a conceptual drawing illustrating a concept.

■ **Distance from the subject**: Is the image a close-up, medium shot, or long shot? Close-ups tend to increase the intensity of the image and suggest the importance of the subject; long shots tend to blend the subject into the background. In the baby photograph opposing phthalates in children's toys (Chapter 1, page 4), the effect of the baby wearing a "poison" bib is intensified by the close-up shot without background. In contrast, the medium shot of the boy holding the toy he has found in the wreckage caused by Typhoon Haiyan (Chapter 6, page 114) focuses on both the boy and his surroundings. While the photo captures the magnitude of the disaster, it also shows the child's interests and his attempt to recover some of his past life.

- **Orientation of the image and camera angle**: Is the camera (or artist) positioned in front of or behind the subject? Is it positioned below the subject, looking up (a low-angle shot)? Or is it above the subject, looking down (a high-angle shot)? Front-view shots, for example, the photo of the fracking protestor (page 153), tend to emphasize the persons being photographed. In contrast, rear-view shots often emphasize the scene or setting. A low-angle perspective tends to make the subject look superior and powerful, whereas a high-angle perspective can reduce the size—and by implication, the importance—of the subject. A level angle tends to imply equality. The low-angle perspective of Katniss Everdeen, the main character of *The Hunger Games,* (page 193) accentuates her heroic stature.

- **Point of view:** Does the camera or artist stand outside the scene and create an objective effect? Or is the camera or artist inside the scene as if the photographer or artist is an actor in the scene, creating a subjective effect?

- **Use of color:** Is the image in color or in black and white? Is this choice determined by the restrictions of the medium, (such as images designed to run in black and white in newspapers) or is it the conscious choice of the photographer or artist? Are the colors realistic or muted? Have special filters been used (a photo made to look old through the use of brown tints)? Are bright colors intended to be catchy and attractive or dominant or disturbing?

- **Compositional special effects:** Is the entire image clear and realistic? Is any portion of it blurred? Is it blended with other realistic or nonrealistic images (a car ad that blends a city and a desert; a body lotion ad that merges a woman and a cactus)? Is the image an imitation of some other famous image such as a classic painting (as in parodies)? The story of the polar bear in the Nissan Leaf ad in Figures 9.6–9.11 and the photo of the young girls trying out the Nerf Rebelle bows in Figure 9.17 make visual associations with popular stories.

- **Juxtaposition of images:** Are several different images juxtaposed, suggesting relationships between them? Juxtaposition can suggest sequential or causal relationships or can metaphorically transfer the identity of a nearby image or background to the subject (as when a bath soap is associated with a meadow). This technique is frequently used in public relations to shape viewers' perceptions of political figures, as when political figures are photographed with American flags or patriotic monuments.

- **Manipulation of images:** Are staged images made to appear real, natural, or documentary-like? Are images altered with airbrushing? Are images actually composites of a number of images (for instance, using images of different women's bodies to create one perfect model in an ad or film)? Are images cropped for emphasis? What is left out? Are images downsized or enlarged?

- **Settings, furnishings, props:** Is the photo or drawing an outdoor or indoor scene? What is in the background and foreground? What furnishings and props, such as furniture, objects in a room, pets, and landscape features, help create the scene? What social associations of class, race, and gender are attached to these settings and props?

FIGURE 9.6 Nissan Leaf ad: Glacier melting and calving ice bergs

FIGURE 9.7 Nissan Leaf ad: Polar bear floating on shrinking sea ice

FIGURE 9.8 Nissan Leaf ad: Polar bear walking on railroad tracks

FIGURE 9.9 Nissan Leaf ad: Polar bear walking along a highway

FIGURE 9.10 Nissan Leaf ad: Polar bear walking through a suburb

FIGURE 9.11 Nissan Leaf ad: Polar bear hugging car owner

▪ **Characters, roles, actions:** Does the photo or drawing tell a story? Are the people in the scene models? Are the models instrumental (acting out real-life roles) or are they decorative (extra and included for visual or sex appeal)? What are the facial expressions, gestures, and poses of the people? What are the spatial relationships of the figures? (Who is in the foreground, center, and background? Who is large and prominent?) What social relationships are implied by these poses and positions? In the "Save the Children" advocacy ad shown in Figure 9.3, the pose of the health worker and the baby—the health worker intently treating the baby and the baby happily trusting the health worker—tells the story of successful health care.

▪ **Presentation of images:** Are images separated from each other in a larger composition or connected to each other? Are the images large in proportion to verbal text? How are images labeled? How does the text relate to the image(s)? Does the image illustrate the text? Does the text explain or comment on the image?

An Analysis of a Visual Argument Using Images

To show you how images can be analyzed, let's examine the advertisement for Nissan's new electric car, the Nissan Leaf. Stills for this television ad are shown in Figures 9.6–9.11. You can see the whole one-minute ad on YouTube, where the fluid sequence of frames gives the full effect. With this ad's debut during a National Football League broadcast in fall 2010, Nissan boldly entered the global controversy over global warming and climate change, casting the iconic polar bear and the Nissan Leaf owner as heroes in a dramatic narrative intended to portray environmental consciousness and responsible consumerism.

This ad links a series of images in a suspenseful story of a long journey culminating in a dramatic encounter. The ad begins with frames of dripping ice melt and a crumbling glacier crashing into the ocean. The next frame shows a polar bear lying on a small floating island of ice, succeeded by a long view of calved icebergs, fragments of the glacier. The camera follows the polar bear swimming, with views of its powerful body above and below the water, until it arrives on land. From there, the polar bear takes a long journey: walking through northern forests; sheltering in a concrete culvert under a train trestle; walking along a train track; padding along a country highway, where it growls at a passing diesel truck; sitting and observing the brilliant lights of a big city at night; traveling across a massive suspension bridge into the city; walking through the city; and finally, walking down a suburban street. In the final frames, a bright blue Nissan Leaf sits in the wide driveway of a comfortable suburban home. Suddenly, the polar bear appears from behind the Nissan Leaf and surprises its owner, who has just come out of his house dressed in a sports coat and carrying a briefcase, presumably heading out for his commute to his white-collar job. As the bear rises on its hind legs, towering above the man, the astonished owner is met not by an attack but by a bear hug: the bear's thank-you for the driver's act of environmental responsibility in buying this electric car. The final frame includes the only text of the ad, which invites viewers to check out the features of the Nissan Leaf on the Web site. A musical soundtrack accompanies the images, with the only other sounds the honk of the truck and the growl of the bear in response. Noticeably absent from this ad is any specific information about the car itself, such as its five-passenger carrying capacity, its zero emissions, and its hundred-mile distance per charge.

The ad uses visual narrative to convey both a causal and an ethical argument. Through vivid, memorable scenes—the glacier calving, the bear afloat, the bear swimming—the ad taps viewers' knowledge of recent scientific accounts of the increased rate of glacial melting and the vanishing sea ice. The ad argues that these events are real, immediate, and threatening. By implication, it argues that the high volume of carbon dioxide emissions from gasoline-powered vehicles—in other words, human actions—has caused this increased rate of melting and destruction of polar bears' habitat. It asks viewers to fill in the links in the causal chain: large amounts of carbon dioxide emissions from internal combustion engines in cars and trucks have contributed to an increase in temperatures, which has sped up the rate at which glaciers and sea ice are melting. This increased rate of melting has in turn decreased the number of seals who usually live on the sea ice and thus reduced the food supply of polar bears. The ad reminds viewers that polar bears are endangered and need human aid. The ad's ethical argument is that humans can help polar bears and the environment by buying electric Nissan Leafs.

The ad's effect is enhanced by its positive *ethos* and its powerful appeals to *pathos*. By making these causal links through bold images and a memorable story, Nissan has staked its claim as a leader in producing alternative-fuel vehicles. In our view, the ad makes brilliant use of visual images, drawing on the most famous environmental icons in the global warming debate: the melting glacier and the polar bear. (See the photograph of the parade polar bear at the beginning of this chapter on page 175.) While news reports of declining polar bear populations arouse concern in some people, numbers can be vague and abstract. Many more people will be stirred by the heroic character of the lone bear making a long journey. This visual narrative taps viewers' familiarity with other animal stories, often featured on Animal Planet and the Discovery Channel, that blend environmental education and entertainment. But the Nissan ad pushes further by creatively drawing on Disney-like, anthropomorphic movies in which a wild creature becomes a friend of humans. Any Inuit will testify that polar bears are intimidating and dangerous, but this ad constructs an environmental fantasy, eliciting viewers' compassion for the heroic bear. It creates a kind of inverted "call of the wild" narrative: Instead of a captured or domesticated animal finding its way back to its wilderness home, this wild creature, endowed with knowledge and filled with gratitude, courageously finds its way to civilization on a mission to thank the Nissan Leaf owner. The ad cultivates warm feelings toward the bear through juxtaposing its isolation against the background of our technologically transformed and urbanized environment—the diesel truck; the concrete culvert; the impressive bridge; the vast, illuminated city; the well-cultivated suburban neighborhood. The ad enhances the character of the bear by showing it take time to watch a delicately flitting butterfly and exchange a glance with a raccoon, a wild creature at home in the city. As viewers are engrossed with the travels of this bear, they wonder, "Where is it going? What will happen?" The genius of the ad is that it casts the bear as an ambassador of the threatened environment and makes viewers care about the bear.

It also converts the Nissan Leaf owner into an environmental hero. The implied ethical argument is that the right moral action is to drive a Nissan Leaf and thus save the environment. Viewers, identifying with the awestruck Nissan owner, will feel, "I want to be an environmental hero, too."

In this sense, the ad follows a problem-solution scenario. Nissan has skillfully enlisted the main symbols of global warming in the service of promoting its new electric car. It has, of course, greatly oversimplified an environmental problem and skirted major issues such as the problem of producing the electricity necessary to charge the Nissan Leaf, the environmental costs of producing the cars themselves, and the drop-in-the-bucket effect of replacing only a tiny portion of gasoline cars with electric vehicles. However, the ad works by suppressing these concerns and implying instead that the individual consumer can make a substantial difference in saving the environment.

■ ■ ■   **FOR CLASS DISCUSSION**   Analyzing Photos and Drawings Rhetorically

Working individually or in groups, imagine that you have been asked to compose a flier advertising a self-defense workshop for women on your university campus. This workshop will include some basic self-defense moves and some fundamentals of martial arts and blocking. Your task is to choose one of the four photos or images in Figures 9.12–9.15 for the poster. Your goal is to get students to notice your poster, appreciate what is at stake in the workshops, and become motivated to sign up. What image might best encourage women to attend? What image might encourage men to urge their female friends or girlfriends to attend?

1. Study the four photos in Figures 9.12 through 9.15, and then answer the following questions:
   a. What camera techniques and composition features do you see in each photo or image? Consider all the composition features described on pages 184–186 and 188 for each image.
   b. What do you think is the dominant impression of each photo? In other words, what is each photo's implicit argument?
2. Once you have analyzed the images, decide which is the most striking or memorable and try to reach consensus about your choice for a rhetorically effective poster.
3. Sometimes designers and ad creators choose cartoonish images to deliver their arguments. You might examine the Chipotle Scarecrow ad that aired during the 2014 Super Bowl (on YouTube), some other cartoon image in an ad, or the War Department's health poster in Figure 9.5 on page 185.
   a. What are the compositional features in this cartoon drawing or ad?
   b. How would you state the argument made by this image?
   c. How does the use of cartoon images affect the *logos*, *ethos*, and *pathos* of the argument?
   d. Why do you think cartoon images were chosen?

FIGURE 9.12 Photo of girl practicing boxing moves

FIGURE 9.13 Photo of a guy in a hoodie

FIGURE 9.14 Drawing of a girl booting a guy

FIGURE 9.15 Photo of woman executing a martial arts move

The Genres of Visual Argument

9.3 To explain the genres of visual argument

We have already mentioned that verbal arguments today are frequently accompanied by photographs or drawings that contribute to the text's persuasive appeal. For example, a verbal argument promoting U.N. action to help AIDS victims in Africa might be accompanied by a photograph of a dying mother and child. However, some genres of argument are dominated by visual elements. In these genres, the visual design carries most of the argumentative weight; verbal text is used primarily for labeling, for focusing the argument's claim, or for commenting on the images. In this section we describe specifically these highly visual genres of argument.

Posters and Fliers

To persuade audiences, an arguer might create a poster designed for placement on walls or kiosks or a flier to be passed out on street corners. Posters dramatically attract and direct viewers' attention toward a subject or issue. They often seek to rally supporters to a strong stance on an issue, and call people to action. For example, during World War II, posters asked Americans to invest in war bonds and urged women to join the workforce in order to free men for active combat. During the Vietnam War, famous posters used slogans such as "Make Love, Not War" or "Girls say yes to boys who say no" to increase national resistance to the war.

The hallmark of an effective poster is the way it focuses and encodes a complex meaning in a verbal-visual text, often with one or more striking images. These images are often symbolic—for example, using children to symbolize family and home, a soaring bird to symbolize freedom, or three firefighters raising the American flag over the World Trade Center rubble on September 11, 2001, to symbolize American heroism, patriotism, and resistance to terrorism. These symbols derive potency from the values they share with their target audience. Posters tend to use words sparingly, either as slogans or as short, memorable directives. This terse verbal text augments the message encoded in an eye-catching, dominant image.

As an example of a contemporary poster, consider the poster on page 193 urging people to see the second *Hunger Games* film, *Catching Fire*. This poster for this popular culture film shows actress Jennifer Lawrence as lead character Katniss Everdeen aiming her weapon of choice, her bow. She is framed by a large version of her mockingjay pin (a symbol from District 12, her home) and a ring of fire. Readers who know Susan Collins's dystopian novels and/or the films know that Katniss appeared in a costume with special-effect flames in the first film and that her defiant spirit sparks the rebellion against the Capital and its repressive government. The impact of the poster is intensified by the angry reds and dark colors and by the centrality and size of the image of Katniss (Jennifer Lawrence) that dominates the poster. The tagline at the top of the poster "Remember who the enemy is" intimates the plotline of the film and calls all potential rebels to be discerning and ready for courageous and risky acts of solidarity.

Fliers and brochures often use visual elements similar to those in posters. An image might be the top and center attraction of a flier or the main focus of the front cover of a brochure. However, unlike posters, fliers and brochures offer additional space for verbal arguments, which often present the writer's claim supported with bulleted lists of reasons. Sometimes pertinent data and statistics, along with testimony from supporters, are placed in boxes or sidebars.

FIGURE 9.16 Poster for *The Hunger Games: Catching Fire*

Public Affairs Advocacy Advertisements

Public affairs advocacy advertisements share with posters an emphasis on visual elements, but they are designed specifically for publication in newspapers and magazines or Web sites and, in their persuasive strategies, are directly analogous to product advertisements. Public affairs advocacy ads are usually sponsored by a corporation or an advocacy organization, often are part of a particular campaign with a theme, and have a more immediate and defined target audience than posters. Designed as condensed arguments aimed at influencing public opinion on civic issues, these ads are characterized by their brevity, audience-based appeals, and succinct, "sound bite" style. Often, in order to sketch out their claim and reasons clearly and concisely, they employ headings and subheadings, bulleted lists, different sizes and styles of type, and a clever, pleasing layout on the page. They usually have an attention-getting slogan or headline such as "MORE KIDS ARE GETTING BRAIN CANCER. WHY?" or "STOP THE TAX REVOLT JUGGERNAUT!" And they usually include a call to action, whether it be a donation, a letter of protest to legislators, or an invitation to join the advocacy group.

The balance between verbal and visual elements in an advocacy advertisement varies. Some advocacy ads are verbal only, with visual concerns focused on document design (for example, an "open letter" from the president of a corporation appearing as a full-page newspaper ad). Other advocacy ads are primarily visual, using images and other design elements with the same shrewdness as advertisements. We looked closely at advocacy ads in this chapter when we examined the StopBullying.gov ad (Figure 9.2) and the Save the Children ad (Figure 9.3). These use text and images in different ways to present their messages.

As another example of a public affairs advocacy ad, consider the ad in Chapter 14, page 305, that attempts to counter the influence of the pro-life movement's growing campaign against abortion. As you can see, this ad is dominated by one stark image: a question mark formed by the hook of a coat hanger. The shape of the hook draws the reader's eye to the concentrated type centered below it. The hook carries most of the weight of the argument. Simple, bold, and harsh, the image of the hanger, tapping readers' cultural knowledge, evokes the dangerous scenario of illegal abortions performed crudely by nonmedical people in the dark backstreets of cities. The ad wants viewers to think of the dangerous last resorts that desperate women would have to turn to if they could not obtain abortions legally. The hanger itself creates a visual pun: As a question mark, it conveys the ad's dilemma about what will happen if abortions are made illegal. As a coat hanger, it provides the ad's frightening answer to the printed question—desperate women will return to backstreet abortionists who use coat hangers as tools.

■ ■ ■   **FOR CLASS DISCUSSION** **Analyzing Posters Rhetorically**

Working individually or in groups, examine the images mentioned here to conduct a rhetorical analysis of them.

1. Some visual arguments gain influence and function by way of intertextuality. By this term, analysts mean the way that a viewer's reading of an image depends on familiarity with a network of "connected" images. Note the social influences

FIGURE 9.17 Photo of young girls with toy bows imitating Katniss Everdeen

and the layering of intertextuality in the photo in Figure 9.17 and the poster for *Catching Fire* on page 193. Readers, viewers, and critics have commented on the mythic qualities of heroine Katniss Everdeen, who as huntress, survivor, and rebel, resembles a Greek goddess, managing her hazardous world largely through her boldness, character, and physical prowess. The novels and films of Susan Collins's *The Hunger Games* have had far-ranging social effects, particularly on the behavior and interests of young girls. Examine the poster for *Catching Fire* on page 193 and the photo of young girls, trying out toymaker Hasbro's new Nerf Rebelle Heartbreaker Exclusive Golden Edge Bow in Figure 9.17. Compare the photo of the young girls with the poster for the film.

a. Analyze the ways that the young girls in the photo reflect the influence of Katniss Everdeen as a role model.

b. What vision of the feminine does the huntress image in the poster exemplify?

2. Examine the poster shown in Figure 9.18 on page 196 that shows a photo of an attractive girl behind the line "HEATHER'S LIFE ENDED TOO SOON." This poster, which appears on the TxtResponsibly.org Web site, reaches out to young drivers and their parents, using both images and text.

a. What visual features of this poster immediately attract your eyes? What principles for effective use of type, layout, color, and image does this ad exemplify?

b. What is the core argument of this ad?

c. Why did Heather's parents choose a large photo of her? How does that photo work with the other photo of a completely mangled car?

d. How does the frankness of the text and the size and use of color of the lettering combine to convey the message of the ad?

e. How would you design a poster warning against texting while driving? Consider questions about its use of type, layout, and image; about the core of its argument; and about its appeals to *ethos, pathos,* and *kairos.*

FIGURE 9.18 Poster argument warning against texting while driving

Cartoons

An especially charged kind of visual argument is the editorial or political cartoon and its extended forms, the comic strip and the graphic novel. Here we focus on political cartoons, which are often mini-narratives portraying an issue dramatically, compactly, and humorously, through images and a few well-chosen words that dramatize conflicts and problems. Using caricature, exaggeration, and distortion, a cartoonist distills an issue down to an image that boldly reveals the creator's perspective on the issue. The purpose of political cartoons is usually satire, or, as one famous cartoonist says, "afflicting the comfortable and comforting the afflicted."* Because they are so condensed and are often connected to current affairs, political cartoons are particularly dependent on the audience's background knowledge of cultural and political events. When political cartoons work well, through their perceptive combination of images and words, they flash a brilliant, clarifying light on a perspective or open a new lens on an issue, often giving readers a shock of insight.

As an illustration, note the cartoon by Milt Priggee in Figure 9.19, which was posted on the cartoon Web site index www.caglecartoons.com. The setting of the cartoon envisions a humorous blend of prehistoric and contemporary times. This cartoon responds to the recent scientific discussions of the creation and development

FIGURE 9.19 Tweeting and evolution cartoon

---

*"The Truth Told in Jest: Interview: Martin Rowson." *Morning Star*. Morning Star Online, 31 July 2007 Web. 6 June 2011.

of the universe and the aging of the Earth. (Note the mention of dark matter, which is a kind of energy-mass concept from physics and astronomy.) However, the main story of the cartoon connects the dinosaur characters with the behavior of people today who go about walking and tweeting, oblivious to anything around them, including dangerous environments. Thus, the cartoon links discussions of evolution to discussions of the contemporary obsession with cell phones and forms of social media.

■ ■ ■ **FOR CLASS DISCUSSION** Analyzing Cartoons

Cartoons can provide insight into how the public is lining up on issues. Choose a current issue such as health care reform, use of drones, dependence on foreign oil, income inequality, or identity theft. Then, using an online cartoon index such as Daryl Cagle's Professional Cartoonists Index (www.cagle.com) or a Web search of your own, find several cartoons that capture different perspectives on your issue.

1. What is the mini-narrative, the main claim, and the use of caricature, exaggeration, or distortion in each?
2. How is *kairos*, or timeliness, important to each cartoon?   ■ ■ ■

Web Pages

So far we have only hinted at the influence of the World Wide Web in accelerating the use of visual images in argument. Multimodal Web pages, with their hypertext design, exhibit the Web's complex mix of text and image, a mix that has changed the way many writers think of argument. The home page of an advocacy site, for example, often has many features of a poster argument, with hypertext links to galleries of images on the one hand and to verbal arguments on the other. These verbal arguments themselves often contain photographs, drawings, and graphics. The strategies discussed in this chapter for analyzing and interpreting visual texts also apply to Web pages.

Constructing Your Own Visual Argument

9.4 To construct your own visual argument

The most common visual arguments you are likely to create are posters, fliers, and public affairs advocacy ads. You may also decide that in longer verbal arguments, the use of visuals or graphics could clarify your points while adding visual variety to your paper. The following guidelines will help you apply your understanding of visual elements to the construction of your own visual arguments.

Guidelines for Creating Visual Arguments

1. **Genre:** Determine where this visual argument is going to appear (on a bulletin board, passed out as a flier, imagined as a one-page magazine or newspaper spread, or as a Web page).
2. **Audience-based appeals:** Determine who your target audience is.
   - What values and background knowledge of your issue can you assume that your audience has?
   - What specifically do you want your audience to think or do after reading your visual argument?
   - If you are promoting a specific course of action (sign a petition, send money, vote for or against a bill, attend a meeting), how can you make that request clear and direct?
3. **Core of your argument:** Determine what clear claim and reasons will form the core of your argument; decide whether this claim and these reasons will be explicitly stated or implicit in your visuals and slogans.
   - How much verbal text will you use?
   - If the core of your argument will be largely implicit, how can you still make it readily apparent and clear for your audience?
4. **Visual design:** What visual design and layout will grab your audience's attention and be persuasive?
   - How can font sizes and styles, layout, and color be used in this argument to create a strong impression?
   - What balance and harmony can you create between the visual and verbal elements of your argument? Will your verbal elements be a slogan, express the core of the argument, or summarize and comment on the image(s)?
5. **Use of images:** If your argument lends itself to images, what photo or drawing would support your claim or have emotional appeal? (If you want to use more than one image, be careful that you don't clutter your page and confuse your message. Simplicity and clarity are important.)
   - What image would be memorable and meaningful to your audience? Would a photo image or a drawing be more effective?
   - Will your image(s) be used to provide evidence for your claim or illustrate a main idea, evoke emotions, or enhance your credibility and authority?

■ ■ ■   **FOR CLASS DISCUSSION**   Developing Ideas for an Advocacy
                                    Ad or Poster Argument

This exercise asks you to do the thinking and planning for an advocacy ad or poster argument to be displayed on your college or university campus. Working individually, in small groups, or as a whole class, choose an issue that is controversial on your campus (or in your town or city), and follow the Guidelines for Creating Visual Arguments on page 199, above to envision the view you want to advocate on that issue. What might the core of your argument be? Who is your target audience? Are you representing a group, club, or other organization? What image(s) might be effective in attracting and moving this audience? Possible issues might be commuter parking; poor conditions in the computer lab; student reluctance to use the counseling center; problems with dorm life; financial aid programs, or intramural sports; ways to improve orientation programs for new students, work-study programs, or travel-abroad opportunities; or new initiatives such as study groups for the big lecture courses or new service-learning opportunities.

Using Information Graphics in Arguments

9.5 To use information graphics rhetorically in arguments

Besides images in the form of photographs and drawings, writers often use quantitative graphics to support arguments using numbers. In Chapter 5 we introduced you to the use of quantitative data in arguments. We discussed the persuasiveness of numbers and showed you ways to use them responsibly in your arguments. With the availability of spreadsheet and presentation programs, today's writers often create and import quantitative graphics into their documents. These visuals—such as tables, pie charts, and line or bar graphs—can have great rhetorical power by making numbers tell a story at a glance. In this section, we'll show you how quantitative graphics can make numbers speak. We'll also show you how to analyze graphics, incorporate them into your text, and reference them effectively.

How Tables Contain a Variety of Stories

Data used in arguments usually have their origins in raw numbers collected from surveys, questionnaires, observational studies, scientific experiments, and so forth. Through a series of calculations, the numbers are combined, sorted, and arranged in a meaningful fashion, often in detailed tables. Some of the tables published by the U.S. Census Bureau, for example, contain dozens of pages. The more dense the table, the more their use is restricted to statistical experts who pore over the data to analyze their meanings. More useful to the general public are midlevel tables contained on one or two pages that report data at a higher level of abstraction.

Consider, for example, Table 9.2, published by the U.S. Census Bureau and based on the 2010 census. This table shows the marital status of people age 15 and older, broken into gender and age groupings, in March 2010. It also provides comparative data on the "never married" percentage of the population in March 2010 and March 1970.

Take a few moments to peruse the table and be certain you know how to read it. You read tables in two directions: from top to bottom and from left to right. Always begin with the title, which tells you what the table contains and includes elements from both the vertical and the horizontal dimensions of the table. In this case the vertical dimension presents demographic categories for people "15 years old and over" for both sexes, for males, and for females. Each of these gender categories is subdivided into age categories. The horizontal dimension provides information about "marital status." Seven of the columns give total numbers (reported in thousands)

TABLE 9.2   Marital Status of People 15 Years and Over by Age and Sex: March 1970 and March 2010 (Numbers in thousands, except for percentages)

Characteristic	Total	Married spouse present	Married spouse absent	Separated	Divorced	Widowed	Never married	Percent never married	March 1970 percent never married
Both Sexes									
Total 15 years old and over	242,047	120,768	3,415	5,539	23,742	14,341	74,243	30.7	24.9
15 to 19 years old	21,079	178	109	151	60	22	20,559	97.5	93.9
20 to 24 years old	21,142	2,655	202	309	195	17	17,765	84.0	44.5
25 to 29 years old	21,445	7,793	406	594	766	60	11,826	55.1	14.7
30 to 34 years old	19,623	10,896	337	632	1,447	72	6,239	31.8	7.8
35 to 44 years old	40,435	25,729	733	1,331	4,697	345	7,599	18.8	5.9
45 to 54 years old	44,373	28,619	703	1,295	6,951	1,080	5,725	12.9	6.1
55 to 64 years old	35,381	23,621	463	763	5,750	1,923	2,861	8.1	7.2
65 years old and over	38,569	21,276	461	465	3,875	10,823	1,668	4.3	7.6
Males									
Total 15 years old and over	117,686	60,384	1,789	2,352	9,981	2,974	40,206	34.2	28.1
15 to 19 years old	10,713	61	55	62	30	8	10,498	98.0	97.4
20 to 24 years old	10,677	946	86	123	49	3	9,469	88.7	54.7
25 to 29 years old	10,926	3,343	220	224	318	21	6,800	62.2	19.1
30 to 34 years old	9,759	5,143	188	246	593	28	3,561	36.5	9.4
35 to 44 years old	20,066	12,614	392	578	1,998	81	4,402	21.9	6.7
45 to 54 years old	21,779	14,280	367	539	3,063	284	3,246	14.9	7.5
55 to 64 years old	16,980	11,958	244	343	2,465	424	1,545	9.1	7.8
65 years old and over	16,786	12,039	237	237	1,464	2,124	685	4.1	7.5
Females									
Total 15 years old and over	124,361	60,384	1,626	3,187	13,760	11,368	34,037	27.4	22.1
15 to 19 years old	10,365	118	55	90	30	13	10,061	97.1	90.3
20 to 24 years old	10,465	1,708	116	185	146	14	8,296	79.3	35.8
25 to 29 years old	10,519	4,451	186	370	448	39	5,026	47.8	10.5
30 to 34 years old	9,864	5,753	150	386	854	44	2,678	27.1	6.2
35 to 44 years old	20,369	13,115	341	753	2,698	264	3,198	15.7	5.2
45 to 54 years old	22,594	14,339	337	756	3,889	794	2,479	11.0	4.9
55 to 64 years old	18,401	11,663	220	420	3,284	1,499	1,315	7.1	6.8
65 years old and over	21,783	9,238	224	227	2,412	8,700	983	4.5	7.7

for March 2010. The eighth column gives the "percent never married" for March 2010, while the last column gives the "percent never married" for March 1970. To make sure you know how to read the table, pick a couple of rows at random and say to yourself what each number means. For example, the first row under "Both sexes" gives total figures for the entire population of the United States age 15 and older. In March 2010 there were 242,047,000 people age 15 and older (remember that the numbers are presented in thousands). Of these, 120,768,000 were married and living with their spouses. As you continue across the columns, you'll see that 3,415,000 people were married but not living with their spouses (a spouse may be stationed overseas or in prison; or a married couple may be maintaining a "commuter marriage" with separate households in different cities). Continuing across the columns, you'll see that 5,539,000 people were separated from their spouses, 23,742,000 were divorced, and 14,341,000 were widowed, and an additional 74,243,000 were never married. In the next-to-last column, the number of never-married people is converted to a percentage: 30.7 percent. Finally, the last column shows the percentage of never-married people in 1970: 24.9 percent. These last two columns show us that the number of unmarried people in the United States rose 5.8 percentage points since 1970.

Now that you know how to read the table, examine it carefully to see the kinds of stories it tells. What does the table show you, for example, about the percentage of married people age 25–29 in 1970 versus 2010? What does it show about different age-related patterns of marriage in males and females? By showing you that Americans are waiting much later in life to get married, a table like this initiates many causal questions for analysis and argument. What happened in American culture between 1970 and 2010 to explain the startling difference in the percentage of married people within, say, the 20–24 age bracket? In 2010 only 16 percent of people in this age bracket were married (we converted "unmarried" to "married" by subtracting 84 from 100). However, in 1970, 55.5 percent of people in this age bracket were married.

Using a Graph to Tell a Story

Table 9.2, as we have seen, tells the story of how Americans are postponing marriage. However, one has to tease out the story from the dense columns of numbers. To focus on a key story and make it powerfully immediate, you can create a graph.

Bar Graphs   Suppose you are writing an argument in which you want to show that the percentage of married women in the 20–29 age bracket has dropped significantly since 1970. You could tell this story through a bar graph (Figure 9.20).

Bar graphs use bars of varying length, extending either horizontally or vertically, to contrast two or more quantities. As with any graphic presentation, you must create a comprehensive title. In the case of bar graphs, titles tell readers what is being compared to what. Most bar graphs also have "legends," which explain what the different features on the graph represent. Bars are typically distinguished from each other by use of different colors, shades, or patterns of crosshatching. The special power of bar graphs is that they can help readers make quick comparisons.

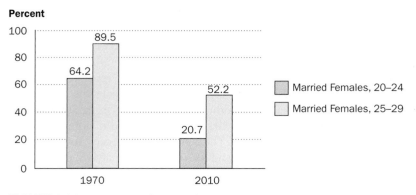

FIGURE 9.20 Percentage of married females ages 20–29, 1970 and 2010

Source: U.S. Census Bureau, *Current Population Survey,* March 2010.

Pie Charts   Another vivid kind of graph is a pie chart or circle graph, which depicts different percentages of a total (the pie) in the form of slices. Pie charts are a favorite way of depicting the way parts of a whole are divided up. Suppose, for example, that you wanted your readers to notice the high percentage of widows among women age 65 and older. To do so, you could create a pie chart (Figure 9.21) based on the data in the last row of Table 9.2. As you can see, a pie chart shows at a glance how the whole of something is divided into segments. However, the effectiveness of pie charts diminishes as you add more slices. In most cases, you'll begin to confuse readers if you include more than five or six slices.

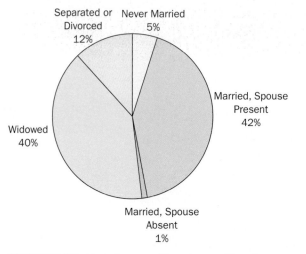

FIGURE 9.21 Marital status of females age 65 and older, 2010

Source: U.S. Census Bureau, *Current Population Survey,* March 2010.

Line Graphs   Another powerful quantitative graphic is a line graph, which converts numerical data into a series of points on a grid and connects them to create flat, rising, or falling lines. The result gives us a picture of the relationship between the variables represented on the horizontal and vertical axes.

Suppose you wanted to tell the story of the rising number of separated/divorced women in the U.S. population. Using Table 9.2, you can calculate the percentage of separated/divorced females in 2010 by adding the number of separated females (3,187,000) and the number of divorced females (13,760,000) and dividing that sum by the total number of females (124,361,000). The result is 13.6 percent. You can make the same calculations for 2000, 1990, 1980, and 1970 by looking at U.S. census data from those years (available on the Web or in your library). The resulting line graph is shown in Figure 9.22.

To determine what this graph is telling you, you need to clarify what's represented on the two axes. By convention, the horizontal axis of a graph contains the predictable, known variable, which has no surprises—what researchers call the "independent variable." In this case the horizontal axis represents the years 1970–2010 arranged predictably in chronological order. The vertical axis contains the unpredictable variable, which forms the graph's story—what researchers call the "dependent variable"—in this case, the percentage of separated or divorced females. The ascending curve tells the story at a glance.

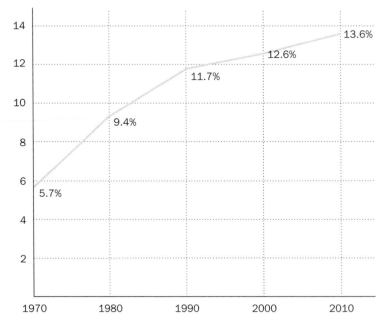

FIGURE 9.22 Percentage of females age 15 and older who were separated or divorced, 1970–2010

Source: U.S. Census Bureau, *Current Population Survey,* March 2010.

Note that with line graphs, the steepness of the slope (and hence the rhetorical effect) can be manipulated by the intervals chosen for the vertical axis. Figure 9.22 shows vertical intervals of 2 percent. The slope could be made less dramatic by choosing intervals of, say, 10 percent and more dramatic by choosing intervals of 1 percent.

Incorporating Graphics into Your Argument

Today, writers working with quantitative data usually use graphing software that automatically creates tables, graphs, or charts from data entered into the cells of a spreadsheet. For college papers, some instructors may allow you to make your graphs with pencil and ruler and paste them into your document.

Designing the Graphic   When you design your graphic, your goal is to have a specific rhetorical effect on your readers, not to demonstrate all the bells and whistles available on your software. Adding extraneous data to the graph or chart or using such features as a three-dimensional effect can often distract from the story you are trying to tell. Keep the graphic as uncluttered and simple as possible and design it so that it reinforces the point you are making.

Numbering, Labeling, and Titling the Graphic   In newspapers and popular magazines, writers often include graphics in boxes or sidebars without specifically referring to them in the text itself. However, in academic and professional workplace writing, graphics are always labeled, numbered, titled, and referred to directly in the text. By convention, tables are listed as "Tables," whereas line graphs, bar graphs, pie charts, or any other kinds of drawings or photographs are labeled as "Figures." Suppose you create a document that includes four graphics—a table, a bar graph, a pie chart, and a photograph. The table would be labeled as Table 1. The rest would be labeled as Figure 1, Figure 2, and Figure 3.

In addition to numbering and labeling, every graphic needs a comprehensive title that explains fully what information is being displayed. Look back over the tables and figures in this chapter and compare their titles to the information in the graphics. In a line graph showing changes over time, for example, a typical title will identify the information on both the horizontal and vertical axes and the years covered. Bar graphs also have a "legend" explaining how the bars are coded if necessary. When you import the graphic into your own text, be consistent in where you place the title—either above the graphic or below it.

Referencing the Graphic in Your Text   Academic and professional writers follow a referencing convention called *independent redundancy*. The general rule is this: The graphic should be understandable without the text; the text should be understandable without the graphic; the text should repeat the most important information in the graphic. An example is shown in Figure 9.23.

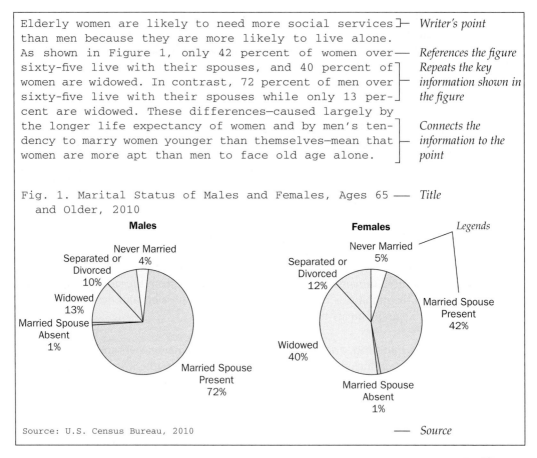

Elderly women are likely to need more social services ⌐— *Writer's point*
than men because they are more likely to live alone.
As shown in Figure 1, only 42 percent of women over— *References the figure*
sixty-five live with their spouses, and 40 percent of⌐ *Repeats the key*
women are widowed. In contrast, 72 percent of men over ⊢ *information shown in*
sixty-five live with their spouses while only 13 per-⌐ *the figure*
cent are widowed. These differences—caused largely by
the longer life expectancy of women and by men's ten-⌐ *Connects the*
dency to marry women younger than themselves—mean that ⊢ *information to the*
women are more apt than men to face old age alone. ⌐ *point*

Fig. 1. Marital Status of Males and Females, Ages 65 — *Title*
    and Older, 2010

Source: U.S. Census Bureau, 2010   — *Source*

FIGURE 9.23 Example of a student text with a referenced graph

Conclusion

In this chapter we have explained the challenge and power of using visuals in arguments. We have examined the components of visual design—use of type, layout, color, and images—and have shown how these components can be used for persuasive effect in arguments. We have also described the argumentative genres that depend on effective use of visuals—posters and fliers, advocacy advertisements, cartoons, and Web pages—and invited you to produce your own visual argument. Finally, we showed you that graphics can tell a numeric story in a highly focused and dramatic way. Particularly, we explained the functions of tables, bar graphs, pie charts, and line graphs, and showed you how to reference graphics and incorporate them into your own prose.

WRITING ASSIGNMENT A Visual Argument Rhetorical Analysis, a Visual   MyWritingLab™
Argument, or a Microtheme Using Quantitative Data

Option 1: Writing a Rhetorical Analysis of a Visual Argument Write a thesis-driven rhetorical analysis essay in which you examine the rhetorical effectiveness of a visual argument, either one of the visual arguments in this text or one specified by your instructor. Unless otherwise stated, direct your analysis to an audience of your class-mates. In your introduction, establish the argumentative conversation to which this argument is contributing. Briefly summarize the argument and describe the visual text. Present your thesis, highlighting two or more rhetorical features of the argument—such as the way the argument appeals to *logos, ethos,* and *pathos*—that you find central to the effectiveness or ineffectiveness of this argument. To develop and support your own points, you will need to include visual features and details (such as color, design, camera angle, framing, and special effects) as well as short quotations from any verbal parts of the argument.

Option 2: Multimodal Assignment: A Public Affairs Advocacy Ad or a Poster Argument Working with the idea of an advocacy ad or poster argument that you explored in For Class Discussion on page 199, use the visual design principles through-out the chapter, the guidelines presented on page 199, your understanding of visual argument and the genre of poster arguments, and your own creativity to produce a visual argument that can be displayed on your campus or in your town or city. Try out the draft of your advocacy ad or poster argument on people who are part of your target audience. Based on these individuals' suggestions for improving the clarity and impact of this visual argument, prepare a final version of your poster argument.

Option 3: Multimodal Assignment: Intertextual Visual Argument Often, visual arguments rely on what scholars call "intertextual associations." By "intertextual" (literally "between texts"), we mean that an image gets its power by drawing on ideas or emotions associated with other images that are part of our cultural background. An example is the photo of the young girls shooting bows (Figure 9.17), in which interpreting the intensity in the girls' faces depends on our cultural knowledge of *The Hunger Games.* Examples of frequently used intertextual images include the Statue of Liberty, the Uncle Sam "I Want You" recruitment poster, Adam and Eve in the garden with an apple or snake, Rosie the Riveter, the raising of the flag on Iwo Jima, and the Rodin sculpture *The Thinker.* Intertextual associations can also be drawn from fairy tales, legends, societal trends, or popular culture. For this assignment, create an idea for a poster or bumper sticker that would depend on an intertextual association for its persuasive effect. Think of an idea or behavior that you would like to promote and then link your persuasive purpose to an image from history, popular culture, or fairy tales that would speak to your audience and enliven your message. Finally, write a short reflection explaining the challenge of creating an intertextual visual argument. Possible ideas for an intertextual visual argument might include silencing cell phones in public places, buying local food, voting for a certain candidate, changing a school policy, supporting or criticizing skateboarders, admiring or mocking video game players, opposing Facebook addiction, defending an art form you value, supporting or criticizing car drivers who are angry at bikers, attacking employers' fixation on dress codes, and so forth.

Option 4: **Multimodal Assignment: Cartoon** Choose a controversial issue important to you and create a single-frame political cartoon that presents your perspective on the issue in a memorable way. Use the cartoon strategies of mini-narrative, caricature, exaggeration, distortion, and the interaction between image and text.

Option 5: **A Microtheme Using a Quantitative Graphic** Write a microtheme that tells a story based on data you select from Table 9.2 or from some other table provided by your instructor or located by you. Include in your microtheme at least one quantitative graphic (table, line graph, bar graph, pie chart), which should be labeled and referenced according to standard conventions. Use as a model the short piece shown in Figure 9.23 on page 206. ▪

MyWritingLab™

Visit Ch. 9 Analyzing Visual Arguments in *MyWritingLab* to complete the For Writing and Discussion and Writing Assignments and to test your understanding of the chapter objectives.

PART FOUR
Arguments in Depth
Types of Claims

This advertisement for Nicolites is one voice in the public controversy over e-cigarettes. The ad claims that e-cigarettes are safer than regular cigarettes but chooses to use the word "smoking" rather than the more sanitized word "vaping." The vapor from an e-cigarette usually includes nicotine (and may have added flavors) but not the tar from cigarettes. However, as the discussion in Chapter 10 on pages 213–215 shows, the safety, healthfulness, and advisability of e-cigarettes are hotly debated issues. Using strategies from Chapter 9 on analyzing visual texts, how do the words and images in this ad work together to make positive claims about e-cigarettes?

An Introduction to the Types of Claims

10

What you will learn in this chapter:

10.1 To identify different claim types and show how each type has characteristic patterns of development

10.2 To use strategies based on claim types to help focus an argument, generate ideas for it, and structure it persuasively

10.3 To be mindful of how different claim types work together in hybrid arguments

---

In Parts One, Two, and Three of this text, we showed how argument entails both inquiry and persuasion. We explained strategies for creating a compelling structure of reasons and evidence for your arguments (*logos*), for linking your arguments to the beliefs and values of your audience (*pathos*), and for establishing your credibility and trustfulness (*ethos*). We also explained how to do a rhetorical analysis of both verbal and visual texts.

Now in Part Four we examine arguments in depth by explaining five types of claims, each type having its own characteristic patterns of development and support. Because almost all arguments use one or more of these types of claims as "moves" or building blocks, knowing how to develop each claim type will advance your skills in argument. The claims we examine in Part Four are related to an ancient rhetorical concept called *stasis*, from a Greek term meaning "stand," as in "to take a stand on something." There are many competing theories of stasis, so no two rhetoricians discuss stasis in exactly the same way. In Part Four, we present a version of stasis theory based on five types of claims. Studying these claim types will increase your flexibility and sophistication as an arguer.

The Types of Claims and Their Typical Patterns of Development

10.1 To identify different claim types and show how each type has characteristic patterns of development

To appreciate what a study of claim types can do, imagine one of those heated but frustrating arguments in which the question at issue keeps shifting. Everyone talks at cross-purposes, each speaker's point unconnected to the previous speaker's. Suppose your heated discussion is about the use of steroids. You might get such a discussion back on track if one person says: "Hold it for a moment. What are we actually arguing about here? Are we arguing about whether steroids are a health risk or whether steroids should be banned from sports? These are two different issues. We can't debate both at once." Whether she recognizes it or not, this person is applying the concept of claim types to get the argument focused.

To understand how claim types work, let's return to the concept of stasis. A stasis is an issue or question that focuses a point of disagreement. You and your audience may agree on the answer to question A and so have nothing to argue about. Likewise you may agree on the answer to question B. But on question C you disagree. Question C constitutes a stasis where you and your audience diverge. It is the place where disagreement begins, where as an arguer you take a stand against another view. Thus you and your audience may agree that steroids, if used carefully under a physician's supervision, pose few long-term health risks but still disagree on whether steroids should be banned from sports. This last issue constitutes a stasis, the point where you and your audience part company.

Rhetoricians have discovered that the kinds of questions that divide people have classifiable patterns. In this text we identify five broad types of claims—each type originating in a different kind of question. The following chart gives you a quick overview of these five types of claims, each of which is developed in more detail in subsequent chapters in Part Four. It also shows you a typical structure for each type of argument. Note that the first three claim types concern questions of truth or reality, whereas the last two concern questions of value. You'll appreciate the significance of this distinction as this chapter progresses.

Claims about Reality, Truth, or the Way Things Are

Claim Type and Generic Question	Examples of Issue Questions	Typical Methods for Structuring an Argument
Definitional arguments: *In what category does this thing belong?* (Chapter 11)	▪ Is solitary confinement cruel and unusual punishment? ▪ Is a skilled video game player an athlete?	▪ Create a definition that establishes criteria for the category. ▪ Use examples to show how the contested case meets the criteria.
Resemblance arguments: *To what is this thing similar?* (Chapter 11)	▪ Is opposition to gay marriage like opposition to interracial marriage? ▪ Is investing in the stock market like gambling?	▪ Let the analogy or precedent itself create the desired rhetorical effect. [or] ▪ Elaborate on the relevant similarities between the given case and the analogy or precedent.

(continued)

Claim Type and Generic Question	Examples of Issue Questions	Typical Methods for Structuring an Argument
Causal arguments: *What are the causes or consequences of this phenomenon?* (Chapter 12)	■ What are the causes of bee colony collapse disorder? ■ What might be the consequences of raising the minimum wage?	■ Explain the links in a causal chain going from cause to effect or summarize experimental studies showing cause or consequence.
Evaluation and ethical arguments: *What is the worth or value of this thing?* (Chapter 13)	■ Is talk therapy a good approach for treating anxiety? ■ Is it ethical to use reproductive technology to make "designer babies"?	■ Establish the criteria for a "good" or "ethical" member of this class or category. ■ Use examples to show how the contested case meets the criteria.
Proposal arguments: *What action should we take?* (Chapter 14)	■ Should colleges abolish the SAT and ACT for admissions? ■ Should the federal government enact a carbon tax?	■ Make the problem vivid. ■ Explain your solution. ■ Justify your solution by showing how it is motivated by principle, by good consequences, or by resemblance to a previous action the audience approves.

■ ■ ■   **FOR CLASS DISCUSSION**   Identifying Types of Claims

Working as a class or in small groups, read the following questions and decide which claim type is represented by each. Sometimes there might be several different ways to classify a claim, so if the question fits two categories, explain your reasoning.

1. Should the president be authorized to employ weaponized drones to kill terrorists?
2. Is taking Adderall to increase concentration for an exam a form of cheating?
3. What would be the economic consequences of a carbon tax aimed at reducing carbon emissions?
4. Is burning the American flag an act of free speech?
5. Were the terrorist attacks of September 11, 2001, more like Pearl Harbor (an act of war) or more like an earthquake (a natural disaster)?
6. How effective is acupuncture in reducing morning sickness?
7. Is acupuncture quackery or real medicine?
8. Should universities ban the use of calculators in calculus exams?
9. Does the rodeo sport of riding bucking horses or bulls constitute cruelty to animals?
10. Why are couples who live together before marriage more likely to divorce than couples who don't live together before marriage?

■ ■ ■

Using Claim Types to Focus an Argument and Generate Ideas: An Example

10.2 To use strategies based on claim types to help focus an argument, generate ideas for it, and structure it persuasively

Having provided an overview of the types of claims, we now show you some of the benefits of this knowledge. First of all, understanding claim types will help you focus an argument by asking you to determine what's at stake between you and your audience. Where do you and your audience agree and disagree? What are the questions at issue? Second, it will help you generate ideas for your argument by suggesting the kinds of reasons, examples, and evidence you'll need.

To illustrate, let's take the recent public controversy about e-cigarettes, which use a battery-powered heating element to vaporize the liquid in a small cartridge. The user inhales the vapor (an act often called "vaping"). Cartridges can be purchased containing various amounts of nicotine or no nicotine at all; flavored liquids (such as apple cinnamon or peach cobbler) are also available. Although there is debate about whether the vapors from e-cigarettes are harmful, everyone agrees that the nicotine-laced liquid itself is poisonous if ingested in its liquid form. In the absence of federal regulations, many states and cities have enacted their own laws about e-cigarettes, often treating them exactly as if they were real cigarettes—banning them from bars, restaurants, and other public places, forbidding their sale to minors, and restricting the ways they can be advertised.

Let's now take the hypothetical case of a city debating a policy on e-cigarettes. Imagine three different writers. Writer 1 wants to ban e-cigarettes, making them subject to the same restrictions as real cigarettes. Writer 2 wants to promote e-cigarettes as a preferred alternative to real cigarettes. Writer 3, a libertarian opposed to the nanny state, wants no restrictions on e-cigarettes other than forbidding sale of nicotine cartridges to minors and making sure that the liquid-containing cartridges are childproof. Let's consider how familiarity with claim types can help each writer generate ideas for his or her argument.

Writer 1: Ban E-Cigarettes

Writer 1, who believes that e-cigarettes are harmful, imagines a somewhat live-and-let-live audience inclined to take no action against e-cigarettes. Her goal is to portray e-cigarettes negatively in order to persuade this audience that e-cigarettes should be banned.

- **Definition argument:** Because regular cigarettes are already banned in public places, Writer 1 wants to place e-cigarettes in the same category as real cigarettes. For part of her argument she can use a definitional strategy, showing that e-cigarettes and regular cigarettes belong in the same category in that they both deliver nicotine extracted from tobacco leaves. She can argue that the differences between e-cigarettes and regular cigarettes, such as one producing smoke and the other vapor, are superficial. What makes them the same is the delivery of nicotine.
- **Resemblance argument:** Using a resemblance strategy, Writer 1 can also show how e-cigarettes are designed to look like regular cigarettes and make smoking

look cool again. You can blow "smoke" rings with the exhaled vapor, just as you can with real tobacco smoke.

▧ **Causal argument:** To increase her negative portrayal of e-cigarettes, Writer 1 can also use a causal strategy. She can argue that e-cigarettes will hook children and teenagers on real cigarettes. She can show how the creation of flavored vapors such as "bubble gum" or "pancake" seem marketed to children and how the availability of cartridges that combine flavored vapors with nicotine give Big Tobacco a new way to create the next generation of nicotine addicts.

▧ **Evaluation argument:** Here Writer 1 will have to summarize and rebut counter-views that e-cigarettes are a good replacement for regular cigarettes. Supporters will say the e-cigarettes are better than regular cigarettes because they produce fewer carcinogens and are thus safer. Writer 1 will need to argue that the negative aspects of e-cigarettes—nicotine addiction and the enticement of children toward smoking—outweigh the increased safety. She can also argue that the propellant ingredients in the cartridges have not yet been proven safe, and she can refer to research showing the liquid itself is extremely poisonous if ingested directly.

▧ **Proposal argument:** The city council should ban e-cigarettes.

This example shows that writers often need to argue issues of reality and truth in order to make claims about values. In this particular case, Writer 1's proposal claim to ban e-cigarettes is based on reasons that are themselves derived from definition, resemblance, and cause: "E-cigarettes should be banned because they contain the same tobacco-derived nicotine as real cigarettes (definition), because they are advertised to make smoking look cool again (resemblance), and because they will hook kids on smoking (cause)."

Writer 2: Promote E-Cigarettes as a Preferred Alternative to Real Cigarettes

Writer 2 shares with his audience a belief that cigarettes are harmful and that smoking should be banned. However, he wants to emphasize the benefits of e-cigarettes to people who already smoke. Like Writer 1, he can use the five claim types to generate strategies for his argument.

▧ **Definition argument:** To portray e-cigarettes more positively, Writer 2 can make the definitional claim that e-cigarettes are **not** the same as real cigarettes and thus belong in a different category. He can argue that the essential trait of real cigarettes is cancer-causing tar derived from the combustion of tobacco leaves. It is the danger of the tar, not the nicotine, that caused the anti-smoking movement in the first place, especially the danger of secondhand smoke to others. By arguing that the delivery of nicotine is a superficial rather than essential criterion for defining cigarettes, he can show that the absence of tar and secondhand smoke makes e-cigarettes essentially different from real cigarettes.

▧ **Resemblance argument:** Using this strategy, Writer 2 can show that although e-cigarettes are essentially different from real cigarettes, the two have pleasing similarities. Vaping provides the same physical and social pleasures as does smoking, but without the harm to self and others.

- **Causal argument:** Writer 2 can also portray e-cigarettes positively through the causal argument that they can save the lives of current smokers by converting them from a dangerous to less dangerous way of getting nicotine. Without condoning nicotine addiction, Writer 2 can point to the positive health consequences of getting a nicotine hit without the carcinogens. Writer 2 can also argue that e-cigarettes can help people stop smoking because they can gradually reduce the nicotine content in the cartridges they purchase.
- **Evaluation argument:** Here Writer 2 can claim that e-cigarettes are better than real cigarettes by arguing that the health benefits of no smoke and tar outweigh the addiction to nicotine, which in itself causes little health risk.
- **Proposal argument:** E-cigarettes should be promoted as a safe alternative to real cigarettes.

Writer 3: Place No Restrictions on E-Cigarettes

Writer 3 is a libertarian who dislikes nanny-state restrictions on our individual freedoms. She wants to argue that the only restrictions on e-cigarettes should be federally mandated childproofing of the cartridges, truth-in-labeling about what is contained in the cartridges, and prevention of sales of nicotine-containing cartridges to minors.

- **Definition argument:** Writer 3, like Writer 2, can argue that e-cigarettes are in a different category from regular cigarettes. They present no proven dangers either to self or to others through secondhand smoke.
- **Resemblance argument:** To celebrate the libertarian endorsement of individual freedom, Writer 3 can show the resemblance between taking a pleasurable hit on an e-cigarette with other pleasures frowned upon by the nanny state—drinking sugary sodas, buying a Big Mac, or owning a muscle car.
- **Causal argument:** Whereas Writer 2 argues that e-cigarettes are safer than regular cigarettes, Writer 3 can argue that nobody has demonstrated any firsthand or secondhand health hazards for e-cigarettes. She can make the additional causal argument that government wants to treat e-cigarettes like regular cigarettes so that they can tax them heavily to produce sin-tax revenue. She can also argue that nanny-state regulations lead to increased loss of personal freedoms and the shutting down of markets for free enterprise.
- **Evaluation argument:** Writer 3 can argue that people should be free to make their own evaluations of e-cigarettes.
- **Proposal argument:** For consenting adults, the city should place no restrictions on e-cigarettes.

Hybrid Arguments: How Claim Types Work Together in Arguments

10.3 To be mindful of how different claim types work together in hybrid arguments

As the e-cigarette example shows, hybrid arguments can be built from different claim types. A writer might develop a proposal argument with a causal subargument in one section, a resemblance subargument in another section, and an evaluation subargument in still

another section. Although the overarching proposal argument follows the typical structure of a proposal, each of the subsections follows a typical structure for its own claim type.

Some Examples of Hybrid Arguments

The following examples show how these combinations of claim types can play out in
actual arguments. (For more examples of these kinds of hybrid arguments, see Chapter 14,
pages 312–313, where we explain how lower-order claims about reality and truth can support
higher-order claims about values.)

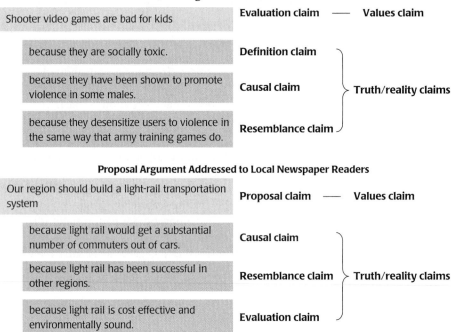

Evaluation Argument Addressed to Parents

| Shooter video games are bad for kids | Evaluation claim — Values claim |

because they are socially toxic.	Definition claim
because they have been shown to promote violence in some males.	Causal claim	Truth/reality claims
because they desensitize users to violence in the same way that army training games do.	Resemblance claim

Proposal Argument Addressed to Local Newspaper Readers

| Our region should build a light-rail transportation system | Proposal claim — Values claim |

because light rail would get a substantial number of commuters out of cars.	Causal claim
because light rail has been successful in other regions.	Resemblance claim	Truth/reality claims
because light rail is cost effective and environmentally sound.	Evaluation claim

■ ■ ■   **FOR WRITING AND DISCUSSION Exploring Different Claim Types**   MyWritingLab™
and Audiences

Individual task: Choose one of the following issues and role-play one of the suggested
authorial purposes. Write out your exploratory ideas for how you might use several of
the claim types to develop your argument (definition, resemblance, cause, evaluation,
proposal). Use as your models our example arguments about e-cigarettes. Imagine an
audience skeptical of your chosen position.

1. Carbon footprint: You want (do not want) the Environmental Protection Agency
   to regulate the amount of carbon dioxide that can be emitted from power plants.
2. Gun restrictions: You want (do not want) the federal government to ban assault
   rifles and high-volume ammunition cartridges.
3. Diet: You want your classmates to adopt (or not adopt) the paleo diet.

4. Minimum wage: You want (do not want) your city or state to adopt as its minimum wage a living wage of $15/hour.

5. Some other issue that you think will be reasonably familiar to your classmates.

Group task: Share with classmates your initial efforts to use the claim types to help generate ideas. What worked for you and what didn't? Where was it useful to think of the category that something belonged in (definition)? For example, is carbon dioxide a "pollutant," a "poison," or a "harmless and natural chemical compound"? Where was it helpful to think about resemblance? Is a paleo diet like a caveman's diet? How about cause? What will be the consequences of raising the minimum wage? How did your thinking about issues of truth or reality help develop evaluation or proposal claims?   ■ ■ ■

An Extended Example of a Hybrid Argument

As the previous examples illustrate, different claim types often serve as building blocks for larger arguments. We ask you now to consider a more extended example. Read the following argument from *Outside Magazine* aimed at enthusiasts of outdoor sports such as hiking, camping, mountain climbing, skiing, biking, and distance running. The magazine's readers are often health-conscious consumers of multivitamins and other diet supplements such as minerals, fish oils, herbals, botanicals, enzymes, antioxidants, amino acids, and other substances often taken as tablets, capsules, powders, energy drinks, or energy bars. In this startling article the writer uses recent scientific studies to make the evaluation claim that these supplements are either "useless" or "worse than useless." Notice how this overall evaluation claim is supported by claims from definition, resemblance, and cause.

Your Daily Multivitamin May Be Hurting You

ALEX HUTCHINSON

Introduces the **evaluation** issue "Are supplements good/bad?"

In JUNE, at this year's European College of Sport Science conference in Barcelona, Mari Carmen Gomez-Cabrera, a physiologist at the University of Valencia and one of the world's leading experts on antioxidants, was debating the merits of supplements with two top researchers. For more than 90 minutes they went back and forth, parsing the accumulated evidence in front of a packed auditorium. Finally, Gomez-Cabrera landed on a provocative question that summarized her position.

Restates **evaluation** issue with implied claim: Supplements are either useless or worse than useless.

The debate, she explained, isn't whether supplements are good or bad for athletes. Rather, it's "are they useless, or are they worse than useless?"

The question may come as a shock to the more than half of Americans who take some sort of dietary supplement—a vast catch-all term that includes everything from vitamins and minerals to herbal remedies to exotic performance boosters like deer-antler spray

Further develops
evaluation claim:
Supplements are bad
because they make
unproven claims and
because they may
come with hazardous
side effects.

Uses **causal
arguments** to
illustrate bad side
effects

Definition claim:
Supplements
belong to one of two
categories: (1) safe but
don't work or (2) work
but have bad side
effects

Develops **definition**
argument by showing
how supplements fit
first category of being
safe but useless

Causal argument
showing bad side
effects (places
supplements in
second category of
being harmful)

Causal argument
showing still more
bad side effects

and glutamine. It's no surprise that the purported muscle-building supplements make unproven claims and may come with hazardous side effects. But in the past few years, Gomez-Cabrera and a growing number of researchers have come to believe that even respectable mainstream supplements such as vitamins C and E suffer from the same basic flaw: few apparent benefits and increasing evidence of negative effects. For example, in July's issue of the *Journal of Physiology,* researchers discovered that resveratrol, an antioxidant in red wine, actually limited the positive effects of cardiovascular exercise—like an increased VO2 max—when taken daily in high concentrations. In July, scientists at the Fred Hutchinson Cancer Research Center found that men with high levels of the omega-3 fatty acid DHA in their blood, often from fish-oil supplements, had a significantly greater risk of prostate cancer.

According to Pieter Cohen, a professor at Harvard Medical School, there are really only two types of sports supplements: those that are safe but don't work, and those that might work but have side effects, especially at higher than normal levels. "If any supplement, no matter how beneficial, has a pharmaceutical effect, it's also got a downside," he says. "There's no way to get around that basic principle."

5   Most supplements stay firmly in the first category. Taking a daily multivitamin, Cohen emphasizes, won't harm you, but it usually won't help either, which is why major health organizations such as the American Heart Association and the American College of Sports Medicine don't recommend supplements to healthy people.

It's not that vitamins and minerals aren't important. If you don't get enough vitamin C, you can get scurvy; without enough iron, you can become anemic; and if you live far enough north to see Russia from your backyard, you may need some extra vitamin D. But all three of these substances have also been linked to negative effects at high doses. Same goes for prolonged use of other common supplements such as vitamin E and calcium. In short, unless tests have shown that you're low in a particular vitamin or mineral, there's no evidence to suggest that you should take a daily supplement.

That rule also applies if you're an athlete who takes supplements because, say, you assume your training requires an antioxidant boost to speed recovery. Gomez-Cabrera and her colleagues at the University of Valencia have shown that antioxidant supplements suppress the oxidative stress that signals your body to adapt and get stronger. The result: regular use of something seemingly innocuous such as vitamin C can actually block gains in endurance-boosting mitochondria.

Causal argument from psychology showing different bad effect: People who take supplements feel they are healthier and thus actually act in less healthy ways.

The balance between risk and return also works in subtler ways, as Wen-Bin Chiou, a psychologist at National Sun Yatsen University in Taiwan, has shown in a series of experiments on a phenomenon called the licensing effect. As part of a battery of tests, subjects were asked to take a pill; half were told the pill was a multivitamin, while the other half were told it was a placebo. In truth, they were all placebos.

In subsequent tests, the subjects who thought they'd taken a vitamin consistently behaved in less healthy ways. When asked to try out a pedometer, they were more likely to choose a shorter walking route; at lunch, they chose less healthy food. In follow-up studies, Chiou has also discovered that smokers who think they've been given a vitamin smoke more, and people who are given a weight-loss supplement are less likely to stick to their diet. The same thing happens when you go to the gym or eat a plate of spinach. The difference is that exercise and vegetables have real benefits, so you've still got a chance to come out ahead. If you take a pill with no benefits, the best you can do is break even.

Brief **resemblance** argument: Taking a vitamin is NOT like eating spinach or going to the gym.

Conclusion

Which brings us back to Gomez-Cabrera in Barcelona. She, of all people, has enormous respect for the powers of micronutrients such as antioxidants—she has devoted her life to studying them. "But if you eat enough fruits and vegetables, five servings a day," she says, "I don't think you need anything else." And if you're not eating like that, then taking a pill isn't a solution. In fact, it may be part of the problem.

As this editorial demonstrates, awareness of different kinds of claims can help you increase your flexibility and effectiveness as an arguer. In the following chapters in Part Four, we discuss each of the claim types in more detail, showing how they work and how you can develop skills and strategies for supporting each type of claim.

MyWritingLab™

Visit Ch. 10 An Introduction to the Types of Claims in *MyWritingLab* to complete the For Writing and Discussion and to test your understanding of the chapter objectives.

Definition and Resemblance Arguments

11

What you will learn in this chapter:

11.1 To explain what is at stake in arguments about definition and resemblance
11.2 To explain four types of categorical arguments
11.3 To explain the criteria-match structure of categorical arguments based on definition
11.4 To use criteria-match reasoning to generate ideas for your own definition argument

Arguments about definition or resemblance concern disputes about what category something belongs to, either directly by definition or indirectly or metaphorically through comparison or resemblance. They are among the most common argument types you will encounter.

Case 1 Are Global Warming Skeptics Like The Outlier Frog In This Cartoon?

This cartoon by award-wining political cartoonist (as well as children's book author) Pat Bagley makes two overlapping resemblance arguments. First, it argues that global warming happens slowly, like a heating pot of water. Second, it argues that the Republican Science Committee, comprised of global warming skeptics, selects its evidence from outlier sources, analogous to the outlier frog in this cartoon. This striking visual analogy makes a resemblance argument against the objectivity of the GOP Science Committee.

Case 2   Is a Frozen Embryo a Person or Property?

An infertile couple conceived several embryos in a test tube and then froze the fertilized embryos for future use. During the couple's divorce, they disagreed about the disposition of the embryos. The woman wanted to use the frozen embryos to try to get pregnant, and the man wanted to destroy them. When the courts were asked to decide what should be done with the embryos, several questions of definition arose: Should the frozen embryos be categorized as "persons," thus becoming analogous to children in custody disputes? Or should they be divided up as "property," with the man getting half and the woman getting the other half? Or should a new legal category be created for them that regards them as more than property but less than actual persons? The judge decided that frozen embryos "are not, strictly speaking, either 'persons' or 'property,' but occupy an interim category that entitles them to special respect because of their potential for human life."*

What Is at Stake in an Argument about Definition and Resemblance?

11.1 To explain what is at stake in arguments about definition and resemblance

Definition and resemblance arguments occur whenever a community disagrees about the category a particular person, thing, act, or phenomenon should be placed in or identified with. Here are some examples:

Issues Involving Categories

Question	Does this specific phenomenon ...	... belong to (or is it similar to) this category?
Is atmospheric carbon dioxide a pollutant?	Atmospheric carbon dioxide	Pollutant
Is LASIK surgery for nearsightedness "medically necessary" surgery or "cosmetic" surgery?	LASIK surgery for nearsightedness	Medically necessary surgery (or cosmetic surgery)
Is women's obsession with thinness today similar in effect to women's footbinding in ancient China?	Women's obsession with thinness	Footbinding in ancient China

Much is at stake when we place things into categories because the category that something belongs to can have real consequences. Naming the category that something belongs to makes an implicit mini-argument.

---

*See Vincent F. Stempel, "Procreative Rights in Assisted Reproductive Technology: Why the Angst?" *Albany Law Review* 62 (1999), 1187.

Consequences Resulting from Categorical Claims

To appreciate the consequences of categorical claims, consider the competing categories proposed for whales in the international controversy over commercial whaling. What category does a whale belong to? Some arguers might say that "whales are sacred animals," implying that their intelligence, beauty, grace, and power mean they should never be killed. Others might argue that "whales are a renewable food resource" like tuna, crabs, cattle, and chickens. This category implies that we can harvest whales for food the same way we harvest tuna for tuna fish sandwiches or cows for beef. Still others might argue that "whales are an endangered species"—a category that argues for the preservation of whale stocks but not necessarily for a ban on controlled hunting of individual whales. Each of these whaling arguments places whales in a separate, different category that implicitly urges the reader to adopt that category's perspective on whaling.

Significant consequences can also result from resemblance claims. Consider the way that media analysts tried to make sense of the September 11, 2001, terrorist attacks on the World Trade Center and the Pentagon by comparing them to different kinds of previous events. Some commentators said, "The September 11 attacks are like Timothy McVeigh's bombing of the Alfred P. Murrah Federal Building in Oklahoma City in 1995"—an argument that framed the terrorists as criminals who must be brought to justice. Others said, "The September 11 attacks are like the 1941 Japanese attack on Pearl Harbor"—an argument suggesting that the United States should declare war on some as-yet-to-be-defined enemy. Still others said, "The September 11 attacks are like an occasionally disastrous earthquake or an epidemic," arguing that terrorists will exist as long as the right conditions breed them and that it is useless to fight them using the strategies of conventional war. Under this analogy, the "war on terror" is a metaphorical war like the "war on poverty" or the "war against cancer." Clearly, each of these resemblance claims had high-stakes consequences. In 2001, the Pearl Harbor claim prevailed, and the United States went to war, first in Afghanistan and then in Iraq. Many critics of these wars continue to say that war is an inappropriate strategy for fighting the "disease of terrorism."

The Rule of Justice: Things in the Same Category Should Be Treated the Same Way

As you can see, the category we place something into—either directly through definition or indirectly through comparison—can have significant implications for people's actions or beliefs. To ensure fairness, philosophers refer to the rule of justice, which states that "beings in the same essential category should be treated in the same way." For example, the problem of how the courts should treat the users or sellers of marijuana depends on the category marijuana belongs to. Marijuana might be placed in the same category as tobacco and alcohol, in which case the possession and sale of marijuana would be legal but subject to regulation and taxes. Or marijuana could be placed in the same category as meth, cocaine, and heroin; in this case, it would be an illegal drug subject to criminal prosecution. Some states have placed marijuana in the same category as penicillin and insulin, making it a legal drug so long as it is obtained from a licensed dispensary with a doctor's prescription. Many states are not happy with any of these categories and are trying to define marijuana in some fourth way. Or to take a more homely example, suppose your professor says that absence from an exam can be excused for emergencies only. How would you define "emergency"? Clearly if you broke your leg on the morning of an exam, you would be excused. But is attending your grandmother's funeral or your best friend's wedding an "emergency"? How about missing an exam because your car wouldn't start? Although your interests might be best served by a broad definition of emergency, your professor might prefer a narrow definition, which would permit fewer exemptions.

The rule of justice becomes especially hard to apply when we consider contested cases marked by growth or slow change through time. At what point does a child become an adult? When does a binge drinker become an alcoholic, an Internet poker player a compulsive gambler, or a fetus a human person? Although we may be able arbitrarily to choose a particular point and declare that "adult" means someone at least eighteen years old or that "human person" means a fetus at conception, or at three months, or at birth, in the everyday world the distinction between child and adult, between fetus and person, between Friday-night poker playing and compulsive gambling seems an evolution, not a sudden and definitive step. Nevertheless, our language requires an abrupt shift between categories. In short, applying the rule of justice often requires us to adopt a digital approach to reality (switches are either on or off, either a fetus is a human person or it is not), whereas our sense of life is more analogical (there are numerous gradations between on and off; there are countless shades of gray between black and white).

As we can see from the preceding examples, the promise of language to structure what psychologist William James called "the buzz and confusion of the world" into an orderly set of categories turns out to be elusive. In most category debates, an argument, not a quick trip to the dictionary, is required to settle the matter.

■ ■ ■ **FOR CLASS DISCUSSION** Applying the Rule of Justice

Suppose your landlord decides to institute a "no pets" rule. The rule of justice requires that all pets have to go—not just your neighbor's barking dog, but also Mrs. Brown's cat, the kids' hamster downstairs, and your own pet tarantula. That is, all these animals have to go, unless you can argue that some of them are not "pets" for purposes of the landlord's "no pets" rule.

1. Working in small groups or as a whole class, define pets by establishing the criteria an animal would have to meet to be included in the category "pets." Consider your landlord's "no pets" rule as the cultural context for your definition.
2. Based on your criteria, which of the following animals is definitely a pet that would have to be removed from the apartment? Based on your criteria, which animals could you exclude from the "no pets" rule? How would you make your argument to your landlord?
   - a German shepherd
   - a small housecat
   - a tiny, well-trained lapdog
   - a gerbil in a cage
   - a canary
   - a tank of tropical fish
   - a tarantula

Types of Categorical Arguments

11.2 To explain four types of categorical arguments

Categorical arguments assert that a disputed phenomenon is (or is not) either a member of a certain category or is like a certain category. Such arguments can be divided into four kinds:

1. **Simple categorical arguments,** in which there is no dispute about the definition of the category.
2. **Definition arguments,** in which there is a dispute about the boundaries of the category and hence of its definition.
3. **Resemblance arguments by analogy,** in which the writer uses metaphor or other figurative language to link the phenomenon to a certain category.
4. **Resemblance arguments by precedent,** in which the arguer claims that one phenomenon or situation is similar to another phenomenon or situation.

Let's look at each in turn.

Simple Categorical Arguments

A categorical argument can be said to be "simple" if there is no disagreement about the definition of the category into which a person, event, or phenomenon is placed. For example, if you make the claim that "Joe is bossy," you are placing him in the category of "bossy people." In this case, you assume that you and the audience agree on what "bossy" means. Your dispute is simply whether Joe meets the criteria for "bossy." To support your claim, you would provide examples of his bossiness (his poor listening skills, his shouting at people, his making decisions without asking the committee). Similarly, if you want to make the simple categorical claim that "low-carb diets are dangerous," you would need to provide evidence of this danger (scientific studies, testimony from doctors, anecdotes, and so forth). The dispute in this case is about low-carb diets, not about the definition of "dangerous." To rebut a simple categorical claim, you would provide counterevidence to show that the person, event, or phenomenon does not meet the criteria for the category.

■ ■ ■ **FOR CLASS DISCUSSION** Supporting and Rebutting Simple Categorical Claims

Working individually or in small groups, consider how you would support the following simple categorical claims. What examples or other data would convince readers that the specified case fits within the named category? Then discuss ways you might rebut each claim.

1. Bottled water is environmentally unfriendly. [That is, bottled water belongs in the category of "environmentally unfriendly substances."]
2. Macklemore is a pure rapper.
3. Americans today are obsessed with their appearance. [That is, Americans belong in the category of "people obsessed with their appearance."]
4. Competitive cheerleading is physically risky.
5. Dinosaurs were warm blooded.

Definition Arguments

Simple categorical arguments morph into definition arguments whenever stakeholders disagree about the boundaries of a category. In the previous exercise, suppose that you had said about Macklemore, "Well, that depends on how you define 'pure rapper.'" The need to define the term "pure rapper" adds a new layer of complexity to your arguments about Macklemore. You are disputing not only specifics about Macklemore but also the definition of "pure rapper" itself.

Full-blown definition arguments occur, then, when the disputants don't agree on the definition of the category into which a person, event, or phenomenon is placed. Consider, for example, the environmental controversy over the definition of *wetland*. Section 404 of the federal Clean Water Act provides for federal protection of wetlands, but it leaves the task of defining *wetland* to administrative agencies and the courts. Currently, about 5 percent of the land surface of the contiguous forty-eight states is potentially affected by the wetlands provision, and 75 percent of this land is privately owned. Efforts to define *wetland* have created a battleground between pro-environment and pro-development or property rights groups. Farmers, homeowners, and developers often want a narrow definition of wetlands so that more property is available for commercial or private use. Environmentalists favor a broad definition in order to protect different habitat types and maintain the environmental safeguards that wetlands provide (control of water pollution, spawning grounds for aquatic species, floodwater containment, and so forth).

The problem is that defining *wetland* is tricky. For example, one federal regulation defines a wetland as any area that has a saturated ground surface for twenty-one consecutive days during the year. But how would you apply this law to a pine flatwood ecosystem that was wet for ten days this year but thirty days last year? And how should the courts react to lawsuits claiming that the regulation itself is either too broad or too narrow? One can see why the wetlands controversy provides hefty incomes for lawyers and congressional lobbyists.

As we will explain in more detail later in this chapter, definition arguments require a "criteria-match" structure in which the arguer must first define the category term by specifying the criteria that must be met for something to be placed in that category. The writer then shows that the disputed person, event, or phenomenon matches those criteria.

Resemblance Argument Using Analogy

Whereas definition arguments claim that a particular phenomenon belongs to a certain category, resemblance arguments simply compare one thing to another. A common kind of resemblance argument uses analogies—imaginative kinds of comparisons often with subtle persuasive effects. If you don't like your new boss, you can say that she's like a Marine drill sergeant or the cowardly captain of a sinking ship. Each of these analogies suggests a different category in which to place your boss, clarifying the nature of your dislike while conveying an emotional charge. The arguer's intention is to transfer the audience's understanding of (or feelings about) the second thing back to the first. The risk of resemblance arguments is that the differences between the two things being compared are often so significant that the argument collapses under close examination.

Sometimes, as in the "My boss is like a Marine drill sergeant" example, arguers use short, undeveloped analogies for quick rhetorical effect. At other times, arguers develop extended analogies that carry a substantial portion of the argument. As an example of an extended analogy, consider the following excerpt from a professor's argument opposing a proposal to require a writing proficiency exam for graduation. In the following portion of his argument, the professor compares development of writing skills to the development of physical fitness.

> A writing proficiency exam gives the wrong symbolic messages about writing. It suggests that writing is simply a skill, rather than an active way of thinking and learning. It suggests that once a student demonstrates proficiency then he or she doesn't need to do any more writing.
>
> Imagine two universities concerned with the physical fitness of their students. One university requires a junior-level physical fitness exam in which students must run a mile in less than 10 minutes, a fitness level it considers minimally competent. Students at this university see the physical fitness exam as a one-time hurdle. As many as 70 percent of them can pass the exam with no practice; another 10–20 percent need a few months' training; and a few hopeless couch potatoes must go through exhaustive remediation. After passing the exam, any student can settle back into a routine of TV and potato chips having been certified as "physically fit."
>
> The second university, however, believing in true physical fitness for its students, is not interested in minimal competency. Consequently, it creates programs in which its students must take one credit physical fitness course each term for the entire four years of the undergraduate curriculum. There is little doubt which university will have the most physically fit students. At the second university, fitness becomes a way of life with everyone developing his or her full potential. Similarly, if we want to improve our students' writing abilities, we should require writing in every course throughout the curriculum.

Thus analogies have the power to get an audience's attention like virtually no other persuasive strategy. But seldom are they sufficient in themselves to provide full understanding. At some point, with every analogy, you need to ask yourself, "How far can I legitimately go with this? At what point are the similarities between the two things I am comparing going to be overwhelmed by their dissimilarities?" Analogies are useful attention-getting devices, but they can conceal and distort as well as clarify.

■ ■ ■   **FOR CLASS DISCUSSION** Developing Analogies

The following exercise will help you clarify how analogies function in the context of arguments. Working individually or in small groups, think of two analogies for each of the following topics. One analogy should urge readers toward a positive view of the topic; the other should urge a negative view. Write each of your analogies in the following one-sentence format:

_____ is like _____: A, B, C … (in which the first term is the contested topic being discussed; the second term is the analogy; and A, B, and C are the points of comparison).

Example

Topic: Cramming for an exam

Negative analogy: Cramming for an exam is like pumping iron for ten hours straight to prepare for a weight-lifting contest: exhausting and counterproductive.

Positive analogy: Cramming for an exam is like carbohydrate loading before a big race: it gives your brain a full supply of facts and concepts, all fresh in your mind.

1. Checking social media constantly
2. Using racial profiling for airport security
3. Using steroids to increase athletic performance
4. Paying college athletes
5. Eating at fast-food restaurants

Resemblance Arguments Using Precedent

Another kind of resemblance argument uses precedent for its persuasive force. An argument by precedent tries to show that a current situation is like a past situation and that therefore a similar action or decision should be taken or reached. You can refute a precedence argument by showing that the present situation differs substantially from the past situation.

Precedence arguments are very common. For example, during the debate about health care reform in the first year of Barack Obama's presidency, supporters of a single-payer, "Medicare-for-all" system pointed to Canada as a successful precedent. Supporters said that since a single-payer system was successful in Canada, it would also be successful in the United States. But opponents also used the Canadian precedent to attack a single-payer system. They pointed to problems in the Canadian system as a reason to reject a Medicare-for-all system in the United States.

A good example of an extended precedence argument can be found in an article entitled "The Perils of Ignoring History: Big Tobacco Played Dirty and Millions Died. How Similar Is Big Food?"* The authors' goal is to place "Big Food" in the same category as "Big Tobacco." The authors argue that the food-processing industry is trying to avoid government regulations by employing the same "dirty tricks" used earlier by Big Tobacco. The authors show how Big Tobacco hired lobbyists to fight regulation, how it created clever advertising to make cigarette smoking seem cool, and how it sponsored its own research to cast doubt on data linking nicotine to lung cancer or asthma to secondhand smoke. The researchers argue that Big Food is now doing the same thing. Through lobbying efforts, coordinated lawsuits, and public relations campaigns, Big Food resists labeling ingredients in food products, casts doubt on scientific evidence about possible carcinogens in processed foods, and uses advertising to create a local, "family farm" image for Big Food. The researchers use this precedence argument to call for stricter government oversight of Big Food.

---

*Kelly D. Brownell and Kenneth E. Warner, "The Perils of Ignoring History: Big Tobacco Played Dirty and Millions Died. How Similar Is Big Food?" *The Milbank Quarterly* 87.1 (2009), 259–294.

■ ■ ■ **FOR CLASS DISCUSSION** **Using Claims of Precedent**

Consider the following claims of precedent, and evaluate how effective you think each precedent might be in establishing the claim. How would you develop the argument? How would you cast doubt on it?

1. To increase alumni giving to our university, we should put more funding into our football program. When University X went to postseason bowls for three years in a row, alumni donations to building programs and academics increased by 30 percent. We can expect the same increases here.
2. Postwar democracy can be created successfully in Afghanistan because it was created successfully in Germany and Japan following World War II.
3. Euthanasia laws work successfully in the Netherlands. Therefore they will work successfully in the United States.   ■ ■ ■

EXAMINING VISUAL ARGUMENTS

MyWritingLab™

Claim about Category (Definition)

This cartoon, by political cartoonist Randy Bish of the *Pittsburgh Tribune Review*, creates a visual pun that makes a categorical argument against heroin. How does Bish's rendering of the letter "r" make a categorical claim? What is that claim? How effective do you find this cartoon in highlighting the seductive danger of heroin addiction?

The Criteria-Match Structure of Definition Arguments

11.3 To explain the criteria-match structure of categorical arguments based on definition

Of the four types of categorical arguments explained in the previous section, definition arguments require the fullest range of argumentative skills. For the rest of this chapter, we'll explain more fully the argumentative moves required to write your own definition argument.

Overview of Criteria-Match Structure

Definition arguments usually have a two-part structure—(1) a definition part that tries to establish the boundaries of the category and (2) a match part that argues whether a given case meets that definition. To describe this structure, we use the term *criteria-match*. Here are two examples:

> **Definition issue:** In a divorce proceeding, is a frozen embryo a "person" rather than "property"?
>
> **Criteria part:** What criteria must be met for something to be a "person"?
>
> **Match part:** Does a frozen embryo meet these criteria?
>
> **Definition issue:** Is this thirty-acre parcel of land near Swan Lake a "wetland"?
>
> **Criteria part:** What criteria must be met for something to be a wetland?
>
> **Match part:** Does this parcel of land meet these criteria?

To show how a definition issue can be developed into a claim with supporting reasons, let's look more closely at a third example:

> **Definition issue:** For purposes of my feeling good about buying my next pair of running shoes, is the Hercules Shoe Company a socially responsible company?
>
> **Criteria part:** What criteria must be met for a company to be deemed "socially responsible"?
>
> **Match part:** Does the Hercules Shoe Company meet these criteria?

Let's suppose you work for a consumer information group that wishes to encourage patronage of socially responsible companies while boycotting irresponsible ones. Your group's first task is to define *socially responsible company*. After much discussion and research, your group establishes three criteria that a company must meet to be considered socially responsible:

> *Your definition:* A company is socially responsible if it (1) avoids polluting the environment, (2) sells goods or services that contribute to the well-being of the community, and (3) treats its workers justly.

The criteria section of your argument would explain and illustrate these criteria.

The match part of the argument would then try to persuade readers that a specific company does or does not meet the criteria. A typical thesis statement might be as follows:

> *Your thesis statement:* Although the Hercules Shoe Company is nonpolluting and provides a socially useful product, it is not a socially responsible company because it treats workers unjustly.

Toulmin Framework for a Definition Argument

Here is how the core of the preceding Hercules definition argument could be displayed in Toulmin terms. Note how the reason and grounds constitute the match argument while the warrant and backing constitute the criterion argument.

Toulmin Analysis of the Hercules Shoe Company Argument

ENTHYMEME

CLAIM The Hercules Shoe Company is not a socially responsible company

REASON because it treats workers unjustly.

GROUNDS

Evidence of unjust treatment:

• Evidence that the company manufactures its shoes in East Asian sweatshops

• Evidence of the inhumane conditions in these shops

• Evidence of hardships imposed on displaced American workers

CONDITIONS OF REBUTTAL
Attacking reasons and grounds

• Possible counter evidence that the shops maintain humane working conditions

• Possible questioning of statistical data about hardships on displaced workers

WARRANT

Socially responsible companies treat workers justly.

BACKING

• Arguments showing that just treatment of workers is right in principle and also benefits society

• Arguments that capitalism helps society as a whole only if workers achieve a reasonable standard of living, have time for leisure, and are not exploited

CONDITIONS OF REBUTTAL
Attacking warrant and backing

Justice needs to be considered from an emerging nation's standpoint:

• The wages paid workers are low by American standards but are above average by East Asian standards.

• Displacement of American workers is part of the necessary adjustment of adapting to a global economy and does not mean that a company is unjust.

As this Toulmin schema illustrates, the warrant and backing constitute the criteria section of the argument by stating and defending "just treatment of workers" as a criterion for a socially responsible company. The reason and grounds constitute the match section of the argument by arguing that the Hercules Shoe Company does not treat its workers justly. How much emphasis you need to place on justifying each criterion and supporting each match depends on your audience's initial beliefs. The conditions of rebuttal help you imagine alternative views and see places where opposing views need to be acknowledged and rebutted.

■ ■ ■   **FOR CLASS DISCUSSION** Identifying Criteria and Match Issues

Consider the following definition claims. Working individually or in small groups, identify the criteria issue and the match issue for each of the following claims.

> **Definition issue:** A Honda assembled in Ohio is (is not) an American-made car.
>
> **Criteria part:** What criteria have to be met before a car can be called "American made"?
>
> **Match part:** Does a Honda assembled in Ohio meet these criteria?

1. American Sign Language is (is not) a "foreign language" for purposes of a college graduation requirement.
2. The violence in *Grand Theft Auto* is (is not) constitutionally protected free speech.
3. Bungee jumping from a crane is (is not) a "carnival amusement ride" subject to state safety inspections.
4. For purposes of a state sales tax on "candy," a Twinkie is (is not) candy.
5. A skilled video game player is (is not) a true athlete.   ■ ■ ■

Creating Criteria Using Aristotelian Definition

When creating criteria for a category, you can often follow the pattern of *Aristotelian definition*. The Aristotelian definitional strategy, regularly used in dictionaries, defines a term by placing it within the next larger class or category and then showing the specific attributes that distinguish the term from other terms within the same category. For example, according to a legal dictionary, *robbery* is "the felonious taking of property" (next larger category) that differs from other acts of theft because it seizes property "through violence or intimidation." Legal dictionaries often provide specific examples to show the boundaries of the term. Here is one example:

> There is no robbery unless force or fear is used to overcome resistance. Thus, surreptitiously picking a man's pocket or snatching something from him without resistance on his part is *larceny,* but not robbery.

Many states specify degrees of robbery with increasingly heavy penalties. For example, *armed robbery* involves the use of a weapon to threaten the victim. In all cases, *robbery* is distinguished from the lesser crime of *larceny,* in which no force or intimidation is involved.

As you can see, an Aristotelian definition of a term identifies specific attributes or criteria that enable you to distinguish it from other members of the next larger class. We created an Aristotelian definition in our example about socially responsible companies. A socially responsible company, we said, is any company (next larger class) that meets three criteria: (1) it doesn't pollute the environment; (2) it creates goods or services that promote the well-being of the community; and (3) it treats its workers justly.

In constructing Aristotelian definitions, you may find it useful to employ the concept of accidental, necessary, and sufficient criteria.

■ An *accidental criterion* is a usual but not essential feature of a concept. For example, armed robbers frequently wear masks, but wearing a mask is an accidental criterion because it has no bearing on the definition of *robbery.* In our example about socially responsible companies, "makes regular contributions to charities" might be an accidental criterion; most socially responsible companies contribute to charities, but some do not. And many socially irresponsible companies also contribute to charities—often as a public relations ploy.

- A *necessary criterion* is an attribute that *must* be present for something to belong to the category being defined. To be guilty of robbery rather than larceny, a thief must have used direct force or intimidation. The use of force is thus a necessary criterion for robbery. However, for a robbery to occur, another criterion must also be met: the robber must also take property from the victim.

- *Sufficient criteria* are all the criteria that must be present for something to belong to the category being defined. Together, the use of force plus the taking of property are *sufficient criteria* for an act to be classified as robbery.

Consider again our defining criteria for a "socially responsible" company: (1) the company must avoid polluting the environment; (2) the company must create goods or services that contribute to the well-being of the community; and (3) the company must treat its workers justly. In this definition, each criterion is necessary, but none of the criteria alone is sufficient. In other words, to be defined as socially responsible, a company must meet all three criteria at once, as the word *and* signals. It is not enough for a company to be nonpolluting (a necessary but not sufficient criterion); if that company makes a shoddy product or treats its workers unjustly, it fails to meet the other necessary criteria and can't be deemed socially responsible. Because no one criterion by itself is sufficient, all three criteria together must be met before a company can be deemed socially responsible.

In contrast, consider the following definition of *sexual harassment* as established by the U.S. Equal Employment Opportunity Commission in its 1980 guidelines:

> Unwelcome sexual advances, requests for sexual favors, and other verbal or physical conduct of a sexual nature constitute sexual harassment when (1) submission to such conduct is made either explicitly or implicitly a term or condition of an individual's employment, (2) submission to or rejection of such conduct by an individual is used as the basis for employment decisions affecting such individual, or (3) such conduct has the purpose or effect of unreasonably interfering with an individual's work performance or creating an intimidating, hostile, or offensive working environment.*

Here each of these criteria is sufficient, but none is necessary. In other words, an act constitutes sexual harassment if any one of the three criteria is satisfied, as the word *or* indicates.

■ ■ ■   **FOR CLASS DISCUSSION** Working with Criteria

Working individually or in small groups, try to determine whether each of the following is a necessary criterion, a sufficient criterion, an accidental criterion, or no criterion for defining the indicated concept. Be prepared to explain your reasoning and to account for differences in points of view.

---

*Quoted in Stephanie Riger, "Gender Dilemmas in Sexual Harassment Policies and Procedures," *American Psychologist* 46 (May 1991), 497–505.

Criterion	Concept to Be Defined
Presence of gills	Fish
Profane and obscene language	R-rated movie
Line endings that form a rhyming pattern	Poem
Disciplining a child by spanking	Child abuse
Diet that excludes meat	Vegetarian
Killing another human being	Murder
Good sex life	Happy marriage

Creating Criteria Using an Operational Definition

In some rhetorical situations, particularly those arising in the physical and social sciences, writers need precise, *operational definitions* that can be measured empirically and are not subject to problems of context and conflicting values and beliefs. A social scientist studying the effects of television on aggression in children needs a precise, measurable definition of *aggression.* Typically, the scientist might measure "aggression" by counting the number of blows a child gives to an inflatable bobo doll over a fifteen-minute period when other play options are available. In our wetlands example, a federal authority created an operational definition of *wetland:* a wetland is a parcel of land that has a saturated ground surface for twenty-one consecutive days during the year.

   Such operational definitions are useful because they are precisely measurable, but they are also limited because they omit criteria that may be unmeasurable but important. Thus, we might ask whether it is adequate to define an *honors student* as someone with a 3.8 GPA or higher or a *successful sex-education program* as one that results in a 25 percent reduction in teenage pregnancies. What important aspects of an honors student or a successful sex-education program are not considered in these operational definitions?

Conducting the Match Part of a Definition Argument

In conducting a match argument, you need to supply examples and other evidence showing that your contested case does (does not) meet the criteria you established in your definition. In essence, you support the match part of your argument in much the same way you would support a simple categorical claim.

   For example, if you were developing the argument that the Hercules Shoe Company is not socially responsible because it treats its workers unjustly, your match section would provide evidence of this injustice. You might supply data about the percentage of shoes produced in East Asia, about the low wages paid these workers, and about the working conditions in these factories. You might also describe the suffering of displaced American workers when Hercules closed its American factories and moved operations to Asia, where the labor is nonunion and cheap. The match section should also summarize and respond to opposing views.

Idea-Generating Strategies for Creating Your Own Criteria-Match Argument

11.4 To use criteria-match reasoning to generate ideas for your own definition argument
In constructing criteria to define your contested term, you can either research how others have defined your term or make your own definitions. If you use the first strategy, you turn to standard or specialized dictionaries, judicial opinions, or expert testimony to establish a definition based on the authority of others. The second strategy is to use your own critical thinking to make your own definition, thereby defining the contested term yourself. This section explains these approaches in more detail.

Strategy 1: Research How Others Have Defined the Term

When you take this approach, you search for authoritative definitions acceptable to your audience yet favorable to your case. When the state of Washington tried to initiate a new sales tax on candy, lawyers and legislators wrestled with a definition. They finally created the following statute available to the public on a government Web site:

What Is the Definition of Candy?

"Candy" is a preparation of sugar, honey, or other natural or artificial sweeteners combined with chocolate, fruits, nuts, or other ingredients or flavorings in the form of bars, drops, or pieces. Candy does not require refrigeration, and does not include flour as an ingredient.

> "Natural or artificial sweeteners" include, but are not limited to, high fructose corn syrup, dextrose, invert sugar, sucrose, fructose, sucralose, saccharin, aspartame, stevia, fruit juice concentrates, molasses, evaporated cane juice, and rice syrup.

> "Flour" includes any flour made from a grain, such as wheat flour, rice flour, and corn flour.

> Items that require "refrigeration," either before or after opening, are not candy. For example, popsicles, ice cream bars, and fruits in sweetened syrups are not candy.

This definition made it easy for state officials to exclude from the "candy tax" any snack food that contained flour. Thus Twinkies, Fruit Loops cereal, and chocolate-covered pretzels were exempt from the tax. But considerable debate occurred over cough drops and halvah (a traditional dessert in India and Mediterranean countries). The state decided to exclude cough drops if the package contained a "drug facts" panel and a list of active ingredients. (Such cough drops were then classified as "over-the-counter drugs.") The state ruled that nut-butter halvah was taxable but that flourbased halvah was not taxable; even so, many kinds of halvah didn't fit neatly into these two categories.

Turning to established definitions is thus a first step for many definition arguments. Common sources of these definitions are specialized dictionaries such as *Black's Law Dictionary*, which form a standard part of the reference holdings of any library. Other sources of specialized definitions are state and federal appellate court decisions, legislative and administrative statutes, and scholarly articles examining a given definition conflict. Lawyers use this research strategy exhaustively in preparing court briefs. They begin by looking at the actual text of laws as passed by legislatures or written by administrative authorities. Then they look at all the court cases in which the laws have been tested and examine the ways courts have refined legal definitions and applied them to specific cases. Using these refined definitions, lawyers then apply them to their own case at hand.

If your research uncovers definitions that seem ambiguous or otherwise unfavorable to your case, you can sometimes appeal to the "original intentions" of those who defined the term. For example, if a scientist is dissatisfied with definitions of *wetlands* based on consecutive days of saturated ground surface, she might proceed as follows: "The original intention of Congress in passing the Clean Water Act was to preserve the environment." What Congress intended, she could then claim, was to prevent development of those wetland areas that provide crucial habitat for wildlife or that inhibit water pollution. She could then propose an alternative definition based on criteria other than consecutive days of ground saturation.

Strategy 2: Create Your Own Extended Definition*

Often, however, you need to create your own definition of the contested term. An effective strategy is to establish initial criteria for your contested term by thinking of hypothetical cases that obviously fit the category you are trying to define and then by altering one or more variables until the hypothetical case obviously doesn't fit the category. You can then test and refine your criteria by applying them to borderline cases. For example, suppose you work at a homeless agency where you overhear street people discuss an incident that strikes you as potential "police brutality." You wonder whether you should write to your local paper to bring attention to the incident.

A Possible Case of Police Brutality

Two police officers confront an inebriated homeless man who is shouting obscenities on a street corner. The officers tell the man to quiet down and move on, but he keeps shouting obscenities. When the officers attempt to put the man into the police car, he resists and takes a wild swing at one of the officers. As eyewitnesses later testified, this officer shouted obscenities back at the drunk man, pinned his arms behind his back in order to handcuff him, and lifted him forcefully by the arms. The man screamed in pain and was later discovered to have a dislocated shoulder. Is this officer guilty of police brutality?

To your way of thinking, this officer seems guilty: An inebriated man is too uncoordinated to be a threat in a fight, and two police officers ought to be able to arrest

---

*The defining strategies and collaborative exercises in this section are based on the work of George Hillocks and his research associates at the University of Chicago. See George Hillocks Jr., Elizabeth A. Kahn, and Larry R. Johannessen, "Teaching Defining Strategies as a Mode of Inquiry: Some Effects on Student Writing," *Research in the Teaching of English* 17 (October 1983), 275–84. See also Larry R. Johannessen, Elizabeth A. Kahn, and Carolyn Calhoun Walter, *Designing and Sequencing Prewriting Activities* (Urbana, IL: NCTE, 1982).

him without dislocating his shoulder. But a friend argues that because the man took a swing at the officer, the police were justified in using force. The dislocated shoulder was simply an accidental result of using justified force.

To make your case, you need to develop a definition of "police brutality." You can begin by creating a hypothetical case that is obviously an instance of "police brutality":

A Clear Case of Police Brutality

A police officer confronts a drunk man shouting obscenities and begins hitting him in the face with his police baton. *[This is an obvious incidence of police brutality because the officer intentionally tries to hurt the drunk man without justification; hitting him with the baton is not necessary for making an arrest or getting the man into the police car.]*

You could then vary the hypothetical case until it is clearly *not* an instance of police brutality.

Cases That Are Clearly Not Police Brutality

Case 1: The police officer handcuffs the drunk man, who, in being helped into the police car, accidentally slips on the curb and dislocates his arm while falling. *[Here the injury occurs accidentally; the police officer does not act intentionally and is not negligent.]*

Case 2: The police officer confronts an armed robber fleeing from a scene and tackles him from behind, wrestling the gun away from him. In this struggle, the officer pins the robber's arm behind his back with such force that the robber's shoulder is dislocated. *[Here aggressive use of force is justified because the robber was armed, dangerous, and resisting arrest.]*

Using these hypothetical cases, you decide that the defining criteria for police brutality are (1) *intention* and (2) use of *excessive force*—that is, force beyond what was required by the immediate situation. After more contemplation, you are convinced that the officer was guilty of police brutality and have a clearer idea of how to make your argument. Here is how you might write the "match" part of your argument:

Match Argument Using Your Definition

If we define police brutality as the *intentional* use of *excessive* force, then the police officer is guilty. His action was intentional because he was purposefully responding to the homeless man's drunken swing and was angry enough to be shouting obscenities back at the drunk (according to eyewitnesses). Second, he used excessive force in applying the handcuffs. A drunk man taking a wild swing hardly poses a serious danger to two police officers. Putting handcuffs on the drunk may have been justified, but lifting the man's arm violently enough to dislocate a shoulder indicates excessive force. The officer lifted the man's arms violently not because he needed to but because he was angry, and acting out of anger is no justification for that violence. In fact, we can charge police officers with "police brutality" precisely to protect us from being victims of police anger. It is the job of the court system to punish us, not the police's job. Because this officer acted intentionally and applied excessive force out of anger, he should be charged with police brutality.

The strategy we have demonstrated—developing criteria by imagining hypothetical cases that clearly do and do not belong to the contested category—gives you a systematic procedure for developing your own definition for your argument.

■ ■ ■ **FOR WRITING AND DISCUSSION** Developing a Definition   MyWritingLab™

Individual task:

1. Suppose you want to define the concept of courage. In each of the following cases, decide whether the person in question is acting courageously or not. In each instance explain your reasoning.

   a. A neighbor rushes into a burning house to rescue a child from certain death and emerges, coughing and choking, with the child in his arms. Is the neighbor courageous?

   b. A firefighter rushes into a burning house to rescue a child from certain death and emerges with the child in her arms. The firefighter is wearing protective clothing and a gas mask. When a newspaper reporter calls her courageous, she says, "Hey, this is my job." Is the firefighter courageous?

   c. A teenager rushes into a burning house to recover a memento given to him by his girlfriend, the first love of his life. Is the teenager courageous?

   d. A parent rushes into a burning house to save a trapped child. The fire marshal tells the parent to wait because there is no chance that the child can be reached from the first floor. The fire marshal wants to try cutting a hole in the roof to reach the child. The parent rushes into the house anyway and is burned to death. Was the parent courageous?

2. Now formulate your own definition of a "courageous act." "An act would be considered courageous if it meets the following criteria: [you specify]."

3. Finally, apply your definition to the following case: An extreme sport enthusiast sets a record for a hang gliding descent from a certain state's highest cliff. Is this record-setting descent a courageous act? Write a paragraph in which you argue that the descent is or is not courageous.

Group task: Share the results from the individual task on courage. Then make up your own series of controversial cases, like those given previously for "courage," for one or more of the following concepts:

a. cruelty to animals
b. child abuse
c. true athlete
d. sexual harassment
e. free speech protected by the First Amendment

Finally, using the strategy of making up hypothetical cases that do and do not belong to each category, construct a definition of your chosen concept.   ■ ■ ■

WRITING ASSIGNMENT A Definition Argument   MyWritingLab™

The assignment for this chapter focuses on definition disputes about categories. Write an essay in which you argue that a borderline or contested case fits (or does not fit) within a given category. In the opening of your essay, introduce the borderline case you will examine and pose your definition question. In the first part of your argument, define the boundaries of your category (criteria) by reporting a definition used by others or by developing your own extended definition. In the second part of your argument (the match), show how your borderline case meets (or doesn't meet) your definition criteria.

Exploring Ideas

Ideally, in writing this argument you will join an ongoing conversation about a definition issue that interests you. What cultural and social issues that concern you involve disputed definitions? In the public arena, you are likely to find numerous examples simply by looking through news stories—for example, the disputes about the definition of "torture" in interrogating terrorist suspects or about "freedom of religion" in debates about religious organizations having to pay for contraception in employees' health insurance. Often you can frame your own definition issues even if they aren't currently in the news. Is using TiVo to avoid TV commercials a form of theft? Is flag burning protected free speech? Is solitary confinement "cruel and unusual punishment"? Is Wal-Mart a socially responsible company? Are voter ID laws racist?

If you have trouble discovering a local or national issue that interests you, you can create fascinating definition controversies among your classmates by asking whether certain borderline cases are "true" or "real" examples of some category: Are highly skilled video game players (race car drivers, synchronized swimmers, marbles players) true athletes? Is a gourmet chef (skilled furniture maker, tagger) a true artist? Is a chiropractor (acupuncturist, naturopathic physician) a "real doctor"? Working as a whole class or in small groups inside or outside class, create an argumentative discussion on one or more of these issues. Listen to the various voices in the controversy, and then write out your own argument.

You can also stimulate definition controversies by brainstorming borderline cases for such terms as *courage* (Is mountain climbing an act of courage?), *cruelty to animals* (Are rodeos [zoos, catch-and-release trout fishing, use of animals for medical research] guilty of cruelty to animals?), or *war crime* (Was the American firebombing of Tokyo in World War II a war crime?).

As you explore your definition issue, try to determine how others have defined your category. If no stable definition emerges from your search, create your own definition by deciding what criteria must be met for a contested case to fit within your category. Try using the strategy for creating criteria that we discussed on pages 235–237 with reference to police brutality. Once you have determined your criteria, freewrite for five or ten minutes, exploring whether your contested case meets each of the criteria.

Identifying Your Audience and Determining What's at Stake

Before drafting your argument, identify your targeted audience and determine what's at stake. Consider your responses to the following questions:

- What audience are you targeting? What background do they need to understand your issue? How much do they already care about it?
- Before they read your argument, what stance on your issue do you imagine them holding? What change do you want to bring about in their views?

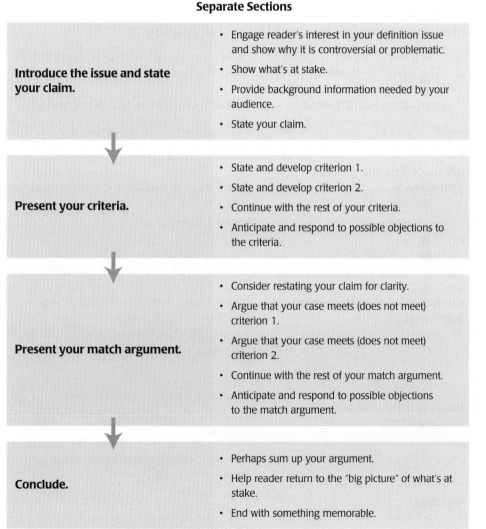

Organization Plan 1: Definition Argument with Criteria and Match in Separate Sections

Introduce the issue and state your claim.	• Engage reader's interest in your definition issue and show why it is controversial or problematic. • Show what's at stake. • Provide background information needed by your audience. • State your claim.
Present your criteria.	• State and develop criterion 1. • State and develop criterion 2. • Continue with the rest of your criteria. • Anticipate and respond to possible objections to the criteria.
Present your match argument.	• Consider restating your claim for clarity. • Argue that your case meets (does not meet) criterion 1. • Argue that your case meets (does not meet) criterion 2. • Continue with the rest of your match argument. • Anticipate and respond to possible objections to the match argument.
Conclude.	• Perhaps sum up your argument. • Help reader return to the "big picture" of what's at stake. • End with something memorable.

- What will they find new or surprising about your argument?
- What objections might they raise? What counterarguments or alternative points of view will you need to address?
- Why does your argument matter? Who might be threatened or made uncomfortable by your views? What is at stake?

Organizing a Definition Argument

As you compose a first draft of your essay, you may find it helpful to know typical structures for definition arguments. There are two basic approaches, as shown in Organization Plans 1 and 2. You can either discuss the criteria and the match separately or interweave the discussion.

Questioning and Critiquing a Definition Argument

A powerful way to stimulate global revision of a draft is to role-play a skeptical audience. The following questions will help you strengthen your own argument or rebut

Organization Plan 2: Definition Argument with Criteria and Match Interwoven

Introduce the issue and state your claim.	• Engage reader's interest in your definition issue and show why it is problematic or controversial. • Show what's at stake. • Provide background information needed by your audience. • State your claim.
Present series of criterion-match arguments.	• State and develop criterion 1 and argue that your case meets (does not meet) the criterion. • State and develop criterion 2 and argue that your case meets (does not meet) the criterion. • Continue with the rest of your criterion-match arguments.
Respond to possible objections to your argument.	• Anticipate and summarize possible objections. • Respond to the objections through rebuttal or concession.
Conclude.	• Perhaps sum up your argument. • Help reader return to the "big picture" of what's at stake. • End with something memorable.

the definition arguments of others. In critiquing a definition argument, you need to appreciate its criteria-match structure because you can question your criteria argument, your match argument, or both.

Questioning Your Criteria

- Could a skeptic claim that your criteria are not the right ones? Could he or she offer different criteria or point out missing criteria?
- Could a skeptic point out possible bad consequences of accepting your criteria?
- Could a skeptic cite unusual circumstances that weaken your criteria?
- Could a skeptic point out bias or slant in your definition?

Questioning Your Match

- Could a skeptic argue that your examples or data don't meet the STAR criteria (see Chapter 5, pages 92–93) for evidence?
- Could a skeptic point out counterexamples or alternative data that cast doubt on your argument?
- Could a skeptic reframe the way you have viewed your borderline case?

READINGS

Our first reading, by student writer Arthur Knopf, grew out of his research into agricultural subsidies and the nutritional content of foods. It was written for the assignment on page 238.

Is Milk a Health Food?

ARTHUR KNOPF (STUDENT)

If asked to name a typical health food, most of us would put milk high on our lists. We've all seen the "Got Milk?" ads with their milk-mustached celebrities or the dairy product campaigns entitled "Milk, It Does a Body Good" or "Body By Milk." These ads, featuring well known athletes or trim celebrities, argue visually that milk helps you grow fit and strong. But if you define "health food" based on science rather than on marketing claims, and if you include in your definition of health food concerns for the planet as well as for individual bodies, then milk might not fit the category of health food at all.

My first criterion for a "health food" is that the food should have a scientifically supported health benefit with minimal risks. Based on the food pyramid from the United States Department of Agriculture (USDA), milk at first glance seems to fit this criterion. On the *MyPyramid* Web site the dairy group (milk, yogurt, cheese) is one of the essential components of a healthy diet (USDA). All elements of the milk group provide calcium, which is important for healthy bones and the prevention of osteoporosis. Dairy products also provide important vitamins. But the Web site entry under the dairy group specifies in a footnote, "Choose fat-free or low-fat milk, yogurt, and cheese." One cup of whole milk, according to the Web site, contains 70 more calories than a cup of skim milk (147 calories compared to 83). The extra 70 calories are potentially harmful saturated fats and sugar, linked to heart disease and obesity. We can say then that "nonfat milk" fits my first criterion for a health food, but that the rest of the milk group may not.

So how do dairy products in general get listed as essential ingredients on the food pyramid rather than just low-fat milk or yogurt? The answer to this question brings us to my second criterion for a health food: Potentially unhealthy aspects of the food should be widely disclosed, not hidden by marketing. Because we are bombarded daily by conflicting nutrition claims, many people turn to the U.S. government for neutral, unbiased information. But the place of dairy products on the USDA food pyramid may be itself a result of marketing. The USDA's mandate isn't directly to promote health, but to promote agriculture and to help farmers flourish economically. In recommending three servings of dairy products per day, the food pyramid serves the interests of dairy farmers by promoting the whole class of dairy products, not just skim milk. According to the Environmental Working Group's Farm Subsidy Primer, the USDA spent

$4.8 billion in dairy subsidies between 1995 and 2009 ("Farm Subsidy Primer"). All these policies invest public dollars to create a steady consumption of dairy products and fundamentally depend on the premise that dairy products are good for us.

As we have seen, skim milk may be good for us but dairy products in general are more problematic. When the fat in whole milk is removed to make skim milk, it is not thrown away. It is used to make high-calorie, high-fat products like cheese and ice cream. Revealing its true ambivalence to public nutrition, the USDA warns against saturated fats in its food pyramid site while simultaneously working with companies like Domino's Pizza to increase the amount of cheese in their products. According to the *New York Times* (Moss), the USDA helped Domino's create a pizza with 40 percent more cheese and paid for a $12 million ad campaign to promote it. The *New York Times* further writes that Americans now consume almost three times as much cheese as we did in 1970. At a time of a national obesity epidemic, the promotion of dairy products either directly or indirectly introduces high-calorie, high-saturated fat foods into our diet while making many persons think they are eating healthfully.

5   Finally, I would like to suggest a third criterion for health food. A true health food should be good not only for our bodies but also for the earth. Milk, as it is currently produced in the United States, clearly does not meet this criterion. According to environmental writer Jim Motavalli, both "the front and rear ends of a cow" compete with coal plant smokestacks and vehicle tail pipes as "iconic" causes of global warming and environmental degradation. Drawing on statistical sources from both the United Nations and the USDA, Motavalli states that livestock in the United States consume 90 percent of the soy crop and more than 70 percent of the corn and grain crops—foods that could otherwise be used for people and could be grown in a more environmentally friendly way. Not only do cattle consume much of the world's grain supply, the need to clear space for grazing contributes to the destruction of rain forests. The other end of the cow, says Motavalli, is equally destructive. While chewing their cuds, cows directly emit methane gas (according to Motavalli, methane has a greenhouse effect 23 times more potent than carbon dioxide) and the concentration of their manure in factory farm sludge ponds produces ammonia, nitrous oxide, and additional methane. According to Motavalli, cows produce a staggering amount of manure ("five tons of waste for every U.S. citizen"), producing 18 percent of the world's greenhouse gases—more than all of the world's cars, trains, and planes. Motavalli also cites additional health risks posed by cows, including dangers of disease from unsafe processing of manure and from antibiotic-resistant bacteria (half of the world's antibiotics are given to cattle instead of humans).

In sum, there is no doubt that skim milk, along with low-fat yogurt and cheese, is a vital source of bone-building calcium and belongs on our list of health foods. But for most people, "milk" evokes dairy products in general, all of which we tend to associate with health. What we don't picture is the extra sugar and saturated fat in whole milk and cheese nor the environmental dangers of the dairy and livestock industries in general. From the perspective of the earth, perhaps dairy products should not be considered a health food at all.

Works Cited

"Farm Subsidy Primer." *Environmental Working Group,* farm.ewg.org/subsidyprimer.php. Accessed 8 Apr. 2016.

Moss, Michael. "While Warning about Fat, U.S. Pushes Cheese Sales." *The New York Times,* 6 Nov. 2010, www.nytimes.com/2010/11/07/us/07fat.html.

Motavalli, Jim. "The Meat of the Matter." *Orlando Weekly,* 31 July 2008, www.orlandoweekly.com/orlando/the-meat-of-the-matter/Content?oid=2273952.

U.S. Department of Agriculture, Center for Nutrition Policy and Promotion. *MyPyramid,* www.cnpp.usda.gov/mypyramid. Accessed 8 Apr. 2016.

Critiquing "Is Milk a Health Food?"

MyWritingLab™

1. Identify the following features of Arthur's essay: (1) his implied definition of "health food"; (2) his criteria for determining whether a borderline case is a health food; (3) his "match" arguments showing whether milk fits each of the criteria.
2. Do you agree with Arthur's criterion that a true health food ought to be good for the planet as well as good for the body?
3. Based on Arthur's argument, do you think the inclusion of dairy products in the USDA's recommendations for a healthy diet is still justified? Visit the USDA's new nutrition Web site, www.choosemyplate.gov. Would you suggest changes to these USDA recommendations? If so, what and why?

The second reading, by student Alex Mullen, was also written for the definition assignment on page 238. Alex's argument was stimulated by class discussions of property ownership in digital environments.

A Pirate But Not a Thief: What Does "Stealing" Mean in a Digital Environment?

ALEX MULLEN (STUDENT)

I am a pirate. In the eyes of the law, I could face serious punishment in fines, up to thousands of dollars, or jail time for my crime. Legally, it matters very little that my crime is one perpetrated by millions of people every year (you yourself may be guilty of it) or that there are far worse offenders out there. But before we get out the noose and head for the yardarm, I think I ought to describe my crime. In my History of Film class we were asked to watch Jean Renoir's *La Grande Illusion.* Now, if you've spent any time searching for 1930s foreign films you will undoubtedly know what a pain it is to find them, and of the twenty or so films we watched for my class a grand total of three were available on streaming sites such as Netflix, Hulu, and YouTube. While there were several copies of this particular film at my

University Library, all had been checked out. I planned to make a journey to the fabled Scarecrow Video (one of the largest rental libraries in the United States), but time was running low at this point. Finally, I broke down and used a person-to-person torrent site to download the film illegally. In the end all the trouble was worthwhile, as *La Grande Illusion* remains one of the greatest films I have ever seen. After watching it several times and writing a brief paper, I deleted the film from my computer. Although I feel that my action was justifiable, many people think what I did was no better than shoplifting and that I am guilty of theft. As a film lover and aspiring filmmaker, I am conflicted on the issue of online piracy. Nevertheless, I contend that what I did wasn't stealing because I deprived no one of either property or profit.

Let's take a step back from online piracy and focus simply on what stealing is in its most basic form. In my mind, stealing is the unlawful taking of another's property or profits without permission. It is the underlying assumption about what makes stealing wrong that needs to be considered. In the case of property, stealing is wrong not because the thief has the property but because the original owner has been deprived of it. The owner's loss causes the wrong, not the thief's gain. To give an example in very simple terms, if you have a phone case and I make a copy of that case (as is quite possible with a 3D printer), you still possess the original case, so no harm has been done to you the owner. However, suppose that you made your living by selling these phone cases. If I made exact duplicates with my 3-D printer and then sold these cases to others, then you could be deprived of profits that might otherwise have been received. Again, the wrong comes from the creator's loss and not the thief's gain.

Now let's focus on my particular example of online piracy. While I concede that piracy has the distinct potential to be stealing, I reject the accusation that all piracy is stealing. Based on the first part of my definition of stealing, my downloading *La Grande Illusion* deprived no consumer or creator of his or her copy of the film. This is why accusations that compare online piracy to shoplifting are false. In the case of shoplifting the owner/creator has one fewer piece of merchandise to make a profit on; with online piracy such loss does not occur because the original copy still exists.

However, the second part of my definition, which focuses on profits, still remains to be examined. Perhaps by downloading the film I have deprived the creators/owners of profits they would normally receive. Let me begin by saying that I never intended to purchase *La Grande Illusion*. While intention does not often register in legal matters, it does have a bearing on the type and degree of wrongdoing. Film industry lawyers often argue that every time a film is pirated the rightful owner is deprived of money because the pirate would have otherwise purchased the film. This claim, however, is fallacious because there is no way to show that these potential consumers would have purchased the film (I certainly wouldn't have). So while we may agree that some of these people would have purchased the film, it would be inaccurate to claim that in all cases piracy directly deprives creators of profit. I argue that what I did in the case of *La Grande Illusion* was more like borrowing than theft. Borrowing a film from a library (or renting it from a video store) has the same basic effect on the owner/creator as online piracy.

That is, a library or video store purchases a copy and then loans it or rents to others. Thus, many persons may not purchase a copy from the owner/creator because they can use this single public or commercial copy. Yet we do not consider borrowing or renting stealing even though it can have the same economic ramification as piracy. To go a step further, any time I borrow a film from a friend I cause the same outcome found so reprehensible in online piracy. In my case, instead of borrowing *La Grande Illusion* from an institution or business, I borrowed it from another individual via the Internet.

5   There is, of course, the counterargument that I could have rented the film from Scarecrow and thus stole profit from this film rental store much loved by film buffs. While it is true that I did not benefit Scarecrow with my patronage (a fact that I partially regret because I do try to support Scarecrow as often as possible), it would be inaccurate to say that I stole from Scarecrow. I am under no obligation to supply them with profits. When I pay money to a rental organization I am not paying for the film; I am paying for the service of being able to use their copy of the film for 24 hours. Had I purchased the film directly from the filmmaker, I would do the same harm to Scarecrow. Thus my not utilizing Scarecrow to obtain *La Grande Illusion* is not theft.

While I understand why the film industry (and also the music industry) views downloading from file-sharing torrent sites as piracy, their motives focus on preserving profits and blur the distinctions among "buying," "renting," and "borrowing." If I owned a DVD version of a movie and loaned it to a friend, no one would object. But if I make the same movie available to a friend via a torrent or file-sharing site, I become a pirate subject to huge fines. The intention is the same, only the format changes. The problem stems from the hazy concept of "ownership" in a digital environment where physical copies are replaced by digital copies. Certainly, we pay to possess digital copies of films, music, and video games, but is this really the same as physical ownership? After all I can lend, rent, or even sell a physical DVD, but such actions are impossible with digital copies without committing piracy. Our consumption of media is evolving rapidly, and while undoubtedly there will always be those who exploit these changes for personal gain, I feel we need to realize that our understanding of ownership, stealing, and illegal use must evolve along with these changes.

Critiquing "A Pirate But Not a Thief: What Does 'Stealing' Mean in a Digital Environment?"   MyWritingLab™

1. Identify the following features of Alex's essay: (1) his definition of "stealing"; (2) his examples to illustrate the definition; (3) his "match" argument showing whether his downloading of the film fits each of the criteria; and (4) his summary of and responses to objections and opposing views.
2. Do you agree with Alex's contention that his downloading the film was an act of "borrowing" rather than "stealing"?
3. What do you see as the major strengths of Alex's argument? How about weaknesses?
4. Do you think that the laws about online piracy should be changed? At what point does online piracy clearly become "stealing"?

Our last reading is an editorial from the *Los Angeles Times* on the day following a controversial decision by the Chicago director of the National Labor Relations Board that gave scholarship-receiving football players at Northwestern University the right to unionize. The decision turns on whether to place football players in the category of "student athlete" or in the category of "paid employee." The editorial illustrates how often definition issues play a role in public controversies.

College Football—Yes, It's a Job

LOS ANGELES TIMES EDITORIAL BOARD

University officials and the NCAA have been reluctant to acknowledge that top-tier college football programs are run these days less as athletic programs than as businesses. But a labor administrator's decision Wednesday that Northwestern University's scholarship football players are, in fact, employees with the right to unionize should get their attention.

This issue has been bubbling for decades as major sports programs evolved from important but ancillary parts of a college's mission into powerful businesses enriched by multimillion-dollar TV contracts and merchandising revenue, all built on the labor of student-athletes who received no compensation beyond scholarships. That might be a workable relationship when the players are truly students whose main focus is on academics. But as the ruling by Peter Sung Ohr, the

National Labor Relations Board's Chicago director, makes clear, scholarship players at Northwestern University are on campus first and foremost to play revenue-generating football. And that, he says, makes them employees.

The logic is clear. The players are accepted first as members of the football team, then as students, Ohr found. Players devote well over 40 hours a week to the team, overwhelming the amount of time they devote to academics. And players sign scholarship "tenders" that define conditions under which they will receive free tuition, room and board, and other support. If players fail to meet the conditions, they lose their scholarships. That, Ohr says, makes them workers. Significantly, Ohr found that non-scholarship players are not workers because they receive no compensation.

It's unclear whether the ruling will apply to other private colleges, such as USC, because Ohr's decision turns on specific circumstances at Northwestern. (The NLRB does not have jurisdiction over public universities such as UCLA.) It's also unclear whether the ruling will survive the anticipated appeals, because, among other issues, the players are not receiving direct wages but grants-in-kind.

What is clear is that the collegiate athletic system generates billions of dollars through the work of people who, if they get paid at all, receive nothing more than free college. No small thing, that, but hardly equitable given the economic scope of top-tier college athletics. This ruling could—and should—force universities and the NCAA to end what has become an exploitative system and make athletic programs subsidiary to the core mission: education.

Critiquing "College Football—Yes It's a Job"   MyWritingLab™

1. What is the implied definition of "employee" in this editorial?
2. How does the editorial make its "match" argument—that is, what evidence is used to support the case that scholarship football players are employees?
3. What is at stake in this argument?

Causal Arguments

12

What you will learn in this chapter:

12.1 To explain and illustrate kinds of causal arguments.

12.2 To explain how different causal mechanisms function in cause/consequence arguments.

12.3 To understand key causal terms and the need to avoid inductive fallacies in causal arguments.

12.4 To write your own cause or consequence argument.

We encounter causal issues all the time. What has caused the declining birth rate among teens in the United States? Why has the dance exercise called Zumba become popular globally? Why are American teens shopping less at traditional teenage clothing stores such as Abercrombie & Fitch and American Eagle Outfitters? Why are white teenage girls seven times as likely to smoke as African American teenage girls? Why do couples who live together before marriage have a higher divorce rate than those who don't? In addition to asking causal questions like these, we pose consequence questions as well: What might be the consequences of installing stricter proof-of-citizenship requirements for voting? What might be the social and economic consequences of establishing public preschool programs? What might be the consequences—expected or unexpected—of expanding commercial use of drones? Often arguments about causes and consequences have important stakes because they shape our view of reality and influence government policies and individual decisions. This chapter explains how to wrestle responsibly with cause/consequence issues to produce effective causal arguments.

Case 1   What Causes Global Warming?

One of the early clues linking global warming to atmospheric carbon dioxide (CO_2) came from side-by-side comparisons of graphs plotting atmospheric carbon dioxide and global temperatures over time. These graphs show that increases in global temperature parallel increases in the percentage of carbon dioxide in the atmosphere. However, the graphs show only a correlation, or link, between increased carbon dioxide and higher average temperature. To argue that an increase in CO_2 could cause global warming, scientists needed to explain the links in a causal chain. They could do so by comparing the earth to a greenhouse. Carbon dioxide, like glass in a greenhouse, lets some of the earth's heat radiate into space but also reflects some of it back to the earth. The higher the concentration of carbon dioxide, the more heat is reflected back to the earth.

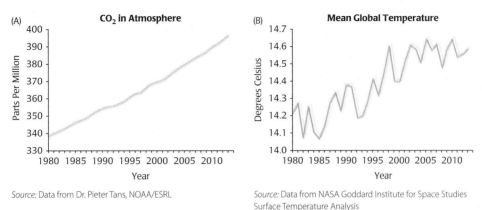

(A) CO$_2$ in Atmosphere

Source: Data from Dr. Pieter Tans, NOAA/ESRL

(B) Mean Global Temperature

Source: Data from NASA Goddard Institute for Space Studies Surface Temperature Analysis

Case 2   What Has Caused the Change in the Rate of Teen Pregnancies in the United State in the Last Five Years?

Although the United States still has the highest rate of teen pregnancies among developed countries, studies show a decline in teen pregnancies since the early 1990s. What has caused this decline? Some economists point to the recession as a major cause, claiming that as the job market has tightened, teens are afraid of not being able to get jobs when encumbered with babies. Other sources emphasize the role of parents in cautioning teens about irresponsible choices concerning sexual behavior and reproduction. A quite different explanation comes from a recent study by the National Bureau of Economic Research analyzing the impact of media images on viewers. This study has found a correlation between the decline in teen pregnancies and the watching of the MTV docudrama *16 and Pregnant* (premiered in 2009) and its spinoff *Teen Moms*. While Parents Television Council and other critics argue that these shows sensationalize and glamorize the lives of the teen moms, researchers, using Nielsen ratings and geographic data on viewership and data from Google Trends and Twitter, found that watching these shows "led to more searches and tweets regarding birth control and abortion, and ultimately led to a 5.7 percent reduction in teen births in the eighteen months" after *16 and Pregnant* first aired.* This study broadens social thinking on the use of reality TV and social media in promoting safe sex, as well as its potential value in addressing other social and health causes.

An Overview of Causal Arguments

12.1 To explain and illustrate kinds of causal arguments.

Typically, causal arguments try to show how one event brings about another. When causal investigation focuses on material objects—for example, one billiard ball striking another—the notion of causality

---

*Melissa S. Kearney and Phillip B. Levine. "Media Influences on Social Outcomes: The Impact of MTV's *16 and Pregnant* on Teen Childbearing," NBER Working Paper No. 19795, National Bureau of Economic Research, January 2014.

appears fairly straightforward. But when humans become the focus of a causal argument, the nature of causality becomes more vexing. If we say that something happened that "caused" a person to act in a certain way, what do we mean? Do we mean that she was "forced" to act in a certain way, thereby negating her free will (as in, an undiagnosed brain tumor caused her to act erratically), or do we mean more simply that she was "motivated" to act in a certain way (as in, her anger at her parents caused her to act erratically)? When we argue about causality in human beings, we must guard against confusing these two senses of "cause" or assuming that human behavior can be predicted or controlled in the same way that nonhuman behavior can. A rock dropped from a roof will always fall at thirty-two feet per second squared, and a rat zapped for turning left in a maze will always quit turning left. But if we raise interest rates, will consumers save more money? If so, how much? This is the sort of question we debate endlessly.

Kinds of Causal Arguments

Arguments about causality can take a variety of forms. Here are three typical kinds:

- **Speculations about possible causes.** Sometimes arguers speculate about possible causes of a phenomenon. For example, whenever a shooter opens fire on innocent bystanders (as in the 2012 Sandy Hook Elementary School massacre or the 2011 attempted assassination of Arizona Representative Gabrielle Giffords in a Tucson parking lot), social scientists, police investigators, and media commentators begin analyzing the causes. One of the most heavily debated shooting incidents occurred in 1999 at Columbine High School in Littleton, Colorado, when two male students opened fire on their classmates, killing thirteen people, wounding twenty-three others, and then shooting themselves. Figure 12.1 illustrates some of the proposed

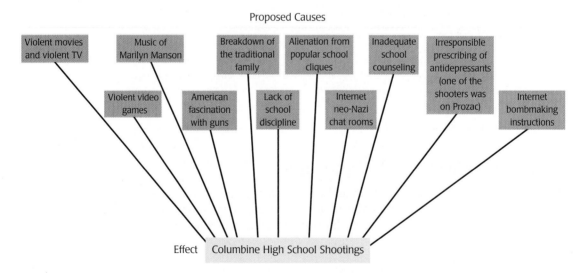

FIGURE 12.1 Speculation about possible causes: Columbine High School massacre

theories for the Columbine shootings. What was at stake was not only our desire to understand the sociocultural sources of school violence but also our desire to institute policies to prevent future school shootings. If a primary cause is the availability of guns, then we might push for more stringent gun control laws. But if the primary cause is the disintegration of the traditional family, the shooters' alienation from high school cliques, or the dangerous side effects of Prozac, then we might seek different solutions.

- **Arguments for an unexpected or surprising cause.** Besides sorting out possible causes of a phenomenon, sometimes arguers try to persuade readers to see the plausibility of an unexpected or surprising cause. This was the strategy used by syndicated columnist John Leo, who wanted readers to consider the role of violent video games as a contributing cause to the Columbine massacre.* After suggesting that the Littleton killings were partly choreographed on video game models, Leo suggested the causal chain shown in Figure 12.2.

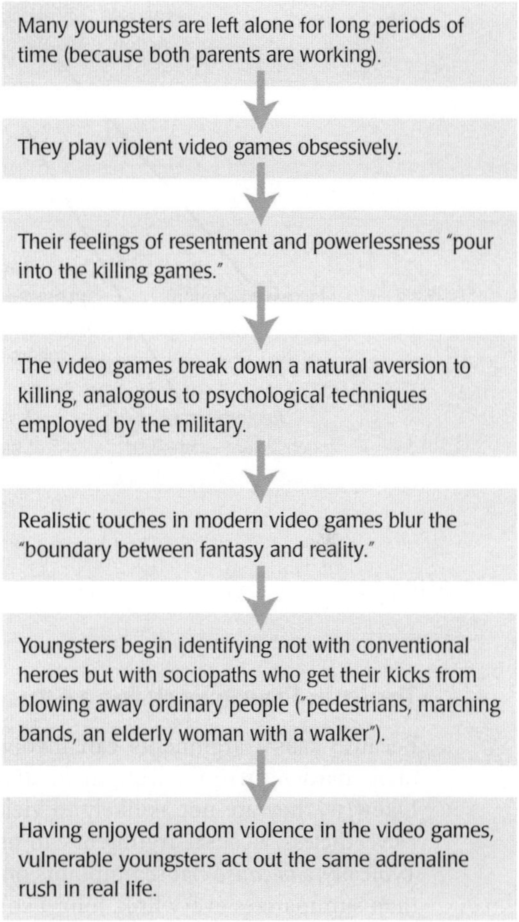

- **Predictions of consequences.** Still another frequently encountered kind of causal argument predicts the consequences of current, planned, or proposed actions or events. Consequence arguments have high stakes because we often judge actions on whether their benefits outweigh their costs. As we will see in Chapter 14, proposal arguments usually require writers to predict the consequences of a proposed action, do a cost/benefit analysis, and persuade readers that no unforeseen negative consequences will result. Just as a phenomenon can have multiple causes, it can also have multiple consequences. Figure 12.3 shows the consequence arguments considered by environmentalists who propose eliminating several dams on the Snake River in order to save salmon runs.

Many youngsters are left alone for long periods of time (because both parents are working).

↓

They play violent video games obsessively.

↓

Their feelings of resentment and powerlessness "pour into the killing games."

↓

The video games break down a natural aversion to killing, analogous to psychological techniques employed by the military.

↓

Realistic touches in modern video games blur the "boundary between fantasy and reality."

↓

Youngsters begin identifying not with conventional heroes but with sociopaths who get their kicks from blowing away ordinary people ("pedestrians, marching bands, an elderly woman with a walker").

↓

Having enjoyed random violence in the video games, vulnerable youngsters act out the same adrenaline rush in real life.

FIGURE 12.2   Argument for a surprising cause: Role of violent video games in the Columbine massacre

---

*John Leo, "Kill-for-Kicks Video Games Desensitizing Our Children," *Seattle Times* 27 April 1999, B4.

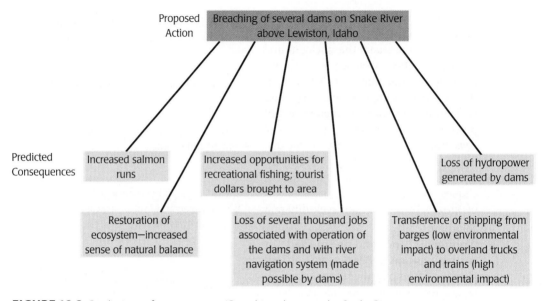

FIGURE 12.3 Predictions of consequences: Breaching dams on the Snake River

Toulmin Framework for a Causal Argument

Because causal arguments can involve lengthy or complex causal chains, they are often harder to summarize in *because* clauses than are other kinds of arguments. Likewise, they are not as likely to yield quick analysis through the Toulmin schema. Nevertheless, a causal argument can usually be stated as a claim with *because* clauses. Typically, a *because* clause pinpoints one or two key elements in the causal chain rather than summarizes every link. John Leo's argument linking the Columbine massacre to violent video games could be summarized in the following claim with a *because* clause:

> Violent video games may have been a contributing cause to the Littleton massacre because playing these games can make random, sociopathic violence seem pleasurable.

Once stated as an enthymeme, the argument can be analyzed using Toulmin's schema. It is easiest to apply Toulmin's schema to causal arguments if you think of the grounds as the observable phenomena at any point in the causal chain and the warrants as the shareable assumptions about causality that join links together.

Toulmin Analysis of the Violent Video Games Argument

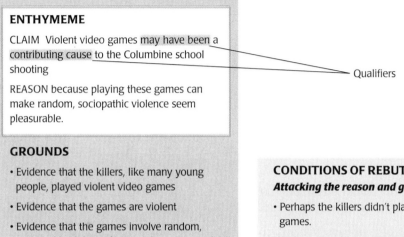

ENTHYMEME

CLAIM Violent video games may have been a contributing cause to the Columbine school shooting

REASON because playing these games can make random, sociopathic violence seem pleasurable.

Qualifiers

GROUNDS

- Evidence that the killers, like many young people, played violent video games
- Evidence that the games are violent
- Evidence that the games involve random, sociopathic violence (not good guys versus bad guys) such as killing ordinary people—marching bands, little old ladies, etc.
- Evidence that young people derive pleasure from these games

CONDITIONS OF REBUTTAL
Attacking the reason and grounds

- Perhaps the killers didn't play violent video games.
- Perhaps the video games are no more violent than traditional kids' games such as cops and robbers.
- Perhaps the video games do not feature sociopathic killing.

WARRANT

If young people derive pleasure from random, sociopathic killing in video games, they can transfer this pleasure to real life, thus leading to the Columbine shooting.

BACKING

- Testimony from psychologists
- Evidence that violent video games desensitize people to violence
- Analogy to military training in which video games are used to "make killing a reflex action"
- Evidence that the distinction between fantasy and reality becomes especially blurred for unstable young people

CONDITIONS OF REBUTTAL
Attacking the warrant and backing

- Perhaps kids are fully capable of distinguishing fantasy from reality.
- Perhaps the games are just fun with no transference to real life.
- Perhaps the games are substantially different from military training games.

■ ■ ■   **FOR WRITING AND DISCUSSION** **Developing Causal Chains**   MyWritingLab™

Individual task:

1. Create a causal chain to show how the item on the left could help lead to the item on the right.

   a. Invention of the automobile   Changes in sexual mores

   b. Popularity of cell phones   Reduction in size and importance of phone directories

   c. Growth of social media around the world   The increase in social activism and political uprisings such as Arab Spring

   d. Millennials' desire for an urban lifestyle   Redesign of cities

   e. Development of way to prevent rejections in transplant operations   Liberalization of euthanasia laws

2. For each of your causal chains, compose a claim with an attached *because* clause summarizing one or two key links in the causal chain—for example, "Millennials' desire for an urban lifestyle is spurring the redesign of cities because Millennials' car- and house-free habits are prompting developers to build new high-density urban communities that offer easy access to work and pleasure."

   Group task: Share your causal claim and *because* clause links with your other class members.   ■ ■ ■

Two Methods for Arguing that One Event Causes Another

12.2 To explain how different causal mechanisms function in cause/consequence arguments.

One of the first things you need to do when preparing a causal argument is to note exactly what sort of causal relationship you are dealing with—a onetime phenomenon, a recurring phenomenon, or a puzzling trend. Here are some examples.

Kind of Phenomenon	Examples
Onetime phenomenon	■ Mysterious disappearance of Malaysia Airlines Flight 370 in March 2014 ■ Firing of a popular teacher at your university ■ 2007 collapse of a freeway bridge in Minneapolis
Recurring phenomenon	■ Eating disorders ■ Road rage ■ Tendency of Chevy Cobalt engines to shut off unexpectedly
Puzzling trend	■ Increase in the number of events counted as Olympic sports ■ Declining audience for TV news ■ Declining populations of both bats and honeybees

With recurring phenomena or with trends, one has the luxury of being able to study multiple cases, often over time. You can interview people, make repeated observations, or study the conditions in which the puzzling phenomenon occurs. But with a onetime occurrence, one's approach is more like that of a detective than a scientist. Because one can't repeat the event with different variables, one must rely only on the immediate evidence at hand, which can quickly disappear. Having briefly stated these words of caution, let's turn now to two main ways that you can argue that one event causes another.

First Method: Explain the Causal Mechanism Directly

The most convincing kind of causal argument identifies every link in the causal chain, showing how an initiating cause leads step by step to an observed effect. A causes B, which causes C, which causes D. In some cases, all you have to do is fill in the missing links. In other cases—when your assumptions about how one step leads to the next may seem questionable to your audience—you have to argue for the causal connection with more vigor.

A careful spelling out of each step in the causal chain is the technique used by science writer Robert S. Devine in the following passage from his article "The Trouble with Dams." Although the benefits of dams are widely understood (they produce pollution-free electricity while providing flood control, irrigation, barge transportation, and recreational boating), the negative effects are less commonly known and understood. In this article, Devine tries to persuade readers that dams have serious negative consequences. In the following passage, he explains how dams reduce salmon flows by slowing the migration of smolts (newly hatched, young salmon) to the sea.

Causal Argument Describing a Causal Chain

Such transformations lie at the heart of the ongoing environmental harm done by dams. Rivers are rivers because they flow, and the nature of their flows defines much of their character. When dams alter flows, they alter the essence of rivers.

Consider the erstwhile river behind Lower Granite (a dam on Idaho's Snake River). Although I was there in the springtime, when I looked at the water it was moving too slowly to merit the word "flow"—and Lower Granite Lake isn't even one of the region's enormous storage reservoirs, which bring currents to a virtual halt. In the past, spring snowmelt sent powerful currents down the Snake during April and May. Nowadays hydropower operators of the Columbia and Snake systems store the runoff behind the dams and release it during the winter, when demand—and the price—for electricity rises. Over the ages, however, many populations of salmon have adapted to the spring surge. The smolts used the strong flows to migrate, drifting downstream with the current. During the journey smolts' bodies undergo physiological changes that require them to reach salt water quickly. Before dams backed up the Snake, smolts coming down from Idaho got to the sea in six to twenty days; now it takes from sixty to ninety days, and few of the young salmon reach salt water in time. The emasculated current is the single largest reason that the number of wild adult salmon migrating up the Snake each year has crashed from predevelopment runs of 100,000–200,000 to what was projected to be 150–750 this year.*

---

*Robert S. Devine, "The Trouble with Dams," *Atlantic* (August 1995), 64–75. The example quotation is from page 70.

Smolts use the river flow to reach the sea.

$\downarrow$

Dams restrict the flow of the river.

$\downarrow$

Before development, a trip that took 6 to 20 days now takes 60 to 90 days.

$\downarrow$

Migrating smolts undergo physiological changes that demand quick access to salt water.

$\downarrow$

Lengthened migration time kills the smolts.

This tightly constructed passage connects various causal chains to explain the decline of salmon runs.

Describing each link in the causal chain—and making each link seem as plausible as possible—is the most persuasive means of convincing readers that a specific cause leads to a specific effect.

Second Method: Infer Causal Links Using Inductive Reasoning

If we can't explain a causal link directly, we often employ a reasoning strategy called *induction*. Through induction we infer a general conclusion based on a limited number of specific cases. For example, if on several occasions you got a headache after drinking red wine but not after drinking white wine, you would be likely to conclude inductively that red wine causes you to get headaches, although you can't explain directly how it does so. However, because there are almost always numerous variables involved, inductive reasoning gives only probable truths, not certain ones.

Three Ways of Thinking Inductively   When your brain thinks inductively, it sorts through data looking for patterns of similarity and difference. In this section we explain three ways of thinking inductively: looking for a common element, looking for a single difference, and looking for correlations.

1. **Look for a common element.** One kind of inductive thinking places you on a search for a common element that can explain recurrences of the same phenomenon. For example, psychologists attempting to understand the causes of anorexia have discovered that many anorexics (but not all) come from perfectionist, highly work-oriented homes that emphasize duty and responsibility. This common element is thus a suspected causal factor leading to anorexia.

2. **Look for a single difference.** Another approach is to look for a single difference that may explain the appearance of a new phenomenon. When infant death rates in the state of Washington shot up in July and August 1986, one event making these two months different stood out: increased radioactive fallout over Washington from the April Chernobyl nuclear meltdown in Ukraine. This single difference led some researchers to suspect radiation as a possible cause of the increase in infant deaths.

3. **Look for correlations.** Still another method of induction is correlation, which means that two events or phenomena tend to occur together but doesn't imply that one causes the other. For example, there is a correlation between nearsightedness and intelligence. (That is, in a given sample of nearsighted people and people with normal eyesight, the nearsighted group will have a somewhat higher mean IQ score.) But the direction of causality isn't clear. It could be that high intelligence causes people to read more, thus ruining their eyes (high intelligence causes nearsightedness). Or it could

be that nearsightedness causes people to read more, thus raising their intelligence (nearsightedness causes high intelligence). Or it could be that some unknown phenomenon, perhaps a gene, is related to both nearsightedness and intelligence. So keep in mind that correlation is not causation—it simply suggests possible causation.

■ ■ ■ **FOR CLASS DISCUSSION**   Developing Plausible Causal Chains Based
on Correlations

Working individually or in small groups, develop plausible causal chains that may explain the relationship between the following pairs of phenomena:

a. A person who registers a low stress level on an electrochemical stress meter — does daily meditation

b. A binge drinker at college parties — has increased risk of becoming a perpetrator or victim of sexual violence

c. A person who grew up in a house with two bathrooms — is likely to have higher SAT scores than a person who grew up in a one-bathroom home

d. A person who takes prescription pain medicine — is more likely to develop dependency on heroin and opiates

e. A member of the National Rifle Association — supports the death penalty

■ ■ ■

EXAMINING VISUAL ARGUMENTS

MyWritingLab™

A Causal Claim

This billboard is part of a Texas campaign to fight sex trafficking. How do both the text and image in this billboard suggest links in a causal chain? Although this ad oversimplifies the complex issue of human trafficking, and some would say it represents only one view of sex workers, how do both the words and the choice of images make powerful appeals to both *logos* and *pathos*?

Key Terms and Inductive Fallacies in Causal Arguments

12.3 To understand key causal terms and the need to avoid inductive fallacies in causal arguments.

Because causal arguments are often easier to conduct if writer and reader share a few specialized terms and concepts, this section explains key terms in causal reasoning and offers ways to avoid inductive fallacies.

A Glossary of Key Terms

- **The problem of oversimplified cause.** One of the great temptations is to look for *the* cause of something, as if a phenomenon had only one cause rather than multiple causes. For example, in recent years the number of persons in the United States sending out Christmas cards has declined substantially. Many commentators attribute the decline to the increasing use of Facebook, which keeps old friends in touch year-round, eliminating the need for holiday "family letters." But there may be other causes also, such as a decline in the number of nuclear families, fewer networks of long-term friends, or generational shifts away from older traditions. When you make a causal argument, be especially careful how you use words such as *all, most, some, the,* or *in part*. For example, to say that *all* the decline in Christmas cards is caused by Facebook is to make a universal statement about Facebook as *the* cause. An argument will be stronger and more accurate if the arguer makes a less sweeping statement: *Some* of the cause for the decline in Christmas cards can be attributed to Facebook. Arguers sometimes deliberately mix up these quantifiers to misrepresent and dismiss opposing views.

- **Immediate and remote causes.** Every causal chain extends backward indefinitely into the past. An immediate cause is the closest in time to the event being examined. Consider the causes for the release of nuclear contaminants around the Fukushima nuclear power plant following the 2011 earthquake off the coast of Japan. The immediate cause was loss of power to the water pumps that cooled the reactor's fuel rods, causing the rods to overheat and partially melt. A slightly less immediate cause (several days earlier) was the earthquake-produced tsunami that had swept away the diesel fuel tanks needed to run the backup generators. These immediate causes can be contrasted with a remote cause—in this case, a late-1960s design decision that used backup diesel generators to power the water pumps in case of an electrical power loss to the reactor facility. Still more remote causes were the economic and regulatory systems in the late 1960s that led to this particular design.

- **Precipitating and contributing causes.** These terms are similar to *immediate* and *remote* causes but don't designate a temporal link going into the past. Rather, they refer to a main cause emerging out of a background of subsidiary causes. If, for example, a husband and wife decide to separate, the *precipitating cause* may be a stormy fight over money, after which one of the partners (or both) says, "I've had enough." In contrast, *contributing causes* would be all the background factors that are dooming the marriage—preoccupation with their careers, disagreement about priorities, in-law problems, and so forth. Note that contributing causes and the precipitating cause all coexist at the same time.

■ **Constraints.** Sometimes an effect occurs because some stabilizing factor—a *constraint*—is removed. In other words, the presence of a constraint may keep a certain effect from occurring. For example, in the marriage we have been discussing, the presence of children in the home may be a constraint against divorce; as soon as the children graduate from high school and leave home, the marriage may well dissolve.

■ **Necessary and sufficient causes.** A *necessary cause* is one that has to be present for a given effect to occur. For example, fertility drugs are necessary to cause the conception of septuplets. Every couple who has septuplets must have used fertility drugs. In contrast, a *sufficient cause* is one that always produces or guarantees a given effect. Smoking more than a pack of cigarettes per day is sufficient to raise the cost of one's life insurance policy. This statement means that if you are a smoker, no matter how healthy you appear to be, life insurance companies will always place you in a higher risk bracket and charge you a higher premium. In some cases, a single cause can be both necessary and sufficient. For example, lack of ascorbic acid is both a necessary and a sufficient cause of scurvy. (Think of those old-time sailors who didn't eat fruit for months.) It is a necessary cause because you can't get scurvy any other way except through absence of ascorbic acid; it is a sufficient cause because the absence of ascorbic acid always causes scurvy.

Avoiding Common Inductive Fallacies that Can Lead to Wrong Conclusions

Largely because of its power, informal induction can often lead to wrong conclusions. You should be aware of two common fallacies of inductive reasoning that can tempt you into erroneous assumptions about causality.

■ *Post hoc* **fallacy:** The *post hoc, ergo propter hoc* fallacy ("after this, therefore because of this") mistakes sequence for cause. Just because event A regularly precedes event B doesn't mean that event A causes event B. The same reasoning that tells us that flipping a switch causes the light to go on can make us believe that low levels of radioactive fallout from the Chernobyl nuclear disaster caused a sudden rise in infant death rates in the state of Washington. The nuclear disaster clearly preceded the rise in death rates. But did it clearly *cause* it? Our point is that precedence alone is no proof of causality and that we are guilty of this fallacy whenever we are swayed to believe that one thing causes another just because it comes first.

■ **Hasty generalization:** The *hasty generalization* fallacy occurs when you make a generalization based on too few cases or too little consideration of alternative explanations: You flip the switch, but the lightbulb doesn't go on. You conclude—too hastily—that the lightbulb has burned out. (Perhaps the power has gone off or the switch is broken.) How many trials does it take before you can make a justified generalization rather than a hasty generalization? It is difficult to say for sure.

Both the *post hoc* fallacy and the hasty generalization fallacy remind us that induction requires a leap from individual cases to a general principle and that it is always possible to leap too soon.

■ ■ ■ **FOR CLASS DISCUSSION** Brainstorming Causes and Constraints

The terms in the preceding glossary can be effective brainstorming tools for thinking of possible causes of an event. For the following events, try to think of as many causes as possible by brainstorming possible *immediate causes, remote causes, precipitating causes, contributing causes,* and *constraints:*

1. Working individually, make a list of different kinds of causes/constraints for one of the following:
    a. Your decision to attend your present college
    b. An important event in your life or your family (a job change, a major move, etc.)
    c. A personal opinion you hold that is not widely shared
2. Working as a group, make a list of different kinds of causes/constraints for one of the following:
    a. Why women's fashion and beauty magazines are the most frequently purchased magazines in college bookstores
    b. Why American students consistently score below Asian and European students in academic achievement
    c. Why large supermarket chains are selling more organic food   ■ ■ ■

WRITING ASSIGNMENT A Causal Argument   MyWritingLab™

12.4 To write your own cause or consequence argument. | Choose an issue about the causes or consequences of a trend, event, or other phenomenon. Write an argument that persuades an audience to accept your explanation of the causes or consequences of your chosen phenomenon. Within your essay you should examine alternative hypotheses or opposing views and explain your reasons for rejecting them. You can imagine your issue either as a puzzle or as a disagreement. If a puzzle, your task will be to create a convincing case for an audience that doesn't have an answer to your causal question already in mind. If a disagreement, your task will be more overtly persuasive because your goal will be to change your audience's views.

Exploring Ideas

Arguments about causes and consequences abound in public, professional, or personal life, so you shouldn't have difficulty finding a causal issue worth investigating and arguing.

In response to a public controversy over why there are fewer women than men on science and math faculties, student writer Julee Christianson argued that culture, not biology, is the primary cause (see pages 265–272). Student writer Carlos

Macias, puzzled by the ease with which college students are issued credit cards, wrote a researched argument disentangling the factors leading young people to bury themselves in debt (see pages 274–277). Other students have focused on causal issues such as these: Why do kids join gangs? What are the consequences of mandatory drug testing (written by a student who has to take amphetamines for narcolepsy)? What has happened since 1970 to cause young people to delay getting married? (This question was initiated by the student's interest in the statistical table in Chapter 9, page 201.)

If you have trouble finding a causal issue to write about, you can often create provocative controversies among your classmates through the following strategies:

- **Make a list of unusual likes and dislikes.** Think about unusual things that people like or dislike. You could summarize the conventional explanations that people give for an unusual pleasure or aversion and then argue for a surprising or unexpected cause. What attracts people to extreme sports? How do you explain the popularity of the paleo diet or of *The Hunger Games*?
- **Make a list of puzzling events or trends.** Another strategy is to make a list of puzzling phenomena and then try to explain their causes. Start with onetime events (a curriculum change at your school, the sudden popularity of a new app). Then list puzzling recurring events (failure of knowledgeable teenagers to practice safe sex). Finally, list some recent trends (growth of naturopathic medicine, increased interest in tattoos). Engage classmates in discussions of one or more of the items on your list. Look for places of disagreement as entry points into the conversation.
- **Brainstorm consequences of a recent or proposed action.** Arguments about consequences are among the most interesting and important of causal disputes. If you can argue for an unanticipated consequence of a real or proposed action, whether good or bad, you can contribute importantly to the conversation. What might be the consequences, for example, of placing "green taxes" on coal-produced electricity; of legalizing marijuana; of overturning *Roe v. Wade*; or of requiring national public service for all young adults?

Identifying Your Audience and Determining What's at Stake

Before drafting your argument, identify your targeted audience and determine what's at stake. Consider your responses to the following questions:

- What audience are you targeting? What background do they need to understand your issue? How much do they already care about it?
- Before they read your argument, what stance on your issue do you imagine them holding? What change do you want to bring about in their views?
- What will they find new or surprising about your argument?
- What objections might they raise? What counterarguments or alternative points of view will you need to address?
- Why does your argument matter? Who might be threatened or made uncomfortable by your views? What is at stake?

Organizing a Causal Argument

At the outset, it is useful to know some of the standard ways that a causal argument can be organized. Later, you may decide on a different organizational pattern, but the standard ways shown in Organization Plans 1, 2, and 3 on pages 263–264 will help you get started.

Plans 2 and 3 are similar in that they examine numerous possible causes or consequences. Plan 2, however, tries to establish the relative importance of each cause or consequence, whereas Plan 3 aims at rejecting the causes or consequences normally assumed by the audience and argues for an unexpected, surprising cause or consequence. Plan 3 can also be used when your purpose is to change your audience's mind about a cause or consequence.

Questioning and Critiquing a Causal Argument

Knowing how to question and critique a causal argument will help you anticipate opposing views in order to strengthen your own. It will also help you rebut another person's causal argument. Here are some useful questions to ask:

- When you explain the links in a causal chain, can a skeptic point out weaknesses in any of the links?
- If you speculate about the causes of a phenomenon, could a skeptic argue for different causes or arrange your causes in a different order of importance?
- If you argue for a surprising cause or a surprising consequence of a phenomenon, could a skeptic point out alternative explanations that would undercut your argument?
- If your argument depends on inferences from data, could a skeptic question the way the data were gathered or interpreted? Could a skeptic claim that the data weren't relevant (for example, research done with lab animals might not apply to humans)?
- If your causal argument depends on a correlation between one phenomenon and another, could a skeptic argue that the direction of causality should be reversed or that an unidentified, third phenomenon is the real cause? ■

Organization Plan 1: Argument Explaining Links in a Causal Chain

Introduce the issue and state your claim.	• Engage reader's interest in your causal issue and show why it is controversial or problematic. • Show what's at stake. • State your claim.
Explain the links in the chain going from cause to effect.	• Explain the links and their connections in order. • Anticipate and respond to possible objections if needed.
Conclude.	• Perhaps sum up your argument. • Return to the "big picture" of what's at stake. • End with something memorable.

Organization Plan 2: Argument Proposing Multiple Causes or Consequences of a Phenomenon

Introduce the issue and state your claim.	• Engage reader's interest in your causal issue and show why it is problematic or controversial. • Show what's at stake. • State your claim.
Propose relative contributions of different causes of a phenomenon or relative importance of different consequences.	• Describe the first possible cause or consequence and explain your reasoning. • Continue with the rest of your causes or consequences. • Arrange causes or consequences in increasing order of importance, significance, or surprise.
Respond to possible objections to your argument (if needed).	• Anticipate and summarize possible objections. • Respond through rebuttal or concession.
Conclude.	• Perhaps sum up your argument. • Return to the "big picture" of what's at stake. • End with something memorable.

Organization Plan 3: Argument Proposing a Surprising Causes or Consequence

Introduce the issue and state your claim.	• Engage reader's interest in your causal issue and show why it is problematic or controversial. • Show what's at stake. • State your claim.

Reject commonly assumed causes or consequences.	• Describe the first commonly assumed cause or consequence and show why you don't think the explanation is adequate. • Continue with the rest of your commonly assumed causes or consequences.

Argue for your surprising cause or consequence.	• Describe your surprising cause or consequence. • Explain your causal reasoning. • Anticipate and respond to possible objections if needed.

Conclude.	• Perhaps sum up your argument. • Return to the "big picture" of what's at stake. • End with something memorable.

READINGS

Our first reading, by student Julee Christianson, was written in response to the assignment in this chapter. Julee was entering an intense public debate about the underrepresentation of women on prestigious math and science faculties, a controversy initiated by Lawrence Summers, then president of Harvard, who suggested the possibility of a genetic cause for this phenomenon. A furious reaction ensued. The Web site of the Women in Science and Engineering Leadership Institute has extensive coverage of the controversy, including Summers's original speech.

Julee's argument illustrates the format and documentation system for a paper following the guidelines of the American Psychological Association (APA).

Why Lawrence Summers Was Wrong: Culture Rather Than Biology

Explains the Underrepresentation of Women in Science and Mathematics

Julee Christianson

December 8, 2008

Why Lawrence Summers Was Wrong: Culture Rather

Than Biology Explains the Underrepresentation of

Women in Science and Mathematics

In 2005, Harvard University's president, Lawrence H. Summers, gave a con-troversial speech that suggested that the underrepresentation of women in tenured positions in math and science departments is partly caused by biological differences. In his address, Summers proposed three hypotheses explaining why women shy away from math and science careers. First, he gave a "high-powered job hypothesis" that stated that women naturally want to start a family and therefore will not have the time or desire to commit to the high-stress workload required for research in math and science. His second hypothesis was that genetic differences between the sexes cause more males than females to have high aptitude for math and science. Lastly, he mentioned the hypothesis that women are underrepresented because of discrimina-tion, but he dismissed discrimination as an insignificant factor. It was Summers's second hypothesis about biological differences that started a heated national debate. The academic world seems split over this nature/nurture issue. Although there is some evidence that biology plays a role in determining math ability, I argue that cul-ture plays a much larger role, both in the way that women are socialized and in the continued existence of male discrimination against women in male-dominated fields.

Evidence supporting the role of biology in determining math ability is effectively presented by Steven Pinker (2005), a Harvard psychologist who agrees with Summers. In his article "The Science of Difference: Sex Ed," Pinker focuses extensively on Summers's argument. According to Pinker, "in many traits, men show greater vari-ance than women, and are disproportionately found at both the low and high ends of the distribution" (p. 16). He explains that males and females have similar average scores on math tests but that there are more males than females in the top and the bottom percentiles. This greater variance means that there are disproportionately more male than female math geniuses (and math dunces) and thus more male than female candidates for top math and science positions at major research universities. Pinker explains this greater variance through evolutionary biology: men can pass on their genes to dozens of offspring, whereas women can pass on their genes to only a few. Pinker also argues that men and women have different brain structures that result in different kinds of thinking. For example, Pinker cites research that shows that on average men are better at mental rotation of figures and mathematical word problems, while women are better at remembering locations, doing mathematical calculations, reading faces, spelling, and using language. Not only do males and females think differently, but they release different hormones. These hormones help shape gender because males release more testosterone and females more estrogen, meaning that men are more aggressive and apt to take risks, while women "are more solicitous to their children" (p. 16). One example Pinker uses to support his biological hypothesis is the case of males born with abnormal genitals and raised as females. These children have more testosterone than normal female children, and many times they show characteristically male interests and behavior. Pinker uses these cases as evidence that no matter how a child is raised, the child's biology determines the child's interests.

Although Pinker demonstrates that biology plays some role in determining math aptitude, he almost completely ignores the much larger role of discrimination and socialization in shaping the career paths of women. According to an editorial from *Nature Neuroscience* (2005), "[t]he evidence to support [Summers's] hypothesis of 'innate difference' turns out to be quite slim" ("Separating," p. 253). The editorial reports that intercultural studies of the variance between boys' and girls' scores on math tests show significant differences between countries. For example, in Iceland girls outscore boys on math tests. The editorial also says that aptitude tests are not very good at predicting the future success of students and that the "SATs tend to underpredict female and over-predict male academic performance" (p. 253). The editorial doesn't deny that men and women's brains work differently, but states that the differences are too small to be blamed for the underrepresentation of women in math and science careers.

If biology doesn't explain the low number of women choosing math and science careers, then what is the cause? Many believe the cause is culture, especially the gender roles children are taught at a very young age. One such believer is Deborah L. Rhode (1997), an attorney and social scientist who specializes in ethics and gender, law, and public policy. Rhode describes the different gender roles females and males are expected to follow from a very young age. Gender roles are portrayed in children's books and television shows. These gender roles are represented by male characters as heroes and problem solvers, while the female characters are distressed damsels. Another example of gender roles is that only a very small number of these shows and books portray working mothers or stay-at-home fathers. Rhodes also discusses how movies and popular music, especially rap and heavy metal, encourage violence and objectify women. As girls grow up, they face more and more gender stereotypes, from toys to

WHY LAWRENCE SUMMERS WAS WRONG   4

magazines. Parents give their boys interactive, problem-solving toys such as chemistry sets and telescopes, while girls are left with dolls. Although more organizations such as the Girl Scouts of America, who sponsor the Web site Girls Go Tech.org, are trying to interest girls in science and math and advertise careers in those fields to girls, the societal forces working against this encouragement are also still pervasive. For example, magazines for teenage girls encourage attracting male attention and the importance of looks, while being smart and successful is considered unattractive. Because adolescents face so many gender stereotypes, it is no wonder that these stereotypes shape the career paths they choose later in life. The gender roles engraved in our adolescents' minds cause discrimination against women later in life. Once women are socialized to see themselves as dependent and not as smart as males, it becomes very difficult to break away from these gender stereotypes. With gender bias so apparent in our society, it is hard for females to have high enough self-confidence to continue to compete with males in many fields.

The effect of socialization begins at a very early age. One study (Clearfield & Nelson, 2006) shows how parents unconsciously send gendered messages to their infants and toddlers. This study examined differences in mothers' speech patterns and play behaviors based on the gender of infants ranging from six months to fourteen months. Although there was no difference in the actual play behavior of male and female infants, the researchers discovered interesting differences in the way mothers interacted with daughters versus sons. Mothers of daughters tended to ask their daughters more questions, encouraging social interaction, whereas mothers of sons were less verbal, encouraging their sons to be more independent. The researchers concluded that "the mothers in our study may have been teaching their infants about gender roles through modeling and reinforcement.... Thus girls may acquire the knowledge that they are 'supposed' to engage in higher levels of interaction with other people and display more verbal behavior than boys.... In contrast, the boys were reinforced for exploring on their own" (p. 136).

One of the strongest arguments against the biological hypothesis comes from a transgendered Stanford neurobiologist, Ben A. Barres (2006), who has been a scientist first as a woman and then as a man. In his article "Does Gender Matter?" Barres states that "there is little evidence that gender differences in [mathematical] abilities exist, are innate or are even relevant to the lack of advancement of women in science" (p. 134). Barres provides much anecdotal evidence of the way women are discriminated against

APA

WHY LAWRENCE SUMMERS WAS WRONG   5

in this male-dominated field. Barres notes that simply putting a male name rather than a female name on an article or résumé increases its perceived value. He also describes research showing that men and women do equally well in gender-blind academic competitions but that men win disproportionately in contests where gender is revealed.

As Barres says, "The bar is unconsciously raised so high for women and minority candidates that few emerge as winners" (p. 134). In one study reported by Barres, women applying for a research grant needed more than twice the productivity of men in order to be considered equally competent. As a female-to-male transgendered person, Barres has personally experienced discrimination when trying to succeed in the science and math fields. When in college, Barres was told that her boyfriend must have done her homework, and she later lost a prestigious fellowship competition to a male even though she was told her application was stronger and she had published "six high-impact papers," while the man that won published only one. Barres even notices subtle differences, such as the fact that he can now finish a sentence without being interrupted by a male.

Barres urges women to stand up publicly against discrimination. One woman he particularly admires as a strong female role model is MIT biologist Nancy Hopkins, who sued the MIT administration for discrimination based on the lesser amount of lab space allocated to female scientists. The evidence from this study was so strong that even the president of MIT publicly admitted that discrimination was a problem (p. 134). Barres wants more women to follow Hopkins's lead. He believes that women often don't realize they are being discriminated against because they have faith that the world is equal. Barres explains this tendency as a "denial of personal disadvantage" (p. 134). Very few women will admit to seeing or experiencing discrimination. Until discrimination and sexism are addressed, women will continue to be oppressed.

As a society, we should not accept Lawrence Summers's hypothesis that biological differences are the reason women are not found in high-prestige tenured jobs in math and science. In fact, in another generation the gap between men and women in math and science might completely disappear. In 2003–2004, women received close to one-third of all doctorates in mathematics, up from 15 percent of doctorates in the early 1980s (American Mathematical Society, 2005). Although more recent data are not yet available, the signs point to a steadily increasing number of women entering the fields of math, science, and engineering. Blaming biology for the lack of women in these fields and refusing to fault our culture is taking the easy way out. Our culture can change.

WHY LAWRENCE SUMMERS WAS WRONG   6

References

American Mathematical Society. (2005, July 6). *Women in mathematics: Study shows gains.* Retrieved from http://www/ams.org/news?news_id=489

Barres, B. A. (2006). Does gender matter? *Nature, 44*(7), 133–136. doi:10.1038/442133a

Clearfield, M. W., & Nelson, N. M. (2006). Sex differences in mothers' speech and play behavior with 6-, 9-, and 14-month-old infants. *Sex Roles, 54*(1–2), 127–137. doi:.10.1007/s11199-005-8874-1

Pinker, S. (2005, February 14). The science of difference: Sex ed. *New Republic. 232,* 15–17.

Rhode, D. L. (1997). *Speaking of sex: The denial of gender inequality.* Cambridge, MA: Harvard University Press.

Separating science from stereotype [Editorial]. (2005). *Nature Neuroscience, 8*(3) 253. doi:10.1038/nn0305-253

Summers, L. H. (2005, January 14). Remarks at NBER conference on diversifying the science and engineering workforce. Retrieved from http://designintelligences .wordpress.com/lawrence-h-summers-remarks-at-nber-conference/

APA

Critiquing "Why Lawrence Summers Was Wrong"   MyWritingLab™

1. The controversy sparked by Harvard president Lawrence Summers's remarks was a highly politicized version of the classic nature/nurture problem. Liberal commentators claimed that women were underrepresented in science because of cultural practices that discouraged young girls from becoming interested in math and science and that blocked female Ph.D.s from advancing in their scientific careers. In contrast, conservative commentators—praising Summers's courage for raising a politically incorrect subject—took the "nature" side of this argument by citing studies pointing to innate cognitive differences between human males and females. How would you characterize Christianson's position in this controversy?

2. How does Christianson handle opposing views in her essay?

3. Do you regard Christianson's essay as a valuable contribution to the controversy over the reasons for the low numbers of women in math and science? Why or why not?

4. How would you characterize Christianson's *ethos* as a student writer in this piece? Does her *ethos* help convince you that her argument is sound? Explain.

Our second reading, by linguist Deborah Fallows, published in the column Wordplay in *The Atlantic* in summer 2013 warns of surprising consequences of a common social phenomenon—multitasking with cell phones.

Papa, Don't Text: The Perils of Distracted Parenting

DEBORAH FALLOWS

Last summer, as my baby grandson and I strolled through the same neighborhood his father and I had strolled through 30 years earlier, I saw that something vital had changed. Back then, adults pushing babies in strollers talked with those babies about whatever came across their path. But these days, most adults engage instead in one-sided conversations on their cellphones, or else text in complete silence.

As a linguist, I wondered whether the time adults spend with their mobile devices might be affecting the way children learn language. Since the technology hasn't been ubiquitous for long, research on this question is scarce. But other research on the effects of adult-child conversation makes a strong case for putting cellphones away when you're around children.

For a study published in the journal *Pediatrics* in 2009, researchers outfitted young children with small digital recorders, which captured the language each child heard and produced. The researchers could then identify and count the two-sided exchanges, or conversational "turns," between children and adults. Subjects were also tested on a range of linguistic measures, from the earliest preverbal behaviors, to nascent phonology and grammar skills, to preliteracy and the integration of complex parts of language.

The children exposed to more conversational give-and-take scored higher at every stage of language proficiency. In essence, the children made greater linguistic strides when adults talked *with* them than when they were simply in the presence of language or even when adults talked *to* them. We learned long ago that children's language abilities and eventual academic success are linked to the sheer volume of words they are exposed to early on. Now we have additional evidence that the quality of linguistic exposure, not just its quantity, matters.

5 Two other studies, reported in the *Proceedings of the National Academy of Sciences* in 2003, looked at the effects of parent-child interactions on very early stages of language production and perception. In one, babbling infants and their mothers were tracked during on-the-floor play-time. Mothers in one group were directed to respond to their babies' vocalizations with smiles and touches, and by moving closer. Mothers in the other group were not cued to respond in the same way. The study found that babies whose moms interacted with them in sync with their babbling soon began to vocalize more, with more complex sounds, and articulated more accurately than the other children.

In the other study, 9-month-old babies, who are in the late stages of locking in to the sound system of their native language, were exposed to mini lessons in Mandarin, to see if they could still learn to discern the sounds of a foreign language. One group of babies was taught by real live Chinese speakers. Another group got lessons from electronic versions of the adults, who appeared either on TV or on audiotape. Infants with live teachers learned to discern the sounds of Mandarin, while those in the group with electronic instruction did not.

These studies suggest that social interaction is important to early language learning. Of course, everyone learns to talk. But how ironic is it that, in this era when child-rearing is the focus of unprecedented imagination, invention, sophistication, and expense, something as simple and pleasurable as conversing with our children can be overlooked? As Dimitri Christakis, one of the authors of the *Pediatrics* paper, put it to me, "You can only do one thing at a time: talk to the baby or talk on the phone."

Critiquing "Papa, Don't Text"   MyWritingLab™

1. According to Deborah Fallows's causal claim in this argument, what is likely to be a serious consequence of adults' texting and cell phone habits?
2. What links and reasoning does Fallows use to develop her causal argument?
3. How does Fallows enlist her professional knowledge as evidence to support her causal claim?
4. What features of this argument—think of its new take on the problem of multi-tasking, for instance—both speak particularly to the readers of *The Atlantic* and convey the stakes and urgency of her argument?

Our final causal argument, by student writer Carlos Macias, examines the phenomenon of credit card debt among college students. Note how Macias intermixes personal experiences and research data in order to make his case.

"The Credit Card Company Made Me Do It!"—The Credit Card Industry's Role in Causing Student Debt

CARLOS MACIAS (STUDENT)

One day on spring break this year, I strolled into a Gap store. I found several items that I decided to buy. As I was checking out, the cute female clerk around my age, with perfect hair and makeup, asked if I wanted to open a GapCard to save 10 percent on all purchases I made at Gap, Banana Republic, and Old Navy that day. She said I would also earn points toward Gap gift certificates in the future. Since I shop at the Gap often enough, I decided to take her up on her offer. I filled out the form she handed me, and within seconds I—a jobless, indebted-from-student-loans, full-time college student with no substantial assets or income whatsoever—was offered a card with a $1000 credit line. Surprised by the speed at which I was approved and the amount that I was approved for, I decided to proceed to both Banana Republic and Old Navy that day to see if there was anything else I might be interested in getting (there was). By the end of the day, I had rung up nearly $200 in purchases.

I know my $200 shopping spree on credit is nothing compared to some of the horror stories I have heard from friends. One of my friends, a college sophomore, is carrying $2000 on a couple of different cards, a situation that is not unusual at all. According to a report in *Forbes* magazine, students with credit cards carry average balances of more than $4,100 by the time they graduate (Nance-Nash). The problem is that most students don't have the income to pay off their balances, so they become hooked into paying high interest rates and fees that enrich banks while exploiting students who have not yet learned how to exercise control on their spending habits.

Who is to blame for this situation? Many people might blame the students themselves, citing the importance of individual responsibility and proclaiming that no one forces students to use credit cards. But I put most of the blame directly on the credit card companies. Credit cards are enormously profitable; according to a *New York Times* article, the industry made $30 billion in pretax profits in 2003 alone (McGeehan). Hooking college students on credit cards is essential for this profit, not only because companies make a lot of money off the students themselves, but because hooking students on cards creates a habit that lasts a lifetime. Credit card companies' predatory lending practices—such as using exploitive advertising, using credit scoring to determine creditworthiness, disguising the real cost of credit, and taking advantage of U.S. government deregulation—are causing many unwitting college students to accumulate high levels of credit card debt.

First of all, credit card companies bombard students with highly sophisticated advertising. College students, typically, are in an odd "in-between" stage where they are not necessarily teens anymore, provided for by their parents, but neither are they fully adults, able to provide entirely for themselves. Many students feel the pressures from family, peers and themselves to assume adult roles in terms of their dress and jobs, not relying on Mom or Dad for help. Card companies know about these pressures. Moreover, college students are easy to target because they are concentrated on campuses and generally consume the same media. I probably get several mailings a month offering me a preapproved credit card. These advertisements are filled with happy campus scenes featuring students wearing just the right clothes, carrying their books in just the right backpack, playing music on their iPods or opening their laptop computers. They also appeal to students' desire to feel like responsible adults by emphasizing little emergencies that college students can relate to such as car breakdowns on a road trip. These advertisements illustrate a point made by a team of researchers in an article entitled "Credit Cards as Lifestyle Facilitators": The authors explain how credit card companies want consumers to view credit cards as "lifestyle facilitators" that enable "lifestyle building" and "lifestyle signaling" (Bernthal et al.). Credit cards make it easy for students to live the lifestyle pictured in the credit card ads.

5   Another contributing cause of high credit card debt for college students is the method that credit card companies use to grant credit—through credit scoring that does not consider income. It was credit scoring that allowed me to get that quadruple-digit credit line at the Gap while already living in the red. The application I filled out never asked my income. Instead, the personal information I listed was used to pull up my credit score, which is based on records of outstanding debts and payment history. Credit scoring allows banks to grant credit cards based on a person's record of responsibility in paying bills rather than on income. According to finance guru Suze Orman, "Your FICO [credit] score is a great tool to size up how good you will be handling a new loan or credit card" (21). Admittedly, credit scoring has made the lending process as a whole much fairer, giving individuals such as minorities and women the chance to qualify for credit even if they have minimal incomes. But when credit card companies use credit scoring to determine college students' creditworthiness, many students are unprepared to handle a credit line that greatly exceeds their ability to pay based on income. In fact, the Center for Responsible Lending, a consumer advocacy organization in North Carolina, lobbied Congress in September 2003 to require credit card companies to secure proof of adequate income for college-age customers before approving credit card applications ("Credit & Prepaid Cards"). If Congress passed such legislation, credit card companies would not be able to as easily take advantage of college students who have not yet learned how to exercise control on their spending habits. They would have to offer students credit lines commensurate to their incomes. No wonder these companies vehemently opposed this legislation.

Yet another contributing cause of high levels of credit card debt is the high cost of having this debt, which credit card companies are especially talented at disguising. As credit card debt increases, card companies compound unpaid interest, adding it to the balance that must be repaid. If this balance is not repaid, they charge interest on unpaid interest. They add exorbitant fees for small slip-ups like making a late payment or exceeding the credit limit. While these costs are listed on statements when first added to the balance, they quickly vanish into the "New Balance" number on all subsequent statements, as if these fees were simply past purchases that have yet to be repaid. As the balance continues to grow, banks spike interest rates even higher. In his 2004 article "Soaring Interest Compounds Credit Card Pain for Millions," Patrick McGeehan describes a "new era of consumer credit, in which thousands of Americans are paying millions of dollars each month in fees that they did not expect . . . lenders are doubling or tripling interest rates with little warning or explanation." These rate hikes are usually tucked into the pages of fine print that come with credit cards, which many consumers are unable to fully read, let alone understand. Usually, a credit card company will offer a very low "teaser rate" that expires after several months. While this industry practice is commonly understood by consumers, many do not understand that credit card companies usually reserve the right to raise the rate at any time for almost any reason, causing debt levels to rise further.

Admittedly, while individual consumers must be held accountable for any debt they accumulate and should understand compound and variable interest and fees, students' ignorance is welcomed by the credit card industry. In order to completely understand how the credit card industry has caused college students to amass high amounts of credit card debt, it is necessary to explain how this vicious monster was let loose during banking deregulation over the past 30 years. In 1978, the Supreme Court opened the floodgates by ruling that the federal government could not set a cap on interest rates that banks charged for credit cards; that was to be left to the states. With Uncle Sam no longer protecting consumers, Delaware and South Dakota passed laws that removed caps on interest rates, in order to woo credit card companies to conduct nationwide business there (McGeehan). Since then, the credit card industry has become one of the most profitable industries ever. Credit card companies were given another sweet deal from the U.S. Supreme Court in 1996, when the Court deregulated fees. Since then, the average late fee has risen from $10 or less, to $39 (McGeehan). While a lot of these fees and finance charges are avoidable if the student pays the balance in full, on time, every month, for college students who carry balances for whatever reason, these charges are tacked on, further adding to the principal on which they pay a high rate of compounded interest. Moreover, the U.S. government has refused to step in to regulate the practice of universal default, where a credit card company can raise the rate they charge if a consumer is late on an unrelated bill, like a utility payment. Even for someone who pays his or her bills in full, on time, 99 percent of the time, one bill-paying slip-up can cause an avalanche of fees and frustration, thanks to the credit card industry.

Credit card companies exploit college students' lack of financial savvy and security. It is no secret that most full-time college students are not independently wealthy; many have limited means. So why are these companies so willing to issue cards to poor college students? Profits, of course! If they made credit cards less available to struggling consumers such as college students, consumers would have a more difficult time racking up huge balances, plain and simple. It's funny that

Citibank, one of the largest, most profitable credit card companies in the world, proudly exclaims "Live richly" in its advertisements. At the rate that it and other card companies collect interest and fees from their customers, a more appropriate slogan would be "Live poorly."

Works Cited

Bernthal, Matthew, et al. "Credit Cards as Lifestyle Facilitators." *Journal of Consumer Research,* vol. 32, no. 1, 2005, pp. 130-45.

"Credit & Prepaid Cards: Our Policy Positions." *Center for Responsible Lending,* 8 Dec. 2015, www.responsiblelending.org/issues/credit-prepaid-cards/credit-prepaid-cards-policy.

McGeehan, Patrick. "Soaring Interest Compounds Credit Card Pain for Millions." *The New York Times,* 21 Nov. 2004, www.nytimes.com/2004/11/21/business/soaring-interest-compounds-credit-card-pain-for-millions.html.

Nance-Nash, Sheryl. "New College Grads: Just Say No to More Debt!" *Forbes,* 8 May 2012, www.forbes.com/sites/sherylnancenash/2012/05/08/new-college-grads-just-say-no-to-more-debt/#41547a517a41.

Orman, Suze. *The Money Book for the Young, Fabulous, and Broke.* Riverhead, 2005.

Critiquing "The Credit Card Company Made Me Do It!"   MyWritingLab™

1. How effective is Macias's argument that the predatory practices of banks and credit card companies are the primary cause of credit card debt among college students?
2. Suppose that you wanted to join this conversation by offering a counterview with a thesis something like this: "Although Macias is partially correct that banks and credit card companies play a role in producing credit card debt among college students, he underestimates other important factors." What would you emphasize as the causes of credit card debt? How would you make your case?

MyWritingLab™

Visit Ch. 12 Causal Arguments in *MyWritingLab* to complete the For Writing and Discussion, Examining Visual Arguments, Critiquing, and Writing Assignments and to test your understanding of the chapter objectives.

Evaluation and Ethical Arguments

13

What you will learn in this chapter:

13.1 To explain and illustrate the difference between categorical and ethical evaluation arguments

13.2 To conduct a categorical evaluation argument using a criteria-match strategy

13.3 To conduct an ethical evaluation argument using principles or consequences

13.4 To be mindful of common problems encountered in evaluation arguments

13.5 To write your own categorical or ethical evaluation argument

---

In our roles as citizens and professionals, we are continually expected to make evaluations and to persuade others to accept them. In this chapter, you will learn to conduct two kinds of evaluation arguments: categorical and ethical. Both have clarifying power to help us make difficult choices about good or bad, right or wrong.

Case 1   How Should We Evaluate the Film *District 9?*

In the film *District 9* (2009), directed by South African Neill Blomkamp and produced by Peter Jackson, a spaceship has stalled out over Johannesburg, South Africa, where it has hovered for several decades. Its starving alien passengers, derogatorily called "The Prawns" for their appearance, have been placed in what has become a crowded, militarized prison ghetto called District 9. As the film begins, South Africans have grown disgusted with and intolerantly fearful of the growing alien population, while corporate powers seek these aliens' technologically advanced bio-weapons. As this poster suggests—based on its "No Humans Allowed" sign, its ominous "You are not welcome here" slogan, and its barbed wire perimeter—the film includes graphic echoes of the racism of apartheid and disturbing depiction of xenophobia, abusive corporate powers, and mistreatment of refugees (the aliens). Nominated for numerous awards, *District 9* has sparked heated evaluation arguments about whether it is a good or a flawed film. Part of the debate focuses on what evaluative criteria to use—a decision that depends on the category into which the film should be placed. Should it be evaluated as a science fiction film, as a corporate espionage thriller, or as a commentary on global social justice? Some critics, for example, have argued that *District 9* is not a great science fiction film, but it is a deeply provocative and moving commentary on social justice.

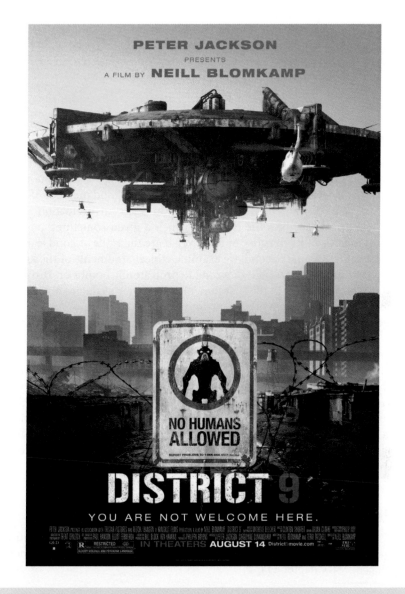

Case 2   What Is a "Good Organ" for a Transplant? How Can an Ill Person Ethically Find an Organ Donor?

In the United States some 87,000 sick people have been waiting as long as six years for an organ transplant, with a portion of these dying before they can find a donor. The problem of organ shortages raises two kinds of evaluation issues. First, doctors are reevaluating the criteria by which they judge a "good" organ—that is, a good lung, kidney, or liver suitable for transplanting. Formerly, people who were elderly or obese or who had engaged in risky behaviors or experienced heart failure or other medical conditions were not considered sources of good organs. Now doctors are reconsidering these sources as well as exploring the use of organs from pigs. Second, the shortage of organs for donation has raised numerous ethical issues: Is it ethical for people to bypass the national waiting list for organs by advertising on billboards and Web sites in search of a volunteer donor? Is it morally right for people to sell their organs? Is it right for patients and families to buy organs or in any way remunerate living organ donors? Some states are passing laws that allow some financial compensation to living organ donors.

An Overview of Categorical and Ethical Evaluation Arguments

13.1 To explain and illustrate the difference between categorical and ethical evaluation arguments

In this chapter we explain strategies for conducting two different kinds of evaluation arguments. First, we examine categorical evaluations of the kind "Is this thing a good member of its class?"[*] (Is Ramon a good leader?) In such an evaluation, the writer determines the extent to which a given something possesses the qualities or standards of its category or class. What are the traits of good leaders? Does Ramon possess these traits? Second, we examine ethical arguments of the kind "Is this action right (wrong)?" (Was it right or wrong to drop atomic bombs on Hiroshima and Nagasaki in World War II?) In these arguments, the writer evaluates a given act from the perspective of some system of morality or ethics.

To see the difference between the two kinds of evaluations, consider the case of terrorists. From a nonethical standpoint, you could make a categorical evaluation by saying that certain people are "good terrorists" in that they fully realize the purpose of the class "terrorist": they cause great anguish and damage with a minimum of resources, and they bring much attention to their cause. In other words, they are good at what they do—terrorism. However, if we want to condemn terrorism on ethical grounds, we have to construct an ethical argument that terrorism is wrong. The ethical question is not whether a person fulfills the purposes of the class "terrorist," but whether it is wrong for such a class to exist. In the rest of this chapter we will explain categorical evaluations and ethical evaluations in more detail.

Constructing a Categorical Evaluation Argument

13.2 To conduct a categorical evaluation argument using a criteria-match strategy

A categorical evaluation uses a criteria-match structure similar to the structure we examined in definition arguments (see Chapter 11).

Criteria-Match Structure of Categorical Evaluations

A typical claim-with-reasons frame for an evaluation argument has the following criteria-match structure:

> This thing/phenomenon is/is not a good member of its class because it meets (fails to meet) criteria A, B, and C.

---

[*]In addition to the term *good*, a number of other evaluative terms involve the same kind of thinking— *effective, successful, workable, excellent, valuable,* and so forth.

Claim: This thing/phenomenon is (is not) a good member of its class.

Criteria: The criteria for being a good member of this class are A, B, and C.

Match: The thing/phenomenon meets (fails to meet) criteria A, B, and C.

The main conceptual difference between an evaluation argument and a definition argument is the nature of the contested category. In a definition argument, one argues whether a particular thing belongs within a certain category. (Is this swampy area a *wetland*?) In an evaluation argument, we know what category something belongs to. For example, we know that this 2008 Chevy Cobalt is a *used car*. For an evaluation argument, the question is whether this 2008 Chevy Cobalt is a *good used car*. Or, to place the question within a rhetorical context, is this 2008 Chevy Cobalt a *good used car for me to buy for college*?

To illustrate the criteria-match structure of an evaluation argument, let's ask whether hydraulic fracturing (commonly called fracking) is a good means for extracting natural gas from shale formations. Supporters of fracking might say, "yes," because it meets three major criteria:

- It is technologically efficient at extracting huge supplies of otherwise untappable natural gas.
- It is cost effective.
- It is environmentally safe.

Opponents might make two counterarguments: First, they might claim that fracking is not environmentally safe. (Safety is still a crucial criterion. Opponents argue that fracking doesn't meet this criterion.) Second, they might argue that fracking, by producing lots of relatively cheap natural gas, removes the urgency from efforts to convert to renewable energy such as solar and wind. Thus it might be cost effective (criterion 2) in the short run, but disastrous in the long run. Page 282 provides a Toulmin analysis of how proponents of fracking might develop their third reason: "Fracking is environmentally safe."

Developing Your Criteria

To help you develop your criteria, we suggest a three-step thinking process:

1. Place the thing you are evaluating in the smallest relevant category so that you don't compare apples to oranges.
2. Develop criteria for your evaluation based on the purpose or function of this category.
3. Determine the relative weight of your criteria.

Let's look at each of these steps in turn.

Step 1: Place the Thing You Are Evaluating in the Smallest Relevant Category
Placing your contested thing in the smallest category is a crucial first step. Suppose, for example, that you want one of your professors to write you a letter of recommendation for a summer job. The professor will need to know what kind of summer job. Are you

TOULMIN ANALYSIS OF THE FRACKING ARGUMENT SUPPORTING ENVIRONMENTAL SAFETY

ENTHYMEME

CLAIM Fracking is a good method for extracting natural gas from shale formations

REASON because it is environmentally safe.

GROUNDS

• Descriptions of safety measures employed by industry

• Descriptions of local, state, and federal regulations aimed at insuring safety

• Summaries of peer-reviewed studies and government studies showing the safety of fracking

• Refutation of anecdotal scare stories told by environmentalists

CONDITIONS OF REBUTTAL

Attacking the reason and grounds

Arguments that fracking is not environmentally safe

• Studies pointing to possible dangers such as contamination of aquifers, earthquakes, flaring of methane, and so forth

• Arguments that local, state, and federal regulations are too loose and unenforced

• Statistics about environmental costs in doing the fracking (huge amounts of required water, recovering contaminated water, use of carbon fuels to run the machinery, and so forth)

WARRANT

Environmental safety is an important criterion for evaluating a method of drilling for natural gas

BACKING

Arguments that safety must be a prime consideration of any business plan. One major accident could undermine public support of fracking. [Backing tries to counter the arguments of environmentalists that business interests put profit ahead of safety.]

CONDITIONS OF REBUTTAL

Attacking the warrant and backing

• Environmentalists will endorse the warrant, but may say that even if fracking is safe, it undermines the urgency of finding alternative energy sources.

• Business interests might want to loosen an insistence on absolute safety by acknowledging that some accidents are inevitable.

applying to become a camp counselor, a law office intern, a retail sales clerk, or a tour guide at a wild animal park in your state? Each of these jobs has different criteria for excellence. Or to take a different example, suppose that you want to evaluate e-mail as a medium of correspondence. To create a stable context for your evaluation, you need to place e-mail in its smallest relevant category. You may choose to evaluate e-mail as a medium for business communication (by contrasting e-mail with direct personal contact, phone conversations, or postal mail), as a medium for staying in touch with high school friends (in contrast, say, to text messaging or Facebook), or as a medium for carrying on a long-distance romance (in contrast, say, to old-fashioned "love letters"). Again, criteria will vary across these different categories.

By placing your contested thing in the smallest relevant class, you avoid the apples-and-oranges problem. That is, to give a fair evaluation of a perfectly good apple, you need to judge it under the class "apple" and not under the next larger class, "fruit," or a neighboring class such as "orange." And to be even more precise, you may wish to evaluate your apple in the class "eating apple" as opposed to "pie apple" because the latter class is supposed to be tarter and the former class juicier and sweeter.

Step 2: Develop Criteria for Your Evaluation Based on the Purpose or Functions of This Category   Suppose that the summer job you are applying for is tour guide at a wild animal park in your state. The functions of a tour guide are to drive the tour buses, make people feel welcome, give them interesting information about the wild animals in the park, make their visit pleasant, and so forth. Criteria for a good tour guide would thus include reliability and responsibility, a friendly demeanor, good speaking skills, and knowledge of the kinds of animals in the wild animal park. In our e-mail example, suppose that you want to evaluate e-mail as a medium for business communication. The purpose of this class is to provide a quick and reliable means of communication that increases efficiency, minimizes misunderstandings, protects the confidentiality of internal communications, and so forth. Based on these purposes, you might establish the following criteria:

A good medium for business communication:

- Is easy to use, quick, and reliable
- Increases employee efficiency
- Prevents misunderstandings
- Maintains confidentiality where needed

Step 3: Determine the relative weight of your criteria   In some evaluations all the criteria are equally important. However, sometimes a phenomenon to be evaluated is strong in one criterion but weak in another—a situation that forces the evaluator to decide which criterion takes precedence. For example, the supervisor interviewing candidates for tour guide at the wild animal park may find one candidate who is very knowledgeable about the wildlife but doesn't have good speaking skills. The supervisor would need to decide which of these two criteria gets more weight.

Making Your Match Argument

Once you've established and weighed your criteria, you'll need to use examples and other evidence to show that the thing being evaluated meets or does not meet the criteria. For example, your professor could argue that you would be a good wildlife park tour guide because you have strong interpersonal skills (based on your work on a college orientation committee), that you have good speaking skills (based on a speech you gave in the professor's class), and that you have quite a bit of knowledge about animals and ecology (based on your major in environmental science).

In our e-mail example, you might establish the following working thesis:

Despite its being easy to learn, quick, and reliable, e-mail is often not an effective medium for business communication because it reduces worker efficiency, leads to frequent misunderstandings, and often lacks confidentiality.

EXAMINING VISUAL ARGUMENTS

MyWritingLab™

An Evaluation Claim

This photograph of Stephen Colbert and Jon Stewart of *The Colbert Report* and *The Daily Show* was taken at the October 30, 2010 "Rally to Restore Sanity 'or Fear,'" on the Washington D.C. National Mall, an event that drew thousands of people. The event followed by two months the "Restoring Honor Rally" led by conservative Fox News talk show celebrity Glenn Beck on August 28, 2010. Political commentators debated whether the Colbert and Stewart rally was simply a satirical entertainment mocking the Beck rally or whether it was serious political activism supporting the liberal left. If your goal was to portray this event as serious political activism, would this photograph be a good image to accompany your argument? What criteria would you establish for selecting a photograph to support your argument that Colbert and Stewart are effective political activists and not simply entertainers?

You could develop your last three points as follows:

- **E-mail reduces worker efficiency.** You can use personal anecdotes and research data to show how checking e-mail is addictive and how it eats into worker time (one research article says that the average worker devotes ten minutes of every working hour to reading and responding to e-mail).
- **E-mail leads to misunderstandings.** Because an e-mail message is often composed rapidly without revision, e-mail can cause people to state ideas imprecisely, to write something they would never say face-to-face, or to convey an unintended tone. You could give a personal example of a high-consequence misunderstanding caused by e-mail.
- **E-mail often lacks confidentiality.** You could provide anecdotal or research evidence of cases in which a person clicked on the "reply to all" button rather than the "reply" button, sending a message intended for one person to a whole group of people. Also, people sometimes forward e-mails without the sender's permission. Finally, e-mail messages are archived forever, so that messages that you thought were deleted may show up years later in a lawsuit.

As these examples illustrate, the key to a successful match argument is to use sufficient examples and other evidence to show how your contested phenomenon meets or does not meet each of your criteria.

■ ■ ■   **FOR CLASS DISCUSSION** Developing Criteria and Match Arguments

The following small-group exercise can be accomplished in one or two class hours. It gives you a good model of the process you can go through in order to write your own categorical evaluation.

1. Choose a specific controversial person, thing, or event to evaluate. To help you think of ideas, try brainstorming controversial members of the following categories: *people* (athletes, political leaders, musicians); *technology* (new car features, phone apps); *media* (a social network, a TV program, a radio station); *government and world affairs* (an economic policy, a Supreme Court decision); *the arts* (a film, a book); *your college or university* (food service, an administrative policy); *the world of work* (a job, a company operation, a dress policy); or any other categories of your choice.
2. Place your controversial person or thing within the smallest relevant class, thus providing a rhetorical context for your argument and showing what is at stake. Do you want to evaluate Harvey's Hamburger Haven in the broad category of *restaurants,* in the narrow category of *hamburger joints,* or in a different narrow category such as *late-night study places*?
3. Make a list of the purpose or function of that class, and then list the criteria that a good member of that class would need to have in order to accomplish the purpose or function. (What is the purpose or function of a hamburger joint versus a late-night study place? What criteria for excellence can you derive from these purposes or functions?)

4. If necessary, rank your criteria from most to least important. (For a late-night study place, what is more important: good ambience, Wi-Fi availability, good coffee, or convenient location?)

5. Provide examples and other evidence to show how your contested something matches or does not match each of your criteria. (As a late-night study place, Carol's Coffee Closet beats out Harvey's Hamburger Haven. Although Harvey's Hamburger Haven has the most convenient location, Carol's Coffee Closet has Wi-Fi, an ambience conducive to studying, and excellent coffee.)

Constructing an Ethical Evaluation Argument

13.3 To conduct an ethical evaluation argument using principles or consequences

A second kind of evaluation argument focuses on moral or ethical issues, which can often merge or overlap with categorical evaluations. For example, many apparently straightforward categorical evaluations can turn out to have an ethical dimension. Consider again the criteria for buying a car. Most people would base their evaluations on cost, safety, comfort, and so forth. But some people may feel morally obligated to buy the most fuel-efficient car, to buy an American car, or not to buy a car from a manufacturer whose labor policies they find morally repugnant. Depending on how large a role ethical considerations play in the evaluation, we may choose to call this an ethical argument based on moral considerations rather than a categorical evaluation based on the purposes of a class or category.

When we are faced with an ethical issue, we must move from arguments of good or bad to arguments of right or wrong. The terms *right* and *wrong* are clearly different from the terms *good* and *bad* when the latter terms mean, simply, "effective" (meets purposes of class, as in "This is a good laptop") or "ineffective" (fails to meet purposes of class, as in "This is a bad cookbook"). But *right* and *wrong* often also differ from what seems to be a moral use of the terms *good* and *bad*. We may say, for example, that sunshine is good because it brings pleasure and that cancer is bad because it brings pain and death, but that is not quite the same thing as saying that sunshine is "right" and cancer is "wrong." It is the problem of "right" and "wrong" that ethical arguments confront.

There are many schools of ethical thought—too many to cover in this brief overview—so we'll limit ourselves to two major systems: arguments from consequences and arguments from principles.

Consequences as the Base of Ethics

Perhaps the best-known example of evaluating acts according to their ethical consequences is utilitarianism, a down-to-earth philosophy that grew out of nineteenth-century British philosophers' concern to demystify ethics and make it work in the practical world. Jeremy Bentham, the originator of utilitarianism, developed the goal of the greatest good for the greatest number, or "greatest happiness," by which he meant the most pleasure for the least pain. John Stuart Mill, another British philosopher, built on Bentham's utilitarianism by using predicted consequences to determine the morality of a proposed action.

Mill's consequentialist approach allows you readily to assess a wide range of acts. You can apply the principle of utility—which says that an action is morally right if it produces a greater net value (benefits minus costs) than any available alternative action—to virtually any situation, and it will help you reach a decision. Obviously, however, it's not always easy to make the calculations called for by this approach because, like any prediction of the future, an estimate of consequences is conjectural. In particular, it's often very hard to assess the long-term consequences of any action. Too often, utilitarianism seduces us into a short-term analysis of a moral problem simply because long-term consequences are difficult to predict.

Principles as the Base of Ethics

Any ethical system based on principles will ultimately rest on moral tenets that we are duty bound to uphold, no matter what the consequences. Sometimes the moral tenets come from religious faith—for example, the Ten Commandments. At other times, however, the principles are derived from philosophical reasoning, as in the case of German philosopher Immanuel Kant. Kant held that no one should ever use another person as a means to his own ends and that everyone should always act as if his acts are the basis of universal law. In other words, Kant held that we are duty bound to respect other people's sanctity and to act in the same way that we would want all other people to act. The great advantage of such a system is its clarity and precision. We are never overwhelmed by a multiplicity of contradictory and difficult-to-quantify consequences; we simply make sure we are following (or not violating) the principles of our ethical system and proceed accordingly.

Example Ethical Arguments Examining Capital Punishment

To show you how to conduct an ethical argument, let's now apply these two strategies to the example of capital punishment. In general, you can conduct an ethical evaluation by using the frame for either a principles-based argument or a consequences-based argument or a combination of both.

Principles-Based Frame: An act is right (wrong) because it follows (violates) principles A, B, and C.

Consequences-Based Frame: An act is right (wrong) because it will lead to consequences A, B, and C, which are good (bad).

A principles-based argument looks at capital punishment through the lens of one or more guiding principles. Kant's principle that we are duty bound not to violate the sanctity of other human lives could lead to arguments opposing capital punishment. One might argue as follows:

Principles-based argument opposing capital punishment: The death penalty is wrong because it violates the principle of the sanctity of human life.

You could support this principle either by summarizing Kant's argument that one should not violate the selfhood of another person or by pointing to certain religious systems such as Judeo-Christian ethics, where one is told, "Vengeance is mine, saith the Lord" or "Thou shalt not kill." To develop this argument further, you might examine two exceptions in which principles-based ethicists may allow killing—self-defense and war—and show how capital punishment does not fall into either category.

Principles-based arguments can also be developed to support capital punishment. You may be surprised to learn that Kant himself—despite his arguments for the sanctity of life—supported capital punishment. To make such an argument, Kant evoked a different principle about the suitability of the punishment to the crime:

> There is no sameness of kind between death and remaining alive even under the most miserable conditions, and consequently there is no equality between the crime and the retribution unless the criminal is judicially condemned and put to death.

Stated as an enthymeme, Kant's argument is as follows:

> *Principles-based argument supporting capital punishment:* Capital punishment is right because it follows the principle that punishments should be proportionate to the crime.

In developing this argument, Kant's burden would be to show why the principle of proportionate retribution outweighs the principle of the supreme worth of the individual. Our point is that a principles-based argument can be made both for and against capital punishment. The arguer's duty is to make clear what principle is being evoked and then to show why this principle is more important than opposing principles.

Unlike a principles-based argument, which appeals to certain guiding maxims or rules, a consequences-based argument looks at the consequences of a decision and measures the positive benefits against the negative costs. Here is the frame that an arguer might use to oppose capital punishment on the basis of negative consequences:

> *Consequences-based argument opposing capital punishment:* Capital punishment is wrong because it leads to the following negative consequences:

- The possibility of executing an innocent person
- The possibility that a murderer who may repent and be redeemed is denied that chance
- The excessive legal and political costs of trials and appeals
- The unfair distribution of executions so that one's chances of being put to death are much greater if one is a minority or is poor

To develop this argument, the reader would need to provide facts, statistics, and other evidence to support each of the stated reasons.

A different arguer might use a consequences-based approach to support capital punishment:

> *Consequences-based argument supporting capital punishment:* Capital punishment is right because it leads to the following positive consequences:

- It may deter violent crime and slow down the rate of murder.
- It saves the cost of lifelong imprisonment.

▓ It stops criminals who are menaces to society from committing more murders.

▓ It helps grieving families reach closure and sends a message to victims' families that society recognizes their pain.

It should be evident, then, that adopting an ethical system doesn't lead to automatic answers to one's ethical dilemmas. A system offers a way of proceeding—a way of conducting an argument—but it doesn't relieve you of personal responsibility for thinking through your values and taking a stand. When you face an ethical dilemma, we encourage you to consider both the relevant principles and the possible consequences the dilemma entails. In many arguments, you can use both principles-based and consequences-based reasoning as long as irreconcilable contradictions don't present themselves.

■ ■ ■ **FOR WRITING AND DISCUSSION: Developing an Ethical Argument** MyWritingLab™

Individual task: Develop a frame for an ethical argument (based on principles, consequences, or both) for or against any two of the following actions. Use the previous examples on capital punishment as a model.

1. Eating meat
2. Using public transportation instead of owning a car
3. Legalizing assisted suicide for the terminally ill
4. Selling organs
5. Allowing concealed weapons on college campuses

Group task: Share your arguments with classmates   ■ ■ ■

Common Problems in Making Evaluation Arguments

13.4 To be mindful of common problems encountered in evaluation arguments

When conducting evaluation arguments (whether categorical or ethical), writers can bump up against recurring problems that are unique to evaluation. In some cases these problems complicate the establishment of criteria; in other cases they complicate the match argument. Let's look briefly at some of these common problems.

▓ **The problem of standards—what is commonplace versus what is ideal:** In various forms, we experience the dilemma of the commonplace versus the ideal all the time. Is it fair to get a ticket for going seventy miles per hour on a sixty-five-mile-per-hour freeway when most of the drivers go seventy miles per hour or faster? (Does what is *commonplace*—going seventy—override what is *ideal*—obeying the law?) Is it better for high schools to pass out free contraceptives to students because students are having sex anyway (what's *commonplace*), or is it better not to pass them out in order to support abstinence (what's *ideal*)?

▓ **The problem of mitigating circumstances:** This problem occurs when an arguer claims that unusual circumstances should alter our usual standards of judgment. Ordinarily, it is fair for a teacher to reduce a grade if you turn in a paper late. But what if you were up all night taking care of a crying baby? Does that count as a *mitigating circumstance* to waive the ordinary criterion? When you argue for mitigating circumstances, you will likely assume an especially heavy burden of proof. People assume the rightness of usual standards of judgment unless there are compelling arguments for abnormal circumstances.

- **The problem of choosing between two goods or two bads:** Often an evaluation issue forces us between a rock and a hard place. Should we cut pay or cut people? Put our parents in a nursing home or let them stay at home, where they have become a danger to themselves? In such cases one has to weigh conflicting criteria, knowing that the choices are too much alike—either both bad or both good.

- **The problem of seductive empirical measures:** The need to make high-stakes evaluations has led many people to seek quantifiable criteria that can be weighed mathematically. Thus we use grade point averages to select scholarship winners, student evaluation scores to decide merit pay for teachers, and combined scores of judges to evaluate figure skaters. In some cases, empirical measures can be quite acceptable, but they are often dangerous because they discount important non-quantifiable traits. The problem with empirical measures is that they seduce us into believing that complex judgments can be made mathematically, thus rescuing us from the messiness of alternative points of view and conflicting criteria.

- **The problem of cost:** A final problem in evaluation arguments is cost. Something may be the best possible member of its class, but if it costs too much, we have to go for second or third best. We can avoid this problem somewhat by placing items into different classes on the basis of cost. For example, a Mercedes will exceed a Kia on almost any criterion, but if we can't afford more than a Kia, the comparison is pointless. It is better to compare a Mercedes to a Lexus and a Kia to an equivalent Ford. Whether costs are expressed in dollars, personal discomfort, moral repugnance, or some other terms, our final evaluation of an item must take cost into account.

WRITING ASSIGNMENT An Evaluation or Ethical Argument   MyWritingLab™

13.5 To write your own categorical or ethical evaluation argument

Write an argument in which you try to change your readers' minds about the value, worth, or ethics of something. Choose a phenomenon to be evaluated that is controversial so that your readers are likely at first to disagree with your evaluation or at least to be surprised by it. Somewhere in your essay you should summarize alternative views and either refute them or concede to them (see Chapter 7).

Exploring Ideas

Evaluation issues are all around us. Think of disagreements about the value of a person, thing, action, or phenomenon within the various communities to which you belong—your dorm, home, or apartment community; your school community, including clubs or organizations; your academic community, including classes you are currently taking; your work community; and your city, state, national, and world communities. Once you have settled on a controversial thing to be evaluated, place it in its smallest relevant category, determine the purposes of that category, and develop your criteria. If you are making an ethical evaluation, consider your argument from the perspective of both principles and consequences.

Identifying Your Audience and Determining What's at Stake

Before drafting your argument, identify your targeted audience and determine what's at stake. Consider your responses to the following questions:

- What audience are you targeting? What background do they need to understand your issue? How much do they already care about it?
- Before they read your evaluation argument, what stance on your issue do you imagine them holding? What change do you want to bring about in their view?
- What will they find new or surprising about your argument?
- What objections might they raise? What counterarguments or alternative points of view will you need to address?
- Why does your evaluation matter? Who might be threatened or made uncomfortable by your views? What is at stake?

Organizing an Evaluation Argument

As you write a draft, you may find useful the following prototypical structures for evaluation arguments shown in Organization Plans 1 and 2 on pages 292 and 293. Of course, you can always alter these plans if another structure better fits your material.

Questioning and Critiquing a Categorical Evaluation Argument

Here is a list of questions you can use to critique a categorical evaluation argument:

Will a skeptic accept my criteria? Many evaluative arguments are weak because the writers have simply assumed that readers will accept their criteria. Whenever your audience's acceptance of your criteria is in doubt, you will need to argue for your criteria explicitly.

Will a skeptic accept my general weighting of criteria? Another vulnerable spot in an evaluation argument is the relative weight of the criteria. How much anyone weights a given criterion is usually a function of his or her own interests relative to your contested something. You should always ask whether some particular group might have good reasons for weighting the criteria differently.

Organization Plan 1: Criteria and Match in Separate Sections

Introduce the issue and state your claim.	• Engage reader's interest in your evaluation issue and show why it is controversial or problematic. • Show what's at stake. • Provide background information needed by your audience. • State your claim.
Present your criteria.	• State and develop criterion 1. • State and develop criterion 2. • Continue with the rest of your criteria. • Anticipate and respond to possible objections to the criteria.
Present your match argument.	• Consider restating your claim for clarity. • Argue that your case meets (does not meet) criterion 1. • Argue that your case meets (does not meet) criterion 2. • Continue with the rest of your match argument. • Anticipate and respond to possible objections to the match argument.
Conclude.	• Perhaps sum up your argument. • Help reader return to the "big picture" of what's at stake. • End with something memorable.

Will a skeptic accept my criteria but reject my match argument? The other major way of testing an evaluation argument is to anticipate how readers may object to your stated reasons and grounds. Will readers challenge you by showing that you have cherry-picked your examples and evidence? Will they provide counterexamples and counterevidence?

Organization Plan 2: Criteria and Match Interwoven

Introduce the issue and state your claim.	• Engage reader's interest in your evaluation issue and show why it is controversial or problematic. • Show what's at stake. • Provide background information needed by your audience. • State your claim.
Present series of criterion-match arguments.	• State and develop criterion 1 and argue that your case meets (does not meet) the criterion. • State and develop criterion 2 and argue that your case meets (does not meet) the criterion. • Continue with the rest of your criterion-match arguments.
Respond to possible objections to your argument.	• Anticipate and summarize possible objections. • Respond to the objections through rebuttal or concession.
Conclude.	• Perhaps sum up your argument. • Help reader return to the "big picture" of what's at stake. • End with something memorable.

Critiquing an Ethical Argument

Ethical arguments can be critiqued through appeals to consequences or principles. If an argument appeals primarily to principles, it can be vulnerable to a simple cost analysis. What are the costs of adhering to this principle? There will undoubtedly be some, or else there would be no real argument. If the argument is based strictly on consequences, we should ask whether it violates any rules or principles, particularly such commandments as the Golden Rule—"Do unto others as you would have others do unto you"—which most members of our audience adhere to. By failing to mention these alternative ways of thinking about ethical issues, we undercut not only our argument but our credibility as well. ■

READINGS

Our first reading, by student writer Lorena Mendoza-Flores, critiques her former high school for the way it marginalizes Hispanic students. Lorena, a physics major in college, has changed the name of her high school and chosen not to reveal her home state.

Silenced and Invisible: Problems of Hispanic Students at Valley High School

LORENA MENDOZA-FLORES (STUDENT)

Every year, thousands of Mexican families come to the United States in order to escape economic hardships in Mexico and hope for better schools for their children. While many American schools try to accommodate immigrant non-native speakers, many immigrant families, according to case study interviews, have increasingly negative perceptions of these attempts (Roessingh). There are action plans to bridge the gap between disadvantaged and advantaged students, yet Hispanic ESL (English as a Second Language) youth continue to perform considerably below that of other students (Good et al.). These problems pose the question: what is wrong with the way our schools treat Hispanic immigrants? Perhaps we could gain some understanding if we looked at a specific school—my own Valley High School in an agricultural region of [name of state]. Valley High School is a perfect example of a school with a growing Hispanic population, well-intentioned teachers, and hopes for their success that simply fall through. The failures at my school include inadequate ESL training for teachers, inadequate counseling for immigrant students, poor multicultural training for all teachers, and failure to value Hispanic identity and provide support for transitioning families.

Despite the fact that the Valley School District has 52 percent Hispanic students, a large percentage of whom have Spanish as their first language and parents who only speak Spanish, the staff at Valley High School is overwhelmingly white with only one Hispanic teacher and only three or four teachers who speak Spanish. Even with a large number of ESL students, Valley High School has not hired teachers who are adequately trained in ESL. There is only one ESL teacher, who is responsible for all the ESL students. They are assigned to regular classes and then go to the ESL classrooms for what is supposed to be extra support. When I've gone into the ESL classroom, I've found students surfing random sites online and the teacher, also the yearbook advisor, working on pages for the annual. Because I was senior editor of the yearbook, he was very open to talking to me about his students, always complaining that they didn't work hard enough even though I could see they weren't being given meaningful work. I was frustrated because it was obvious that the ESL classroom did not engage either the students or the teacher. The students' language progress remained stagnant, while the expectations of standardized testing became increasingly more demanding, dooming ESL students to failure.

Another problem is inadequate counseling for Hispanic students and inadequate methods of assessing their progress so they can be placed in the right classes. When immigrant students need help, teachers often recruit other students to address their needs. As a student mentor, I was called upon a few times to speak with students about their performance in class. In one particular situation, the math teacher called me in to talk to a student who had decided to drop out. The teacher was visibly concerned for the student's welfare but didn't have any means for understanding or addressing the student's issues. The student told me that he did not feel like he belonged at school. The lack of adequate counseling sent the message that immigrant students were not worth fighting for to stay in our school.

Additionally, when students enter the school, their skills in other coursework are not taken into consideration. All ESL students are placed in the basic Math and English courses and while they might move down, sometimes as far as being placed in special education classes, they're never moved up. A student's aptitude in math or science may never get recognized in the four years that he or she is in high school because the ESL students move as a single group and take just about all coursework together. Their status as ESL students becomes the sole determinant of their identity as a student within the school system, and they are not given the same considerations and levels of attention required to grow and develop academically. Personally, I have fallen victim to our school's overlooking of student progress. When I entered the Valley School District in 8th grade, I had already taken several years of algebra and tested far above other students in my grade. At my previous school in another district, I had surpassed the school's highest level of math. In fact, my 5th–7th grade math instructor had to find advanced online material for me so that I could keep progressing. Entering the Valley School District, however, I regressed two years. Even though I communicated to both my math teacher and the counselor that I was being placed too low and that the nearby high school had several higher-level courses, I was kept in the same class. The next year, I was shocked to see that two 8th grade white students were in my 9th grade geometry class; the system had catered to them while it had denied to me an acknowledgement of the same earned achievement. I felt dismissed because I was Hispanic.

5   A third problem is that outside of the ESL classroom, in the regular classroom settings, teachers are often untrained in how to create safe multicultural dialogue. One time in sociology my teacher asked the class why the Hispanic students were performing so much worse than white students. I tried to explain that our support was inadequate. I stated that since most Hispanic students came from immigrant backgrounds, our parents weren't able to help us maneuver through the school system. In doing our homework, we had no one to turn to, and if the instructions were unclear, we did not have access to a resource such as an English speaking parent, something that many white students and faculty never even thought about when

considering this gap in performance. When I started talking about these things, white students around the room started becoming upset. They argued that they were hard workers and didn't have their parents do their homework for them. Obviously, my point was not to dismiss their efforts but to emphasize that these are two different worlds we're living in. Coming from an immigrant background, I and my fellow Hispanic students undoubtedly had more obstacles to overcome every step of the way. What was most troubling about this situation was that at no point did my sociology teacher step up and defend the validity of my arguments. Teachers need to know how to facilitate these multicultural clashes by helping make injustices more visible rather than marginalizing someone for bringing up uncomfortable issues.

Finally, Valley High School does little to honor cultural identity or reach out to immigrant families. My senior year I was president of the International Club (the only club at our school that had lots of immigrant student participation). Without my consent, or that of the members, my advisor began a transition to convert the International Club into the InterAct club affiliated with the community's Rotaract Club (part of Rotary). While this new connection with the Rotary would provide more funding, the only club that was primarily made up of Hispanic members was now being taken over by one sponsored by an all-white organization. In this transition, our advisor had pre-elected leaders to move it forward (also all white). By the time I graduated, the transition was well under way. In fact, on Cinco de Mayo, International Club's major event every year, our club members realized that our advisor didn't think this event was worth our time. As the only Mexican teacher, this advisor did not even advocate for the desires of our community. Ultimately, she turned her back on the members, and the following year InterAct became a primarily white club just like every other club at school.

The loss of a club supporting Hispanic students is matched by failure to create a welcoming environment for Hispanic parents and families. When immigrant parents come to the school, they have to wait around until they can find a translator if they want to speak to a teacher or administrator. Usually this interpreter is another student, creating awkward moments for parents who don't want to discuss their children's problems in front of another student. The school occasionally does try to reach out to Hispanic parents by holding Hispanic Nights where all the events are held in Spanish. However, all the other school events are held only in English. Considering that the school population is more than half Hispanic, the absence of any interpreters makes it clear the school thinks of itself as white. In addition, there are no translators at larger school events such as academic award nights or sporting banquets. As a result, immigrant parents and families feel isolated from the school and unwelcomed.

Debate remains over the exact or best procedures for helping immigrant ESL students successfully integrate into schools, but what is not debated is that these students deserve equal opportunities to learn and grow. Just as any other student, immigrant students should meet the demanding academic standards needed for higher education, but first they must have adequate support. It is essential that schools support educational reforms that address the problem areas apparent at Valley High School. Particularly, schools need to hire qualified ESL instructors, provide adequate counseling for immigrant students, enable teachers to develop multicultural sensitivity and skills at handling ethnic conflict, and provide outreach to immigrant families while valuing their culture.

Works Cited

Good, Mary Ellen, et al. "Latino English Language Learners: Bridging Achievement and Cultural Gaps between Schools and Families." *Journal of Latinos & Education,* vol. 9, no. 4, 2010, pp. 321-39.

Roessingh, Hetty. "The Teacher Is the Key: Building Trust in ESL High School Programs." *Canadian Modern Language Review,* vol. 62, no. 4, 2006, pp. 563-90.

Critiquing "Silenced and Invisible: Problems of Hispanic Students at Valley High School"   MyWritingLab™

1. What criteria does Lorena Mendoza-Flores use to evaluate her high school's treatment of Hispanic students?
2. For evidence, Lorena uses primarily personal experiences, anecdotes, and observations. How effective do you find this evidence in developing the match part of her argument?
3. If Lorena were to identify the real name of her former high school and send the argument directly to the principal and to the city newspaper, how do you think it would be received?
4. How effectively does Lorena make appeals to *logos, ethos*, and *pathos*?

Our second reading, by student writer Christopher Moore, grew out of class discussions about what constitutes a "good news medium" and about whether today's college students are informed about the news.

Information Plus Satire: Why *The Daily Show* and *The Colbert Report* Are Good Sources of News for Young People

CHRISTOPHER MOORE (STUDENT)

Media commentators often complain that college-age students, along with much of the older population, are uninformed about the news. Fewer people today read mainstream newspapers or watch network news than in the past. Hard-core news junkies often get their news online from blog sites or from cable news. Meanwhile, less informed people use social networking tools like Twitter and Facebook for instant, unofficial news, often about popular culture or their favorite celebrities. Another possible source of news is *The Daily Show* and *The Colbert Report*. By presenting information and entertainment together, these shows attract a young audience, especially college-age students who shy away from newspapers or news networks like Fox or CNN. But are these actually good news sources? I will argue that they are, especially for a young audience, because they cover each day's important news and because their satire teaches viewers how to read the news rhetorically. The content on these shows provides up-to-date news stories and compels consumers to recognize that all news has an angle of vision demanding thoughtful processing, not simply blind consumption.

The first thing a good news source does is keep consumers up-to-date on the most important worldwide news. Since *The Daily Show* and *The Colbert Report* both air every weekday except Friday, they constantly present viewers with up-to-date news. Furthermore, all broadcasts are available online, as well as archived—if you missed Tuesday's episode, it's easy to backtrack so that you can stay current. Content published in these shows is trimmed to about 22 minutes (to allow for commercial time), so only the most pertinent information is presented. Consider, for example, the content published in January and February of 2011, which focused almost exclusively on the revolutions in Egypt and the volatile political climate in Tunisia. In these episodes, the shows pulled information from different news sources, both liberal and conservative, showing clips, news anchor commentary, or primary sources just the way other news sources do. In one episode during the turmoil in the Middle East, Stewart interviewed CNN reporter Anderson Cooper, who had just returned from reporting on the revolution from inside Egypt. Viewers watching Stewart might have had more insight into the controversial issues surrounding these revolutions than watchers of network news.

Skeptics, however, may argue that *The Daily Show* and *The Colbert Report* aren't providing real news but just satire. After all, the shows air on Comedy Central. Yet even a satirist needs material to satirize, and these satires always focus on current events, politics, or social trends. Moreover, watching *The Daily Show* offers deeper coverage than many network news programs because it focuses on what is most significant or important in the news. Whereas network news broadcasts tend to move quickly toward sports, weather, humanitarian "feel good" stories, or "breaking news" such as fires, robberies, or traffic accidents, Stewart and Colbert keep their satirical focus on major events with social or political significance.

The satirical methods used by Stewart and Colbert lead to my second and most important reason that *The Daily Show* and *The Colbert Report* are good sources of news: The satire teaches audiences how to "read" the news rhetorically. Unlike conventional news sources, the satire in these two shows unmasks the way that traditional news is packaged and framed, encouraging viewers to be skeptical of news. The satire in these shows functions by pointing out a news source's angle of vision, which promotes specific ideologies and presents news with an agenda. Consider the satirical character played by Stephen Colbert, who presents at one moment a far-right conservative ideology, only to compromise these beliefs at the next moment. His dramatization helps viewers see how rhetorical strategies create an angle of vision. For example, in an interview with Julian Assange, the founder of WikiLeaks, Colbert told his audience that he would show two versions of the interview: one of the unaltered footage and one that deliberately edited the footage to serve an agenda. Network news programs often employ the same tactics as Colbert, but in a much more subtle fashion. Editing may be one strategy, but opinion show hosts like Bill O'Reilly and other conservative news commentators employ a variety of tactics, like selective interviewing, cherry-picking news topics, following "fair and balanced" news with tacit conservative thinking, or any number of other methods. Showing the two versions of Colbert's interview is just one example that reminds viewers that information can be manipulated, presented out of context, edited, or reshaped. Foregrounding these strategies helps viewers criticize and analyze the news they digest.

5   The satire on these shows also points out the absurdities and pretensions of politicians, media commentators, and other public figures. An episode that discussed the Wisconsin labor protests in early 2011 focused on newly elected Republican Governor Scott Walker's decision to slash union benefits and collective bargaining rights to cover deficits in the state budget. When protestors took to the streets, Stewart showed clips from CNN, MSNBC, and CBS that called these protests "inspired by" or "having strong parallels to" revolutionary political action in Egypt or Cairo. However, Stewart rejected this comparison. He pointed out that "no citizens have died, no reporters have been abused, and Republican Governor Scott Walker was elected with 52 percent of the vote—dictators like Mubarak typically hold about 92 percent favor." Stewart's point, in other words, is that comparing two dissimilar things, as traditional news media had done, is unjust to both the Wisconsin protestors and the Tunisian and Egyptian rebels. It belittles those Tunisians or Egyptians who had the courage to raise their voices against dictators just as it distorts the very different political and economic issues and motivations at work in Wisconsin.

       Satire also points out inconsistencies in news reporting, or the logical pitfalls into which politicians regularly stumble. In a skit in which Jon Stewart interviewed a conservative political candidate, he exposed inconsistencies in ideological views about when life begins. On the abortion issue, the candidate argued that life begins at conception, but on constitutional issues of citizenship, he argued that life begins at birth. Stewart took these two conflicting Republican ideologies and used a humorous either/or fallacy to show their inconsistency. Stewart argued that Obama was conceived by his mother in Hawaii. Therefore, if pro-life Republicans believe life begins at conception, then logically Obama is a natural citizen of Hawaii. Either Obama is a citizen, or life does not begin at conception, contradicting the fundamental right-to-life belief. Arguments like these help show how poorly constructed arguments or logical fallacies are common tools of news media for political discussions, facilitating a certain agenda or ideological perspective.

       Viewers of *The Daily Show* or *The Colbert Report* will not get the same kind of news coverage that they would get from reading hard-copy news or an online newspaper, but they learn a healthy skepticism about the objective truthfulness of news. To many young people, entering a discussion on current affairs can be intimidating. Both Stephen Colbert and Jon Stewart make it easier for younger audiences to analyze the rhetorical dimension of news stories, thus allowing the viewer to see bias and angle of vision. The use of satire is a means of allowing entertainment and information to mingle together on a critical level. These approaches to delivering news are energizing, providing an alternative to lackluster news sources that can make us feel like we're drowning in a sea of information. The conservative Fox News commentator Bill O'Reilly once called my generation "a bunch of stone slackers" who sit at home unengaged in politics and watching *The Daily Show* and *The Colbert Report.* Yeah, right. But I wonder, where did he get his information?

Critiquing "Information Plus Satire"   **MyWritingLab**™

1. Christopher Moore's first criterion for a good news source is that it should keep viewers up-to-date with significant and important news rather than with ephemeral events like traffic accidents or celebrity divorces. Do you agree with Moore that *The Daily Show* and *The Colbert Report* keep viewers up-to-date with important news?
2. Moore's second criterion is the thought-provoking claim that a good news source teaches viewers to read the news rhetorically. What does he mean by reading the news rhetorically? How does he make his case? Are you persuaded?

Our final readings represent two different ethical arguments emerging from recent research on therapeutic cloning at the Oregon Health and Sciences University. The first article, by Judith Daar and Erez Aloni, appeared as an op-ed piece in the *Los Angeles Times* on March 21, 2014. Judith Daar, a professor of both law and medicine, is a member of the Ethics Committee of the American Society for Reproductive Medicine. Her co-author Erez Aloni is a professor at Whittier Law School. The second article appeared a year earlier (May 17, 2013) in *National Review*. It was written by Catholic writer Samuel Aquila, the archbishop of the Archdiocese of Denver, Colorado.

Three Genetic Parents—For One Healthy Baby

JUDITH DAAR AND EREZ ALONI

Since January, a new California law allows for a child to have more than two legal parents. But children are still limited to two genetic parents. That could change soon, if the Food and Drug Administration approves human clinical trials for a technique known as mitochondrial replacement, which would enable a child to inherit DNA from three parents.

News of the pending application has caused a kind of panic not seen since Dolly the sheep was cloned, raising the possibility of a single genetic parent. But far from being the end of the human race as we know it, the technique might be a way to prevent hundreds of mitochondrial-linked diseases, which affect about one in 5,000 people.

The idea of multi-person reproductive collaborations is not new. Over the last several decades we have acclimated to various forms of assisted reproductive technologies. Indeed, in the U.S. about 75,000 infants are born each year to parents who enlist the aid of egg donors, sperm donors or gestational carriers. These methods, however, still involve the "traditional" merger of DNA from one male and one female

Mitochondrial replacement would alter this two-genetic-parent model by introducing a third set of DNA into the procreative process. The technique would enable women who carry harmful mutations in their mitochondria to have a child without those harmful mutations. As with all human reproduction, the child would carry a combination of genes from one male and one female. However, in this technique, the nucleus of the mother's egg would be injected into a "third parent's" nucleus-free egg containing healthy mitochondrial DNA. As a result, the child would inherit the characteristics of the original male and female but have healthy mitochondria from a third person.

5 Experiments employing the technique conducted on monkeys resulted in healthy offspring that did not carry the harmful mutation. Now, a team at Oregon Health and Sciences University is seeking approval from the FDA to begin human clinical trials.

It seems likely that, if it is proved safe and effective, mitochondrial replacement will eventually join the panoply of techniques facilitating the birth of healthy children through assisted conception. But it should be no surprise that the new technology is causing a furor.

The introduction of assisted reproductive technologies has followed a predictable pattern: initial panic followed by widespread condemnation, followed by gradual acceptance as a technique becomes more widespread. In the 1950s, when reports of pregnancies using donor sperm first appeared in medical journals, lawmakers declared the process "mechanical adultery" and sought its criminalization. Early reports of success with in vitro fertilization in the 1970s provoked editorials that decried the process as totally immoral. In the 1990s, the introduction of pre-implantation diagnosis of genetic diseases provoked allegations of a war on disabled individuals.

Today, detractors remain, but the methods have been embraced as the standard of care in reproductive medicine. Once a technique proves safe and effective, its ability to assist in the birth of

healthy children generally paves the way for public approval.

For some, the introduction of a third genetic parent is alarming because the novel genetic configuration could be embedded in the child's DNA in perpetuity, with unknown implications for future generations. But the panic also rests in part on simple discomfort with upending the notion of genetic parenthood involving just two people.

10 A similar anxiety seized the public this year after California authorized judges to recognize more than two people as a child's lawful parents. The law grew out of a horrendous situation in which the court's inability to recognize a third parent diverted a young child into foster care. Though it's hardly on par with the scientific breakthrough represented by mitochondrial replacement, the so-called three-parent law stirred deep fears about the durability of traditional family life in the modern era.

But the fears about three-parent possibilities—both genetic and legal—are likely to subside as people realize that they are aimed at one goal: the well-being of children. The California law orders judges to recognize three parents when not doing so "would otherwise be detrimental to the child." And mitochondrial replacement will be employed to avoid transmission of a heritable disease. If the "power of three" has the ability to improve a child's well-being, isn't that something worth embracing?

The "Therapeutic Cloning" of Human Embryos

SAMUEL AQUILA

Oscar Wilde's *The Picture of Dorian Gray* is the sort of timeless morality tale students read as an antidote, or at least an objection, to the hedonism that seems to follow naturally from youthful ideas about immortality.

The story is familiar to many: Dorian Gray is a narcissist who wishes that a portrait of him—his copy in paint—would age in his place. His wish comes true, and though his life is corrupted by a pursuit of pleasure, only his painted visage bears the effects. Dorian himself is visibly unscathed, though the novel's fatal climax exposes a soul rendered ugly by a life of egoistic debauchery.

The Picture of Dorian Gray took on a particular prescience yesterday. Scientists at Oregon Health and Science University reported a successful incidence of cloning, one that relied on the same method that researchers used 17 years ago to clone Dolly the sheep. This week, the cloned embryos were not sheep; they were human beings. The work is heralded as the success of "therapeutic cloning."

We will hear a lot about therapeutic cloning in the news this week. Researchers distinguish between "therapeutic cloning," which creates embryos in order to harvest their stem cells, and "reproductive cloning," which has the intention of a live birth. The Oregon researchers insist that theirs was not an act of "reproductive cloning."

5   But the distinction is spurious. *Both* types of cloning are reproductive. Both bring a new human being into existence. In fact, so-called therapeutic cloning is the more heinous because the process is intended to create life, exploit it, and then destroy it.

Consider what the cloning breakthrough means. Scientists have discovered how to create perfect human copies, to be used for the sole purpose of growing tissue in the effort to combat disease, and then these copies will be destroyed. From a scientific perspective, this breakthrough could solve, among other problems, that of tissue rejection or a delay that renders organ transplant unfeasible. From the standpoint of materialism, there has been no greater advance in regenerative medicine. Through therapeutic cloning, a person's health can be enhanced immeasurably—and only the copy, the embryo, will suffer the effects.

The problem is that the embryo is not merely a copy. The embryo is not an extension of the patient who donated the DNA, a cell bank to be utilized without consequence. The embryo, though genetically identical, is a new manifestation of human life, endowed by its very being with dignity. The embryo is a human being.

The humanity of the cloned embryo will be aggressively denied in the weeks to come. Though human life demonstrably begins at the embryonic stage of development, the created embryo will be presented as a collection of tissue, a biological tabula rasa from which organs can be grown. Scientists will seek more funding, and the Dickey Amendment, which prohibits federal funding for the creation of cloned embryos, will be attacked.

In 1968, Pope Paul VI warned in *Humanae Vitae* that the sexual revolution, beginning with a cultural acceptance of the contraceptive mentality, would lead to a wholesale denial of human dignity and the family. Now we are cloning embryos to destroy them. It will be only a matter of time before therapeutic cloning will cede to reproductive cloning. If we don't seriously contemplate the ethical consequences of therapeutic cloning now, eventually cloned human beings will be born in America.

The "progress" of therapeutic cloning will not be victimless. But the victims will be hidden from sight, tucked away in the dark like Dorian's decaying portrait.

The first class of victims, and the ones most pressing on our consciences, will be the embryos: brought into existence to be used, and then killed. If nurtured, as in a womb, these embryos would grow into fetuses, and then infants, and then children. They are, no matter their size, human beings. But because they are small and have no voice and offer such tremendous possibility, they will be ignored.

10   The embryos will be a class of human beings created only to be exploited and discarded.

The second class of victims will be the rest of us. We will be the ones remaining healthy and making progress and defeating disease—all by means of killing. We will be the ones who appear beautiful, while our souls embrace the most harrowing kind of social utilitarianism and darkness. If we ignore the problem, as we have done with contraception and abortion, we will only sink into a more violent depravity, like the one that befell vain Dorian Gray. We will be the ones whose portrait grows ever uglier, and who grow ever closer to madness.

Critiquing "Three Genetic Parents—For One Healthy Baby" and "The 'Therapeutic Cloning' of Human Embryos"   MyWritingLab™

1. In "Three Genetic Parents—For One Healthy Baby," Daar and Aloni note that news coming from cloning research at Oregon Health and Science University "has caused a kind of panic not seen since Dolly the sheep was cloned." An example of this panic is the earlier *National Review* article by Archbishop Aquila. Summarize Aquila's objection to both therapeutic and reproductive cloning. What rhetorical strategies do Daar and Aloni use to counter the objections of those like Archbishop Aquila?
2. Identify in both articles examples of arguments from consequence and arguments from principle used either to support the authors' claims or to summarize opposing claims.
3. Aquila acknowledges the health benefits of therapeutic cloning, particularly its potential for curing or preventing certain diseases. He recognizes also that many people will consider therapeutic cloning a moral good because it produces good consequences. To make his case for the moral evil of cloning, he creates an analogy argument based on Oscar Wilde's gothic novel *The Picture of Dorian Gray*. Explain how this analogy functions. What does Aquila compare to what?

MyWritingLab™

Visit Ch. 13 Evaluation and Ethical Arguments in *MyWritingLab* to complete the For Writing and Discussion, Examining Visual Arguments, Critiquing, and Writing Assignments and to test your understanding of the chapter objectives.

Proposal Arguments

14

What you will learn in this chapter:

14.1 To explain the special features and concerns of proposal arguments

14.2 To use a problem-solution-justification structure to develop proposal arguments

14.3 To use heuristic strategies to develop supporting reasons for your proposal argument

14.4 To use words and images to create an advocacy poster or advertisement

14.5 To write your own proposal argument

Proposal arguments are essential for the workings of a free and open society. A proposal argument motivates its audience to recognize a problem and then proposes a solution to the problem. When effective, proposal arguments call an audience to action. Whether you are writing a grant proposal to seek funding for a research project, a practical proposal for remedying a problem at your workplace, or a policy proposal to address a national issue, proposal arguments are among the most important kinds of writing you will ever be called upon to produce.

Case 1   Should the Supreme Court Overturn *Roe v. Wade?*

Among the most heated debates in the United States is whether the due process and privacy protections of the Fourteenth Amendment can be extended to a woman's right to an abortion. The right-to-life movement has intensified its efforts to restrict access to abortions at the state level and to overturn *Roe v. Wade* in the U.S. Supreme Court. Meanwhile, pro-choice advocates such as Planned Parenthood have vigorously defended a woman's right to an abortion. Both sides make effective use of visual arguments. Right-to-life groups frequently use posters showing ultrasound images of unborn babies (often not using the word "fetus"). The poster on the following page, sponsored by Planned Parenthood, features a starkly black question mark that on second look is seen to be made from a coat hanger. It makes an implied proposal claim ("Abortion should remain legal") and supports it with a consequence argument: If abortions are outlawed, women will have abortions anyway—using coat hangers instead of medically safe procedures. The image of the coat hanger (reminiscent of horror stories about abortions prior to *Roe v. Wade*) appeals simultaneously to *logos* and *pathos*.

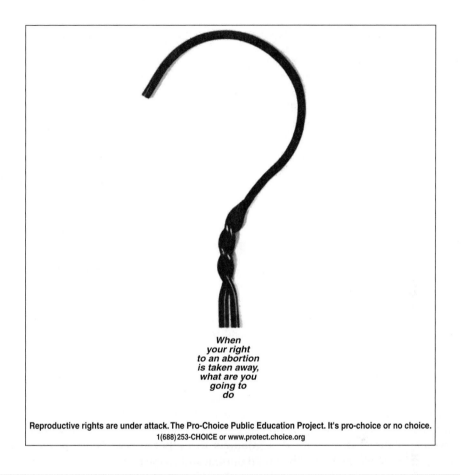

When
your right
to an abortion
is taken away,
what are you
going to
do

Reproductive rights are under attack. The Pro-Choice Public Education Project. It's pro-choice or no choice.
1(688)253-CHOICE or www.protect.choice.org

Case 2   How Should the United States Reduce the Carbon Footprint of Automobiles?

The concern for climate change—combined with the high price of gasoline—has increased the popularity of small, energy-efficient cars. Much debated among policy makers is the role that federal or state governments should play in further promoting a green transportation system. Some argue that the government should stay out of free markets, letting buyers decide for themselves what kinds of cars they want to buy. Others argue that free markets do not currently make gasoline consumers pay for the "externalities" of gasoline consumption—particularly the cost to the environment of loading more carbon into the atmosphere. Concerned citizens have proposed dozens of ideas for reducing the carbon footprint of cars and trucks. Among the proposals are the following: placing a "green tax" on gasoline; requiring auto manufacturers to increase the fuel efficiency of their fleets; giving tax credits for buying a fuel-efficient car; increasing incentives for carpooling or taking public transportation; increasing the cost of parking; charging different gas prices at the pump (with higher prices for less fuel-efficient cars); retrofitting cars to burn natural gas; and rebuilding cities so that housing is closer to worksites.

The Special Features and Concerns of Proposal Arguments

14.1 Explain the special features and concerns of proposal arguments

Although proposal arguments are the last type of argument we examine, they are among the most common arguments that you will encounter or be called on to write. The essence of proposal arguments is that they call for action. In reading a proposal, the audience is enjoined to make a decision and then to act on it—to *do* something. Proposal arguments are sometimes called *should or ought* arguments because those helping verbs express the obligation to act. They typically have a three-part structure: (1) description of a problem, (2) proposed solution, and (3) justification for the proposed solution. In the justification section of your proposal argument, you develop *because* clauses of the kinds you have practiced throughout this text.

Practical Proposals versus Policy Proposals

For instructional purposes, we distinguish between two kinds of proposal arguments—*practical proposals,* which propose an action to solve some kind of local or immediate problem, and *policy proposals,* which propose a broad plan of action to solve major social, economic, or political problems affecting the common good. A student's proposal to build bike paths on campus would be an example of a practical proposal. In contrast, an argument that the United States should abolish the income tax would be a policy proposal.

The primary difference is the narrowness versus breadth of the concern. *Practical* proposals are narrow, local, and concrete; they focus on the nuts and bolts of getting something done in the here and now. They are often concerned with the exact size of a piece of steel, the precise duties of a new person to be hired, or a close estimate of the cost of paint or computers to be purchased. *Policy* proposals, in contrast, are concerned with the broad outline and shape of a course of action, often on a regional, national, or even international issue. What government should do about overcrowding of prisons would be a problem addressed by policy proposals. How to improve the security alarm system for the county jail would be addressed by a practical proposal.

Learning to write both kinds of proposals is valuable. Researching and writing a *policy* proposal is an excellent way to practice the responsibilities of citizenship, which require the ability to understand complex issues and to weigh positive and negative consequences of policy choices. In your professional life, writing *practical* proposals may well be among your most important duties on the job. Effective proposal writing is the lifeblood of many companies and also constitutes one of the most powerful ways you can identify and help solve problems.

Toulmin Framework for a Proposal Argument

The Toulmin schema is particularly useful for proposal arguments because it helps you support your proposal with reasons linked to your audience's beliefs, assumptions, and values. Suppose that your university is debating whether to banish fraternities and sororities. Suppose further that you are in favor of banishing the Greek system. One of your arguments is that eliminating the Greek system will improve your university's academic reputation. The following chart shows how you might use the Toulmin schema to make this line of reasoning as persuasive as possible.

Toulmin Analysis of the Greek System Argument

ENTHYMEME

CLAIM Our university should eliminate the Greek system

REASON because doing so will improve our university's academic reputation.

GROUNDS

Evidence that eliminating the Greek system will improve our academic reputation:

- Excessive party atmosphere of some Greek houses emphasizes social life rather than studying—we are known as a party school.
- Last year the average GPA of students in fraternities and sororities was lower than the GPA of non-Greek students.
- New pledges have so many house duties and initiation rites that their studies suffer.
- Many new students think about rush more than about the academic life.

WARRANT

It is good for our university to achieve a better academic reputation.

BACKING

- The school would attract more serious students, leading to increased prestige.
- Campus would be more academically focused and attract better faculty.
- Losing the "party-school" reputation would put us in better light for taxpayers and legislators.
- Students would graduate with more skills and knowledge.

CONDITIONS OF REBUTTAL
Attacking the reason and grounds

- Many of the best students are Greeks. Last year's highest-GPA award went to a sorority woman, and several other Greeks won prestigious graduate school scholarships.
- Statistics on grades are misleading. Many houses had a much higher average GPA than the university average. Total GPA was brought down by a few rowdy houses.
- Many other high-prestige universities have Greek systems.
- There are ways to tone down the party atmosphere on campus without abolishing the Greek system.
- Greeks contribute significantly to the community through service projects.

CONDITIONS OF REBUTTAL
Attacking the warrant and backing

- No one will argue that it is not good to have a strong academic reputation.
- However, skeptics may say that eliminating sororities and fraternities won't improve the university's academic reputation but will hurt its social life and its wide range of living options.

Special Concerns for Proposal Arguments

In their call for action, proposal arguments entail certain emphases and audience concerns that you don't generally face with other kinds of arguments. Let's look briefly at some of these special concerns.

- **The need for presence.** To persuade people to *act* on your proposal, particularly if the personal or financial cost of acting is high, you must give your argument presence as well as intellectual force. By *presence* we mean an argument's ability to grip your readers' hearts and imaginations as well as their intellects. You can give presence to an argument through appeals to *pathos,* such as effective use of details, provocative statistics, dialogue, illustrative narratives, and compelling examples that show the reader the seriousness of the problem you are addressing or the consequences of not acting on your proposal.
- **The need to overcome people's natural conservatism.** Another difficulty with proposals is the innate conservatism of all human beings, whatever their political persuasion, as suggested by the popular adage "If it ain't broke, don't fix it." The difficulty of proving that something needs fixing is compounded by the fact that frequently the status quo appears to be working. So sometimes when writing a proposal, you can't argue that what we have is bad, but only that what we could have would be better. Often, then, a proposal argument will be based not on present evils but on the evils of lost potential. And getting an audience to accept lost potential may be difficult indeed, given the inherently abstract nature of potentiality.
- **The difficulty of predicting future consequences.** Further, most proposal makers will be forced to predict consequences of their proposed action. As the "law of unintended consequences" suggests, few major decisions lead neatly to their anticipated results without surprises along the way. So when we claim that our proposal will lead to good consequences, we can expect our audience to be skeptical.
- **The problem of evaluating consequences.** A final problem for proposal writers is the difficulty of evaluating consequences. In government and industry, managers often use a *cost-benefit analysis* to reduce all consequences to a single-scale comparison, usually money. Although this scale may work well in some circumstances, it can lead to grotesquely inappropriate conclusions in other situations. Just how does one balance the environmental benefits of a green tax on gasoline against the suffering of drivers who can't afford to get to work? Also a benefit for one group often entails a cost for others. For example, a higher minimum wage will benefit low-wage workers but at a cost to consumers, who must pay higher prices, or to other low-wage workers who get laid off.

These, then, are some of the general difficulties facing someone who sets out to write a proposal argument. Although these difficulties may seem daunting, the rest of this chapter offers strategies to help you overcome them and produce a successful proposal.

EXAMINING VISUAL ARGUMENTS

MyWritingLab™

A Proposal Claim

This photo of a dead baby albatross on a Pacific island near an albatross nesting ground resembles the photos taken by environmental photographer Chris Jordan in his well-known 2009 exhibit entitled "Midway: Message from the Gyre." The purpose of that exhibit was to draw attention to the effects of the increasing volumes of ocean garbage on albatrosses, who mistake the garbage for food. How could this photo be used to generate concern and activism regarding this environmental problem? The colorful, plastic-filled carcass of the baby albatross creates a complex appeal to *pathos* in the way that it illustrates the problem. What verbal text would you use to interpret the message of the photo and call people to action?

Developing a Proposal Argument

14.2 Use a problem-solution-justification structure to develop proposal arguments

Writers of proposal arguments must focus in turn on three main phases or stages of the argument: showing that a problem exists, explaining the proposed solution, and offering a justification.

Convincing Your Readers that a Problem Exists

There is one argumentative strategy generic to all proposal arguments: calling your reader's attention to a problem. In some situations, your intended audience may already be aware of the problem and may have even asked for solutions. In such cases, you do not need to develop the problem extensively or motivate your audience to solve it. But in most situations, awakening your readers to the existence of a problem—a problem they may well not have recognized before—is your first important challenge. You must give your problem presence through anecdotes, telling statistics, or other means that show readers how the problem affects people or otherwise has important stakes. Your goal is to gain your readers' intellectual assent to the depth, range, and potential seriousness of the problem and thereby motivate them to want to solve it.

Typically, the arguer develops the problem in one of two places—either in the introduction prior to the presentation of the arguer's proposed solution or in the body of the paper as the first main reason justifying the proposed solution. In the second instance the writer's first *because* clause has the following structure: "We should do this action *because* it addresses a serious problem."

Here is how one student writer gave presence to a proposal, addressed to the chair of the mathematics department at her school, calling for redesign of the first-year calculus curriculum in order to slow its pace. She wants the chair to see the problem from her perspective.

Example Passage Giving Presence to a Problem

For me, who wants to become a high school math teacher, the problem with introductory calculus is not its difficulty but its pace. My own experience in the Calculus 134 and 135 sequence last year showed me that it was not the learning of calculus that was difficult for me. I was able to catch on to the new concepts. My problem was that it went too fast. Just as I was assimilating new concepts and feeling the need to reinforce them, the class was on to a new topic before I had full mastery of the old concept.... Part of the reason for the fast pace is that calculus is a feeder course for computer science and engineering. If prospective engineering students can't learn the calculus rapidly, they drop out of the program. The high dropout rate benefits the Engineering School because they use the math course to weed out an overabundance of engineering applicants. Thus the pace of the calculus course is geared to the needs of the engineering curriculum, not to the needs of someone like me, who wants to be a high school mathematics teacher and who believes that my own difficulties with math—combined with my love for it—might make me an excellent math teacher.

By describing the fast pace of the math curriculum from the perspective of a future math teacher rather than an engineering student, this writer brings visibility to a problem. What before didn't look like a problem (it is good to weed out weak engineering majors) suddenly became a problem (it is bad to weed out future math teachers). Establishing herself as a serious student genuinely interested in learning calculus, she gave presence to the problem by calling attention to it in a new way.

Showing the Specifics of Your Proposal

Having decided that there is a problem to be solved, you should lay out your thesis, which is a proposal for solving the problem. Your goal now is to stress the feasibility of your solution, including costs. The art of proposal making is the art of the possible. To be sure, not all proposals require elaborate descriptions of the implementation process. If you are proposing, for example, that a local PTA chapter buy new tumbling mats for the junior high gym classes, the procedures for buying the mats will probably be irrelevant. But in many arguments the specifics of your proposal—the actual step-by-step methods of implementing it—may be instrumental in winning your audience's support.

You will also need to show how your proposal will solve the problem either partially or wholly. Sometimes you may first need to convince your reader that the problem is solvable and not something intractably rooted in "the way things are," such as earthquakes or jealousy. In other words, expect that some members of your audience will be skeptical about the ability of any proposal to solve the problem you are addressing. You may well need, therefore, to "listen" to this point of view in your refutation section and to argue that your problem is at least partially solvable.

In order to persuade your audience that your proposal can work, you can follow any one of several approaches. A typical approach is to use a causal argument to show that your solution is feasible. Another approach is to use a resemblance argument to show how similar proposals have been successful elsewhere. Or, if similar things have failed in the past, you try to show how the present situation is different.

Convincing Your Readers that the Benefits of Your Proposal Outweigh the Costs

The justification phase of a proposal argument will need extensive development in some arguments and minimal development in others, again depending on your particular problem and the rhetorical context of your proposal. If your audience already acknowledges the seriousness of the problem you are addressing and has simply been waiting for the right solution to come along, then your argument will be successful, so long as you can convince your audience that your solution will work and that it won't cost too much. Such arguments depend on the clarity of your proposal and the feasibility of its being implemented.

But what if the costs are high? What if your readers don't think the problem is serious? What if they don't appreciate the benefits of solving the problem or the bad consequences of not solving it? In such cases you have to develop persuasive reasons for enacting your proposal. You may also have to determine who has the power to act on your proposal and apply arguments directly to that person's or agency's immediate interests. You need to know to whom or to what your power source is beholden or responsive and what values your power source holds that can be appealed to. You're looking, in short, for the best pressure points.

Using Heuristic Strategies to Develop Supporting Reasons for Your Proposal

14.3 Use heuristic strategies to develop supporting reasons for your proposal argument

To help you find supporting reasons for your proposal—the pressure points that will move your audience—we offer two heuristic strategies. (A *heuristic* is an exploratory problem-solving technique or invention aid that helps you generate ideas.) We call these heuristics the "claim types" strategy and the "stock issue" strategy.

The "Claim Types" Strategy

In Chapter 10 we explained how evaluation and proposal claims often use claims about category, cause, or resemblance for their supporting reasons. This fact leads to a powerful idea-generating strategy based on arguments from category (particularly from a category of actions that adhere to a certain principle), on arguments from consequences, or on arguments from resemblance. This "claim types" strategy is illustrated in the following chart:

Explanation of Claim Types Strategy for Supporting a Proposal Claim

Claim Type	Generic Template	Example from Biotechnology Issue
Argument from principle or category	We should do this action ▪ because doing so adheres to this good principle [or] ▪ because this action belongs to this good category	We should support genetically modified foods ▪ because doing so values scientific reason over emotion [or] ▪ because genetically modified foods are safe [belong to the category of safe things]
Argument from consequences	▪ because this action will lead to these good consequences	▪ because biotech crops can reduce world hunger ▪ because biotech crops can improve the environment by reducing use of pesticides
Argument from resemblance	▪ because this action has been done successfully elsewhere [or] ▪ because this action is like this other good action	▪ because genetic modification is like natural crossbreeding that has been accelerated [or] ▪ because genetic modification of food is like scientific advancements in medicine

Before we give you some simple strategies for using this approach, let's illustrate it with another example.

The United States should levy a "carbon tax" on carbon-based fuels.

▪ Because such a tax accords with the free-market principle that the price of a good should reflect the full cost of production (category/principle)
▪ Because such a tax will accelerate the transition to cleaner fuels and thus help reduce global warming (cause/consequence)
▪ Because this approach is similar to the market-based tax on sulfur emissions that helped solve the problem of acid rain (resemblance)

Note how each of these supporting reasons appeals to the value system of different kinds of voters. The writer argues that a carbon tax belongs to the category of things that use free market principles (particularly valued by conservative, pro-business voters); that it will lead to the good consequence of reducing global warming (valued particularly by environmentalists and others worried about climate change); and that it is similar to something that has already proved successful (the market-based approach to fighting acid rain, which has been hailed by both liberals and conservatives). The claim types strategy for generating ideas is easy to apply in practice. The following chart shows you how.

Suggestions for Applying the Claim Types Strategy to Your Proposal

Claim Type	Your Goal	Thinking Strategy
Argument from principle or category	Show how your proposed action follows a principle valued by your audience or belongs to a category valued by your audience.	Think of how your proposed action adheres to an audience-valued rule or principle or belongs to an audience-valued category (for example, "doing this action is kind, just, constitutional, appropriately restrained, safe, efficient," and so forth).
Argument from consequences	Show how your proposed action will lead to consequences valued by your audience.	Brainstorm consequences of your proposal and identify those that the audience will agree are good.
Argument from resemblance	Show how your proposed action has been done successfully elsewhere or is like another action valued by your audience.	Find analogies that compare your proposed action to something the audience already values or find previous places or times that your proposed action (or something similar to it) has been done successfully.

■ ■ ■   **FOR WRITING AND DISCUSSION Generating Ideas Using the Claim MyWritingLab™ Types Strategy**

Individual task: Use the strategies of principle/category, consequence, and resemblance to create *because* clauses that support each of the following claims. Try to have at least one *because* clause from each of the claim types, but generate as many reasons as possible. Don't worry about whether any individual reason exactly fits the category. The purpose is to stimulate thinking, not fill in the slots.

Example

Congress should not pass gun control laws (proposal claim)

- because the Second Amendment guarantees the right to own guns (principle or category)
- because owning a gun allows citizens to protect themselves, their homes, and their loved ones from intruders (consequence)

- because laws to ban guns will be as ineffective as laws to ban alcohol during Prohibition (resemblance)

1. Colleges should require a service learning course for graduation.
2. Restaurants should be required to post calorie counts and other ingredient information for all menu items.
3. Division-I college athletes should receive salaries.
4. Alcohol should not be allowed on campus.
5. Parents should be heavily taxed for having more than two children.

Group task: Share your efforts with classmates. Then, working in small groups or a whole class, repeat the exercise, taking the opposite position on each issue.   ▪ ▪ ▪

The "Stock Issues" Strategy

Another effective heuristic for a proposal argument is to ask yourself a series of questions based on the "stock issues" strategy. Suppose, for example, you wanted to develop the following argument: "In order to solve the problem of students who won't take risks with their writing, the faculty should adopt a pass/fail method of grading in all writing courses." The stock issues strategy invites the writer to consider "stock" ways (that is, common, usual, frequently repeated ways) that such arguments can be conducted.

Stock issue 1: *Is there really a problem here that needs to be solved?* Is it really true that a large number of student writers won't take risks in their writing? Is this problem more serious than other writing problems such as undeveloped ideas, lack of organization, and poor sentence structure? This stock issue invites the writer to convince her audience that a true problem exists. Conversely, an opponent to the proposal may argue that a true problem does not exist.

Stock issue 2: *Will the proposed solution really solve this problem?* Is it true that a pass/fail grading system will cause students to take more risks with their writing? Will more interesting, surprising, and creative essays result from pass/fail grading? Or will students simply put less effort into their writing? This stock issue prompts a supporter to demonstrate that the proposal will solve the problem; in contrast, it prompts the opponent to show that the proposal won't work.

Stock issue 3: *Can the problem be solved more simply, without disturbing the status quo?* An opponent of the proposal may agree that a problem exists and that the proposed solution might solve it. However, the opponent may say, "Are there not less radical ways to solve this problem? If we want more creative and risk-taking student essays, can't we just change our grading criteria so that we reward risky papers and penalize conventional ones?" This stock issue prompts supporters to show that *only* the proposed solution will solve the problem and that no minor tinkering with the status quo will be adequate. Conversely, opponents will argue that the problem can be solved without acting on the proposal.

Stock issue 4: *Is the proposed solution really practical? Does it stand a chance of actually being enacted?* Here an opponent to the proposal may agree that the proposal would work but contends that it involves pie-in-the-sky idealism. Nobody will vote to change the existing system so radically; therefore, it is a waste of our time to debate it. Following this prompt, supporters would have to argue that pass/fail grading is workable and that enough faculty members are disposed to it that the proposal is worth debating. Opponents may argue that the faculty is so traditional that pass/fail has utterly no chance of being accepted, despite its merits.

Stock issue 5: *What will be the unforeseen positive and negative consequences of the proposal?* Suppose we do adopt a pass/fail system. What positive or negative consequences may occur that are different from what we at first predicted? Using this prompt, an opponent may argue that pass/fail grading will reduce the effort put forth by students and that the long-range effect will be writing of even lower quality than we have now. Supporters would try to find positive consequences—perhaps a new love of writing for its own sake rather than for the sake of a grade.

■ ■ ■ **FOR CLASS DISCUSSION** Brainstorming Ideas for a Proposal

The following collaborative task takes approximately two class days to complete. The exercise takes you through the process of creating a proposal argument.

1. In small groups, identify and list several major problems facing students in your college or university.
2. Decide among yourselves which are the most important of these problems and -rank them in order of importance.
3. Take your group's number one problem and explore answers to the following questions. Group recorders should be prepared to present their group's answers to the class as a whole:

   a. Why is the problem a problem?
   b. For whom is the problem a problem?
   c. How will these people suffer if the problem is not solved? (Give specific examples.)
   d. Who has the power to solve the problem?
   e. Why hasn't the problem been solved up to this point?
   f. How can the problem be solved? (That is, create a proposal.)
   g. What are the probable benefits of acting on your proposal?
   h. What costs are associated with your proposal?
   i. Who will bear those costs?
   j. Why should this proposal be enacted?
   k. Why is it better than alternative proposals?
4. As a group, draft an outline for a proposal argument in which you

   a. describe the problem and its significance.
   b. propose your solution to the problem.
   c. justify your proposal by showing how the benefits of adopting that proposal outweigh the costs.
5. Recorders for each group should write their group's outline on the board and be prepared to explain it to the class.

■ ■ ■

Proposal Arguments as Advocacy Posters or Advertisements

14.4 Use words and images to create an advocacy poster or advertisement

A frequently encountered kind of proposal argument is the one-page newspaper or magazine advertisement often purchased by advocacy groups to promote a cause. Such arguments also appear as Web pages or as posters or fliers. These condensed advocacy arguments are marked by their bold, abbreviated, tightly planned format. The creators of these arguments know they must work fast to capture our attention, give presence to a problem, advocate a solution, and enlist our support. Advocacy advertisements frequently use photographs, images, or icons that appeal to a reader's emotions and imagination. In addition to images, they often use different type sizes and styles. Large-type text in these documents frequently takes the form of slogans or condensed thesis statements written in an arresting style. To outline and justify their solutions, creators of advocacy ads often put main supporting reasons in bulleted lists and sometimes enclose carefully selected facts and quotations in boxed sidebars. To add an authoritative *ethos,* the arguments often include fine-print footnotes and bibliographies. (For more detailed discussion of how advocacy posters and advertisements use images and arrange text for rhetorical effect, see Chapter 9 on visual argument.)

Another prominent feature of these condensed, highly visual arguments is their appeal to the audience through a direct call for a course of action: go to an advocacy Web site to find more information on how to support the cause; send an e-mail to a decision maker or political representative; vote for or against the proposition or the candidate; or donate money to a cause.

An example of a student-produced advocacy poster is shown in Figure 14.1. Here, environmental studies student Janie Bube urges residents of her city to build rain gardens to help solve the problem of excess stormwater. At the top of this poster, Janie uses a photo of a flood she took during her internship fieldwork to give the problem presence. She then offers her proposed solution, made visually appealing by another of her own photos—a neighborhood rain garden. She offers three reasons to justify the choice of rain gardens, asserting why and how rain gardens work. The final lines of the poster give readers a Web site for more information. The rhetorical effect of the text, image, and layout is to attract readers' attention, remind them of the problem, and push them toward adopting her proposed solution.

WRITING ASSIGNMENT   A Proposal Argument   MyWritingLab™

14.5 To write your own proposal argument

Option 1: A Practical Proposal Addressing a Local Problem   Write a practical proposal offering a solution to a local problem. Your proposal should have three main sections: (1) description of the problem, (2) proposed solution, and (3) justification. Proposals are usually accompanied by a *letter of transmittal*— a one-page business letter that introduces the proposal to its intended audience and provides some needed background about the writer. Document design is important in practical proposals, which are aimed at busy people who have to make many decisions under time constraints. An effective design helps establish the writer's *ethos* as a quality-oriented professional and helps make the reading of the proposal as easy as possible. For a student example of a practical proposal, see Megan Johnson's argument on pages 322–325.

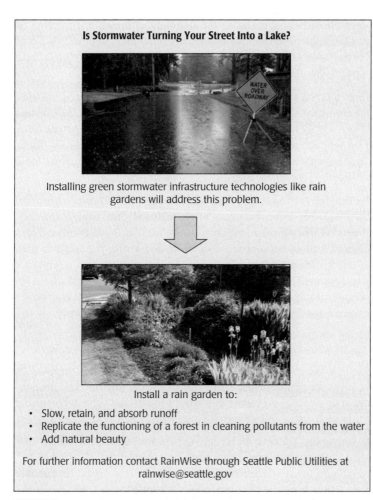

Is Stormwater Turning Your Street Into a Lake?

Installing green stormwater infrastructure technologies like rain gardens will address this problem.

Install a rain garden to:

- Slow, retain, and absorb runoff
- Replicate the functioning of a forest in cleaning pollutants from the water
- Add natural beauty

For further information contact RainWise through Seattle Public Utilities at rainwise@seattle.gov

FIGURE 14.1 Student advocacy poster

Option 2: A Policy Proposal as a Guest Editorial   Write a two- to three-page policy proposal suitable for publication as a feature editorial in a college or city newspaper, on an appropriate Web site, or in a publication associated with a particular group, such as a church newsletter or employee bulletin. The voice and style of your argument should be aimed at readers of your chosen publication or Web site. Your editorial should have the following features:

1. The identification of a problem (Persuade your audience that this is a genuine problem that needs solving; give it presence.)
2. A proposal for action that will help alleviate the problem
3. A justification of your solution (the reasons why your audience should accept your proposal and act on it)

Option 3: A Researched Argument Proposing Public Policy   Write an eight- to twelve-page proposal argument as a formal research paper, using researched data for development and support. In business and professional life, this kind of research proposal is often called a *white paper*, which recommends a course of action internally within an organization or externally to a client or stakeholder. An example of a researched policy proposal is student writer Ivan Snook's "Flirting with Disaster: An Argument against Integrating Women into the Combat Arms," on pages 326–330.

Option 4: Multimedia Project: A One-Page Advocacy Poster or Advertisement   Using the strategies of visual argument discussed in Chapter 9 and on pages 316–317 of this chapter, create a one-page advocacy advertisement urging action on a public issue. Your advertisement should be designed for publication in a newspaper or Web site or for distribution as a poster or flier. For an example of a student-produced advocacy poster, see Janie Bube's poster shown in Figure 14.1 on page 317.

Option 5: Multimedia Project: A Proposal Speech with Visual Aids   Deliver a proposal argument as a prepared but extemporaneous speech of approximately five to eight minutes, supported with visual aids created on presentation software such as PowerPoint or Prezi. Your speech should present a problem, propose a solution, and justify the solution with reasons and evidence. Use visual aids to give "presence" to the problem and to enhance appeals to *logos*, *ethos*, and *pathos*. Good aids use visual strategies to create encapsulated visual arguments; they are not simply bullet point outlines of your speech. Sandy Wainscott's speech outline and selected PowerPoint slides (pages 333–335) illustrate this genre.

Exploring Ideas

Because *should or ought* issues are among the most common sources of arguments, you may already have ideas for proposal issues. To think of ideas for practical proposals, try making an idea map of local problems you would like to see solved. For initial spokes, try trigger words such as the following:

- Problems at my university (dorms, parking, registration system, financial aid, campus appearance, clubs, curriculum, intramural program, athletic teams)
- Problems in my city or town (dangerous intersections, ugly areas, inadequate lighting, parks, police policy, public transportation, schools)
- Problems at my place of work (office design, flow of customer traffic, merchandise display, company policies)
- Problems related to my future career, hobbies, recreational time, life as a consumer, life as a homeowner

If you can offer a solution to the problem you identify, you may make a valuable contribution to some phase of public life.

To find a topic for policy proposals, stay in touch with the news, which will keep you aware of current debates on regional and national issues. Also, visit the Web sites of your congressional representatives to see what issues they are currently investigating and debating. You might think of your policy proposal as a white paper for one of your legislators.

Once you have decided on a proposal issue, we recommend you explore it by trying one or more of the following activities:

- Explore ideas by using the claim types strategy (see pages 312–314).
- Explore ideas by using the "stock issues" strategy (see pages 314–315).
- Explore ideas using the eleven questions (3a–3k) on page 316.

Identifying Your Audience and Determining What's at Stake

Before drafting your argument, identify your targeted audience and determine what's at stake. Consider your responses to the following questions:

- What audience are you targeting? What background do they need to understand your problem? How much do they already care about it? How could you motivate them to care?
- After they read your argument, what stance do you imagine them holding? What change do you want to bring about in their view or their behavior?
- What will they find uncomfortable or threatening about your proposal? Particularly, what costs will they incur by acting on your proposal?
- What objections might they raise? What counterarguments or alternative solutions will you need to address?
- Why does your proposal matter? What is at stake?

Organizing a Proposal Argument

When you write your draft, you may find it helpful to have at hand an organization plan for a proposal argument. The plan on page 320 shows a typical structure for a proposal argument. In some cases, you may want to summarize and rebut opposing views before you present the justification for your own proposal.

Designing a One-Page Advocacy Poster or Advertisement

As an alternative to a traditional written argument, your instructor may ask you to create a one-page advocacy advertisement. The first stage of your invention process should be the same as that for a longer proposal argument. Choose a controversial public issue that needs immediate attention or a neglected issue about which you want to arouse public passion. As with a longer proposal argument, consider your audience in order to identify the values and beliefs on which you will base your appeal.

When you construct your argument, the limited space available demands efficiency in your choice of words and in your use of document design. Your goal is to have a memorable impact on your reader in order to promote the action you advocate. The following questions may help you design and revise your advocacy ad:

1. How could photos or other graphic elements establish and give presence to the problem?
2. How can type size, type style, and layout be used to present the core of your proposal, including the justifying reasons, in the most powerful way for the intended audience?
3. Can any part of this argument be presented as a memorable slogan or catchphrase? What key phrases could highlight the parts or the main points of this argument?
4. How can document design clarify the course of action and the direct demand on the audience this argument is proposing?
5. How can use of color enhance the overall impact of your advocacy argument? (Note: One-page advertisements are expensive to reproduce in color, but you might make effective use of color if your advocacy ad were to appear as a poster or Web page.)

Designing PowerPoint Slides or Other Visual Aids for a Speech

In designing visual aids, your goal is to increase the persuasive effect of your speech rather than to demonstrate your technical wizardry. A common mistake with PowerPoint presentations is to get enamored with the program's bells and whistles. If you find yourself thinking about special effects (animations, fade-outs, flashing letters) rather than about "at a glance" visual appeals to *logos or pathos*, you may be on the wrong track. Another common mistake is to use slides simply to project a bullet point outline of your speech. Our best advice in designing slides is thus to "think visual argument."

Organization Plan for a Proposal Argument

Introduce and develop the problem.	• Engage readers' interest in your problem. • Provide background, including previous attempts to solve the problem. • Give the problem "presence" by showing who is affected and what is at stake. • Argue that the problem is solvable (optional).
Present your proposed solution to the problem.	• First, state your proposal concisely to serve as your thesis statement or claim. • Then, explain the specifics of your proposal.
Justify your proposed solution through a series of supporting reasons.	• Restate your claim and forecast your supporting reasons. • Present and develop reason 1. • Present and develop reason 2. • Present and develop additional reasons.
Respond to objections or to alternative proposals.	• Anticipate and summarize possible objections or alternative ways to solve the problem. • Respond appropriately through rebuttal or concession.
Conclude.	• Sum up your argument and help readers return to the "big picture" of what's at stake. • Call readers to action. • End with something memorable.

In terms of visual argument, effective presentation slides can usually be placed in three design categories:

- Slides using images (photographs, drawings) to enhance *pathos* or to create a snapshot for visual clarity of a concept (*logos*)
- Slides using graphs or other visual displays of numbers to make numeric arguments
- Slides using bulleted (all-text) subpoints for evidence

All the strategies for visual arguments discussed in Chapter 9 and in this chapter under "Proposal Arguments as Advocacy Posters or Advertisements" (pages 316–317) apply equally to presentation slides.

In most cases, the "title" of the slide should put into words the "take-away point" of the slide—a verbal summary of the slide's visual argument. Most rhetoricians suggest that the title of a slide be a short sentence that makes a point rather than just a topic phrase.

Topic as Title (Weak)	Point as Title (Strong)
Coal and the Environment	Burning Coal Produces Dangerous Greenhouse Gases
The Effect of Money on Happiness	More Money Doesn't Mean More Happiness

Student writer Sandy Wainscott follows these principles in her speech and accompanying PowerPoint slides, shown on pages 333–335. ■

Questioning and Critiquing a Proposal Argument

As we've suggested, proposal arguments need to overcome the innate conservatism of people, the difficulty of anticipating all the consequences of a proposal, and so forth. What questions, then, can we ask about proposal arguments to help us anticipate these problems?

Will a skeptic deny that my problem is really a problem? Be prepared for skeptics who aren't bothered by your problem, who see your problem as limited to a small group of people, or who think you are exaggerating.

Will a skeptic doubt the effectiveness of my solution? A skeptic might agree that your problem is indeed important and worth solving, but might not be convinced that your solution will work. For these skeptics, you'll need to provide evidence that your solution is feasible and workable. Also be prepared for skeptics who focus on the potential negative or unintended consequences of your proposed solution.

Will a skeptic think my proposal costs too much? The most commonly asked question of any proposal is simply, "Do the benefits of enacting the proposal outweigh the costs?" Be wary of the (understandable) tendency to underestimate the costs and exaggerate the benefits of a proposal. Honesty will enhance your *ethos.*

Will a skeptic suggest counterproposals? Once you've convinced readers that a problem exists, they are likely to suggest solutions different from yours. It only makes sense to anticipate alternative solutions and to work out ways to argue why your solution is better. And who knows, you may end up liking the counterproposal better and changing your mind about what to propose!

READINGS

Our first reading, by student writer Megan Johnson, is a practical proposal addressing the problem of an inequitable meal plan on her campus—one that she claims discriminates against women. As a practical proposal, it uses headings and other elements of document design aimed at giving it a finished and professional appearance. When sent to the intended audience, it is accompanied by a single-spaced letter of transmittal following the conventional format of a business letter.

A Practical Proposal

MEGAN JOHNSON (STUDENT)

Ms. Jane Doe
Vice-President for Budgeting and Finance
Certain University
Certain City
Certain State, Zip

Dear Ms. Doe:

Enclosed is a proposal that addresses our university's minimum meal plan requirements for students living on campus. My proposal shows the problems associated with this requirement and suggests a workable solution for the university.

The enclosed proposal suggests a modest plan for allowing students to use their campus cards to purchase items off campus. Currently, students are required to purchase a minimum meal plan of $1,170, even though women eat less than men and often have to donate unspent meal funds back to the university. This proposal would give students the option to spend some of their meal plan money off campus. The benefits of my plan include more fairness to women students, fewer incentives toward binge eating, more opportunities for student bonding, and better relations with the nearby business community.

Through web research, I have discovered that other universities have systems in place similar to what I am proposing. I hope that my proposal is received well and considered as a workable option. A change in the minimum meal plan requirement might make our university a more desirable option for more prospective students as well as ultimately benefit the general welfare of the current student body.

Thank you for your time.

Sincerely,
Megan Johnson (Student)

A Proposal to Allow Off-Campus Purchases with a University Meal Card, Submitted by Megan Johnson (Student)

Problem

The problem with this university's required meal plan is that it is too large for many students, particularly women. For example, at the end of Winter Quarter, my final balance on my meal card was $268.50, all of which, except for $100, I had to donate back to the university. As the current system stands, students have to purchase a minimum meal plan for living on campus. The minimum meal plan totals $1,170 per quarter. During the academic year an amount of $100 may be rolled into the next quarter. At the end of the quarter any remaining funds, excluding the $100, will be removed from the meal plan. Therefore, if students do not spend the money on their meal plans, it will be wasted. As a woman, I am frustrated about having to decide whether to give my money back to the university or to use up my meal card by binge eating at the end of each quarter.

Proposed Solution

I propose that our university create a system in which students are able to use their campus meal plans at local businesses off campus such as local drug stores, grocery stores, and restaurants. As I will note later in this proposal, other universities have such a system, so the technical difficulties should be easy to solve. Basically, the card works as a debit card loaded with the amount of money the student places on the card. Local businesses would swipe a student's card the same way as the on-campus food service currently does, deducting the current charge against the amount still available on the card. It would probably be possible to limit the total number of dollars available for spending off campus.

Justification

My proposal would allow on-campus residential students to use some of their meal plan money on groceries, on non-food related items such as toiletries, or on an occasional off-campus meal at a local restaurant. This proposal would resolve the problem of gender bias in the current system, promote opportunities for more bonding among students, and ultimately help create a healthier student body. Moreover, it would show the university's commitment to its students' welfare.

First of all, the current meal plan policy tends to discriminate against women. All students on campus are required to have a minimum meal plan, even though men and women have clearly different eating habits. Men tend to eat much more than women and frequently have to add money to their meal plans to get through the quarter. In contrast, many women, like myself, don't use up their prepaid amounts. For example, my friend James ran out of his meal plan by the eighth week of the quarter whereas my roommate Blaire still had over $400 left on her card at the end of the quarter. She and I, like many other women, will have to donate our money back to the school. Therefore, women often feel cheated out of their money while men do not. It is discriminatory to require all students, regardless of gender, to have the same minimum meal plan. However, if the university is going to require all students to have the same minimum meal plan, then the university needs to give women more options to spend their money on things other than food purchased in the school dining halls.

5   In addition, my proposal would create more opportunities for bonding. For example, it would allow persons who love to cook, such as me, to use the residence hall kitchens to create "home-cooked meals" for floor mates, thus creating more friendships among students. Personally, I have had the pleasure of helping create such bonds among the women on my floor by cooking a "family dinner" in our floor's kitchen. The aroma of the roasted chicken and homemade mashed potatoes drew the students on the fifth floor into the lounge. After our shared dinner, it seemed as if our floor felt more comfortable being around each other in a more family-like way. I think that cooking on campus gives students a sense of comfort that they do not get when they go to the dining halls and have food pre-made for them. While I would love to cook dinner for my floor more often, the bottom line is that ingredients are too expensive to pay for on my regular credit card when I have already purchased from the university more food than I can eat. If the school were to implement a system where we could use a portion of our meal plans off campus, students would be able to buy groceries from local stores and to put to better use the kitchens already built into the residence halls.

In addition to creating closer bonds between students, an off-campus option for our meal cards would help women eat more healthfully. The current system promotes bad eating habits causing women to overeat or even to binge in order to use up their extra meal plan money. For example, with the left over money on my card at the end of Fall Quarter, I bought cases of energy drinks which are filled with high fructose corn syrup and other empty calories. As another example, my friend Amber purchases multiple meals such as pizza and a burger for dinner because she doesn't want to waste her money. Overeating is obviously unhealthy and could eventually lead to an increase in obesity or eating disorders. However, if students were able to use their meal card off campus, they could buy items such as shampoo or other toiletries, which would be more beneficial for women than overeating to avoid losing money.

Despite all these benefits of a new meal plan system, some administrators might be skeptical of the benefits and focus on the drawbacks instead. The biggest drawback is the potential loss of revenue to food services. As it is now, women help subsidize food costs for men. Without that subsidy, the food service might not be able to break even, forcing them to raise food costs for everyone. I don't have the financial expertise to know how to compute these costs. Clearly, however, other universities have thought about these issues and decided that allowing students to spend some of their food money off campus was a benefit worth providing for students. For example, the University of Texas, the University of Minnesota, and the University of Florida allow their meal cards to be used as debit cards at local businesses. As stated on their website, the University of Texas has a system called Bevo Bucks in which students can "purchase food, goods and services at participating locations, both on and off campus" by loading money onto their ID cards. Also according to the University of Minnesota's website, students have a system called FlexDine connected to their ID cards. FlexDine gives students the "convenience … [to eat] at PAPA JOHN's for residence hall residents." If other schools can implement off campus use of dining cards, then the plan is feasible. It might also be possible to limit the number of dollars that could be spent each quarter off campus in order to assure a minimum level of revenue for the food service.

Even if my proposal would be costly in terms of lost revenue to the food service, the benefits of my plan might still outweigh the costs. A revised meal card system might become a recruiting point for prospective students because they would feel as if the university is more personalized to fit the students' needs rather than just the university's needs. My proposal might help prospective students see how close the students at our university are and might draw more students to apply here. (Our website and view books could even include pictures of students cooking in the resident hall kitchens or eating at a local restaurant.) Moreover local off-campus businesses would welcome the opportunity for more student customers and might offer special promotions for students. A new meal card system might even improve the relationship between the university and the surrounding community.

Based on all these reasons, I believe that the university community as a whole would benefit if my proposal were enacted. The new plan would be especially appreciated by women students, many of whom now subsidize the food costs of men. In addition, the new system would bring students closer together by encouraging more creative use of the residence hall kitchens for community meals and by reducing the incentive toward binge eating at the end of each quarter. Finally, if other universities can use this system then our university should be able to use it as well. Although the food service may lose money to local businesses, the university would ultimately benefit by creating a more flexible and attractive meal option— especially for women—and by showing administrative concern for student welfare.

Critiquing "A Proposal to Allow Off-Campus Purchases with a MyWritingLab™ University Meal Card"

1. In your own words, summarize briefly the problem that Megan Johnson addresses, her proposed solution, and her justifying reasons.
2. Megan addresses her proposal to Ms. Jane Doe, an administrator who has the power to change policy. To what extent does Megan develop audience-based reasons that resonate for this audience of university administrators? How effectively does she anticipate and respond to objections her audience might raise?
3. How does Megan establish a positive *ethos* in this argument? To what extent does she appeal to *pathos* as well as *logos*?
4. How effective is Megan's proposal?

Our second reading, by student writer Ivan Snook, is a researched public policy proposal written in response to the option 3 assignment on pages 317–318. Snook's argument is based both on library and Internet research and on personal experience (he is a returning veteran who served as a Marine infantry soldier in Iraq). It is formatted as a formal research paper using the documentation style of the Modern Language Association (MLA).

Ivan Snook

Dr. Johnson

Argumentative Writing

March 31, 2014

Flirting with Disaster: An Argument Against Integrating
Women into the Combat Arms

In 2005 I was a rifleman for the elite 1st Reconnaissance Battalion in Iraq.
My deployment was not all bad. When we returned to Camp Fallujah to repair our
humvee we ate great chow, enjoyed good entertainment, and drank contraband vodka.
I never had a girlfriend, though. I was too busy working in my all-male infantry unit.
At the time I wished we had a few girls in the unit. What can I say? I wanted female
companionship like the guys in non-combat jobs had. But I realized that women could
never serve in the infantry because of the negative impact of boyfriend/girlfriend
dramatics on unit morale, cohesiveness, and ultimately combat effectiveness.

However, America's civilian leadership recently moved towards integrating
women into frontline combat arms units such as infantry, tanks, and artillery. In
January, 2014, Secretary of Defense Leon Panetta lifted the Pentagon's policy on
all-male combat arms occupations. "The department's goal . . . is to ensure that the
mission is met with the best qualified and most capable people, regardless of gender,"
he said. "I'm not talking about reducing the qualifications for the job—if they can
meet the qualifications for the job, then they should have a right to serve" (qtd. in
Michaels and Vanden Brook). President Obama expanded upon Panetta's sentiment
by saying, "Every American can be proud *that our military will grow even stronger*,
with our mothers, wives, sisters, and daughters playing a greater role in protecting
this country we love" (qtd. in Michaels and Vanden Brook, emphasis mine.)

If this policy change will indeed strengthen our military, every American should
support it. However, no one has specified how integrating women into the combat
arms will strengthen our military. I wholeheartedly agree with integrationists who
claim that women can meet the rigorous physical and mental requirements for frontline
combat. Any CrossFit has at least half a dozen women more physically and mentally
fit than some of my Marine brothers in arms. If those were the sole criteria by which
we evaluate infantrymen, I would endorse integration. But, how an individual soldier
affects the combat unit as a whole must be considered. The great military theorist Carl

von Clausewitz coined the term "friction" to represent the "[c]ountless minor incidents ... [that] combine to lower the general level of performance [of the military machine]." He continues, "We should bear in mind that none of its components is of one piece: each part is composed of individuals, every one of whom retains his potential of friction." Therefore, we must not judge individual soldiers only by their individual physical capabilities, but also by their impact on the unit as a whole.

Introducing women to previously all-male combat units means introducing the friction of romantic relationships. Petty jealousies and other dramatic relational issues combine to lower the general level of performance. In 1997, the non-profit global policy think tank RAND Corporation studied how romantic relationships affect coed military units. The study reported that such relationships "sexualize" the work environment, making it "difficult for colleagues to regard one another as just coworkers. Thus, the cohesion of the unit is negatively affected" (Harrell and Miller 81). One respondent complained, "The [cafeteria] ... at night looks more like a singles club or promenade deck than a cafeteria [for a military unit]." Another said, "I get tired of seeing a junior enlisted female and her boyfriend [at the cafeteria]. ... This place is like high school all over again. Everyone is dating others. To me this is not the military. We are here to do a job not meet our spouse. Guys seem more worried about getting a girl than doing their job" (Harrell and Miller 81-82).

Integrationists claim the military's high level of discipline coupled with strict rules against fraternization will prevent romantic relationships. However, those strict rules have always been in place and have never worked. During the Gulf War, 5 percent of deployed women were sent home early due to pregnancy. The Navy sends home on average 10 percent of deployed female sailors for the same reason. The USS *Theodore Roosevelt,* one of America's largest aircraft carriers, lost 45 of its 300 female sailors to pregnancy leave and became one of the many U.S. Navy ships to earn the nickname "The Love Boat" (Browne 246). My point is not about morality. These statistics demonstrate that despite strict rules against fraternization, 18-25 year olds succumb to their natural urges. What else should one expect when young adults are locked away on ship or deployed to Afghanistan for months at a time? It is analogous to locking the doors on a coed college dormitory for a year and making rules against sex. It is preposterous to expect 18-25 year olds to work, live, and relax together in such close proximity and expect no romantic relationships to sprout.

These problems are more than just trifling lovers' quarrels. They affect a serious decline in performance and can lead to a total breakdown of command structure. In 2005, Brian Kates of the *New York Daily News* visited Camp Bucca, a military prison in Southern Iraq, which he described as a drunken "out-of-control frat party." "In front of a cheering male audience, two young women wearing only bras and panties threw themselves into a mud-filled plastic kiddie pool and rolled around in a wild wrestling match." Sergeant Emil Ganim, who refereed the match, said other non-commissioned officers "had been lending out their rooms for soldiers to have sex." These were not just young privates, either. A witness told investigators that a drunken first sergeant and master sergeant, two high-ranking non-commissioned officers, were in attendance (Kates). Although Camp Bucca was far away from any actual fighting, it is safe to assume similar sexual antics and command structure breakdowns will occur in coed frontline combat units whose members confront their own mortality on a daily basis.

Still, Camp Bucca is not the worst case scenario. The military is currently battling an epidemic of rape and sexual assault. A study conducted by the Department of Veterans' Affairs reported that one-third of female veterans say they were victims of rape or attempted rape. A third of those claim they were raped multiple times, and 14 percent claim they were gang raped (Browne). Introducing females to frontline combat units will only exacerbate the problem. Dr. David Grossman, one of the world's foremost experts on human aggression and the psychology of combat, has explained how combat stress affects human sex drive. He analogizes the human body's ability to cope with stress to a bathtub: it can hold only so much water before overflowing. When our body overflows with stress the midbrain releases hormones causing a fight or flight response, often followed by a dramatic change in hunger and sex drive. Grossman writes, "Some people lose their appetite for food in response to stress, but many have an enhanced craving to eat. In the same way, some individuals can lose their sex drive in response to great stress, but other people experience a tremendous sex drive, especially after a combat situation in which they were triumphant" (275). Frontline combat is fueled by stress hormones, and the potential for a woman to be sexually assaulted is very high. An inter-unit sexual assault costs the unit two soldiers: the victim is typically transferred to a new unit, the assaulter is sent to prison. Replacing two comrades integrated in a tight-knit unit with two new recruits is a difficult blow to a unit's esprit de corps and trust members have in one another. Thus, to put at risk a female soldier's sexual well-being is to also put at risk her unit's combat ability.

Snook 4

Rather than respond to the physiological realities of preparing for and engaging in combat, integrationists such as CNN's Maren Leed deflect to a false analogy connecting integration of women to past arguments against integrating minorities and homosexuals. Regarding minorities, race is a social construct not a biological difference. Whereas the military somewhat successfully trained its men to not act on racial prejudices, it is improbable that 18-25 year old men can be trained to be not sexually attracted to women. Regarding homosexuals, one homosexual has little effect on a group of heterosexuals, but one female can have a significant impact on a large group of stress hormone driven heterosexual men.

Another integrationist argument is that changes in modern warfare already put women in combat. They say modern warfare is "asymmetric" and attacks can come from anywhere. It is true that women have served in combat in Afghanistan and Iraq, but integrationists erroneously believe the nature of warfare has evolved beyond traditional frontlines. Every American military engagement since World War II has been a limited war, but that does not mean all future wars will be. The wars our military must prepare to fight are global conflicts where combat troops face well-armed and well-trained enemies on traditional frontlines.

Perhaps the most important argument made by integrationists, and one to which I am sympathetic, concerns fairness and equity. It is extremely difficult to be promoted to General without infantry training. Some may say the Army should change its promotion policy, but this would harm overall morale. Frontline troops more enthusiastically follow leaders who are sharing, or have at one time shared, the toils and dangers of war. Thus, high-ranking female officers hit a glass ceiling because no such experience is available to them. However, there is an alternative to break through this glass ceiling without making all combat units coed. The U.S. Army National Guard consists of every imaginable combat arms occupation. If they were opened to aspirant female soldiers, they would have access to the necessary experience for advancement to the military's upper echelon and have the option of transferring from the National Guard to active duty. General John Vessey began his illustrious career in the National Guard infantry and was later selected as Chairman of the Joint Chiefs of Staff. This compromise would give women the opportunity to get infantry training while still protecting our active duty frontline infantry units from the unnecessary friction caused by romantic relationships.

Snook 5

Although some outsiders call terms like friction, morale, and unit cohesion mere buzzwords, to the Marines they mean life or death. Coed infantry is a parlous experiment with too much at stake. The restriction against women joining the infantry must be reinstated before the policy becomes entrenched and the negative side effects of romantic relationships deteriorate our fighting ability. I fully support gender equality, and I am proud of the brave women in the Marines, Army, Navy, and Air Force who have sacrificed so much defending this country I love. But when one considers the ultimate mission of the military, which is to win wars, we must not risk losing the cohesion of combat units when there is no exigent reason to do so except for the sake of expanding military career opportunities for women.

Snook 6

Works Cited

Browne, Kingsley. *Co-Ed Combat: The New Evidence That Women Shouldn't Fight the Nation's Wars.* Sentinel, 2007.

Clausewitz, Carl von. *On War.* Translated by Michael Howard and Peter Paret, Princeton UP, 1984.

Grossman, David. *On Combat: The Psychology and Physiology of Deadly Conflict in War and in Peace.* 3rd ed., Warrior Science, 2008.

Harrell, Margaret C., and Laura L. Miller. "New Opportunities for Military Women: Effects Upon Readiness, Cohesion, and Morale." *RAND Corporation,* 1 Jan. 1997, www.rand.org/pubs/monograph_reports/MR896.html.

Kates, Brian. "Out of Control at Camp Crazy! Female Soldiers Dress Down & Get Dirty for Mud Romps." *New York Daily News,* 6 Feb. 2005, www.nydailynews.com/archives/news/control-camp-crazy-female-soldiers-dress-dirty-mud-romps-g-s-wild-article-1.590262.

Leed, Maren. "Will Infantry Men Accept Women as Peers?" *CNN,* 26 Jan. 2013, www.cnn.com/2013/01/25/opinion/leed-women-in-infantry.

Michaels, Jim, and Tom Vanden Brook. "Women, Men Must Meet Same Combat Standards in Military." *USA Today,* 25 Jan. 2013, www.usatoday.com/story/news/world/2013/01/24/women-in-combat-briefing/1861887.

Critiquing "Flirting with Disaster: An Argument Against Integrating Women into the Combat Arms"

1. What is Ivan Snook's major reason for not integrating women into the combat arms? What evidence does he provide in support of his argument? Do you find that evidence persuasive?
2. What opposing or alternative views does Snook summarize? How effectively does Snook respond to these views?
3. Snook offers as a counterproposal a way that women could get infantry training (for purposes of career advancement) without having to make all infantry units coed. How effective do you find his counterproposal?
4. How effective is Snook's use of audience-based reasons? How would you evaluate his overall appeal to *logos, ethos*, and *pathos*?

Our third reading, from the Save-Bees.org Web site, is the one-page paid advocacy advertisement on page 332. Working in conjunction with other environmental organizations such as Beyond Pesticides, the Center for Food Safety, and Pesticide Action Network, the Save the Bees organization advocates a moratorium on pesticides that are killing off bees. The Web site itself demonstrates how the Internet can be enlisted for education and advocacy. It solicits support for a petition directed to the United States Environmental Protection Agency calling for an immediate discontinuation in the use of certain toxic chemicals deadly to bees. On the Web, this advocacy ad shows a list of organizations in support of this moratorium.

Critiquing the Save the Bees Advocacy Ad

1. How does this advocacy advertisement give "presence" to the problem with bees?
2. What solution does the ad propose for helping the bees? Why hasn't this solution already been adopted? What action does the ad ask readers to take?
3. What reasons and evidence does this advocacy ad provide to persuade readers to take action? How effective is this evidence?
4. How does this proposal argument appeal to personal interest as well as environmental values? How would you say appeals to *logos, ethos*, and *pathos* work together in this advocacy piece?

Our fourth reading, by student Sandy Wainscott, illustrates option 5, a proposal speech supported by visual aids. We have reproduced Sandy's outline for her speech, along with her scripts for the introduction and conclusion. (Although she delivered the body of the speech extemporaneously from her outline, she scripted the introduction and conclusion to reduce nervousness.) We have also reproduced four of her ten PowerPoint slides. She used these four slides to introduce each of the four main points shown on the outline. Note how she has constructed her slides as visual arguments supporting a main point (stated in the slide title).

Bees can't wait 5 *more* years.

And neither can we.

Honey bees, native bees and other pollinators are responsible for 1 out of every 3 bites of food we eat. Bees pollinate 71 of the 100 crops that make up 90% of the world's food supply. Many fruits and vegetables, including apples, blueberries, strawberries, carrots and broccoli, as well as almonds and coffee, rely on bees. These beneficial insects are critical to maintaining our diverse food supply.

Honey bee populations have been in alarming decline since 2006. Widespread use of a new class of toxic pesticides, neonicotinoids, is a significant contributing factor. In addition to killing bees outright, research has shown that even low levels of these dangerous pesticides impair bees' ability to learn, to find their way back to the hive, to collect food, to produce new queens, and to mount an effective immune response.

This week, 15 countries are imposing a two-year restriction on the use of several of these chemicals. Meanwhile, the United States is **stalling**.

The U.S. Environmental Protection Agency estimates it will be **2018, 5 years from now,** before it makes a decision on this deadly class of pesticides.

Bees can't wait 5 more years – they are dying now. The U.S. Environmental Protection Agency has the power and responsibility to protect our pollinators. Our nation's food system depends on it.

HELP PROTECT FOOD CHOICES

Save-Bees.org

Why McDonald's Should Sell Meat and Veggie Pies: A Proposal to End Subsidies for Cheap Meat

SANDY WAINSCOTT (STUDENT)

Script for Introduction: McDonald's hamburgers are popular because they're satisfying and pretty darn cheap. But I will argue that the hamburger is cheap because the American taxpayer subsidizes the cost of meat. Uncle Sam pays agribusiness to grow feed corn while not requiring agribusiness to pay the full cost for water or for cleaning up the environmental damage caused by cattle production. If meat producers had to recover the true cost of their product, the cost of meat would be substantially higher, but there would be offsetting benefits: a healthier environment, happier lives for cows and chickens, and healthier diets for all of us.

1. Meat is relatively cheap partly because taxpayers help feed the cows.
   a. U.S. taxpayers give farmers money to grow feed corn, which is fed to cows.
   b. U.S. taxpayers provide farmers with cheap water.
2. Cheap meat threatens health.
   a. Factory-style farms significantly reduce effectiveness of antibiotics.
   b. Antibiotic-resistant pathogens are potentially huge killers.
   c. Factory farms are likely sources of new swine and bird flus.
   d. Meat-related food poisoning harms millions of people per year with thousands of deaths.
3. Cheap meat hurts the environment.
   a. Factory farms create 130 times more sewage than humans.
   b. Animal farming contributes more to global warming than all forms of human transportation combined.
   c. Farming uses much of the world's land and water.
4. Cheap meat requires cruelty to animals.
   a. Ninety-eight percent of egg-laying hens in the U.S. spend their entire lives in stacked cubicle cages with 9-inch sides.
   b. Cruel conditions also exist for pigs and cows.

Script for Conclusion: If we quit giving farmers taxpayer subsidies and required them to pay for the pollution they cause, the cost of meat would be much higher—but with great benefits to our health and to our environment. A restaurant like McDonald's would likely adjust its menus. McDonald's would move the burger off its 99 cent menu and replace it with something like a meat pie, a similarly warm, quick, and satisfying choice, but with a lower proportion of meat than a burger. In a fair market, we should have to pay more for a hamburger than for a meat pie or a stir fry. But we would have the benefit of a healthier Earth.

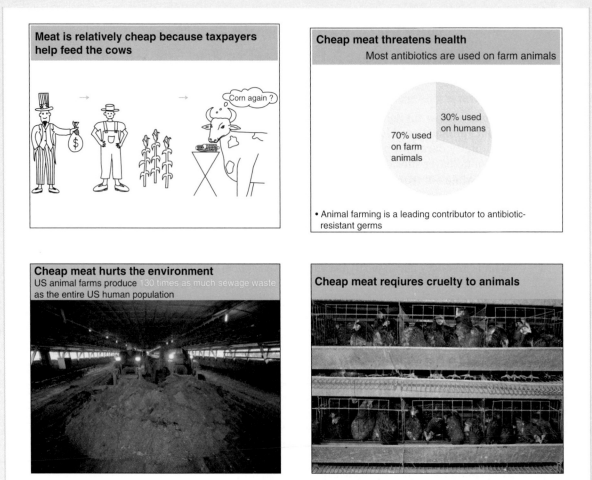

FIGURE 14.2   Sandy's PowerPoint Slides Used to Introduce Main Points

Critiquing "Why McDonald's Should Sell Meat and Veggie Pies: A Proposal to End Subsidies for Cheap Meat"

MyWritingLab™

1. Although it is common to design PowerPoint slides that use topics and bullets to reproduce the speaker's outline, most public speaking experts prefer the approach that Sandy takes in this speech. She uses photographs, drawings, and graphics to create a visual argument that reinforces rather than simply reproduces the verbal message of her speech. How do her slides operate visually to create arguments from both *logos* and *pathos*?

2. Note that the top heading of each slide is a complete sentence making a point rather than a topic phrase without a subject and verb. For example, the

top-left slide in Figure 14.2 might have had the heading "Cheap Meat" or "Role of Subsidies." Do you agree with most experts, who would say that the complete-sentence version ("Meat is relatively cheap because taxpayers help feed the cows") is more effective? Why or why not?

3. How effective do you find Sandy's speech?

Our final reading appeared in the *Wall Street Journal* on February 19, 2011. The authors are both professors of entomology at Wageningen University in the Netherlands. In 2007, Marcel Dicke was awarded the NWO-Spinoza award, often called the Dutch Nobel Prize. He gives speeches (summaries of which are available on the Web) arguing that humans should eat insects rather than meat as one solution to the environmental degradation caused by the meat industry. Coauthor Arnold Van Huis coordinates a research consortium of scientists investigating the nutritional value of insects. He also gives cooking classes featuring bug recipes.

The Six-Legged Meat of the Future

MARCEL DICKE AND ARNOLD VAN HUIS

At the London restaurant Archipelago, diners can order the $11 Baby Bee Brulee: a creamy custard topped with a crunchy little bee. In New York, the Mexican restaurant Toloache offers $11 chapulines tacos: two tacos stuffed with Oaxacan-style dried grasshoppers.

Could beetles, dragonfly larvae and water bug caviar be the meat of the future? As the global population booms and demand strains the world's supply of meat, there's a growing need for alternate animal proteins. Insects are high in protein, B vitamins and minerals like iron and zinc, and they're low in fat. Insects are easier to raise than livestock, and they produce less waste. Insects are abundant. Of all the

known animal species, 80% walk on six legs; over 1,000 edible species have been identified. And the taste? It's often described as "nutty."

Worms, crickets, dung beetles—to most people they're just creepy crawlers. To Brooklyn painter and 5 art professor Marc Dennis, they're yummy ingredients for his Bug Dinners.

The vast majority of the developing world already eats insects. In Laos and Thailand, weaver-ant pupae are a highly prized and nutritious delicacy. They are prepared with shallots, lettuce, chilies, lime and spices and served with sticky rice. Further back in history, the ancient Romans considered beetle larvae to be gourmet fare, and the Old Testament mentions eating

crickets and grasshoppers. In the 20th century, the Japanese emperor Hirohito's favorite meal was a mixture of cooked rice, canned wasps (including larvae, pupae and adults), soy sauce and sugar.

Will Westerners ever take to insects as food? It's possible. We are entomologists at Wageningen University, and we started promoting insects as food in the Netherlands in the 1990s. Many people laughed—and cringed—at first, but interest gradually became more serious. In 2006 we created a "Wageningen—City of Insects" science festival to promote the idea of eating bugs; it attracted more than 20,000 visitors.

Over the past two years, three Dutch insect-raising companies,

which normally produce feed for animals in zoos, have set up special production lines to raise locusts and mealworms for human consumption. Now those insects are sold, freeze-dried, in two dozen retail food outlets that cater to restaurants. A few restaurants in the Netherlands have already placed insects on the menu, with locusts and mealworms (beetle larvae) usually among the dishes.

Insects have a reputation for being dirty and carrying diseases—yet less than 0.5% of all known insect species are harmful to people, farm animals or crop plants. When raised under hygienic conditions—eating bugs straight out of the backyard generally isn't recommended—many insects are perfectly safe to eat.

Meanwhile, our food needs are on the rise. The human population is expected to grow from six billion in 2000 to nine billion in 2050. Meat production is expected to double in the same period, as demand grows from rising wealth.

Pastures and fodder already use up 70% of all agricultural land, so increasing livestock production would require expanding agricultural acreage at the expense of rain forests and other natural lands. Officials at the United Nations Food and Agriculture Organization recently predicted that beef could become an extreme luxury item by 2050, like caviar, due to rising production costs.

Raising insects for food would avoid many of the problems associated with livestock. For instance, swine and humans are similar enough that they can share many diseases. Such co-infection can yield new disease strains that are lethal to humans, as happened during a swine fever outbreak in the Netherlands in the late 1990s. Because insects are so different from us, such risks are accordingly lower.

10   Insects are also cold-blooded, so they don't need as much feed as animals like pigs and cows, which consume more energy to maintain their body temperatures. Ten pounds of feed yields one pound of beef, three pounds of pork, five pounds of chicken and up to six pounds of insect meat.

Insects produce less waste, too. The proportion of livestock that is not edible after processing is 30% for pork, 35% for chicken, 45% for beef and 65% for lamb. By contrast, only 20% of a cricket is inedible.

Raising insects requires relatively little water, especially as compared to the production of conventional meat (it takes more than 10 gallons of water, for instance, to produce about two pounds of beef). Insects also produce far less ammonia and other greenhouse gases per pound of body weight. Livestock is responsible for at least 10% of all greenhouse gas emissions.

Raising insects is more humane as well. Housing cattle, swine or chickens in high densities causes stress to the animals, but insects like mealworms and locusts naturally like to live in dense quarters. The insects can be crowded into vertical stacked trays or cages. Nor do bug farms have to be restricted to rural areas; they could sprout up anywhere, from a suburban strip mall to an apartment building. Enterprising gourmets could even keep a few trays of mealworms in the garage to ensure a fresh supply.

The first insect fare is likely to be incorporated subtly into dishes, as a replacement for meat in meatballs and sauces. It also can be mixed into prepared foods to boost their nutritional value—like putting mealworm paste into a quiche. And dry-roasted insects can be used as a replacement for nuts in baked goods like cookies and breads.

15 We continue to make progress in the Netherlands, where the ministry of agriculture is funding a new $1.3 million research program to develop ways to raise edible insects on food waste, such as brewers' grain (a byproduct of beer brewing), soyhulls (the skin of the soybean) and apple pomace (the pulpy remains after the juice has been pressed out). Other research is focusing on how protein could be extracted from insects and used in processed foods.

Though it is true that intentionally eating insects is common only in developing countries, everyone already eats some amount of insects. The average person consumes about a pound of insects per year, mostly mixed into other foods. In the U.S., most processed foods contain small amounts of insects, within limits set by the Food and Drug Administration. For chocolate, the FDA limit is 60 insect fragments per 100 grams. Peanut butter can have up to 30 insect parts per 100 grams, and fruit juice can have five fruit-fly eggs and one or two larvae per 250 milliliters (just over a cup). We also use many insect products to dye our foods, such as the red dye cochineal in imitation crab sticks, Campari and candies. So we're already some of the way there in making six-legged creatures a regular part of our diet.

Not long ago, foods like kiwis and sushi weren't widely known or available. It is quite likely that in 2020 we will look back in surprise at the era when our menus didn't include locusts, beetle larvae, dragonfly larvae, crickets and other insect delights.

Critiquing "The Six-Legged Meat of the Future"   MyWritingLab™

1. On page 308 we note that a problem faced by all proposal writers is "the need to overcome people's natural conservatism." Their readers' natural conservatism is a major constraint for coauthors Dicke and Van Huis ("Hey, I've never eaten bugs before! If four-legged meat was good enough for my parents, it's good enough for me!") How do the authors use the appeals of *logos, ethos,* and *pathos* to try to overcome this natural conservatism?

2. Although this journalistic piece does not have a tightly closed-form structure with transitions and because clauses marking each reason, it still provides a logical progression of separate reasons in support of eating insects. Convert this argument into a bulleted list of because clauses in support of the claim "Westerners should eat insects as a major source of protein."

3. Are you persuaded by this argument? Would you try some mealworm spaghetti or a handful of fried crickets? Why or why not?

MyWritingLab™

Visit Ch. 14 Proposal Arguments in *MyWritingLab* to complete the For Writing and Discussion, Examining Visual Arguments, Critiquing, and Writing Assignments and to test your understanding of the chapter objectives.

SECTION TWO

Rhetoric Supplement

An Introduction to Inquiry

(material from Linda McMeniman's *From Inquiry to Argument*)

Read the following selection carefully, then respond as indicated below:

> Imagine that you enter a parlor. You come late. When you arrive, others have long preceded you, and they are engaged in a heated discussion, a discussion too heated for them to pause and tell you exactly what it is about. In fact, the discussion had already begun long before any of them got there, so that no one present is qualified to retrace for you all the steps that had gone before. You listen for a while until you decide that you have caught the tenor of the argument: then you put in your oar. Someone answers; you answer him; another comes to your defense; another aligns himself against you.... However, the discussion is interminable. The hour grows late, you must depart. And you do depart, with the discussion still in progress.

> —Kenneth Burke, *The Philosophy of Literary Form*

Writer's Journal

In your notebook, write informally to explain the meaning of the passage. Then describe its effects on you and express any other responses you may have. Strive for an entry of at least 150 words.

From Inquiry ...

Let's begin with the term *inquiry,* a simple word, one we all know how to use. If you examine the following uses of *inquiry* (and its relative, *to inquire*), some may strike you as more appropriate than others:

1. Sal inquired about the penalty for late payment of his gas bill.
2. Judith made an inquiry as to the location of the restroom.
3. The House of Representatives began an inquiry into the states' enforcement of highway traffic laws.
4. The counterman inquired what flavor ice cream I wanted.

If you discuss your responses with classmates, you might discover you agree— that in sentences 1 and 3 *inquiry* works well, but that in 2 and 4 it seems artificial or awkward. In these sentences, you may prefer *asked* as less grand, less affected. Or perhaps you disagree because you can envision a scene or context for sentences 2 and 4 that calls for a special, more elevated word than *ask*. You can agree, however, that the word *inquiry* and the act of *inquiring* are not about asking just any question; an inquiry is more self-conscious, more intentional.

A look in the dictionary reveals that the word *inquiry* shares the same Latin root as *question*: *quaerere*, meaning "to seek." The prefix *in* serves as an intensifier, so we might say that inquire is built from its roots to mean "to seek intensely." In the actual definition, an inquiry is said to be a "question or query" or "a close examination of some matter in a quest for information or truth."

I like this last definition because the phrase "quest for information or truth" reflects the deepest purpose of academic life, the discovery of explanations that will endure—at least until the next inquiry. And "close examination" implies study and research, processes that flow beneath and animate all the teaching and talking, paper writing and e-mailing, reading and note taking that form the day-to-day activities in higher education.

But this definition doesn't tell us much about the context of inquiry or about its inspiration. Why bother to inquire? What creates the need to know?

The Motives for Inquiry

Consider a time when you made an intensive search for knowledge. Make a list of such times. Do these occasions have anything in common? What motivated your need to know?

Often, the search for information or "truth" results from a problem, an impending decision, a conflict between possible choices, or some other controversial situation. The need may be immediate and practical. Perhaps someone whose father has developed cataracts wants information about eye disease in order to understand possible treatments.

Or the need may be to plan for the future. A student may be about to make the life-altering decision to attend college and so collects and studies many college catalogues in order to make the most appropriate choice. A county might study traffic patterns over the course of the workday and workweek so that future road improvements can be planned.

Or the necessary information may be more abstract: solving a societal problem such as a rise in high school dropout rates requires analyzing and perhaps conducting numerous studies of adolescent behavior, the educational system, family dynamics, and so forth.

So an inquiry implies certain things: a problem, dilemma, or controversial issue, first of all, and a community that has a stake in resolving that problem.

The Context of Inquiry

Such a community can be official, such as a township, a civic or professional group, or a university. But many communities or groups of people linked by a common interest or situation are informal and unofficial. Cliques in a high school, recreational groups such as golfers or quilters, and fans of the ballet or progressive jazz are examples.

Any group that uses discourse—that is, any form of written or spoken communication—to maintain itself, articulate and solve group problems, and otherwise assist its own cohesiveness and identity is called a **discourse community**. Members of discourse communities—and we are all members of several—base their interactions with each other on the discourse expectations of the group. The discourse community is an active collaborator in any member's use of language, providing a vocabulary and expected styles of discussing and handling issues of concern and even limiting or defining acceptable topics. Such a community has conventions for discussing, analyzing, and proving ideas and for addressing conflicts.

A high school clique may evolve a trademark vocabulary that reaffirms its identity and may develop customary ways of discussing academic work, friendships, romances, and other topics. Inside jokes can be cued with a few words, and greeting or parting may involve signature phrases or gestures. To a certain extent, any member's behavior and talk, both subject and style, will be based on the group's expectations.

A town-council meeting will also be characterized by a customary discourse. Some characteristics of its discourse will be common to town-council meetings throughout the United States, for local government officials and politically active citizens constitute an informal national discourse community. Most likely, the discussion will be sprinkled with technical terms or jargon derived from various professional domains: the law, real estate, health and public safety, and so on. The discourse will be generally polite and somewhat formal but probably will include informal segments in which humorous asides and little in-jokes lighten the mood. Discourse will follow an agenda, the shape of which may be mandated by law or determined by custom. Proceedings will follow parliamentary procedure to a greater or lesser extent. Decisions will be made by the head official or the council through voice vote, secret ballot, or consensus as local law requires or as is customary.

It is fair to say that any inquiry a person conducts occurs within the web of a discourse community, and it involves interaction with that community. Individual inquiries require dialogue, perhaps oral, perhaps written. How a problem is defined, how study and research are performed, and what counts as a result or solution are all determined by our linguistic and social environment. Discourse communities limit their members to the discourse formulations within them; but discourse communities also open pathways for members by providing conventions of wording and expression and patterns of thought out of which understanding is built.

As Gregory Clark writes, "Using language is necessarily an act of collaboration through which we create the meaning we share, a socially constructed meaning that is inherently incomplete".

Asking Questions

16

material from Richard E. Miller and Ann Jurecic's *Habits of the Creative Mind*

"There are no bad questions": this is an incantation repeated year in and year out in classrooms across the country. It represents a well-intentioned effort to establish a comfortable learning environment, but it's a hard sell, since teachers and students alike know that not only are there bad questions, but there are whole categories of questions that are unwelcome in the classroom. There are questions most teachers dread—the intrusively personal question, the cynical question, and the do-you-mind-repeating-what-you-just-said question, to name a few—and there are questions most students dread, such as the teacher's guess-what-I'm-thinking question, the teacher's fill-in-the-blank question, and the question that exposes the student who asked it to ridicule.

Rather than make the demonstrably false assertion that there are no bad questions, we prefer to ask: What is a good question? In this section, we introduce you to two of our favorite question posers, the hosts of *Radiolab*. We also propose an alternative to the thesis-driven writing project: writing your way to a question. And we look at how to prepare for an interview-based project. Questions you hear, questions produced by your own speculative writing, questions you put to others: we give you three different contexts for considering the roles that context, expertise, research, and curiosity play in the production of good questions.

On Asking Questions

We're devoted fans of *Radiolab*, a radio show and podcast on which the hosts, Jad Abumrad and Robert Krulwich, invite listeners to join them "on a curiosity bender." Abumrad is a composer by training and won a MacArthur Fellowship in 2011 for his work on the show, while Krulwich is a science correspondent with over three decades of broadcast experience. Working together, they make the exercise of being curious about the world *sound* like an exciting adventure.

In each show, Abumrad and Krulwich assume the air of happy amateurs who delight in having simple questions open up complex realities. They typically begin with a big question—about science, the arts, medicine, philosophy, or some other aspect of human experience—and then spend an hour exploring a range of responses to the question they've posed. The questions they ask often express an open-minded wonder about the world: Why do we sleep? What is color? What is race? How do we assign blame? To help them with their explorations, they always turn to experts, but they never take what the experts have to say as the final word on the matter. They question, provoke, and at times openly disagree with their guests and with each other.

There's a common pattern in most *Radiolab* shows: Abumrad and Krulwich move back and forth between questions, big ideas, interviews, and stories, inevitably leading their listeners to new problems and new questions, and revealing in the process that the issue they started with is more complicated than it first seemed. We admire how they move from simple wonder to complex possibilities, and we like that multiple answers, insights, and solutions are entertained along the way. We also like that *Radiolab* sounds beautiful. It's important to recognize that the creative soundscapes Abumrad and Krulwich produce are more than mere entertainment. In every episode, they demonstrate how curiosity can generate beauty as well as answers and ideas.

What we admire most about *Radiolab* is that the hosts manage to express in sound and language the whole spectrum of habits of the creative mind. You can hear Abumrad's creativity as a composer in the ways he uses sound to represent ideas that might otherwise remain too abstract for listeners to grasp. You can hear how open both men are to ambiguity, the unknown, and discovery as Abumrad and Krulwich talk their way through the implications of what they're learning. You can also hear their attention to and engagement with ideas, information, and expertise in the questions they ask. And you can hear their reflectiveness as thoughts digress, reverse, and surprise. Most of all, you can hear their boundless curiosity at work in the shape and progress of each episode.

We'd like you to listen to two episodes of *Radiolab*—one scripted, one open ended—so that you can hear what curiosity as a habit of mind sounds like.

Practice Session One

Listening   In "An Equation for Good," a chapter in *Radiolab's* "The Good Show" podcast, Abumrad and Krulwich consider an open-ended question that has puzzled evolutionary biologists since Charles Darwin first advanced his theory that species evolve through struggle and competition. If the "fittest" survive through tooth-and-claw rivalry, how can we explain kindness, generosity, and altruism?

Find a quiet place where you can listen to "An Equation for Good" without interruption; the podcast is about 22 minutes long. Use headphones or earbuds so you don't miss a thing.

Next, listen to the podcast again, this time pausing it when necessary to write down the questions Abumrad and Krulwich ask; this is likely to take more than 30 minutes. Keep track of where each question leads. What people and sources do Abumrad and Krulwich turn to for answers? What stories do they tell? Is there a logic to the overall shape of the show? An aesthetic?

Writing   Spend at least 30 minutes creating a visual map that illustrates the development of the hosts' thinking as "An Equation for Good" unfolds. When do their ideas move in a straight line? When do their questions cause a change in direction? Do they ever take wrong turns? If so, are any of the resulting digressions useful? By the end of "An Equation for Good," how far have Abumrad and Krulwich traveled? What do they conclude about the status of the definition of *evolution* as "the survival of the fittest"? (Note: You might want to experiment with making your map "move"; feel free to use presentation and/or animation software to bring your map to life.)

After you've created your map, pause to reflect on what you've learned. What does your map reveal about Abumrad and Krulwich's methods? Could someone else look at your map and understand what you've learned about how the show is structured? If not, how is what you've produced a map?

Practice Session Two

Listening   Next, we'd like you to listen to the *Radiolab* podcast "Secrets of Success," a conversation between Robert Krulwich and Malcolm Gladwell, author of *The Tipping Point, Blink,* and *Outliers.* This podcast shows how questions unfold when a curious person talks at length to a single expert, trying to understand the development and reach of the expert's ideas while also puzzling through whether to accept the expert's conclusions.

Find a quiet place where you can listen without interruption; the interview is about 25 minutes long. Don't forget your earbuds.

When you're done, set aside more than 30 minutes to listen to the podcast again, this time pausing to write down the questions and other prompts Krulwich uses to get Gladwell to explain his ideas about talent, practice, passion, and success.

Writing   Set aside at least 30 minutes to create another map that illustrates the unfolding conversation between Gladwell and Krulwich. When does Krulwich move the discussion in a straight line? When does he seem to change direction? Do any apparent digressions end up looping back to serve the main argument? Are there other digressions that take the conversation off track? Are you convinced by Gladwell's responses to Krulwich's questions?

Practice Session Three

Reflecting   After you've created maps for both "An Equation for Good" and "Secrets of Success," look at them side by side. Spend at least 30 minutes considering what they show you about how curiosity works and how understanding and arguments develop. What do you see that helps you to think about how you might compose a curiosity-driven essay or podcast about a big question like "How can we explain why humans sometimes go out of their way to help strangers?" or "Is there a secret to success?" What are some open-ended questions you'd like to read, listen, or write about?

Explore

We're drawn to works of nonfiction that are question-driven. The podcast *Radiolab* asks questions about anything and everything, including time, tumors, blame, mosquitos, quicksand, and the power of music. While *Radiolab* jumps from topic to topic, the captivating podcast *Serial* devotes twelve episodes to one subject—an investigation into whether a man was wrongfully imprisoned for the 1999 murder of a Maryland teen.

Law professor Ruthann Robson asks questions about a different kind of case, one that emerges after she is misdiagnosed with cancer, suffers through chemotherapy and medical mistreatment, and then considers both what her life is worth, and what matters more to her than money.

Radiolab. Podcast.
Robson, Ruthann. "Notes from a Difficult Case." *In Fact: The Best of Creative Nonfiction.*
    Ed. Lee Gutkind. New York: Norton, 2005. 226–44. Print.
Serial. Season One. Podcast.

On Writing to a Question

What's writing for? In school, the most common answer given to that question is, "To make a point." And so in school one practices having a point that can be succinctly stated in a thesis statement. "Writing is for making points" is itself an example of a succinct thesis statement.

We think the requirement to *start* an essay by committing to a thesis is a good way to kill curiosity. It turns writing into a mindless fill-in-the-blank exercise: Thesis? Check. Three examples? Check. Conclusion that summarizes the previous three paragraphs? Check. This approach to writing is a machine for arguing the obvious; it does not use writing as a tool for thinking new thoughts or for developing ideas that are new to the writer.

For your writing to become a mode of learning for you, you must begin in a state of not-knowing rather than committing yourself to a claim you came up with before you've done any curiosity-driven research. In the "Curiosity at Work" profiles in this book, we showcase a wide range of nonfiction writers who use writing as a mode of learning. Consider the divergent cases of Donovan Hohn and Rebecca Skloot.

Donovan Hohn, a high school English teacher, was reading a student's paper when he first learned about the plastic bath toys—yellow ducks, green frogs, blue turtles, and red beavers—that began washing ashore in Alaska and Australia in the early 1990s. Curious, he began to do some research online. Caught up in the mysteries, he left his job and traveled the earth to follow the path of the toys. He recorded his journey of discovery in his book *Moby-Duck*.

Rebecca Skloot was sixteen years old and taking a biology class when she learned that the first human cells ever grown in a lab were from an African American woman named Henrietta Lacks. Skloot wanted to know more about Lacks, but her teacher had no additional information, and at the time Skloot couldn't find anything more in the library. Many years later, when Skloot decided to become a writer, she tracked down Lacks's family and pieced together Henrietta Lacks's history and the history of her cell line. Then Skloot wrote the best-selling book *The Immortal Life of Henrietta Lacks*.

Neither of these writers began with a thesis that they then set out to prove. Rather, each started with a question and pushed past simplistic discussions of pollution or racism to develop a deeper, richer understanding of the situation's complexity. But where did the questions that Donovan and Skloot began with come from? Were the questions the result of inspiration or just dumb luck?

While there's always an element of chance in any research project, we think you learn how to ask the kinds of questions that stick with you for years by cultivating the habit of generating questions. How does this process work? Once you've developed the habit of generating questions about things that are taken for granted and about things unknown, you will find that you have many questions to choose from and many possible paths to explore. Some questions will seem more important than others, some will nag at you, and some will seem urgent; the very best questions will have all of these attributes.

To help our students develop the intertwined habits of curiosity and questioning, we've adopted a drafting strategy that throws out the familiar essay form. We ask our students instead to write frequent short papers in response to readings, and we tell them that these papers should not contain thesis statements.

At first they're baffled. How can you even begin an essay without a thesis? We tell them to just go ahead and give it a try. We instruct them to look in the assigned readings for moments when an author

- says something surprising or confusing;
- makes an unexpected connection;
- presents a provocative example;
- uses a familiar term in a new or peculiar way;
- or poses an idea or argument that is difficult to accept.

Freed from having to begin with a thesis statement, our students use their responses to readings to puzzle through surprising, confusing, or provocative passages. Consequently, when they write, they aren't reporting what the author said and then agreeing or disagreeing with it; they are focusing on interesting moments in which they sense a tension between their own thoughts, knowledge, or expectations and what an author has written.

Once they've written their way through a passage or a series of passages, we ask them to conclude their response papers with a reflection on what they've figured out over the course of developing their responses. Ideally, their exploration of moments of tension leads them to a compelling question or questions, which they pose in the final sentences of their responses. These should be questions that they can't presently answer and that require more thought, reading, and research—questions they are truly curious about and *want* to answer.

Right now you might be wondering, what's the point of writing to a question you can't answer? Isn't exposing your own ignorance the exact opposite of what you should be doing in school? Good questions!

We think there are many good reasons to use informal writing and drafting to arrive at a compelling question. When you write about passages or ideas in a text or set of texts that confuse or interest you, you are learning to use writing as a tool for thinking. And you'll see that writers discover what they think not *before* they write but *in the act* of writing. You'll also learn how to take more risks with your thinking. Ending with a question you don't know the answer to may feel uncomfortable at first—as if you're revealing a weakness. But openly confronting what you don't know is an essential part of learning to write well. Paradoxically, by writing to a question in a draft, you'll learn how to generate a truly interesting thesis. Once you've drafted a question that you're genuinely curious about, you're ready for the next step: figuring out how to respond to that question. Your response will be a thesis that's worth writing and reading about. Writing to a question also gives you practice with the essential habits of the creative mind: curiosity, openness to new ways of thinking, engagement with learning, and intellectual adventurousness.

Practice Session One

Reflecting   Are you a curious person? Do you express your curiosity most often in school, among your friends, at work, or elsewhere? You may not know the answers to these questions, so we'd like you to pay attention to your own curiosity for a week. Take notes every day, keeping an account of when, where, and how you pose questions, whether out loud to others or silently to yourself.

At the end of the week, spend at least 30 minutes reviewing your notes and learning about your own curiosity. When and where were you most curious? How often did you ask questions in classes? Did you pose more questions in one class or another? Did you ask questions as you read, jotting questions in the margins or in your notes? What was your most vivid experience of curiosity-driven learning in the past week? Was it in school or elsewhere?

Practice Session Two

Reading   In the list of suggested readings in this essay's "Explore" section, on page 349, each writer presents his or her central question in the article's subtitle: "What Should Medicine Do When It Can't Save Your Life?"; "Did American Conservationists in Africa Go Too Far?"; "Why Are We So Fat?"; "Is It a Crime?" Read one of the suggested readings, paying attention to how the writer answers the question posed in the subtitle. Trace how the writer's answer to the main question develops as the piece progresses.

Spend 30 minutes taking notes on how the answer to the question unfolds. Does the writer reverse or qualify your expectations? Are additional questions posed, explicitly or implicitly, that shift the direction of the writer's inquiry or reshape your understanding of the issue?

Reflecting   In our essay, we describe how we ask our students to write to a question. Now we want you to give it a try.

Return to the reading you selected and review it, looking for moments in the argument that catch your attention—passages that are surprising or confusing, make an unexpected connection, present a provocative example, use a term in a new or peculiar way, or pose an idea or argument that is difficult to accept. Then write a draft in which you explore three or more parts of the reading that you find interesting or baffling—places where you feel friction between the text and your own thoughts, knowledge, or expectations.

In the final paragraph of your draft, reflect on what you've learned about the ideas or argument in the reading you selected, and pose a question that has emerged from your work with the passages you've chosen. The standard for assessing the quality of the question you've generated is this: Do you genuinely want to answer it?

Writing   Having arrived at an interesting question, you can now write an essay that allows you to develop your thoughts and figure out your answer. Bring a version of your question into your essay's title or subtitle, as the writers of the suggested readings do. Then go about answering it, working with the reading you selected and the passages you wrote about, as well as any other passages that now seem relevant.

Explore

At the beginning of Practice Session Two, we draw your attention to the subtitles of the essays listed below: each one poses a difficult question and each question leads readers into realms of ambiguity, uncertainty, and ethical confusion. It's unlikely these writers began with their questions already formed; they began instead with challenging cases: a pregnant mother who learns she is going to die; a conservation effort that leads to killings; a graph that shows an explosion in American obesity in the 1980s; a man who forgot to drop his toddler off at daycare and the terrible consequences that followed. Only after much reading, researching, drafting, and revising did the big issues crystalize: How should medicine treat the dying? What is the human cost of protecting endangered species? What has caused an "epidemic" of obesity? And can a terrible mistake also be a crime?

Gawande, Atul. "Letting Go: What Should Medicine Do When It Can't Save Your Life?" *New Yorker*. 2 Aug. 2010. Web.
Goldberg, Jeffrey. "The Hunted: Did American Conservationists in Africa Go Too Far?" *New Yorker*. 5 April 2010. Web.
Kolbert, Elizabeth. "XXXL: Why Are We So Fat?" *New Yorker*. 20 July 2009. Web.
Weingarten, Gene. "Fatal Distraction: Forgetting a Child in the Backseat of a Car Is a Horrifying Mistake. Is It a Crime?" *Washington Post*. 8 March 2009. Web.

Exigence

17

Academic Writing Program, University of Maryland

What Is "Exigence," and Why Do I Need to Know?

How many times have you written something—or read something—that just didn't seem to have much of a reason for being (aside, perhaps, from getting a grade in a class)? Although this problem certainly arises outside the classroom, it plagues the writing most students do in school. Perhaps your research paper leaves the impression of being unrelated to anyone or anything in the "real world," or your essay just doesn't seem to go anywhere or do anything important. We can probably all think of times when a reader's most honest response to our writing would reasonably have been "So what? Why should I care about this?"

Writing that fails to answer the "so what?" question lacks what is known as **exigence**. That is, it fails to convey the urgency, importance, usefulness, timeliness, or interest of its subject for its particular audience. Readers are likely to become bored because they find the writing pointless. Isn't that the last thing we want our readers, including our professors, to think? On the other hand, writing that establishes exigence gives its readers a genuine reason to keep reading.

Kairos and *Chronos* and Exigence

In Ancient Greece, there were two different concepts of time. *Chronos* expressed quantifiable, linear, time; it's the source of our word "chronological," for example. But they also conceived a term that expressed a sense of circumstance or situation. That word, *kairos*, is more akin to a sense of quality of time rather than quantity of time. We might think of it more in the sense of "the right time" or a "window of opportunity." And it is to this sense of *kairos* that exigence refers. When something has exigence, it is taking advantage of the right time, the right place, of a sense of urgency or advantage or appropriateness.

Intrinsic and Extrinsic Exigence

Writers must always be conscious of exigence as they compose, but because exigence is related to the audience and the situation, it often seems to exist outside of the writer's control. There are, in other words, situations that seem to have an **extrinsic** sense of exigence; the situation itself presents all the urgency and appropriateness, seeming to demand a response. For example, if there is a terrible natural catastrophe in, say, California, we expect the

President to make some remarks about it. In that case, it seems to be the situation that calls for a response. Not only does it call for a response, but it calls for a certain kind of response. We can imagine what we would deem appropriate or inappropriate for the President to say in such a situation. In the workplace, assigned work provides the exigence for writing a report or a memo. In these cases, the exigence comes from the situation; so long as you attend to the subject at hand, you will have established the exigence for your discourse for that audience. (While this kind of situation might seem to "naturally" demand a response, the idea that a situation in endowed with essential exigence is thought by many to be questionable; instead, they suggest that there are social or situational reasons why we expect certain responses, why some things seem to "be" news and others are not).

In contrast to situations with a strong sense of extrinsic exigence, other situations seem to need to have exigence created for them. That will be the case with most of your writing. While indeed you are responding to a situation outside of your own making—that is, you are responding to a requirement set up by the instructor of your course—beyond that exigence you should also consider creating a sense of urgency and need for your writing. We refer to the author creating the exigence as a situation of **intrinsic** exigence; that is, the exigence is created within the composition rather than in the situation outside of the writing. How do you fashion such an opening, such a sense of urgency or demand for your argument? By showing your readers that a problem exists, that there is a situation that demands their attention, that you will discuss something they will find interesting and applicable to their lives.

Can You Give Me an Example?

Let's start with a typical example from *The Washington Post*. When the paper runs a story evaluating twenty brands of bottled water, the writer of the article may begin by explaining, "Since last week, when the federal government released studies showing that tap water in forty states is polluted, there has been a run on bottled water. What are the better brands?" Why does a story about bottled water begin this way? With his lead-in, the writer has shown the audience that his story addresses a problem that may affect them: much tap water is polluted, so they are probably changing to bottled water right now—shouldn't they know which is the best buy? Thus, the writer creates exigence for his story.

In academic writing, a writer might begin by referencing past works written on a topic, or with a review of the literature, or a review of what past scholars have said, on a given topic. The writer does this to establish exigence in the scholarly debate on the topic: people in the field are talking about it, and the writer is adding a new dimension to the conversation. An article in *College Composition and Communication* on using technology in the classroom aimed at an audience of writing teachers and scholars, for example, might begin by referring to recent articles on the topic published in journals of the field. The writer might then show what his article adds to the conversation about teaching with technology. Or, a writer might show that no one else has talked about a topic, and create exigence that shows how this new view adds to the field. For example, an article in a history journal on a lesser-known historical figure might begin by showing how this figure has been ignored in past scholarship and then by establishing the importance of this figure to understanding a particular point in history. Writers publishing in scholarly journals provide exigence that shows how their work is adding to the academic conversations in the field.

Now let's look back at the opening paragraphs of this discussion of exigence. You will find that we began by identifying a need or problem that affects our audience: students. We assumed that as students, you would find this problem pressing enough to read about our proposed solution. If you felt that this discussion was worth reading, for a reason other than passing a quiz, perhaps we have proven our point?

In these cases, the writers have taken steps to create an impression of exigence *for their readers,* even though the writers themselves naturally believe that the problems they are addressing are obviously both real and pressing. The point is that writers must begin with language that leads readers to believe that they should care.

When Do I Establish Exigence? Do I Just Need a Catchy Introduction?

Exigence should be apparent throughout a paper, and the first place it would appear is the introduction. When a reader finds that she has something at stake in a particular argument, issue, or decision, she will read on. In the first several sentences, it is essential to pull your reader in with a brief and clear picture of how your topic is relevant to her experience or self-interest.

Since you only have a few moments to catch a reader's attention, you should try to establish exigence early on. But readers may continue asking "So what?" as they read; if your writing continues to provide an answer to this question, they will continue reading. Thus, establishing exigence goes beyond writing a clever or captivating introduction. Solid exigence should reside behind your thesis statement, and every other statement in your text, because it keeps your readers' needs in mind. It is a factor guiding your selection of information to include and information to discard. It is a factor determining the order in which information is disclosed, and the way your writing is introduced and concluded. Exigence tells the writer and the reader what the importance behind the work is, providing focus and giving a sense of force or drive behind the words.

Let's consider the possible differences between a catchy introduction and the establishment of exigence. An introduction to a paper arguing for research funds for cystic fibrosis could be a sad story about a child with cystic fibrosis. The story could be a pathetic appeal to readers which could provide the "hook" that encourages them to continue reading past the first paragraph or two. In fact, the story could be an important supporting argument for your thesis. But it may not be enough to convince readers that they have a stake in the issue. What would be enough? Maybe the articulation of a problem marked by an urgency: thousands of children each year are born with this debilitating disease.

This brings us to a very important distinction in persuasive writing. There is a subtle difference between compelling your readers to read and persuading your readers to hold a position or to change their minds or to act for change. For the writing you do in this class, then, think of your interesting introduction and your established exigence as two separate things that work together. But remember that your argument needs both an interesting introduction to engage readers and established exigence to convince them that they have a stake in the issue about which you are writing.

Using the Five Canons of Rhetoric as Steps in the Process of Writing

Academic Writing Program, University of Maryland

18

Have you ever had the experience of sitting with a blank sheet of paper (or a blank computer screen) before you and being unable to make any progress on a writing task that you are trying to accomplish? Does it seem that there are just too many things to think about? That you don't know where to start? As surprising as it might sound, even experienced writers feel this way sometimes. There's no shame in admitting it: writing is hard work. Effectively putting thoughts down on paper requires great effort and careful consideration; you must think about what you want to say, what order you want to say it in, what wording or style you want to use. It can often seem overwhelming.

Classical rhetoricians, who wanted to systematize the process of writing speeches, developed a pattern for steps in the writing process, so that speech writers could proceed in an organized fashion and consider everything necessary for composing a good speech. This pattern became known as the "parts" or **canons** of rhetoric. One influential version of this pattern included five canons: invention, arrangement, style, memory, and delivery. This structure can also be adapted to other types of composition besides speeches, as long as we keep in mind the distinctions between composing oral speeches and composing typewritten papers.

Invention: Generating Arguments

Of all the steps in the writing process, invention is probably the hardest—and the most important. Invention is the crucial first step of determining what to put in your paper. One reason it can be so hard to figure out what we want to say is that we often take for granted that good writing has to be "original" in the sense of saying something the likes of which has never been said before. When taken to an extreme, this notion almost makes it seem as if good writing appears magically out of thin air. In reality, good writing can indeed be original, but classical rhetoricians recognized that real originality has less to do with trying to produce something from nothing, and more to do with working with what you already have and making it better. After all, when entrepreneurs "invent" a new tool or labor-saving device, they work with materials that are already available; they don't just magically create something from nothing. Similarly, classical rhetoricians imagined "invention" as a process of "finding" ideas that already exist—appropriately enough, since the word "invent" really means "come upon" or "find." Thinking about writing in this way can make the writing process less intimidating, since you're no longer under pressure to come up with something absolutely new. It doesn't mean that there's no room for originality or creativity. On the contrary, some of the most original and creative writing owes a great deal to ideas and writings that came before it.

So how exactly do you go about "inventing" an argument? There are several options available. You may already be familiar with the method called **brainstorming**, in which you jot down a list of words, phrases, or ideas on a sheet of paper as they come to you, not worrying (at least at first) whether everything fits together neatly; this process can give you a place to start. There's also the technique known as **freewriting**, in which you try to write continuously for a set period of time, not worrying about things like grammar and sentence structure. Using methods such as these, you may come up with some things that you may eventually choose not to include in the final draft of your paper, but the more material that you can generate using invention exercises, the more potential material you will have to choose from when you are deciding what belongs and what doesn't.

Arrangement: Organizing Arguments

So you've figured out what you want to say. Does it matter what order you say it in? With respect to argumentative writing, we can definitely say yes. The order in which you present your material can have a significant impact on the success or failure of your writing. To take one example, let's say you have three main points, two of which the audience might find strongly convincing, but one of which is weaker and less convincing. Should you save the best for last, and therefore present the weakest point first? That might cause your audience to lose interest early on, thinking that all your points will be as ineffective as the first one. Or do you leave the weakest point for last? That might be problematic too, since the last point is often the one most likely to be remembered by the reader, and you don't want the reader to walk away dwelling on your weakest point. In such a situation, many experts recommend a sort of "sandwich" structure in which the weakest point comes in between the two stronger ones. The point is that when you write your own papers, you must make decisions about how best to organize your material, keeping in mind the audience and purpose of your writing.

In addition to thinking about how to present your main points, it's also necessary to consider how to begin and end the paper, as well as what other structural features your paper might need. Papers that jump right into their main points with no background or context are generally not successful or even interesting to readers, since readers need to know why the topic is important before they can make sense of what a writer is arguing about that topic. The same goes for papers that end too suddenly. For this reason, a very basic pattern of writing arrangement consists of an introduction, body (where the main points are explained in detail), and conclusion. For longer papers (such as the final paper that you will write this semester), you will learn about an expanded version of the basic arrangement pattern. This version, called the "parts of a full argument," is especially helpful when you have more than a few sentences of background information, and when you must think about how to organize both your own supporting points and your refutation of opposing points. In the end, it's important to keep in mind that usually there is no single correct way to set up a paper. Instead, a different range of options is available in each case, and you as the writer must decide which option is best for the audience you are trying to reach and the purpose you are trying to achieve.

Style: Expressing Arguments

How you say something can be as important as what you say. Language can be a tricky thing, because it presents us with a seemingly endless range of potential problems. Some words have more than one meaning, and you want your readers to be clear about what meaning you intend. Different words can have the same meaning; or, more likely, they have meanings that are very similar but with slightly different connotations, and you will need to think carefully about which is the right one to use in a given situation.

To add to the complexity, no single variety of any language can be used in all possible situations. The language appropriate to a formal event would be inappropriate in a more casual context. The style a writer uses on a particular occasion may be influenced by things like dialect, slang, jargon, and colloquialisms, or it may be carefully crafted to be as neutral as possible. We have all probably wished at one time or another that language were simple, that there were only one single, correct word for each object or idea, so that there would never be any confusion or ambiguity. It might seem as if that would make writing (and indeed, all communication) much easier.

Looked at another way, however, the complexity of language presents us with a great opportunity. Different forms of language exist both because people themselves are different and because the same people can use different forms of language depending on the situation. Thus, the complexities inherent in language are best seen from a rhetorical perspective as possibilities available for a given audience and situation. The study of style, the consideration of how best to express one's own ideas to a specific audience in a particular situation, is empowering because it gives us the chance to make choices for ourselves, to choose our words just as we choose our method of organization. How formal should you be? What tone do you want to express in your writing? Will your audience understand jargon if you use it? Does your audience expect conciseness, or does the complexity of your content require you to present some information in two or three different ways?

To help you think about these and other stylistic issues, a number of language skills are built into the writing curriculum. Practicing these skills can help you develop your own written style, enabling you to make choices about emphasizing ideas in different ways, using figures of speech to create patterns and support your arguments, and combining sentences so that your writing flows more smoothly. In essence, style is about learning what options are available, so that you can use your own creativity to make the most effective choices in your writing.

Memory: Storing Arguments

Since classical rhetoricians were concerned primarily with composing speeches that would be delivered before an audience (and in an era without teleprompters), they devoted a considerable amount of thought to techniques that would help speakers memorize their points and arguments so that they could deliver them without having to look at notes. Such techniques often included mnemonic devices and "tricks" to aid memorization. For the composition of typewritten papers, memorization for oral delivery usually does not play a prominent role, but memory—in the sense of where typewritten arguments are *stored*—is still important. Think of what we mean when we talk about a computer's "memory," for example. Today, a number of technologies are available that allow us to store documents with ease, and it is to our advantage to make use of them. It goes without saying that you should save a copy of a paper that you are working on. But it pays to save *multiple* copies of really important documents (including ones that will be turned in for a grade), since accidents happen—files can be corrupted, disks can get erased, hard drives can crash, flash drives can get lost, and so on. To be on the safe side, you may even want to take the precaution of saving your paper to an email attachment that is stored in your email system; that way, even if your own hardware fails at some point, you still have a version of your paper on email that you can access. You may also find it helpful to deliberately save multiple versions of a single paper. For example, it's difficult to undo a major change to your draft if you don't have an earlier version saved. So you should consider at least saving a file copy of your rough draft and a separate copy of your final draft, so that you can access both versions electronically if you decide that it's useful to do so. Not only can using these labor-saving techniques help you out of potentially disastrous computer malfunctions, but they can also make the overall writing process flow more smoothly.

Delivery: Publishing and Formatting Arguments

"Delivery" originally referred to the act of delivering speeches orally before a live audience. Being an effective speaker usually means speaking loudly enough and at the right speed so that the audience can easily hear and follow the speech, enunciating clearly and according to the audience's standards for public speech, and perhaps using gestures to emphasize a point. But even in writing, delivery is important. For writing, we can think of delivery in two aspects: how an argument is transmitted to an audience, and how a typewritten argument is formatted.

When a speech is delivered orally before a live audience, the audience simply hears it as the speaker delivers it. But if your argument is typewritten, how would your audience physically receive it? For example, if you imagined writing your paper to "every citizen of the United States," how would you ensure that every citizen in the country could read your argument? It's obviously impractical to imagine mailing a copy of your argument to everyone in the country. Could you have it published in a venue in which everyone could read it? You might imagine having it published in a widely-read newspaper or magazine, but realistically, there's no newspaper or magazine that is read by *every* person in the country. How about publishing it online? Even then, it is worth considering that some American citizens don't have access to the internet.

In many cases, thinking about issues like these can prompt you to reconsider your audience, to narrow it down in order to make your argument more effective. For example, even if you are writing about an issue with a national scope—say, what to do about illegal immigration—that doesn't mean that your argument should be written to every citizen of the U.S. Your argument is more likely to be successful if you focus. For example, if you decide that you want to focus on the effect of the immigration debate on American presidential campaigns, then you could write your paper to scholars of government and politics, and emphasize the aspects of the issue that are most interesting to them. Since they are experts in political science, they would be able to put your argument to better use in advancing the national debate on immigration and politics than the "average" American citizen would; many of the latter might not only disagree with what you're arguing, they might even lack interest in the political side of the issue. By choosing to deliver your argument by having it published in a political science journal (such as *The Journal of Politics*), or even by imagining that you would distribute copies to your instructor and fellow students in the Government and Politics course that you're taking this semester, you can use the concept of delivery to narrow your audience and be more confident that the audience will be interested in your scholarly approach to the topic.

Thinking about where you would publish your argument is helpful for conceptualizing your audience, but within the context of ENGL 101, you will be designing your papers so that a special set of overhearers—your instructor and (in draft workshops) your fellow students—can read it. Thus, your paper must be formatted so that these readers can understand your argument. Formatting requirements that might seem minor are really a matter of audience expectation. For example, consider how your experience of reading a textbook, such as this one, would change if it were printed in tiny type, in a strange script or Old English style font, or, worse, if it were handwritten. Would you bother to read it? Would you even be able to read it? This is why most teachers have standard requirements for what papers should look like. For example, double-spacing your papers and leaving one-inch margins allows your teacher to make comments on your paper that will help you understand both what you did well and what you could improve on. Page numbers help readers find their way around the paper. And using a clear, standard format for citing your sources helps readers track down additional information and helps you establish yourself as a valid participant in a public or scholarly debate.

Other seemingly minor issues with potentially substantial impact also relate to delivery and format. Printing problems can happen to anybody, but when a writer turns in a paper with printing that obviously hasn't been aligned correctly, or that is far too light because of ink problems, it makes the paper—and the writer—look bad. If you submitted such a document to an audience other than your teacher (if, for example, you submitted a resume with that problem to potential employers), your readers wouldn't be inclined to take it seriously, and there is no reason why your teacher is obligated to do so, either. That's why you should print out your paper ahead of time so that you can correct any printing problems that may arise. And don't fall into the habit of handing in your paper as a jumble of loose sheets; you should staple your paper together (or at the very least paper-clip it) so that your teacher doesn't have to keep track of loose paper. Finally, perhaps the most important part of delivery is turning in your paper when it's due. Even the most brilliant argument cannot achieve its intended purpose if it's not delivered at the right time.

For these reasons, you will be expected to follow formatting guidelines in your papers. Your teacher will include information about formatting requirements on his or her course policies.

Seeing the Parts of Rhetoric as a Whole

This five-part pattern is a useful tool, but it should be used with flexibility. Ideally, an orderly writing process would treat invention first, then arrangement, then style, then memory, and finally delivery. But in reality, good writers keep all of them in mind throughout the composing process. In the middle of considering arrangement, you may discover that your paper seems unbalanced and that you need to add another main point, which sends you back to the invention process to find more material. Also, the parts can overlap; arrangement and style can be closely related, especially when you consider the layout of sentences within a paragraph. The parts of rhetoric, then, are not meant to be rigid and inhibiting. Instead, they are simply terms and concepts for things that writers need to think about under any circumstances. They give you a way of structuring the process of writing; just keep in mind that this structure can be adaptable and open-ended.

Invention—Generating Ideas with Stasis Theory

19

Academic Writing Program, University of Maryland

One way to invent something to say is to think about the kinds of questions people might ask about a subject. Just as classical rhetorical theory offers a system for the process of writing, it also offers a system for inventing or analyzing what's at issue in any debate. This system is called **stasis theory**. Stasis theory can help you come up with ways to argue and it can help you understand the ways others are arguing. The term *stasis* comes from a Greek term that means "a stand," as in "taking a stand." For the Greeks, who literally pictured their arguments, the arguer envisioned where "to stand" in a particular debate. The best translation here might be "issue," as in understanding what is "at issue" in a controversy. That's a phrase you might hear in a news report covering a topic; the reporter, having introduced the topic and offered some information, might begin to delineate "what's at issue" in the topic by saying what various participants or factions in the debate think and what kinds of questions come up in the matter. When you are thinking about a topic for a composition, it can be useful to imagine yourself as a reporter looking at some problem and beginning to think about what's at issue, where the controversies are, where you may take a stand.

Stasis theory presents us with categories or questions to pose in understanding a debate or understanding where there is debate or disagreement in an issue. There are many theories about how many categories of the stases there are; some theorists use slightly different categories than the ones we have included here. In general, the stases and the questions they pose are these:

Stasis	Questions
Conjecture (or fact/ definition, or essence/ existence)	Did it happen? Does it exist? What is it? How is it defined?
Cause/Effect	How did it get this way? What caused this to happen? What are/will be the effects of this?

Value	Is it a good or bad thing? Is it right or wrong, honorable or dishonorable? Is it better or worse, more or less desirable than any alternatives? Should it be sought out or avoided?
Action	What should we do about this? What actions are possible? What proposals shall we make about it?
Jurisdiction	Who should handle this matter? Who has the right to decide this matter?

Staking a Claim with Stasis Theory

Perhaps you want to write about an experience you had with the police last year. One day, you were driving home from a friend's house, and you saw police lights flashing in your rearview mirror. You were pulled over, and the white police officer looked at you suspiciously and asked to see your license. Too afraid to ask what this was about, you just complied. Later that night, you heard that a crime had been committed not far from where you were stopped, and the suspect was vaguely described as a young African American man. You too are a young African American man. When you tell the story to some friends, they say that you were stopped for DWB—driving while black.

How can you begin inquiry into this experience? There's no doubt that it occurred—you were definitely stopped. But what other possible questions arise here. Think about stasis theory. What can you call what happened to you—was it routine police work? racial profiling? Why did it happen? Was it a good or bad thing it happened? Was it reasonable or unreasonable? Should you do something about it? What could be done about it? Is it up to you as an individual to do something about it, or should you look to others to respond? If you use these questions from stasis theory, you can find what about the issue interests you and focus on that in your inquiry.

Or perhaps one of the experiences you cherish most from your childhood was listening to stories from your grandmother. She told stories about everything—about when she was a small girl on a farm during the Great Depression, about when your dad was born, stories she made up, stories she heard herself as a young girl. But how can you write about this in terms of an argument of inquiry? Again, you might use the questions from stasis theory to help you think about whether there are any issues to consider here. Again, there's no disputing that this happened, but you can again think about definitions—were the stories your grandmother told you just stories, or could they be considered folklore? Why do we tell stories? Is it to pass along values, or just for entertainment? What effect did these stories have on you? What effect does storytelling have on children (or cultures) in general? Is hearing stories a good thing? Is it better for children to hear stories from family than, say, to watch television or see movies? Should we encourage the telling of stories among families? How should we encourage storytelling? Who should do such encouraging, if we agree it should be done?

Writing a Rhetorical Analysis

20

Academic Writing Program, University of Maryland

One of the best ways to engage a text rhetorically is to look at how an author utilizes the rhetorical appeals to persuade his or her audience. This may be done either by looking at a single persuasive text or by looking at two persuasive texts that tackle the same topic. To demonstrate how a rhetorical analysis might be written, we have chosen to discuss two arguments on the topic of gay straight alliance clubs from the April 14, 2000 issue of *CQ Researcher*.

At Issue: Should High Schools Permit "Gay-Straight Alliance" Clubs?

Yes

Jim Anderson
Communications Director, Gay, Lesbian and Straight Education Network

WRITTEN FOR *THE CQ RESEARCHER*

Considerable media attention has been paid over the past few months, to gay-straight alliance (GSA) controversies in Utah, Louisiana and Orange County, Calif. In each instance, school boards either considered or took action to prevent students from exercising their federally protected right under the Equal Access Act.

While these battles and controversies have been intriguing, it is, perhaps, more interesting to consider the stories that have not made the news.

Little attention has been paid to the approximately 700 gay-straight alliances that are currently meeting in high schools from coast-to-coast. These school communities accepted or embraced the students and their efforts, and not as a result of judicial mandate. Instead, they recognized their professional, if not moral, responsibility to do so.

Should other high schools permit the creation of gay-straight alliances? To answer the question, we need to define gay-straight alliances and to discuss why students are forming them in

"Should High Schools Permit Gay-Straight Alliance Clubs?" by Jim Anderson and Peter LaBarbera, reprinted from *The CQ Researcher* 10, no. 14 (April 14, 2000), by permission of Congressional Quarterly, Inc.

such numbers. A gay-straight alliance is formed by lesbian, gay, bisexual and transgender (LGBT) students and their straight classmates. These students join together to support one another and to address concerns about the misinformation and ignorance that too often result in anti-gay harassment or violence at school.

Their concerns are well-founded. Studies by the federal Centers for Disease Control and Prevention (CDC) show that lesbian, gay and bisexual students are more than four times as likely as their heterosexual classmates to be threatened with or injured by a weapon while at school.

The Gay, Lesbian and Straight Education Network found similarly disturbing trends. In a recent national survey, we found that 61 percent of LGBT students experience verbal harassment, 27 percent physical harassment and 14 percent outright physical assault while at school.

This harassment and isolation may negatively affect students' self-esteem and school performance. Such experiences may explain why national mainstream organizations such as the American Counseling Association and the National Association of Social Workers have recently endorsed gay-straight alliances.

Every student is entitled to a supportive, safe and affirming learning environment. With this goal in mind, we urge schools not only to permit gay-straight alliances but also to encourage and foster their existence.

No

Peter LaBarbera
Senior Analyst, Family Research Council

WRITTEN FOR *THE CQ RESEARCHER*
School districts should not allow the formation of gay-straight alliances on their campuses. These groups, where they already exist, have become de facto homosexuality booster clubs—causing unnecessary divisions and distractions and subjecting the entire student body to one-sided propaganda. Moreover, they are part of a movement that promotes radical identities and dangerous sexual practices to vulnerable, confused teens.

The gay-straight alliances are part of an ingenious strategy by pro-homosexuality and transsexuality groups like the Gay, Lesbian and Straight Education Network (GLSEN) to inject their unhealthy sexual and gender ideologies into the classroom. Students rally around the "rights" of gay, bi or even trans (transgender) classmates who, it is true, are ostracized and sometimes mistreated by their peers.

But while GLSEN and other groups have artfully "spun" the issue of youth homosexuality into one of "discrimination," it is really about behavior and parents' rights to guide their children's moral decisions.

In Massachusetts, taxpayers subsidize the formation of gay-straight alliances—there are now 185— through state grants for GSA projects.

Across the country, educators are wasting valuable school time by allowing GSAs to promote extreme notions to the entire student body. Students rarely get to hear the other side of the debate, and they fear expressing their opposition to homosexuality because of the schools' politically correct embrace of homosexuality.

The National Education Association, the American Civil Liberties Union, GLSEN and their allies promote GSAs in the name of school "safety." But schools shouldn't promote homosexual identities to troubled kids when studies show that homosexual males have drastically shorter life spans. This is due to the risky sexual behavior that flourishes in the promiscuous "gay" world. At a March conference sponsored by GLSEN's Boston affiliate, speakers from the state's Education Department approvingly discussed "queer sex" acts to an audience made up mostly of students ages 14–21.

Parents must resist an agenda that uses schools' authority to confirm impressionable youth in harmful lifestyles. As one former homosexual has noted, "From every medical and health aspect—up to and including the probability of becoming infected with AIDS—it is tragic, even criminal, to lead a child into homosexuality because he or she showed some degree of confusion in adolescence."

Rhetorical Analysis—Understanding the Appeals

Quick, which of the two arguments is more convincing? Jim Anderson's in favor of high schools permitting gay straight alliance clubs or Peter LaBarbera's opposing high schools' decisions to allow gay straight alliance clubs? The answer you arrive at by performing a rhetorical analysis could be that either author's argument is stronger for its intended audience. Your goal in the rhetorical analysis is to assess each author's effectiveness in using the three rhetorical appeals and to conclude that one author's argument is more effective overall for its intended audience because of the way that author uses one, two, or all three rhetorical appeals.

Before we proceed, we must identify each author's intended audience. Although both writers, Jim Anderson and Peter LaBarbera, composed their arguments for the *CQ Researcher*, and their audiences share certain traits, it is also clear from reading the two arguments that the authors have two very different audiences in mind. What traits do the two authors' audiences share? We can determine these by looking at the authors' joint publication choice: the *CQ Researcher*. *CQ Researcher* is published weekly in print, and offered forty-four times a year online to libraries, universities, and researchers who subscribe, and it attempts to give in depth coverage to a single topic each issue. In addition to each edition featuring a bibliography, each edition features a pair of opposing arguments from politicians, academics, or people connected by their vocations to the issue. Both Anderson's and LaBarbera's audiences, therefore, are interested in topics of debate, either because they are politically minded or because they are pursuing research on a particular topic: in this case, gay-straight alliance clubs. Anderson's and LaBarbera's audiences are also similar in that they would be made up of adults voting-age and older and would include all races and both genders. There is, however, an important characteristic that differentiates the two authors' intended audiences: degree of partisanship. Whereas Jim Anderson, who supports gay-straight alliance clubs in high schools, attempts to convince those who are neutral and perhaps slightly opposed to his position as well as supporters, Peter LaBarbera is addressing exclusively those who support his position. LaBarbera's choice is problematic, given the fact that the readers of the *CQ Researcher* cover every pole of the liberal to conservative spectrum. He will have to be careful to avoid offending those who disagree with his position. Now we are ready for the next stage of the rhetorical analysis: an evaluation of each author's use of the rhetorical appeals.

Let's begin by comparing the two authors' extrinsic ethos. Extrinsic ethos refers to the credibility that an author possesses outside of the argumentative text itself. Jim Anderson is the Communications Director of the Gay, Lesbian and Straight Education Network. Based upon his position and his organizational affiliation, what level of credibility should we attach to Anderson outside of the argument? The nature of his position and his role as director of communications leads us to conclude both that he is trained and well educated and that he is frequently called upon to communicate with the press and the public. This suggests strong extrinsic ethos. His organizational affiliation, in contrast, points to exactly what position he will be taking: supporting gay-straight alliance clubs. Although this does not necessarily translate as weak extrinsic ethos, it does mean that Anderson will have to work to convince a neutral or opposing audience that he is not biased. Peter LaBarbera is the Senior Analyst for the Family Research Council, a conservative think tank. Even if you did not know that the Family Research Council is a conservative think tank, the phrase "family research" should clue you in to what stand LaBarbera will be taking on the question of whether high schools should permit gay-straight alliance clubs. Similarly to Anderson, LaBarbera will have to work to convince a neutral or opposing audience that he is not biased in terms of character. LaBarbera's title and position indicates that he is an expert in tabulating, compiling, and assessing data. In this regard, LaBarbera's extrinsic ethos is strong.

In order to grasp Jim Anderson's intrinsic ethos, we need to ask a series of questions. Is he fair-minded? Does he cite knowledgeable authorities and provide outside evidence to back his claims? Does he treat the opposing side with respect? Anderson succeeds in all three of these endeavors, and avoids alienating an opposing audience, because he is careful to build his credibility slowly, over the course of his entire argument. He uses the first three paragraphs to set up the question that he asks in the opening sentence of the fourth paragraph: "Should other high schools permit the creation of gay straight alliances?" (321) By asking this question overtly, he is suggesting to an opposing audience that support for gay straight alliance clubs is not a foregone conclusion and that it is a stance that must be carefully considered before being defended. He proceeds to justify a need for a definition of gay-straight alliance clubs and offers a warrant for why those clubs have become necessary (victimization of gay students). He then calls upon the statistical findings of two national organizations, one of which is his own: the federal Centers for Disease Control and Prevention and the Gay, Lesbian and Straight Education Network. Finally, after invoking the support of the American Counseling Association and the National Association of Social Workers, he makes an ethical plea: "Every student is entitled to a supportive, safe, and affirming learning environment" (321). Once he has presented a full defense of gay straight alliance clubs, he is comfortable stating the position that he would like his audience to take: "not only to permit gay straight alliances but also to encourage and foster their existence" (321).

Peter LaBarbera's intrinsic ethos, in contrast, is poor, not because of the position he is taking but because of the way he addresses the opposing side. His overriding disrespect for the proponents of gay straight alliance clubs can be seen in two different ways: through his use of language and characterization, and through his use of quotation marks. Consider the diction or word choice that LaBarbera incorporates in the opening sentence of the second paragraph: "The gay-straight alliances are part of an ingenious strategy by pro-homosexuality and transsexuality groups like the Gay, Lesbian and Straight Education Network (GLSEN) to inject their unhealthy sexual and gender ideologies into the classroom" (321). In choosing words like "ingenious" to describe the opponents' method, "inject" to describe how organizations supporting gay rights get their information into the classrooms, and "unhealthy" to describe the "ideologies" that organizations like GLSEN promote, LaBarbera risks alienating both readers who have not yet made up their mind about gay straight alliance clubs and supporters of gay civil rights. LaBarbera's use of quotation marks presents an even greater chance that he will lose the support of an opposing or neutral audience. Consider the first instance where LaBarbera uses quotation marks. LaBarbera writes:

> Students rally around the "rights" of gay, bi, or even trans (transgender) classmates, who, it is true, are ostracized and sometimes mistreated by their peers. (321)

Any credibility that LaBarbera might gain by the concession that he makes at the end of the sentence (that gays are "sometimes mistreated") is undermined by his decision to put quotation marks around the word *rights*. The reader may wonder, "Does LaBarbera believe that gays, bisexuals, and transsexuals do not deserve rights?" On multiple occasions later in LaBarbera's argument, he uses quotation marks in a manner that calls into question whether he respects his opposing audience. For example, he writes that "GLSEN and other groups have artfully `spun' the issue of youth homosexuality into one of `discrimination'" (321). Does he not believe that what gays face is discrimination? Each instance where LaBarbera comes across as unnecessarily antagonistic may solidify a neutral or opposing reader's opinion that LaBarbera disrespects the opposing side. The end result is that LaBarbera may lose credibility in all but the staunchest supporter's mind.

Ethos is not the only measure of whether a piece of persuasive writing is weak or strong. In fact, "many rhetoricians . . . have considered pathos the strongest of the appeals." Whereas in terms of ethos, Anderson's argument is stronger, in terms of pathos, LaBarbera's argument is stronger. LaBarbera excels in making the audience fear for the morality of students. One way in which he does this is by identifying gay straight alliance clubs as a threat. LaBarbera concludes his opening paragraph by suggesting that "[gay straight alliance clubs] are part of a movement that promotes radical identities and dangerous sexual practices to vulnerable, confused teens" (321). Even if we disagree with LaBarbera's stance, we must recognize the emotional impact of his word choices: "a movement," "radical identities," "dangerous sexual practices," and "vulnerable, confused teens." Each phrase asks LaBarbera's audience to feel the same concern that he feels regarding the implementation of gay straight alliance clubs. Jim Anderson, on the other hand, does not take full advantage of the fact that he is making an argument that is based upon empathizing (and sympathizing) with the plight of gay and bisexual students, who are "more than four times as likely as their heterosexual classmates to be threatened with or injured by a weapon while at school" (321). Although Anderson provides a statistic, he could have also made the statistic personal by identifying one such victim of anti-gay or anti-bisexual harassment by name if that person was willing.

In terms of logos, Anderson and LaBarbera adopt completely different strategies; and it is up to you to make the case that one of the strategies is more successful. Anderson begins by giving a context for an argument on the topic of gay straight alliance clubs. He then proceeds to offer a definition of gay straight alliances that suggests the twofold purpose of such organizations is to open up communication between homosexuals and heterosexuals and to help spread awareness of the obstacles that many gay students face. He waits until the final sentence of his argument to state the position that he would like his audience to take (in support of gay straight alliances), but not until he makes an assertion that few teachers and parents would disagree with: "Every student is entitled to a supportive, safe, and affirming learning environment" (321). LaBarbera, in contrast, opens with the thesis or position that he wants his audience to support: "School districts should not allow the formation of gay straight alliances on their campuses" (321). He proceeds to attach as much negativity and long-term risk as he can to the effect of high schools allowing gay straight alliance clubs to form.

Ultimately, if you conclude in your rhetorical analysis that Jim Anderson's argument supporting gay straight alliance clubs is stronger, you are most likely building your case on Anderson's effective use of ethos, whereas if you conclude that LaBarbera's argument opposing gay straight alliance clubs is more persuasive you are building your case both on LaBarbera's substantial use of pathos and on the fact that his intended audience supports his position.

Rhetorical Analysis and Stasis Theory— Determining What's at Issue in a Text

You already know something about **stasis theory**, about the categories of questions for thinking about what is at issue in a topic. When you do rhetorical analysis, particularly of a persuasive text, it's important to know what arguments are being made, and one way to recognize the arguments is to think of what kinds of issues are being discussed.

Determining "what's at issue" in a debate is crucial to understanding the topic, proceeding with research, and finding a solution. But arguers rarely stop to identify the kind of issue they are debating. Imagine two educators disagreeing over whether a national school exit test should come at the end of the eighth or twelfth grades. They will probably not stop to tell their audience, "The issue we are debating here concerns what course of action to take." Yet the reader analyzing their arguments needs to have a general system for describing what kind of issue is being addressed.

The first four stases are "hierarchical", meaning they build on each other and there must be agreement in an earlier stasis before there can be agreement in a later one. So, for example, before two historians can agree about the **causes** of terrorism, they must agree not only that terrorism exists (a matter of **conjecture**) but also on how to **define** it. Similarly, before two policy analysts can agree on a proposal of how to deal with terrorism, they must agree that it exists (**fact**), on how exactly it should be **defined**, on what **causes** and **effects** it has, and on its **value**. Then they can debate a plan of **action**. The stasis of **jurisdiction** stands outside this hierarchy but it can relate to any of the other questions. Thus before the policy that the analysts working for the executive branch agree upon can be implemented, it must be agreed that it is the executive branch that has a right to make such decisions.

First Stasis: Conjecture (or Fact and Definition)

The questions in this stasis concern the existence, nature, and attributes of subjects. Arguments about whether something existed or exists, happened or is happening belong in this stasis. Some disagreements concern how or whether a potential "fact" can be verified, and some disagreements go deeper and question whether the status of "fact" is even possible in some cases.

Identifying facts can depend on prior definitions. We saw this with the recent recategorization of Pluto. Because there was disagreement on what constituted a planet, there was disagreement about which bodies in space should be categorized as planets. Once the definition was changed, the categorization was changed.

There are other instances when arguers agree on some set of "facts" but disagree on how they should be labeled or characterized. For example, we may agree that a friend of ours has taken a car, but disagree on whether to call that fact "borrowing" or "stealing."

Second Stasis: Cause

If we agree that something exists or happened, we may next naturally question what brought it about. Causes are usually matters of probable argument rather than factual demonstration when people are involved, since it is usually impossible to recreate human events in order to test a causal hypothesis, while controlling all the potentially influential variables.

Predictions—forecasts of what will happen—are essentially questions about cause since our speculations about what might happen depend on what causes we think could bring about a certain effect, whether we think those causes are likely to occur, and whether we agree upon what kinds of effects a certain event might cause.

Third Stasis: Value (or Quality or Evaluation)

Many perspectives can gather around questions of quality and value. What quality does the thing have? Is it good or bad of its kind, beautiful or ugly, moral or immoral, or at any of the fine gradations between these extremes? These disagreements can also concern what kind of evaluation to make in the first place. Should a person, a politician for example, be judged only in one area of performance, or for character overall? Should a work of art be evaluated morally, or only aesthetically?

Often participants in a discussion about values find they actually share the same values but disagree over how to weight or order them according to importance in a given case. They must use some key value to help them create a hierarchy of other values from most to least important.

Fourth Stasis: Action

If we agree that a situation exists and we evaluate it negatively, we next naturally ask what, if anything, can be done about it. (In fact, one argumentative strategy pushes to action as the issue under debate, as though agreement existed on the preceding issues. Rebuttal then requires moving the issue back down the stases.)

There can be many different arguments over what the best possible course of action might be. Thus arguments in this stasis frequently concern feasibility and trade-offs. We can often agree on what should be done ideally, but not on what is actually possible given the available resources. We can also debate who has the authority or responsibility to take action; in fact, some arguments for courses of action spend much of their time trying to "create" an audience that will act.

We can also agree that a situation exists and evaluate it positively, concurring that we'd like to see the situation maintained (although others might argue against us). Maintaining the *status quo* and arguing that we *should* maintain it also belong within the action stasis.

Questions of Jurisdiction

During an argument in any of the preceding stases, but particularly in questions of evaluation and action, someone may challenge someone else's right to conduct or even to participate in the discussion. Does a particular group have the right to make decisions about the issue? Is one group interfering in another's domain? How do we determine the appropriate forum in which to conduct the argument?

Jurisdictional arguments can be raised in many kinds of controversies. Is it America's right to evaluate China's human rights policies? Do certain powers belong to Congress, to the States, or to the people? Who has the right to decide what a person can do with his or her body? Because such questions do not directly tackle the arguments advanced within the four stases outlined above, they form a separate stasis. Jurisdiction, however, does not follow the first four stases in sequential order. Instead, it is a kind of underlying stasis which attempts to shift the conversation to a different forum or to redistribute the authority for making decisions about the subject. It is ultimately a question of who can debate and who can decide.

The Rhetoric of "Setting an Issue"

Classifying an issue according to its stasis is a useful stage in the arts of inquiry, discussion, and argument. Arguers making or responding to a case can try to set or change the issue to their advantage.

The order of the stases (from fact and definition to cause, to value, to action) is an important feature of the system since it reveals the consequences of setting an issue in a certain stasis. Setting an issue in the third or fourth stasis, for example, frequently assumes agreement in the first or second; in some situations that agreement may be unwarranted. An arguer may propose action for a situation that the audience has yet to identify as a problem. The audience is pressured to see the situation as a problem, however, simply because a solution has been proposed. Similarly, in some situations and with some audiences, arguing in the first or second stasis will immediately create agreement in the third or fourth. For example, a case for the disappearance of a certain species of fish (first stasis) will function with some very receptive audiences as a call to action (fourth stasis). So setting the issue in a particular stasis can be a powerful rhetorical strategy.

Let's look at the pair of articles from *CQ Researcher*. The way they are presented underscores the point here about stasis theory: the whole section is titled "AT ISSUE". What is "at issue" in the overriding question "Should high schools permit 'gay-straight' alliance clubs?" In which stasis is that question? That's pretty simple—should it be done is a question of **action**. But are the articles only discussing action? Let's consider them with more depth.

Jim Anderson's "yes" argument begins with points that related to the fact/definition stasis: he points out that there has been "considerable media attention" to this subject, and that school boards have considered or taken action. He doesn't dispute anything there, he just says what has happened. He makes a point that is in the stasis of fact/definition, but it's not a controversial point, as far as he is concerned.

He then goes on to say that what is more interesting is what hasn't made the news (paragraph two), and that's the "approximately 700 gay-straight alliance" clubs that are already meeting. Again, he's making a point about the existence of these clubs, but that's not what's controversial. He notes that "These school communities accepted or embraced the students and their efforts, and not as a result of judicial mandate. Instead, they recognized their professional, if not moral, responsibility to do so." In terms of the stases, he's suggesting *why* schools formed these clubs (that's a point about cause/effect), and saying that the cause was professional and/or moral duty. That last part sounds a lot like value, and it's a good example of how cause/effect and value are very intertwined. He's stating the idea that forming these clubs was morally right. Certainly someone could interject their own perspective here and say no, they are not, but Anderson is not arguing this point—he makes this move and believes his audience agrees, because he doesn't argue this point.

Then, in paragraph four, he raises the question of whether there should be more of these clubs in other high schools. We can see there that he has moved to action after making some presumptions about existence, cause and value. But then he makes an interesting move. From that question about action—"Should other high schools permit the creation of gay-straight alliances"—he jumps back to the definition stasis and the causal stasis, saying that "To answer the question, we need to define gay-straight alliances and to discuss why students are forming them in such numbers.' What's the rhetorical effect of the way he is arranging these arguments so far?

Anderson offers a definition of these alliances in the rest of paragraph four. Is the definition particularly controversial? Would we say he is making an argument with this definition? Why or why not? Is his definition of the alliances purely definitional, or does he pull in elements of cause/effect and value as well? How does he do this? Why might he be doing it?

In the next three paragraphs, Anderson builds his argument with arguments from various authorities, using statistics to make his case. All of these are examples of arguments that state the existence of threats and harassment, which point out arguments in cause/effect stasis: the statistics prove that these threats exist, and these threats have an effect ("This harassment and isolation may negatively affect students' self-esteem and school performance"). He also makes subtle value arguments here—the affects are negative, the trends are disturbing.

Anderson ends the argument with a clear statement of action, dependent on a sentence that has to do with fact/definition, cause, and value: "Every student is entitled [the idea that students are entitled to something harkens back to the idea that our rights exist] to a supportive, safe and affirming learning environment" [the implication is that such an environment will have an effect on students; furthermore, the implication is that it will be a positive affect]. Based on arguments of fact/definition, cause/effect and value, Anderson makes his argument: yes, these clubs should exist.

If we think about it, it makes sense that any argument about an action should be made on points about cause/effect and value—we generally decide that we want to do things because we believe they will have positive effects. We have coffee in the morning because we believe it will have an effect (it will caffeinate us) and that effect will be good (it will make us alert). Anderson has used the hierarchy of the stases—whether consciously or not—to establish this argument about an action he favors. The extent to which he goes into each point has to do with the constraints of his rhetorical situation: his audience, the genre, the source, the limitations of space.

Exercise

Look at Peter LaBarbera's "no" argument about gay-straight alliance clubs. Does he, like Anderson, make arguments in other stases to construct his point that the clubs should not be permitted in high schools? How can you compare their arguments using the way each constructs points in the various stases? Does LaBarbera use one stasis more than others to make his point?

Stasis Theory— Identifying the Issues and Joining the Debate

21

Academic Writing Program, University of Maryland

Without a sense of what is at issue in a disagreement, it can be difficult to decide where to begin one's own argument or to determine what even counts as arguable within a particular discourse. In his book *Political Communication*, Dan Hahn suggests that one reason there is apathy in American politics is because it is hard to find one's way into a debate:

> Anybody who has ever arrived late to a cocktail party knows how difficult it is to catch up. Every conversation you try to join is confusing. You don't know what has already been said, so you don't know what you should say. Sometimes you plunge in, only to have somebody say, "Yes, that was what Bill was saying a few minutes ago." After a few such embarrassing incidents, you learn either to keep your mouth shut or to change the subject as soon as you enter the group.
>
> Unfortunately, those are also the two options most people take when becoming aware of politics. Nobody bothers to explain what the societal conversation has already covered (although history courses try to do so). Nobody brings you "up to snuff" on the nature of the controversies, what the various sides are, and why people on those sides take the positions they do. All too many people conclude that politics is too complicated and give up.[1]

Perhaps you have felt this way when reading about a topic. Stasis theory offers a system for finding your way in, for getting "up to snuff" on a debate. The stases are like sorting bins for issues and questions. No matter what the subject, the issues can be put into one or more of the five categories described below. (Note that, collectively, the categories are called **stases**; each individual category is called a **stasis**.) If you keep these categories in mind while you read about a subject, you will find it easier to identify the separate issues in the discourse about it. Later, as you begin to fashion your own arguments, knowing where people tend to agree and disagree will assist you in knowing how to start and how to rebut counterarguments that assume agreement where it does not, in fact, exist.

---

[1] Hahn, Dan F. *Political Communication: Rhetoric, Government, and Citizens.* 2nd ed. State College, PA: Strata Publishing, Inc.: 2003.

As you prepare your stasis grid, you can use stasis theory to both anticipate debates and to recognize them when you see them.

The Stases in a Debate

We often wonder how the stases will help us as writers once we have figured out what to write about. Since we know the stases work as sorting bins to classify different types of arguments, and we know how to decide which stasis applies to our opposing arguments, we can use this to devise a thesis that confronts our opposition in the right mode. But do the stases have any use to us as writers after we've formulated our thesis? The answer is an emphatic "yes!"

To understand how they are useful, we must first understand how the stases function differently in a large, multi-faceted debate as opposed to their use in our own individual arguments. In a large debate, we can trace the stases through the issues by posing them as a series of questions:

- Does X exist? How do we define X?
- What causes X? What are the consequences of X?
- Is X therefore a good thing or bad thing? Are the benefits of X worth the costs?
- What should we do about X? Should we implement X?
- Who decides any of these questions about X?

In doing this, we can map the arc of the debate, identify the points at which opposing sides are in disagreement, and decide where we, as participants, should intervene in the debate. For example, we may map the debate over same-sex marriage:

- How do we define marriage?
- What are the consequences of applying or ignoring that definition?
- Are the benefits of these consequences worth the costs?
- Should we legalize same-sex marriage?
- Who should make this decision—states, the federal government, a popular vote?

The Stases in Your Argument

When you as a writer sit down to say your piece about this issue, you may realize a couple of things. First, you may notice that the two major parties in the debate don't agree in any of the stases, so even though the debate is bogged down in definitional issues, the public discourse is centered on action. Second, you may notice that in order to establish your action claims, you must first establish your value claims, which in turn rely on the answer to the cause and consequence questions, which themselves require a definition to work from. Each question depends on the answer reached in the previous stasis.

Suddenly, you have to tackle five major questions instead of one, but fortunately, they're already organized into a logical sequence for you. Thus, in constructing your own argument, you can use the procedure of moving through the stases as an organizational technique. Depending on your position, then, a basic outline might look like one of these:

Definition: Marriage, a love bond between two consenting adults, is a fundamental right.

Consequence: By denying same-sex partners marriage, we are consequently withholding their human rights.

Evaluation: These human rights are more important than archaic traditions based on procreation.

Action (thesis):   We should legalize same-sex marriage.

-or-

Definition: Marriage is a procreative bond and a privilege.

Consequence: By extending these rights to same-sex couples, we de-emphasize the role of parenting and break down the family structure.

Evaluation: Upholding traditional family structures is more important than granting special rights to couples whose bond is not for the purpose of procreation.

Action (thesis):   We should reserve marriage for heterosexual couples.

Notice that taking this debate through the stases in both your own position and the opposing position or positions is also useful for invention. Here, for example, someone supporting same-sex marriage would notice that by starting with marriage as primarily procreative in purpose, the opposing side potentially paints itself into a corner, unless it is willing to stipulate that infertile heterosexuals cannot properly marry. Since few opponents of same-sex marriage are willing to go that far, the supporter now has a useful point of refutation. Someone opposing same-sex marriage, on the other hand, would notice that the definition they start with may lead them to a position they do not in fact hold, and therefore will want to modify their definition.

You will surely find that your argument is more complex than this: perhaps your definitional argument will require a few paragraphs, and your evaluation argument may require a few more. You may want to add a jurisdiction component to your action argument, or propose a compromise that bridges more than one position. Still, by following the shape of the larger debate using the stases, you will find that the logic of your argument follows more smoothly, and, if well managed, more convincingly.

When you read through your research, you may notice that individual authors often work through these stases, even though an author's thesis will focus on one stasis. As you read the articles you have found for your writing project, try to locate each article's thesis, identify its stasis, and then work backwards. Ask yourself whether the author builds an argument by using the conclusions drawn in the previous stasis. By analyzing how other authors work through the stases, you may well find yourself devising a claim structure for your own argument.

How to Use the Lines of Argument to Generate Claims and Discussion

22

Academic Writing Program, University of Maryland

This handout describes the rhetorical work of eight strategies for argument and offers examples of each.

1. **Premise-based claims:** Premise-based claims use *since or because* in order to respond openly to the overarching thesis.

   Example: Because we have agreed that women and men are able to engage in all types of work with the same rigor and expertise, we should support the passing of the ERA.

2. **Correlative claims:** Correlative claims are straightforward cause and effect based claims that can be written using the structure, *if x then y*.

   Example: If we create stronger and more stringent laws regarding purchasing guns, then the government would at least make a move to respond to the rampant gun violence in our country.

3. *A fortiori* **claims:** A *fortiori* claims are probability-based claims that take one of the following two shapes

   a. If something occurs when it is not likely, it will almost certainly occur when it is likely.

   b. If something does not occur when it is likely, it will almost certainly not occur when it is not likely.

   Example: If misreporting on criminal cases such as rape occurs with careful guidelines regarding how to treat both the details of the case and the victim, misreporting will almost certainly occur if no such guidelines are in place.

4. **Partitioning the subject:** Partitioning the subject involves establishing the conditions under which a stance should be adopted or an action should be mobilized. If all conditions exist, the stance should be adopted and the act should be made. If one or more of the conditions do not exist, the stance should be rejected and the action should not be mobilized.

Example: UMD should change its policy regarding recycling on the conditions that fraternities and sororities sign the recycling agreement and if the bars on campus agree to refrain from serving plastic, disposable cups.

5. **Arguments from consistency**: Arguing on the basis of consistency involves arguing for an approach that is in line with a practice or policy already accepted or in place and/or with a belief people already hold.

Example: If professional athletes were expected to follow the same drug testing policies and protocols as collegiate athletes, then the occurrence of steroid use would diminish.

6. **Arguments from simile and metaphor:** Drawing comparisons through metaphors enables the reader to see comparisons between and draw connections between two unlikely pairs.

Example: If we see argument as war, then we will not think about building bridges with the people we are in conversation with but rather trying to "win" and convincing others to do things "our way."

7. **Arguments from exigence:** Arguments from exigence articulate the temporal importance of an issue and call readers attention to the issue at this time.

Example: Due to the fact that our representative will be voting on a bill regarding gun violence next month, we need to respond to, refine, and submit this proposal immediately.

8. **Arguments from popularity:** Arguments from popularity invoke the popularity or lack of popularity of the position to support its value and worth.

Example: Everyday millions of people update their Facebook accounts; while they think their updates are private and that no one other than their intended audience can access this information, this is not the case.

9. **Arguments from superiority:** Arguments from superiority invoke the relative superiority of one position compared to alternatives.

Example: While offering self-defense classes to women to prevent sexual assault is targeting the potential victim or survivor rather than the perpetrator, these classes provide important ways for women to gain confidence and feel some modicum of protection.

Developing Argument Paragraphs

23

Academic Writing Program, University of Maryland

Below are opening sentences from which you can construct whole paragraphs. Complete the paragraphs by adding sentences which fulfill the specified logical function. To stimulate your thinking and to practice using transitions, you can begin each sentence with a transition word that specifies the relation.

Example

1. *The University of Maryland should expand its computer labs.*
2. [Restatement] *That is, the University should buy 500 more computers and should open two new labs.*
3. [Premise] *The University should take this step because the labs are currently overcrowded.*
4. [Exemplification] *For instance, in the months of April and May, when many students have papers due, the average wait at the WAM labs is two hours.*
5. [Addition (to Premise)] *Moreover, many labs are not even open at night, the time when most students need to use computers.*
6. [Conclusion] *Therefore, the University must make expanding the WAM labs a priority.*

Paragraph #1

1. The University of Maryland should provide more parking for students.

2. [Premise]

3. [Premise (a "because" phrase backing up the preceding premise, not the opening sentence)]

4. [Conclusion]

5. [Concession]

6. [Nevertheless]

Paragraph #2

1. The federal government should censor violence on television.

2. [Premise]

3. [Addition]

4. [Exemplification]

5. [Concession]

6. [Nevertheless]

7. [Conclusion]

Paragraph #3

1. Violence on television should remain unregulated.

2. [Restatement]

3. [Conclusion]

4. [Addition]

5. [Contrast]

6. [Conclusion]

SECTION THREE

Style

Concision

24

material from Joseph M. Williams and Joseph Bizup's
Style: The Basics of Clarity and Grace, 5th ed.

> *I spare both my reader's time and my own, by couching my sense in as few words as I can.*
>
> —John Wesley

Understanding Concision

You write more clearly when you match your characters and actions to your subjects and verbs, when you get the right characters into topics and the right words under stress, when you motivate readers with well-crafted introductions, and when you frame your paragraphs, sections, and documents to help readers grasp their global coherence. But readers may still think your prose is a long way from graceful if it's anything like this:

> In my personal opinion, it is necessary that we should not ignore the opportunity to think over each and every suggestion offered.

That writer matched characters with subjects and actions with verbs, but in too many words: opinion is always personal, so we don't need *personal*, and since this statement is opinion, we don't need *in my opinion. Think over* and *not ignore* both mean *consider. Each and every* is redundant. A suggestion is by definition offered. In fewer words:

- We should consider each suggestion.

Though not yet shapely or elegant, that sentence at least has the virtue of compactness, or as we'll call it, *concision.*

Diagnosis and Revision

Six Principles of Concision

When I edited that sentence about suggestions, I followed six principles:

1. Delete words that mean little or nothing.
2. Delete words that repeat the meaning of other words.

3. Delete words implied by other words.
4. Replace a phrase with a word.
5. Change negatives to affirmatives.
6. Delete useless adjectives and adverbs.

Those principles are easy to state but hard to follow, because you have to inch your way through every sentence you write, cutting here, compressing there, and that's labor intensive. Those six principles, though, can guide you in that work.

1. **Delete meaningless words.** Some words are verbal tics that we use as unconsciously as we clear our throats:

kind of	actually	particular	really	certain	various
virtually	individual	basically	generally	given	practically

Productivity **actually** depends on **certain** factors that **basically** involve psychology more than **any particular** technology.

   ▪ Productivity depends on psychology more than on technology.

2. **Delete doubled words.** Early in the history of English, writers got into the habit of pairing a French or Latin word with a native English one, because foreign words sounded more learned. Most paired words today are just redundant. Among the common ones:

full and complete	hope and trust	any and all
true and accurate	each and every	basic and fundamental
hope and desire	first and foremost	various and sundry

3. **Delete what readers can infer.** This redundancy is common but hard to identify, because it comes in so many forms.

   Redundant Modifiers Often, the meaning of a word (italicized) implies its modifier (boldfaced):

   Do not try to *predict* those **future** events that will **completely** *revolutionize* society, because **past** *history* shows that it is the **final** *outcome* of minor events that **unexpectedly** *surprises* us more.

   ▪ Do not try to predict revolutionary events, because history shows that the outcome of minor events surprises us more.

   Some common redundancies:

terrible tragedy	various different	free gift
basic fundamentals	future plans	each individual
final outcome	true facts	consensus of opinion

Redundant Categories Every word implies its general category, so you can usually cut a word that names it (boldfaced):

> During that *period* **of time,** the *membrane* **area** became *pink* **in color** and *shiny* **in appearance.**
>
> ▪ During that *period,* the *membrane* became *pink* and *shiny.*

In doing that, you may have to change an adjective into an adverb:

> The holes must be aligned in an *accurate* **manner.**
>
> ▪ The holes must be aligned *accurately.*

Sometimes you change an adjective into a noun:

> The county manages the *educational* **system** and *public recreational* **activities.**
>
> ▪ The county manages *education* and *public recreation.*

Here are some general nouns (boldfaced) often used redundantly:

large in **size**	round in **shape**	honest in **character**
unusual in **nature**	of a strange **type**	**area** of mathematics
of a bright **color**	at an early **time**	in a confused **state**

General Implications This kind of wordiness is even harder to spot, because it can be so diffuse:

> Imagine someone trying to learn the rules for playing the game of chess.

Learn implies *trying, playing the game* implies *rules,* chess is a game. So more concisely,

> Imagine learning the rules of chess.

4. **Replace a phrase with a word.** This redundancy is especially difficult to fix, because you need a big vocabulary and the wit to use it. For example:

> As you carefully read what you have written to improve wording and catch errors of spelling and punctuation, the thing to do before anything else is to see whether you can use sequences of subjects and verbs instead of the same ideas expressed in nouns.

That is,

▪ As you edit, first replace nominalizations with clauses.

I compressed five phrases into five words:

carefully read what you have written	→	edit
the thing to do before anything else	→	first
use X instead of Y	→	replace
nouns instead of verbs	→	nominalizations
sequences of subjects and verbs	→	clauses

I can offer no principle that tells you when to replace a phrase with a word, much less give you the word. I can point out only that you often can, and that you should be alert for opportunities to do so—which is to say, try.

Here are some common phrases (boldfaced) to watch for. Note that some of these let you turn a nominalization into a verb (both italicized):

We must explain **the reason for** the *delay* in the meeting.

▦ We must explain **why** the meeting is *delayed.*

Despite the fact that the data were checked, errors occurred.

▦ **Even though** the data were checked, errors occurred.

In the event that you finish early, contact this office.

▦ **If** you finish early, contact this office.

In a situation where a class closes, you may petition to get in.

▦ **When** a class closes, you may petition to get in.

I want to say a few words **concerning the matter of** money.

▦ I want to say a few words **about** money.

There is a need for more careful *inspection* of all welds.

▦ You **must** *inspect* all welds more carefully.

We **are in a position** to make you an offer.

▦ We **can** make you an offer.

It is possible that nothing will come of this.

▦ Nothing **may** come of this.

Prior to the *end* of the training, apply for your license.

▦ **Before** training *ends*, apply for your license.

We have noted a **decrease/increase in** the number of errors.

▦ We have noted **fewer/more** errors.

5. **Change negatives to affirmatives.** When you express an idea in a negative form, not only must you use an extra word: *same → not different*, but you also force readers to do a kind of algebraic calculation. These two sentences, for example, mean much the same thing, but the affirmative is more direct:

Do not write in the negative.   →   Write in the affirmative.

You can rewrite most negatives:

not careful	→	careless	not many	→	few
not the same	→	different	not often	→	rarely
not allow	→	prevent	not stop	→	continue
not notice	→	overlook	not include	→	omit

Do not translate a negative into an affirmative if you want to emphasize the negative. (Is that such a sentence? I could have written, *Keep a negative sentence when....*)

Some verbs, prepositions, and conjunctions are implicitly negative:

Verbs	*preclude, prevent, lack, fail, doubt, reject, avoid, deny, refuse, exclude, contradict, prohibit, bar*
Prepositions	*without, against, lacking, but for, except*
Conjunctions	*unless, except when*

You can baffle readers if you combine *not* with these negative words. Compare these:

Except when you have **failed** to submit applications **without** documentation, benefits will **not** be **denied**.

▪ You will receive benefits only if you submit your documents.

▪ To receive benefits, submit your documents.

And you baffle readers completely when you combine explicitly and implicitly negative words with passives and nominalizations:

There should be **no** submission of payments **without** notification of this office, **unless** the payment does **not** exceed $100.

Do not **submit** payments if you have not **notified** this office, unless you are **paying** less than $100.

Now revise the negatives into affirmatives:

▪ If you pay more than $100, notify this office first.

6. **Delete adjectives and adverbs.** Many writers can't resist adding useless adjectives and adverbs. Try deleting every adverb and every adjective before a noun, then restore *only* those that readers need to understand the passage. In this passage, which ones should be restored?

> At the heart of the argument culture is our habit of seeing issues and ideas as ~~absolute and irreconcilable~~ principles ~~continually~~ at war. To move beyond this ~~static and limiting~~ view, we can remember the ~~Chinese~~ approach to yin and yang. They are two principles, yes, but they are conceived not as ~~irreconcilable polar~~ opposites but as elements that coexist and should be brought into balance. ~~as much as possible~~ As sociolinguist Suzanne Wong Scollon notes, "Yin is always present in and changing into yang and vice versa." How can we translate this ~~abstract~~ idea into ~~daily~~ practice?
>
> —Deborah Tannen, *The Argument Culture*

Here's the point: Readers think you write concisely when you use only enough words to say what you mean.

1. Delete words that mean little or nothing.
2. Delete words that repeat the meaning of other words.
3. Delete words implied by other words.
4. Replace a phrase with a word.
5. Change negatives to affirmatives.
6. Delete useless adjectives and adverbs.

Redundant Metadiscourse

Metadiscourse as language that refers to the following:

- The writer's intentions: *to sum up, candidly, I believe*
- Directions to the reader: *note that, consider now, as you see*
- The structure of the text: *first, second, finally, therefore, however*

Everything you write needs metadiscourse, but too much buries your ideas:

> The last point I would like to make is that in regard to men–women relationships, it is important to keep in mind that the greatest changes have occurred in how they work together.

Only nine of those thirty-four words address men–women relationships:

> men-women relationships . . . greatest changes . . . how they work together.

The rest is metadiscourse. When we prune the metadiscourse, we tighten the sentence:

> The greatest changes in men–women relationships have occurred in how they work together.

Now that we see what the sentence says, we can make it still more direct:

> ▥ Men and women have changed their relationships most in how they work together.

How writers use metadiscourse varies by field, but you can usually cut these two types:

1. **Metadiscourse That Attributes Your Ideas to a Source** Don't announce that something has been *observed*, *noticed*, *noted*, and so on; just state the fact:

   > High divorce rates **have been observed** to occur in areas that **have been determined to have** low population density.

   > ▥ High divorce rates occur in areas with low population density.

2. **Metadiscourse That Announces Your Topic** The boldface phrases tell your reader what your sentence is "about":

   > **This section introduces another** problem, that of noise pollution. **The first thing to say about it is** that noise pollution exists not only . . .

   Readers catch the topic more easily if you reduce the metadiscourse:

   > ▥ **Another** problem is noise pollution. **First**, it exists not only . . .

   Two other constructions call attention to a topic, usually one already mentioned in the text:

   > **In regard to** a vigorous style, the most important feature is a short, concrete subject followed by a forceful verb.

   > **So far as** China's industrial development **is concerned**, it has long surpassed that of Japan.

   But you can usually work those topics into a subject:

   > ▥ **The most important fe**ature of a vigorous style is a short, concrete subject followed by a forceful verb.

   > ▥ **China** has long surpassed Japan's industrial development.

Hedges and Intensifiers

Another kind of metadiscourse reflects the writer's certainty about what she is claiming. *Hedges* qualify your certainty; *intensifiers* increase it. Both can be redundant when used excessively. But they can also be useful, because they signal how well you balance caution and confidence and therefore influence how readers judge your character.

Hedges

These are common hedges:

Adverbs	*usually, often, sometimes, almost, virtually, possibly, allegedly, arguably, perhaps, apparently, in some ways, to a certain extent, somewhat, in some/certain respects*
Adjectives	*most, many, some, a certain number of*
Verbs	*may, might, can, could, seem, tend, appear, suggest, indicate*

Too much hedging sounds mealy-mouthed, like this:

There **seems to be some** evidence to **suggest** that **certain** differences between Japanese and Western rhetoric **could** derive from historical influences **possibly** traceable to Japan's cultural isolation and Europe's history of cross-cultural contacts.

On the other hand, only a fool or someone with massive historical evidence would make an assertion as flatly certain as this:

This evidence **proves** that Japanese and Western rhetorics differ because of Japan's cultural isolation and Europe's history of cross-cultural contacts.

In most academic writing, we more often state claims closer to this (note my own hedging; compare the more assertive, *In academic writing, we state claims like this*):

- This evidence **suggests** that **aspects** of Japanese and Western rhetoric differ because of Japan's cultural isolation and Europe's history of cross-cultural contacts.

The verbs *suggest* and *indicate* let you state a claim about which you are less than 100-percent certain but confident enough to propose:

- The evidence **indicates** that some of these questions remain unresolved.

- These data **suggest** that further studies are necessary.

Even confident scientists hedge. This next paragraph introduced the most significant breakthrough in the history of genetics, the discovery of the double helix of DNA.

If anyone was entitled to be assertive, it was Crick and Watson. But they chose to be diffident (note, too, the first-person *we*; hedges are boldfaced):

> We **wish to suggest a** [not *the*] structure for the salt of deoxyribose nucleic acid (DNA).... A structure for nucleic acid has already been proposed by Pauling and Corey.... **In our opinion,** this structure is unsatisfactory for two reasons: (1) **We believe** that the material which gives the X-ray diagrams is the salt, not the free acid.... (2) **Some** of the van der Waals distances **appear** to be too small.
>
> —J. D. Watson and F. H. C. Crick,
> "Molecular Structure of Nucleic Acids"

Intensifiers

These are common intensifiers:

Adverbs	*very, pretty, quite, rather, clearly, obviously, undoubtedly, certainly, of course, indeed, inevitably, invariably, always*
Adjectives	*key, central, crucial, basic, fundamental, major, principal, essential*
Verbs	*show, prove, establish, as you/we/everyone knows/can see, it is clear/ obvious that*

The most common intensifier is the absence of a hedge. In this case, less is more. The first sentence below has no intensifiers at the blanks, but neither does it have any hedges, and so it seems like a strong claim:

_____ Americans believe that the federal government is _____ intrusive and _____ authoritarian.

▪ **Many** Americans believe that the federal government is **often** intrusive and **increasingly** authoritarian.

Confident writers use intensifiers less often than they use hedges because they want to avoid sounding as assertive as this:

> For a century now, **all** liberals have argued against **any** censorship of art, and **every** court has found their arguments so **completely** persuasive that **not a** person **any** longer remembers how they were countered. As a result, today, censorship is **totally** a thing of the past.

Some writers think that kind of aggressive style is persuasive. Quite the opposite. If you state a claim moderately, readers are more likely to consider it thoughtfully:

> For **about** a century now, **many** liberals have argued against censorship of art, and **most** courts have found their arguments persuasive **enough** that **few** people **may** remember **exactly** how they were countered. As a result, today, censorship is **virtually** a thing of the past.

Some claim that a passage hedged that much is wordy and weak. Perhaps. But it does not come on like a bulldozer. It leaves room for a reasoned and equally moderate response.

Here's the point: You need some metadiscourse in everything you write, especially metadiscourse that guides readers through your text, words such as *first, second, therefore, on the other hand*, and so on. You also need some metadiscourse that hedges your certainty, words such as *perhaps, seems, could*, and so on. The risk is in using too much.

Cohesion and Coherence

material from Joseph M. Williams and Joseph Bizup's
Style: The Basics of Clarity and Grace, 5th ed.

25

> *If he would inform, he must advance regularly from Things known to things unknown, distinctly without Confusion, and the lower he begins the better. It is a common Fault in Writers, to allow their Readers too much knowledge: They begin with that which should be the Middle, and skipping backwards and forwards, 'tis impossible for any one but he who is perfect in the Subject before, to understand their Work, and such an one has no Occasion to read it.*
>
> —Benjamin Franklin

Understanding Connections

So far, I've discussed clarity as if we could achieve it just by mapping characters and actions onto subjects and verbs. But readers need more than individually clear sentences before they think a passage "hangs together." These two passages, for example, say much the same thing but feel very different:

1a. The basis of our American democracy—equal opportunity for all—is being threatened by college costs that have been rising fast for the last several years. Increases in family income have been significantly outpaced by increases in tuition at our colleges and universities during that period. Only the children of the wealthiest families in our society will be able to afford a college education if this trend continues. Knowledge and intellectual skills, in addition to wealth, will divide us as a people, when that happens. Equal opportunity and the egalitarian basis of our democratic society could be eroded by such a divide.

■ 1b. In the last several years, college costs have been rising so fast that they are now threatening the basis of our American democracy—equal opportunity for all. During that period, tuition has significantly outpaced increases in family income. If this trend continues, a college education will soon be affordable only by the children of the wealthiest families in our society. When that happens, we will be divided as a people not only by wealth, but by knowledge and intellectual skills. Such a divide will erode equal opportunity and the egalitarian basis of our democratic society.

The first seems choppy, even disorganized; the second seems more connected.

But like the word *clarity*, the words *choppy*, *disorganized*, and *connected* refer not to the words on the page but to how they make us *feel*. What is it about the *arrangement* of words in (1a) that makes us feel we are moving through it in fits and starts? Why does (1b) seem to flow more easily? We base those judgments on two aspects of word order:

- We judge a sequence of sentences to be *cohesive* based on how each sentence ends and the next begins.
- We judge a whole passage to be *coherent* based on how all the sentences in a passage cumulatively begin. (Here I discuss the coherence of passages; in Chapter 26, I discuss the coherence of whole documents.)

Cohesion

The Sense of Flow

Avoid passives. If we always did, we would choose the active verb in sentence (2a) over the passive in (2b):

2a. The collapse of a dead star into a point perhaps no larger than a marble **CREATES**$_{active}$ a black hole.

2b. A black hole **IS CREATED**$_{passive}$ by the collapse of a dead star into a point perhaps no larger than a marble.

But we might choose otherwise in context. Consider:

[1]Some astonishing questions about the nature of the universe have been raised by scientists studying black holes in space. [2a]**The collapse of a dead star into a point perhaps no larger than a marble creates a black hole.** [3]So much matter compressed into so little volume changes the fabric of space around it in puzzling ways.

[1]Some astonishing questions about the nature of the universe have been raised by scientists studying black holes in space. [2b]**A black hole is created by the collapse of a dead star into a point perhaps no larger than a marble.** [3]So much matter compressed into so little volume changes the fabric of space around it in puzzling ways.

In context, our sense of "flow" calls not for (2a), the sentence with the active verb, but for (2b), the one with the passive.

The reason is clear: the last four words of the first sentence introduce an important character—*black holes in space*. But with sentence (2a), the next concepts we hit are *collapsed stars* and *marbles*, information that seems to come out of nowhere:

[1]Some astonishing questions about the nature of the universe have been raised by scientists studying **black holes in space**. [2a]**The collapse of a dead star into a point perhaps no larger than a marble** creates . . .

If we follow sentence (1) with (2b), the sentence with the passive verb, we feel those sentences connect more smoothly, because now the first words in (2b) repeat what we just read at the end of (1):

[1]. . . studying **black holes in space**. [2b]**A black hole** is created by the collapse of a dead star . . .

Note too that the passive lets us put at the *end* of sentence (2b) words that connect it to the *beginning* of sentence (3):

> [1] . . . black holes in space. [2b]A black hole is created by the collapse of a dead star into **a point perhaps no larger than a marble.** [3]**So much matter compressed into so little volume** changes the fabric of space around it in puzzling ways.

Here's the point: Sentences are *cohesive* when the last few words of one set up information that appears in the first few words of the next. That's what gives us our experience of flow. And in fact, that's the biggest reason the passive is in the language: to let us arrange sentences so that they flow from one to the next easily.

Diagnosis and Revision: Old Before New

In sentences, readers prefer to encounter old, familiar information before they encounter new, unfamiliar information. So:

1. **Begin sentences with information familiar to your readers.** Readers get that familiar information from two sources. First, they remember words from the sentences they just read. That's why in our example about black holes, the beginning of (2b) coheres with the end of (1), and the beginning of (3) coheres with the end of (2b). Second, readers bring to a sentence a general knowledge of its content. We would not be surprised, for example, to find the next sentence (4) begin like this:

    > . . . changes the fabric of space around it in puzzling ways. [4]**Astronomers have reported** that . . .

The word *astronomers* did not appear in the preceding sentence, but since we are reading about space, we wouldn't be surprised by a reference to them.

2. **End sentences with information readers cannot predict.** Readers always prefer to read what's new and complex *after* they read what's familiar and simple.

    You can more easily see when others fail to observe this old-before-new principle than when you do, because after you've worked on your own ideas for a while, they all seem familiar—to you. But hard as it is to distinguish old from new in your own writing, you have to try, because readers want to begin sentences with information that is familiar to *them*, and only then move on to information that is new.

Here's the point: So far, we have identified three main principles of clarity. Two are about sentences:

- Make main characters the subjects of sentences.
- Make important actions verbs.

The third is about sentences as well, but it also explains how sentences flow together:

■ Put old information before new information.

These principles usually complement one another, but if you have to choose among them, favor the third. The way you organize old and new information determines how cohesive readers will find your writing. And for readers, a passage's overall *cohesion* trumps the *clarity* of individual sentences.

Coherence

A Sense of the Whole

When you create cohesive flow, you take the first step toward helping readers feel that your prose hangs together. But they will judge you to be a competent writer only when they feel that your writing has *coherence*, a quality different from cohesion. It's easy to confuse the words *cohesion* and *coherence* because they sound alike.

- Think of *cohesion* as pairs of sentences fitting together the way individual pieces of a jigsaw puzzle do (recall the black hole sentences).
- Think of *coherence* as seeing what all the sentences in a piece of writing add up to, the way all the pieces in a puzzle add up to the picture on the box.

This next passage has good cohesive flow because we move from one sentence to the next without a hitch:

> Sayner, Wisconsin, is the snowmobile capital of the world. The buzzing of snowmobile engines fills the air, and their tanklike tracks crisscross the snow. The snow reminds me of Mom's mashed potatoes, covered with furrows I would draw with my fork. Her mashed potatoes usually make me sick—that's why I play with them. I like to make a hole in the middle of the potatoes and fill it with melted butter. This behavior has been the subject of long chats between me and my analyst.

Though its individual sentences are cohesive, that passage as a whole is incoherent. (It was created by six different writers, one of whom wrote the first sentence, with the other five sequentially adding one sentence, knowing only the immediately preceding one.) It is incoherent for three reasons:

1. The subjects of the sentences are entirely unrelated.
2. The sentences share no common themes or ideas.
3. The paragraph has no one sentence that states what the whole passage is about.

I will discuss the third point in Chapter 26. The rest of this chapter focuses on the first point, shared subjects.

Subjects, Topics, and Coherence

For 500 years, English teachers have defined *subject* in two ways:

1. the "doer" of the action
2. what a sentence is "about," its main topic

The subjects of many sentences are not doers. Here, for example, the subject is an action: *The **explosion** was loud.* Here it is a quality: ***Correctness** is not writing's highest virtue.* Here it is just a grammatical placeholder: ***It** was a dark and stormy night.*

But also flawed is that second definition: *a subject is what a sentence is about.* It is flawed because often, the subject of a sentence doesn't state its main topic, the idea that the rest of the sentence "comments" on. That "topicalizing" function can be performed by other parts of a sentence. For example, none of the main subjects in these sentences name their topics:

- The main subject of the next sentence (italicized) is *it*, but the topic of the sentence (boldfaced) is *your claim*, the object of the preposition *for*:

  It is impossible for **your claim** to be proved.

- The subject of this sentence is *I*, but its topic is *this question*, the object of *to*:

  In regard to **this question**, *I* believe more research is needed.

- The subject of this sentence is *it*, but its topic is *our proposal*, the subject of a verb in a subordinate clause:

  It is likely that **our proposal** will be accepted.

- The subject of this sentence is *no one*, but its topic is *such results*, a direct object shifted to the front for emphasis:

  Such results *no one* could have predicted.

Diagnosis and Revision: Topics

As with issues of clarity, you can't predict how readers will judge the flow of your writing just by reading it, because you know it too well. You must analyze it more objectively. This passage feels choppy, out of focus, even disorganized:

> Consistent ideas toward the beginnings of sentences help readers understand what a passage is generally about. A sense of coherence arises when a sequence of topics comprises a narrow set of related ideas. But the context of each sentence is lost by seemingly random shifts of topics. Unfocused paragraphs result when that happens.

Here's how to diagnose and revise such passages:

1. **Diagnose**
   a. Underline the first seven or eight words of every sentence in a passage, stopping if you hit the main verb.

b. If you can, underline the first five or six words of every clause in those sentences.

<u>Consistent ideas toward the beginnings of sentences</u>, especially in their subjects, help readers understand <u>what a passage</u> is generally about. A <u>sense of coherence</u> arises when <u>a sequence of topics</u> comprises a narrow set of related ideas. But <u>the context of each sentence</u> is lost by seemingly random shifts of topics. <u>Unfocused, even disorganized paragraphs</u> result when that happens.

2. **Analyze**

a. Do the underlined words constitute a relatively small set of related ideas? Even if *you* see how they are related, will your readers? For that passage, the answer is no.

b. Do the underlined words name the most important characters, real or abstract? Again, the answer is no.

3. **Rewrite**

a. In most (not necessarily all) of your sentences, use subjects to name their topics.

b. Be sure that those topics are, in context, familiar to your readers.

Here is that passage revised, with the new subjects boldfaced.

Readers understand what a passage is generally about when **they** see consistent ideas toward the beginnings of sentences, especially in their subjects. **They** feel a passage is coherent when **they** read a sequence of topics that focuses on a narrow set of related ideas. But when topics seem to shift randomly, **readers** lose the context of each sentence. When **that** happens, **they** feel they are reading paragraphs **that** are unfocused and even disorganized.

Now the subjects form a strong topic string: *readers, they, they, they, topics, readers, that, they [readers].*

Avoiding Distractions at the Beginning of a Sentence

It's hard to begin a sentence well. Readers want to get to a subject/topic quickly, but too often we begin sentences in ways that keep readers from getting there. It's called *throat-clearing*. Throat-clearing typically begins with metadiscourse that connects a sentence to the previous one, with transitions such as *and, but,* or *therefore*:

And therefore . . .

We then add a second kind of metadiscourse that expresses our attitude toward what is coming, words such as *fortunately, perhaps, allegedly, it is important to note, for the most part,* or *politically speaking*:

And therefore, it is important to note . . .

Then we indicate time, place, or manner:

And therefore, it is important to note that, in Eastern states since 1980 . . .

Only then do we get to the subject/topic:

> And, therefore, it is important to note that, in Eastern states since 1980, **acid rain** has become a serious problem.

When you open several sentences with distractions like that, your readers have a hard time seeing not just what each sentence is about, but the focus of a whole passage. When you find a sentence with lots of words before its subject/topic, revise:

▪ Since 1980, therefore, **acid rain** has become a political problem in the Eastern states.

Here's the point: In most of your sentences (not necessarily all), start with the subject and make that subject the topic of the sentence.

Learning to write clear sentences is hard enough. Even more demanding is assembling those sentences into a passage that is both cohesive and coherent. We can bring together these principles about old and new and strings of consistent topics with the principles about characters as subjects and actions as verbs:

Fixed	Topic		
Variable	Familiar	New	
Fixed	Subject	Verb	_____
Variable	Character	Action	_____

Global Coherence

material from Joseph M. Williams and Joseph Bizup's
Style: The Basics of Clarity and Grace, 5th ed.

26

> *The two capital secrets in the art of prose composition are these:—1st, the philosophy of transition and connection, or the art by which one step in an evolution of thought is made to arise out of another: all fluent and effective composition depends on the connections;—2^ndly, the way in which sentences are made to modify each other; for, the most powerful effects in written eloquence arise out of this reverberation, as it were, from each other in a rapid succession of sentences.*
>
> —Thomas De Quincey

Understanding How Frameworks Shape Reading

Create an introduction that can do two things:

- Motivate your readers by stating a problem that they care about.
- Frame the rest of your document by stating the point and key concepts that you will develop in what follows.

In this chapter, I explain how that second point applies to all the parts of your document—its sections, subsections, and even paragraphs. Like the term *clear*, the term *coherent* doesn't refer to anything we find on the page. Coherence is an experience we create for ourselves as we make our own sense out of what we read.

What we look for on the page are signals that help us know what parts of our prior knowledge to bring to the text and how we can integrate what we read with the knowledge we have. You help your readers do that by building those signals into your writing deliberately. This chapter explains how to do that.

Forecasting Themes to Create Coherence

In Chapter 25 we looked at those features that help readers create "local" coherence in short passages. But readers need more to grasp the coherence of a whole document. To help them achieve that coherence, you can use a by-now-familiar principle: begin each document, its sections, and subsections with a short, easily grasped segment that states the point and introduces the themes that readers use to organize the rest. Then, in the body, support, develop, or explain the point and themes stated in the first part.

To help readers grasp the coherence of a document and its sections, follow these six principles:

For the document:

1. Readers must know where the introduction ends and the body begins as well as where each section ends and the next begins. Identify the start of each new section with a heading that includes the key themes for that section (see 5 below). If your field does not use headings, delete them for the final draft.
2. At the end of the introduction, readers look for the document's main point/solution to the problem, which should state the main themes developed in the rest. If you have good reason to save your main point for the conclusion, put at the end of the introduction a sentence that promises the point to come *and* states the main themes.
3. In the body, readers look for the concepts announced as themes at the end of the introduction, using them to organize their understanding of the whole. Be sure that you repeat those themes regularly.

For each section and subsection:

4. Readers look for a short segment that introduces the section or subsection.
5. At the end of that introductory segment, readers look for a sentence that states both the point of the section and the specific concepts you will develop as distinctive themes for that section.
6. In the body of the section, readers look for the concepts announced as themes at the end of the introductory segment, using them to organize their understanding of that section. Be sure that you repeat them regularly.

In the limited space we have here, I can't illustrate these principles with entire documents, or even long sections. I have to use paragraphs and ask you to relate their structure to a whole section of a document.

For example, read this:

> 1a. Thirty sixth-grade students wrote essays that were analyzed to determine the effectiveness of eight weeks of training to distinguish fact from opinion. That ability is an important aspect of making sound arguments of any kind. In an essay written before instruction began, the writers failed almost completely to distinguish fact from opinion. In an essay written after four weeks of instruction, the students visibly attempted to distinguish fact from opinion, but did so inconsistently. In three more essays, they distinguished fact from opinion more consistently, but never achieved the predicted level of performance. In a final essay written six months after instruction ended, they did no better than they did in their preinstruction essays. Their training had some effect on their writing during the instruction period, but it was inconsistent, and six months after instruction it had no measurable effect.

The first few sentences introduce the rest, but we don't see in them the key concepts that follow: *inconsistently, never achieved, no better, no measurable effect*. Those terms are crucial to the *point* of the whole and help organize the rest. Worse, we don't get to that point until we get to the end of the passage: training had no long-term effect. And so as we read, the passage seems to ramble—until the end, when we learn what we need to know to make sense of it retrospectively. But that takes more effort than we should have to expend.

Compare this version:

> 1b. In this study, thirty sixth-grade students were taught to distinguish fact from opinion. They did so successfully during the instruction period, but the effect was inconsistent and less than predicted, and six months after instruction ended, the instruction had no measurable effect. In an essay written before instruction began, the writers failed almost completely to distinguish fact from opinion. In an essay written after four weeks of instruction, the students visibly attempted to distinguish fact from opinion, but did so inconsistently. In three more essays, they distinguished fact from opinion more consistently, but never achieved the predicted level of performance. In a final essay written six months after instruction ended, they did no better than they did in their preinstruction essay. We thus conclude that short-term training to distinguish fact from opinion has no consistent or long-term effect.

In (1b), we quickly grasp that the first two sentences introduce what follows. And in the second sentence, we see two things: both the point of the passage (underlined) and its key terms (boldfaced):

> 1b. In this study, thirty sixth-grade students were taught to distinguish fact from opinion. <u>They did so successfully during the instruction period, but the **effect was inconsistent and less than predicted**, and six months after instruction ended, the instruction had **no measurable effect**</u>.

Consequently, we feel the passage hangs together better and we read it with more understanding.

Now imagine two documents: in one, the point of each section and the whole appears at its *end* (as in 1a) and what openings there are do not introduce the key terms that follow; in the other, each point appears in an *introductory* segment to every paragraph, section, and of the whole (as in 1b). Which would be easier to read and understand? The second, of course.

Keep in mind this principle: put the point sentence at the *end* of the short opening segment; make it the *last* sentence that your reader reads before starting the longer, more complex segment that follows.

- In a paragraph, the introductory segment might be just a single sentence, so by default, it will be the last sentence readers read before they read what follows. If the paragraph has a two-sentence introduction (as did 1b), be sure the point of the paragraph is the *second* sentence, still making it the last thing readers read before they read the rest.
- For sections, your introduction might be a paragraph or more. For a whole document, you might need several paragraphs. Even in those cases, put your point sentence at the end of that introductory segment, no matter how long it is. Make your point the last thing readers read before they begin reading the longer, more complex segments that follow.

Some inexperienced writers think that if they tip off their main point in their introduction, readers will be bored and not read on. Not true. If you motivate readers with an interesting problem, they will want to see how you address it.

Here's the point: To write a document that readers will think is coherent, open every section, subsection, and the whole with a short, easily grasped introductory segment. At the end of that opening segment, put a sentence that states both the point of the unit and the key themes that follow. Such *point sentences* constitute the outline of your document, its logical structure. If readers miss them, they may judge your writing to be incoherent.

Two More Requirements for Coherence

We can make sense of almost anything we read if we know its points. But to make full coherent sense of a passage, we must see two more things.

1. **Readers must see how everything in a section or whole is relevant to its point.** Consider this passage:

   We analyzed essays written by sixth-grade students to determine the effectiveness of training in distinguishing fact from opinion. In an essay written before training, the students failed almost completely to distinguish fact and opinion. These essays were also badly organized in several ways. In the first two essays after training began, the students attempted to distinguish fact from opinion, but did so inconsistently. They also produced fewer spelling and punctuation errors. In the essays four through seven, they distinguished fact from opinion more consistently, but in their final essay, written six months after completion of instruction, they did no better than they did in their first essay. Their last essay was significantly longer than their first one, however. Their training thus had some effect on their writing during the training period, but it was inconsistent and transient.

   What are those sentences about spelling, organization, and length doing there? When readers can't see the relevance of sentences to a point, they are likely to judge what they read as being incoherent.

   I am sorry to say that I can't give you a simple rule of relevance, because it's so abstract a quality. I can only list its most important kinds. Sentences are relevant to a point when they offer these:

   - background or context
   - points of sections and the whole
   - reasons supporting a point
   - evidence, facts, or data supporting a reason
   - an explanation of reasoning or methods
   - consideration of other points of view

2. **Readers must see how the parts of your document are ordered.** Readers want to see not just how everything they read is relevant to a point but what principle is behind the order of your document's parts. We look for three kinds of order: chronological, coordinate, and logical.

- **Chronological** This is the simplest order, from earlier to later (or vice versa), as a narrative or as cause and effect. Signal time with *first, then, finally*; signal cause and effect with *as a result, because of that*, and so on. The passage about the essay research was chronologically organized.
- **Coordinate** Two or more sections are coordinate when they are like pillars equally supporting a common roof. *There are three reasons why . . .* Order those sections so that their sequence makes sense to your reader—by importance, complexity, and so on—then signal that order with words and phrases such as *first, second, also, another, more important, in addition*, and so on. That's how this section on order is organized.
- **Logical** This is the most complex order: by example and generalization (or vice versa), premise and conclusion (or vice versa), or by assertion and contradiction. Signal logic with *for example, on the other hand, it follows that . . . .*

On Paragraphs

It would be easy to say that all paragraphs should follow these principles:

- Begin with one or two short, easily grasped sentences that frame what follows.
- State the point of the paragraph (in traditional terms its *topic sentence*) in the last sentence of its introduction. If the introduction is just one sentence, it will be its point, by default.
- Toward the end of that point sentence, name the key themes that thread through what follows.

The problem is, not all paragraphs follow that tidy structure, and we get through most of the ones that don't just fine. We can ignore short paragraphs that serve special functions, such as providing a transition or an aside, because we have no problem reading (or writing) them. But many substantial paragraphs of six or seven sentences or more seem to have no evident principle of design. Even so, we can see in most of them some kind of opening segment that frames the rest of the paragraph. It might not include its *point*—that may come later, usually at its end. But the first sentence or two will set up what follows, introducing its key terms. And that is usually enough to help us make sense of what is to come.

For example, compare these two paragraphs:

2a. The team obtained exact sequences of fossils—new lines of antelopes, giraffes, and elephants developing out of old and appearing in younger strata, then dying out as they were replaced by others in still later strata. The most specific sequences they reconstructed were several lines of pigs that had been common at the site and had developed rapidly. The team produced family trees that dated types of pigs so accurately that when they found pigs next to fossils of questionable age, they could use the pigs to date the fossils. By mapping every fossil precisely, the team was able to recreate exactly how and when the animals in a whole ecosystem evolved.

2b. By precisely mapping every fossil they found, the team was able to recreate exactly how and when the animals in a whole ecosystem evolved. They charted new lines of antelopes, giraffes, and elephants developing out of old and appearing in younger strata, then dying out as they were replaced by others in still later strata. The most exact sequences they reconstructed were several lines of pigs that had been common at the site and had developed rapidly. The team produced family trees that dated types of pigs so accurately that when they found pigs next to fossils of questionable age, they could use the pigs to date the fossils.

Paragraph (2a) makes its point in the last sentence; paragraph (2b) in its first sentence. But in the context of an otherwise coherent text about fossil hunters and their work, we wouldn't have a big problem understanding (2a).

And that only emphasizes why it is so important to introduce the sections and subsections of your document clearly, accurately, and helpfully. If your readers begin a section knowing its point, they can make their way through a few paragraphs that are less than perfect. But if they don't know what your paragraphs add up to, then no matter how well written they are individually, your readers may well feel lost.

A Basic Principle of Clarity

This basic principle applies to individual sentences, to substantive paragraphs, to sections and subsections, and to wholes:

> Readers are more likely to judge as clear any unit of writing that opens with a short segment that they can easily grasp and that frames the longer and more complex segment that follows.

- In a simple sentence, that short, easily grasped segment is a subject/topic. Compare these two:

  3a. <u>Resistance in Nevada against its use as a waste disposal site</u> has been heated.

  3b. <u>Nevada</u> has heatedly resisted its use as a waste disposal site.

- In a complex sentence, that short, easily grasped segment is a main clause that expresses the point of its sentence. Compare these two:

  4a. Greater knowledge of pre-Columbian civilizations and the effect of European colonization destroying their societies by inflicting on them devastating diseases has led to a historical reassessment of Columbus' role in world history.

  4b. <u>Historians are reassessing Columbus' role in world history,</u> because they know more about pre-Columbian civilizations and how European colonization destroyed their societies by inflicting on them devastating diseases.

The point of sentence (4a) is buried at its end. In (4b), the opening clause states the *main point* of the sentence, its most important claim: *Historians are reassessing Columbus' role.* . . . That claim is then supported by the longer and more complex clause that follows.

- In a paragraph, that short, easily grasped unit is an introductory sentence or two that both expresses the point of the paragraph and introduces its key concepts. Compare these two paragraphs:

5a. Thirty sixth-grade students wrote essays that were analyzed to determine the effectiveness of eight weeks of training to distinguish fact from opinion. That ability is an important aspect of making sound arguments of any kind. In an essay written before instruction began, the writers failed almost completely to distinguish fact from opinion. In an essay written after four weeks of instruction, the students visibly attempted to distinguish fact from opinion, but did so inconsistently. In three more essays, they distinguished fact from opinion more consistently, but never achieved the predicted level. In a final essay written six months after instruction ended, they did no better than they did in their pre-instruction essay. Their training had some effect on their writing during the instruction period, but it was inconsistent, and six months after instruction it had no measurable effect.

5b. <u>In this study, thirty sixth-grade students were taught to distinguish fact from opinion. They did so **successfully** during the instruction period, but the effect was **inconsistent** and **less than predicted**, and six months after instruction ended, the instruction had **no measurable effect**</u>. _{opening segment/point} In an essay written before instruction began, the writers failed almost completely to distinguish fact from opinion. In an essay written after four weeks of instruction, the students visibly attempted to distinguish fact from opinion, but did so inconsistently. In three more essays, they distinguished fact from opinion more consistently, but never achieved the predicted level. In a final essay written six months after instruction ended, they did no better than they did in their pre-instruction essay. We thus conclude that short-term training to distinguish fact from opinion has no consistent or long term effect.

Paragraph (5a) has no clearly distinguished opening unit, and it does not announce the key themes of the paragraph. Paragraph (5b) has a clearly marked opening unit that states the point, and it clearly announces the key themes of the paragraph.

- In a section or subsection, that short, easily grasped unit may be just a paragraph; in longer units, it will be proportionally longer. Even so, at its end it expresses the point of its unit and introduces the key concepts that follow. There is not enough space here to illustrate how that principle applies to a passage several paragraphs long, but it is easy to imagine.
- In a whole document, that introductory unit might be one or more paragraphs long, perhaps even a few pages. Even so, it is usually substantially shorter than the rest, and in a sentence at its end, it states the point of the whole document and introduces its key concepts.

Diagnosis and Revision: Global Coherence

To diagnose how well you have helped your readers create a coherent understanding of your document, start by diagnosing and revising your introduction. Then do this:

1. **In the body of the document, circle the key themes and other words that refer to the same concepts.** If you cannot find where your document has repeated its connecting ideas, neither will your readers.
2. **Draw a line after the introductory segment of each section and subsection.** If you cannot quickly locate where you set up a section, neither will your readers.

3. **Underline the sentence(s) that state(s) the main point of the section and box its most important words that you did not circle in step 1.** That point is what the rest of the section will support and the boxed words are the key concepts that the section will develop as its distinct themes.
4. **In the body of the section, put a box around that section's themes and other words that refer to the same concepts.** If you cannot find where your section has repeated its connecting ideas, neither will your readers.

Remember, if you get your beginnings right, you will take your readers most of the way home.

The Costs and Benefits of Cookie-Cutter Writing

Some writers fear that patterns like these will inhibit their creativity and bore their readers. That's a reasonable concern, if you are writing a literary essay that explores your own thoughts as you have them, for readers who have the time and patience to follow the twists and turns of your thinking. If you are writing that kind of essay for that kind of reader, go to it. Don't tie yourself to what I've said here.

On most occasions, however, most of us read less for aesthetic pleasures than to understand what we need to know. You help readers toward this end when you follow the principles of clarity and coherence we've looked at in this book.

Such writing may seem cut and dried—to *you*, because *you* will be so conscious of the forms you followed. But it earns the gratitude of readers who have too little time to read, understand, and remember everything they must and who will, in any event, focus more on understanding the substance of your writing than on critiquing its form.

Language Varieties

material from Jeanne Fahnestock's *Rhetorical Style: The Uses of Language in Persuasion*

27

> *I used to sit in class and listen to the terms come floating down the room like paper airplanes. Geology was called a descriptive science, and with its pitted outwash plains and drowned rivers, its hanging tributaries and starved coastlines, it was nothing if not descriptive.*
>
> —JOHN MCPHEE, Basin and Range

Classical rhetoricians listed criteria for effective language choices based ultimately on audience reception. With alterations in emphasis, the same criteria reappear in manual after manual over the centuries: rhetorically effective language displays **correctness, clarity, forcefulness,** and **appropriateness**. The first quality has to do with language that is well formed grammatically; in inflected languages. words need correct case markers. The second standard, clarity, means that the speaker's or writer's choices are understandable; they convey a comprehensible meaning to the intended audience. The final quality, forcefulness, has to do with finding the memorable or striking expression that will reinforce the rhetor's message. Later sections will consider the standard of forcefulness or effectiveness in more detail. In this chapter, the criterion highlighted is **appropriateness**.

Rhetorical appropriateness is a notion ultimately tied to a culture's norms of propriety, of proper behavior according to circumstances (McKenna 2006). For the limited purposes of this chapter, appropriate language is defined as language that fits the audience, the rhetor, the subject, and the situation. In rhetorical manuals, appropriateness was discussed in terms of three levels of style: the **simple** or **low**, the **middle**, and the **grand** or **high** ([Cicero] 1981, 253–63: Cicero, 1998, 319–21). The simple style was conversational and colloquial, suitable for friendly exchanges and comic accounts: the grand was highly formal and ornate, appropriate for the highest, most serious and intense topics. In between these two was the middle style, which conveyed an unmarked, neutral stance, fitted for straight narration and exposition.

The notion of levels of style is still useful, but it intersects with other ways of assessing appropriateness, and the notion of "appropriateness" itself has been expanded and particularized by contemporary writers on the social dimensions of language use. Sociolinguists examine how people adjust their language according to the status, age, or intimacy differences among interlocutors and to their mutual activity or subject matter, as well as to whether the

mec
peo
use
sis (
lang
bee
can
to tl
wri
stat

Low, Mi

As
app
lish
the
are
ma
and
eve
tha
sha
or
sag
vu
to
W
"w
his
ho
tha

gu
Sta
cia
bu
se
ev

fe
ra
le
as
bu

is one among a set of official languages, including South Africa, India, Pakistan, and Nigeria. Within any area where English is spoken there will be further variants, or *regiolects*, spoken in defined geographical regions. Within the United States itself, local variants (e.g., western, southern, New England) have distinctive lexical items that are amply documented in the *Dictionary of American Regional English*. A New England *johnnycake* (fried or baked cornmeal) is a Southern *hoecake*; a Midwesterner's *pop* is a New Yorker's *soda*. Using regionalisms can be a sign of accommodation or identification with the audience, or a sign marking the speaker's distance. But more than the odd localism, dialect differences are largely matters of what is popularly called *accent*, the way words are pronounced. Presidents Bill Clinton and George W. Bush spoke with the distinctive regional accents of Arkansas and Texas respectively; they could exaggerate or mute these distinctive features to some extent for effect. Both tended to sound more regional when speaking less formally, off-the-cuff.

Groups of people inhabiting the same geographical region may still use different varieties of English if they come from different social, racial, or ethnic groups. These varieties, sometimes referred as *sociolects*, have been documented by sociolinguists, and anyone working with a text using such a variant needs to study it carefully. Perhaps the most extensively examined language variety in the United States, African American Vernacular English (AAVE), has special phonetic and grammatical features (see Dillard 1973; McWhorter 2001). Its earlier forms may overlap with southern and rural speech patterns, but AAVE also varies by region and has changed over time. Other sociolects (or sometimes *ethnolects*) arise among groups living in concentrated communities, as, for example, the English spoken in South Philly versus the English spoken in the Mainline suburbs west of Philadelphia. A general principle accounts for all regiolects and sociolects: people who live together and who are isolated from surrounding groups tend to develop and perpetuate their own form of language. Intensity of interaction can even isolate generations living in the same geographical and social spaces, creating generational dialects. However, pressure from the mass media, a mass form of "living together," works against all these language varieties.

Idiolects

The ways of describing language varieties so far—levels of usage from the colloquial to the formal to dialects—concern language features shared by communities of various sizes and types. But finally, within all of the languages and varieties, spoken or written, each person retains a set of language habits that are unique to that person. This personal pattern of usage is called an *idiolect*. Arguably, if a sizable batch of an individual's speech and writing were submitted to statistical analysis for diagnostic features, and if norms of usage were established for those features, idiosyncratic patterns would emerge. Everyone has favorite words, ways of phrasing things, and tendencies to structure sentences in certain ways; these patterns amount to a profile of frequencies for these features. These individual patterns are presumably so reliable that statisticians have used them to argue for authorship in disputed cases, the most famous being Frederick Mosteller and David Wallace's identification of James Madison as the author of unattributed numbers of the Federalist Papers (Salsburg 2002, 130–31). That there is an irreducible individuality in language use is an enabling premise in literary stylistics; great writers, literary analysts would argue, are worth examining for their unique or even extraordinary linguistic signatures, or, in other words, for their idiolects.

Registers: Occupation, Avocation, Discipline

In addition to levels of usage and geographical/dialectical differences, another dimension of appropriate language use has to do with what linguists and discourse analysts call **register**, a subset of language tied to a particular activity or situation. Registers do not rise to the level of distinctness of dialects; they require special terms and phrases and occasionally distinctive speech patterns, but not alternate grammars. Most adults command several registers or "languages" appropriate for different circumstances. They slip into one special language on the job, another when they discuss sports with friends, another when they are worshipping. Some occupations and professions require highly specialized language practices from their members, to the point that analysts often describe the "language of air traffic controllers" or the "language of naval fighter pilots."[1] Registers also vary in their range of applicability, in the breadth or narrowness of the audiences and situations they are appropriate for, and in their typical mode of transmission. Some are primarily spoken, sometimes requiring special pronunciation (e.g., auctioneers), and others primarily written, requiring unique sentence forms and formatting (e.g., the Emergency Medical Technician repertoire of phrases for filling out forms).

Disciplinary registers include the special lexicon and special ways of talking and writing in a field of learning. Taking a course in a discipline, like astronomy or accounting or rhetoric, requires learning the special vocabulary and verbal mannerisms of that discipline. In the epigraph to this chapter, John McPhee records the experience of being exposed to the specialist lexicon of geology, whose terms sail over his head in the lecture hall (1980, 24). Dictionaries mark words that are appropriate to disciplinary contexts with **subject labels**. In the *American Heritage Dictionary*, for example, *pioneer* has a fourth meaning labeled *Ecology*, "an animal or plant species that establishes itself in a previously barren environment"; *resonance* has a second meaning labeled *Physics*, a third *Acoustics*, a fourth *Linguistics*, a fifth *Medical*, and a sixth *Chemistry*, and there is not much overlap among them. To learn the meaning and proper usage of disciplinary terms is one facet of learning a subject matter. (This text, for instance, is in part an elaborate dictionary of disciplinary terms for rhetorical stylistics.)

While disciplinary registers can be more or less adequately captured in textbooks and glossaries, occupational registers are more difficult to pin down. An occupational register is a fluid subset of the language, but it is nevertheless recognizable because of the repeating who, where, when, and why of its use. The language of law enforcement is a case in point. When the police describe a crime in an official manner, they use a special vocabulary, a "police register." They *conduct an investigation*, they refer to a *suspect* and a *perpetrator*. In the last few years they have adopted a new term, person of interest, as a way to designate an individual they wish to question. The police also have their own legally determined taxonomy of crimes: *aggravated assault, armed robbery, vehicular homicide, breaking and entering*. They use the passive voice frequently: *The suspect was apprehended/has been arrested*. Some law enforcement terms have entered wider usage, such as *dui = driving under the influence*. The terms that police officers use when filling out official reports are not, however, the same as their slang, the informal spoken discourse they use with each other.[2]

The medical professions are another occupational area with a highly specialized but constantly changing vocabulary. Here the terms of art come in part from the disciplines mastered by medical professionals: anatomy, neurology, cardiology, etc. Other terms come from the considerable technical apparatus and pharmacological resources that medical professionals rely on (producing, for example, acronyms like *MRI, NSAID, EEG*), and still others derive from the insurance constraints, legal conditions, and even physical settings that medical professionals work in. Fire and rescue personnel and emergency medical technicians (EMTs) also have registers with highly formulaic phrases. The language of medical and rescue personnel has been criticized as impersonal or even evasive, but these special languages can be thought of as linguistic insulation or as verbal robotic arms, necessary for people whose daily work requires them to handle danger, pain, and death.

Other occupations with highly developed registers include information technology, fashion design and merchandising, publishing, stock trading, and finance. The technical terms for specialized objects and activities in these fields can be the residue of many centuries, as in sheepherding or weaving, or they can be deliberately created new words referring to a constant stream of new developments, as in computing or biotechnology. Working in any of these professions can require a period of initiation that is in part an apprenticeship in how to use a special language. Yet even someone who goes to work at an entry-level job in a fast-food restaurant or a record store or a branch bank will also, within a week or two, learn a specialized set of terms and phrases for the common gear and activity of that particular working environment. All that is required to bring about a special register, an insiders' language, is a coherent and persisting environment and a mutual activity.

All occupational, avocational, and disciplinary registers share certain features or tendencies that create problems in accommodation when specialists communicate with outsiders. First, they have a high proportion of technical terms referring to things that most people have no occasion to refer to and making distinctions that most people have no need to make; the vocabularies are *elaborated* in certain areas of meaning.[3] Thus the average person *cooks* dinner, or at most *roasts, fries, boils,* and *bakes*, but chefs who make a living cooking also *braise, sauté, poach, parboil, caramelize, reduce, render, flame*, and so on. Importing these terms into nonspecialist discourse often requires translation.

Second, a specialist's register may use apparently common words in very restricted senses. Paradoxically, these familiar-looking words are among the most difficult for the uninitiated to understand. For example, the following testimonial from a satisfied customer appeared in *Cabela's Hunting, Fishing and Outdoor Gear Catalog* in the blurb for a special camera that can take flash pictures when an animal trips an infrared sensor. It appeared next to two pictures, one of a deer caught in a flash and another of two hunters with a dead buck:

Your trail camera was invaluable to me in patterning this giant East Texas whitetail. After getting photos of him in July at two different locations I set my stand on a ridge about half way in between. On the first morning with proper rattling conditions, I was able to bring him right under my tree. (*Cabela's* 2003, 345)

This text seems highly accessible, and yet two of its terms are not being used in ways a general reader would understand: *patterning* and *rattling* It is written by a hunter for hunters, and the special meanings of these two terms in this context are not recorded in dictionaries.[4] Such apparently common words with arcane meanings are among the most misleading and difficult in a special register.[5]

Genre and Register

Stable registers, with their co-occurring sets of language features, develop in recurring situations from people in the same types of roles communicating on the same subjects. But registers can also be studied from another perspective, that of types of discourse or texts, or, in other words, of **genres**. In fact, by definition genres are genres because they have consistent language features or registers, and they have these consistent features because they are "gelled" responses to recurring rhetorical situations (Miller 1984). Examples of genres with distinctive registers abound: rental contracts, horoscopes, advice columns, recipes, sports stories—each tends to use a consistent lexicon and predictable sentence patterns. A rhetorical analyst taking a large sample of discourse from any recurring situation will be able to identify consistent register features, though many will involve syntactic and structural elements beyond the word choice features noted so far. Consider as a genre with a distinct register the "species description" found in texts such as bird guides. Here is a sample from Roger Tory Peterson's *Eastern Birds* (4th ed.):

TREE SWALLOW *Iridoprocne bicolor* 5–6" (13–15 cm)

Steely blue-green-black above, *clear white below*. Immature with dusky brown back and incomplete breastband may be confused with Rough-winged swallow (dingy throat) or Bank Swallow (complete breastband). Tree swallow glides in circles, ending each glide with 3 or 4 quick flaps and a short climb.

Voice: Note, *cheet* or *chi-veet*. A liquid twitter. Song, *weet, trit, weet*, repeated with variations.

Range: Alaska, Canada to California, cen.-e, U.S. Winters from s. U.S. to Cen. America. [...] Habitat: Open country near water; marshes, meadows, streams, lakes, wires. Roosts in reeds. Nests in holes in dead trees, snags, birdhouses (1980, 204).

The genre of the "species identification:" with its missing articles and its emphasis on descriptive adjectives in predictable categories, is perhaps one influence on what has become a distinct genre on its own: the personal ad in newspapers.

Cheetah with Attitude

SWF, 38, 5'2", 135 lbs, N/S, never married, no kids, Irish-Italian brown-eyed beauty. Enjoys dancing, music, dinner.

Fun and Four-Wheeling

SBM, 20, N/S, 6'1", 190 lbs, muscular, wavy hair, dark brown eyes, loving, caring, outgoing, adventurous, likes four-wheeling, (*The Philadelphia Inquirer,* August 1, 2003, W34–W35)

Genres then, as rhetorical accommodations to recurring situations, determine registers, and hybrid or evolved genres carry traces of the registers of their sources.

Shifting and Mixing Language Varieties

What is the rhetorical payoff for attention to language varieties ? The use of a particular level, dialect, or register can indicate a rhetor's awareness of the language appropriate to a subject, situation, and audience. Usually a text stays at an appropriate level or in a particular register: legalese for a legal document, formal academic prose for a scholarly article. Part of the description of its rhetorical effectiveness will then be an assessment of the overall appropriateness of the language to the rhetor's ethos, audience, situation, and genre.

Often, however, and quite deliberately, speakers and writers shift into a different language variety. In a single word, phrase, or sentence they suddenly depart from the prevailing dialect, register, or level and switch to another. Such departures draw attention to themselves by violating the surrounding norm, often with persuasive consequences. Stephen Jay Gould, for example, wrote the following in an article published in *Natural History* on the German poet Goethe's biological theories.

> In particular, Goethe argued for a primacy of imaginative and integrative hypotheses over building toward generality by factual accumulation in the "neutral" mode. (This is a dangerous method, easily leading to dogmatism, unreality, improper respect for the empirical record, and all the speculative excesses less politely known as bullshit.) (1991, 18).

Most of the key words in this passage come from the formal academic level: *primacy, integrative, hypothesis, generality, factual, accumulation, suggestion, explanation.* But ending the parenthesis is a word labeled *obscene* in the *American Heritage Dictionary.* Yet here it appears in a reputable publication.[6] Gould, of course, makes it obvious that he knows he is radically shifting levels by marking his choice as "less politely known." By doing so, he draws attention to the denigrated status of speculation beyond the evidence in the sciences. It is as far down in the value scale as *bullshit* is in the language scale.

Rhetors may also create notable effects with a **register shift**. The following passage comes from a press briefing by then Chairman of the Joint Chiefs of Staff Colin Powell at the beginning of the Persian Gulf War, January 23, 1991. Like most of those speaking in an official role, Powell has multiple audiences: members of the media, his professional peers in the military, the U.S. public, and, in this case somewhat unusually, the enemy on the eve of battle. Powell was providing an overview of what the U.S. Army's tactics would be.

> Let me turn now to the Iraqi Army in the Kuwaiti theater of operations. As the secretary [Secretary of Defense, Dick Cheney] pointed out, this is a large combined-arms army. It has tanks, it has personnel carriers, it has air defense guns, it has very redundant resilient communications between the different operating echelons of the army.

It has stockages of food, ammunition and parts with the army in theater, and they have a very elaborate supply system coming down from the interior of the country to sustain that army. Our strategy to go after this army is very, very simple. First, we're going to cut it off, and then we're going to kill it. (1991, A11)

Powell begins notably in an official, professional military register. He speaks of a *theatre of operations*, he calls the Iraqi army in Kuwait a *combined-arms* force and lists their resources (*tanks, personnel carriers, air defense guns,* not using the more common adjective *anti-aircraft*). This army's redundant resilient communications connect its different operating echelons. It has *stockages*, not *stocks* or *supplies*, of food, as well as *ammunition* with the *army in theatre*. All these are terms typical of an official military report. The summation in this register in then followed by the succinct statement of strategy: "First we're going to cut it off and then we're going to kill it," rendered in non-specialist colloquial words from the OE core. The combination of technical assessment and straight forward intention is, as it was no doubt intended to be, a projection of competence and a brutal warning.

While a shift involves the insertion of a word or phrase that comes from another discourse niche, **register mixing** is more extensive. It involves writing part of a text in one language variety and part in another. Register mixes often indicate attempts to reach multiple audiences, and they are common in documents required by law to address several audiences. Money market fund managers, for example, must issue semiannual reports that address both uninitiated shareholders and others with more financial expertise. The following opening paragraphs from such a report illustrate the solution:

> The first six months of 2003 were a good period for both stocks and bonds. Interest rates continued to fall and stock prices rose broadly. In addition, new tax cut legislation was enacted and corporate earnings showed signs of improvement.
>
> American Balanced Fund posted a total return of 10.0% for the six-month period ended June 30. The fund outpaced the Lipper Balanced Fund Index, which had a total return of 8.9%. Stocks, as measured by Standard & Poor's 500 Composite Index, gained 11.8%. Bonds, as measured by the Lehman Brothers Aggregate Bond Index, rose 3.9%. The market indexes are unmanaged. (American Balanced Fund 2003, 1).

The first paragraph here gives the message in very general terms; the second presents the same information again in more detail and in specialist's terms for the more knowledgeable.

Language Varieties and Humor

A staple source of humor is the unexpected, the violation of a norm or a pattern. A person expects to sit down and confidently backs up; then someone pulls the chair away and—pratfall! Similarly, suddenly pulling away the expected language in a text, the prevailing level or register secured in a genre, produces a linguistic pratfall, a potential source of humor. Laughs may follow when a topic is discussed in an unexpected or inappropriate register, the serious for the trivial or vice versa. Switching to an unpredictable register is the source of chuckles in the following sketch from Woody Allen's *Without Feathers.*

A Brief, Yet Helpful, Guide to Civil Disobedience

In perpetrating a revolution, there are two requirements: someone or something to revolt against and someone to actually show up and do the revolting. Dress is usually casual and both parties may be flexible about time and place but if either faction fails to attend, the whole enterprise is likely to come off badly. In the Chinese Revolution of 1650 neither party showed up and the deposit on the hall was forfeited. (1972, 111).

The humor here (if it takes) comes from recognizing the abrupt switches between levels and registers. The opening phrasing seems to begin a straightforward discussion of a political concept, but by the end of the first sentence, the inappropriate word choice is noticeable. The second sentence uses the register of an etiquette book. The two registers of politics and etiquette then clash in the third sentence, and the rest of the piece continues to interweave these registers, treating revolutions as a matter of correct or incorrect behavior—a compounding that could be taken as a rather trenchant criticism of political posing. Somewhat different is the "register mayhem" of P.J.O' Rourke that produces humor in the following, which originally appeared in *Automobile Magazine*.

There is a select class of motor vehicles with the worst fuel economy in the world. We had seven of them. Our job was to take these splendid gobble wagons and drive like hell.

In a Rolls-Royce Silver Spirit III, a Dodge Viper, a Ferrari 512 TR, a Chevrolet Suburban, a Jaguar XJ12, a Mercedes S600, and a Ford F-150 Lightning pickup truck, we broiled the left lane, we spanked the map. From Ann Arbor across Ontario—that province masquerading as a Mulsanne straight—we wheeled with throttles open. We sped through the alarming cleanliness of Toronto and along the shore of the mare nostrum of hockey and up the St. Lawrence to the froggy delights of Montreal. We skedaddled over rural Quebec and dashed into the wilderness of Maine, where every river, lake, and mountain peak is named after an item of clothing from L.L. Bean. All the while we were staying in swell hostelries and posh country inns, eating meals so rich and toothsome that our waistlines were becoming air bag parodies, smoking fat Havana cigars that cost as much as a pair of shoes and smell the same when lit, and drinking Scotch older than George Stephanopoulos. (O'Rourke 1995, 187–88)

From the special names for car models to the Latin *mare nostrum* (= our sea, the Roman name for the Mediterranean) to the countrified *skedaddle* to the faux British upper-crusty *swell hostelries* and *posh country inns* to the insider's term *Mulsanne straight* from the Le Mans racing course, the style here careens around the registers the way the cars were driven. This eclectic style, exciting the mind with echoes of different registers, is the signature of frenetic modern humor.[7]

Spoken versus Written Style

In his overview of register in *Stylistics* (1983), G. W. Turner includes *mode of delivery* in speech or writing as a key variable influencing language choice. This issue of spoken versus written language has received considerable attention from psycholinguists, sociolinguists, discourse analysts, and composition specialism and an impressive body of scholarship is available marking these distinctions. The differences can only be selectively reviewed here. To concentrate on word choice issues, Wallace Chafe and Jane Danielewicz (1987) find less lexical variety in spontaneous speech (both in conversations and in unplanned lectures delivered to small classes) than in written texts. The ratio of different words to total words, which they call the type/token ratio, shows that since writers have time to choose their words, they use a greater variety. Chafe and Danielewicz believe that this difference does not come from differences in context, purpose, or subject matter but is an invariable difference based on the method of text production. They also find that informal hedges, phrases such as *kind of* and *sort of,* are more common in speech and completely absent in the academic discourse in their sample. Speakers also use the all-purpose pronouns *it, that,* and *this,* often in "global references" to large stretches of preceding text. They use frequent contractions and more coined words.

These features do not match the characterization of speech in the rhetorical tradition. There the concern is with *planned* speech, with deliberately prepared and often practiced oral performance, which may even originate from a written text. Prepared rhetorical orators are not searching for words, unless they are doing so deliberately. Hence, prepared speech belongs toward the written end of the speech/writing continuum. Furthermore, a rhetorical education, especially as it is described by Quintilian, aimed to produce fluent extemporaneous speakers who commanded *facilitas,* the ability to speak readily and appositely on any occasion. This *facilitas,* a sign of social astuteness, is far from the conversation studied by discourse analysts.

From the perspective of rhetorical stylistics, a more speech-like or a more written style are options that rhetors can choose in *either* medium. They can even vary between these styles on a single occasion, moving the counter, as it were, along different spots on the continuum, and it is this movement, this perceptible change of styles, that in itself creates effects. Martin Luther King Jr., for example, mixed oral and written features in some of his speeches. The "I Have a Dream" speech represents rehearsed preparation in an orally inflected written style, but a speech like "I've Been to the Mountaintop" shows movement between written planning and spoken spontaneity. Delivered to a group of ministers and supporters to promote the cause of striking sanitation workers, the speech opens with a prepared *fantasia* in the most formal rhetorical tradition: "And you know, if I were standing at the beginning of time, with the possibility of taking a general and panoramic view of the whole of human history up to now, and the Almighty said to me, 'Martin Luther King, which age would you like to live in?'" King then offers a series of visions, saying after each, "But I wouldn't stop there," until he comes to his own era of a global "human rights revolution." This passage then follows:

> I can remember—I can remember when Negroes were just going around as Ralph has said, so often, scratching where they didn't itch, and laughing when they were not tickled. But that day is all over. We mean business now, and we are determined to gain our rightful place in God's world.

> And that's all this whole thing is about. We aren't engaged in any negative protest and in any negative arguments with anybody. We are saying that we are determined to be men. We are determined to be people. We are saying that we are God's children. And that we don't have to live like we are forced to live. (1968)

In this section, King turns to a different style displaying the features that Chafe, Danielewicz, and others define as diagnostic of speech. He is redundant without serving emphasis in the repeated "I can remember—I can remember," a digressive move within the speech that marks off this segment from the preceding. He is mindful of someone immediately present and a previous speaker, Ralph Abernathy. He uses pro- verbial sayings like "scratching where you don't itch" and the formulaic "we mean busi- ness." Contractions abound, though not in every place they might occur (e.g., *were not tickled* instead of *weren't tickled* to match *didn't itch*). The clauses, or what Chafe calls "intonational units," are relatively short—certainly shorter than those in the immedi- ately preceding paragraph. King also uses the vague globally referring pronouns sum- ming up previous points: "And *that's* all *this whole thing* is about."

King's variation is typical of successful platform speakers who alternate between more written and prepared versus more spontaneous language features. The *writerly* sections show that the speaker has prepared for the occasion, a mark of respect for the audience and the situation. The more speech-like and hence spontaneous-sounding remarks show that the speaker is moved by the moment, mentally engaged, and respon- sive to those immediately present.

Crafting Counterarguments

28

Academic Writing Program, University of Maryland

When we craft effective counterarguments, there are two moves we generally make. The first move is the *concession*, and it's the moment where we demonstrate that we understand the claims being made about some topic. These claims may be in common knowledge (who did what?) or they may be made by specific people (who asserts what?). The concession signals to a reader that the claims being presented are going to be challenged, and, as such, what follows the concession in a counterargument is the *counter*. In the counter, we present a new claim which makes the argument that the initial claim in the concession does not present the whole story. What follows here are some tips for how to signal concessions and counters and some tips on how to present the claims in the concession to make the counter movement more effective.

The Concession

When we concede, we show that we know the argument being made. The stronger we show that we know the argument being made, the more effective the counter-argument will be. If someone is able to echo back to you a version of your argument that you agree with and then goes ahead and explains what they disagree with, this makes for a stronger counter-argument. It doesn't provide a space for someone to interrupt and say, "But that's not a fair representation at all!" Since we want a strong counter-argument, we need to first focus on making a strong concession.

There are many ways we can signal concession, and both professional and novice writers tend to use similar sorts of phrasing to make these signals. Here are a few frequent signals for concession in academic writing:

Although X	*Although the construction was invited by the community…*
While X	*While community invited the construction…*
Yes, X	*Yes, the situation required the community to immediately call for construction…*
X is right in saying that Y	*The company is right in saying that the construction was invited by the community….*
I grant that X	*I grant that the construction was invited by the community*

417

I concede that X	*I concede that the construction was invited by the community*
I admit that X	*I admit that the construction was invited by the community*
I understand that X	*I understand that the construction was invited by the community*
X's claim that Y is compelling	*The company's claim that it came because it was invited is compelling…*
True, X	*True, the community invited the construction*
Clearly X,	*Clearly, the community invited the construction*
Obviously, X	*Obviously, the community invited the construction*
Of course, X	*Of course, the community invited the construction*
Certainly, X	*Certainly, the community invited the construction*

In each of these cases, we are presented with some presupposed statement which is perceived to be agreeable. In this example, it's a straight forward statement—that the community invited a construction company to perform some task, but the signaling words mark to the reader that this position will be countered. Again, the more agreeable the statement being conceded, the stronger the counter. This is the rhetorical form of the counterargument.

The Counter

In the two-part move of the "concede + counter" formula, the counter performs the role presenting the argument. It works from at least one shared premise, found in the concession, and from this, it presents an argument that pushes against the beliefs held by some people who may believe that the statement in the concession is unproblematic. Like concessions, counters have markers, too. Following from above, here are some of the most popular ways academic writers signal that they are countering statements:

Yet,	*Yet, the community was never given an estimate on the cost or timeline of the construction*
Nevertheless,	*Nevertheless, the company never gave the community an estimate for the cost of the project or the time it would take to complete.*
Still,	*Still, the company took advantage of the situation by beginning the project before offering an estimate or a timeline.*
Regardless,	*Regardless, the community would have never agreed to the bill the company would eventually charge*
At the same time,	*At the same time, the community was unaware of the company's plans*
But	*But no one in the community had agreed to the conditions of the construction*
However	*However, the company did not make its plans or costs clear to the community*

In the counter, a new statement is brought into the argument. This statement will most likely be elaborated on to some degree, either as the topic of a paragraph or as the topic of a sentence or two following the counter. As a result, we produce the counter argument, which can be a sentence, a few sentences, a paragraph, or a series of paragraphs that begin with a concession and end with an elaboration of a counter. Here are some examples of different levels of counterarguments. The concessions here are in **bold** and the counters are <u>underlined</u>:

> Sentence: ***While*** *community invited the construction,* the company, <u>however,</u> did not make its plans or costs clear to the community.

> Sentences: ***True,*** *the community invited the construction.* <u>*Nevertheless,*</u> *the company never gave the community an estimate for the cost of the project or the time it would take to complete.*

> Paragraph: ***I concede that*** *the construction was invited by the community.* <u>*Regardless,*</u> *the community would have never agreed to the bill the company would eventually charge. The company should have known that the community would not be able to pay the exorbitant fees charged. If the community was given an invoice before the construction or warned about the time, labor, and cost of the construction, it would have certainly turned down the company's offer and looked elsewhere for service.*

Part of the challenge of creating counterargument is not only figuring out what sorts of strong and representative statements to put in the concession but also figuring out how to match the counter with the concession. Here, writers need to think about efficacy and the goals of persuasion. We can sometimes produce very effective arguments that come off as more polemical than persuasive. That is, we may lose sight of the fact that we are trying to persuade our audience, not ridicule them for believing in the statement we concede. When we come across as overly aggressive, the very people we are trying to win over may become hesitant to entertain our point of view. The goal of the counter, then, is not to viciously tear down or break apart what is proposed in the concession but to get our audiences to see that there are potential problems. And we don't want to insult our audience's intelligence while we forward our own arguments and points of view. Aggression doesn't often make for good persuasion.

Putting Sources in Dialogue

Now that we have a sense of how counterarguments are formed, we can start to think about how we can use the "concede + counter" formula to enter into dialogue with our sources. Since what we concede is a claim or statement, we can use claims or statements from sources we interact with in our academic writing. This requires us to integrate a source into the concession. The concession marker, the author marker, and the claim or statement that is being conceded can be arranged in various ways. Here are a few examples. In each, the Concession marker is <u>underlined,</u> the author marker is **in bold,** and the claim or statement being conceded is <u>double underlined</u>.

> <u>*Although*</u> ***Dreyfus's claim that*** <u>*computers can't approach the complexity of human thought may be true,*</u>

> _While it's true that,_ **to quote Bill Clinton,** _"there's no single, solitary example that [signing the bill to end Glass-Steagall] had anything to do with the financial crash,"_
>
> _Much of a child's learning depend, of course, on_ **what Piaget calls** _"factors of educational and cultural transmission"_...

From these examples, we can see different ways we can integrate our sources into our concessions. Each statement and each source who believes in each statement can now be countered. In the following examples, concessions are <u>underlined</u> and counters are in **bold**

> (A paper on Google's DeepMind machine learning project counters the claim that artificial intelligence cannot approach human cognition)
>
> <u>Although Dreyfus claims that computers can't approach the complexity of human thought may be true,</u> **Google DeepMind has nevertheless shown us that computers may be able to aid us in performing certain risky and complex tasks, often times with more accuracy.**
>
> (A paper on the relationship between the government's allowing of unregulated banking practices and the rise of financial crises counters politicians' claims that the lack of regulation and rise of financial crises are related)
>
> _While it's true that, to quote Bill Clinton, "there's no single, solitary example that [signing the bill to end Glass-Steagall] had anything to do with the financial crash,"_ **still there is evidence that there is a relationship between the singing of Glass-Steagall and the financial crash when we observe trends that arose as a result of Glass-Steagall.**
>
> (A paper on the effects of attention on cognitive development and learning in children counters the claim that learning should be studied in moments of educational and cultural transmission)
>
> _Much of a child's learning depend, of course, on_ **what Piaget calls** _"factors of educational and cultural transmission."_ **Nevertheless, to get a fuller understanding of children's ability to learn, it's necessary to look at other factors of cognitive development, such as the roles executive control and attention play the developing mind.**

We can easily imagine where these counterarguments would fit into a paragraph or how these counter arguments may give rise to full paragraphs arguing against certain positions held by certain authorial sources (philosophers, politicians, education theorists). Notice that when we introduce authorial sources, we treat these claims and statements in the same way as we did above: with charity. The stronger we can paraphrase, summarize, and accurately represent a held position, the stronger our counter will be.

In each counterargument presented above, the goal was not to call the authorial source or people who believe such sources wrong—or at least not completely wrong—but instead to demonstrate that, despite the positions held by some, our arguments still are able to stand. This allows us to respect our audiences' intelligence while still attempting to persuade them if they are, in fact, the kind of person who believes in the view being conceded and the proper audience to listen to and follow through an argument. What the counterargument does is allow us to bring together and engage with various viewpoints, while forwarding our own. We enter into dialogue with a position held by a source, and in doing so, we show that we are able to provide something to the academic discourse community we are engaging with.

Convention and Deviation

29

material from Chris Holcomb and M. Jimmie Killingsworth's *Performing Prose: The Study and Practice of Style*

Conventions are patterns mutually recognizable to performer and audience, crystallizations of audience expectations in certain rhetorical situations: beginning a musical production with an overture, ending a Catholic mass with a benediction, structuring a pop song by alternating between verse and chorus. In written media, it is conventional to begin a letter with the greeting "Dear Somebody," for example. Other conventions include the kind of guidelines given in any editorial style guide: whether to place a comma before *and* in a series, whether to use single or double quotation marks, whether to capitalize all words or only the first word in titles, and so on. These conventions amount to rules but vary from style to style (American to British, or MLA to ABA, for example). They also change over time, sometimes from year to year.

Even more variable are the conventions of rhetorical style, which many authors seem to ignore altogether. Such conventions include the use of the passive voice in scientific writing, the use of overview paragraphs at the beginning of news stories, and the use of "once upon a time" to signal the beginning of a fairy tale.

Stylistic conventions help writers manage their relationships with readers, placing them in a comfortable frame of mind by meeting previously established expectations. But in many genres of writing, such as the personal essay, readers expect not only to be comforted but also to be surprised occasionally by what the author says and the way it is said. Surprise involves violating, transgressing, or suspending other expectations. Figures of speech often violate the conventional meaning of a word's denotative, dictionary definition. Love is not a rose, after all, despite what poets and country singers say. To take another example, some authors of historical narratives create a sense of drama, a you-are-there intensity, by slipping into the present tense even though convention requires the use of past tense. Autobiographers usually narrate in the first person, but a few famous examples, such as *The Education of Henry Adams,* use third person "he, she, or they" instead of the conventional "I" to create an odd sense of pseudo-objectivity. The Mexican writer Carlos Fuentes narrates his novella *Aura* in the second person "you" to create a creepy feeling' of personal investment for the reader. The word linguists use for such stylistic adventures is "deviation." For some, deviation from a linguistic norm is the definition of style itself, at least in the literary or rhetorical sense.

This chapter invites you to think about style as the interplay of convention and deviation. How you follow convention and deviate from it in prose performances will largely determine the tone of your work—the attitude you display toward the audiences and subject matter of your work.

Convention

A good place to start is with the concept of rigidity (see Kostelnick and Hassett). Rigid conventions often masquerade as rules, especially among novice writers and their teachers: never start a sentence with *and*, never end a sentence with a preposition, never use the first person in formal writing. These conventions are often taken as matters of grammar, not style. But in fact they are regularly violated by the best writers and speakers of English. Why do they persist? The short answer is that they serve the needs of some community of writers and readers. Teachers may find it useful to reserve the use of *and* as a compounding conjunction to be used between independent clauses. By prohibiting students from using it as a sentence opener, they keep the word separate from another class of words—conjunctive adverbs like *however, moreover,* and *thus*. By prohibiting students from ending on a preposition, they teach the formal use of relative pronouns, especially the troublesome *who* and *whom*; instead of "He is the man I spoke of," you have to say, "He is the man of whom I spoke." By prohibiting first person, the teacher forces students into the variations of formal academic writing, notably the use of impersonal pronouns such as *one* and the passive voice. If the goal is to move students from a set of colloquial conventions of speech to a set of formal conventions of writing, these "rules" can work nicely.

Often teachers are unaware of these goals, and they themselves come to think of the conventions as unbreakable rules. They are simply passing on what they were taught. Conventions generally work this way. They are reinforced by habitual usage and often serve to mark social boundaries. Students who know and use the conventions of "Standard Edited English" get marked as "educated" or "advanced" by their teachers. Students who have not formed these habits get marked as "at risk" or somehow deficient. Linguists have worked for decades to get teachers to see deviation from these norms as indications of difference instead of deficiency. Students may be bringing dialectical or second-language patterns into English class that have a perfectly good logic of their own, but a logic different from that of Standard Edited English. Moreover, some scholars argue that the stylistic and rhetorical differences these students bring to academic writing may in fact invigorate their prose and lead to productive innovation (see Balester, for example).

Outside of English class, conventions also arise from habitual use and serve to create and maintain social boundaries and distinctions. The use of "sir" and "ma'am" as a form of address in the south is an-interesting case, made even more interesting in places like Texas because of the large number of Spanish speakers. Southerners of the old school were taught to address their elders as "sir" and "ma'am" (a contraction of "madam"). This formality has disappeared in many places, but gets reinforced in Texas, perhaps because of the Spanish influence. "Sir" (or "señor") gets used primarily as a deferential form. We say "sir" not only to elders but to strangers and to bosses and customers as a sign of respect. If a middle-aged man buys a shirt at the local department store and a young clerk waits on him, it is conventional for the clerk to say, "Thank you, sir" at the end of the transaction. This usage says, in effect, "I am in your service and I am showing you respect as my elder." If the older man responds, "Thank YOU, sir," he confuses the relationships of age and service. Such a deviant response may communicate dissatisfaction with what he considers to be antidemocratic conventions involving age and service. Maybe he wants everybody to be equal, so he insists that if the clerk calls him sir, he's going to return the same honor. The young interlocutor may understand this message, or he may think the old fellow just made a mistake. Maybe he's a foreigner, the clerk might think, from Japan or New Jersey.

The problem of sexist and racist language is an obvious case of convention clashing with changing social norms. Until recently, the use of the masculine pronoun was considered conventional when the gender of the antecedent was unclear, as in the sentence "Every student should bring his book." As the problem of inequality between men and women became a political issue in the ongoing process of democracy, people began to question the convention and said, "Every student should bring his or her book." Now the so-called indefinite masculine is banned in most editorial styles, such as MLA. What name to give social groups also comes under scrutiny. Do you say Negro, black, or African American? Mexican, Mexican American, Hispanic, or Latino/a? Homosexual, gay, or queer? Most of these terms are embattled as the process of democratic inclusion continues in the public performance of language.

In these cases, conventions that had been invisible, seemingly part of the fabric of language, are revealed as conventions that can be opened to variation. Like the social activist, the inventive stylist creates subtle shifts in the audience's habitual sense of conventional language to put forward a special agenda. The stylistic innovator wants to open the audience's awareness to new linguistic possibilities that in turn suggest new ways of seeing the world or new perspectives of thought.

Conventions of Readability

Textbooks on style have their own conventions of advising students on how to improve their prose. The standard is usually called "readability."

When critics and editors say a writer's prose is "readable" (or "clear" or "lucid" or "user-friendly"), they can mean many different things. Back in the 1960s and 1970s, analysts tried to develop readability formulas such as the Flesch Readability Index, which is still used to determine grade-level readability in school textbooks and in some journalism. The formulas tend to be based on such easily countable (and programmable) features as sentence length and word length. These random measures rarely satisfy experts in stylistic analysis.

If you look through the best books on stylistic clarity, such as those by Richard Lanham and Joseph Williams, a few general and more variable characteristics of readable prose emerge:

- It is active.
- It flows.

- It organizes for emphasis.
- It uses familiar language.
- It is concise.

Let's consider these features one at a time on the way to both acknowledging their usefulness and questioning their status as rigid rather than flexible conventions of prose performance.

It is Active

Active prose involves three things: it is in the active voice, it puts human beings in the subject position whenever possible, and it uses a high percentage of action verbs.

Active Voice. English sentences have two voices: active and passive. Active voice says, "I will take out the trash." Passive says, "The trash will be taken out." Active voice: "You should now enter the data." Passive: "The data should now be entered."

In active voice, the subject position is filled with the person or thing actually performing the action, the active agent: "Bob recorded the information." In passive voice, the subject position is taken by what would be an object in active voice: "The information was recorded by Bob." The active agent may even drop entirely out of the sentence: "The information was recorded."

Though passive voice is perfectly grammatical and at times very useful, research has shown that it sometimes requires readers to perform an extra step in comprehending the information. In one study, researchers watched while small business owners tried to make sense of federal tax instructions. They were told to talk aloud while they worked through the instructions. Time and again, when they came upon a sentence like "The information should now be recorded," they would say something like "OK, now I'm supposed to record the information," or "Am I supposed to do the recording myself?" The researchers concluded that a step would be saved if the instructions used the active voice ("Now you should record the information") or simply the imperative ("Now record the information") (Flower, Hayes, and Swarts, 51–68).

The passive voice is preferred in some styles, notably in scientific prose. The presence of too many active agents can be distracting in this kind of writing. If, in a lab report, you were to write, "The assistant recorded the data," the emphasis would be all wrong. It doesn't matter who records the data. The data and the act of recording are the important things. So the passive is preferred: "The data were recorded." Scientific prose is "objective" in the sense that objects are emphasized over human subjects.

Human subjects. The downside of this "objective style" is that passive voice obscures who is doing what. Even in scientific writing, the habit of writing passive sentences can create confusion. In our example below, notice how hard it is to distinguish between findings reported in the literature and the authors' own findings, even with the parenthetical references to the names of researchers:

> The existence of a singularity phenomenon (SP) has been verified many times (Smith, 1984; Jones, 1988). But the exact nature of the event remains unclear. The possibility that it actually camprises two or three distinct phenomena was raised by research using

electron-optical methods (Jones,1989; Rama,1990). With the introduction of laser-based methodology (Rama et al., 1992), the hypothesis can be reconsidered.

Our revision uses more active voice and connects agents to the actions they perform, clarifying who is responsible for each action:

> The research of Smith (1984) and Jones (1988) verified the existence of a singularity phenomenon (SP) but did not go very far in specifying its exact nature. Later researchers used electron-optical methods to show that the events observed in the first experiments may actually comprise two or three distinct phenomena (Jones, 3989; Rama, 1992). Using the laser-based methodology introduced by Rama et al. (1992), we were able to establish that the SP is in fact a single, though complex, phenomenon.

Sorting out who does what in this manner can even prevent confusion and keep the reader moving through the material.

Action verbs. Think about your experience in reading stories. Narrative moves you forward, but description may slow you down. Description favors the use of "to be" verbs (*am, are, is, was, were,* and so forth). Writers who use "to be" too. often create a descriptive prose that favors nouns over verbs. "The committee's first task," you might write, "involved the determination of the proper orientation of the buildings." Notice how nouns like "determination" and "orientation" are formed from simpler action verbs, "determine" and "orient." Such words are called "nominalizations." Some writing guides call them "shun words" because of the "-tion" ending and because they should be shunned whenever possible. To revise a sentence like this one, turn the nominalizations back into verbs and find a grammatical subject for each: "The committee first determined how the buildings should be oriented," or "The committee first determined how they should orient the buildings."

It Flows

To create prose that flows, you need to write sentences that fit together in a cohesive structure. Cohesion results from overlapping old and new information in each sentence, paragraph, and section of a document (see J. Williams, chapter 3; also Kolln, chapter 1).

Remember that a sentence is composed of a subject and a predicate. The subject presents a topic, and the predicate (the part with the verb) makes a comment about the topic. In cohesive prose the topic relates to information that has already been presented, whereas the comment carries the writing forward to new information. Three possible patterns will develop:

- An overlapping, woven pattern with each subject taking up the information presented in the previous predicate.
- A pattern in which a single topic is repeated as the subject in consecutive sentences.
- A pattern that blends the first two.

If we represent each bit of information as a letter in the alphabet (A, B, C, D. . .), then the patterns will look something like this:

- A—B. B—C. C—D.
- A—B. A—C. A—D.
- A—B. B—C. B—D.

Consider a set of simple sentence that fail to follow any of these patterns. Because each subject introduces new information, the paragraph does not flow:

> The sales team (A) left the St. Louis meeting with many new ideas for promoting the project (B), Wilcox (C) liked the-direct mail approach (D). Customers (E) can be located by mailing lists purchased from professional organizations (F). Then we (G) can send them a brochure on the product (H).

Here's a revision that improves cohesion by creating a flow of overlapping information:

> The sales team (A) left the St. Louis meeting with many new ideas for promoting our product (B). Oar favorite (B) was the direct mail approach (C), Direct mailing (C) is best for companies like ours that have a good idea of who will buy the product (D). Additional customers (D) can be located by mailing lists purchased from professional organizations (E). These lists (E) will boost the number of people who receive a product brochure (F).

There is a drawback to this woven pattern: because the subject (although carried over from the previous predicate) changes with each sentence, the result can seem a bit scattered. To give their prose a tighter focus, writers will often use the second pattern listed above and repeat a single subject across consecutive sentences (J. Williams 85). Here David Quammen largely adheres to this pattern while explaining how wild dogs were first domesticated by humans:

> Wild dogs (A) were welcomed as scavengers, it seems, to the fringes of those nomad camps (B). The dogs (A) cleaned up what would otherwise stink and draw flies (C). When a camp was moved they (A) tagged along as walking garbage Disposalls (D). [They (A) were] [t]-olerated at a distance (E). Eventually they (A) became familiar and permanent (F). (*Flight 65*)

Even more common is a blending of the two patterns, writers using the first to switch focus from one topic to another, and the second to keep it centered on a single one:

> Let's say you've (A) created a network television series for the 2006-2007 season (B). It's (B) beautifully calibrated to appeal to the only viewers of any value to advertisers: young people (C). It's (B) about a family of migrant lifeguards (D). They (D) travel beaches all over the world in revealing swimwear, saving lives and drinking popular beverages (B). They (D) have a soon to be famous catchphrase, which they use in the face of any adversity: "You can't stop progress" (F). (Hauck A15)

For a variation within any of these patterns, you can put the old information in an introductory phrase or clause instead of in the subject itself, as Munro does in a passage we considered earlier:

> A small screen (A) hung over his head (B). On the screen (A) a bright jagged line (C) was continually being written (D). (Munro 307)

The important thing is to begin with the old and lead toward the new.

The same is true for transitions between paragraphs, sections, chapters, and even whole documents. For example, a literature review at the beginnings of an essay shows how previous research flows into the information presented in the current article.

It Organizes for Emphasis

Readability improves when you put the most general and most important information in positions of emphasis, where hurried readers will look first, such as the beginning and end of organizational units. Positions of emphasis include the following:

- The title
- The abstract or summary at the beginning and list of conclusions at the end of a document (if available)
- Any list or item set of from the rest of the text
- Headings, figure and table lists, and captions (if available)
- The first and last page of every section or chapter (in a long work)
- The first and (less frequently) the last sentence in each paragraph

The positioning in paragraphs is particularly important because all prose has paragraphs even if the other items are missing. The first sentence of each paragraph should answer the question, "What is the point of this paragraph?" (Williams 97).

This *point sentence*, often called a topic sentence, gets the most attention from busy readers, many of whom read the first sentence of a paragraph before they decide to read the rest. They are like newspaper readers, who start with the headline, then read the first sentence, and finally, if their interest holds, the whole article. Journalists caught on to this reading trend years ago and began to use the well-known "pyramid structure" in organizing news articles.

One exception to the "rule of firsts" is in the sentence itself. The most important information (the news) tends to come last in the sentence (as discussed in our treatment of flow).

It Uses Familiar Language

George Orwell once said never to use a fancy term where an ordinary word will do. The idea is to create an open style, accessible to the greatest number of readers. Even readers with a large vocabulary appreciate the simplest possible language in a style that reserves unfamiliar language for special nuances of meaning. In other words, nobody—or perhaps only the smallest percentage of your readers (such as your high school English teacher)—wants to be impressed by your command of the language; rather, they want to know what you have to say. According to the conventions of readability, your style should seem effortless to read. It should not require the reader to stop and puzzle over the meaning of a word, or even to stop too long to admire your usage.

One of the most common kinds of language that hampers readability is technical jargon. Certainly it's fine to use the technical terminology of a specialized research field to show your identity with that field. Economists, education specialists, literary critics, and physicists all have their own technical jargon. As a kind of shorthand, jargon terms are useful. They save space and time. Biologists pack more than a hundred years of evolutionary theory into the term "natural selection." Computer engineers have co-opted the term "interface" from biology to describe the combined techniques and technologies that users employ to make a computer work. Literary critics who use a term like "mimesis" allude to Aristotle and the long tradition of poetical theory rooted in classical Greece. But jargon has a self-limiting effect on your audience. Knowledgeable members of your in-group will find jargon-filled prose fluent, but others wifl find it an obstruction to their reading comprehension. Even people who are highly educated in another field have difficulty because they do not often use the term or use it in a different way. The key is to be aware of the possible effects of jargon on your audience, then select, define, and explain words accordingly. Also consider keeping the density of specialized language low, even in specialized discourse.

Using unexplained technical jargon outside the field in which people understand it shows disrespect for your audience. The tone you project suggests pomposity and arrogance. Worse yet is the use of merely inflated language—obscure or rarely used words. Why say "rubbish receptacle" when you mean "trash can"? Examples of pompous words substituted for simple ones include *endeavor* rather than *try*, *utilize* rather than *use*, *termination* rather than *end*, and *subsequent to* rather than *after*.

It Is Concise

The term *wordiness* can mean many things. It does not refer simply to long passages or ones with a lot of words. Sometimes you need a lot of words. The point is to make your prose economical, getting the most out of every word and phrase, never using more words than what you need to get the message across with the right tone

Wordiness, then, refers to unnecessary words, or unnecessarily big and pompous words, or sentences that drag on pointlessly. Here are a few guidelines for reducing wordiness (based on Rawlins' treatment of economic style in *The Writer's Way;* see also Williams, *Style* 116–33).

- Cut out pretentious language. You can usually do without impressive-sounding, pseudo-academic phrases such as *fundamentally, it is important to note that . . . , the fact is that . . . , or it is a commonly held assumption that . . . .*
- Reduce redundancy. Planned repetition may be highly effective in oral presentations, but it is quickly overdone in writing. Also avoid redundant pairs of words (*basic and fundamental, question and problems, hopes and desires*), redundant modifiers (*true facts, final outcome*), and redundant categories (*period of time, red in color, slimy to the touch*).
- Look for the news in every phrase, sentence, and paragraph. In a sentence such as "The project is profitable and scientifically valid," the only important words may be "profitable" and "scientifically valid." Can you work those into another sentence?
- Reduce transitional words and phrases. As long your paragraphs are well structured (moving from old to new information in a woven pattern), you can often eliminate such expressions as *moreover, furthermore, thus,* and *therefore.*

Deviation (Using an Arbitrary Norm)

Under normal conditions, the conventions of readability will serve your needs as a working writer. Even so, you should not think of these guidelines as a sure-fire formula for effective performance. A study of the best writers will show that, while they follow these guidelines a high percentage of the time, they deviate in ways that make their work unique and rhetorically engaging. They follow clear principles. The writers themselves may not be able to articulate these principles, but an observant prose analyst or stylist can usually derive good reasons for deviations. The advantage of analyzing prose to discover principles for stylistic variation is that, when you come to write yourself, you don't have to treat every decision as a new one. You can begin to theorize a number of possible moves in any given sentence based on your experience as an analyst of other people's writing.

Assuming that rhetorical style involves deviation from a norm, our first problem as prose analysts is defining the norm. One approach is to designate an arbitrary norm. Let's say, for example, that the norm follows the guidelines for readability we have developed in this chapter: the language should be active, fluent, organized for emphasis, familiar, and concise. We might also add that normal diction is constituted by the first definition of a given word in a standard dictionary. We'll notice some problems with these guidelines immediately in that even so simple a norm becomes something of a moving target. As we move from region to region, what is considered denotative and familiar will shift, for example; the same is true for historical shifts. But in general, we can use this norm to begin to pick out and discuss possible deviations.

Consider the following sample from Edward. Abbey's 1971 essay "Canyonlands and Compromises":

> Like the network of new highways proposed for the canyon country, these power plants are meant not for current needs but for "anticipated" needs. "Planning for growth," it's called. The fact that planning for growth encourages growth, even forces growth, would not be seen as a serious objection by the majority of Utah-Arizona businessmen and government planners. They believe in growth. Why? Ask any cancer cell why it believes in growth. (393)

A few of the deviations that might make the hurried reader pause and mull over the language, or at least register it subliminally, include the following:

1. The phrase "network of new highways," a metaphor. Unlike a metaphor such as "web of new highways," which connotes something natural, "network" suggests an elaborate technological system.
2. The predicate "are meant not for current needs but for 'anticipated needs'" the syntax of which involves passive voice, inversion of positive and negative complements, and use of quotation marks. Passive voice allows the writer to put "roads" in the subject position for emphasis and provides cohesion with the previous sentence; the inversion puts "anticipated needs" at the end of the sentence so that it can be explained further in the next sentence. So both of these seeming deviations ultimately serve the goals of readability—*flow*, to be precise. The quotation marks around material not clearly taken from another source serve to distance the author from the quoted phrase, creating irony.

3. The sentence "'Planning for growth,' it's called," the syntax of which involves an inversion of the verb and complement, as well as quotation, contraction, and the substitution of the expletive "it" for a human agent in subject position. Putting the complement first makes the transition to the previous sentence; the quotation sets up the troublesome phrase to be interpreted later in the passage; the contraction creates an informality typical of the author's persona (the informal, natural man); the omission of the agent keeps the focus on the idea of "growth," which is being criticized. It also suggests (and this is an interpretive stretch) that anyone who uses the phrase is inhuman in one sense or another.

4. The phrase "cancer cell," a metaphor that identifies economic growth with the spread of cancer cells. The author urges the reader toward a new perspective by associating something usually considered positive (economic growth) with something considered bad to the point of being terrifying and life-threatening (cancer).

Thus we can use deviations from arbitrary norms—Abbey's use of irony, metaphor, and other variations—to bring stylistic characteristics to the foreground for analysis. in the following chapters, we will continue to develop a vocabulary for discussing such deviations. But even without the specialized vocabulary, you should be able to pick out deviations from the norm of readability conventions, such as Abbey's "cancer cell" metaphor and his backwards sentence, "'Planning for growth,' it's called."

Deviation (Using a Community Norm)

The problem with using arbitrary norms is that the method doesn't account for historical and cultural differences. 'Using the terms developed in chapter 1, we can say that with this kind of analysis, we remain within the textual arena and do not advance to the social and cultural arenas of performance. An approach more sensitive to shifts in the arena of performance involves analyzing deviations by beginning with a community norm, a style that is characteristic of a particular group of writers and readers. You can then point out deviations within the work of a subgroup or individual writer.

In the scientific community, for example, it is conventional to write impersonally, avoiding first-person references and obscuring human subjects by the use of indirect and passive sentences; nouns and strings of noun modifiers predominate over variety in the use of action verbs, adjectives, and adverbs; conciseness is greatly valued, aided by the use of technical terminology, which constitutes a kind of insider shorthand. But conciseness yields to the value of precision, so that repetition of key words and phrases is preferred if there is any chance of ambiguity; hedging and qualification are common manifestations of caution in interpreting data. Here's a typical sample from the field of environmental toxicology:

> Nonpoint source pollution can be defined as the diffuse input of pollutants that occurs in addition to inputs from undeveloped land of similar genesis. . . . Agricultural nonpoint sources of pollution significantly altered water quality in 68% of the drainage basins in the United States, and in nearly 90% of the drainage basins in the north central region of the United States. . . . Agricultural sources are probably the major contributors of suspended and dissolved solids, nitrogen, phosphorus and associated biochemical oxygen demand loadings in U.S. waters. (quoted in Killingsworth and Palmer 119)

Consider a slight deviation from this style, a sample from the famous 1953 paper in the journal *Nature* by James Watson and Francis Crick announcing the double-helix structure of DNA—a contribution for which they won the Nobel Prize:

> We wish to suggest a structure for the salt of deoxyribose nucleic acid (D.N.A.). This structure has novel features which are of considerable biological interest.
>
> A structure for nucleic acid has already been proposed by Pauling and Corey1. They kindly made their manuscript available to us in advance of publication. Their model consists of three intertwined chains, with the phosphates near the fibre axis, and the bases on the outside. In our opinion, this structure is unsatisfactory for two reasons:
>
> (1) We believe that the material which gives the X-ray diagrams is the salt, not the free acid. Without the acidic hydrogen atoms it is not clear what forces would hold the structure together, especially as the negatively charged phosphates near the axis will repel each other. (2) Some of the van der Waals distances appear to be too small.
>
> Another three-chain structure has also been suggested by Fraser (in the press). In his model the phosphates are on the outside and the bases on the inside, linked together by hydrogen bonds. This structure as described is rather ill-defined, and for this reason we shall not comment on it.
>
> We wish to put forward a radically different structure for the salt of deoxyribose nucleic acid. This structure has two helical chains each coiled round the same axis (see diagram). We have made the usual chemical assumptions, namely, that each chain consists of phosphate diester groups joining β-D-deoxyribofuranose residues with 3′, 5′ linkages. The two chains (but not their bases) are related by a dyad perpendicular to the fibre axis. Both chains follow right-handed helices, but owing to the dyad the sequences of the atoms in the two chains run in opposite directions. . . . (Watson and Crick np)

The authors preserve many key features of scientific style, notably the technical terminology and frequent use of the passive voice. But the use of first-person plural "we" works to emphasize the originality of the discovery and to distinguish this work from that of other scientists working on the same problem. The greater frequency of action verbs adds a sense of urgency and excitement to the presentation.

Watson and Crick are unusually gifted stylists who, not surprisingly, often irritated their fellow scientists and have been criticized for egotistically trumpeting their own originality. Both wrote memoirs in later years that capitalized on their fame and showed their ability to appeal to a wider audience. Watson's book *The Double Helix* has become a classic in the genre known as science writing or scientific journalism, nonfictional accounts of scientific research and theory written for a general audience of educated readers.

Below is a paragraph from *The Double Helix* describing one of the many steps in Watson's reasoning that ultimately led to the discovery of the structure of DNA, Watson speaks forthrightly throughout the book of the emotions involved in the search, the ego conflicts, and the competitive drive behind scientific research. In the chapter that includes our sample, he writes thus of the reaction to his views by one of his colleagues: "Rosy by then was hardly able to control her temper, and her voice rose as she told me that the stupidity of my remarks would be obvious if I would stop blubbering and look at her X-ray evidence" (105). Need we say that in formal scientific writing we rarely hear of human emotions or encounter such diction as "stupidity" and "blubbering."

Notice how Watson narrates with gusto, using the first-person singular, placing human beings in subject positions, and favoring active verbs, He calls people by their first names and includes details about his personal experience—the English weather, his means of transportation, his worry over his colleague's acceptance, and so on—that would all be edited out in even the most stylistically deviant scientific report:

> Afterwards, in the cold, almost unheated train compartment, I sketched on the blank edge of my newspaper what I remembered of the B pattern. Then as the train jerked toward Cambridge, I tried to decide between two and three-chain models. As far as I could tell, the reason the King's group did not like two chains was not foolproof. It depended upon the water content of the DNA samples, a value they admitted might be in great error. Thus by the time I had cycled back to college and climbed over the back gate, I had decided to build two-chain models. Francis would have to agree. Even though he was a physicist, he knew that important biological objects come in pairs. (Watson 108)

In this kind of writing, Watson has not just deviated from the conventions of scientific style; he has decamped entirely, switching genres of discourse. Instead of a scientific report, he is writing a personal memoir. Compared to writers in that genre, his style is not especially deviant. Now he's a storyteller, writing like a novelist or an autobiographer. The audience of novels and memoirs thrives on juicy gossip, strong emotions, and plenty of vivid detail about personal experience.

Genres are discourses that follow a pattern that gets repeated over and over again, a rhetorical situation that keeps coming up, a writer addressing an audience that wants something fairly predictable to occur. A detective novel has a crime that must be solved; a tragedy has a hero who must experience a tragic fall; a how-to book gives steps toward completing a task, These conventional forms, like all conventions, involve audience expectations in matters of style and delivery. People read scientific reports to further their own research; people read scientific memoirs to gain insight into the lives of scientists and a general knowledge of important idea. Each rhetorical situation fosters an appropriate style. For this reason, even so skilled a scientific writer and essayist as Stephen Jay Gould may seem naive when he argues the following:

> I deeply deplore the equation of popular writing with pap and distortion for two main reasons. First, such a designation imposes a crushing professional burden on scientists (particularly young scientists without tenure) who might like to try their hand at this expansive style. Second, it denigrates the intelligence of millions of Americans eager for intellectual stimulation without patronization. If we writers assume a crushing mean of mediocrity and incomprehension, then not only do we have contempt for our neighbors, but we also extinguish the light of excellence. The "perceptive and intelligent" layperson is no myth. They exist in millions—a low percentage of Americans perhaps, but a high absolute number with influence beyond their proportion in the population. (12)

In suggesting that popular science writing and professional scientific reports need not be separated so widely as they are in the minds of most scientists, Gould has neglected the social and cultural arenas of stylistic performance. Any discussion of deviation involves locating the text in question within a particular genre and arena of performance and then designating the audience expectations within those limits.

Authors use conventional styles to project identity with various social and cultural groups—or they break ranks by deviating from those styles or decamping to another style and genre.

Exercises

1. Rate the effectiveness of the following passage using the five criteria for readable prose: it is active, it flows, it organizes for emphasis, it uses familiar language, and it is concise. Be precise and point to specific words and structures:

> The committee's first task involved the determination of the proper orientation of the buildings. Landscape designs were drawn up by the committee next. There was a disagreement among several members over the placement of trees and shrubs around the perimeter of the parking lot. This nonconformity of opinion was resolved, however, in a short period of time. The topic of zoning laws was the next item of concern on the agenda to which the committee then turned its attention.

Now revise the passage, improving its readability.

2. The movie review is a well-established genre with fairly stable conventions, especially in terms of structure: there's typically a "lead" that captures readers' interests and hints toward the reviewer's overall assessment of the film, followed by a plot summary of the film (without giving the ending away!), and then a more detailed evaluation of the movie's merits. Of course there's room for structural deviation (changing up the order, for instance, or blending the plot summary with the evaluation), but most reviews have these three parts. More variable is the style in which the review is delivered, and those variations often depend on the venue in which the review is published: a review appearing in the *New Yorker*, for instance, will likely differ stylistically from one found in *Rolling Stone* or *Entertainment Weekly*.

Find two short reviews of the same movie (the *Movie Review Query Engine* at http://www.mrqe.com lists reviews from dozens of publications). First, analyze these reviews in terms of the three-part convention we outlined above. Do the reviews contain all three elements? How are they arranged? Do either or both of the writers go outside the box in terms of organization? If so, why? Then using the norm of the dictionary standard and readability guidelines from this chapter, point out how these two reviews differ stylistically. Consider the rhetorical purposes for these differences, and be sure to identify relevant textual features throughout.

3. Write your own movie review. Or if you're not a film buff, pick something else to review (a restaurant, a book, a new computer product). Whatever you pick, begin with the three-part structure we described in exercise 2 and the readability guidelines covered in this chapter as rough maps to the organization and style of your review. Then look for opportunities to deviate in terms of either structure or style. These deviations should be "motivated"—that is, they should serve some purpose. Follow your review with a short analysis in which you describe several key moments where you either adhered to conventions or departed from them.

4. Write a brief comment about convention and deviation in one or two of the quotations in your commonplace book. Be prepared to discuss your examples in class or in a small group. Here are a couple of examples:

> *Quotation:* The continent is covered by an ocean of engine noise. (Wendell Berry, quoted in Finch and Elder 724)
>
> *Comment:* Berry uses a figure of speech that deviates from the dictionary meaning of "ocean." By definition an ocean cannot cover a continent. By creating this "unnatural" situation and by using a natural image to describe a mechanical problem (engine noise)— comparing the size and the roar of the ocean to noise pollution—he hints ironically at how extensive and contrary to nature the noise is.

> *Quotation:* The smell of Funk Island is the smell of death. It is probably the source of the island's name, which in various languages means "to steam," "to create a great stench," "to smoke"; it may also mean "fear." The island certainly smells ghastly. No battlefield could ever concentrate such a coalition of dead and dying. (Franklin Russell, quoted in Finch and Elder 609)

> *Comment*: Russell uses etymology and dictionary definitions of "funk" to describe the island, then augments his description with a deviation, a kind of negative comparison: no battlefield was ever this bad.

Strengthening and Weakening Claims as a Rhetorical Strategy

Academic Writing Program, University of Maryland

Certain qualifying words help us alter the degree of force of a statement that we express. A qualifier is a word or phrase—usually an adverbial or a verb that takes a casual complement—that expresses certainty or reservation about the strength of a claim. When a qualifier expresses certainty and thus boosts our conviction in a claim's strength, we call it a "booster." When it protects a claim's certainty by broadening the conditions for it to be true we call it a "hedge." Each have their place in academic writing.

UNQUALIFIED: President Nixon resigned as a result of the Watergate cover-up.

HEDGED: President Nixon may have resigned possibly as a result of the Watergate cover-up.

BOOSTED: President Nixon resigned, of course, as a result of the Watergate cover-up.

Boosters	Hedges
Will	May/might
Of course	Perhaps
Obvious(ly)	Possibly
Surely	Could
The fact that	Suggests that
Indeed	Assume(s)
Shows	Seems to
Makes explicit	Tends to
States	Appears to
Demonstrates	Looks as if
Proves	Alludes to
Clearly/It is clear	Indicates
Claim	Suppose
Consistently	(Most) often
Exactly	Almost
Perpetually	Virtually
Very	Somewhat

Extremely	To a certain degree/extent
Invariably	In many cases
Indeed	In a way
Central	Centered around
Literally	Almost
Undoubtedly	Questionably
Know	Guess
Assert	Think
Certainly	Just
Always	Usually

Activity

- Have students come with a paragraph defining their research topic problem expressing why it's an important topic to inquire.
- Break up into groups of two.
- On a separate piece of paper have students find and write three boosted claims from their partner's work (e.g. *it has always been the case, it's undeniable that, most important*).
- On the back of the sheet change these sentences into hedged claims (*e.g. it may have been the case, it may be that, perhaps important*). Note: If students cannot find boosted claims have them find hedged claims.
- Next to each sentence have students mark whether they are strengthening or weakening the initial claim and indentify how such claims are being weakened or strengthened
- Questions for class conversation: Statements of exigence often have boosted claims. Sometimes these boosted claims can come off as hyperbolic and untrustworthy. In the writing you looked at what boosts came across as untrustworthy? Why? How do boosts affect how your audience responds to a claim? What's the relationship between making claims and stating exigence? Can we state exigence without boosting our claims? Why or why not?

Readings on Revision and Reflection

Shitty First Drafts

31

by Anne Lamott

Born in San Francisco in 1954, Anne Lamott is a graduate of Goucher College in Baltimore and is the author of six novels, including Rosie *(1983),* Crooked Little Heart *(1997),* All New People *(2000), and* Blue Shoes *(2002). She has also been the food reviewer for California magazine, a book reviewer for* Mademoiselle, *and a regular contributor to* Salon's *"Mothers Who Think." Her nonfiction books include* Operating Instructions: A Journal of My Son's First Year *(1993), in which she describes her adventures as a single parent, and* Tender Mercies: Some Thoughts on Faith *(1999), in which she charts her journey toward faith in God.*

In the following selection, taken from Lamott's popular book about writing, Bird by Bird *(1994), she argues for the need to let go and write those "shitty first drafts" that lead to clarity and sometimes brilliance in our second and third drafts.*

—Joseph Harris

Now, practically even better news than that of short assignments is the idea of shitty first drafts. All good writers write them. This is how they end up with good second drafts and terrific third drafts. People tend to look at successful writers who are getting their books published and maybe even doing well financially and think that they sit down at their desks every morning feeling like a million dollars, feeling great about who they are and how much talent they have and what a great story they have to tell; that they take in a few deep breaths, push back their sleeves, roll their necks a few times to get all the cricks out, and dive in, typing fully formed passages as fast as a court reporter. But this is just the fantasy of the uninitiated. I know some very great writers, writers you love who write beautifully and have made a great deal of money, and not one of them sits down routinely feeling wildly enthusiastic and confident. Not one of them writes elegant first drafts. All right, one of them does, but we do not like her very much. We do not think that she has a rich inner life or that God likes her or can even stand her. (Although when I mentioned this to my priest friend Tom, he said you can safely assume you've created God in your own image when it turns out that God hates all the same people you do.)

Very few writers really know what they are doing until they've done it. Nor do they go about their business feeling dewy and thrilled. They do not type a few stiff warm-up sentences and then find themselves bounding along like huskies across the snow. One writer I know tells me that he sits down every morning and says to himself nicely, "It's not like you don't have a choice, because you do—you can either type, or kill yourself." We all often feel like we are pulling teeth, even those writers whose prose ends up being the most natural and fluid. The right words and sentences just do not come pouring out like ticker tape most of the time. Now, Muriel Spark is said to have felt that she was taking dictation from God every morning—sitting there, one supposes, plugged into a Dictaphone, typing away, humming. But this is a very hostile and aggressive position. One might hope for bad things to rain down on a person like this.

For me and most of the other writers I know, writing is not rapturous. In fact, the only way I can get anything written at all is to write really, really shitty first drafts.

The first draft is the child's draft, where you let it all pour out and then let it romp all over the place, knowing that no one is going to see it and that you can shape it later. You just let this childlike part of you channel whatever voices and visions come through and onto the page. If one of the characters wants to say, "Well, so what, Mr. Poopy Pants?," you let her. No one is going to see it. If the kid wants to get into really sentimental, weepy, emotional territory, you let him. Just get it all down on paper because there may be something great in those six crazy pages that you would never have gotten to by more rational, grown-up means. There may be something in the very last line of the very last paragraph on page six that you just love, that is so beautiful or wild that you now know what you're supposed to be writing about, more or less, or in what direction you might go—but there was no way to get to this without first getting through the first five and a half pages.

I used to write food reviews for *California* magazine before it folded. (My writing food reviews had nothing to do with the magazine folding, although every single review did cause a couple of canceled subscriptions. Some readers took umbrage at my comparing mounds of vegetable puree with various ex-presidents' brains.) These reviews always took two days to write. First I'd go to a restaurant several times with a few opinionated, articulate friends in tow. I'd sit there writing down everything anyone said that was at all interesting or funny. Then on the following Monday I'd sit down at my desk with my notes and try to write the review. Even after I'd been doing this for years, panic would set in. I'd try to write a lead, but instead I'd write a couple of dreadful sentences, XX them out, try again, XX everything out, and then feel despair and worry settle on my chest like an x-ray apron. It's over, I'd think calmly. I'm not going to be able to get the magic to work this time. I'm ruined. I'm through. I'm toast. Maybe, I'd think, I can get my old job back as a clerk-typist. But probably not. I'd get up and study my teeth in the mirror for a while. Then I'd stop, remember to breathe, make a few phone calls, hit the kitchen and chow down. Eventually I'd go back and sit down at my desk, and sigh for the next ten minutes. Finally I would pick up my one-inch picture frame, stare into it as if for the answer, and every time the answer would come: all I had to do was to write a really shitty first draft of, say, the opening paragraph. And no one was going to see it.

So I'd start writing without reining myself in. It was almost just typing, just making my fingers move. And the writing would be terrible. I'd write a lead paragraph that was a whole page, even though the entire review could only be three pages long, and then I'd start writing up descriptions of the food, one dish at a time, bird by bird, and the critics would be sitting on my shoulders, commenting like cartoon characters. They'd be pretending to snore, or rolling their eyes at my overwrought descriptions, no matter how hard I tried to tone those descriptions down, no matter how conscious I was of what a friend said to me gently in my early days of restaurant reviewing. "Annie," she said, "it is just a piece of *chicken*. It is just a bit of *cake*."

But because by then I had been writing for so long, I would eventually let myself trust the process—sort of, more or less. I'd write a first draft that was maybe twice as long as it should be, with a self-indulgent and boring beginning, stupefying descriptions of the meal, lots of quotes from my black-humored friends that made them sound more like the Manson girls than food lovers, and no ending to speak of. The whole thing would be so long and incoherent and hideous that for the rest of the day I'd obsess about getting creamed by a car before I could write a decent second draft. I'd worry that people would read what I'd written and believe that the accident had really been a suicide, that I had panicked because my talent was waning and my mind was shot.

The next day, I'd sit down, go through it all with a colored pen, take out everything I possibly could, find a new lead somewhere on the second page, figure out a kicky place to end it, and then write a second draft. It always turned out fine, sometimes even funny and weird and helpful. I'd go over it one more time and mail it in.

Then, a month later, when it was time for another review, the whole process would start again, complete with the fears that people would find my first draft before I could rewrite it.

Almost all good writing begins with terrible first efforts. You need to start somewhere. Start by getting something—anything—down on paper. A friend of mine says that the first draft is the down draft—you just get it down. The second draft is the up draft—you fix it up. You try to say what you have to say more accurately. And the third draft is the dental draft, where you check every tooth, to see if it's loose or cramped or decayed, or even, God help us, healthy.

■ ■ ■   **FOR CLASS DISCUSSION**

1. Lamott says that the perceptions most people have of how writers work is different from the reality of the work itself. She refers to this in the first paragraph as "the fantasy of the uninitiated." What does she mean?

2. In the paragraph beginning "But because by then I had been writing for so long . . . ," Lamott refers to a time when, through experience, she "eventually let [herself] trust the process—sort of, more or less." She is referring to the writing process, of course, but why "more or less"? Do you think that her wariness is personal, or is she speaking for all writers in this regard? Explain.

3. From what Lamott has to say, is writing a first draft more about the product or the process? Do you agree in regard to your own first drafts? Explain.   ■ ■ ■

Revising

material from *Rewriting: How to Do Things with Texts* by
Joseph Harris

FIRST DRAFT OF PAPER INADVERTENTLY BECOMES FINAL DRAFT, *EU-GENE, OR—The first draft of an English 140 paper by University of Oregon sophomore Marty Blain ultimately became the final draft, Blain reported Monday. "I was gonna keep working on it and add a bunch of stuff about how the guy who wrote [*The Great Gatsby]* was affected by a lot of the stuff going on around him," she said. "But then I was like, fuck it." Blair said that she spent the time that would have been devoted to revision watching* Friends *in her dorm's TV lounge.*

—*The Onion*, September 27, 2000

I'm dying for some action
I'm sick of sitting 'round here trying to
write this book.

—Bruce Springsteen, "Dancing in the Dark"

So far in this book I've offered you four moves for rewriting—for making the words, ideas, and images of others part of your own project as a writer. In this last chapter, I propose some ways of using those moves in *revising*—that is, in rethinking, refining, and developing—your own work-in-progress as writer. *Revising* is thus a particular form of what throughout this book I've called *rewriting*; it names the work of returning to a draft of a text you've written in order to make your thinking in it more nuanced, precise, suggestive, and interesting.

My method here will be to work in the mode of the previous four chapters—to ask what it might mean to come to terms with, forward, counter, or take the approach of your own text-in-progress. My hope is that doing so will allow me offer a view of revising that, on the one hand, doesn't reduce it to a mere fiddling with sentences, to editing for style and correctness, but that also, on the other hand, avoids lapsing into mystical exhortations for risk taking or critical self-awareness or some other vague but evidently desirable quality of mind. My aim is instead to describe revising as a knowable practice, as a consistent set of questions you can ask of a draft of an essay that you are working on:

- *What's your project?* What do you want to accomplish in this essay? (Coming to Terms)
- *What works?* How can you build on the strengths of your draft? (Forwarding)

- *What else might be said?* How might you acknowledge other views and possibilities? (Countering)
- What's next? What are the implications of what you have to say? (Taking an Approach)

While these questions are straightforward, they are not easy. Revising is the sort of thing that is fairly simple to describe but very hard to do well—like playing chess, or serving in tennis, or teaching a class. It is also an activity that tends to be hidden from view. As readers we usually come upon texts in their final form—with many of the hesitations, repetitions, digressions, false starts, alternative phrasings, inconsistencies, speculations, infelicities, and flat-out mistakes of earlier drafts smoothed over, corrected, or erased. Another way to put this is to say that finished texts tend to conceal much of the labor involved in writing them. Since we rarely get to see the early drafts of most published texts, it can often seem as though other writers work, as it were, without ever blotting a line, confidently progressing through their texts from start to finish, paragraph to paragraph, chapter to chapter, as if they were speaking them aloud. This one-draft view of writing is reinforced by most movie and TV depictions of writers at work, as we watch them quickly type perfectly balanced and sequenced sentences until, with a sigh of satisfaction, they pound out THE END or press SEND. It is also a view inculcated by the pace and structure of American schooling, whose frequent exams reward students who can produce quick clean essays on demand. A result is that much of what little instruction that does get offered in writing tends to focus on questions of correctness. Handbooks are filled with advice on proofreading and teachers downgrade for mistakes in grammar and spelling.

But while the moments of both inspiration and correction, of creating a text and fixing its errors, are well marked in our culture, the work of revision, of rethinking and reshaping a text, is rarely noted. With the exception of a few literati who, in anticipation of future biographies and critical editions, seem to save all their papers, early, drafts tend to get cleared off the desk or deleted from the hard drive once a project is finished, or even as it is being written. In fact, one of the few places where you can readily trace how a project evolves from one draft to the next—and thus make the labor of writing it more visible—is in a university writing course. Several of the examples in this chapter are thus drawn, with their permission, from the writings of students in courses I have taught. Each is an example of a student working with—commenting on, analyzing, rethinking—a draft of his or her own writing. For that is perhaps the key challenge of revising, to find a way to step outside of your own thinking and to look at the text you are working on as another reader might. But before looking at strategies for revising in detail, let me briefly distinguish it from two other important forms of work on an academic essay.

Drafting, Revising, Editing

For most academic writers, work on a piece begins long before they sit down at a keyboard or desk and continues well past their first attempts at putting their thoughts into prose. They tend, that is, to imagine a text they are writing less as a performance (which is what an exam calls for) and more as a work-in-progress, as an ongoing project that they can add to and reshape over time. And while the working habits of individual writers are too varied to be generalized into a single process of composing, you can think of the labor of writing as involving:

- Drafting, or generating text.
- Revising, or working with the text you've created, rethinking and reshaping what you want to say.
- Editing, or working on your text as an artifact, preparing the final version of your document.

The three form an intuitive sequence: First, you move from ideas to words on the screen or page; next you reconsider and rework what you've written, often with the help of responses from readers; and, finally, you edit, design, and format your final document. In practice, though, these forms of work tend to be overlapping and recursive: Most writers do some amount of revising and editing as they draft (although it is usually wise not to invest too much time in polishing a passage before you know for sure if you will even include it in the final version of your text); serious revision almost always involves the drafting of some new prose; and the careful editing of a piece can often lead back into a more extensive revising of it.

By far the most elusive of these three forms of work is drafting—or what is sometimes called *invention*. Trying to figure out something to write about has been the frustration of writing students—and their teachers—for decades. Stephen King puts the problem with his usual plainspoken acuity in his novel Misery—in which the writer of a popular series of paperback romances is held hostage by a demented fan and forced to write a new book to her liking. (In other words, the novel is about a writing class.) Here are the thoughts of King's captive author as he desperately tries to get started on his new book:

> Another part of him was furiously trying out ideas, rejecting them, trying to combine them, rejecting the combinations. He sensed this going on but had no direct contact with it and wanted none. It was dirty down there in the sweatshops.
>
> He understood what he was doing now as TRYING TO HAVE AN IDEA. TRYING TO HAVE AN IDEA wasn't the same thing as GETTING AN IDEA. GETTING AN IDEA was a more humble way of saying *I am inspired, or Eureka! My muse has spoken!* . . .
>
> This other process—TRYING TO HAVE AN IDEA—was nowhere near as exalted or exalting, but it was every bit as mysterious and every bit as necessary. Because when you were writing a novel you almost always got roadblocked somewhere, and there was no sense in trying to go until you HAD AN IDEA.

INTERTEXTS

Steven King, *Misery* (New York: Signet, 1988), 119–20.

> His usual procedure when it was necessary to HAVE AN IDEA was to put on his coat and go for a walk. He recognized walking as good exercise, but it was boring. If you didn't have someone to talk to while you walked, a book was a necessity. But if you needed to HAVE AN IDEA, boredom could be to a roadblocked novel what chemotherapy was to a cancer patient.

I can't claim to have all that much to say about how to begin writing an essay. For me, like King, the deep origins of words and ideas seem more often than not mysterious and untraceable. But King does also offer us a number of useful ways of thinking about this mystery. First, he points to the importance of seizing hold of those ideas that do somehow come to you. The volume next to the one you were looking for on the library shelf, the comment from another class that continues to echo in your head, the connection you notice between the papers and books that happen to be sitting on your desk, the song or movie that a text reminds you of-work on an essay often begins with such serendipities. Second, King notes the value of patience, of knowing when you're stalled, when you simply need to take a break. Similarly, he speaks of the usefulness of boredom, of letting ideas percolate. Finally, he suggests that a writer often needs to start not from a moment of inspiration (*eureka!*) but from the need to work through a conceptual problem or roadblock. Indeed, I'd suggest that most academic writing begins with such questions rather than insights, with difficulties in understanding rather than moments of mastery.

What I hope I can tell you more about is how to revise a text you've begun to write, to work with the words you've started to put on the page, or screen. Perhaps the most common mistake that student writers make is to slight the work of revising—either by trying to conceive and draft an entire text from start to end in a single sitting, without pausing to consider alternate (and perhaps more interesting) ways of developing their ideas, or by worrying so much about issues of editing and correctness that they hardly allow themselves to think about anything else at all. (It is only too possible, as any writing teacher can tell you, to create a text that is wonderfully designed, phrased, formatted, edited, and proofread—but that says almost nothing.) Many students enter college without really ever having been asked to rethink their views on an issue or to: restructure the approach they've taken in an essay. They've been trained in how to find and fix mistakes, and perhaps even in how to respond to specific questions about a draft posed by their teacher. But their final drafts are essentially the same as their first ones—only cleaner, smoother, more polished. They have been taught how to edit but not how to revise.

In revising, the changes you make to a text are connected. They form a plan of work. For instance, if in reworking the introduction to an essay, you realize that you also need to change the order of the paragraphs that follow it, then you are revising. Or if dealing with a new example also requires you to adjust some of your key words or concepts, you are revising. Or if in rethinking the implications of your argument at the end of an essay, you also begin to see a stronger way of beginning it, you are revising. And so on. In revising, one change leads to others. You edit sentences; you revise essays.

The changes you make in editing tend to be ad hoc and local. To edit is to fine-tune a document. Proofreading is the extreme case: You simply correct a typo or a mistake in punctuation and move on. Nothing else needs to be done; no other changes need to be made. Similarly, you can often edit for style, recast the wording of a particular sentence to make it more graceful or clear, without having to alter much (or anything) else in the paragraph of which it is part. You can even sometimes insert a sentence or two in a paragraph—to add an example, clarify a point, answer a question—while making few or no other changes to it. Indeed I've seen entire blocks of text dropped into an essay without sending any ripples at all into the paragraphs before or after it, but rather leaving the original flow of ideas serenely undisturbed. The aim of revising is to rethink the ideas and examples that drive your thinking in an essay; the aim of editing is to improve the flow and design of your document. Both forms of work are important. But simply editing a text that needs to be rethought and revised is like waxing a car that needs repairs to its engine.

Tracking Revision

You can begin to see how the work of revising differs from that of editing by mapping the changes you make in moving from one draft of an essay to the next. Most word processing programs have a "track changes" or "compare documents" tool that you can use to record the changes you make in keyboarding a new version of an essay. Using this tool allows you to mark where you

- Add to
- Delete
- Move (cut and paste)
- Rework (select and type over)
- Reformat a text you are working on.

You can of course also note and mark such changes by hand; the software simply cuts down on some of the drudgery involved.

Revising an essay is complex and difficult intellectual work. But it is work not only with ideas but text. You can't just think changes to an essay; you need to *make* them. (This is a lesson I've learned to my chagrin only too many times—as paragraphs that seemed to flow clearly in my mind when I was in the shower or out for a walk with the dogs somehow become muddled and intractable when I sit down to type, them out.) At some point, that is, you have to translate plans and ideas into the material labor of adding, cutting, moving, reworking, or reformatting text. While revising clearly involves more than keyboarding, all of the work you do in rethinking a text will find its final expression in' some combination of those five functions. Tracking the changes you make in keyboarding a new draft of an essay can thus help make the conceptual work you've done in revising more visible.

Let me offer an example. Here is the opening paragraph of the first draft of an essay written by Abhijit Mehta, a student in a writing course, in response to an assignment that asked him to describe some' of the distinctive ways a particular group makes use of language—to reflect on how they give their own spin, as it were, to the meanings of certain words. Abhijit decided to write on the vocabulary of his own field of study, mathematics:

> The Strange Language of Math
>
> As our society becomes more dependant on technology, the work of mathematicians and physicists comes closer to everyday experience. In order to have a basic understanding of many modern issues and technologies, people need to become more familiar with the language of, math and science. However, mathematicians and physicists have a tendency to use common words in a strange way. In math and physics, *nice, elegant, trivial, well-behaved, charm, flavor, strange,* and *quark* all have meanings that can be very different from their everyday meanings. Mathematicians and physicists often use common words to express ideas that are very complex.

INTERTEXTS

Abhijit Mehta, "the Playful Language of Math" (1st and 2nd drafts), unpublished essay, Duke University, 2002.

The rest of the essay follows the plan laid out in this paragraph, as Abhijit goes on to discuss the particular meanings mathematicians give to each of the terms he mentions—*nice, elegant, trivial,* and so on—in the order that he lists them. What the readers of his first draft told Abhijit, though, was that while in creating this catalogue of odd usages he had assembled the materials for an interesting essay, he hadn't yet suggested what those specialized uses told us about the culture of math. Indeed, the problem with the draft is hinted at in its title, which simply says that the language of math is "strange" but doesn't specify *how*. His readers thus asked Abhijit for a more precise sense of the attitudes and values that lay behind the usages he discussed. What *kind* of "strangeness" connected the ways mathematicians used these words?

Hard questions, but it turned out that Abhijit had answers to them. Here is the opening of his second and revised draft.

> The Playful Language of Math
> As our society becomes more dependent on technology, the work of mathematicians and physicists comes closer to everyday experience. In order to have a basic understanding of many modern issues and technologies, people need to become more familiar with the language of math and science. However, mathematicians and physicists have a tendency to use common words to describe complex things. In math and physics, *nice, elegant, trivial, well-behaved, charm, flavor, strange,* and *quark* all have meanings that can be very different from their everyday meanings. The migration of these words from common usage to their specialized usage conveys some of the playful attitude that mathematicians and physicists have towards abstract, complex problems.

And here is a version that maps the keyboarding changes between the two paragraphs. Words ~~deleted~~ from the first draft are struck through; text <u>added</u> to the second draft is underlined.

> The ~~Strange~~ <u>Playful</u> Language of Math
> As our society becomes more ~~dependant~~ <u>dependent</u> on technology, the work of mathematicians and physicists comes closer to everyday experience. In order to have a basic understanding of many modern issues and technologies, people need to become more familiar with the language of math and science. However, mathematicians and physicists have a ~~tendancy~~ <u>tendency</u> to use common words ~~in a strange way~~ <u>to describe complex things</u>. In math and physics, *nice, elegant, trivial, well-behaved, charm, flavor, strange,* and *quark* all have meanings that can be very different from their everyday meanings. ~~Mathematicians and physicists often use common words to express ideas that are very complex.~~ <u>The migration of these words from common usage to their specialized usage conveys some of the playful attitude that mathematicians and physicists have towards abstract, complex problems.</u>

This map of changes shows that Abhijit was working on at least three different levels in moving from his first to second draft: At the most mundane level, he did some proofreading and corrected the spellings of *dependent* and *tendency*. Such work is simple correction, necessary but uninteresting. On a second level, he also edited for clarity and concision, combining two sentences that say almost the same thing in his first draft (mathematicians have a "tendancy to use common words in a strange way" and "often

use common words to express ideas that are very complex") into a single briefer statement in the second ("a tendency to use common words to express complex things").
But while such editing helps the flow of this particular paragraph, its impact does not
extend beyond it. While intelligent and helpful, it remains a local edit, unconnected to
a larger pattern of revision throughout the essay.

The third level of work—what I would call *revision*—involves such a pattern and
plan of change. By far the most ambitious change that Abhijit makes in his second draft
is to move, in both his revised title and new last sentence, from a nebulous description
of the language of math as "strange" to a more precise view of it as *playful*. These two
changes signal an important shift in his project as a writer—from offering a simple
catalogue of some of the strange ways that mathematicians use words to making an
argument about the unexpected playfulness of the field, as evidenced by its vocabulary.
In the rest of his revised essay, Abhijit goes on to identify two ways in which the playfulness of mathematicians comes into view—one in their unconventional use of common
words like *nice* or *trivial* and the other in their choice of exotic and fanciful terms like
quark to describe their concepts and discoveries. This allows him to conclude his piece
by contesting the cultural stereotype of the math nerd or computer geek as a humorless
drone. In short, for Abhijit the notion of play becomes a generative concept, an idea that
leads to other ideas, that he uses to structure and develop the revised version of his essay.

When students in the courses I teach hand in a revised draft of an essay, I require
them to include with it another copy of their text on which they track all the changes
they have made in moving from one draft to the next and, more important, highlight
those changes that are central to their plan of revision. I then ask them to refer to
this map in writing a brief reflection on their aims and strategies in revising. (See the
Projects box "Mapping Your Approach" below in this chapter for the guidelines I offer
students for creating this map and reflection.) And so, for instance, a version of Abhijit's
opening paragraph that boldfaced changes in **revising** (as contrasted with local proofreading or editing changes) might look something like this:

> The ~~Strange~~ **Playful** Language of Math
> As our society becomes more ~~dependant~~ <u>dependent</u> on technology, the work of mathemati-
> cians and physicists comes closer to everyday experience. In order to have a basic under-
> standing of many modern issues and technologies, people need to become more familiar
> with the language of math and science. However, mathematicians and physicists have a
> ~~tendancy~~ <u>tendency</u> to use common words ~~in a strange way~~ <u>to describe complex things</u>. In
> math and physics, *nice, elegant, trivial, well-behaved, charm, flavor, strange,* and *quark* all
> have meanings that can be very different from their everyday meanings. ~~Mathematicians
> and physicists often use common words to express ideas that are very complex~~. **The mi-
> gration of these words from common usage to their specialized usage conveys some of
> the playful attitude that mathematicians and physicists have towards abstract, complex
> problems.**

Those points throughout the rest of his revised essay where Abhijit returned to and
developed the idea of the playful attitude of math would then also be boldfaced.

My aim here is not to denigrate the work of proofreading or editing. There is
almost always a moment near the end of work on an essay when the most serious

task that remains for you to do is to recheck and format your document with as much thought and care as you can give. (There was yet one more draft of Abhijit's essay to come, for instance, in which he noted in his opening paragraph that he would discuss *two* forms of playfulness in math, as well as made other local refinements to his prose.) Nor am I especially invested in advocating one particular method of mapping revision. What I do hope to have shown here, however, is how the local task of editing sentences and paragraphs differs in tangible and practical ways from the more global work of rethinking an essay. If in tracking the changes you've made to the draft of an essay, you can't point to a series or pattern of changes linked by an idea, then you haven't revised, you've only edited. With this sense of revising as rethinking in mind, then, let me turn to the four questions I proposed earlier.

What's Your Project? Coming to Terms With a Draft

It may seem the most banal of advice to suggest that in composing an essay you should have a good sense of your overall aim in writing, of what you want to achieve in your work, but there are at least two reasons why this truism proves harder to act upon than it might at first appear. First, while academic writers tend to begin with problems that they want to investigate, with texts that intrigue or puzzle or somehow fascinate them, their essays, when completed, need not simply to pose questions but also to respond to them. You may begin work on a project simply with the goal of finding out more about a certain subject or thinking your way through a particular set of issues, but in writing about that subject you need to articulate a stance, to establish a position of your own. The orientation of your work, that is, needs to shift as you make your way through a project. (The writing researcher and teacher Linda Flower has called this moving from *writer-based* to *reader-based* prose.) Second, you will often find that your ideas evolve over the course of writing, particularly when you are at work on an ambitious or complex project. Digressions morph into key lines of argument; examples don't quite seem to work as planned; apercus become central ideas; afterthoughts prove more interesting than the ideas they followed; a reader's comment makes you think about your subject in unexpected ways; a small shift in phrasing leads into unforeseen avenues of thought. These are not problems to be avoided in working on an essay; they are moments to be anticipated and used.

> **INTERTEXTS**
>
> Linda Flower, *Problem Solving Strategies for Writing in College and the Community*, 4th ed. (New York: Heinle, 1997).

Your project as a writer is thus something you are likely to need to rethink throughout the process of working on an essay. You may find it especially useful to revisit your purposes in writing, when you have completed close to a full draft of an essay. I have often found, in rereading my work at such moments, that I seem to be looking at a different piece than the one I thought I had set out to write. The question, then, is whether to rethink what I've written in order to adhere to my original plan or to revise the plan to better describe what I've ended up writing. The answer is usually some mix of both, as my sense of my project as a whole evolves alongside my attempts to write my way through particular problems and examples.

But to test your project against your draft in such a way you need a precise and detailed account of what your aims in writing actually are. You need, that is, to come to terms with your own work. And, as I suggested in the first chapter, this involves not simply restating something like your "main idea" but rather describing your project in writing—your goals, the materials you're working on, and the moves you make with those materials. I thus often require students in my courses, once they have completed a draft of an essay, to write a brief *abstract* of their work as it then stands. (A version of this assignment appears in the Projects box "Coming to Terms with Your Own Work-in-Progress" at the end of the first chapter.) In writing such an abstract your goal should not be to reintroduce your essay but to summarize its gist for someone who has not read it. You want, that is, to write a piece that describes your essay from the outside, that distills what you have to say into as clear and pointed a form as possible.

For example, if I were to abstract the second section of this chapter—"Drafting, Revising, Editing"—I might say something like this:

> In this section I define three forms of work that go into producing an essay: *drafting*, *revising*, and *editing*. I suggest that while our culture both romanticizes the labor of drafting and fetishizes the importance of editing for correctness, the work of revision, of rethinking writing, often goes unnoticed and undervalued. After a brief account of the mysteries of drafting (with the help of Stephen King), I argue for distinguishing the local changes of editing from the *global* work of revising.

As my use of italics suggests, one aim of an abstract is to bring forward the key terms and ideas of an essay. And as the main verbs of my sentences indicate ("I define;' "I suggest:' and "I argue"), another goal is to identify its line of thought, the moves its writer makes. (It is up to you as my reader, of course, to decide how well I have managed to catch the gist of the previous section and what aspects of it I may have glossed over or distorted.)

The point of writing an abstract of your own work is to push you to think about the essay you are writing on two levels: (1) your project as a whole; and (2) how you develop your line of thinking. In one sense, of course, it trivializes the complexities of an essay to reduce them to a single page or paragraph, but it's also a problem if you can't offer a lucid overview of your aims in writing. If it simply seems impossible to summarize an essay that you are in the process of drafting, this may be a sign that you haven't yet quite figured out what you want to say in it. On the other hand; you also want there to be a sense of surprise and nuance in how you write out your ideas, from sentence to sentence and paragraph to paragraph, that eludes complete summary—or otherwise there will be no reason for anyone to read through your piece as whole. Forcing yourself to write an abstract of an essay you've drafted can help you move between these levels, to see where your prose advances your project effectively and where it does not. Sometimes you may find that you need to rethink how you talk about your project in order to catch up with the actual work you've done in your draft. And you are also likely to find, on a practical level, that many of the sentences you compose for your abstract end up as part of your next draft, signaling key moves or points in your argument.

PROJECTS   Making a Revising Plan

One reason, I suspect, that many writers end up simply· editing rather than revising their work-in-progress is that they approach the task haphazardly, simply trying to fix mistakes or infelicities in their texts as they happen to come across them, without ever forming a larger sense of what they want to accomplish through making such changes. To counter this tendency to fine-tune rather than rewrite, I ask students in my courses, after they've gotten feedback on a piece they are writing, to form a plan for revising their work-in-progress. We then discuss these plans before they actually begin work on the next draft of their essays. In developing their revising plans, I ask students first to write an abstract of what they have drafted so far and then:

> Offer a brief but specific plan for revision. Try as much as you can at this point to describe the substance or content of the changes you want to make. See if you can answer the following questions as precisely as you can:

> - Which comments from your readers—either written on your draft or offered during a workshop—have you found most useful in rethinking your essay?
> - If you plan to add to what you've written so far, what will you say and where will it go?
> - If you now plan to revise your project in writing, how will you do so? If you want to work with any different ideas or examples, what will they be? ■

In coming to terms with a draft, it is also often useful to counterpose the sort of overview of an essay provided by an abstract with the more narrative working through of it offered by a *sentence outline*. To create such an outline, you simply need to go through an essay, summarizing each of its paragraphs or sections in a single sentence. The result should be a kind of quick-paced version of your essay, in which it becomes clear how each of your moves and examples follows upon the other (or, sometimes, where they fail to do so). The trick in writing such a sentence outline is much like that in composing an abstract—you want to write new prose (rather than simply highlighting phrases from your text) and you want to focus less on the topics of your paragraphs than on what you are trying to do in them, on the moves you are making as a writer. And so, for instance, if I were to outline the previous section of this chapter, "Tracking Revision," I might produce something like this:

> I begin by suggesting that there are five basic types of changes that you can make in revising an essay: adding, deleting, moving, reworking, and reformatting. I then suggest that while revision can't be reduced to keyboarding, tracking keyboarding changes can make the conceptual work that goes into revising more visible. I then offer the first and second drafts of the opening paragraph of Abhijit's essay as an example of how to track changes and think about them. I start by reproducing his first draft and suggesting that there was a problem with the vagueness of "strange" as a descriptor for the language of math. Then I reproduce his second draft, first as plain text (so that readers don't get confused by all those strikeovers and underlines) and then with changes marked. Next I argue that this map of revision shows Abhijit working on three levels: proofreading, editing, and revision. I suggest that revision differs from editing in being *systematic* and *generative*, and reproduce yet one more version of Abhijit's second draft with revising changes boldfaced. Finally, I set up the

next sections of the chapter by saying that I will now try to offer four strategies for rewriting (and not simply editing) your own work-in-progress.

I'll again leave it to you as my reader to decide how effective an outline of the preceding section this may be. But even though my example here is of an outline of a section in its final form, I hope you can begin to get a sense of how you could use this technique to identify moments in a text that you might want to rethink and rework. (They would be those points where you find yourself saying something like: "Well, what *am* I really trying to do here?" or "How does *this* sentence or idea follow from *that* one?") I've argued throughout this book that the strong use of the work of other writers needs to be grounded in a generous understanding of their projects. The same principle applies to your own work-in-progress. Before revising an essay, you need to articulate a clear sense of your aims in writing, so you can then assess what is working in your text and what is not.

What Works? Revising as Forwarding

An irony of revising is that writers often become so preoccupied with fixing what isn't going right in a text that they neglect to build on what is. The upshot of such attempts at remediation is often not a more interesting essay but simply one that is a little less weak in revising you want not only to deal with the problems of a draft but also to develop its strengths. And so, when students in my courses read and respond to one another's work, I ask them to mark both those passages that strike them as especially strong and those that they have questions or worries about. (The usual code is a straight line for <u>strengths</u> and a wavy<add wavy line under "wavy"> one for questions. You can, of course, use this system in rereading and marking your own drafts as well as in responding to the work of others.) This simple form of marking a text offers writers a map of their work that identifies those passages that their readers liked, posed questions about, or were simply indifferent toward-that no one made any particular note of. While the instinct of many writers is to let such unmarked passages stand—after all, no one has signaled them out as a problem—this third category of (non-) response more often than not points to passages that they may want to cut or abbreviate, since it is prose that has failed to draw the interest, one way or the other, of any of their readers.

You will probably want to spend most of your time reworking or developing those moments in a text that your readers have marked for either praise or question. Note that it's not always a bad sign for readers to have questions about a certain point or passage in an essay. This often means that there is something there worth thinking about, puzzling over, working through. Indeed, you can sometimes find a section of an essay both compelling and troubling at once—and I have many times seen readers mark some of the most interesting passages in an essay with both straight and wavy lines! The point is to identify those moments that have most drawn the attention of readers and to see how you can build on them, bring them forward in your next draft.

Another question to ask is *where* readers mark a draft as interesting or intriguing. Often enough, you may find that several of your readers seem engaged by a sentence that appears in the middle of a paragraph in a middle page of your essay—that is, in a

INTERTEXTS

I learned this simple and useful code of commenting on drafts, along with many other strategies of response, from Peter Flbow's remarkable and enduring guide to running a writer's workshop, *Writing without Teachers*, 2nd ed. (New York: Oxford University Press, 2000).

spot where it might well have been missed. In revising you may thus want to consider positioning that idea more prominently— perhaps at the start of the paragraph or even shifted to the opening of your essay. Or you may learn that your readers think that your most interesting work comes at the very end of your essay, on its last page or so. In such a case, you may want to see what happens if you begin your next draft with those closing ideas and see where doing so takes your thinking. This is in fact advice that I have given to many writers. The value of writing an early draft of an essay can sometimes lie in the chance it gives you to think your way through to the point, sometimes at the very end of your draft, where you've finally figured out what is you want to say. Often the best way to build on that work is not to try to salvage the fumblings of your first pages but to continue to forge ahead, to begin your next draft from the point where you ended your first.

What Else Might Be Said? Revising as Countering

Writers are often urged to anticipate the questions that readers might ask about their work, usually so that they can then preempt any possible objections to what they are trying to argue. While this advice makes some sense, it suffers from imagining the writing of an essay as the staking out of a position in a pro-con debate, and thus tends to lock a writer into defending a fixed point of view. But there is another, and I think more interesting, way of countering your own work-in-progress, and that is not simply to ask what possible objections might be raised to your work but also what alternative lines of thought you might want to pursue. You want to read a draft of an essay in ways that open up the possibilities of what you might say rather than lock you into a particular perspective. In revising you thus need to learn how to look at your work-in-progress not simply as a finished (or nearly finished) artifact but also as a source of ideas, a starting point for more writing.

Sometimes revising involves reworking existing text, but many other times it consists of following through on an idea or an aside, building on a suggestive turn of phrase, or taking your essay in an unplanned direction. In writing there are often moments when the best thing to do is to start over—except that you won't really be starting over, but rather beginning with an idea that's grabbed you in the midst of your work on an essay, or with a new sense of where you want to go in your thinking, or even with just a few key terms or examples that you've gleaned from the experience of working on your first draft. For instance, here is how Charles Jordan described how he rethought and redrafted an essay he was writing on Thomas Bell's novel *Out of This Furnace* for an undergraduate course in critical reading:

> My paper didn't simply evolve from a mediocre paper to an acceptable one (as I suspect most of my classmates' papers did). Rather, instead of just improving on the same paper, I wrote one with a completely different point. I started out focusing on the cyclic nature of

the workers' lives and their experiences, and how the cycle was a perpetual one in which those who were in this class were trapped. However, going from first to second draft, I was asked to find something I could say at the end (or at least the middle) of my analysis that I couldn't say at the beginning. I said that I thought that my analysis validated the statement that the experiences and struggles of those in this working class actually came to define the class of people in this novel. I included something to that effect briefly in my conclusion, and in a few other places throughout the paper. However, I began to realize (not only on my own but also through the help of readers) that my initial argument of the "endless cycle" was weak, and evidence was scarce and hard to find. . . . What started out being an insightful one or two line statement in my paper started seeming more and more like an interesting argument I could make, which would also be stronger (due to more evidence). So, my paper metamorphosed from a paper trying to prove the existence of this cycle into a paper trying to show that Bell tries to define this class of workers by their struggles and sacrifices. So the major change in my paper was that my arguments and examples were then framed to support this new thesis. Also, I reworded a lot of awkward phrases, and added a few more examples. . . . Besides the fact that the main argument in the paper was changed, all the other changes I made were minor, and mostly technical.

> **INTERTEXTS**
>
> Charles Jordan, "Reflection on Writing," unpublished essay, Duke University, 2001.
> The essay that Charles describes in this reflection was on Thomas Bell, *Out of This Furnace* (Pittsburgh: University of Pittsburgh Press, 1976).

What Charles has to say here reminds me of the passage I quoted earlier by Stephen King. Both contrast the "minor and technical" work of piecing a text together with the more central problem of finding and developing its key ideas—although Charles usefully shows how such ideas can emerge not only through happenstance (as King suggests) but also through a process of talk and revision. But there is a kind of boldness, a willingness to set aside what isn't working and to build on what is, that underlies the views of both writers. Rather than simply trying to pull together evidence for a line of thought that he had begun to realize was mediocre, Charles chose the riskier path of developing another idea. I admire that. The aim of revising should not be simply to fix up or refine a text but to develop and extend what it has to say—to make your writing more precise, nuanced, inventive, and surprising. The best form of countering a work-in-progress allows for new lines of thought to emerge.

What's Next? Revising as Looking Ahead

One of the most difficult problems in writing involves figuring out how to close an essay or chapter or book before you've simply begun to repeat yourself. There's a familiar kind of academic essay that says almost everything it has to say in its first few pages—that begins, as it were, with its conclusions, laying out its thesis so mordantly in its opening paragraphs that its writer is left with little to do in the rest of the piece but to offer a set of supporting examples for points he or she has already made. The principal aim of such writing sometimes seems to be to ensure that there will be no surprises beyond the first page or two, that everything will follow the initial plan and argument as set out by the writer. The conclusions of such essays thus tend to be almost wholly ornamental, bookends whose task is simply to restate what has come before.

I have no quarrel with the need 'to define a clear plan of work for an essay or book. You want readers to know what your project is, to have a sense of where you're headed in your thinking and what you see as at stake in your writing. (See the Project box "Mapping Your Approach".) But you also want to *develop* a line of thinking in an essay, to explore its contradictions and stuck points and ambiguities, not simply to stake out a fixed position and defend it. You want to be able to say something at the end of an essay that you couldn't say at its start, that your work in the previous pages has made possible.

A good question to ask of a draft of an essay that you are writing, then, is at what point do you simply start to restate what you've said before? For that is where you will want to bring the piece to a close. And if your experience is like mine, you may often find in rereading a draft that you have written several pages past the point where you might have ended it. I have many times found myself wondering how to conclude a piece, only to find that I already had—although without yet realizing it. You want to finish a piece not with a ceremonial flourish, a restatement of what has come before, but with a look ahead, a gesture toward work to come, a new question or idea or insight to be followed.

PROJECTS   Mapping Your Approach

You may find the metaphor of a *map* useful in clarifying the approach you want to take in a piece of writing. Think of this map as having two parts: an overview and road signs. The former is a passage near the start of your piece that states where you are headed in your thinking and how you will get there. For example, *In this essay I argue that . . . First, I look at . . . Then I call on . . .* An overview is often a revised version of the sort of abstract I talked about before. Road signs are brief markers throughout your text that indicate the moves you are making as a writer. In a longer piece, road signs may be section headings (as in the chapters of this book). In a shorter essay, they may be signaled by metatextual phrases like *An example of this problem is . . .* or *Some implications of this stance are . . .* or *By way of concluding, let me . . .*

First, read through your text and highlight its overview and road signs. Then, check to see if your overview really describes your essay as it now stands. Sometimes you end up in different place at the end of a piece than you thought you were headed toward at its start. Sometimes you find alternate lines of inquiry. Sometimes you simply wander off track. If your overview and essay don't correspond with each other, decide which you want to change.

Finally, check to see if you have clearly marked the turns of thought throughout your text. If you list your subheads and/or metatextual phrases, these should offer a workable outline of your essay. If not, then you may need to mark the steps of your thinking more clearly. ▇

A powerful close to an essay or book responds to two questions: *So what?* and *What's next?* By this I don't mean that such questions are posed! explicitly—they rarely are—but that readers should finish a text with a strong sense of how they have been asked to change what they feel or believe, as well as of what would be involved in continuing to think along the lines 'you have proposed, of what it would mean for them to take on *your* approach. In revising, then, you want to ask yourself the same question as you consider how to close an essay: How might this piece point toward new work, new writing?

It is an ambitious question—and one that you need to work toward answering throughout the whole of your essay and not simply at its conclusion. But it is not an impossible question to ask or answer. For instance, in an early draft of an analysis of the term *sketchy*, an adjective then in common use at both Duke and many other college campuses, Justin Lee concluded with this paragraph:

> Sketchy has become more than a word used in 'context at Duke to refer to unsure ideas. It has become a transformer itself—reshaping people's attitudes and thoughts. As a sort of personal character modifier, *sketchy* is now a powerful integrity-altering word that forms a powerful impact.

While this is not a terrible close to an essay, it failed to get at the idea driving the work that Justin had done throughout his piece—which was that there was something suspect about a term, *sketchy*, that could be used to indicate vague disapproval of almost anything, without ever really indicating what the grounds for that disapproval were. And what could a reader do with the vague idea that sketchy somehow had a "powerful impact" on the "integrity" of its users? What did his analysis point toward? It was hard to say. So this is how Justin revised his closing paragraph:

> *Sketchy* has become more than a word used in context at Duke to refer to unsure ideas. It has become a transformer itself—reshaping people's attitudes and thoughts. As a sort of personal character modifier, *sketchy* is an influential character-altering word that carries a powerful impact. What I have come to discover through the course of this paper is that sketchy is also at times a less than ideal word to use. Ironically, its strength is also its weakness. To see this connection clearly, think about what makes *sketchy* a perfect word sometimes—its vagueness does. *Sketchy* carries an almost deliberate non-committal interpretation, in that it has such a wide range of uses. This means that people can say it without actually "totally taking a side,' so to speak, allowing someone to voice an opinion, but also not requiring that person to "lay all of his cards down." It permits a person to half commit to a conviction without totally coming out. . . . People never really know how strongly a person is using it in context; therefore, people never know what to make of it. For this reason, the word sketchy is itself "sketchy," according to the definition and application it has taken on at Duke University—and should be used with caution.

In this new closing Justin not only offers a pointed criticism of the use of *sketchy* as a way of "half committing" yourself to an opinion but also suggests a self-reflexive mode of analysis in which you apply the values of a term to itself. Is *sketchy* itself sketchy? How cool is cool? Is it shady to call someone else shady? Justin is thus doing new work until the very end of his piece, rather than simply concluding by restating what he has already said

INTERTEXTS

Justin Lee, "Sketchy: A Transformer of Personal Character," unpublished essay (2nd and 3rd drafts), Duke University 2002.

(as was the case in his first closing passage). And in doing so, he invites his readers to continue the work he has begun, to take up his approach, to write in his spirit.

You can imagine the work of revision, then, at its most ambitious, as pushing beyond the space of a single essay, as advancing a project whose ideas, aims, and possibilities spill over the bounds of a single piece and point toward further writing. That is what the first four chapters of this book are about: extending and rewriting the work of others. But you can also rewrite your own work in this interesting and difficult sense— to use one essay to fuel the next, to conclude not by wrapping things up but by pointing toward new lines of inquiry, by setting new tasks for yourself as a writer. Here's how another Duke undergraduate, Emily Murphy, put it in reflecting on her work on an essay in which she tried to connect the idea of "cultural capital," as formulated by a number of social theorists, to her own experiences in trying to reach out to people from other social classes. (These experiences included spending a number of days without money or shelter in order to gain some insight into the lives of homeless persons.)

> For some reason, I have a feeling that this is not the final draft of this paper—I imagine that I will revisit it again throughout my life. Therefore, although it is completely "revised" for now, it is doubtful that that is the final version. When the assignment was first given, I brainstormed lots of semi-related ideas, but I wasn't sure how I could connect them reasonably. I honestly did not think that I would use my homeless story in my piece, but when I told the story to my group, they became fascinated by it. I decided to write about being homeless and somehow relate it to our educational system, comparing myself with Cary and Kovacic. However, when I wrote the paper, I started discussing "cultural capital"—a term which I had previously just thrown around. I have learned about this term in several classes, but I have never truly considered the "cultural capital" of my high school. Once I started brainstorming, it was difficult to stop. I realized that 'I need to be specific, citing many examples. At this point, I knew that my paper could logically discuss my homeless experience in terms of "cultural capital." The paper began to take shape. When I presented it, I realized that I needed to reword some sentences because of my tone. I didn't want to appear that I was over-generalizing—after all, I am really just trying to discuss my own situation. Even though I tried to make this clear, I still feel that the paper could be easily criticized for its overgeneralization. Throughout this week, I have continued to think of more examples or semi-related topics. It was difficult for me to actually turn in the final draft because I kept on wanting to add more. Finally, my roommate looked at me and said: "You're obsessing Em, turn it in." At this point, I do like this draft. However, I also know that I will probably write a slightly different draft after my experiences student teaching this summer. This paper will follow me, hopefully expanding and altering through time—it will be interesting to compare drafts. My roommate knows me well—I do obsess.

INTERTEXTS

Emily Murphy, "Reflection on Class and Cultural Capital," unpublished essay, Duke University, 2001.

Emily eloquently describes her essay here as "following" her, its shape and ideas shifting as she herself changes as a person and writer. But you might just as readily describe your project as a writer as something that is always a few steps ahead of you— that is, as something you are always reaching *toward*, only to find, at the very point you think you have at last come to the end of work on an essay or book, that there is still more writing to be done.

I've tried throughout this book to describe rewriting as an active and generous use of the work of others, an attempt to keep the conversation going, *to add* to what other writers and intellectuals have thought and said about a subject. My aim here in this chapter has been to suggest how in revising you might look similarly at your own work-in-progress—that is, to view a draft of an essay not as something to be patched or fixed but as a starting point for new work, for further talk and writing. I've tried, that is, to offer a view of academic writing as a *social* practice, as a form of intellectual work that is always rooted in a set of ongoing conversations, and that is always looking to push such talk another step forward. Even so, I'm aware that I've said fairly little so far about the actual social context in which much of this work takes place—that is, about the college or university writing course. In the afterword, then, I share some of my ideas about designing and teaching courses in academic writing. But while I address this section to my fellow teachers, I hope that my brief sketch of the pace and rhythm, the feel and tone, of the sort of courses I try to teach will be of interest to students as well.

PROJECTS Reflecting on Revision

When students in a course I am teaching are ready to turn in the final version of an essay, I also ask them to reflect on the work they have done over the last several weeks in drafting, revising, and editing their projects. Here is what I ask them to give me:

Along with the revised and final version of your essay, I'd like you to turn in a set of materials that trace the progress of your work in writing it. These materials will take some time and care to get ready. Please submit a folder with the following materials:

- The archival version of your essay.

- A version of your essay on which you highlight the changes you have made in moving from your first to second draft—marking those points where you have added to, cut, shifted, reworked, or reformatted your text. You can use the "compare documents" function in Microsoft Word to do much of this work, but you are likely to find that you also need to use colored pens to mark or clarify certain kinds of changes. Include a key to reading your highlights (e.g., green for added text, blue for cuts, etc.)

- In addition to tracking these changes, you should also identify a series of connected moves that you have made in rethinking your essay—that is, to point to a *pattern* of revision that runs through your piece. Mark this pattern clearly you should be able to point to at least three or four linked changes at various points in your essay and to name the idea that connects them.

- A copy of the previous drafts of your essay, along with the comments of your readers on those drafts.

- Any revising plans you have created during your work on your essay.

- A brief but specific reflection on how your project has developed over the last few weeks. Drawing on the map of changes you've' made, and especially the series of moves in revision you've identified, talk about the aims and strategies that have directed your work in drafting and revising your essay. How did your project in writing evolve over time? How did you come up with and carry through on your plan for revising? What went according to plan and what surprised you? If you have the opportunity to return to this piece, what further work might you want to do on it? ■

The Maker's Eye: Revising Your Own Manuscripts

33

by Donald M. Murray

Born in Boston, Massachusetts, in 1924, Donald M. Murray taught writing for many years at the University of New Hampshire, his alma mater. He has served as an editor at Time *magazine, and he won the Pulitzer Prize in 1954 for editorials that appeared in the* Boston Globe. *Murray's published works include novels, short stories, poetry, and sourcebooks for teachers of writing, like* A Writer Teaches Writing *(1968),* The Craft of Revision *(1991), and* Learning by Teaching *(1982), in which he explores aspects of the writing process.* Write to Learn, *(6th ed., 1998), a textbook for college composition courses, is based on Murray's belief that writers learn to write by writing, by taking a piece of writing through the whole process, from invention to revision.*

In the following essay, first published in the Writer *in October 1973 and later revised for this text, Murray discusses the importance of revision to the work of the writer. Most professional writers live by the maxim that "writing is rewriting." And to rewrite or revise effectively, we need to become better readers of our own work, open to discovering new meanings, and sensitive to our use of language. Murray draws on the experiences of many writers to make a compelling argument for careful revising and editing.*

When students complete a first draft, they consider the job of writing done— and their teachers too often agree. When professional writers complete a first draft, they usually feel that they are at the start of the writing process. When a draft is completed, the job of writing can begin.

That difference in attitude is the difference between amateur and professional, inexperience and experience, journeyman and craftsman. Peter F. Drucker, the prolific business writer, calls his first draft "the zero draft"—after that he can start counting. Most writers share the feeling that the first draft, and all of those which follow, are opportunities to discover what they have to say and how best they can say it.

To produce a progression of drafts, each of which says more and says it more clearly, the writer has to develop a special kind of reading skill. In school we are taught to decode what appears on the page as finished writing. Writers, however, face a different category of possibility and responsibility when they read their own drafts. To them the words on the page are never finished. Each can be changed and rearranged, can set off a chain reaction of confusion or clarified meaning. This is a different kind of reading which is possibly more difficult and certainly more exciting.

Writers must learn to be their own best enemy. They must accept the criticism of others and be suspicious of it; they must accept the praise of others and be even more suspicious of it. Writers cannot depend on others. They must detach themselves from their own pages so that they can apply both their caring and their craft to their own work.

Such detachment is not easy. Science-fiction writer Ray Bradbury supposedly puts each manuscript away for a year to the day and then rereads it as a stranger. Not many writers have the discipline or the time to do this. We must read when our judgment may be at its worst, when we are close to the euphoric moment of creation.

Then the writer, counsels novelist Nancy Hale, "should be critical of everything that seems to him most delightful in his style. He should excise what he most admires, because he wouldn't thus admire it if he weren't . . . in a sense protecting it from criticism." John Ciardi, the poet, adds, "The last act of the writing must be to become one's own reader. It is, I suppose, a schizophrenic process, to begin passionately and to end critically, to begin hot and to end cold; and, more important, to be passion-hot and critic-cold at the same time."

Most people think that the principal problem is that writers are too proud of what they have written. Actually, a greater problem for most professional writers is one shared by the majority of students. They are overly critical, think everything is dreadful, tear up page after page, never complete a draft, see the task as hopeless.

The writer must learn to read critically but constructively, to cut what is bad, to reveal what is good. Eleanor Estes, the children's book author, explains: "The writer must survey his work critically, coolly, as though he were a stranger to it. He must be willing to prune, expertly and hard-heartedly. At the end of each revision, a manuscript may look . . . worked over, torn apart, pinned together, added to, deleted from, words changed and words changed back. Yet the book must maintain its original freshness and spontaneity."

Most readers underestimate the amount of rewriting it usually takes to produce spontaneous reading. This is a great disadvantage to the student writer, who sees only a finished product and never watches the craftsman who takes the necessary step back, studies the work carefully, returns to the task, steps back, returns, steps back, again and again. Anthony Burgess, one of the most prolific writers in the English-speaking world, admits, "I might revise a page twenty times." Roald Dahl, the popular children's writer, states, "By the time I'm nearing the end of a story, the first part will have been reread and altered and corrected at least 150 times. . . . Good writing is essentially rewriting. I am positive of this."

Rewriting isn't virtuous. It isn't something that ought to be done. It is simply something that most writers find they have to do to discover what they have to say and how to say it. It is a condition of the writer's life.

There are, however, a few writers who do little formal rewriting, primarily because they have the capacity and experience to create and review a large number of invisible drafts in their minds before they approach the page. And some writers slowly produce finished pages, performing all the tasks of revision simultaneously, page by page, rather than draft by draft. But it is still possible to see the sequence followed by most writers most of the time in rereading their own work.

Most writers scan their drafts first, reading as quickly as possible to catch the larger problems of subject and form, and then move in closer and closer as they read and write, reread and rewrite.

The first thing writers look for in their drafts is *information*. They know that a good piece of writing is built from specific, accurate, and interesting information. The writer must have an abundance of information from which to construct a readable piece of writing.

Next writers look for *meaning* in the information. The specifics must build to a pattern of significance. Each piece of specific information must carry the reader toward meaning.

Writers reading their own drafts are aware of *audience*. They put themselves in the reader's situation and make sure that they deliver information which a reader wants to know or needs to know in a manner which is easily digested. Writers try to be sure that they anticipate and answer the questions a critical reader will ask when reading the piece of writing.

Writers make sure that the *form* is appropriate to the subject and the audience. Form, or genre, is the vehicle which carries meaning to the reader, but form cannot be selected until the writer has adequate information to discover its significance and an audience which needs or wants that meaning.

Once writers are sure the form is appropriate, they must then look at the *structure,* the order of what they have written. Good writing is built on a solid framework of logic, argument, narrative, or motivation which runs through the entire piece of writing and holds it together. This is the time when many writers find it most effective to outline as a way of visualizing the hidden spine by which the piece of writing is supported.

The element on which writers spend a majority of their time is *development*. Each section of a piece of writing must be adequately developed. It must give readers enough information so that they are satisfied. How much information is enough? That's as difficult as asking how much garlic belongs in a salad. It must be done to taste, but most beginning writers underdevelop, underestimating the reader's hunger for more information.

As writers solve development problems, they often have to consider questions of *dimension*. There must be a pleasing and effective proportion among all the parts of the piece of writing. There is a continual process of subtracting and adding to keep the piece of writing in balance.

Finally, writers have to listen to their own voices. *Voice* is the force which drives a piece of writing forward. It is an expression of the writer's authority and concern. It is what is between the words on the page, what glues the piece of writing together. A good piece of writing is always marked by a consistent, individual voice.

As writers read and reread, write and rewrite, they move closer and closer to the page until they are doing line-by-line editing. Writers read their own pages with infinite care. Each sentence, each line, each clause, each phrase, each word, each mark of punctuation, each section of white space between the type has to contribute to the clarification of meaning.

Slowly the writer moves from word to word, looking through language to see the subject. As a word is changed, cut or added, as a construction is rearranged, all the words used before that moment and all those that follow that moment must be considered and reconsidered.

Writers often read aloud at this stage of the editing process, muttering or whispering to themselves, calling on the ear's experience with language. Does this sound right—or that? Writers edit, shifting back and forth from eye to page to ear to page. I find I must do this careful editing in short runs, no more than fifteen or twenty minutes at a stretch, or I become too kind with myself. I begin to see what I hope is on the page, not what actually is on the page.

This sounds tedious if you haven't done it, but actually it is fun. Making something right is immensely satisfying, for writers begin to learn what they are writing about by writing. Language leads them to meaning, and there is the joy of discovery, of understanding, of making meaning clear as the writer employs the technical skills of language.

Words have double meanings, even triple and quadruple meanings. Each word has its own potential of connotation and denotation. And when writers rub one word against the other, they are often rewarded with a sudden insight, an unexpected clarification.

The maker's eye moves back and forth from word to phrase to sentence to paragraph to sentence to phrase to word. The maker's eye sees the need for variety and balance, for a firmer structure, for a more appropriate form. It peers into the interior of the paragraph, looking for coherence, unity, and emphasis, which make meaning clear.

I learned something about this process when my first bifocals were prescribed. I had ordered a larger section of the reading portion of the glass because of my work, but even so, I could not contain my eyes within this new limit of vision. And I still find myself taking off my glasses and bending my nose toward the page, for my eyes unconsciously flick back and forth across the page, back to another page, forward to still another, as I try to see each evolving line in relation to every other line.

When does this process end? Most writers agree with the great Russian writer Tolstoy, who said, "I scarcely ever reread my published writings, if by chance I come across a page, it always strikes me: all this must be rewritten; this is how I should have written it."

The maker's eye is never satisfied, for each word has the potential to ignite new meaning. This article has been twice written all the way through the writing process [. . .]. Now it is to be republished in a book. The editors made a few small suggestions, and then I read it with my maker's eye. Now it has been re-edited, re-revised, re-read, and re-re-edited, for each piece of writing to the writer is full of potential and alternatives.

A piece of writing is never finished. It is delivered to a deadline, torn out of the typewriter on demand, sent off with a sense of accomplishment and shame and pride and frustration. If only there were a couple more days, time for just another run at it, perhaps then . . .

■ ■ ■   **FOR CLASS DISCUSSION**

1. How does Murray define *information* and meaning? Why is the distinction be-
    tween the two terms important?
2. According to Murray, at what point(s) in the writing process do writers become
    concerned about the individual words they are using? What do you think Murray
    means when he says that "language leads [writers] to meaning"?
3. The phrase "the maker's eye" appears in Murray's title and in several places
    throughout the essay. What do you suppose he means by this? Consider how the
    maker's eye could be different from the reader's eye.
4. According to Murray, when is a piece of writing finished? What, for him, is the
    function of deadlines?   ■ ■ ■

Making Meaning Clear: The Logic of Revision

by Donald M. Murray

Donald M. Murray. Professor of English at the University of New Hampshire and a Pulitzer Prize editorial writer, has been director of freshman English and now supervises a university-wide composition course. He is the author of A Writer Teaches Writing *as well as articles, poems, novels, and juvenile nonfiction books. He was writing consultant to the Boston* Globe *and is consultant to the Providence* Journal-Bulletin, *the* News Observer *and the Raleigh* Times, *and other newspapers.*

The writer's meaning rarely arrives by room-service, all neatly laid out on the tray. Meaning is usually discovered and clarified as the writer makes hundreds of small decisions, each one igniting a sequence of consideration and reconsideration.

Revision is not just clarifying meaning, it is discovering meaning and clarifying it while it is being discovered. That makes revision a far more complicated process than is usually thought—and a far simpler process at the same time.

It is complicated because the writer cannot just go to the rule book. Revision is not a matter of correctness, following the directions in a manual. The writer has to go back again and again and again to consider what the writing means and if the writer can accept, document, and communicate that meaning. In other words, writing is not what the writer does after the thinking is done; writing is thinking.

This also makes revision simpler. There is a logic to the process. The writer needs only a draft, a pen, and a brain. Each editorial act must relate to meaning. That is the primary consideration that rules each editorial decision. Considerations of audience, structure, tone, pace, usage, mechanics, typography are primarily decided on one issue: do they make the meaning clear?

The process of revision—what the reviser does—is fairly simple. The writer cuts, adds, reorders, or starts over. Each of these acts fits into a sequence most of the time. The writer solves the problems of meaning, and those solutions make it possible to solve the problems of order, and those solutions make it possible to solve the problems of voice.

Unfortunately, many teachers—and, I have discovered recently, many newspaper editors—do not understand the logic of revision and, therefore, do not encourage or even allow revision. They pounce on first draft writing and make corrections.

Since most writers have not discovered their meaning in their first draft, the corrections editors make must come from the editors' own preconception of what the writing should mean. It comes from the editors' own experience, their own research, their own prejudices. They work in ignorance of the writer's intentions and take the writing away from the writer.

When editors or teachers kidnap the first draft, they also remove the responsibility for making meaning from the writer. Writing becomes trivialized, unchallenging, unauthoritative, impersonal, unimportant.

Hemingway told us, "Prose is architecture, not interior decoration...." Premature correction by a teacher or an editor must focus mainly on the decoration, the cosmetics of writing. Of course, writers must spell correctly, must follow the conventions of language that make meaning clear. But the writer must do it in relation to the writer's meaning through the medium of the writer's own voice. Writing is too important to be corrected by the book; it must be corrected in relation to meaning.

When revision is encouraged, not as a punishment but as a natural process in the exploration of the text to discover meaning, then many basic writers become motivated to revise. It is a slow but miraculous process. The basic writers spot a hint of meaning that surprises them. Usually the meaning is in a primitive form at the time it is first shared with a teacher or fellow student. Basic writers are urged on. Soon they do not revise to become correct, they revise to discover their individual meaning, to hear their own voices making those meanings clear, and to hear their readers' delight as an unexpected meaning is recognized as true.

The making of meaning through revision is a logical craft. Once a student has made meaning, the process can be repeated. It is not an act of magic anymore than magic acts are; it is a matter of tuning an engine, kneading dough, sewing a dress, building a shelf. The act of revision allows the writer to take something that was not and make it something that is; it allows the writer to achieve the satisfaction of completion, closure.

Revision can be the most satisfying part of teaching composition if the teacher is willing to let go. The composition teacher must wean the student. The teacher must give the responsibility for the text to the writer, making clear again and again that it is the student, not the teacher, who decides what the writing means.

The best way for teachers to reveal exploration in revision is by writing in public on the blackboard, or by using an overhead projector, allowing the students to see how writing struggles to find what it has to say. The teacher should not consciously write badly; the teacher should write as well as possible. That will produce copy that is quite bad enough to deserve revision.

The teacher who writes in public will expose the fact that writing often does not come clear; in fact, syntax often breaks down just at the point where a new or significant meaning is beginning to break out of its shell. That meaning has an awkward and clumsy time of it, but if the writer listens carefully and nurtures the meaning, it may grow into significance. Or it may not. It may have to be put aside. But first it has to be understood before it can be rejected. Teachers who are willing to share evolving writing will find their class willing to share in a workshop where everyone is trying to help the writer discover and clarify the evolving meaning.

I have internalized a checklist that follows the logic of revision. It may be helpful to consider this checklist, but each teacher should work to develop a new checklist with each class. Neither my checklist nor anyone else's checklist should be taken as gospel. The checklist should be formulated while the class experiences the process of making meaning clear.

The principles that underlie my checklist are:

- *Build on strength*. The writer searches the text for the meaning that is being developed by the writing and looks for what is working to make it work better. Revising is not so much a matter of correction as it is a matter of discovering the strength of the text and extending that strength.
- *Cut what can be cut*. An effective piece of writing has a single dominant meaning, and everything in the text must advance that meaning.
- *Simplicity is best*. This does not mean writing in pidgin English, merely sending a telegram to the reader. It does mean making the writing as simple as it can be for what is being said. The message may be complex, and that may require linguistic or rhetorical complexity, but that complexity should always be the simplest way to communicate the complexity.
- *The writing will tell you how to write*. In revising I do not look to rule books, to models from other writers, to what I have written before, or how I have written it. The answers to the problems of this piece of writing lie in the evolving text. I have faith that if I read carefully—if I listen to my own developing voice—I will discover what I have to say.

My checklist requires at least three different kinds of reading—for focus, form and voice. This does not mean that I read the text three times; it is possible that the readings overlap and I read it only a couple of times. Most times I read it many more times. There is no ideal number of readings. I read it enough times to discover what I have to say.

During each of the readings I keep my eye and my ear on the single dominant meaning that is evolving from the text. A good piece of writing, I believe, says only one thing. Or to put it in a different way, the many things that are said in a piece of writing all add up to a single meaning.

Here is my internal checklist articulated:

Focus. First I read the text as fast as possible, trying to keep my pen capped, trying to see it from a distance the way the reader will so I can ask myself the larger questions of content and meaning. I do not do this "first" reading, of course, until I have the meaning of the writing in mind. In other words, I have to have a focus before I can work on *the* focus. If, in each stage of the reading, the meaning does not become clearer and clearer, I go back and discover a potential meaning that can be brought into focus. The questions I ask are:

- *What does the piece of writing mean?* If it is not clear, I will take the time to write a sentence that makes the meaning clear, that achieves what Virginia Woolf calls, "the power of combination," that contains the tensions within the piece of writing in a single statement.
- *Are all the reader's questions answered?* Many times I will brainstorm the questions that the reader will inevitably ask of the text.

- *Is new information needed?*
- *Is the piece built on undocumented assumptions?* Sometimes I will actually write down my assumptions to see if they make sense or stand up as a firm foundation for the piece.
- *Is the genre appropriate to the meaning?* One of my novels started out as a series of articles. By genre I mean fiction, poetry, or the larger categories of non-fiction—personal narrative, familiar essay, argument, exposition.
- *Are there any tangents that can be cut loose?* I used to have much more trouble getting rid of those wonderful pieces of evidence or examples of writing that really did not relate to the meaning. Hannah Lees taught me how to solve this problem. For years I wrote one paragraph to a page, then played solitaire with these paragraphs, arranging and re-arranging them until they made a single meaning.
- *Is there a section that should be a separate piece of writing?*
- *Is each point supported by convincing evidence?* Sometimes I actually role-play a reader. It is always a specific person I know who does not agree with me and who I believe does not like me. I want to confront my enemies and defeat them before the writing is published.
- *Is the piece long enough to satisfy the reader?* Most writers underwrite, and I am no exception. The tendency is to say it and not to give the reader enough room for the reader to discover the meaning.
- *Is the piece short enough to keep the reader involved?* The piece of writing must develop its own energy, its own momentum. If my mind wanders during this first quick reading, the reader's certainly will.

Form. Next, I read the text again, a bit more slowly, only uncapping my pen when a marginal note is necessary, trying to look at the text as a sequence of chunks of writing, perhaps chunks of meaning. I am no longer looking at the text as a whole, although I am aware of the territory now, and I am trying to keep myself free of the concern with detail, for a premature involvement with the details of language may keep me from evaluating the questions of form. The questions I ask are:

- *Is the title on target?* Years ago when I could put my own heads on editorials, I found that the effort to write a title is worth the trouble. I may draft as many as a hundred titles, for each one is a way of discovering meaning, and I can draft a number of titles in almost slivers of time. At this stage of the revision process I check to make sure that the title relates to the meaning as that meaning has now evolved.
- *Does the lead catch the reader in three seconds—or less?* I hear rumors of good pieces of writing that have poor leads or beginnings, but I have not been able to find any from professional writers. The first few lines of a piece of writing establish the tone, the voice, the direction, the pace, the meaning. I check once more to make sure that the lead will entice the reader.
- *Does the lead deliver on its contract with the reader?* The lead must be honest. It must relate to the meaning that will evolve through the text.
- *Does the piece answer the reader's questions at the point the reader will ask them?* This is the key to effective organization. Again and again I will ask the questions the reader will ask, even if they are the questions I do not want the reader to ask,

and then number them in the order the reader will ask them. A good piece of writing does not need transitional phrases. The information arrives when the reader can use it. The reader's questions and their order can be anticipated.

■ *How can I get out of the way of the reader and show rather than tell?* Orwell instructed writers that they should be like a pane of glass through which the reader sees the subject. I do not want the reader to be impressed with my writing; my arrogance is greater than that. I want the reader to receive the evidence in such a direct fashion that it will cause the reader to think the way I want the reader to think. I want to show so effectively that the reader will see my meaning as inevitable.

■ *Is there an effective variety of documentation?* Most of us fall into a pattern using quotations, citations, anecdotes, statistics, personal experience—whatever we feel comfortable using or whatever we think we do well. The documentation, of course, should be what works best for the point being documented.

■ *Does the pace reinforce the meaning?* The reader should be allowed to absorb each point before moving on to the next one. I tend to write and to teach too intensively; I have to remember to give the reader room.

■ *Does the pace provide the energy to carry the reader forward?*

■ *Are the dimensions appropriate to the meaning?* The size of each section should be in proportion to other sections.

■ *Does the end echo the lead and fulfill its promise?*

Voice. At last, I read the text slowly, line by line, my pen uncapped. I usually read the text many times within this category, generally working from the larger issue of voice down to paragraphs to sentences to phrases to single words. This is the most satisfying part of revision. There is a single meaning. It will change and develop and become clearer, but there is a focus, there is an order, and there is the chance to work with language, to combine my voice with the voice that is evolving from the draft. The questions I then ask are:

■ *Can the piece be read aloud?* Does it sound as if one person is talking to one person? Reading is a private experience, a human contact from one single person to another single person. I think that effective writing should be conversational. Sometimes the conversation is more formal than others, but it should never be stuffy, pretentious, or incapable of being read aloud by the writer.

■ *Are important pieces of specific information at the ends and beginnings of key sentences, paragraphs, sections, and the entire piece itself?* The 2-3-1 principle of emphasis can do as much as anything else to sharpen up prose and make meaning clear: the second most important point of emphasis is at the beginning; the least important piece of emphasis is at the middle, and the greatest point of emphasis is at the end.

■ *Does each paragraph make one point?*

■ *Does each paragraph carry a full load of meaning to the reader?*

■ *Do the paragraphs vary in length in relation to meaning—the shorter the more important the information?*

■ *Are the paragraphs in order?* If the reader's questions are answered when they will be asked, formal transitions will not be needed.

- *Does the reader leave each sentence with more information than the reader entered it?*
- *Are there sentences that announce what will be said or sum up what has been said and, therefore, can be cut?*
- *Are most sentences subject-verb-object sentences?* At least most sentences that carry the essence of meaning should be direct sentences. The interesting work done in sentence-combining has too often confused this issue. Of course sentences should be combined, but the strength and vigor of the language still lies in simple, direct subject-verb-object sentences. These are the sentences, short and to the point, that will communicate.
- *Are there clauses that get in the way of meaning?* Many sentences have to be reordered so that the meaning comes clear. This usually means that sentences have to be read aloud again and again until the information in the sentence appears at the moment that the reader can use it.
- *Are the verbs active and strong enough to drive the meaning forward?* The verbs are the engines of meaning, and during revision the writer must give priority to finding verbs that are accurate and provide energy.
- *Has the right word been found?* Many times we try to use two almost right words in the hope that we will trap the meaning between them. That does not work. Mark Twain said, "The difference between the right word and the almost-right word is the difference between lightning and a lightning-bug." He was right. Revision is the search for the exactly right word.
- *Does the meaning depend on verbs and nouns, not adverbs and adjectives?* The right word is rarely an adjective or an adverb. Again, the meaning is not caught best in the crush between adjective and noun, or adverb and verb. I always feel a tiny sense of failure when I use an adjective or an adverb. I have failed to find the right noun or the right verb.
- *Is there sexist or racist language that should be changed?*
- *Can the writing be more specific?*
- *Are there unnecessary -lys, -ings, thats, and woulds that should be cut?* Each writer must develop a list of linguistic interferences with meaning. I find when I do professional ghost-editing that merely cutting the *-lys*, the *-ings*, the *thats*, the *woulds*—and yes, the unnecessary verb *be*—will make an obscure text start to come clear.
- *Is every fact checked?*
- *Is every word spelled correctly?*
- *Is there anything I can do to make the writing simple? clear? graceful? accurate? fair?*

Do I formally ask all of these questions of myself in every piece of writing I do? Of course not. These concerns are internalized, and they overlap. The process is recursive. I discover meaning by language. I work back and forth from meaning to focus to form to voice and from voice to form to focus to meaning.

The process is, however, logical. Everything on the page must reveal meaning. Every word, every space between words, is put on the page or left on the page because it develops the meaning of the piece of writing.

This checklist cannot be dumped on the beginning or the remedial writer, but it can be used by the teacher to establish priorities. The student has to learn that writing is a search for meaning, and once a potential meaning is found, it may be clarified through the process of revision.

There is a simple guiding logic to revision, and every question of spelling, usage, structure, mechanics, style, content, documentation, voice, pace, development, must be answered in terms of meaning.

Think of a workman who moves in close, measuring, marking, sawing, fitting, standing back to examine the job, moving back in close to plane, chisel, mark and fit, standing back again to study the task, moving in close to nail the piece in place, stepping back for another look, moving in close to set the nails, another step back, another look, then in close to hide the nail holes, to sand, stepping back to make sure the sanding is complete, then in close at last to apply the finish.

Actually the workman probably moved in close many more times before finishing the task and certainly stepped back many times to see the job entire. And so does the writer, working between word and meaning.

What the student can discover is that this process is logical; it can be understood. An effective piece of writing is produced by a craft. It is simply a matter of working back and forth between focus, form, and voice until the meaning is discovered and made clear.

When We Dead Awaken: Writing as Re-Vision

35

by Adrienne Rich

Ibsen's "When We Dead Awaken" is a play about the use that the male artist and thinker—in the process of creating culture as we know it—has made of women, in his life and in his work; and about a woman's slow struggling awakening to the use to which her life has been put. Bernard Shaw wrote in 1900 of this play:

> [Ibsen] shows us that no degradation ever devized or permitted is as disastrous as this degradation; that through it women can die into luxuries for men and yet can kill them; that men and women are becoming conscious of this; and that what remains to be seen as perhaps the most interesting of all imminent social developments is what will happen "when we dead awaken".[1]

It's exhilarating to be alive in a time of awakening consciousness; it can also be confusing, disorienting, and painful. This awakening of dead or sleeping consciousness has already affected the lives of millions of women, even those who don't know it yet. It is also affecting the lives of men, even those who deny its claims upon them. The argument will go on whether an oppressive economic class system is responsible for the oppressive nature of male/female relations, or whether, in fact, the sexual class system is the original model on which all the others are based. But in the last few years connections have been drawn between our sexual lives and our political institutions, which are inescapable and illuminating. The sleepwalkers are coming awake, and for the first time this awakening has a collective reality; it is no longer such a lonely thing to open one's eyes.

Re-vision—the act of looking back, of seeing with fresh eyes, of entering an old text from a new critical direction—is for us more than a chapter in cultural history: it is an act of survival. Until we can understand the assumptions in which we are drenched we cannot know ourselves. And this drive to self-knowledge, for woman, is more than a search for identity: it is part of her refusal of the self-destructiveness of male-dominated society. A radical critique of literature, feminist in its impulse, would take the work first of all as a clue to how we live, how we have been living, how we have been led to imagine ourselves, how our language has trapped as well as liberated us; and how we can begin to see—and therefore live—afresh. A change in the concept of sexual identity is essential if we are not going to see the old political order re-assert itself in every new revolution. We need to know the writing of the past, and know it differently than we have ever known it; not to pass on a tradition but to break its hold over us.

For writers, and at this moment for women writers in particular, there is the challenge and promise of a whole new psychic geography to be explored. But there is also a difficult and dangerous walking on the ice, as we try to find language and images for a consciousness we are just coming into, and with little in the past to support us. I want to talk about some aspects of this difficulty and this danger.

Jane Harrison, the great classical anthropologist, wrote in 1914 in a letter to her friend Gilbert Murray:

> By the by, about "Women," it has bothered me often—why do women never want to write poetry about Man as a sex—why is Woman a dream and a terror to man and not the other way around? . . . Is it mere convention and propriety, or something deeper?[2]

I think Jane Harrison's question cuts deep into the myth-making tradition, the romantic tradition; deep into what women and men have been to each other; and deep into the psyche of the woman writer. Thinking about that question, I began thinking of the work of two 20th-century women poets, Sylvia Plath and Diane Wakoski. It strikes me that in the work of both Man appears as, if not a dream, a fascination and a terror; and that the source of the fascination and the terror is, simply, Man's power—to dominate, tyrannize, choose, or reject the woman. The charisma of Man seems to come purely from his power over her and his control of the world by force, not from anything fertile or life-giving in him. And, in the work of both these poets, it is finally the woman's sense of *herself*—embattled, possessed—that gives the poetry its dynamic charge, its rhythms of struggle, need, will, and female energy. Convention and propriety are perhaps not the right words, but until recently this female anger and this furious awareness of the Man's power over her were not available materials to the female poet, who tended to write of Love as the source of her suffering, and to view that victimization by Love as an almost inevitable fate. Or, like Marianne Moore and Elizabeth Bishop, she kept human sexual relationships at a measured and chiselled distance in her poems.

One answer to Jane Harrison's question has to be that historically men and women have played very different parts in each others' lives. Where woman has been a luxury for man, and has served as the painter's model and the poet's muse, but also as comforter, nurse, cook, bearer of his seed, secretarial assistant and copyist of manuscripts, man has played a quite different role for the female artist. Henry James repeats an incident which the writer Prosper Merimee described, of how, while he was living with George Sand,

> he once opened his eyes, in the raw winter dawn, to see his companion, in a dressing-gown, on her knees before the domestic hearth, a candlestick beside her and a red *madras* round her head, making bravely, with her own hands, the fire that was to enable her to sit down betimes to urgent pen and paper. The story represents him as having felt that the spectacle chilled his ardor and tried his taste; her appearance was unfortunate, her occupation an inconsequence, and her industry a reproof-the result of all of which was a lively irritation and an early rupture."[3]

I am suggesting that the specter of this kind of male judgment, along with the active discouragement and thwarting of her needs by a culture controlled by males, has created problems for the woman writer: problems of contact with her-self, problems of language and style, problems of energy and survival.

In rereading Virginia Woolf's *A Room Of One's Own* for the first time in some years, I was astonished at the sense of effort, of pains taken, of dogged tentative-ness, in the tone of that essay. And I recognized that tone. I had heard it often enough, in myself and in other women. It is the tone of a woman almost in touch with her anger, who is determined not to appear angry, who is *willing* herself to be calm, detached, and even charming in a roomful of men where things have been said which are attacks on her very integrity. Virginia Woolf is addressing an audience of women, but she is acutely conscious—as she always was—of being over-heard by men: by Morgan and Lytton and Maynard Keynes and for that matter by her father, Leslie Stephen. She drew the language out into an exacerbated thread in her determination to have her own sensibility yet protect it from those masculine presences. Only at rare moments in that essay do you hear the passion in her voice; she was trying to sound as cool as Jane Austen, as Olympian as Shakespeare, because that is the way the men of the culture thought a writer should sound.

No male writer has written primarily or even largely for women, or with the sense of women's criticism as a consideration when he chooses his materials, his theme, his language. But to a lesser or greater extent, every woman writer has written for men even when, like Virginia Woolf, she was supposed to be addressing women. If we have come to the point when this balance might begin to change, when women can stop being haunted, not only by "convention and propriety" but by internalized fears of being and saying themselves, then it is an extraordinary moment for the woman writer—and reader.

I have hesitated to do what I am going to do now, which is to use myself as an illustration. For one thing, it's a lot easier and less dangerous to talk about other women writers. But there is something else. Like Virginia Woolf, I am aware of the women who are not with us here because they are washing the dishes and looking after the children. Nearly fifty years after she spoke, that fact remains largely unchanged. And I am thinking also of women whom she left out of the picture altogether—women who are washing other people's dishes and caring for other people's children, not to mention women who went on the streets last night in order to feed their children. We seem to be special women here, we have liked to think of ourselves as special, and we have known that men would tolerate, even romanticize us as special, as long as our words and actions didn't threaten their privilege of tolerating or rejecting us according to *their* ideas of what a special woman ought to be. An important insight of the radical women's movement, for me, has been how divisive and how ultimately destructive is this myth of the special woman, who is also the token woman. Every one of us here in this room has had great luck—we are teachers, writers, academicians; our own gifts could not have been enough, for we all know women whose gifts are buried or aborted. Our struggles can have meaning only if they can help to change the lives of women whose gifts—and whose very being—continue to be thwarted.

My own luck was being born white and middle-class into a house full of books, with a father who encouraged me to read and write. So for about twenty years I wrote for a particular man, who criticized and praised me and made me feel I was indeed "special." The obverse side of this, of course, was that I tried for a long time to please him, or rather, not to displease him. And then of course there were other men—writers, teachers—the Man, who was not a terror or a dream but a literary master and a master in other ways less easy to acknowledge. And there were all those poems about women, written by men: it seemed to be a given that men wrote poems and women frequently inhabited them. These women were almost always beautiful, but threatened with the loss of beauty, the loss of youth—the fate worse than death. Or, they were beautiful and died young, like Lucy and Lenore. Or, the woman was like Maud Gonne, cruel and disastrously mistaken, and the poem reproached her because she had refused to become a luxury for the poet.

A lot is being said today about the influence that the myths and images of women have on all of us who are products of culture. I think it has been a peculiar con-fusion to the girl or woman who tries to write because she is peculiarly susceptible to language. She goes to poetry or fiction looking for *her* way of being in the world, since she too has been putting words and images together; she is looking eagerly for guides, maps pos-sibilities; and over and over in the "words' masculine persuasive force" of literature she comes up against something that negates everything she is about: she meets the image of Woman in books written by men. She finds a terror and a dream, she finds a beauti-ful pale face, she finds La Belle Dame Sans Merci, she finds Juliet or Tess or Salomé, but precisely what she does not find is that absorbed, drudging, puzzled, sometimes inspired creature, herself, who sits at a desk trying to put words together.

So what does she do? What did I do? I read the older women poets with their pecu-liar keenness and ambivalence: Sappho, Christina Rossetti, Emily Dickinson, Elinor Wylie, Edna Millay, H.D. I discovered that the woman poet most admired at the time (by men) was Marianne Moore, who was maidenly, elegant, intellectual, discreet. But even in reading these women I was looking in them for the same things I had found in the poetry of men, because I wanted women poets to be the equals of men, and to be equal was still confused with sounding the same.

I know that my style was formed first by male poets: by the men I was reading as an undergraduate—Frost, Dylan Thomas, Donne, Auden, MacNiece, Stevens, Yeats. What I chiefly learned from them was craft. But poems are like dreams: in them you put what you don't know you know. Looking back at poems I wrote before I was 21, I'm startled because beneath the conscious craft are glimpses of the split I even then experienced between the girl who wrote poems, who defined herself in writing poems, and the girl who was to define herself by her relation-ships with men. "Aunt Jennifer's Tigers," written while I was a student, looks with deliberate detachment at this split.

Aunt Jennifer's tigers stride across a screen,
Bright topaz denizens of a world of green.
They do not fear the men beneath the tree;
They pace in sleek chivalric certainty.

Aunt Jennifer's fingers fluttering through her wool
Find even the ivory needle hard to pull.
The massive weight of Uncle's wedding band
Sits heavily upon Aunt Jennifer's hand.

When Aunt is dead, her terrified hands will lie
Still ringed with ordeals she was mastered by.
The tigers in the panel that she made
Will go on striding, proud and unafraid.[4]

In writing this poem, composed and apparently cool as it is, I thought I was creating a portrait of an imaginary woman. But this woman suffers from the opposition of her imagination, worked out in tapestry, and her life-style, "ringed with ordeals she was mastered by." It was important to me that Aunt Jennifer was a person as distinct from myself as possible—distanced by the formalism of the poem, by its objective, observant tone—even by putting the woman in a different generation.

In those years formalism was part of the strategy—like asbestos gloves, it allowed me to handle materials I couldn't pick up barehanded. (A later strategy was to use the persona of a man, as I did in "The Loser.") I finished college, published my first book by a fluke, as it seemed to me, and broke off a love affair. I took a job, lived alone, went on writing, fell in love. I was young, full of energy, and the book seemed to mean that others agreed I was a poet. Because I was also deter-mined to have a "full" woman's life, I plunged in my early twenties into marriage and had three children before I was thirty. There was nothing overt in the environment to warn me: these were the '50's, and in reaction to the earlier wave of feminism, middle-class women were making careers of domestic perfection, working to send their husbands through professional schools, then retiring to raise large families. People were moving out to the suburbs, technology was going to be the answer to everything, even sex; the family was in its glory. Life was extremely private; women were isolated from each other by the loyalties of marriage. I have a sense that women didn't talk to each other much in the fifties—not about their secret emptinesses, their frustrations. I went on trying to write; my second book and first child appeared in the same month. But by the time that book came out I was already dissatisfied with those poems, which seemed to me mere exercises for poems I hadn't written. The book was praised, however, for its "gracefulness"; I had a marriage and a child. If there were doubts, if there were periods of null depression or active despairing, these could only mean that I was ungrateful, insatiable, perhaps a monster.

About the time my third child was born, I felt that I had either to consider myself a failed woman and a failed poet, or to try to find some synthesis by which to understand what was happening to me. What frightened me most was the sense of drift, of being pulled along on a current which called itself my destiny, but in which I seemed to be losing touch with whoever I had been, with the girl who had experienced her own will and energy almost ecstatically at times, walking around a city or riding a train at night or typing in a student room. In a poem about my grandmother I wrote (of myself): "A young girl, thought sleeping, is certified dead."[5] I was writing very little, partly from fatigue, that female fatigue of suppressed anger and the loss of contact with her own being; partly from the discontinuity of female life with its attention to small chores, errands, work that others constantly undo, small children's constant needs. What I did write was unconvincing to me; my anger and frustration were hard to acknowledge in or out of poems because in fact I cared a great deal about my husband and my children. Trying to look back and understand that time I have tried to analyze the real nature of the conflict. Most, if not all, human lives are full of fantasy—passive day-dreaming which need not be acted on. But to write poetry or fiction, or even to think well, is not to fantasize, or to put fantasies on paper. For a poem to coalesce, for a character or an action to take shape, there has to be an imaginative transformation of reality which is in no way passive. And a certain freedom of the mind is needed—freedom to press on, to enter the currents of your thought like a glider pilot, knowing that your motion can be sustained, that the buoyancy of your attention will not be suddenly snatched away. Moreover, if the imagination is to transcend and transform experience it has to question, to challenge, to conceive of alternatives, perhaps to the very life you are living at that moment. You have to be free to play around with the notion that day might be night, love might be hate; nothing can be too sacred for the imagination to turn into its opposite or to call experimentally by another name. For writing is re-naming. Now, to be maternally with small children all day in the old way, to be with a man in the old way of marriage, requires a holding-back, a putting-aside of that imaginative activity, and seems to demand instead a kind of conservatism. I want to make it clear that I am *not* saying that in order to write well, or think well, it is necessary to become unavailable to others, or to become a devouring ego. This has been the myth of the masculine artist and thinker; and I repeat, I do not accept it. But to be a female human being trying to fulfill traditional female functions in a traditional way is in direct conflict with the subversive function of the imagination. The word traditional is important here. There must be ways, and we will be finding out more and more about them, in which the energy of creation and the energy of relation can be united. But in those earlier years I always felt the conflict as a failure of love in myself. I had thought I was choosing a full life: the life available to most men, in which sexuality, work, and parenthood could coexist. But I felt, at 29, guilt toward the people closest to me, and guilty toward my own being.

I wanted, then, more than anything, the one thing of which there was never enough: time to think, time to write. The fifties and early sixties were years of rapid revelations: the sit-ins and marches in the South, the Bay of Pigs, the early anti-war movement, raised large questions—questions for which the masculine world of the academy around me seemed to have expert and fluent answers. But I needed desperately to think for myself—about pacifism and dissent and violence, about poetry and society and about my own relationship to all these things. For about ten years I was reading in fierce snatches, scribbling in notebooks, writing poetry in fragments; I was looking desperately for clues, because if there were no clues than I thought I might be insane. I wrote in a notebook about this time:

> Paralyzed by the sense that there exists a mesh of relationships—e.g. between my anger at the children, my sensual life, pacifism, sex, (I mean sex in its broadest significance, not merely sexual desire)—an interconnectedness which, if I could see it, make it valid, would give me back myself, make it possible to function lucidly and passionately. Yet I grope in and out among these dark webs.

I think I began at this point to feel that politics was not something: "out there" but something "in here" and of the essence of my condition.

In the late '50's I was able to write, for the first time, directly about experiencing myself as a woman. The poem was jotted in fragments during children's naps, brief hours in a library, or at 3 a.m. after rising with a wakeful child. I despaired of doing any continuous work at this time. Yet I began to feel that my fragments and scraps had a common consciousness and a common theme, one which I would have been very unwilling to put on paper at an earlier time because I had been taught that poetry should be "universal," which meant, of course, non-female. Until then I had tried very much *not* to identify myself as a female poet. Over two years I wrote a 10-part poem called "Snapshots of a Daughter-in-Law," in a longer, looser mode than I'd ever trusted myself with before. It was an extraordinary relief to write that poem. It strikes me now as too literary, too dependent on allusion; I hadn't found the courage yet to do without authorities, or even to use the pronoun "I"—the woman in the poem is always "she." One section of it, No. 2, concerns a woman who thinks she is going mad; she is haunted by voices telling her to resist and rebel, voices which she can hear but not obey.

The poem "Orion," written five years later, is a poem of reconnection with a part of myself I had felt I was losing—the active principle, the energetic imagination, the "half-brother" whom I projected, as I had for many years, into the constellation Orion. It's no accident that the words "cold and egotistical" appear in this poem, and are applied to myself. The choice still seemed to be between "love"—womanly, maternal love, altruistic love—a love defined and ruled by the weight of an entire culture; and egotism—a force directed by men into creation, achievement, ambition, often at the expense of others, but justifiably so. For weren't they men, and wasn't that their destiny as womanly love was ours? I know now that the alternatives are false ones-that the word "love" is itself in need of re-vision.

There is a companion poem to "Orion," written three years later, in which at last the woman in the poem and the woman writing the poem become the same person. It is called "Planetarium," and it was written after a visit to a real planetarium, where I read an account of the work of Caroline Herschel, the astronomer, who worked with her brother William, but whose name remained obscure, as his did not.

In closing I want to tell you about a dream I had last summer. I dreamed I was asked to read my poetry at a mass women's meeting, but when I began to read, what came out were the lyrics of a blues song. I share this dream with you because it seemed to me to say a lot about the problems and the future of the woman writer, and probably of women in general. The awakening of consciousness is not like the crossing of a frontier—one step, and you are in another country. Much of woman's poetry has been of the nature of the blues song: a cry of pain, of victimization, or a lyric of seduction. And today, much poetry by women—and prose for that matter—is charged with anger. I think we need to go through that anger, and we will betray our own reality if we try, as Virginia Woolf was trying, for an objectivity, a detachment, that would make us sound more like Jane Austen or Shakespeare. We know more than Jane Austen or Shakespeare knew: more than Jane Austen because our lives are more complex, more than Shakespeare because we know more about the lives of women, Jane Austen and Virginia Woolf included.

Both the victimization and the anger experienced by women are real, and have real sources, everywhere in the environment, built into society. They must go on being tapped and explored by poets, among others. We can neither deny them, nor can we rest there. They are our birth-pains, and we are bearing ourselves. We would be failing each other as writers and as women, if we neglected or denied what is negative, regressive, or Sisyphean in our inwardness.

We all know that there is another story to be told. I am curious and expectant about the future of the masculine consciousness. I feel in the work of the men whose poetry I read today a deep pessimism and fatalistic grief; and I wonder if it isn't the masculine side of what women have experienced, the price of masculine dominance. One thing I am sure of: just as woman is becoming her own mid-wife, creating herself anew, so man will have to learn to gestate and give birth to his own subjectivity—something he has frequently wanted woman to do for him. We can go on trying to talk to each other, we can sometimes help each other, poetry and fiction can show us what the other is going through; but women can no longer be primarily mothers and muses for men: we have our own work cut out for us.

The Loser

A MAN THINKS OF THE WOMAN HE ONCE LOVED: FIRST, AFTER HER WEDDING,
AND THEN NEARLY A DECADE LATER.

I
I kissed you, bride and lost, and went
home from that bourgeois sacrament,
your cheek still tasting cold upon
my lips that gave you benison
with all the swagger that they knew—
as losers somehow learn to do.
Your wedding made my eyes ache; soon
the world would be worse off for one
more golden apple dropped to ground
without the least protesting sound,
and you would windfall lie, and we
forget your shimmer on the tree.

Beauty is always wasted: if
not Mignon's song sung to the deaf,
at all events to the unmoved.
A face like yours cannot be loved
long or seriously enough.
Almost, we seem to hold it off.

II
Well, you are tougher than I thought.
Now when the wash with ice hangs taut

this morning of St. Valentine,
I see you strip the squeaking line,
your body weighed against the load,
and all my groans can do no good.

Because you are still beautiful,
though squared and stiffened by the pull
of what nine windy years have done.
You have three daughters, lost a son.
I see all your intelligence
flung into that unwearied stance.

My entry is of no avail.
I turn my head and wish him well
who chafed your beauty into use
and lives forever in a house
lit by the friction of your mind.
You stagger in against the wind.

ADRIENNE RICH 1958[6]

Orion

Far back when I went zig-zagging
through tamarack pastures
you were my genius, you
my cast-iron Viking, my helmed
lion-heart king in prison.
Years later now you're young

my fierce half-brother, staring
down from that simplified west
your breast open, your belt dragged down
by an oldfashioned thing, a sword
the last bravado you won't give over
though it weighs you down as you stride

and the stars in it are dim
and maybe have stopped burning.
But you burn, and I know it;
as I throw back my head to take you in
an old transfusion happens again:
divine astronomy is nothing to it.

Indoors I bruise and blunder,
break faith, leave ill enough
alone, a dead child born in the dark.
Night cracks up over the chimney,
pieces of time, frozen geodes
come showering down in the grate.

A man reaches behind my eyes
and finds them empty
a woman's head turns away
from my head in the mirror
children are dying my death
and eating crumbs of my life.

Pity is not your forte.
Calmly you ache up there
pinned aloft in your crow's nest,
my speechless pirate!
You take it all for granted
 and when I look you back

it's with a starlike eye
shooting its cold and egotistical spear
where it can do least damage.
Breathe deep! No hurt, no pardon
out here in the cold with you
you with your back to the wall.

ADRIENNE RICH 1965[7]

Snapshots of a Daughter-in-Law

2.
Banging the coffee-pot into the sink
she hears the angels chiding, and looks out
past the raked gardens to the sloppy sky.
Only a week since They said: *Have no patience.*

The next time it was: *Be insatiable.*
Then: *Save yourself; others you cannot save.*
Sometimes she's let the tapstream scald her arm,
a match burn to her thumbnail,

or held her hand above the kettle's snout
right in the woolly steam. They are probably angels,
since nothing hurts her anymore, except
each morning's grit blowing into her eyes.

ADRIENNE RICH 1958–1960[8]

Planetarium

THINKING OF CAROLINE HERSCHEL, 1750–1848, ASTRONOMER, SISTER OF WILLIAM; AND OTHERS

A woman in the shape of a monster
a monster in the shape of a woman
the skies are full of them

a woman   'in the snow
among the Clocks and instruments
or measuring the ground with poles'

in her 98 years to discover
8 comets

she whom the moon ruled
like us
levitating into the night sky
riding the polished lenses

Galaxies of women, there
doing penance for impetuousness
ribs chilled
in those spaces   of the mind

An eye,
        'virile, precise and absolutely certain'
        from the mad webs of Uranisborg

                        encountering the NOVA

every impulse of light exploding
from the core
as life flies out of us

        Tycho whispering at last
        'Let me not seem to have lived in vain'

What we see, we see
and seeing is changing

the light that shrivels a mountain
and leaves a man alive

Heartbeat of the pulsar
heart sweating through my body

The radio impulse
pouring in from Taurus

    I am bombarded yet   I stand

I have been standing all my life in the
direct path of a battery of signals
the most accurately transmitted most
untranslateable language in the universe
I am a galactic cloud so deep   so involuted
that a light wave could take 15
years to travel through me   And has
taken   I am an instrument in the shape
of a woman trying to translate pulsations
into images   for the relief of the body
and the reconstruction of the mind.

ADRIENNE RICH 1968[9]

Notes

1. G. B. Shaw, *The Quintessence of Ibsenism* (Hill and Wang, 1922), p. 139.
2. J. G. Stewart, *Jane Ellen Harrison: A Portrait from Letters* (London, 1959), p. 140.
3. Henry James, "Notes on Novelists" in *Selected Literary Criticism of Henry James*, ed. Morris Shapira (London: Heineman, 1963), pp. 157–58.
4. Adrienne Rich, *A Change of World* (Yale University Press, 1951). Quoted by permission of the author.
5. "Halfway," in *Necessities of Life* (W. W. Norton and Company, 1966), p. 34.
6. *Snapshots of a Daughter-in-Law: Poems, 1954–1962.* Copyright © 1956, 1957, 1958, 1959, 1960, 1961, 1962, 1963, 1967 by Adrienne Rich Conrad. Reprinted by permission of W. W. Norton and Company, Inc.
7. *Leaflets: Poems, 1965–1968.* Copyright © 1969 by W. W. Norton and Company, Inc. Reprinted by permission of W. W. Norton and Company, Inc.
8. *Snapshots of a Daughter-in-Law* (see note 6).
9. *The Will to Change: Poems, 1968–1970.* Copyright © by W. W. Norton and Company, Inc. Reprinted by permission of W. W. Norton and Company, Inc.

Revision Strategies of Student Writers and Experienced Adult Writers

by Nancy Sommers

Nancy Sommers, formerly Director of Composition at the University of Oklahoma, is now Adjunct Assistant Professor at New York University. She has taught writing at Boston University, the Harvard Graduate School of Business Administration, and the Polaroid Corporation. An NCTE Promising Researcher for her studies of the processes of revising, she is writing a research monograph on revision.

Although various aspects of the writing process have been studied extensively of late, research on revision has been notably absent. The reason for this, I suspect, is that current models of the writing process have directed attention away from revision. With few exceptions, these models are linear; they separate the writing process into discrete stages. Two representative models are Gordon Rohman's suggestion that the composing process moves from prewriting to writing to rewriting and James Britton's model of the writing process as a series of stages described in metaphors of linear growth, conception—incubation—production.[1] What is striking about these theories of writing is that they model themselves on speech: Rohman defines the writer in a way that cannot distinguish him from a speaker and Britton bases his theory of writing on what he calls (following Jakobson) the "expressiveness" of speech.[2] Moreover, Britton's study itself follows the "linear model" of the relation of thought and language in speech proposed by Vygotsky, a relationship embodied in the linear movement "from the motive which engenders a thought to the shaping of the thought, *first* in inner speech, *then* in meanings of words, and *finally* in words". What this movement fails to take into account in its linear structure—"first . . . then . . . finally"—is the recursive shaping of thought by language; what it fails to take into account is *revision*. In these linear conceptions of the writing process revision is understood as a separate stage at the end of the process—a stage that comes after the completion of a first or second draft and one that is temporally distinct from the prewriting and writing stages of the process.[3]

The linear model bases itself on speech in two specific ways. First of all, it is based on traditional rhetorical models, models that were created to serve the spoken art of oratory. In whatever ways the parts of classical rhetoric are described, they offer "stages" of composition that are repeated in contemporary models of the writing process. Edward Corbett, for instance, describes the "five parts of a discourse"—*inventio, dispositio, elocutio, memoria, pronuntiatio*—and, disregarding the last two parts since "after rhetoric came to be concerned mainly with written discourse, there was no further need to deal with them,"[4] he produces a model very close to Britton's conception [*inventio*], incubation [*dispositio*], production [*elocutio*]. Other rhetorics also follow this procedure, and they do so not simply because of historical accident. Rather, the process represented in the linear model is based on the irreversibility of speech. Speech, Roland Barthes says, "is irreversible":

> "A word cannot be retracted, except precisely by saying that one retracts it. To cross out here is to add: if I want to erase what I have just said, I cannot do it without showing the eraser itself (I must say: '*or rather. . .*' '*I expressed myself badly. . .*'); paradoxically, it is ephemeral speech which is indelible, not monumental writing. All that one can do in the case of a spoken utterance is to tack on another utterance."[5]

What is impossible in speech is *revision*: like the example Barthes gives, revision in speech is an afterthought. In the same way, each stage of the linear model must be exclusive (distinct from the other stages) or else it becomes trivial and counterproductive to refer to these junctures as "stages."

By staging revision after enunciation, the linear models reduce revision in writing, as in speech, to no more than an afterthought. In this way such models make the study of revision impossible. Revision, in Rohman's model, is simply the repetition of writing; or to pursue Britton's organic metaphor, revision is simply the further growth of what is already there, the "pre-conceived" product. The absence of research on revision, then, is a function of a theory of writing which makes revision both superfluous and redundant, a theory which does not distinguish between writing and speech.

What the linear models do produce is a parody of writing. Isolating revision and then disregarding it plays havoc with the experiences composition teachers have of the actual writing and rewriting of experienced writers. Why should the linear model be preferred? Why should revision be forgotten, superfluous? Why do teachers offer the linear model and students accept it? One reason, Barthes suggests, is that "there is a fundamental tie between teaching and speech," while "writing begins at the point where speech becomes *impossible*."[6] The spoken word cannot be revised. The possibility of revision distinguishes the written text from speech. In fact, according to Barthes, this is the essential difference between writing and speaking. When we must revise, when the very idea is subject to recursive shaping by language, then speech becomes inadequate. This is a matter to which I will return, but first we should examine, theoretically, a detailed exploration of what student writers as distinguished from experienced adult writers *do* when they write and rewrite their work. Dissatisfied with both the linear model of writing and the lack of attention to the process of revision, I conducted a series of studies over the past three years which examined the revision processes of student writers and experienced writers to see what role revision played in their writing processes. In the course of my work the revision process was redefined as *a sequence of changes in a composition—changes which are initiated by cues and occur continually throughout the writing of a work.*

Methodology

I used a case study approach. The student writers were twenty freshmen at Boston University and the University of Oklahoma with SAT verbal scores ranging from 450–600 in their first semester of composition. The twenty experienced adult writers from Boston and Oklahoma City included journalists, editors, and academics. To refer to the two groups, I use the terms *student writers* and *experienced writers* because the principal difference between these two groups is the amount of experience they have had in writing.

Each writer wrote three essays, expressive, explanatory, and persuasive, and rewrote each essay twice, producing nine written products in draft and final form. Each writer was interviewed three times after the final revision of each essay. And each writer suggested revisions for a composition written by an anonymous author. Thus extensive written and spoken documents were obtained from each writer.

The essays were analyzed by counting and categorizing the changes made. Four revision operations were identified: deletion, substitution, addition, and reordering. And four levels of changes were identified: word, phrase, sentence, theme (the extended statement of one idea). A coding system was developed for identifying the frequency of revision by level and operation. In addition, transcripts of the interviews in which the writers interpreted their revisions were used to develop what was called a *scale of concerns* for each writer. This scale enabled me to codify what were the writer's primary concerns, secondary concerns, tertiary concerns, and whether the writers used the same scale of concerns when revising the second or third drafts as they used in revising the first draft.

Revision Strategies of Student Writers

Most of the students I studied did not use the terms *revision* or *rewriting*. In fact, they did not seem comfortable using the word *revision* and explained that revision was not a word they used, but the word their teachers used. Instead, most of the students had developed various functional terms to describe the type of changes they made. The following are samples of these definitions:

> *Scratch Out and Do Over Again*: "I say scratch out and do over, and that means what it says. Scratching out and cutting out. I read what I have written and I cross out a word and put another word in; a more decent word or a better word. Then if there is somewhere to use a sentence that I have crossed out, I will put it there."
>
> *Reviewing*: "Reviewing means just using better words and eliminating words that are not needed. I go over and change words around."

Reviewing: "I just review every word and make sure that everything is worded right. I see if I am rambling; I see if I can put a better word in or leave one out. Usually when I read what I have written, I say to myself, 'that word is so bland or so trite,' and then I go and get my thesaurus."

Redoing: "Redoing means cleaning up the paper and crossing out. It is looking at something and saying, no that has to go, or no, that is not right."

Marking Out: "I don't use the word rewriting because I only write one draft and the changes that I make are made on top of the draft. The changes that I make are usually just marking out words and putting different ones in."

Slashing and Throwing Out: "I throw things out and say they are not good. I like to write like Fitzgerald did by inspiration, and if I feel inspired then I don't need to slash and throw much out."

The predominant concern in these definitions is vocabulary. The students understand the revision process as a rewording activity. They do so because they perceive words as the unit of written discourse. That is, they concentrate on particular words apart from their role in the text. Thus one student quoted above thinks in terms of dictionaries, and, following the eighteenth century theory of words parodied in *Gulliver's Travels*, he imagines a load of things carried about to be exchanged. Lexical changes are the major revision activities of the students because economy is their goal. They are governed, like the linear model itself, by the Law of Occam's razor that prohibits logically needless repetition: redundancy and superfluity. Nothing governs speech more than such superfluities; speech constantly repeats itself precisely because spoken words, as Barthes writes, are expendable in the cause of communication. The aim of revision according to the students' own description is therefore to clean up speech; the redundancy of speech is unnecessary in writing, their logic suggests, because writing, unlike speech, can be reread. Thus one student said, "Redoing means cleaning up the paper and crossing out." The remarkable contradiction of cleaning by marking might, indeed, stand for student revision as I have encountered it.

The students place a symbolic importance on their selection and rejection of words as the determiners of success or failure for their compositions. When revising, they primarily ask themselves: can I find a better word or phrase? A more impressive, not so cliched, or less hum-drum word? Am I repeating the same word or phrase too often? They approach the revision process with what could be labeled as a "thesaurus philosophy of writing"; the students consider the thesaurus a harvest of lexical substitutions and believe that most problems in their essays can be solved by rewording. What is revealed in the students' use of the thesaurus is a governing attitude toward their writing: that the meaning to be communicated is already there, already finished, already produced, ready to be communicated, and all that is necessary is a better word "rightly worded." One student defined revision as "redoing"; "redoing" meant "just using better words and eliminating words that are not needed." For the students, writing is translating: the thought to the page, the language of speech to the more formal language of prose, the word to its synonym. Whatever is translated, an original text already exists for students, one which need not be discovered or acted upon, but simply communicated.[7]

The students list repetition as one of the elements they most worry about. This cue signals to them that they need to eliminate the repetition either by substituting or deleting words or phrases. Repetition occurs, in large part, because student writing imitates—transcribes—speech: attention to repetitious words is a manner of cleaning speech. Without a sense of the developmental possibilities of revision (and writing in general) students seek, on the authority of many textbooks, simply to clean up their language and prepare to type. What is curious, however, is that students are aware of lexical repetition, but not conceptual repetition. They only notice the repetition if they can "hear" it; they do not diagnose lexical repetition as symptomatic of problems on a deeper level. By rewording their sentences to avoid the lexical repetition, the students solve the immediate problem, but blind themselves to problems on a textual level; although they are using different words, they are sometimes merely restating the same idea with different words. Such blindness, as I discovered with student writers, is the inability to "see" revision as a process: the inability to "review" their work again, as it were, with different eyes, and to start over.

The revision strategies described above are consistent with the students' understanding of the revision process as requiring lexical changes but not semantic changes. For the students, the extent to which they revise is a function of their level of inspiration. In fact, they use the word *inspiration* to describe the ease or difficulty with which their essay is written, and the extent to which the essay needs to be revised. If students feel inspired, if the writing comes easily, and if they don't get stuck on individual words or phrases, then they say that they cannot see any reason to revise. Because students do not see revision as an activity in which they modify and develop perspectives and ideas, they feel that if they know what they want to say, then there is little reason for making revisions.

The only modification of ideas in the students' essays occurred when they tried out two or three introductory paragraphs. This results, in part, because the students have been taught in another version of the linear model of composing to use a thesis statement as a controlling device in their introductory paragraphs. Since they write their introductions and their thesis statements even before they have really discovered what they want to say, their early close attention to the thesis statement, and more generally the linear model, function to restrict and circumscribe not only the development of their ideas, but also their ability to change the direction of these ideas.

Too often as composition teachers we conclude that students do not willingly revise. The evidence from my research suggests that it is not that students are unwilling to revise, but rather that they do what they have been taught to do in a consistently narrow and predictable way. On every occasion when I asked students why they hadn't made any more changes, they essentially replied, "I knew something larger was wrong, but I didn't think it would help to move words around." The students have strategies for handling words and phrases and their strategies helped them on a word or sentence level. What they lack, however, is a set of strategies to help them identify the "something larger" that they sensed was wrong and work from there. The students do not have strategies for handling the whole essay. They lack procedures or heuristics to help them reorder lines of reasoning or ask questions about their purposes and readers. The students view their compositions in a linear way as a series of parts. Even such potentially useful concepts as "unity" or "form" are reduced to the rule that a composition, if it is to have form, must have an introduction, a body, and a conclusion, or the sum total of the necessary parts.

The students decide to stop revising when they decide that they have not violated any of the rules for revising. These rules, such as "Never begin a sentence with a conjunction" or "Never end a sentence with a preposition," are lexically cued and rigidly applied. In general, students will subordinate the demands of the specific problems of their text to the demands of the rules. Changes are made in compliance with abstract rules about the product, rules that quite often do not apply to the specific problems in the text. These revision strategies are teacher-based, directed towards a teacher-reader who expects compliance with rules—with pre-existing "conceptions"—and who will only examine parts of the composition (writing comments about those parts in the margins of their essays) and will cite any violations of rules in those parts. At best the students see their writing altogether passively through the eyes of former teachers or their surrogates, the textbooks, and are bound to the rules which they have been taught.

Revision Strategies of Experienced Writers

One aim of my research has been to contrast how student writers define revision with how a group of experienced writers define their revision processes. Here is a sampling of the definitions from the experienced writers:

Rewriting: "It is a matter of looking at the kernel of what I have written, the content, and then thinking about it, responding to it, making decisions, and actually restructuring it."

Rewriting: "I rewrite as I write. It is hard to tell what is a first draft because it is not determined by time. In one draft, I might cross out three pages, write two, cross out a fourth, rewrite it, and call it a draft. I am constantly writing and rewriting. I can only conceptualize so much in my first draft—only so much information can be held in my head at one time; my rewriting efforts are a reflection of how much information I can encompass at one time. There are levels and agenda which I have to attend to in each draft."

Rewriting: "Rewriting means on one level, finding the argument, and on another level, language changes to make the argument more effective. Most of the time I feel as if I can go on rewriting forever. There is always one part of a piece that I could keep working on. It is always difficult to know at what point to abandon a piece of writing. I like this idea that a piece of writing is never finished, just abandoned."

Rewriting: "My first draft is usually very scattered. In rewriting, I find the line of argument. After the argument is resolved, I am much more interested in word choice and phrasing."

Revising: "My cardinal rule in revising is never to fall in love with what I have written in a first or second draft. An idea, sentence, or even a phrase that looks catchy, I don't trust. Part of this idea is to wait a while. I am much more in love with something after I have written it than I am a day or two later. It is much easier to change anything with time."

Revising: "It means taking apart what I have written and putting it back together again. I ask major theoretical questions of my ideas, respond to those questions, and think of proportion and structure, and try to find a controlling metaphor. I find out which ideas can be developed and which should be dropped. I am constantly chiseling and changing as I revise."

The experienced writers describe their primary objective when revising as finding the form or shape of their argument. Although the metaphors vary, the experienced writers often use structural expressions such as "finding a framework," "a pattern," or "a design" for their argument. When questioned about this emphasis, the experienced writers responded that since their first drafts are usually scattered attempts to define their territory, their objective in the second draft is to begin observing general patterns of development and deciding what should be included and what excluded. One writer explained, "I have learned from experience that I need to keep writing a first draft until I figure out what I want to say. Then in a second draft, I begin to see the structure of an argument and how all the various sub-arguments which are buried beneath the surface of all those sentences are related." What is described here is a process in which the writer is both agent and vehicle. "Writing," says Barthes, unlike speech, "develops like a seed, not a line,"[8] and like a seed it confuses beginning and end, conception and production. Thus, the experienced writers say their drafts are "not determined by time," that rewriting is a "constant process," that they feel as if (they) "can go on forever." Revising confuses the beginning and end, the agent and vehicle; it confuses, *in order to find*, the line of argument.

After a concern for form, the experienced writers have a second objective: a concern for their readership. In this way, "production" precedes "conception." The experienced writers imagine a reader (reading their product) whose existence and whose expectations influence their revision process. They have abstracted the standards of a reader and this reader seems to be partially a reflection of themselves and functions as a critical and productive collaborator—a collaborator who has yet to love their work. The anticipation of a reader's judgment causes a feeling of dissonance when the writer recognizes incongruities between intention and execution, and requires these writers to make revisions on all levels. Such a reader gives them just what the students lacked: new eyes to "review" their work. The experienced writers believe that they have learned the causes and conditions, the product, which will influence their reader, and their revision strategies are geared towards creating these causes and conditions. They demonstrate a complex understanding of which examples, sentences, or phrases should be included or excluded. For example, one experienced writer decided to delete public examples and add private examples when writing about the energy crisis because "private examples would be less controversial and thus more persuasive." Another writer revised his transitional sentences because "some kinds of transitions are more easily recognized as transitions than others." These examples represent the type of strategic attempts these experienced writers use to manipulate the conventions of discourse in order to communicate to their reader.

But these revision strategies are a process of more than communication; they are part of the process of *discovering meaning* altogether. Here we can see the importance of dissonance; at the heart of revision is the process by which writers recognize and resolve the dissonance they sense in their writing. Ferdinand de Saussure has argued that meaning is differential or "diacritical," based on differences between terms rather than "essential" or inherent qualities of terms. "Phonemes," he said, "are characterized not, as one might think, by their own positive quality but simply by the fact that they are distinct."[9] In fact, Saussure bases his entire *Course in General Linguistics* on these differences, and such differences are dissonant; like musical dissonances which gain their significance from their relationship to the "key" of the composition which itself is determined by the whole language, specific language (parole) gains its meaning from the system of language (langue) of which it is a manifestation and part. The musical composition—a "composition" of parts—creates its "key" as in an overall structure which determines the value (meaning) of its parts. The analogy with music is readily seen in the compositions of experienced writers: both sorts of composition are based precisely on those structures experienced writers seek in their writing. It is this complicated relationship between the parts and the whole in the work of experienced writers which destroys the linear model; writing cannot develop "like a line" because each addition or deletion is a reordering of the whole. Explicating Saussure, Jonathan Culler asserts that "meaning depends on difference of meaning."[10] But student writers constantly struggle to bring their essays into congruence with a predefined meaning. The experienced writers do the opposite: they seek to discover (to create) meaning in the engagement with their writing, in revision. They seek to emphasize and exploit the lack of clarity, the differences of meaning, the dissonance, that writing as opposed to speech allows in the possibility of revision. Writing has spatial and temporal features not apparent in speech—words are recorded in space and fixed in time—which is why writing is susceptible to reordering and later addition. Such features make possible the dissonance that both provokes revision and promises, from itself, new meaning.

For the experienced writers the heaviest concentration of changes is on the sentence level, and the changes are predominantly by addition and deletion. But, unlike the students, experienced writers make changes on all levels and use all revision operations. Moreover, the operations the students fail to use—reordering and addition—seem to require a theory of the revision process as a totality—a theory which, in fact, encompasses the *whole* of the composition. Unlike the students, the experienced writers possess a non-linear theory in which a sense of the whole writing both precedes and grows out of an examination of the parts. As we saw, one writer said he needed "a first draft to figure out what to say," and "a second draft to see the structure of an argument buried beneath the surface." Such a "theory" is both theoretical and strategical; once again, strategy and theory are conflated in ways that are literally impossible for the linear model. Writing appears to be more like a seed than a line.

Two elements of the experienced writers' theory of the revision process are the adoption of a holistic perspective and the perception that revision is a recursive process. The writers ask: what does my essay as a *whole* need for form, balance, rhythm, or communication. Details are added, dropped, substituted, or reordered according to their sense of what the essay needs for emphasis and proportion. This sense, however, is constantly in flux as ideas are developed and modified; it is constantly "reviewed" in relation to the parts. As their ideas change, revision becomes an attempt to make their writing consonant with that changing vision.

The experienced writers see their revision process as a recursive process—a process with significant recurring activities—with different levels of attention and different agenda for each cycle. During the first revision cycle their attention is primarily directed towards narrowing the topic and delimiting their ideas. At this point, they are not as concerned as they are later about vocabulary and style. The experienced writers explained that they get closer to their meaning by not limiting themselves too early to lexical concerns. As one writer commented to explain her revision process, a comment inspired by the summer 1977 New York power failure: "I feel like Con Edison cutting off certain states to keep the generators going. In first and second drafts, I try to cut off as much as I can of my editing generator, and in a third draft, I try to cut off some of my idea generators, so I can make sure that I will actually finish the essay." Although the experienced writers describe their revision process as a series of different levels or cycles, it is inaccurate to assume that they have only one objective for each cycle and that each cycle can be defined by a different objective. The same objectives and sub-processes are present in each cycle, but in different proportions. Even though these experienced writers place the predominant weight upon finding the form of their argument during the first cycle, other concerns exist as well. Conversely, during the later cycles, when the experienced writers' primary attention is focused upon stylistic concerns, they are still attuned, although in a reduced way, to the form of the argument. Since writers are limited in what they can attend to during each cycle (understandings are temporal), revision strategies help balance competing demands on attention. Thus, writers can concentrate on more than one objective at a time by developing strategies to sort out and organize their different concerns in successive cycles of revision.

It is a sense of writing as discovery—a repeated process of beginning over again, starting out new—that the students failed to have. I have used the notion of dissonance because such dissonance, the incongruities between intention and execution, governs both writing and meaning. Students do not see the incongruities. They need to rely on their own internalized sense of good writing and to see their writing with their "own" eyes. Seeing in revision—seeing beyond hearing—is at the root of the word *revision* and the process itself; current dicta on revising blind our students to what is actually involved in revision. In fact, they blind them to what constitutes good writing altogether. Good writing disturbs: it creates dissonance. Students need to seek the dissonance of discovery, utilizing in their writing, as the experienced writers do, the very difference between writing and speech—the possibility of revision.

Acknowledgment

The author wishes to express her gratitude to Professor William Smith, University of Pittsburgh, for his vital assistance with the research reported in this article and to Patrick Hays, her husband, for extensive discussions and critical editorial help.

Notes

1. D. Gordon Rohman and Albert O. Wlecke, "Pre-writing: The Construction and Application of Models for Concept Formation in Writing," Cooperative Research Project No. 2174, U.S. Office of Education, Department of Health, Education, and Welfare; James Britton, Anthony Burgess, Nancy Martin, Alex McLeod, Harold Rosen, *The Development of Writing Abilities (11–18)* (London: Macmillan Education, 1975).
2. Britton is following Roman Jakobson, "Linguistics and Poetics," in T. A. Sebeok, *Style in Language* (Cambridge, Mass: MIT Press, 1960).
3. For an extended discussion of this issue see Nancy Sommers, "The Need for Theory in Composition Research," *College Composition and Communication*, 30 (February, 1979), 46–49.
4. *Classical Rhetoric for the Modern Student* (New York: Oxford University Press, 1965), p. 27.
5. Roland Barthes, "Writers, Intellectuals, Teachers," in *Image-Music-Text*, trans. Stephen Heath (New York: Hill and Wang, 1977), pp. 190–191.
6. "Writers, Intellectuals, Teachers," p. 190.
7. Nancy Sommers and Ronald Schleifer, "Means and Ends: Some Assumptions of Student Writers," *Composition and Teaching*, II (in press).
8. *Writing Degree Zero in Writing Degree Zero and Elements of Semiology*, trans. Annette Lavers and Colin Smith (New York: Hill and Wang, 1968), p. 20.
9. *Course in General Linguistics*, trans. Wade Baskin (New York, 1966), p. 119.
10. Jonathan Culler, *Saussure* (Penguin Modern Masters Series; London: Penguin Books, 1976), p. 70.

Thirteen (Lucky!) Strategies for Revision

37

Academic Writing Program, University of Maryland

"The beautiful part of writing is that you don't have to get it right the first time, unlike, say, a brain surgeon."

—Robert Cormier

1. Synthesize your feedback from the entire semester.

Gather all the essays you wrote over the course of the semester. Be sure to collect the versions that have your teacher's and peers' comments on them. Take time to read through all of the feedback you got from peers and your teacher, looking for patterns. What keeps popping up? What's consistently strong and what do you consistently need to improve? What issues keep appearing? Make a list of the recurrent themes or issues. You can take time to address each of these issues when you revise.

2. Write a reverse outline of your essay.

- Re-read the essay you plan to revise.
- In the margins of your essay, jot down a one-sentence summary of each paragraph.
- On a separate page, compose a "reverse" outline of your essay by listing the (one-sentence) primary argument for each paragraph.
- Read your reverse outline. As you do so, answer the following: where are ideas out of place? What can you rearrange? Where do your ideas flow logically and where is there a gap in logic? Where do your ideas seem connected and/or disconnected? What seems to be extraneous information that you can omit? Where do you need new material?
- Based on your reverse outline, make a plan for how you can reorganize your essay, what you can omit, what you can expand, etc.
- See "Rewriting" (Joseph Harris, in this collection) for more details on how to compose a reverse outline.

3. Write a plan of action.

Before jumping into your revision, write a plan of action. Include the three main elements or issues you plan to tackle. This might include adding a new section with additional research, starting the conclusion from scratch, or re-writing all of your topic sentences to match your new thesis. Having a pre-determined plan of action will help keep you on track as you try to make substantive revisions.

4. Start a new document file for the revision.

Instead of revising your essay in the same MS Word document, click "Save As" and start a new document. Give it a new title with a draft number and/or date (such as InquiryEssay2 or PositionPaper-11.1.13). This may sound obvious, but saving into a new document will enable you to delete text, copy/paste and make major changes without losing your original work. It is easier to make substantive revisions when you have multiple (similar) versions of your essay saved with different titles.

5. Find a new reader for your essay, one that is NOT in your class.

A new reader can read the essay with fresh eyes, interests, and questions. Think of asking your sibling, friend, roommate, parent, grandparent, colleague, etc., to read your essay. People who aren't in your class sometimes give better feedback about what's missing and what works/doesn't based on their sense of the piece as a whole.

6. Revisit the stases.

Go back to stasis theory. Ask yourself: can I approach this topic and essay more effectively if I argue or inquire in a different stasis? If your first draft argues or inquires in the value stasis, for example, you might try to approach the issue through cause/effect. If you argue about the actions that should be taken to address an issue, you might consider the definition stasis. Think about where the real controversy in your issue lies. How might changing the stasis strengthen your argument or refocus your entire essay?

7. Play "What If."

Review the essay that you plan to revise with the question "what if" in mind. Here are the types of questions you might ask of yourself and your writing:

- What if my conclusion became my introduction?
- What if I made this point my central claim?
- What if I used this source instead of another?
- What if I offered my experience in this way instead of that way?

As you explore these what if questions, you should also consider how the changes would then affect the rest of the essay.

8. Work on thesis and support away from the essay.

Rather than working on the essay itself, focus your attention solely on your thesis statement or central inquiry question. Write your thesis or central question in a new document or on a separate paper. Focusing only on that thesis or question, consider the following: given the stated thesis, what does my audience expect to learn? What is interesting or exciting to me about my thesis? How might I make this more specific? Does this thesis have a worthy counterargument or not? How might I rewrite or reconsider the thesis statement in light of what I have learned since writing the original essay?

9. Identify what's "good" and what you want to keep.

Free-write about what is essentially "good" about your paper. What is it that you want to preserve or save? This may be a central idea or point that forms the "heartbeat" of the paper, or it may be specific passages of text that form a foundation. It's important to know what's worth saving before you start changing things up. Furthermore, identifying this "good" part might also enable you to envision new and better supporting claims or see that the central point of the essay could shift from the previous idea to this new "good" idea. It also makes it easier to delete entire paragraphs or passages, which can be an important part of revision.

10. Return to research and source use.

Now that you are more experienced researchers, can you return to the way that you chose, interpreted, and "forwarded" (to use Joseph Harris's term) your sources? Did you give ample credit when due? Do you need to differentiate more between your ideas and the ideas of others? Is there better evidence, after your extensive research, to support your central question or argument? Are there places where you could do more research and find better sources?

11. Radically rearrange your paper.

Break out the scissors and tape. Cut apart your draft into paragraphs or chunks and tape them back together in a new order. Re-label sections and craft new transitions between them. Consider what happens to the essay if a different part of the essay becomes the introduction—what now needs to go? What could stay? How would this material that remains need to be reframed?

12. Summarize and revise.

Write a one-paragraph summary or abstract of your paper. Then, consider these questions: What's included in the summary? What's left out? After composing your summary and considering your abstract, turn back to your paper and consider what you should keep, emphasize, take out, or restructure to make the argument clearer or more effective.

13. What else? What's next?

Consider the question, what else could happen in this paper? What else could you say about this subject or in support of this argument? Also consider the question, what's next? What's the next level or stage for this paper and how might you take it there?

Substantive Revision in Process: The Effects of Breast Cancer Awareness Month

38a

Academic Writing Program, University of Maryland

*The following essay "The Effects of National Breast Cancer Awareness Month" demonstrates effective and substantive revisions. The first version of the essay shown below is the final polished essay. In the second version of the essay shown on **ps. 498–501**, you can see the changes the writer made to the original draft of the essay. As the marked-up draft reveals, this Argument of Inquiry essay was revised to focus the central question and to sharpen the writer's use of personal experience. This revision shows how making substantive changes such as these have a ripple effect and strengthen the entire essay.*

The Effects of National Breast Cancer Awareness Month

National Breast Cancer Awareness Month (NBCAM) is ubiquitous with the month of October. Multitudes of organizations come together to find a cure for breast cancer across the world by, as said by the Susan G. Komen foundation, "ground-breaking research, community health outreach, advocacy and programs in more than 50 countries" (About Us). The movement focuses specifically on prevention and early detection via mammograms, in addition to spreading hope and support to women diagnosed with all stages of cancer. Breast cancer is an extremely pervasive disease: there were around 232,340 new cases diagnosed in 2013, and there are around 2.8 million breast cancer survivors (Breast Cancer Overview). NBCAM and the breast cancer awareness movement itself touch millions of lives each year, leading to many questions about the positive and negative aspects of the movement.

Most families in the United States have had breast cancer touch their lives. My own experience relies heavily on my aunt, who was diagnosed around 5 years ago. When my aunt was first diagnosed, she became extremely active in the breast cancer awareness movement. She would often thank her mammogram for saving her life, and appreciate the movement for giving her the knowledge and tools to take charge of her cancer. After she had successfully fought off the cancer, however, my aunt began to question the inescapable presence of the movement. I remember her asking, what about other cancers? This only heightened when my grandmother was diagnosed with Stage IV pancreatic cancer. No one had known what signs and symptoms to look for, and by the time the cancer was detected it was too late. Could this have been prevented if more had been known about pancreatic cancer? What makes the breast cancer movement stand out among the rest?

Breast cancer awareness takes on many roles. With around 750 million dollars designated to research by the National Institute of Health (Langerth), and millions more being raised by foundations such as Susan G. Komen for the Cure, there is no shortage of research into developing advanced treatments and detection tests. While breast cancer is only the third most common type of cancer, following lung and prostate, it receives the largest amount of funding (Cancer Research Funding). If so much money is being funneled into breast cancer research by the government and other organizations, how are alternative awareness movements fairing? Experience has shown me that fundraising for other advocacy groups is not very widespread, and the amount of money allocated is nowhere near as great. While March is Colorectal Cancer Awareness Month, a disease that kills around 10,000 more people per year than breast cancer (Langerth), there are much fewer attempts to advocate for patients than breast cancer. NIH only allocates around 256 million dollars per year toward research of colorectal cancer. This leads me to question: Why is NBCAM so successful? How can other awareness movements learn from NBCAM?

NBCAM has, in general, successfully increased prevention, treatment knowledge, and research funding (Glynn et al). At its core, the breast cancer awareness movement advocates for women afflicted with a deadly disease. The medical community, however, frequently debates over whether breast cancer awareness detracts from the knowledge and prevention of other diseases. A very distinct "pink culture" defines the breast cancer awareness movement. If something can be sold, it has likely been pink washed. This has greatly impacted the public's perception of breast cancer, and their understanding of the risks. The prevalence of breast cancer related products and keeps breast cancer at the forefront of the public's mind. A study by Glynn et al examined internet searches for the terms 'breast cancer,' 'lung cancer,' and 'prostate cancer' to better understand awareness of each disease. Glynn et al determined that, "on average breast cancer research activity was significantly higher in every month of the year versus the other two cancers." The effects of breast cancer awareness have spread beyond NBCAM; while other awareness movements have remained stagnate.

This debate over breast cancer awareness has brought to light the many sides of NBCAM. On one side, as said by RN and PhD holder Debra M. Wujcik, "the pink ribbon is just an opener for frank discussion." Without breast cancer awareness, other advocacy groups may not have the public's attention. The conversation started by NBCAM allows for other groups to join in and gain precedence. In other ways, however, the breast cancer awareness movement has monopolized advertising and created a superficial atmosphere (Orensein 7). By stressing the importance of mammograms and knowledge of symptoms, NBCAM has managed to pinpoint the public's focus one on specific disease, as opposed to advocating for overall health. As Gylnn et al states, the medical community often finds that "the attention being given to breast cancer, in terms of both research time and money, is leading to a concomitant neglect of research into other malignancies." Has the attention garnered by NBCAM hindered the growth of other awareness groups?

What is the cause of discrepancies between cancer knowledge? Women obtain the majority of their cancer information from popular media, as opposed to their physicians. The disproportionate amount of information on breast cancer found in mass media greatly skews women's judgment of risk factors, for example, in many cases; they believe that breast cancer is the leading cause of death in women (Healton et al). As Healton et al state, there is a "real-world lack of messages that promote accurate perceptions about cancer mortality," including breast cancer. This lack of information presented to women explains their ignorance of other cancer awareness groups. It also brings to light many more questions about advocacy groups in general. How can other awareness groups spread their message when the media is filled with scaretactics?

My aunt, now a breast cancer survivor of five years, is still continuously dissecting NBCAM. She is extremely active in the movement, but also cautious to not exclude a much more holistic picture of health. Breast cancer awareness is extremely multifaceted, but also presents an extremely limited view of cancer advocacy. NBCAM causes variety of effects that must be researched in much more depth to truly understand its constructive and destructive qualities. NBCAM can either hinder alternative advocacy groups from spreading preventative knowledge, or begin a dialogue between the media and the public concerning health. In some way, all cancer advocacy groups are impacted by the dominance of NBCAM. How can these other groups lean to grow and expand? My own cautious opinion is that breast cancer awareness has opened doors that will allow other cancer advocacy groups to attempt the same success, perhaps by following in the footsteps of NBCAM.

Bibliography

"About Us." *Susan G. Komen.* n.p. 2013. Web. 7 Dec 2013.

"Breast Cancer Overview" *Cancer.org.* American Cancer Society, n.d. Web. 30 Oct. 2013.

"Cancer Research Funding." *National Cancer Institute.* n.p. 2012. Web. 9 Dec 2013.

Glynn, W. Ronan, Kelly, C. John, Coffery, Norma, Sweeney, J. Karl, and Kerin, J. Michael. "The Effect of Breast Cancer Awareness Month on Internet Search Activity – A Comparison with Awareness Campaigns for Lung and Prostate Cancer." *BioMed Central.* 2011. Electronic.

Healton, Cheryl G, Ellen R. Gritz, Kevin C. Davis, Ghada Homsi, Kristen McCausland, M L. Haviland, and Donna Vallone. "Women's Knowledge of the Leading Causes of Cancer Death." *Nicotine &; Tobacco Research.* 9.7 (2007): 761-768. Print.

Jacobsen, D. Grant and Jacobsen, H. Kathyrn. "Health Awareness Campaigns and Diagnosis Rates: Evidence from National Breast Cancer Awareness Month." *Journal of Economic Health* 30. (2011): 55-61. Print.

Langerth Robert. "Too Much Breast Cancer Awareness?" *n.p.* Forbes, 13 Oct. 2010. Web. 20 Oct 2013.

Orenstein, Peggy. "Our Feel-Good War on Breast Cancer." *n.p.* New York Times Magazine, 25 April 2013. 20 Oct. 2013.

Substantive Revision in Process: The Effects of Breast Cancer Awareness Month

Academic Writing Program, University of Maryland

~~54A~~

54B

English 101

~~10 October~~11 December 2013

The Effects of National Breast Cancer Awareness Month~~: What are the Effects?~~

~~Every October,~~ National Breast Cancer Awareness Month (NBCAM) ~~saturates~~is ubiquitous with the ~~United States~~month of ~~America.~~ ~~Many~~October. Multitudes of organizations~~;~~ ~~such as~~ come together to fnd a cure for breast cancer across the world by, as said by the Susan G. Komen foundation, ~~come together to fundraise~~"ground-breaking research, community health outreach, advocacy and ~~raise awareness, all with a unifying message of fnding a cure and increasing knowledge of~~ programs in more than 50 countries" (About Us). The movement focuses specifcally on prevention ~~methods.~~ ~~The awareness movement focuses on~~ and early ~~screening and~~ detection ~~by way of~~via mammograms, ~~which, according to Peggy Orenstein, "remains an unquestioned pillar" in the breast cancer movement (Orenstein 1).~~in addition to spreading hope and support to women diagnosed with all stages of cancer. Breast cancer is an extremely pervasive disease: there were around 232,340 new cases diagnosed in 2013, and there are ~~currently~~around 2.8 million breast cancer survivors (Breast Cancer Overview). ~~The extensiveness of~~ NBCAM ~~makes it~~and the ~~largest~~breast cancer awareness movement itself touch millions of lives each year, leading to many questions about the positive and negative aspects of ~~any cancer or disease~~the movement.

Most families in the United States have had breast cancer touch their lives. My own experience ~~with breast cancer~~ relies heavily on my aunt, ~~a survivor of fve~~who was diagnosed around 5 years ago. When my aunt was frst diagnosed, ~~my mother participated in the Susan G. Komen Race for the Cure. I gained frsthand experience with~~ she became extremely active in the breast cancer awareness ~~by helping my mother attempt to raise the funds required to complete the walk. The insight I gained gave me a huge appreciation for~~

~~the love and hope being poured into the~~ movement. ~~In high school, I spearheaded the October awareness month with~~ She would often thank her mammogram for saving her life, and appreciate the movement for giving her the knowledge and tools to take charge of her cancer. After she had successfully fought off the cancer, however, my aunt began to question the inescapable presence of the movement. I remember her asking, what about other cancers? This only heightened when my grandmother was diagnosed with Stage IV pancreatic cancer. No one had known what signs and symptoms to look for, and by the ~~National Honors Society. We organized fundraisers, and attempted to get~~time the ~~school involved with raising awareness for sisters, mothers, and anyone potentially at risk. My personal experience with fundraising for~~ cancer was detected it was too late. Could this have been prevented if more had been known about pancreatic cancer? What makes the breast cancer ~~has left me extremely interested and curious about the effects of NBCAM.~~ movement stand out among the rest?

Breast cancer awareness ~~is multi-faceted. NBCAM raises funds that further~~ takes on many roles. With around 750 million dollars designated to research ~~into a pivotal disease, potentially impacting millions of lives. As shown by Robert Langerth,~~by the National Institute of Health ~~designates around 750 million dollars to~~ (Langerth), and millions more being raised by foundations such as Susan G. Komen for the Cure, there is no shortage of research into developing advanced treatments and detection tests. While breast cancer ~~research.~~is only the third most common type of cancer, following lung and prostate, it receives the largest amount of funding (Cancer Research Funding). If so much money is being funneled into breast cancer research by the government and other organizations, how are alternative awareness movements fairing? Experience has shown me that~~, while other awareness movements do exist, they are not~~ as widespread ~~or ubiquitous as the breast cancer movement. At my school, while October brought about a multitude of pink worn by sporting teams and students, as well as~~ fundraising~~; there were no organized attempts to raise awareness~~ for other ~~diseases.~~advocacy groups is not very widespread, and the amount of money allocated is nowhere near as great. While March is Colorectal Cancer Awareness Month, a disease that kills around 10,000 more people per year than breast cancer ~~per year~~(Langerth), ~~I never personally learned any information or participated in any fundraising~~there are much fewer attempts to advocate for patients than breast cancer. NIH only allocates around 256 million dollars per year toward research of colorectal cancer. This leads me to question: Why is NBCAM so successful? How can other awareness movements learn from NBCAM?

~~It is widely accepted that the breast cancer awareness movement has~~NBCAM has, in general, successfully increased prevention, ~~treatment~~streatment knowledge, and research funding (Glynn et al). ~~The breast cancer movement, at~~ At its core, ~~is an attempt to advocate~~the breast cancer awareness movement advocates for women ~~and~~afflicted with a deadly disease. ~~There is a debate, however, in the~~ The medical community, however, frequently debates over whether breast cancer awareness detracts from the knowledge and prevention of other ~~cancers. Breast cancer repeatedly receives more attention in print and television media, in addition to~~ adiseases. A very distinct "pink culture" ~~which surrounds the cancer (Glynn et al).~~defnes the breast cancer awareness movement. If something can be sold, it has likely been pink washed. This ~~not only~~

~~detracts from other cancers, but also potentially has negative consequences for~~has greatly impacted the public's perception of breast cancer, and their understanding of the risks. The prevalence of breast cancer related products and keeps breast cancer ~~patients themselves. By looking at Internet~~at the forefront of the public's mind. A study by Glynn et al examined internet searches for the terms 'breast cancer,' 'lung cancer,' and 'prostate ~~cancer;~~cancer' to better understand awareness of each disease. Glynn et al determined that, "on average breast cancer research activity was signifcantly higher in every month of the year versus the other two cancers." ~~This shows that the~~The effects of ~~NBCAM~~breast cancer awareness have spread beyond ~~the month of October;~~NBCAM; while other awareness movements have remained stagnate.

~~The many aspects of~~This debate over breast cancer awareness ~~lead~~has brought to ~~an important debate over~~light the ~~importance and infuence~~many sides of NBCAM. On one side, as said by RN and ~~PHD~~PhD holder Debra M. Wujcik ~~states,~~ "the pink ribbon is just an opener for frank discussion." ~~Breast~~Without breast cancer awareness ~~opens many doors, and not just for breast cancer. In addition to raising critical funds for a cure, NBCAM starts a~~, other advocacy groups may not have the public's attention. The conversation ~~about~~started by NBCAM allows for other ~~cancer awareness movements and~~groups to join in and gain precedence. In other ways, however, the breast cancer awareness movement has monopolized advertising and ~~superfcially raised awareness~~created a superfcial atmosphere (Orensein 7). By stressing the importance of mammograms and knowledge of symptoms, NBCAM has managed to pinpoint the public's focus ~~one~~ on specifc disease, as opposed to advocating for overall health. As ~~Glynn~~Gylnn et al states, ~~some people fnd~~the medical community often fnds that "the attention being given to breast cancer, in terms of both research time and money, is leading to a concomitant neglect of research into other malignancies." ~~My own cautious opinion is that breast cancer awareness has opened doors that~~Has the attention garnered by NBCAM hindered the growth of other awareness groups?

What is the cause of discrepancies between cancer knowledge? Women obtain the majority of their cancer information from popular media, as opposed to their physicians. The disproportionate amount of information on breast cancer found in mass media greatly skews women's judgment of risk factors, for example, in many cases; they believe that breast cancer is the leading cause of death in women (Healton et al). As Healton et al state, there is a "real-world lack of messages that promote accurate perceptions about cancer mortality," including breast cancer. This lack of information presented to women explains their ignorance of other cancer awareness groups. It also brings to light many more questions about advocacy groups in general. How can other awareness groups spread their message when the media is flled with scare-tactics?

My aunt, now a breast cancer survivor of fve years, is still continuously dissecting NBCAM. She is extremely active in the movement, but also cautious to not exclude a much more holistic picture of health. Breast cancer awareness is extremely multifaceted, but also presents an extremely limited view of cancer advocacy. NBCAM causes variety of effects that must be researched in much more depth to truly understand its constructive and destructive qualities. NBCAM can either hinder alternative advocacy groups from spreading preventative knowledge, or begin a dialogue between the media and the public concerning health. In some way, all cancer advocacy groups are impacted by the dominance of NBCAM. How can these other groups lean to grow and expand? My own cautious opinion is that breast cancer awareness has opened doors that will allow other cancer advocacy groups to attempt the same success, perhaps by following in the footsteps of NBCAM.

~~Works Cited~~

Bibliography

"About Us." *Susan G. Komen.* n.p. 2013. Web. 7 Dec 2013.
"Breast Cancer Overview" *Cancer.org.* American Cancer Society, n.d. Web. 30 Oct. 2013. "Cancer Research Funding." *National Cancer Institute.* n.p. 2012. Web. 9 Dec 2013.
Glynn, W. Ronan, Kelly, C. John, Coffery, Norma, Sweeney, J. Karl, and Kerin, J. Michael. "The Effect of Breast Cancer Awareness Month on Internet Search Activity – A Comparison with Awareness Campaigns for Lung and Prostate Cancer." *BioMed Central.* 2011. Electronic.
Healton, Cheryl G, Ellen R. Gritz, Kevin C. Davis, Ghada Homsi, Kristen McCausland, M L. Haviland, and Donna Vallone. "Women's Knowledge of the Leading Causes of Cancer Death." *Nicotine &; Tobacco Research.* 9.7 (2007): 761–768. Print.
Jacobsen, D. Grant and Jacobsen, H. Kathyrn. "Health Awareness Campaigns and Diagnosis Rates: Evidence from National Breast Cancer Awareness Month." *Journal of Economic Health* 30. (2011): 55–61. Print.
Langerth Robert. "Too Much Breast Cancer Awareness?" *n.p.* Forbes, 13 Oct. 2010. Web. 20 Oct 2013.
Orenstein, Peggy. "Our Feel-Good War on Breast Cancer." *n.p.* New York Times Magazine, 25 April 2013. 20 Oct. 2013.

~~Audience Analysis~~

~~Readers of this essay would primarily be highly educated doctors and other medical professionals who are interested in the funding and awareness breast cancer generates. These readers are already extremely knowledgeable about the scientifc and clinical aspect of breast cancer. They would understand the term mammogram, an early detection test for breast cancer, all well as greatly know the positives and negatives of the test. Their feelings on breast cancer awareness are potentially mixed. They could understand the need for funding, and be grateful for the awareness breast cancer brings for all diseases. They could wish that awareness could be spread around more, hoping for funds in various other felds. This essay is attempting to inform these professionals about the different stances and spark and interest in advocacy. This could be published in a medical magazine, to raise interest in common readers, perhaps patients or those affected by cancer, as well.~~

What Makes for a Substantive Revision?

Academic Writing Program, University of Maryland

What makes for a substantive revision? We ask that the revision you make to the project of your choice be "substantive," but what exactly we mean by substantive may be elusive. Throughout the semester, you have been getting feedback from your instructor and your peers, and some of this feedback focuses on editorial concerns, like correcting your MLA citation style or making sure you are following standard punctuation practices for academic writing. If you focus on these changes, you are *not focusing* on substantive revision but instead you are focusing on editorial concerns.

To begin to think about making substantive changes to your work, you first need to think about how your paper could have been better. You may want to read your instructor's comments at the end of your paper and look for suggestions regarding what could be improved or what interesting directions you could take your paper if you were given another chance to resubmit. You may want to go back to the library and see if you can find any new research on your topic. You may want to think more about inventing new persuasive appeals to help strengthen your argument, or you may think about tailoring your paper to a particular kind of academic audience that was unforeseen when you were initially writing your original project. All of these require you to make *substantive* revision. In other words, in order to complete the revised project, you need to add substance to your original piece—add something new, something meaningful and helpful for making your essay better, stronger, even more impactful. Extending this point, you may *take away* material that was not working and replacing it with ideas and arguments that do.

While substantive revisions require concentrated and creative thinking, planning a substantive revision ought not to be anxiety inducing. Throughout the semester, you have been learning various revision strategies, most of which are helpful for creating substantive revisions. If you stop to think about the rhetorical terminology you have learned so far, you have grounds for generating ideas for a substantive revision. You may think about stasis, for example. What stases did you cover in your initial project? Which stases were overlooked? What could addressing the overlooked stases do for your argument? If you are looking at earlier projects, you may consider readdressing them with concepts that you learned later in the semester, concepts like *counterarguments, arrangement, enthymemes and appeals to reason, appeals to emotion, appeals to character, global coherence*, or even the idea of *kairos*. You may consider taking out entire paragraphs and replacing them with new ones that better reflect your new audience awareness and argumentative skills. Use the rhetorical vocabulary you have learned in this class as a springboard into the thought process of planning a substantive revision.

A final note: Often, when going through the process of making substantive revisions, you may discover something new about your own writing. You may disagree with some choices you made earlier and modify some claims that you proposed. You may even find yourself arriving at a conclusion different from the one you initially argued. This is completely normal. This, too, is part of the process of making substantive revisions. So long as you think of your new contributions as not only meaningful but also impactful—so long as you think of your paper as potentially changing and changing significantly based on your new contributions—you are on the right path in developing a substantive revision. The point is not to rewrite your entire paper but to re-envision even a portion of it in such a way that the overall impact is that of a new argument.

What Makes a Strong Reflective Essay?

Academic Writing Program, University of Maryland

In your Revision and Reflection assignment, you not only revise, but you also reflect on your revision process. What makes for a good reflective essay? Much of what makes for a good reflection depends on describing aspects specific to your thinking, writing, and revision practices and processes. The key for the assignment is that you (1) identify the changes that you made, and (2) explain why these changes made sense to you as you strove to make substantive and effective improvements to your essay.

Reflection is a vital step in improving one's practices—and not just in writing. Regardless of context, the work of reflection and of attending closely to the choices we make encourages us to recognize those choices as options in future situations. Reflection helps us develop a sense of what works and what does not, leading us to new practices, strategies, and ways of thinking about past, present, and future situations. With regards to writing, revision and reflection go hand-in-hand, so much so that some writers keep "craft journals" in which they map out their reactions to the drafts they have written and use those reactions to set goals for their next drafts. This means that, in writing, reflection does not just happen after one has finished and submitted a piece (whether for grade or publication), but also concurrently with the process of drafting and revision so that the writer can scrutinize the choices she has made and determine if the choices really serve the goals and purposes she established.

In short, *revision and reflection inform each other*, revision telling us what to reflect on and reflection telling us what to revise and why our efforts at revision have succeeded. The two are entwined, essentially so, with reflection especially allowing for deliberate, goal-oriented revision rather than haphazard or minimal changes that might fail to attend to global concerns. Even more, careful reflection allows us to better take our learning into our hands. Instead of hoping that we will just learn things by way of osmosis and be able to draw up them in future situations, we use reflection to deliberately analyze what we have done and signal the specific strategies we want to carry forward, increasing the likelihood that we'll be able to later call upon them when needed.

To help you think about good reflection practices, below you will find some patterns and habits of mind that are often present in excellent reflections on revision processes.

Tell Us What You <u>Did</u>: The Tense of Reflection

Your reflection should center on what you've accomplished in your revision and the decisions you have made, which means that a key part of the reflection process is looking back on the revisions you have made. Like how painters need to step away and come back to their paintings in order to reevaluate their work, your reflections should also have a reflective distance from the time of initially making your revisions. One of the clearest markers of excellent reflections is a sustained, descriptive focus on the past.

Excellent reflections are more likely to use past tense verbs and focus on past time events. The kinds of concepts that you might focus on may vary. You'll want to describe the choices you made in your revisions (e.g. "I *created* a new paragraph to discuss the article about Governor Pat McCoy's stance on liberal arts . . . "). You'll want to discuss why you made these choices (e.g. ". . . because I *wanted* the evidence part of the paper to be about the different stances . . . "). And, you'll want to offer justification for the necessity of these choices ("I *did* not think the original *captured* the true essence of the primary article..."). Excellent reflective writers keep the focus on the past, thinking about past choices and the reasons why these past choices were made. This focus on the past should help you to think more thoroughly and with more justification about your revisions. Moreover, a concentrated and sustained focus on the past—past comments from instructors, past writing experiences, past choices made, past changes and justifications for those changes—is a large part of what it means to reflect.

Offer Textual Evidence: An Engagement with Your Writing

Excellent reflections make explicit engagements with the texts under revision as well as the texts that are catalyzing the revision process. Strong reflective writers do this kind of work because by engaging closely with their writing, teacher's commentary, and peer responses (among other materials) reveals they are thinking about what they have done and what others have suggested and the reflective writer is responding specifically to past writing and suggestion. She is focusing on particular writing ideas and thinking them through as possibilities for revision.

Thus, you'll want to be specific when you discuss my comments on your project, your reflective memos, your research, and your revisions. Furthermore, you'll want to be specific about what and why you revised what you did. Therefore, you'll want to include sentences that operate like this:

- On page 3, I made X changes for Y reasons;
- When you made X comment on my Rhetorical Analysis assignment, I realized W; therefore I did Z in my revision.
- My new research made me think about X, so I revised the argument on page 5 in this way (X) for these reasons (Y).

Focus on "Big" Issues: Center Reflections (and Revisions) on Major Concerns

Similar to a focus on the project itself and on particular changes, excellent reflections are more likely to discuss specific rhetorical concepts learned throughout the semester. These concepts generally have to do with argumentation:

- making claims,
- engaging in analysis,
- strengthening supporting arguments,
- bolstering the exigence of the topic and/or position,
- considering the audience,
- crafting rhetorical appeals,
- organizing and arranging points,
- eradicating ineffective claims,
- incorporating new evidence, and
- writing with style.

Excellent reflections focus on these concerns because their revisions hinge on "big" ideas and concerns: the writer is now composing strong arguments that will make persuasion more probable for a specific reader. Excellent reflective writers (and revisers) also think about how they have revised their writing in order to better accomplish their goals. They realize that there is no one way to do this, so they think of the available means of persuasion in a given context with a particular audience; they revise accordingly and their reflections explain why they *chose* the available means that they did.

In sum, your reflective writing should reveal all of the hard and complex thinking and writing you engaged in as you moved through the revision process. It should make clear to the reader not only that you made particular changes to your essay but that you made these changes with *rhetorical* thoughtfulness and care.

Readings on Academic Writing and Linguistic Diversity

"Should Writers Use They Own English?"

41

by Vershawn Ashanti Young

What would a composition course based on the method I urge look like? [...] First, you must clear your mind of [the following . . .]: "We affirm the students' right to their own patterns and varieties of language—the dialects of their nurture or whatever dialects in which they find their own identity and style."

—Stanley Fish, "What Should Colleges Teach? Part 3."

Cultural critic Stanley Fish come talkin bout—in his three-piece *New York Times* "What Should Colleges Teach?" suit—there only one way to speak and write to get ahead in the world, that writin teachers should "clear [they] mind of the orthodoxies that have taken hold in the composition world" ("Part 3"). He say dont no student have a rite to they own language if that language make them "vulnerable to prejudice"; that "it may be true that the standard language is [...] a device for protecting the status quo, but that very truth is a reason for teaching it to students" (Fish "Part 3").

Lord, lord, lord! Where do I begin, cuz this man sho tryin to take the nation back to a time when we were less tolerant of linguistic and racial differences. Yeah, I said racial difference, tho my man Stan be talkin explicitly bout language differences. The two be intertwined. Used to be a time when a black person could get hanged from the nearest tree just cuz they be black. And they fingers and heads (double entendre intended) get chopped off sometimes. Stanley Fish say he be appalled at blatant prejudice, and get even madder at prejudice exhibited by those who claim it dont happen no mo (Fish "Henry Louis Gates"). And it do happen—as he know—when folks dont get no jobs or get fired or whatever cuz they talk and write Asian or black or with an Applachian accent or sound like whatever aint the status quo. And Fish himself acquiesce to this linguistic prejudice when he come saying that people make theyselves targets for racism if and when they dont write and speak like he do.

But dont nobody's language, dialect, or style make them "vulnerable to prejudice." It's ATTITUDES. It be the way folks with some power perceive other people's language. Like the way some view, say, black English when used in school or at work. Black English dont make it own-self oppressed. It be negative views about other people usin they own language, like what Fish expressed in his *NYT* blog, that make it so.

508

This explain why so many bloggers on Fish's *NYT* comment page was tryin to school him on why teachin one correct way lend a hand to choppin off folks' tongues. But, let me be fair to my man Stan. He prolly unware that he be supportin language discrimination, cuz he appeal to its acceptable form–standard language ideology also called "dominant language ideology" (Lippi-Green). Standard language ideology is the belief that there is one set of dominant language rules that stem from a single dominant discourse (like standard English) that all writers and speakers of English must conform to in order to communicate effectively. Dominant language ideology also say peeps can speak whateva the heck way they want to—BUT AT HOME!

Dont get me wrong, Fish aint all wrong. One of his points almost on da money—the one when he say teachers of writin courses need to spend a lot of time dealin straight with writin, not only with topics of war, gender, race, and peace. But he dont like no black English and Native American rhetoric mixing with standard English. Yeah, he tell teachers to fake like students have language rites. He say,

> If students infected with the facile egalitarianism of soft multiculturalism declare, "I have a right to my own language," reply, "Yes, you do, and I am not here to take that language from you; I'm here to teach you another one." (Who could object to learning a second language?) And then get on with it. (Fish "Part 3")

Besides encouraging teachers to be snide and patronizing, Fish flat out confusin (I would say he lyin, but Momma say be nice). You cant start off sayin, "disabuse yo'self of the notion that students have a right to they dialect" and then say to tell students: "Y'all do have a right." That be hypocritical. It further disingenuous of Fish to ask: "Who could object to learning a second language?" What he really mean by this rhetorical question is that the "multiculturals" should be thrilled to leave they own dialect and learn another one, the one he promote. If he meant everybody should be thrilled to learn another dialect, then wouldnt everybody be learn in everybody's dialect? Wouldnt we all become multidialectal and pluralingual? And that's my exact argument, that we all should know everybody's dialect, at least as many as we can, and be open to the mix of them in oral and written communication (Young).

See, dont nobody all the time, nor do they in the same way subscribe to or follow standard modes of expression. Everybody mix the dialect they learn at home with whateva other dialect or language they learn afterwards. That's how we understand accents; that's how we can hear that some people are from a Polish, Spanish, or French language background when they speak English. It's how we can tell somebody is from the South, from Appalachia, from Chicago or any other regional background. We hear that background in they speech, and it's often expressed in they writin too. It's natural (Coleman).

But some would say, "You cant mix no dialects at work; how would peeps who aint from yo hood understand you?" They say, "You just gotta use standard English." Yet, even folks with good jobs in the corporate world dont follow no standard English. Check this out: Reporter Sam Dillon write about a survey conducted by the National Commission on Writing in 2004. He say "that a third of employees in the nation's blue-chip companies wrote poorly and that businesses were spending as much as $3.1 billion annually on remedial training" (A23).

Now, some peeps gone say this illustrate how Fish be rite, why we need to be teachin mo standard grammar and stuff. If you look at it from Fish view, yeah it mean that. But if you look at it from my view, it most certainly dont mean that. Instead, it mean that the one set of rules that people be applyin to everybody's dialects leads to perceptions that writers need "remedial training" or that speakers of dialects are dumb. Teachin speakin and writin prescriptively, as Fish want, force people into patterns of language that aint natural or easy to understand. A whole lot of folk could be writin and speakin real, real smart if Fish and others stop using one prescriptive, foot-long ruler to measure the language of peeps who use a yard stick when they communicate.

Instead of prescribing how folks should write or speak, I say we teach language descriptively. This mean we should, for instance, teach how language functions within and from various cultural perspectives. And we should teach what it take to understand, listen, and write in multiple dialects simultaneously. We should teach how to let dialects comingle, sho nuff blend together, like blending the dialect Fish speak and the black vernacular that, say, a lot—certainly not all—black people speak.

See, people be mo pluralingual than we wanna recognize. What we need to do is enlarge our perspective about what good writin is and how good writin can look at work, at home, and at school. The narrow, prescriptive lens be messin writers and readers all the way up, cuz we all been taught to respect the dominant way to write, even if we dont, cant, or wont ever write that one way ourselves. That be hegemony, Internalized oppression, Linguistic self-hate. But we should be mo flexible, mo acceptin of language diversity, language expansion, and creative language usage from ourselves and from others both in formal and informal settings. Why? Cuz nobody can or gone really master *all* the rules of any language or dialect.

So, what happen when peeps dont meet the dominant language rules? Well, some folks can get away with not meeting those rules while others get punished, sometimes severely, for not doing so. Let me go a lil mo way with this: Even university presidents and highly regarded English professors dont always speak and write in the dominant standard, even when they believe they do.

Remember when Fish put former Harvard President Lawrence Summers on blast in 2002? What had happened was, Summers called professor Cornell West to his office and went straight off on the brotha for writin books everybody could read, for writin clear, accessible scholarship. Summers apologized after the media got involved, sayin: "I regret any faculty member leaving a conversation feeling they are not respected" (qtd. in Fish, "Say It Ain't So"). Fish say: "In a short, 13-word sentence, the chief academic officer of the highest ranked university in the country, and therefore in the entire world, has committed three grammatical crimes, failure to mark the possessive case, failure to specify the temporal and the causal relationships between the conversations he has and the effects he regrets, and failure to observe noun-pronoun agreement" ("Say It Ain't So").

But get this: Fish's correction of Summers is suspect, according to a grammar evaluation by linguist Kyoko Inoue (2002). Inoue say, "What the writer/speaker says (or means) often controls the form of the sentence." She say Summers' *intent* make his sentence clear and understandable, not rules from the grammar police-man.

But Fish gone ignore Inoue again, as he did back then in 2002. Fish gone say that the examples of Summers and the corporate workers show reasons why we should teach mo standard grammar, that if corporations and high ranked universities got folks who cant write rite, we gotta do a better job of teachin the rules. And since most of those workers are white, he gone also say he not supportin prejudice. He dont like it when whites dont speak rite, just the same as he dont like it when Latinos not speakin rite. Race aint got nothin to do with it, he gone add. It be only about speakin and writin standard English. He say his words apply to everybody not just to those who be wantin "a right to they own language."

But here what Fish dont get: Standard language ideology insist that minority people will never become an Ivy League English department chair or president of Harvard University if they dont perfect they mastery of standard English. At the same time the ideology instruct that white men will gain such positions, even with a questionable handle of standard grammar and rhetoric (I think here of the regular comments made about former President Bush's bad grammar and poor rhetoric). Fish respond that this the way our country is so let's accept it. I say: "No way, brutha!"

Also, Fish use his experience teachin grad students as evidence for his claim. He say his grad students couldnt write a decent sentence. Well, they wrote good enuff in they essays to get into grad school, didnt they? And most grad schools admit students by committee, which mean some of his colleagues thought the grad students could write rite. But it sound like Fish sayin he the only one who could judge what good writin is—not his colleagues. What is Fish really on, what is he really tryin to prove?

I, for one, sho aint convinced by Fish. I dont believe the writin problems of graduate students is due to lack of standard English; they problems likely come from learnin new theories and new ways of thinkin and tryin to express that clearly, which take some time. New ideas dont always come out clear and understandable the first few times they expressed. And, further, grad students also be tryin too hard to sound smart, to write like the folk they be readin, instead of usin they own voices.

In my own experience teachin grad students, they also tend to try too hard to sound academic, often using unnecessary convoluted language, using a big word where a lil one would do, and stuff. Give them students some credit, Fish! What you should tell them is there be more than one academic way to write rite. Didnt yo friend Professor Gerald Graff already school us on that in his book *Clueless in Academe* (2003)? He say he tell his students to be bilingual. He say, say it in the technical way, the college-speak way, but also say it the way you say it to yo momma—in the same paper. Now that's some advice!

But Fish must dont like this advice. He say that we should have students to translate the way they talk into standard English on a chalk board. He say, leave the way they say it to momma on the board and put the standard way on paper. This is wrongly called code switching. And many teachers be doin this with they students. And it dont work. Why? Cuz most teachers of code switching dont know what they be talkin bout. Code switching, from a linguistic perspective, is not translatin one dialect into another one. It's blendin two or mo dialects, languages, or rhetorical forms into one sentence, one utterance, one paper. And not all the time is this blendin intentional, sometime it unintentional. And that's the point. The two dialects sometime naturally, sometime intentionally, co-exist! This is code switching from a linguistic perspective: two languages and dialects co-existing in one speech act (Auer).

But since so many teachers be jackin up code switching with they "speak this way at school and a different way at home," we need a new term. I call it CODE MESHING!

Code meshing is the new code switching; it's mulitdialectalism and pluralingual-ism in one speech act, in one paper.

Let me drop some code meshing knowledge on y' all.

Code meshing what we all do whenever we communicate—writin, speakin, what-eva. Code meshing blend dialects, international languages, local idioms, chat-room lingo, and the rhetorical styles of various ethnic and cultural groups in both formal *and* informal speech acts.

This mode of communication be just as frequently used by politicians and profes-sors as it be by journalists and advertisers. It be used by writers of color to compose full-length books; and it's sometimes added intentionally to standard English to make the point that there aint no one way to communicate.

Code meshing also be used to add flavor and style, like journalist Tomas Palermo do in the excerpt below from his interview with Jamal Cooks, professor of Education. In his online article "Rappin about Literacy Activism," Palermo write:

> Teachers frequently encounter him on panels with titles like "The Expanding Canon: Teaching Multicultural Literature In High School." But the dude is also hella down to earth. He was in some pretty successful "true-school" era hip-hop recording groups [...]. Meet the man who made it his passion to change the public education game, one class at a time.

With vernacular insertions such as "but the dude is also hella down to earth" (not to mention beginning a sentence with the conjunction *but*) and adding the colloquial *game* to "public education," the article, otherwise composed in mono-dialect standard English, shift into a code meshed text.

Here some mo examples:

(1) Iowa Republican Senator Chuck Grassley sent two tweets to President Obama in June 2009 (Werner). His messages blend together common txtng abbrvs., standard English grammar and a African American rhetorical technique:

> First Tweet: "Pres Obama you got nerve while u sightseeing in Paris to tell us 'time to deliver' on health care. We still on skedul/even workinWKEND."
> Second Tweet: "Pres Obama while u sightseeing in Paris u said 'time to delivr on healthcare' When you are a 'hammer' u think evrything is NAIL I'm no NAIL."

(2) Professor Kermit Campbell uses multiple dialects to compose *Gettin' Our Groove On* (2005), a study of college writing instruction. In it he say:

> Middle class aspirations and an academic career have rubbed off on me, fo sho, but all hell or Texas gotta freeze over befo you see me copping out on a genuine respect and love for my na-tive tongue. [...] That's from the heart, you know. But I don't expect a lot of folks to feel me. (3)

(3) Chris Ann Cleland, a real estate agent from Virginia, express disappointment about President Obama's economic plan in an interview with the *Washington Post* (Rich):

> "Nothing's changed for the common guy," she said. "I feel like I've been punked."

(4) Referencing Cleland's remark, the title of *New York Times* columnist Frank Rich's Op-ed article asks: "Is Obama Punking Us?" Rich writes in the last paragraph of his article:

> "The larger fear is that Obama might be just another corporatist, punking voters much as the Republicans do when they claim to be all for the common guy."

The contraction "nothing's," the colloquial phrase "common guy," and the vernacular expression "punked," are neither unusual nor sensational. Yet, when these examples get compared to the advice giving about code switching, you get a glaring contradiction.

Students be told that vernacular language should be reserved for the playground with friends or at a picnic with neighbors, and that standard English be used by professionals at work, in academic writing, and when communicating with important officials. However, the colloquial language of two white, middle-aged professionals (Cleland and Rich), which appears in two of our nations most highly regarded newspapers prove this aint so, at least not no mo and prolly never was. The BIG divide between vernacular and standard, formal and informal be eroding, if it aint already faded. And for many, it's a good thing. I know it sho be for me.

The Internet, among other mass media, as well as the language habits of America's ever-growing diverse ethnic populations be affecting how everybody talk and write now, too. A term like "punked," which come from black culture to describe someone getting tricked, teased, or humiliated, used to be taboo in formal communication as was black people wearin braided hair at work in the 1980s. The professional world has become more tolerant of black hair styles. And that same world not only toleratin but incorporatin, and appropriatin, black language styles.

Actor Ashton Kutcher popularized the term "punked" with his hit TV show of the same title. That's probably how the word seeped into the parlance of suburban professionals ("I feel punked"; "Obama [...] punking voters"), although it still retains it colloquial essence.

Fish may reply, "But these examples be from TV and journalism; those expressions wont fly in academic or scholarly writing." But did you read Campbell's book, Fish? What about Geneva Smitherman's *Talkin and Testifyin* (1977)? Is you readin this essay? Campbell blends the grammars and rhetorical styles of both black English and so-called standard English, along with the discourse of Rap and Hip Hop. He also blend in oral speech patterns (with the phonological representation of words like "fo sho" and "befo"). And his book is published by an academic press and marketed to teachers of English. Campbell just one of many academics—professors of language and writin studies, no less—who code mesh.

Still, Fish may say, "Yeah, but look, they paid their dues. Those professors knew the rules of writin before they broke them." To this objection, Victor Villanueva, a Puerto Rican scholar of American studies, as well as language and literacy, point to "writers of color who have been using the blended form [...] from the get-go" (351). As he put it, "The blended form is our dues" (351). They dont have to learn to the rules to write rite first; the blended form or code meshing is writin rite.

This brings us back to Senator Grassley's tweets. It's obvious he learned some cool techno-shorthand (e.g., "WKEND" and "delivr"). He also uses both the long spelling of *you* and the abbrv. "u" in the same line. "We still on skedul" is a complete sentence; the backslash ("/") that follow it function like a semicolon to connect the emphatic fragment to the previous thought. And the caps in "WKEND" and "NAIL" pump up the words with emphasis, which alleviates the need for formal exclamation marks.

Grassley's message be a form of loud-talking—a black English device where a speaker indirectly insults an authority figure. The authority figure is meant to overhear the conversation (thus loud-talking) so that the insult can be defended as unintentional. Grassley sent the message over his Twitter social network but he address Obama. He wanna point out what seem like a contradiction: If healthcare reform is so important to Obama, why is he sightseeing in Paris?

Grassley didnt send no standard English as a tweet. Twitter allow messages with 140 characters. The standard English question—If healthcare reform is so important to Obama, why is he sightseeing in Paris?—is 80 characters. Why didnt Grassley use this question or compose one like it? Cuz all kinds of folks know, understand, and like code meshing. So Grassley code meshed.

Code meshing be everywhere. It be used by all types of people. It allow writers and speakers to bridge multiple codes and modes of expression that Fish say disparate and unmixable. The metaphorical language tool box be expandin, baby.

Plus code meshing benefit everybody.

In the 1970's linguist William Labov noted that black students were ostracized because they spoke and wrote black dialect. Yet he noted that black speakers were more attuned to argumentation. Labov say that "in many ways [black] working-class speakers are more effective narrators, reasoners, and *debaters* than many middle-class [white] speakers, who temporize, qualify, and lose their argument in a mass of irrelevant detail" (qtd in Graff 37).

So when we teach the rhetorical devices of blacks we can add to the writing proficiency of whites and everybody else. Now, that's something, aint it? Code meshing use the way people already speak and write and help them be more rhetorically effective. It do include teaching some punctuation rules, attention to meaning and word choice, and various kinds of sentence structures and some standard English. This mean too that good writin gone look and sound a bit different than some may now expect.

And another real, real, good result is we gone help reduce prejudice. Yes, mam. Now that's a goal to reach for.

Works Cited

Auer, Peter. *Code-Switching in Conversation: Language, Interaction and Identity*. New York: Routledge, 1988.

Campbell, Kermit. *Gettin' Our Groove On: Rhetoric, Language, and Literacy for The Hip Hop Generation*. Detroit: Wayne State University Press, 2005.

Coleman, Charles F. "Our Students Write with Accents. Oral Paradigms for ESD Students." *CCC* 48.4 (1997): 486–500.

Dillon, Sam. "What Corporate America Can't Build: A Sentence." *New York Times* 7 Dec, 2004: A23.

Fish, Stanley. "Henry Louis Gates: Déjà Vu All Over Again." *Opinionator: Exclusive Online Commentary From The Times. The New York Times,* 24 July 2009. <http://opinion-ator.blogs.nytimes.com/2009/07/24/henry-louis-gates-deja-vu-all-over-again/>.

—. "Say It Ain't So." *Chronicle of Higher Education.* 21 June 2002. <http:// chronicle. com/article/ Say-It-Ain-t-So/46137>.

—. "What Should Colleges Teach?" *Opinionator: Exclusive Online Commentary From The Times.* The New York Times, 24 Aug. 2009. <http://fish,blogs.nytimes.com/2009/08/24/what-should-colleges-teach/>.

—. "What Should Colleges Teach? Part 2." *Opinionator: Exclusive Online Commentary From The Times.* The New York Times, 31 Aug. 2009. <http://fish.blogs.nytimes.com/2009/08/31/what-should-colleges-teach-part-2/>.

—. "What Should Colleges Teach? Part 3." *Opinionator: Exclusive Online Commentary From The Times.* The New York Times, 7 Sept. 2009. <http://fish.blogs.nytimes.com/2009/09/07/what-should-colleges-teach-part-3/>.

Graff, Gerald. *Clueless in Academe: How Schooling Obscures the Life of the Mind.* New Haven: Yale University Press, 2003.

Inoue, Kyoko. "A Linguist's Perspective on Teaching Grammar." Unpublished paper. University of Illinois at Chicago. Oct. 2002.

Lippi-Green, Rosina. *English with an Accent: Language, Ideology and Discrimination in the United States.* London: Routledge, 1997.

Palermo, Tomas. "Rappin about Literacy Activism." *WireTap Online Magazine.* 13 July 2007. <http://www.wiretapmag.org/education/43160/>.

Rich, Frank. "Is Obama Punking Us?" *New York Times* 9 Aug. 2009: WK8.

Smitherman, Geneva. *Talkin and Testifyin: The Language of Black America.* Detroit: Wayne State University Press, 1977.

Villanueva, Victor. "Personally Speaking: Experience as Evidence in Academic Discourse." *Rhetoric Review* 25.3 (2006): 348–352.

Werner, Erica. "Grassley Lashes Out at Obama Via Twitter." *Gazette* [Cedar RapidsIowa City, IA] 8 June 2009, F: 1A.

Young, Vershawn. *Your Average Nigga: Performing Race, Literacy, and Masculinity.* Detroit: Wayne State University Press, 2007.

Vershawn Ashanti Young performs his solo show *Your Average Nigga.* based on his book of the same title, around the nation. He has edited two collections: *Code Meshing as World English* (forthcoming 2011, NCTE Press) and *From Bourgeois to Boojie: Black Middle-Class Performances* (Forthcoming 2011, Wayne State UP). He is completing another monograph: *The New Equality: Gender Anxiety and the Politics of Racial Performance.*

Recommended Citation

Young, Vershawn A. "Should Writers Use They Own English?." *Iowa Journal of Cultural Studies* 12 (2010): 110–117.

Available at: http://ir.uiowa.edu/ijcs/vol12/iss1/10 (accessed 2-19-2016).

<http://opinionator.blogs.nytimes.com/2009/08/31/what-should-colleges-teach>.

—. "What Should Colleges Teach? Part 3." *Opinionator: Exclusive Online Commentary From The Times.* The New York Times, 7 Sept. 2009. 30 April 2010 <http://opinionator. blogs.nytimes. com/2009/09/07/ what-should-colleges-teach>.

Rée, Jonathan. "The Translation of Philosophy." *New Literary History* 32.2 (2001). 223–57.

Venuti, Lawrence. *The Translator's Invisibility: a History of Translation.* London, New York: Routledge, 1995.

How to Tame a Wild Tongue

42

material from Gloria Anzaldúa's *Borderlands/La Frontera: The New Mestiza*

"We're going to have to control your tongue," the dentist says, pulling out all the metal from my mouth. Silver bits plop and tinkle into the basin. My mouth is a motherlode.

The dentist is cleaning out my roots. I get a whiff of the stench when I gasp. "I can't cap that tooth yet, you're still draining," he says.

"We're going to have to do something about your tongue," I hear the anger rising in his voice. My tongue keeps pushing out the wads of cotton, pushing back the drills, the long thin needles. "I've never seen anything as strong or as stubborn," he says. And I think, how do you tame a wild tongue, train it to be quiet, how do you bridle and saddle it? How do you make it lie down?

> "Who is to say that robbing a people
> of its language is less violent than war?"
>
> —Ray Gwyn Smith[1]

I remember being caught speaking Spanish at recess—that was good for three licks on the knuckles with a sharp ruler. I remember being sent to the corner of the classroom for "talking back" to the Anglo teacher when all I was trying to do was tell her how to pronounce my name. "If you want to be American, speak 'American.' If you don't like it, go back to Mexico where you belong."

"I want you to speak English. *Pa' hallar buen trabajo tienes que saber hablar el inglés bien. Qué vale toda tu educación si todavía hablas inglés con un 'accent,'*" my mother would say, mortified that I spoke English like a Mexican. At Pan American University, I, and all Chicano students were required to take two speech classes. Their purpose: to get rid of our accents.

Attacks on one's form of expression with the intent to censor are a violation of the First Amendment. *El Anglo con cara de inocente nos arrancó la lengua.* Wild tongues can't be tamed, they can only be cut out.

Overcoming the Tradition of Silence

Ahogadas, escupimos el oscuro.
Peleando con nuestra propia sombra
el silencio nos sepulta.

En boca cerrada no entran moscas. "Flies don't enter a closed mouth" is a saying I kept hearing when I was a child. *Ser habladora* was to be a gossip and a liar, to talk too much. *Muchachitas bien criadas*, well-bred girls don't answer back. *Es una falta de respeto* to talk back to one's mother or father. I remember one of the sins I'd recite to the priest in the confession box the few times I went to confession: talking back to my mother, *hablar pa' 'trás, repelar. Hacicona, repelona, chismosa*, having a big mouth, questioning, carrying tales are all signs of being *mal criada*. In my culture they are all words that are derogatory if applied to women—I've never heard them applied to men.

The first time I heard two women, a Puerto Rican and a Cuban, say the word "*nosotras*," I was shocked. I had not known the word existed. Chicanas use *nosotros* whether we're male or female. We are robbed of our female being by the masculine plural. Language is a male discourse.

> And our tongues have become
> dry the wilderness has
> dried out our tongues and
> we have forgotten speech.
>
> —Irena Klepfisz[2]

Even our own people, other Spanish speakers *nos quieren poner candados en la boca*. They would hold us back with their bag of *reglas de academia*.

Oyé como ladra: el lenguaje de la frontera

Quien tiene boca se equivoca.

—*Mexican saying*

"*Pocho*, cultural traitor, you're speaking the oppressor's language by speaking English, you're ruining the Spanish language," I have been accused by various Latinos and Latinas. Chicano Spanish is considered by the purist and by most Latinos deficient, a mutilation of Spanish.

But Chicano Spanish is a border tongue which developed naturally. Change, *evolución, enriquecimiento de palabras nuevas por invención o adopción* have created variants of Chicano Spanish, *un nuevo lenguaje. Un lenguaje que corresponde a un modo de vivir.* Chicano Spanish is not incorrect, it is a living language.

For a people who are neither Spanish nor live in a country in which Spanish is the first language; for a people who live in a country in which English is the reigning tongue but who are not Anglo; for a people who cannot entirely identify with either standard (formal, Castillian) Spanish nor standard English, what recourse is left to them but to create their own language? A language which they can connect their identity to, one capable of communicating the realities and values true to themselves—a language with terms that are neither *español ni inglés*, but both. We speak a patois, a forked tongue, a variation of two languages.

Chicano Spanish sprang out of the Chicanos' need to identify ourselves as a distinct people. We needed a language with which we could communicate with ourselves, a secret language. For some of us, language is a homeland closer than the Southwest—for many Chicanos today live in the Midwest and the East. And because we are a complex, heterogeneous people, we speak many languages. Some of the languages we speak are:

1. Standard English
2. Working class and slang English
3. Standard Spanish
4. Standard Mexican Spanish
5. North Mexican Spanish dialect
6. Chicano Spanish (Texas, New Mexico, Arizona and California have regional variations)
7. Tex-Mex
8. *Pachuca* (called *caló*)

My "home" tongues are the languages I speak with my sister and brothers, with my friends. They are the last five listed, with 6 and 7 being closest to my heart. From school, the media and job situations, I've picked up standard and working class English. From Mamagrande Locha and from reading Spanish and Mexican literature, I've picked up Standard Spanish and Standard Mexican Spanish. From *los recién llegados*, Mexican immigrants, and *braceros*, I learned the North Mexican dialect. With Mexicans I'll try to speak either Standard Mexican Spanish or the North Mexican dialect. From my parents and Chicanos living in the Valley, I picked up Chicano Texas Spanish, and I speak it with my mom, younger brother (who married a Mexican and who rarely mixes Spanish with English), aunts and older relatives.

With Chicanas from *Nuevo México* or *Arizona* I will speak Chicano Spanish a little, but often they don't understand what I'm saying. With most California Chicanas I speak entirely in English (unless I forget). When I first moved to San Francisco, I'd rattle off something in Spanish, unintentionally embarrassing them. Often it is only with another Chicana *tejana* that I can talk freely.

Words distorted by English are known as anglicisms or *pochismos*. The *pocho* is an anglicized Mexican or American of Mexican origin who speaks Spanish with an accent characteristic of North Americans and who distorts and reconstructs the language according to the influence of English.[3] Tex-Mex, or Spanglish, comes most naturally to me. I may switch back and forth from English to Spanish in the same sentence or in the same word. With my sister and my brother Nune and with Chicano *tejano* contemporaries I speak in Tex-Mex.

From kids and people my own age I picked up *Pachuco*. *Pachuco* (the language of the zoot suiters) is a language of rebellion, both against Standard Spanish and Standard English. It is a secret language. Adults of the culture and outsiders cannot understand it. It is made up of slang words from both English and Spanish. *Ruca* means girl or woman, *vato* means guy or dude, *chale* means no, *simón* means yes, *churo* is sure, talk is *periquiar, pigionear* means petting, *que gacho* means how nerdy, *ponte águila* means watch out, death is called *la pelona*. Through lack of practice and not having others who can speak it, I've lost most of the *Pachuco* tongue.

Chicano Spanish

Chicanos, after 250 years of Spanish/Anglo colonization have developed significant differences in the Spanish we speak. We collapse two adjacent vowels into a single syllable and sometimes shift the stress in certain words such as *maíz/maiz, cohete/cuete*. We leave out certain consonants when they appear between vowels: *lado/lao, mojado/mojao*. Chicanos from South Texas pronounced *f* as *j* as in *jue (fue)*. Chicanos use "archaisms," words that are no longer in the Spanish language, words that have been evolved out. We say *semos, truje, haiga, ansina,* and *naiden*. We retain the "archaic"*j*, as in *jalar,* that derives from an earlier *h*; (the French *halar* or the Germanic *halon* which was lost to standard Spanish in the 16th century), but which is still found in several regional dialects such as the one spoken in South Texas. (Due to geography, Chicanos from the Valley of South Texas were cut off linguistically from other Spanish speakers. We tend to use words that the Spaniards brought over from Medieval Spain. The majority of the Spanish colonizers in Mexico and the Southwest came from Extremadura— Hernán Cortés was one of them—and Andalucía. Andalucians pronounce *ll* like a *y*, and their *d*'s tend to be absorbed by adjacent vowels: *tirado* becomes *tirao*. They brought *el lenguaje popular, dialectos y regionalismos.*[4])

Chicanos and other Spanish speakers also shift *ll* to *y* and *z* to s.[5] We leave out initial syllables, saying *tar* for *estar, toy* for *estoy, hora* for ahora (*cubanos* and *puertorriqueños* also leave out initial letters of some words.) We also leave out the final syllable such as *pa* for *para*. The intervocalic *y*, the *ll* as in *tortilla, ella, botella*, gets replaced by *tortia* or *tortiya, ea, botea*. We add an additional syllable at the beginning of certain words: *atocar* for *tocar, agastar* for *gastar*. Sometimes we'll say *lavaste las vacijas*, other times *lavates* (substituting the *ates* verb endings for the *aste*).

We use anglicisms, words borrowed from English: *bola* from ball, *carpeta* from carpet, *máchina de lavar* (instead of *lavadora*) from washing machine. Tex-Mex argot, created by adding a Spanish sound at the beginning or end of an English word such as *cookiar* for cook, *watchar* for watch, *parkiar* for park, and *rapiar* for rape, is the result of the pressures on Spanish speakers to adapt to English.

We don't use the word *vosotros/as* or its accompanying verb form. We don't say *claro* (to mean yes), *imagínate,* or *me emociona,* unless we picked up Spanish from Latinas, out of a book, or in a classroom. Other Spanish-speaking groups are going through the same, or similar, development in their Spanish.

Linguistic Terrorism

Deslenguadas. Somos los del español deficiente. We are your linguistic nightmare, your linguistic aberration, your linguistic *mestizaje*, the subject of your *burla*. Because we speak with tongues of fire we are culturally crucified. Racially, culturally and linguistically *somos huérfanos*—we speak an orphan tongue.

Chicanas who grew up speaking Chicano Spanish have internalized the belief that we speak poor Spanish. It is illegitimate, a bastard language. And because we internalize how our language has been used against us by the dominant culture, we use our language differences against each other.

Chicana feminists often skirt around each other with suspicion and hesitation. For the longest time I couldn't figure it out. Then it dawned on me. To be close to another Chicana is like looking into the mirror. We are afraid of what we'll see there. *Pena.* Shame. Low estimation of self. In childhood we are told, that our language is wrong. Repeated attacks on our native tongue diminish our sense of self. The attacks continue throughout our lives.

Chicanas feel uncomfortable talking in Spanish to Latinas, afraid of their censure. Their language was not outlawed in their countries. They had a whole lifetime of being immersed in their native tongue; generations, centuries in which Spanish was a first language, taught in school, heard on radio and TV, and read in the newspaper.

If a person, Chicana or Latina, has a low estimation of my native tongue, she also has a low estimation of me. Often with *mexicanas y latinas* we'll speak English as a neutral language. Even among Chicanas we tend to speak English at parties or conferences. Yet, at the same time, we're afraid the other will think we're *agringadas* because we don't speak Chicano Spanish. We oppress each other trying to out-Chicano each other, vying to be the "real" Chicanas, to speak like Chicanos. There is no one Chicano language just as there is no one Chicano experience. A monolingual Chicana whose first language is English or Spanish is just as much a Chicana as one who speaks several variants of Spanish. A Chicana from Michigan or Chicago or Detroit is just as much a Chicana as one from the Southwest. Chicano Spanish is as diverse linguistically as it is regionally.

By the end of this century, Spanish speakers will comprise the biggest minority group in the U.S., a country where students in high schools and colleges are encouraged to take French classes because French is considered more "cultured." But for a language to remain alive it must be used.[6] By the end of this century English, and not Spanish, will be the mother tongue of most Chicanos and Latinos.

So, if you want to really hurt me, talk badly about my language. Ethnic identity is twin skin to linguistic identity—I am my language. Until I can take pride in my language, I cannot take pride in myself. Until I can accept as legitimate Chicano Texas Spanish, Tex-Mex and all the other languages I speak, I cannot accept the legitimacy of myself. Until I am free to write bilingually and to switch codes without having always to translate, while I still have to speak English or Spanish when I would rather speak Spanglish, and as long as I have to accommodate the English speakers rather than having them accommodate me, my tongue will be illegitimate.

I will no longer be made to feel ashamed of existing. I will have my voice: Indian, Spanish, white. I will have my serpent's tongue—my woman's voice, my sexual voice, my poet's voice. I will overcome the tradition of silence.

> My fingers
> move sly against your palm
> Like women everywhere, we speak in code . . . .
>
> —Melanie Kaye/Kantrowitz [7]

"Vistas," corridos, y comida: My Native Tongue

In the 1960s, I read my first Chicano novel. It was *City of Night* by John Rechy, a gay Texan, son of a Scottish father and a Mexican mother. For days I walked around in stunned amazement that a Chicano could write and could get published. When I read *I Am Joaquín*[8] I was surprised to see a bilingual book by a Chicano in print. When I saw poetry written in Tex-Mex for the first time, a feeling of pure joy flashed through me. I felt like we really existed as a people. In 1971, when I started teaching High School English to Chicano students, I tried to supplement the required texts with works by Chicanos, only to be reprimanded and forbidden to do so by the principal. He claimed that I was supposed to teach "American" and English literature. At the risk of being fired, I swore my students to secrecy and slipped in Chicano short stories, poems, a play. In graduate school, while working toward a Ph.D., I had to "argue" with one advisor after the other, semester after semester, before I was allowed to make Chicano literature an area of focus.

Even before I read books by Chicanos or Mexicans, it was the Mexican movies I saw at the drive-in—the Thursday night special of $1.00 a carload—that gave me a sense of belonging. "*Vámonos a las vistas*," my mother would call out and we'd all—grandmother, brothers, sister and cousins—squeeze into the car. We'd wolf down cheese and bologna white bread sandwiches while watching Pedro Infante in melodramatic tear-jerkers like *Nosotros los pobres*, the first "real" Mexican movie (that was not an imitation of European movies). I remember seeing *Cuando los hijos se van* and surmising that all Mexican movies played up the love a mother has for her children and what ungrateful sons and daughters suffer when they are not devoted to their mothers. I remember the singing-type "westerns" of Jorge Negrete and Miguel Aceves Mejía. When watching Mexican movies, I felt a sense of homecoming as well as alienation. People who were to amount to something didn't go to Mexican movies, or *bailes* or tune their radios to *bolero, rancherita*, and *corrido* music.

The whole time I was growing up, there was *norteño* music sometimes called North Mexican border music, or Tex-Mex music, or Chicano music, or *cantina* (bar) music. I grew up listening to *conjuntos*, three- or four-piece bands made up of folk musicians playing guitar, *bajo sexto*, drums and button accordion, which Chicanos had borrowed from the German immigrants who had come to Central Texas and Mexico to farm and build breweries. In the Rio Grande Valley, Steve Jordan and Little Joe Hernández were popular, and Flaco Jiménez was the accordion king. The rhythms of Tex-Mex music are those of the polka, also adapted from the Germans, who in turn had borrowed the polka from the Czechs and Bohemians.

I remember the hot, sultry evenings when *corridos*—songs of love and death on the Texas-Mexican borderlands—reverberated out of cheap amplifiers from the local *cantinas* and wafted in through my bedroom window.

Corridos first became widely used along the South Texas/Mexican border during the early conflict between Chicanos and Anglos. The *corridos* are usually about Mexican heroes who do valiant deeds against the Anglo oppressors. Pancho Villa's song, "*La cucaracha*," is the most famous one. *Corridos* of John F. Kennedy and his death are still very popular in the Valley. Older Chicanos remember Lydia Mendoza, one of the great border *corrido* singers who was called *la Gloria de Tejas.* Her "*El tango negro,*" sung during the Great Depression, made her a singer of the people. The everpresent *corridos* narrated one hundred years of border history, bringing news of events as well as entertaining. These folk musicians and folk songs are our chief cultural mythmakers, and they made our hard lives seem bearable.

I grew up feeling ambivalent about our music. Country-western and rock-and-roll had more status. In the 50s and 60s, for the slightly educated and *agringado* Chicanos, there existed a sense of shame at being caught listening to our music. Yet I couldn't stop my feet from thumping to the music, could not stop humming the words, nor hide from myself the exhilaration I felt when I heard it.

There are more subtle ways that we internalize identification, especially in the forms of images and emotions. For me food and certain smells are tied to my identity, to my homeland. Woodsmoke curling up to an immense blue sky; woodsmoke perfuming my grandmother's clothes, her skin. The stench of cow manure and the yellow patches on the ground; the crack of a .22 rifle and the reek of cordite. Homemade white cheese sizzling in a pan, melting inside a folded *tortilla.* My sister Hilda's hot, spicy *menudo, chile colorado* making it deep red, pieces of *panza* and hominy floating on top. My brother Carito barbecuing *fajitas* in the backyard. Even now and 3,000 miles away, I can see my mother spicing the ground beef, pork and venison with *chile.* My mouth salivates at the thought of the hot steaming *tamales* I would be eating if I were home.

Si le preguntas a mi mamá, "¿Qué eres?"

> "Identity is the essential core of who we are as individuals, the conscious experience of the self inside."
>
> —Kaufman[9]

Nosotros los Chicanos straddle the borderlands. On one side of us, we are constantly exposed to the Spanish of the Mexicans, on the other side we hear the Anglos' incessant clamoring so that we forget our language. Among ourselves we don't say *nosotros los americanos, o nosotros los españoles, o nosotros los hispanos.* We say *nosotros los mexicanos* (by *mexicanos* we do not mean citizens of Mexico; we do not mean a national identity, but a racial one). We distinguish between *mexicanos del otro lado* and *mexicanos de este lado.* Deep in our hearts we believe that being Mexican has nothing to do with which country one lives in. Being Mexican is a state of soul—not one of mind, not one of citizenship. Neither eagle nor serpent, but both. And like the ocean, neither animal respects borders.

> *Dime con quien andas y te diré quien eres.*
> (Tell me who your friends are and I'll tell you who you are.)
>
> —Mexican saying

Si le preguntas a mi mamá, "¿Qué eres?" te dirá, "Soy mexicana." My brothers and sister say the same. I sometimes will answer *"soy mexicana"* and at others will say *"soy Chicana" o "soy tejana."* But I identified as *"Raza"* before I ever identified as *"mexicana"* or "Chicana."

As a culture, we call ourselves Spanish when referring to ourselves as a linguistic group and when copping out. It is then that we forget our predominant Indian genes. We are 70 to 80% Indian.[10] We call ourselves Hispanic[11] or Spanish-American or Latin American or Latin when linking ourselves to other Spanish-speaking peoples of the Western hemisphere and when copping out. We call ourselves Mexican-American[12] to signify we are neither Mexican nor American, but more the noun "American" than the adjective "Mexican" (and when copping out).

Chicanos and other people of color suffer economically for not acculturating. This voluntary (yet forced) alienation makes for psychological conflict, a kind of dual identity—we don't identify with the Anglo-American cultural values and we don't totally identify with the Mexican cultural values. We are a synergy of two cultures with various degrees of Mexicanness or Angloness. I have so internalized the borderland conflict that sometimes I feel like one cancels out the other and we are zero, nothing, no one. *A veces no soy nada ni nadie. Pero hasty cuando no lo soy, lo soy.*

When not copping out, when we know we are more than nothing, we call ourselves Mexican, referring to race and ancestry; *mestizo* when affirming both our Indian and Spanish (but we hardly ever own our Black ancestry); Chicano when referring to a politically aware people born and/or raised in the U.S.; *Raza* when referring to Chicanos; *tejanos* when we are Chicanos from Texas.

Chicanos did not know we were a people until 1965 when Cesar Chavez and the farmworkers united and *I Am Joaquín* was published and *la Raza Unida* party was formed in Texas. With that recognition, we became a distinct people. Something momentous happened to the Chicano soul—we became aware of our reality and acquired a name and a language (Chicano Spanish) that reflected that reality. Now that we had a name, some of the fragmented pieces began to fall together—who we were, what we were, how we had evolved. We began to get glimpses of what we might eventually become.

Yet the struggle of identities continues, the struggle of borders is our reality still. One day the inner struggle will cease and a true integration take place. In the meantime, *tenemos que hacerla lucha. ¿Quién está protegiendo los ranchos de mi gente? ¿Quién está tratando de cerrar la fisura entre la india y el blanco en nuestra sangre? El Chicano, sí, el Chicano que anda como un ladrón en su propia casa.*

Los Chicanos, how patient we seem, how very patient. There is the quiet of the Indian about us.[13] We know how to survive. When other races have given up their tongue, we've kept ours. We know what it is to live under the hammer blow of the dominant *norteamericano* culture. But more than we count the blows, we count the days the weeks the years the centuries the eons until the white laws and commerce and customs will rot in the deserts they've created, lie bleached. *Humildes* yet proud, *quietos* yet wild, *nosotros los mexicanos*-Chicanos will walk by the crumbling ashes as we go about our business. Stubborn, persevering, impenetrable as stone, yet possessing a malleability that renders us unbreakable, we, the *mestizas* and *mestizos*, will remain.

Good Enough Writing: What Is Good Enough Writing, Anyway?

43

by Lynn Z. Bloom

Good enough student writing isn't bad, it isn't great. And although it ultimately isn't good enough, it's what many of us will settle for much of the time. Although many American colleges and universities claim to strive for excellence, they will be reasonably contented with Bs. For most have adopted a de facto standard for college-level writing: whatever is good enough to warrant (note that I do not say merit) a B in whatever course it is written for at that particular school is good enough writing. Yes, this definition is pragmatic, rather than utopian. Its contours are determined locally, rather than nationally, by individual teachers in individual classes—though more exacting teachers or "hard graders" may continue to measure against the ideal.[1]

Yet we can discuss the concept of good enough writing in general because B is the standard grade in American undergraduate education in general, and in composition courses as well.[2] It is widely based on the following characteristics. B-level writing is college-level writing that exemplifies the following characteristics judged according to local standards. B-level writing is good enough to satisfy first-year writing standards and to meet norms of acceptable writing in more advanced classes. It is thus good enough to serve as the lingua franca for writing throughout the writer's home institution, and presumably, to meet the standard for writing beyond that college—the larger community, and the student's future professional world. If this writing is also good enough to satisfy the student writer's own expectations, so much the better, but that's an unexpected bonus, not a given. Although the following definition is embedded in a discussion of first-year composition, the features of good enough writing are equally discernable in academic writing required in any other college course up, down, or across the curriculum except for creative writing, which is beyond the scope of this discussion.

As I will explain in this essay, good enough writing is characterized by a clutch of Academic Virtues. These include: Rationality; Conformity, Conventionality—which is attained by using Standard English, following the rules, and otherwise maintaining proper academic decorum; *Self-Reliance, Responsibility, Honesty; Order; Modesty* in form and style; *Efficiency*, and *Economy*. When accompanied by *Punctuality*, turning the papers in on time, according to the demands of the academic schedule, a great deal of student writing that meets these criteria—perhaps most of it—should be good enough to receive a good enough grade, a B, in most institutions.[3] (Nevertheless, any teacher—and we have all met them—can override the norm using individual or idiosyncratic criteria, such as "Any paper with more than three spelling errors gets an F.")

Many teachers would also insist on evidence of "the ability to discuss and evaluate abstract ideas" as crucial to college-level writing (Sullivan 384). Critical thinking is more variable than the tidier Academic Virtues, more dependent on the individual teacher's expectations and frames of reference, and often difficult to measure. It will be addressed in the last two sections of this essay. Otherwise, my analysis assumes that although we say we value and expect critical thinking, when awarding the final grade we cave on this quality. If throughout the semester we have received a preponderance of technically and politically correct papers that reflect all the other Virtues, we will deem that writing good enough for a B.

Although composition studies handbooks and rhetorics hold out the Platonic ideals of excellence, particularly when their illustrations are from professional writers, classroom teachers perforce read these through the realistic lenses of "good enough." The label, "good enough writing," is an analogue of British psychoanalyst D. W. Winnicott's concept of the "good enough mother," neither negligent nor a smother-mother, but good enough to provide adequate physical and psychological nurture that will ensure the development of a distinctive individual, a healthy child (17–19). Most of us tend to teach to the class average (or slightly above, but still within B range), yet oddly enough, given the tacit acceptance throughout the country of this pervasive concept, it has never been given a label that stuck.[4] Like Moliére's Bourgeois Gentleman, who was delighted to finally have a label to acknowledge that he had been speaking prose all his life, the label "good enough writing" tells us what we've been teaching our students to do all along. Now we know what to call the resulting work; if good enough writing is not the best outcome, it is certainly the normative practice that we tolerate.

The Characteristics of Good Enough Writing

Rationality

The academy purports to be nothing if not rational—a virtue as old as Aristotle. The academic writer, from student on up to faculty researcher, is constrained to write rationally, to produce nonfiction prose usually construed as expository or argumentative writing, critical or otherwise. This must be organized according to a logical plan or purpose and proceed by a series of logical steps from its initial premise to a logical conclusion. In pursuing this goal—the logical consequence of the five-paragraph theme construed as a heuristic rather than a template—the writer is expected and advised in all the Handbooks[5] to be reasonable, balanced, fair-minded, and "respectful of the feelings of [the] audience," to "avoid rhetorical fallacies" and "learn from others' arguments." Thus the writer should be able to "distinguish fact from opinion," "take a position" and "make claims" derived from "supporting evidence" based on "verifiable and reliable facts." He or she should "respond to diverse views," considering "at least two sides of the issue under discussion" (Glenn, Miller, and Webb 502–27).

Although ethical and emotional appeals receive a nod (a paragraph apiece in this 876-page book), the emphasis throughout the *Handbook*, as in the course it sustains, is on the rational. *Emotion* and *passion*—which might signal the operation of a host of nonrational elements—are not indexed; *play* refers only to the literary genre. The dead seriousness that dominates academic discourse, allegedly the epitome of rationality, must prevail. William H. Gass contends that the article (or essay) as a genre—and by extrapolation, most academic writing—is far less rational than it purports to be, that it is in fact a "veritable Michelin of misdirection; for the article pretends that everything is clear, that its argument is unassailable, that there are no soggy patches, no illicit inferences, no illegitimate connections; it furnishes seals of approval and underwriters' guarantees" (25). In point of fact, as all researchers and writing teachers know, every piece of academic writing has a point of view and presents an argument, explicit or implicit, and evidence to reinforce the author's bias. Just because a piece of writing sounds objective (including, say, the essay you are reading right now) doesn't mean that it is; though one can—and should, in a rational universe—be fair, one can never be objective.

Conformity, Conventionality

Conformity, conventionality, and their consequent predictability are the necessary hallmarks of respectable academic writing. Academic readers expect academic writing to exhibit decorum and propriety appropriate in style and thought to the academic universe in general and to their discipline in particular. Teachers expect students to use Standard English, and follow the rules (see, for instance, Sullivan 385); and maintain decorum of thought as well as expression. Thus, as will be clear from the following discussion, the authors of good enough papers must color—and think—within the party lines, however loosely or tightly they are drawn at any given institution. However clearly or vaguely these are spelled out at any given school, most students are acculturated to understand them. When they don't—if, for instance, they are from another culture or their first language is not English and even if they know the words they don't understand the music—their failure to conform may land them in big trouble, as the following discussion reveals.

Adherence to Standard English and Rules

No matter how informal or slangy one's speech may be outside of class, teachers and textbooks and college standards concur on the importance of Standard English as the lingua franca for writing in the academy (again, creative writing excepted), reinforced by conventional grammar, mechanics, and spelling. Failure to follow the rules will result in papers that are not good enough, no matter what other virtues they exhibit. Although the National Council of Teachers of English (NCTE) manifesto on "Students' Right to Their Own Language"—a defense of nonstandard English, among other things—was promulgated in 1974 and is still on the books, teachers detest error and devote much effort to stamping it out, as Connors and Lunsford's research in "Frequency of Formal Errors" reveals. Likewise, Mina Shaughnessy's sensitive analysis of the "stunningly unskilled," error-laden writing of thousands of open admissions students in *Errors and*

Expectations leads ultimately to the expectation that sensitive, insightful teachers will assume that their students are "capable of learning" what they themselves have learned, and what they now teach—Standard English (292). Three semesters of basic writing will, if done right, give students Standard English facility with syntax, punctuation, grammar, spelling, vocabulary, "order and development," and "academic forms" (285–86). Though Mike Rose's equally sympathetic work, *Lives on the Boundary*, identifies many pitfalls that must be overcome on the road to successful academic writing, he shares Shaughnessy's vision of the ultimate goal. And, as David Bartholomae argues in "Inventing the University," when entering students have learned to talk the talk, they can walk the walk.

So taken for granted is this normative view of language that it is manifested from kindergarten through college in workbooks, grammar and usage tests, and spelling lists. Standard usage and grammar are addressed today in college and admissions (and exit) testing and placement. But these are the end of the line that now—as a consequence of the highly problematic, very politicized No Child Left Behind legislation—begins with mandatory testing in the primary grades and continues as long as the child remains in school. Despite objections from individual teachers and professional educational organizations, the law of the land reinforces adherence to the rules.

Decorum

Student writing must stay within the decorous boundaries of expression, and—for many teachers—suitable (however they define it) parameters of thought and ideas, even at the risk of hypocrisy. Sarah Freedman's classic research reveals that students whose writing is seen as insubordinate—too friendly, familiar, casual, presumptive of equal status with the teacher—may be penalized with lower grades (340–42). Making academic and professional norms explicit, *Harbrace* emphasizes that "respectful writers do not use homophobic" or racist or sexist language, and are "sensitive to ability, age, class, religion, and occupation" (287–89). Although the advice is couched in terms of language—"avoid the stereotyping that careless use of language can create" (289)—its implications are clear: if the writer's true sentiments are subversive or transgressive, they should be suppressed in the writing.

Students socialized in American high schools arrive in college with an understanding of the deep as well as surface meaning of many types of writing assignments. Most of them steer clear of the cultural undertow in which they might drown, even when to do so means evading the underlying moral issues—a potential breach of ethics far more serious than surface impropriety. The heated discussion of "Queers, Bums, and Magic," a gay-bashing paper in which the Kuwait-born student author also confesses to urinating on and beating up a homeless person in "San Fagcisco," makes it clear that students who violate the prevailing moral imperatives, whether by intention or in innocence, run the risk of incurring the teacher's wrath or even legal sanctions that could get them thrown out of school, into jail, or both (Miller; see my discussion in "The Good, the Bad, and the Ugly").

Self-Reliance, Responsibility, Honesty

Composition teachers, ever Emersonian in spirit, stress the importance of self-reliance, despite the constraints on independent thought and language imposed in the interests of decorum. "Your work must be your *own* work," we say, even in collaborative classrooms. "*Yours* is the most important voice in a paper that has your name on it," echoes the *Harbrace* (264). Yet, paradoxically, teachers distrust the personal voice (except in narratives), which signals ownership of the subject. And teachers emphatically discount the unsubstantiated opinion. Indeed, the most elaborate discussion of a single topic in the *Harbrace*, 16.6 percent of the total, is devoted to finding, using, and citing sources responsibly (548–693); the most responsible writing, students might well infer, is that which is most heavily and accurately cited. The emphasis on citations is also intended to nip irresponsibility in the bud. From sea to shining sea, as proscribed by decrees and honor codes throughout American colleges and universities, plagiarism and piracy, now complicated and confounded by the easy accessibility of materials on the Web, are the writer's cardinal sins. The *Harbrace* epitomizes and updates conventional wisdom, beginning with a harsh opening sally: "Taking someone's words or ideas and presenting them as your own leaves you open to criminal charges" (597). This is followed by, "In the film, video, music, and software businesses, this sort of theft is called *piracy*. In publishing and education, it is called *plagiarism* or *cheating*. Whatever it is called, it is illegal" (597). The ensuing discussion again typifies the paradox of, requiring students to be self-reliant in finding and using sources while simultaneously distrusting them to do this accurately or, more particularly, honestly: "Although it is fairly easy to copy material from a Web site or even purchase a paper on the Web, it is just as easy for a teacher or employer to locate that same material on the Web and determine that it has been plagiarized" (598–99). Gotcha!

Order

Most arenas of the academy, except those encouraging artistic creativity, depend on order—in calendars and schedules, procedures, and written documents. The academic world runs better when the participants can know, respect, and follow a predictable, conspicuous pattern. Thus good enough writing is reasonably well organized. Writing that looks disorganized is as disreputable as disorderly conduct, for disorder implies mental laxity, if not downright confusion, and shows disrespect for one's readers. We even like to see the organizational scaffolding; witness the popularity of PowerPoint presentations that threaten to become caricatures of order, arrangement made explicit in a series of short sentences or sentence fragments. Five paragraph themes likewise serve as their own caricature.

Nevertheless, the late Richard Marius's views on order in *A Writer's Companion* represent the academic norm. He asserts that "A Good Essay Gets to the Point Quickly" and "Stays with Its Subject" (47–53). It is well integrated and does not drift without clear purpose from item to item. Thus, says Marius, "A good essay will march step by step to its destination. Each step will be clearly marked; it will depend on what has gone before, and it will lead gracefully to what comes afterward" (53). Marius's advice, the antithesis of postmodernism, is proffered more categorically than, for instance, that of Strunk and White, who say, "Choose a suitable design and hold to it" (#12) (15). Their realistic analysis accommodates both the necessity of good design and the vagaries of the procedures by which it may be attained: "A basic structural design underlies every kind of writing. Writers will in part follow this design, in part deviate from it, according to their skills, their needs, and *the unexpected events that accompany the act of composition*" [italics mine]. Writing, they say, "to be effective, must follow closely the thoughts of the writer, but not necessarily the order in which those thoughts occur. This calls for a scheme of procedure." However, they add, "In some cases, the best design is no design, as with a love letter, which is simply an out-pouring" (15). Nevertheless, academic necessity puts most teachers in Marius's camp; students write no love letters on our watch.

Modesty in Form and Style

Good enough writers are advised to keep out of sight, even while taking responsibility for their own ideas. For good enough writing is moderate and temperate, its qualities of style, form, and tone quiet, steady, and inconspicuous. This is a pragmatic response to the ethos of the academy, for academics expect papers to be written in the form, language, and style appropriate to their respective discipline. When they are reading for substance, they cannot afford to be distracted by departures from conventions of form, or language that calls attention to itself, what my agriculture colleagues object to as "flowery writing."

To violate the normative literary conventions of the discipline in which one is writing is to mark the writer as either highly naive or very unprofessional. Or so the academy believes.[6] Thus *Harbrace* identifies the particular conventions and illustrates them with sample papers: "Writing about literature follows certain special conventions" ("Use the full name of the author of a work in your first reference and only the last name in all subsequent references"); "Reports in the social sciences follow prescribed formats to present evidence"—along the lines of introduction, definitions, methods and materials, results, discussion and critique; and "Writing in the natural sciences is impartial and follows a prescribed format" to ensure that the experiments can be replicated (694–703).

The sense of style conveyed in Polonius's advice to Laertes ("rich, not gaudy"; "familiar, but by no means vulgar") is reiterated today in the rules of Strunk and White, who together constitute the American Polonius: "*Place yourself in the background*" (#1) (70); "*Do not inject opinion*" (#17) (79–80). It would be as hard for anyone educated in American schools in the past thirtyfive years to escape the influence of advice embodied in *The Elements of Style* (itself a direct descendant of conventional eighteenth-century advice) or its analogues as it would for any post–World War II American baby to escape the influence of Benjamin Spock's *Baby and Child Care*. "The approach to style," say these books, "is by way of plainness, simplicity, orderliness, sincerity" (Strunk and White 69). This precept governs much of the normative stylistic advice to students: "*Be clear*" (#16); "*Prefer the standard to the offbeat*" (#21); "*Avoid fancy words*" (#14); "*Use figures of speech sparingly*" (#18). And be patriotic: "*Avoid foreign languages*" (#20) (70–81).

The author's individual, human voice is generally not welcome, particularly in papers written by teams of authors, as in the hard sciences, where convention dictates anonymity. Yet when the first person is permitted, Gass observes that such writing must appear voiceless, faceless, "complete and straightforward and footnoted and useful and certain" even when it is not, its polish "like that of the scrubbed step" (25). This suppression of the self, that might otherwise be manifested in the individual writer's voice and distinctive features of syntax and vocabulary, has the effect of making a given piece of academic writing sound like every other piece in the same field. For a single writer's voice to speak out would be to speak out of turn, and thus be regarded as immodest—calling attention to the speaker rather than where it properly belongs, on the subject.[7] The emergence of the authorial self, a necessary attribute of personal writing, may be one reason curmudgeonly diehard academic critics dislike and distrust this genre.

Efficiency, Economy

Good enough academic writers squander neither time nor words. Concepts such as George Orwell's "Never use a long word where a short one will do" and "If it is possible to cut a word out, always cut it out" (176) and Strunk and White's "Omit needless words"—"a sentence should contain no unnecessary words, a paragraph no unnecessary sentences" (23)—govern American textbooks and much of our red-penciling. In *A Writer's Companion*, Richard Marius reiterates, "Write Efficiently. Here is one of the fundamentals of modern English style: Use as few words as possible to say what you want to say" (10). Efficient prose, direct, honest, and to the point, enables readers to be efficient, as well, "without having to back up time and again to read it again to see what it means" (11). Although this advice could be interpreted as designed to produce a svelte body of Word Watchers in, say, advertising or the sciences, it seems just as likely to meet good enough writers where they live—writing to fulfill the letter of the required assignment (forget about its spirit) and get on with the more engaging aspects of their lives beyond the paper at hand.

By this criterion, the writer's ideal composing process would be equally efficient. I question how often the ideal is actually met, for it is antithetical to the unruly, wasteful, disorderly means by which creation usually occurs, even in good enough writing. Thus, although Lunsford and Connors in the second edition of *The St. Martin's Handbook*, for example, accurately explain that the writing process is "repetitive, erratic," recursive, "and often messy," rather than proceeding "in nice, neat steps," they hold out the hope that "writing can be a little like riding a bicycle: with practice the process becomes more and more automatic" (3–4). To the extent that process follows format, this may be true. It may be possible to write on automatic pilot if writers are working with predetermined forms of academic and professional writing, such as research reports, business memos, literature reviews, lab reports, and writing against deadlines where time is truly money. Nevertheless, by the fifth edition, Lunsford has abandoned this concept: "It is inaccurate to envision a single writing process. There are, in fact, as many different writing processes as there are writers—more if you consider that individual writers vary their writing processes each time they sit down to write!" (32).

Whereas economy and efficiency are subordinated, if not suppressed, in Lunsford's commentary, these concepts drive *Harbrace's* discussion of writing against real-world deadlines. In what is likely a reflection of the writing process of many good enough students, *Harbrace* considers the fact that "[i]t may sometimes be necessary to abbreviate the writing process," and therefore to cut corners by narrowing "the topic to a manageable scope" and drawing on one's store of academic or experiential knowledge—"but stay away, if possible, from a topic that requires much research" (482). Check the topic and approach with your instructor; do the best you can in the time allotted, emphasizing the main points and a strong conclusion; proofread. And " [s]ubmit your work on time" (483).

Punctuality

The academic and business worlds must run like clockwork in order to function well. Only selected creative writers and major thinkers—Proust and James Joyce come to mind—are expected to meet Matthew Arnold's criterion of "the best that has been known and thought in the world," and allowed by the workaday world (to which they are sublimely indifferent) to take their sweet time about attaining this standard of excellence. But for the good enough student writer this is irrelevant; a balance must be struck between procrastination and production. If the writing produced against deadlines is simply good enough to do the job but no better, that's all right for most people, most institutions, most of the time. When the Muse must report for duty on time, at least the work gets written.

The Upshot

If student papers meet all these criteria, are they guaranteed a B? Probably yes, for teachers oriented to the universe of good enough papers. But, as I indicated at the outset, not necessarily. Teachers for whom some criteria or types of error weigh more heavily than others, or who employ other local or institutional norms, may mark down or fail students who don't measure up. (As in the use of sentence fragments. Which I've now done twice in the same paragraph. So flunk me!) Teachers who value critical thinking, originality, discovery, experimentation, and other attributes of creativity—striking metaphors, dazzling language, a powerful individual voice—may also downgrade papers that are unoriginal, vacuous, faceless, voiceless, or otherwise bland. Let us examine why, for these teachers, good enough writing is simply not good enough.

The Consequences of Being Good Enough: What's Missing and What's Possible

We get what we ask for, a plethora of procedural virtues. Thus we get student writing that is rational, well-organized, decorous, modest, and efficient; that plays by the rules of Standard English and academic discourse; that follows the disciplinary conventions of form and style, and is turned in on time. Handbooks, rhetorics, dictionaries, usage directives, study guides and checklists, tests reaffirm these academic values and virtues. Student writing that meets the letter of these expectations should, in many venues, be good enough to earn the B that all involved in the transaction—students, teachers, their institutions—will settle for. By and large, these are the qualities we can teach and reinforce. If, as a consequence, student papers—at least, on the introductory level—also seem predictable, pedestrian, perhaps boring, well, maybe we're implicitly asking for this as well.

Beginning students can learn the conventions before they gain the knowledge and authority that will enable them to make genuine intellectual contributions to the ongoing dialogue in their field. Whether this writing could ever become better than good enough—supply the adjective—amazing, engaging, groundbreaking, earthshaking, or exciting in a myriad of other wonderful ways may be beyond our capacity to teach. But maybe not. Students may just have to cross the great divide between As and Bs on their own—but we would be remiss as teachers if we didn't try to help them on the ascent.

Beyond this great divide are, of course, the characteristics missing from the list of those that constitute good enough writing. These include: evidence of the writer's critical thinking; grappling with multiple, perhaps contradictory, sources and ideas; questioning both authority and one's own convictions; experimentation with genre, language, and other attributes of form, style, persona, and voice. Any and all of these have the potential to transform a good enough paper into a great one. In the process, student writers must transform, transcend, violate, or ignore a number of the attributes of good enough writing. In this section I address some of the possibilities for writing that could change the meaning of "good enough" from the merely acceptable to the genuinely good.

Because these attributes of genuinely good writing are much more variable, they are more difficult to categorize and to define, although we—and our students—know them when we see them. Whether these can be taught to first-year student writers is de-batable, but students can certainly be exposed to the concepts. Success depends in part on how automatically the students can deal with the essentials of good enough writing so they can concentrate on the more challenging and creative aspects of the as-signment at hand. Success depends also on the teacher's own appreciation of, understanding of, and ability to write with creative, confrontational, or otherwise original thinking and expression, for it's hard if not impossible to teach what one cannot do. All my life I have advocated writing in the genres we teach, for ourselves and our students (see "Why Don't We Write What We Teach?"). After writing a dissertation that was a critical analysis of the methodology of literary biography ("How Literary Biographers Use Their Subjects' Works"), I wrote the biography of America's best-known living author, Benjamin Spock, to learn firsthand what I could about writing biography (see "Growing Up"). It turns out that I learned a lot. Long experience as a teacher and author of textbooks convinces me that students write best about literature when they write as insiders, creators of texts in the genre, mode, and even the sensibility of the work they are studying.

Indeed, today many Readers, which are textbook collections of articles and essays, complement the readings with demanding assignments intended to "draw on students' creative imaginations and analytical skills to turn them from passive consumers into active producers of critical and creative texts" (Scholes, Comley, and Ulmer v)—an application of Scholes's theory articulated in *Textual Power*. Among the more thoroughgoing are Scholes, Comley, and Ulmer's *Text Book*: *Writing through Literature*, now in its third edition (2002), Bartholomae and Petrosky's *Ways of Reading*, the seventh edition also published in 2004, and my own books, including current editions of *The Essay Connection, The Arlington Reader,* and *Inquiry*, although, it would be possible for imaginative teachers to create such transformative writing assignments from nearly any contemporary textbook.

Whereas outsiders read and write as aliens trying to secondguess the teacher's understanding of unapproachable iconic texts; insiders are reading and writing "through literature," as Scholes et al. explain, to produce original texts of their own. Space does not permit here a comprehensive analysis of the scope, variety, depth, and level of difficulty of assignments intended to transform student writers from outsiders to insiders. There is room, however, to briefly illustrate this pedagogical philosophy with some of my own assignments from "Coming of Age in American Autobiography," a course I have taught recently to honors firstyear students and (in a separate course) to upperclass undergraduates. The central readings in each course are six canonical American autobiographies: Benjamin Franklin's *Autobiography*, Frederick Douglass's *Narrative*, Thoreau's *Walden*, Annie Dillard's *American Childhood*, Richard Wright's *Black Boy*, and Maxine Hong Kingston's *Woman Warrior*. To enable the students "to identify some of the issues and problems of the autobiographers's art—as readers, critics, and writers" (one of the course aims), I ask them in discussion and in writing to "examine the ways autobiographers see themselves (and others) and shape their vision and self-presentation—as children in an idyllic or problematic era; as members of a particular gender, social class or ethnic, regional, or racial group; as people fulfilling particular destinies or roles; as individuals in family, occupational, or other group contexts." They do this, however, not as ventriloquists of high culture criticism, which would put them in the conventional roles of outsiders trying to unlock iconic texts and characters, but insiders trying to recreate these figures through interpreting the subjects' self-interpretations, central ideas, milieus; psychological, intellectual, and social growth and development.

Thus one assignment requires students to work in pairs to "[w]rite a dialogue between Franklin and Douglass in which they discuss, debate, and ultimately define the meaning(s) of one of the following concepts as it pertains to either coming of age as an individual or as a nation (or both): independence, self-reliance, defiance of authority, citizenship, maturity, contributions to/engagement in the larger society." Another assignment asks pairs of students to " [d]esign a 21st century house for Thoreau, in an appropriate setting. One of you (as Annie Dillard) is the decorator. The other is the environmental engineer and landscaper. Remembering Frank Lloyd Wright's dictum, 'form follows function,' this dwelling and its environment should reflect, be symbolic of the predominant values of the people involved. You may include a drawing, floor plan, sketches, photos, whatever, ad lib." Of course, to fully experience autobiography as a genre, it is essential for the students to write one on the theme of the course: "Tell a true story with yourself as the central character—of some experience; event; relationship with a person or group; recognition of a belief or value system; or other phenomenon that was pivotal in your coming of age and/or understanding of the world."

Other briefer writings involve keeping a Thoreauvian journal, telling a joke Dillard's family would appreciate, making a list in the style of Richard Wright, and constructing a Kingstonesque cautionary tale.

The students lit up when they read these papers—every single one—aloud to their primary audience, the class; their discussions were energetic, enthusiastic, and engaged. So it was not surprising that when I asked the students to evaluate each assignment individually, they loved "trying new modes of writing and getting into the heads of the authors we were reading." With the exception of one paper, we all loved the results: varied, imaginative, on target, and—a bonus for me—virtually unplagiarizable because they are so specifically geared to the texts and context of the course. (Surprisingly, none of the twenty-four chapters in Buranen and Roy's otherwise comprehensive *Perspectives on Plagiarism* addresses writing assignments.) As one student commented, "I was pleasantly surprised with the assignments. I liked them a great deal more than the simple, mechanical, and stereotypical critical papers I was used to." The autobiography, assigned two-thirds of the way through the class (I shared my own "Living to Tell the Tale"), was voted "the best paper of the year," and further validation of insider writing: "It gave everyone a hands-on experience with the genre. While I found writing about myself exceedingly difficult, this assignment gave me a great appreciation of the subject matter of this course."

There are other types of real-world writing assignments so thoroughly embedded in innovative course material that they require extensive original investigation and very careful writing and revising—much of it conducted in groups. Linda Flower in *The Construction of Negotiated Meaning* and Thomas Deans in *Writing Partnerships: Service-Learning in Composition* explore a variety of writing courses and projects that ask students and teachers to situate their work and their writing in disciplinary as well as wider nonacademic communities with which the classes form partnerships (Deans 9). The writings thus become reports, bulletins, brochures, operating manuals, position statements, case studies, and a host of other materials described in the four programs Deans examines in detail, as well as in the appendix of courses offered in sixty-one other schools (219–44; see also Deans's textbook, *Writing and Community Action*). The students are described as highly invested in their work, which is perforce original and usually takes a great deal of time, because the students have to learn to understand the subject to which it pertains and the contexts in which it will be read. Much of it, intended for business, professional, or community audiences, has to be technically proficient. Whether it is intellectually innovative as well, or essentially only good enough is beside the point of Flower's and Deans's research, though the students have considerable incentive, encouragement, and models to make their writing clear, accurate, and to the point.

Truly Good Enough Writing

It should be apparent by now that in the final analysis good enough writing may not really be good enough at all, even if, as realists, we're willing to settle for it. If we're good enough teachers, are we only good enough to help students navigate the upward (and sometimes slippery) slope, but not good enough to get them to the summit? Should we, dare we, ask more of ourselvesas teachers? As innovative writers who understand from the inside out how to break the mold? If not, can we ask more 'of our students? If so, if we do fulfill our escalating demands on ourselves, perhaps our students still won't want to scale the peak. But, with creative assignments and latitudinarian pedagogy, we can set that vision before them, point them in the right direction, coach them for the climb, and expect the best. When we get it, that writing will truly be good enough.

Notes

1. For instance, in "What Is 'College-Level' Writing?" Patrick Sullivan reports that his informal survey of community college faculty and administrators reveals their common understanding that what is "'college- level' at one institution [is]clearly not college-level at others" (383).

2. *Evaluation and the Academy*, Rosovsky and Hartley's thoroughgoing survey of the research literature from the 1960s through the mid-1990s provides comprehensive evidence to demonstrate that large-scale surveys show that "the number of A's increased nearly four fold" during this time, from "7 percent in 1969 to 26 percent in 1993, and that the number of C's declined 66 percent (from 25 percent in 1969 to 9 percent in 1993)"; that "across all institutional types GPA's rose approximately 15–20 percent from the mid-1960s through the mid-1990s," by which time "the average grade (formerly a C) resided in the B- to B range. More recent research [1995] across all types of schools shows that only between 10 percent and 20 percent of students receive grades lower than a B-A" (p. 5 includes the authors' extensive citations).

3. Some portions of the discussion below are adapted from my analysis of "Freshman Composition as a Middle-Class Enterprise," though here the orientation is different.

4. A literature search reveals only a single, fleeting use of the concept, likewise derived from Winnicott, by Peter Elbow: "By 'good enough writing,' I do not mean mediocre writing with which we cannot be satisfied. But I do not mean excellent writing, either. . . . In my view, the concept is particularly appropriate for required writing courses where many students are there under duress and are more interested in satisfying the requirement acceptably than in achieving excellence. (Can we hold that against them?) Yet in elective writing courses, 'good enough writing' is also appropriate because students there are more ready to develop their own autonomous standards" (87).

5. I am using as the source of normative advice *The Writer's Harbrace Handbook* (Glenn, Miller, and Webb), the 2004 descendant of the ubiquitous ur-Harbrace, with thirty-nine editions 1941–98, a status warranted by its longevity and ascendancy in the market for years.

6. For example, to claim in a paper of literary criticism on Shakespeare that "Shakespeare was a great writer," though true, is considered a mark of critical naiveté, for everyone (however that is determined) knows this. Nevertheless,

if a noted critic were to make that claim, the cognoscenti would attribute this apparent banality to extreme sophistication—since the critic couldn't possibly be that naive—and try to puzzle out what arcane meaning she or he intended by making such an obvious statement.

7. *Harbrace*, surprisingly, says that "The first person is typically used" in literary analyses (718), though a brief survey of the industry standard, *PMLA*, reveals that of eight substantive articles in the January 2003 issue, only three (by John Carlos Rowe, Lori Ween, and Michael Bérubé) used the first person, Rowe and Ween very sparingly and impersonally: "I admit there is a tendency" (Rowe 78); "I will mention only" (Rowe 83); "I extend to the marketing of novels James Twichell's observation" (Ween 92). This seemingly idiosyncratic advice is not borne out by other widely used handbooks, Lunsford's *St. Martin's Handbook*, fifth edition (2003); Kirszner and Mandell's *Brief Handbook*, fourth edition (2004); or Hacker's *Writer's Reference*, fifth edition (2003).

Works Cited

Arnold, Matthew. "The Function of Criticism at the Present Time." 1865. *The Norton Anthology of English Literature*. Ed. Stephen Greenblatt. 8th ed. Vol. 2. New York: Norton, 2006.

Bartholomae, David. "Inventing the University." *Writing on the Margins: Essays on Composition and Teaching*. Boston: Bedford/St. Martin's, 2005. 60–85.

Bartholomae, David, and Tony Petrosky. *Ways of Reading: An Anthology for Writers*. 7th ed. Boston: Bedford/St. Martin's, 2004.

Bérubé, Michael. "American Studies without Exceptions." *PMLA* 118.1 (Jan. 2003): 103–13.

Bloom, Lynn Z., ed. *The Essay Connection: Readings for Writers*. 8th ed. Boston: Houghton Mifflin, 2007.

——. "Freshman Composition as a Middle-Class Enterprise." *College English* 58.6 (1996): 654–75.

——. "The Good, the Bad, and the Ugly: Ethical Principles for (Re)Presenting Students and Student Writing in Teachers' Publications." *Writing on the Edge* 13.2 (2003): 67–82.

——. "Growing Up with Doctor Spock: An Auto/Biography." *alb: Auto/Biography Studies 8.2* (1993): 271–85.

——. "Living to Tell the Tale: The Complicated Ethics of Creative Nonfiction." *College English* 65.3 (2003): 278–89.

——. "Why Don't We Write What We Teach? And Publish It?" 1990. *Composition Theory for the Postmodern Classroom*. Ed. Gary A. Olson and Sidney I. Dobrin. Albany: SUNY P, 1994. 143–55.

Bloom, Lynn Z., and Louise Z. Smith, eds. *The Arlington Reader: Canons and Contexts*. Boston: Bedford, 2003.

Bloom, Lynn Z., Edward M. White, and Shane Borrowman, eds. *Inquiry: Questioning, Reading, Writing*. 2nd ed. New York: PrenticeHall, 2003.

Buranen, Lise, and Alice M. Roy, eds. *Perspectives on Plagiarism and Intellectual Property in a Postmodern World*. Albany:SUNYP,1999.

Connors, Robert, and Andrea Lunsford. "Frequency of Formal Errors in Current College Writing, or Ma and Pa Kettle Do Research." *College Composition and Communication 39* (1988): 395–409.

Deans, Thomas. *Writing and Community Action: A Service-Learning Rhetoric and Reader.* New York: Longman, 2003.

——. *Writing Partnerships: Service-Learning in Composition.* Urbana, IL: NCTE, 2000.

Elbow, Peter. "Writing Assessment in the 21st Century: A Utopian View." *Composition in the Twenty-First Century: Crisis and Change.* Ed. Lynn Z. Bloom, Donald A. Daiker, and Edward M. White. Carbondale: Southern Illinois UP, 1996.47–62.

Flower, Linda. *The Construction of Negotiated Meaning: A Social Cognitive Theory of Writing.* Carbondale: Southern Illinois UP, 1994.

Freedman, Sarah Warshauer. "The Registers of Student and Professional Expository Writing: Influences on Teachers' Responses." *New Directions in Composition Research.* Ed. Richard Beach and L. S. Bridwell. New York: Guilford, 1984. 334–47.

Gass, William H. "Emerson and the Essay." *Habitations of the Word: Essays.* New York: Simon & Schuster, 1985. 9–49.

Glenn, Cheryl, Robert Keith Miller, and Suzanne Strobeck Webb. *Hodges' Harbrace Handbook.* 15th ed. Boston: Thomson/ Wadsworth, 2004.

Hacker, Diana. *Writer's Reference*, 5th ed. Boston: Bedford, 2003.

Kirszner, Laurie G., and Stephen R. Mandell. *The Brief Handbook.* 4th ed. Boston: Thomson/ Heinle, 2004.

Lunsford, Andrea. *The St. Martin's Handbook.* 5th ed. New York: St. Martin's, 2003.

Lunsford, Andrea, and Robert Connors. *The St. Martin's Handbook.* 2nd ed. New York: St. Martin's, 1992.

Marius, Richard. *A Writer's Companion.* 4th ed. Boston: McGraw-Hill, 1999.

Miller, Richard. "Fault Lines in the Contact Zone." *College English 56* (1994): 389–408.

Moliére, Jean-Baptiste. *The Bourgeois Gentleman.* Trans. J. Miller and H. Baker. Mineola, NY: Dover, 2001.

National Council of Teachers of English. NCTE Position Statement: "On the Students' Right to Their Own Language." 1974. 6 June 2006 <http://www.ncte.org/about/over/positions/category/lang/107502.htm>.

Orwell, George. "Politics and the English Language." 1946. *A Collection of Essays by George Orwell.* Garden City, NY: Doubleday, 1954. 162–77.

Rose, Mike. *Lives on the Boundary: The Struggles and Achievements of America's Underprepared.* New York: Free Press, 1989.

Rosovsky, Henry, and Matthew Hartley. *Evaluation and the Academy: Are We Doing the Right Thing?* Cambridge, MA: American Academy of Arts and Sciences, 2002.

Rowe, John Carlos. "Nineteenth-Century Literary Culture and Transnationality." PMLA 118.1 (Jan. 2003): 78–89.

Scholes, Robert. *Textual Power: Literary Theory and the Teaching of English.* New Haven: Yale UP, 1985.

Scholes, Robert, Nancy R. Comley, and Gregory L Ulmer. *Text Book: Writing through Literature.* 3rd ed. Boston: Bedford/St. Martin's, 2002.

Shaughnessy, Mina P. *Errors and Expectations: A Guide for the Teacher of Basic Writing.* New York: Oxford UP, 1977.

Strunk, William, and E. B. White. *The Elements of Style.* 1979. 4th ed. Boston: Allyn and Bacon, 2000.

Sullivan, Patrick. "What Is 'College-Level' Writing?" *Teaching English in the Two-Year College.* 30.4 (2003): 374–90.

Ween, Lori. "This Is Your Book: Marketing America to Itself," *PMLA* 118.1 (Jan. 2003): 90–102.

Winnicott, D. W. "The Relationship of a Mother to Her Baby at the Beginning." *The Family and Individual Development.* New York: Basic Books, 1965. 15–20.

SECTION SIX

Other Readings

Letter from Birmingham Jail

by Martin Luther King, Jr.

16 April 1963

My Dear Fellow Clergymen:

While confined here in the Birmingham city jail, I came across your recent statement calling my present activities "unwise and untimely." Seldom do I pause to answer criticism of my work and ideas. If I sought to answer all the criticisms that cross my desk, my secretaries would have little time for anything other than such correspondence in the course of the day, and I would have no time for constructive work. But since I feel that you are men of genuine good will and that your criticisms are sincerely set forth, I want to try to answer your statement in what I hope will be patient and reasonable terms.

I think I should indicate why I am here in Birmingham, since you have been influenced by the view which argues against "outsiders coming in." I have the honor of serving as president of the Southern Christian Leadership Conference, an organization operating in every southern state, with head-quarters in Atlanta, Georgia. We have some eighty-five affiliated or-ganizations across the South, and one of them is the Alabama Christian Movement for Human Rights. Frequently we share staff, educational and financial resources with our affiliates. Several months ago the affiliate here in Birmingham asked us to be on call to engage in a nonviolent direct-action program if such were deemed necessary. We readily consented, and when the hour came we lived up to our promise. So I, along with several members of my staff, am here because I was invited here. I am here because I have organizational ties here.

But more basically, I am in Birmingham because injustice is here. Just as the prophets of the eighth century B.C. left their villages and carried their "thus saith the Lord" far beyond the boundaries of their home towns, and just as the Apostle Paul left his village of Tarsus and carried the gospel of Jesus Christ to the far corners of the Greco-Roman world, so am I compelled to carry the gospel of freedom beyond my own home town. Like Paul, I must constantly respond to the Macedonian call for aid.

Moreover, I am cognizant of the interrelatedness of all communities and states. I cannot sit idly by in Atlanta and not be concerned about what hap-pens in Birmingham. Injustice anywhere is a threat to justice everywhere. We are caught in an inescapable network of mutuality, tied in a single garment of destiny. Whatever affects one directly, affects all indirectly. Never again can we afford to live with the narrow, provincial "outside agitator" idea. Anyone who lives inside the United States can never be considered an outsider anywhere within its bounds.

5   You deplore the demonstrations taking place in Birmingham. But your statement, I am sorry to say, fails to express a similar concern for the conditions that brought about the demonstrations. I am sure that none of you would want to rest content with the superficial kind of social analysis that deals merely with effects and does not grapple with underlying causes. It is unfortunate that demonstrations are taking place in Birmingham, but it is even more unfortunate that the city's white power structure left the Negro community with no alternative.

In any nonviolent campaign there are four basic steps: collection of the facts to determine whether injustices exist; negotiation; self-purification; and direct action. We have gone through all these steps in Birmingham. There can be no gainsaying the fact that racial injustice engulfs this community. Birmingham is probably the most thoroughly segregated city in the United States. Its ugly record of brutality is widely known. Negroes have experienced grossly unjust treatment in the courts. There have been more unsolved bombings of Negro homes and churches in Birmingham than in any other city in the nation. These are the hard, brutal facts of the case. On the basis of these conditions, Negro leaders sought to negotiate with the city fathers. But the latter consistently refused to engage in good-faith negotiation.

Then, last September, came the opportunity to talk with leaders of Birmingham's economic community. In the course of the negotiations, certain promises were made by the merchants—for example, to remove the stores' humiliating racial signs. On the basis of these promises, the Reverend Fred Shuttlesworth and the leaders of the Alabama Christian Movement for Human Rights agreed to a moratorium on all demonstrations. As the weeks and months went by, we realized that we were the victims of a broken promise. A few signs, briefly removed, returned; the others remained.

As in so many past experiences, our hopes had been blasted, and the shadow of deep disappointment settled upon us. We had no alternative except to prepare for direct action, whereby we would present our very bodies as a means of laying our case before the conscience of the local and the national community. Mindful of the difficulties involved, we decided to undertake a process of self-purification. We began a series of workshops on nonviolence, and we repeatedly asked ourselves: "Are you able to accept blows without retaliating?" "Are you able to endure the ordeal of jail?" We decided to schedule our direct-action program for the Easter season, realizing that except for Christmas, this is the main shopping period of the year. Knowing that a strong economic-withdrawal program would be the by-product of direct action, we felt that this would be the best time to bring pressure to bear on the merchants for the needed change.

Then it occurred to us that Birmingham's mayoral election was coming up in March, and we speedily decided to postpone action until after election day. When we discovered that the Commissioner of Public Safety, Eugene "Bull" Connor, had piled up enough votes to be in the run-off, we decided again to postpone action until the day after the run-off so that the demonstrations could not be used to cloud the issues. Like many others, we waited to see Mr. Connor defeated, and to this end we endured postponement after postponement. Having aided in this community need, we felt that our direct-action program could be delayed no longer.

10   10 You may well ask: "Why direct action? Why sit-ins, marches and so forth? Isn't negotiation a better path?" You are quite right in calling for negotiation. Indeed, this is the very purpose of direct action. Nonviolent direct action seeks to create such a crisis and foster such a tension that a community which has constantly refused to negotiate is forced to confront the issue. It seeks so to dramatize the issue that it can no longer be ignored. My citing the creation of tension as part of the work of the nonviolent-resister may sound rather shocking. But I must confess that I am not afraid of the word "tension." I have earnestly opposed violent tension, but there is a type of constructive, nonviolent tension which is necessary for growth. Just as Socrates felt that it was necessary to create a tension in the mind so that individuals could rise from the bondage of myths and half-truths to the unfettered realm of creative analysis and objective appraisal, so must we see the need for nonviolent gadflies to create the kind of tension in society that will help men rise from the dark depths of prejudice and racism to the majestic heights of understanding and brotherhood.

The purpose of our direct-action program is to create a situation so crisis-packed that it will inevitably open the door to negotiation. I therefore concur with you in your call for negotiation. Too long has our beloved Southland been bogged down in a tragic effort to live in monologue rather than dialogue.

One of the basic points in your statement is that the action that I and my associates have taken in Birmingham is untimely. Some have asked: "Why didn't you give the new city administration time to act?" The only answer that I can give to this query is that the new Birmingham administration must be prodded about as much as the outgoing one, before it will act. We are sadly mistaken if we feel that the election of Albert Boutwell as mayor will bring the millennium to Birmingham. While Mr. Boutwell is a much more gentle person than Mr. Connor, they are both segregationists, dedicated to maintenance of the status quo. I have hope that Mr. Boutwell will be reasonable enough to see the futility of massive resistance to desegregation. But he will not see this without pressure from devotees of civil rights. My friends, I must say to you that we have not made a single gain in civil rights without determined legal and nonviolent pressure. Lamentably, it is an historical fact that privileged groups seldom give up their privileges voluntarily. Individuals may see the moral light and voluntarily give up their unjust posture; but, as Reinhold Niebuhr has reminded us, groups tend to be more immoral than individuals.

We know through painful experience that freedom is never voluntarily given by the oppressor; it must be demanded by the oppressed. Frankly, I have yet to engage in a direct-action campaign that was "well timed" in the view of those who have not suffered unduly from the disease of segregation. For years now I have heard the word "Wait!" It rings in the ear of every Negro with piercing familiarity. This "Wait" has almost always meant "Never." We must come to see, with one of our distinguished jurists, that "justice too long delayed is justice denied."

We have waited for more than 340 years for our constitutional God-given rights. The nations of Asia and Africa are moving with jetlike speed toward gaining political independence, but we still creep at horse-and-buggy pace toward gaining a cup of coffee at a lunch counter. Perhaps it is easy for those who have never felt the stinging darts of segregation to say, "Wait." But when you have seen vicious mobs lynch your mothers and fathers at will and drown your sisters and brothers at whim; when you have seen hate-filled policemen curse, kick, and even kill your black brothers and sisters; when you see the vast majority of your twenty million Negro brothers smothering in an airtight cage of poverty in the midst of an affluent society; when you suddenly find your tongue twisted and your speech stammering as you seek to explain to your six-year-old daughter why she can't go to the public amusement park that has just been advertised on television, and see tears welling up in her eyes when she is told that Funtown is closed to colored children, and see ominous clouds of inferiority beginning to form in her little mental sky, and see her beginning to distort her personality by developing an unconscious bitterness toward white people; when you have to concoct an answer for a five-year-old son who is asking: "Daddy, why do white people treat colored people so mean?"; when you take a cross-country drive and find it necessary to sleep night after night in the uncomfortable corners of your automobile because no motel will accept you; when you are humiliated day in and day out by nagging signs reading "white" and "colored"; when your first name becomes "nigger," your middle name becomes "boy" (however old you are) and your last name becomes "John," and your wife and mother are never given the respected title "Mrs."; when you are harried by day and haunted by night by the fact that you are a Negro, living constantly at tiptoe stance, never quite knowing what to expect next, and are plagued with inner fears and outer resentments; when you are forever fighting a degenerating sense of "nobodiness"—then you will understand why we find it difficult to wait. There comes a time when the cup of endurance runs over, and men are no longer willing to be plunged into the abyss of despair. I hope, sirs, you can understand our legitimate and unavoidable impatience.

15   You express a great deal of anxiety over our willingness to break laws. This is certainly a legitimate concern. Since we so diligently urge people to obey the Supreme Court's deci-sion of 1954 outlawing segregation in the public schools, at first glance it may seem rather paradoxical for us consciously to break laws. One may well ask: "How can you advocate breaking some laws and obeying others?" The answer lies in the fact that there are two types of laws: just and unjust. I would be the first to advocate obeying just laws. One has not only a legal but a moral responsibility to obey just laws. Conversely, one has a moral responsibility to disobey unjust laws. I would agree with St. Augustine that "an unjust law is no law at all."

Now, what is the difference between the two? How does one determine whether a law is just or unjust? A just law is a man-made code that squares with the moral law or the law of God. An unjust law is a code that is out of harmony with the moral law. To put it in the terms of St. Thomas Aquinas: An unjust law is a human law that is not rooted in eternal law and natural law. Any law that uplifts human personality is just. Any law that degrades human personality is unjust. All segregation statutes are unjust because segregation distorts the soul and damages the personality. It gives the segregator a false sense of superiority and the segregated a false sense of inferiority. Segregation, to use the terminology of the Jewish philosopher Martin Buber, substitutes an "I–it" relationship for an "I–thou" relationship and ends up relegating persons to the status of things. Hence, segregation is not only politically, economically and sociologically unsound, it is morally wrong and sinful. Paul Tillich has said that sin is separation. Is not segregation an existential expression of man's tragic separation, his awful estrangement, his terrible sinfulness? Thus it is that I can urge men to obey the 1954 decision of the Supreme Court, for it is morally right; and I can urge them to disobey segregation ordinances, for they are morally wrong.

Let us consider a more concrete example of just and unjust laws. An unjust law is a code that a numerical or power majority group compels a minority group to obey but does not make binding on itself. This is *difference* made legal. By the same token, a just law is a code that a majority compels a minority to follow and that it is willing to follow itself. This is *sameness* made legal.

Let me give another explanation. A law is unjust if it is inflicted on a minority that, as a result of being denied the right to vote, had no part in enacting or devising the law. Who can say that the legislature of Alabama which set up that state's segregation laws was democratically elected? Throughout Alabama all sorts of devious methods are used to prevent Negroes from becoming registered voters, and there are some counties in which, even though Negroes constitute a majority of the population, not a single Negro is registered. Can any law enacted under such circumstances be considered democratically structured?

Sometimes a law is just on its face and unjust in its application. For instance, I have been arrested on a charge of parading without a permit. Now, there is nothing wrong in having an ordinance which requires a permit for a parade. But such an ordinance becomes unjust when it is used to maintain segregation and to deny citizens the First-Amendment privilege of peaceful assembly and protest.

20   I hope you are able to see the distinction I am trying to point out. In no sense do I advocate evading or defying the law, as would the rabid segregationist. That would lead to anarchy. One who breaks an unjust law must do so openly, lovingly, and with a willingness to accept the penalty. I submit that an individual who breaks a law that conscience tells him is unjust, and who willingly accepts the penalty of imprisonment in order to arouse the conscience of the community over its injustice, is in reality expressing the highest respect for law.

Of course, there is nothing new about this kind of civil disobedience. It was evidenced sublimely in the refusal of Shadrach, Meshach and Abednego to obey the laws of Nebuchadnezzar, on the ground that a higher moral law was at stake. It was practiced superbly by the early Christians, who were willing to face hungry lions and the excruciating pain of chopping blocks rather than submit to certain unjust laws of the Roman Empire. To a degree, academic freedom is a reality today because Socrates practiced civil disobedience. In our own nation, the Boston Tea Party represented a massive act of civil disobedience.

We should never forget that everything Adolf Hitler did in Germany was "legal" and everything the Hungarian freedom fighters did in Hungary was "illegal." It was "illegal" to aid and comfort a Jew in Hitler's Germany. Even so, I am sure that, had I lived in Germany at the time, I would have aided and comforted my Jewish brothers. If today I lived in a Communist country where certain principles dear to the Christian faith are suppressed I would openly advocate disobeying that country's antireligious laws.

I must make two honest confessions to you, my Christian and Jewish brothers. First, I must confess that over the past few years I have been gravely disappointed with the white moderate. I have almost reached the regrettable conclusion that the Negro's great stumbling block in his stride toward freedom is not the White Citizen's Counciler or the Ku Klux Klanner, but the white moderate, who is more devoted to "order" than to justice; who prefers a negative peace which is the presence of tension to a positive peace which is the presence of justice; who constantly says, "I agree with you in the goal you seek, but I cannot agree with your methods of direct action"; who paternalistically believes he can set the timetable for another man's freedom; who lives by a mythical concept of time and who constantly advises the Negro to wait for a "more convenient season." Shallow understanding from people of good will is more frustrating than absolute misunderstanding from people of ill will. Luke-warm acceptance is much more bewildering than outright rejection.

I had hoped that the white moderate would understand that law and order exist for the purpose of establishing justice and that when they fail in this purpose they become the dangerously structured dams that block the flow of social progress. I had hoped that the white moderate would understand that the present tension in the South is a necessary phase of the transition from an obnoxious negative peace, in which the Negro passively accepted his unjust plight, to a substantive and positive peace, in which all men will respect the dignity and worth of human personality. Actually, we who engage in nonviolent direct action are not the creators of tension. We merely bring to the surface the hidden tension that is already alive. We bring it out in the open, where it can be seen and dealt with. Like a boil that can never be cured so long as it is covered up but must be opened with all its ugliness to the natural medicines of air and light, injustice must be exposed, with all the tension its exposure creates, to the light of human conscience and the air of national opinion before it can be cured.

25   In your statement you assert that our actions, even though peaceful, must be condemned because they precipitate violence. But is this a logical assertion? Isn't this like condemning a robbed man because his possession of money precipitated the evil act of robbery? Isn't this like condemning Socrates because his unswerving commitment to truth and his philosophical inquiries precipitated the act by the misguided populace in which they made him drink hemlock? Isn't this like condemning Jesus because his unique God-consciousness and never-ceasing devotion to God's will precipitated the evil act of crucifixion? We must come to see that, as the federal courts have consistently affirmed, it is wrong to urge an individual to cease his efforts to gain his basic constitutional rights because the quest may precipitate violence. Society must protect the robbed and punish the robber.

I had also hoped that the white moderate would reject the myth concerning time in relation to the struggle for freedom. I have just received a letter from a white brother in Texas. He writes: "All Christians know that the colored people will receive equal rights eventually, but it is possible that you are in too great a religious hurry. It has taken Christianity almost two thousand years to accomplish what it has. The teachings of Christ take time to come to earth." Such an attitude stems from a tragic misconception of time, from the strangely irrational no-tion that there is something in the very flow of time that will inevitably cure all ills. Actually, time itself is neutral; it can be used either destructively or constructively. More and more I feel that the people of ill will have used time much more effectively than have the people of good will. We will have to repent in this generation not merely for the hateful words and actions of the bad people but for the appalling silence of the good people. Human progress never rolls in on wheels of inevitability; it comes through the tireless efforts of men willing to be co-workers with God, and without this hard work, time itself becomes an ally of the forces of social stagnation. We must use time creatively, in the knowledge that the time is always ripe to do right. Now is the time to make real the promise of democracy and transform our pending national elegy into a creative psalm of brotherhood. Now is the time to lift our national policy from the quicksand of racial injustice to the solid rock of human dignity.

You speak of our activity in Birmingham as extreme. At first I was rather disappointed that fellow clergymen would see my nonviolent efforts as those of an extremist. I began thinking about the fact that I stand in the middle of two opposing forces in the Negro community. One is a force of complacency, made up in part of Negroes who, as a result of long years of oppression, are so drained of self-respect and a sense of "somebodiness" that they have adjusted to segregation; and in part of a few middle-class Negroes who, because of a degree of academic and economic security and because in some ways they profit by segregation, have become insensitive to the problems of the masses. The other force is one of bitterness and hatred, and it comes perilously close to advocating violence. It is expressed in the various black nationalist groups that are springing up across the nation, the largest and best-known being Elijah Muhammad's Muslim movement. Nourished by the Negro's frustration over the continued existence of racial discrimination, this movement is made up of people who have lost faith in America, who have absolutely repudiated Christianity, and who have concluded that the white man is an incorrigible "devil."

I have tried to stand between these two forces, saying that we need emulate neither the "do-nothingism" of the complacent nor the hatred and despair of the black nationalist. For there is the more excellent way of love and nonviolent protest. I am grateful to God that, through the influence of the Negro church, the way of nonviolence became an integral part of our struggle.

If this philosophy had not emerged, by now many streets of the South would, I am convinced, be flowing with blood. And I am further convinced that if our white brothers dismiss as "rabble-rousers" and "outside agitators" those of us who employ nonviolent direct action, and if they refuse to support our nonviolent efforts, millions of the Negroes will, out of frustration and despair, seek solace and security in black-nationalist ideologies—a development that would inevitably lead to a frightening racial nightmare.

30   Oppressed people cannot remain oppressed forever. The yearning for freedom eventually manifests itself, and that is what has happened to the American Negro. Something within has reminded him of his birthright of freedom, and something without has reminded him that it can be gained. Consciously or unconsciously, he has been caught up by the *Zeitgeist*, and with his black brothers of Africa and his brown and yellow brothers of Asia, South America and the Caribbean, the United States Negro is moving with a sense of great urgency toward the promised land of racial justice. If one recognizes this vital urge that has engulfed the Negro community, one should readily understand why public demonstrations are taking place. The Negro has many pent-up resentments and latent frustrations, and he must release them. So let him march; let him make prayer pilgrimages to the city hall; let him go on freedom rides—and try to understand why he must do so. If his repressed emotions are not released in nonviolent ways, they will seek expression through violence; this is not a threat but a fact of history. So I have not said to my people: "Get rid of your discontent." Rather, I have tried to say that this normal and healthy discontent can be channeled into the creative outlet of nonviolent direct action. And now this approach is being termed extremist.

But though I was initially disappointed at being categorized as an extremist, as I continued to think about the matter I gradually gained a measure of satisfaction from the label. Was not Jesus an extremist for love: "Love your enemies, bless them that curse you, and persecute you." Was not Amos an extremist for justice: "Let justice roll down like waters and righteousness like an ever-flowing stream." Was not Paul an extremist for the Christian gospel: "I bear in my body the marks of the Lord Jesus." Was not Martin Luther an extremist: "Here I stand; I cannot do otherwise, so help me God." And John Bunyan: "I will stay in jail to the end of my days before I make a butchery of my conscience." And Abraham Lincoln: "This nation cannot survive half slave and half free." And Thomas Jefferson: "We hold these truths to be self-evident, that all men are created equal . . . ." So the question is not whether we will be extremists, but what kind of extremists we will be. Will we be extremists for hate or for love? Will we be extremists for the preservation of injustice or for the extension of justice? In that dramatic scene on Calvary's hill three men were crucified. We must never forget that all three were crucified for the same crime—the crime of extremism. Two were extremists for immorality, and thus fell below their environment. The other, Jesus Christ, was an extremist for love, truth and goodness, and thereby rose above his environment. Perhaps the South, the nation and the world are in dire need of creative extremists.

I had hoped that the white moderate would see this need. Perhaps I was too optimistic; perhaps I expected too much. I suppose I should have realized that few members of the oppressor race can understand the deep groans and passionate yearnings of the oppressed race, and still fewer have the vision to see that injustice must be rooted out by strong, persistent and determined action. I am thankful, however, that some of our white brothers in the South have grasped the meaning of this social revolution and committed them-selves to it. They are still all too few in quantity, but they are big in quality. Some—such as Ralph McGill, Lillian Smith, Harry Golden, James McBride Dabbs, Ann Braden and Sarah Patton Boyle—have written about our struggle in eloquent and prophetic terms. Others have marched with us down nameless streets of the South. They have languished in filthy, roach-infested jails, suffering the abuse and brutality of policemen who view them as "dirty nigger-lovers." Unlike so many of their moderate brothers and sisters, they have recognized the urgency of the moment and sensed the need for powerful "action" antidotes to combat the disease of segregation.

Let me take note of my other major disappointment. I have been so greatly disappointed with the white church and its leadership. Of course, there are some notable exceptions. I am not unmindful of the fact that each of you has taken some significant stands on this issue. I commend you, Reverend Stallings, for your Christian stand on this past Sunday, in welcoming Negroes to your worship service on a nonsegregated basis. I commend the Catholic leaders of this state for integrating Spring Hill College several years ago.

But despite these notable exceptions, I must honestly reiterate that I have been disappointed with the church. I do not say this as one of those negative critics who can always find something wrong with the church. I say this as a minister of the gospel, who loves the church; who was nurtured in its bosom; who has been sustained by its spiritual blessings and who will remain true to it as long as the cord of life shall lengthen.

35   When I was suddenly catapulted into the leadership of the bus protest in Montgomery, Alabama, a few years ago, I felt we would be supported by the white church. I felt that the white ministers, priests and rabbis of the South would be among our strongest allies. Instead, some have been outright opponents, refusing to understand the freedom movement and misrepresenting its leaders; all too many others have been more cautious than courageous and have remained silent behind the anesthetizing security of stained-glass windows.

In spite of my shattered dreams, I came to Birmingham with the hope that the white religious leadership of this community would see the justice of our cause and, with deep moral concern, would serve as the channel through which our just grievances could reach the power structure. I had hoped that each of you would understand. But again I have been disappointed.

I have heard numerous southern religious leaders admonish their worshipers to comply with a desegregation decision because it is the law, but I have longed to hear white ministers declare: "Follow this decree because integration is morally right and because the Negro is your brother." In the midst of blatant injustices inflicted upon the Negro, I have watched white churchmen stand on the sideline and mouth pious irrelevancies and sanctimonious trivialities. In the midst of a mighty struggle to rid our nation of racial and economic injustice, I have heard many ministers say: "Those are social issues, with which the gospel has no real concern." And I have watched many churches commit themselves to a completely otherworldly religion which makes a strange, un-Biblical distinction between body and soul, between the sacred and the secular.

I have traveled the length and breadth of Alabama, Mississippi and all the other southern states. On sweltering summer days and crisp autumn mornings I have looked at the South's beautiful churches with their lofty spires pointing heavenward. I have beheld the impressive outlines of her massive religious-education buildings. Over and over I have found myself asking: "What kind of people worship here? Who is their God? Where were their voices when the lips of Governor Barnett dripped with words of interposition and nullification? Where were they when Governor Wallace gave a clarion call for defiance and hatred? Where were their voices of support when bruised and weary Negro men and women decided to rise from the dark dungeons of complacency to the bright hills of creative protest?"

Yes, these questions are still in my mind. In deep disappointment I have wept over the laxity of the church. But be assured that my tears have been tears of love. There can be no deep disappointment where there is not deep love. Yes, I love the church. How could I do otherwise? I am in the rather unique position of being the son, the grandson, and the great-grandson of preachers. Yes, I see the church as the body of Christ. But, oh! How we have blemished and scarred that body through social neglect and through fear of being nonconformists.

40   There was a time when the church was very powerful—in the time when the early Christians rejoiced at being deemed worthy to suffer for what they believed. In those days the church was not merely a thermometer that recorded the ideas and principles of popular opinion; it was a thermostat that transformed the mores of society. Whenever the early Christians entered a town, the people in power became disturbed and immediately sought to convict the Christians for being "disturbers of the peace" and "outside agitators." But the Christians pressed on, in the conviction that they were "a colony of heaven," called to obey God rather than man. Small in number, they were big in commitment. They were too God-intoxicated to be "astronomically intimidated." By their effort and example they brought an end to such ancient evils as infanticide and gladiatorial contests.

Things are different now. So often the contemporary church is a weak, ineffectual voice with an uncertain sound. So often it is an archdefender of the status quo. Far from being disturbed by the presence of the church, the power structure of the average community is consoled by the church's silent—and often even vocal—sanction of things as they are.

But the judgment of God is upon the church as never before. If today's church does not recapture the sacrificial spirit of the early church, it will lose its authenticity, forfeit the loyalty of millions, and be dismissed as an irrelevant social club with no meaning for the twentieth century. Every day I meet young people whose disappointment with the church has turned into outright disgust.

Perhaps I have once again been too optimistic. Is organized religion too inextricably bound to the status quo to save our nation and the world? Perhaps I must turn my faith to the inner spiritual church, the church within the church, as the true *ekklesia* and the hope of the world. But again I am thankful to God that some noble souls from the ranks of organized religion have broken loose from the paralyzing chains of conformity and joined us as active partners in the struggle for freedom. They have left their secure congregations and walked the streets of Albany, Georgia, with us. They have gone down the highways of the South on tortuous rides for freedom. Yes, they have gone to jail with us. Some have been dismissed from their churches, have lost the support of their bishops and fellow ministers. But they have acted in the faith that right defeated is stronger than evil triumphant. Their witness has been the spiritual salt that has preserved the true meaning of the gospel in these troubled times. They have carved a tunnel of hope through the dark mountain of disappointment.

I hope the church as a whole will meet the challenge of this decisive hour. But even if the church does not come to the aid of justice, I have no despair about the future. I have no fear about the outcome of our struggle in Birmingham, even if our motives are at present misunderstood. We will reach the goal of freedom in Birmingham and all over the nation, because the goal of America is freedom. Abused and scorned though we may be, our destiny is tied up with America's destiny. Before the pilgrims landed at Plymouth, we were here. Before the pen of Jefferson etched the majestic words of the Declaration of Independence across the pages of history, we were here. For more than two centuries our forebears labored in this country without wages; they made cotton king; they built the homes of their masters while suffering gross injustice and shameful humiliation—and yet out of a bottomless vitality they continued to thrive and develop. If the inexpressible cruelties of slavery could not stop us, the opposition we now face will surely fail. We will win our freedom because the sacred heritage of our nation and the eternal will of God are embodied in our echoing demands.

45   Before closing I feel impelled to mention one other point in your statement that has troubled me profoundly. You warmly commended the Birmingham police force for keeping "order" and "preventing violence." I doubt that you would have so warmly commended the police force if you had seen its dogs sinking their teeth into unarmed, nonviolent Negroes. I doubt that you would so quickly commend the policemen if you were to observe their ugly and inhumane treatment of Negroes here in the city jail; if you were to watch them push and curse old Negro women and young Negro girls; if you were to see them slap and kick old Negro men and young boys; if you were to observe them, as they did on two occasions, refuse to give us food because we wanted to sing our grace together. I cannot join you in your praise of the Birmingham police department.

It is true that police have exercised a degree of discipline in handling the demonstrators. In this sense they have conducted themselves rather "nonviolently" in public. But for what purpose? To preserve the evil system of segregation. Over the past few years I have consistently preached that nonviolence demands that the means we use must be as pure as the ends we seek. I have tried to make clear that it is wrong to use immoral means to attain moral ends. But now I must affirm that it is just as wrong, or perhaps even more so, to use moral means to preserve immoral ends. Perhaps Mr. Connor and his policemen have been rather nonviolent in public, as was Chief Pritchett in Albany, Georgia, but they have used the moral means of nonviolence to maintain the immoral end of racial injustice. As T. S. Eliot has said: "The last temptation is the greatest treason: To do the right deed for the wrong reason."

I wish you had commended the Negro sit-inners and demonstrators of Birmingham for their sublime courage, their willingness to suffer and their amazing discipline in the midst of great provocation. One day the South will recognize its real heroes. They will be the James Merediths, with the noble sense of purpose that enables them to face jeering and hostile mobs, and with the agonizing loneliness that characterizes the life of the pioneer. They will be old, oppressed, battered Negro women, symbolized in a seventy-two-year-old woman in Montgomery, Alabama, who rose up with a sense of dignity and with her people decided not to ride segregated buses, and who responded with ungrammatical profundity to one who inquired about her weariness: "My feets is tired, but my soul is at rest." They will be the young high school and college students, the young ministers of the gospel and a host of their elders, courageously and nonviolently sitting in at lunch counters and willingly going to jail for conscience' sake. One day the South will know that when these disinherited children of God sat down at lunch counters, they were in reality standing up for what is best in the American dream and for the most sacred values in our Judaeo-Christian heritage, thereby bringing our nation back to those great wells of democracy which were dug deep by the founding fathers in their formulation of the Constitution and the Declaration of Independence.

Never before have I written so long a letter. I'm afraid it is much too long to take your precious time. I can assure you that it would have been much shorter if I had been writing from a comfortable desk, but what else can one do when he is alone in a narrow jail cell, other than write long letters, think long thoughts and pray long prayers?

If I have said anything in this letter that overstates the truth and indicates an unreasonable impatience, I beg you to forgive me. If I have said anything that understates the truth and indicates my having a patience that allows me to settle for anything less than brotherhood, I beg God to forgive me.

50   I hope this letter finds you strong in faith. I also hope that circumstances will soon make it possible for me to meet each of you, not as an integrationist or a civil-rights leader but as a fellow clergyman and a Christian brother. Let us all hope that the dark clouds of racial prejudice will soon pass away and the deep fog of misunderstanding will be lifted from our fear-drenched communities, and in some not too distant tomorrow the radiant stars of love and brotherhood will shine over our great nation with all their scintillating beauty.

Yours for the cause of Peace and Brotherhood

MARTIN LUTHER KING, JR.

Credits

Text

Page 5. Juan Lucas

Pages 22, 23, 36, 37, 44. Trudie Makens

Page 33. James Surowiecki, "The Pay is Too Damn Low," *The New Yorker*. Reprinted with permission of the Chris Calhoun Agency.

Page 40. Michael Saltsman, "To Help the Poor, Move Beyond 'Minimum Gestures," Huffington Post. Reprinted by permission of the author.

Page 55. Pearson Education

Pages 66, 81, 82. Carmen Tieu

Page 129. Trudie Makens, "Bringing Dignity to Workers: Make the Minimum Wage a Living Wage"

Page 140. Colleen Fontana, "An Open Letter to Robert Levy in Response to His Article 'They Never Learn.'" Used by permission.

Page 145. Lauren Shinozuka, "The Dangers of Digital Distractedness"

Page 149: Monica Allen, "An Open Letter to Christopher Eide in response to His Article 'High-Performing Charter Schools Can Close the Opportunity Gap'"

Page 159. Kathryn Jean Lopez, "Egg Heads," *National Review*. (c) 1998 National Review, Inc. Reprinted by permission.

Page 171. Zachary Stumps, "A Rhetorical Analysis of Ellen Goodman's 'Womb for Rent.'" Reprinted with permission of the author.

Page 217. Alex Hutchinson, "Your Daily Multivitamin May Be Hurting You—The Debate Is On: Just Useless, or Truly Dangerous?" *Outside Magazine*, Oct. 8, 2013. Used with permission.

Page 242. John Bean

Page 244. Alex Mullens, "A Pirate but Not a Thief: What Does 'Stealing' Mean in a Digital Environment?" Reprinted by permission of the author.

Page 257. LA Times Editorial Board, "College Football…Yes, It's a Job." Reprinted by permission of *LA Times*.

Page 257. "Buying Sex Causes Sex Trafficking" from Free the Captives. Used by permission.

Page 266. Julee Christianson, "Why Lawrence Summers Was Wrong." Used by permission.

Page 272. Deborah Fallows, "Papa, Don't Text: The Perils of Distracted Parenting." (c) 2013 The Atlantic Media Co., as first published in *The Atlantic* Magazine. All rights reserved. Distributed by Tribune Content Agency, LLC

Page 274. Carlos Macias, "'The Credit Card Company Made Me Do It!'—The Credit Card Industry's Role in Causing Student Debt." Used by permission.

Page 294. Lorena Mendoza-Flores, "Silenced and Invisible: Problems of Hispanic Students at Valley High School"

Page 297. Christopher Moore, "Information Plus Satire: Why The Daily Show and The Colbert Report Are Good Sources of News for Young People." Reprinted with permission.

Page 300. Judith Daar, "Three Genetic Parents for One Healthy Baby," *Los Angeles Times,* March 21, 2014. Reprinted with permission of the author.

Page 302. Samuel Aquila, "The 'Therapeutic Cloning' of Human Embryos," *National Review,* May 17, 2013. Reprinted with permission.

Page 322. Megan Johnson, "A Practical Proposal"

Page 326. Ivan Snook, "Flirting with Disaster: An Argument Against Integrating Women into the Combat Arms." Reprinted by permission of the author.

Page 333. Sandy Wainscott, "Why McDonald's Should Sell Meat and Veggie Pies: A Proposal to End Subsidies for Cheap Meat." Used by permission.

Page 335. Marcel Dicke and Arnold Van Huis, "The Six-Legged Meat of the Future," *The Wall Street Journal*, February 19, 2011. Reprinted with permission.

Section Two—Rhetoric Supplement

Page 340, Chapter 15. "An Introduction to Inquiry," taken from *From Inquiry to Argument* by Linda McMeniman.

Page 350, Chapter 17. "Exigence," reprinted by permission of the Academic Writing Program, University of Maryland.

Page 353, Chapter 18. "Using the Five Canons of Rhetoric as Steps in the Process of Writing," reprinted by permission of the Academic Writing Program, University of Maryland.

Page 359, Chapter 19. "Invention—Generating Ideas with Stasis Theory," reprinted by permission of the Academic Writing Program, University of Maryland.

Page 361, Chapter 20. "Writing a Rhetorical Analysis," reprinted by permission of the Academic Writing Program, University of Maryland.

Page 361. "Should High Schools Permit Gay-Straight Alliance Clubs?" by Jim Anderson and Peter LaBarbera, reprinted from *The CQ Researcher* 10, no. 14 (April 14, 2000), by permission of Congressional Quarterly, Inc.

Page 371, Chapter 21. "Stasis Theory—Identifying the Issues and Joining the Debate," reprinted by permission of the Academic Writing Program, University of Maryland.

Section Four—Readings on Revision and Reflection

Page 438, Chapter 31. "Shitty First Drafts," by Anne Lamott, reprinted from *Bird by Bird* (1995), by permission of Random House, Inc.

Page 441, Chapter 32. "Revising," by Joseph Harris, reprinted from *Rewriting: How to Do Things with Texts* (2006), by permission of Utah State University Press.

Page 458, Chapter 33. "The Maker's Eye: Revising Your Own Manuscripts," by Donald M. Murray, reprinted from *The Writer* (1973), Rosenberg Group.

Page 463, Chapter 34. "Making Meaning Clear: The Logic of Revision," by Donald M. Murray, reprinted by permission from the *Journal of Basic Writing* 3.3 (fall, winter 1981).

Page 470, Chapter 35. "When We Dead Awaken: Writing as Re-Vision," by Adrienne Rich, reprinted from *On Lies, Secrets, and Silence: Selected Prose 1966–1978* (1995), W.W. Norton & Company, Inc.

Page 482, Chapter 36. "Revision Strategies of Student Writers and Experienced Adult Writers," by Nancy Sommers, reprinted from *College Composition and Communication*, Edition 31.4 (1980), National Council of Teachers of English.

Page 492, Chapter 37. "Thirteen (Lucky!) Strategies for Revision," reprinted by permission of the Academic Writing Program, University of Maryland.

Page 542. "Letter from Birmingham Jail" by Dr. Martin Luther King Jr. (1963). The Heirs to the Estate of Martin Luther King Jr., c/o Writers House as agent for the proprietor.

Images

Page 1. AP Photo/StephanSavoia

Page 4. United Steelworkers Union

Page 6. Top, GHoneywell Design. Bottom, AP Photo/Hans Pennink.

Page 7. www.cartoonstock.com

Page 20. Employment Policies Institute. Reprinted with permission.

Page 21. www.cartoonstock.com

Index